ISBN 978-1-5285-0354-9
PIBN 10931174

INDEX

TO THE

ENGLISH POETS.

VOLUME I.

Vol. LVII.

INDEX

TO THE

ENGLISH POETS.

VOLUME THE FIRST.

LONDON:

PRINTED BY J. NICHOLS;

FOR C. BATHURST, J. BUCKLAND, W. STRAHAN, J. RIVING-
TON AND SONS, T. DAVIES, T. PAYNE, L. DAVIS, W. OWEN,
B. WHITE, S. CROWDER, T. CASLON, T. LONGMAN,
B. LAW, E. AND C. DILLY, J. DODSLEY, J. WILKIE,
J. ROBSON, J. JOHNSON, T. LOWNDES, T. BECKET,
G. ROBINSON, T. CADELL, J. NICHOLS, F. NEW-
BERY, T. EVANS, J. RIDLEY, R. BALDWIN,
G. NICOL, LEIGH AND SOTHEBY, J. BEW,
N. CONANT, J. MURRAY, W. FOX, J. BOWEN.

MDCCLXXX.

Israel. P & 2
Lit
Albert Brune -
1815 - 1935

ADVERTISEMENT.

THE following Index is a fynoptical view of the Englifh Poets in thefe particulars; namely, in prudential, moral and religious fentences; in remarkable proverbial fayings, either of a ludicrous or ferious turn; in chatacters of celebrated perfons, both ancient and modern; in defcriptions of places and countries, and in accounts of remarkable events, either in the natural or political world, and of the ancient cuftoms or antiquities; in critical obfervations on poets and poetry, by Dryden, Addifon, Pope, &c. with ftrong remonftrances againft the vile proftitution of the gift of heaven to impure and immoral purpofes:

the

the whole in the words of the poets, when they could conveniently be brought within the compass of a line, and in the very arrangement of their words, in order to preserve entire the harmony and emphasis of the sentence, more especially in the proverbial sayings, which are much of the same nature with the sententious, differing only in point of authority, the latter being the result of the observation of the wise and learned, and expressed with dignity; but the former, that of the vulgar, and generally as vulgarly expressed, yet equally true with the sententious. Proverbial sayings could not well be disarranged, without spoiling them, or at least making them sound harsh to an ear unaccustomed to an unusual arrangement. When a quality stands alone, without the express mention of its subject, either person or thing,

but

but which it neceſſarily implies, it is in all languages, both learned and unlearned, taken ſubſtantively; it may therefore lead the ſentence, according to the general rule of index-making; namely, that a ſubſtantive is always to be the leading word; the truth of which will be conſidered hereafter. For inſtance, we ſay, the *virtuous, the vicious,* &c. with reſpect to perſons; and with reſpect to a thing, *the good, the ill, the vain,* &c. *of life.* When quality and ſubject are both expreſſed together, I conſider them as one word; both on account of their neceſſary connection; and eſpecially, becauſe the ſtreſs of the ſentence turns upon them: I therefore ſcruple not to make them the leading words: Dryden, for inſtance, to mention no other, ſays, *lively faith bears aloft the mind:* if the above rule, namely that

of always making a ſubſtantive to lead
the ſentence, be made an invariable and
univerſal rule, it will neceſſarily ex-
clude, from a place in an index, very
many important ſentences, which are
without a ſubſtantive. Dryden again
ſays, *write well, or not at all:* I there-
fore ſcrupled not to make a verb the
leading word; or even an adverb, if
uſed emphatically; for inſtance, *greatly
wiſe to talk with our paſt hoars,* Young.
I endeavoured all along, in the arrange-
ment, to form ſome connection between
the articles under the ſame alphabetical
head, unleſs where they happen to be
contradictory, and which the order of
the alphabet, and not their connection,
brought together.

INDEX

TO THE

ENGLISH POETS.

N. B. When the poet is in one volume only, the number denotes the page: when in more volumes than one, the firſt number, ſeparated by a colon, denotes the volume; the ſecond, the page of that volume.

ABBREVIATIONS EXPLAINED.

Add. Addiſon; Aken. Akenſde; A. Phil. Ambroſe Philips; Black. Blackmore; Buck. Buckingham; Butl. Butler; Coll. Collins; Cong. Congreve; Cow. Cowley; Den. Denham; Dor. Dorſet: Dry. Dryden; Fent. Fenton; Hal. Halifax; Ham. Hammond; Lanſ. Lanſdowne; Lytt. Lyttelton; Mall. Mallet; Milk. Milton; Ot. Otway; Parn. Parnell; Phil. John Philips; Pom. Pomfret; Pope il. od. Pope's Iliad and Odyſſey; Roch. Rocheſter; Roſc. Roſcommon; Rowe L. Rowe's Lucan; Sav. Savage; Shen. Shenſtone; Som. Somervile; Step. Stepney; Thom. Thomſon; Tick. Tickell; Wall. Waller; Yal. Yalden.

A

ABANTES. their uncommon length of hair, Pope il. 1: 88
   Abbeys put down,   Den. 11
Abdael, character of,   Dry. 1: 193
Abdiel, zeal of,   Mil. 1: 166

Ariel, reception of in heaven,   *Milt.* 1 : 174

Abel, murder of, in vision,   *Milt.* 2 : 100

Abelard,   *Pope* 1 : 184

———— ill-fated youth,   *Prior* 2 : 58

Aberdeen, univerfity, founder of,   *Mall.* 171

Abijah attempts in vain to recover the ten tribes,   *Cow.* 2 : 127

Abimelec, ambition of,   *Cow.* 2 : 257

Abra, the favourite of Solomon,   *Prior* 2 : 142

———— the Georgian Sultana,   *Coll.* 239

Abraham called,   *Milt.* 2 : 123

———————— in his feed the world bleffed,   *Milt.* 2 : 124

————— friend of God, muft bear the deftin'd load, *Prior* 2 : 179

Abfalom and Achitophel,   *Dry.* 1 : 125

———— character of,   *Dry.* 1 : 126, 141

————— engages in rebellion,   *Dry.* 1 : 149

Abfence,   { *Cong.* 53
                                                       { *Shen.* 125

———— death to thofe who love,   *Pope* 1 : 37

Abftinence lean and fallow,   *Milt.* 3 : 146

Abfurdities, grand climacterical,   *Young* 2 : 113

Abundance is the mifer's doom,   *Young* 3 : 270

Abufe, unhallowed licence of,   *Mall.* 257

Abyfs of endlefs woe,   *Pom.* 338

Academia, fchool of Plato,   *Akin.* 89.

Acamus and Pyrous from Thracia come,   *Pope il.* 1 : 101

Accents, where to place,   *Rofc.* 1 : 221

Account, Anacreontic,   *Cow.* 1 : 143

———— balanced,   *Watts* 262

Achaia, women of, and men no more,   *Pope il.* 1 : 77

Achaemenides, ftory of,   *Add.* 47

                                                       Achaeme nides,

Achæmenides, adventures of, *Garth* 129

————— ———— ftory of, *Dry.* 6 : 28

Achelous and Hercules *Gay* 1 : 311

————— his horn facred to plenty, *Gay* 1 : 315

Acheron, flaming gulf, *Pope od.* 3 : 271

Acheson to the Dean, *Swift* 2 : 159

————'s, Dean at, *Swift* 2 : 54

Achillas pierc'd Pompey's breaft, *Rowe L.* 357

———— partner-ruffian, in Pompey's fall, *Hughes* 303

———— meets his juft fate, *Hughes* 311

Achilles, fwift-footed fon of Peleus, *Phil.* 18

———— wrath, fpring of woes to Greece, *Pope il.* 1 : 37

———— fuch was the will of Jove, *Pope il.* 1 : 37

———— the fierce, the fearlefs, and the brave, *Pope il.* 1 : 77

———— knows no fears, *Pope il.* 2 : 101

———— launced fifty veffels for Ilion's fhore, *Pope il.* 2 : 106

———— who can match, muft be more than man, *Pope il.* 2 : 320

———— that iron-heart, inflexibly fevere, *Pope il.* 2 : 328

———— a lion, not a man. *Pope il.* 2 : 328

———— flaughters wide in impotence of pride, *Pope il.* 2 : 328

———— flower of war, *Fent.* 268

———— fhield and bulwark of the Grecian hoft, *Tick.* 174

———— pride of Greece, and bulwark of our hoft, *Pope il.* 1 : 49

———— full fifty fhips commands, *Pope il.* 1 : 94

———— entertains the Grecian embaffy, *Pope il.* 1 : 274

———— rejects their propofal, *Pope il.* 1 : 279

———— firft of men, but not a match for gods, *Pope il.* 2 : 245

———— to the gods refigned, to reafon yield, *Pope* 1 : 46

———— abfent, was Achilles ftill, *Pope il.* 2 : 277

———— *his courfers of immortal breed,* *Pope il.* 2 : 105

B 2

Achilles, like wind in speed,   *Pope il.* 2: 105

———— and Myrmidons thrice go round Patroclus, *il.* 289

———— facrifices animals and men to Patroclus, *Pope il.* 2: 296.

———— makes libations to the winds,   *Pope il.* 2: 297

———————————— to Paroclus,   *Pope il.* 2: 298

———— gathers Patroclus' bones into an urn,   *Pope il.* 2: 299

———— comforted by Thetis on his death,   *Pope il.* 2: 174

———— fo fhall fall,   *Pope il.* 2: 174

———— fhield of, defcribed,   *Pope il.* 2: 137, feq.

———— finifhed wrath, the Greeks accept   *Pope il.* 2: 197

———— terrour of the plain,   *Pope il.* 2: 215

———— long loft to battle, fhone in arms,   *Pope il.* 2: 215

———— puts on his armour,   *Pope il.* 2: 208

———— fpear of, an afh entire,   *Pope il.* 2: 209

———— ftood, all grim with duft,   *Pope il.* 2: 232

———— drags the body of Hector,   *Pope il.* 2: 279

———— fear the juft Gods,   *Conz.* 36

———— relents at the prayer of Priam,   *Pope il.* 2: 348

———— grants Priam a truce of twelve days,   *Pope il.* 2: 354

———— and Cygnus, fight of,   *Dry.* 4: 79

———— impatient, rafh, inexorable, proud,   *Rofc.* 264

———— fteel-proof,   *Butl.* 1: 105

———— for his wench, like tall-boy, wept,   *Prior* 2: 47

Achitophel, character of,   *Dry.* 1: 130, feq.

———— ftirs up Abfalom to rebel,   *Dry.* 1: 133

Achoreus, with gentleft manners fraught,   *Rowe L.* 350

———— told how much Egypt to Pompey was indebted, *ib.* 350

Acis and Galatea,   *Gay* 1: 300

    'phemus and Galatea,   *Dry.* 4: 124

        'or to Pallas,   *Dry.* 7: 3, 5.

                                              Acontius

Acontius to Cydippe,   *Duke* 155

Acquaintance not many but choice,   *Cow.* 1: 75

————— invaders of our time,   *Cow.* 2: 294

Acres unnumbered, arable, and green,   *Pope od.* 4: 172

Acronycal rising, what,   *Dry.* 5: 271

Acroftic land, a province in,   *Dry.* 2: 116

Actaeon transformed,   *Add.* 150

Action, fuccefs gives it all its comelinefs,   *Som.* 313

———— caufes and beginning of,   *Pope od.* 3: 21

———— intrigue of,   *Pope od.* 3: 22, feq.

———— unraveling of,   *Pope od.* 3: 26

———— time of,   *Pope od.* 3: 27

———— of the epic, to be fingle,   *Pope od.* 3: 3

———— to traverfe,   *Butl.* 2: 105

Actions not always fhew the man,   *Pope* 2: 99

———— generous meet a bafe reward,   *Parn.* 83

———— from a brute necefiity cannot be wife,   *Black.* 163

Acts, things reduced to,   *Butl.* 1: 11

Adam, offspring of heaven and earth,   *Milt.* 2: 12

———— and Eve, character of,   *Milt.* 1: 110, feq.

———— encompafied by the beafts,   *Milt.* 1: 112

———— and Eve daily labour of,   *Milt.* 1: 146

———— relates his creation,   *Milt.* 1: 239

———— had fpeech and reafon,   *Milt.* 1: 240

———— firft fleep of,   *Milt.* 1: 240

———— dream of,   *Milt.* 1: 240, feq.

———— fcarce tafting life, was of joy bereaved,   *Prior* 2: 177

———— bewailing ftill his haplefs choice,   *Prior* 2: 178

———— younger fon, firft fruit of death,   *Prior* 2: 178

———— won to eat forbidden fruit,   *Milt.* 2: 36

B 3

Adam,

Adam, fondnefs for Eve,   *Milt.* 2 : 33, 34

———— reafon of, difturbed,   *Milt.* 2 : 34

———— fin of, affects all nature, *Milt.* 2 : 36

———— and Eve, mutual reproaches of, *Milt.* 2 : 41, 42

———— charges Eve with his guilt, *Milt.* 2 : 49

———— gave names from natures of things, *Den.* 102

———— and Eve covered with fkins, *Den.* 52

———— regret on leaving paradife, *Milt.* 2 : 95

———— doomed,   *Milt.* 2 : 51, 52

———— fubmiffive to his doom, *Milt.* 2 : 97

———— and Eve burn in luft, *Milt.* 2 : 37

———— cover their nakednefs, *Milt.* 2 : 39 •

————'s ale, pure element, *Prior* 2 : 246

Adder, wifdom of,   *Milt.* 3 : 38

Adderbury, on lying in Rochefter's bed there, *Pope* 1 : 358

Addifon, prologue to Tender Hufband, *Add.* 216

———— epilogue to Britifh Enchanters, 218

———— St. Cecilia,   31, 219

———— an ode,   222, 225

———— an hymn,   223, 207

———— paraphrafe, Pfalm 23d, 229

———— the play-houfe,   230

———— on Lady Manchefter, 234

———— Cato, a tragedy,   251

———— verfes to, on his Cato, 237, feq.

———— Campaign,   51

———— to Kneller,   213

———— prologue to Phaedra, 215

———— tranflation of Cowley's epitaph, 68

———— Englifh poets,   34

        Addifon

INDEX

Addiſon to Burnet,   96
——— tranſlation from Horace,   100
——— letter to Halifax,   40
——— eſſay on Georgics,   200
——— fourth Georgic,   17
——— tranſlations from Ovid,   125
——— Latin poems of,   69
——— on peace reſtored,   72
——— deſcription of Barometer,   78
——— battle of Pygmies and Cranes,   81
——— reſurrection,   86
——— bowling-green,   82
——— to Dr. Hannes,   93
——— puppet-ſhew,   85
——— to his Majeſty,   9
——— to Somers,   7
——— to Montague,   71
——— to Dryden,   5
——— Milton imitated,   46
——— no whiter page remains than his,   Pope 2 : 225
——— from the taſte obſcene reclaims our youth, Pope 2 : 225
——— ſets the paſſions on the ſide of truth,   Pope 2 : 225
——— pours each human virtue in the heart,   Pope 2 : 225
——— on death of,   Tick. 187
——— gone for ever, take this long adieu,   Tick. 188
——— turn from ill, a frail and feeble heart,   Tick. 189
——— a candid cenſor and a friend ſevere,   Tick. 190
——— verſes to,   Som. 174
——— Ardenna's groves ſhall boaſt,   Som. 176
——— letter on his death,   Young 1 : 239

Addison early bloom'd amid the learned train, *Young* 1 : 239

Adieu to all but Gay alone, *Pope* 1 : 356

———— I bid to all the sex of queens, *Aken.* 348

Admiral, Waller, to, *Wall.* 44

Admire we then the trade of fools for gold ? *Pope* 2 : 204

Adolphus, with imperial splendor gay, *Hughes* 41

Adonis, now my sorrow, once my pleasure, *Hughes* 168

———— transform'd, arose a flower, *Hughes* 169

———— and, smiling, grac'd the plain, *Hughes* 169

Adrastus king of Argos, *Pope* 1 : 305

———— descent of, *Pope* 1 : 305

Adrian to his soul, imitated, *Prior* 1 : 157

Adriel, character of, *Dry.* 1 : 154

Adventurous Muse, *Watts* 206

Adverse winds untied by Ulysses' companions, *Pope od.* 3 : 252

Adversity, hymn to, *Gray* 335

———————— tamer of the human breast, *Gray* 335

———————— virtue, stern, rugged nurse of, *Gray* 335

———————— leaves us leisure to be good, *Gray* 335

———————— severe instructor, but the best, *Som.* 330

———————— right reason's ever faithful friend, *Som.* 330

———————— to thee our haughty passions bend, *Som.* 330

———————— hardens some souls, *Dry.* 2 : 23

———————— fiery trials of, *Cow.* 1 : 191

Advice, progress of, *Shen.* 172

———— thrown away on avarice, *Som.* 323

———— ratify the best for public good, *Pope il.* 1 : 269

Adulterate Christs already rise, *Pom.* 346

Adultery rampant, *Resc.* 256

Aerial knights and combats in the skies, *Tick.* 131

Ægis,

Ægis, Jove's immortal shield,   *Pope il.* 1: 84

———— —— enormous shield,   *Pope il.* 2: 76

Ægypt. See Egypt.

Æneas, the draught of Peleus' and Laertes' son,   *Pitt* 311

———— Ulysses' conduct and Achilles' fire,   *Pitt* 311

———— brings the Dardans,   *Pope il.* 1: 100

———— delivered by Venus,   *Pope il.* 1: 164

———— wound of, cured,   *Pope il.* 1: 169

———— warned by Hector to escape,   *Dry.* 5: 363

———— carries off his father,   *Dry.* 5: 383

———— leads Ascanius in his hand,   *Dry.* 5: 383

———— driven on Sicily,   *Dry.* 6: 72

———— hospitably received,   *Dry.* 6: 73

———— celebrates funeral games,   *Dry.* 6: 74

———— builds a city for the aged,   *Dry.* 6: 104

———— sails for Italy,   *Dry.* 6: 109

———— arrives at an African port,   *Dry.* 5: 319

———— entertained by Dido,   *Dry.* 5: 341

———— relates his adventures,   350

———— voyage to Thrace,   *Dry.* 6: 2

———— —— to Delos,   *Dry.* 6: 5

———— consults the oracle,   *Dry.* 6: 6

———— settles in Crete,   *Dry.* 6: 8

———— sails for Italy,   *Dry.* 6: 10

———— lands in Sicily,   *Dry.* 6: 27

———— entertained by Helenus,   *Dry.* 6: 17

———— warned to quit Carthage,   *Dry.* 6: 47

———— prepares for his voyage,   *Dry.* 6: 50

———— voyage of continued,   *Garth* 124

———— descent to hell,   *Garth* 125

                   Æneas,

Æneas, arrival of in Italy,   *Garth* 136

———— arrives at Cumae,   *Dry.* 6 : 112

———— consults the Sibyl,   *Dry.* 6 : 116

———— lands at the mouth of the Tiber,   *Dry.* 6 : 158

———— plucks off the golden bow,   *Dry.* 6 : 123

———— ferried over Styx,   *Dry.* 6 : 131

———— descendants pass in review,   *Dry.* 6 : 147

———— begs succours of Evander,   *Dry.* 6 : 202

———— received kindly,   *Dry.* 6 : 202

———— shield of,   *Dry.* 6 : 224

———— on, shall devolve the reign,   *Pope il.* 2 : 225

———— rescued by Neptune,   *Pope il.* 2 : 225

———— secure, no Grecian force transcends his own,   *ib.* 225

———— erects a trophy,   *Dry.* 7 : 1

———— buries his slain companions,   *Dry.* 7 : 2

———— deplores Pallas' death,   *Dry.* 7 : 3

———— sends home Pallas' body,   *Dry.* 7 : 4

———— bids him the last farewel,   *Dry.* 7 : 6

———— grants a truce for burying the dead,   *Dry.* 7 : 7

———— prayer of,   *Dry.* 7 : 55

———— and Turnus, like two bulls,   *Dry.* 7 : 82

———— wounded,   *Dry.* 7 : 63

———— leaves the field,   *Dry.* 7 : 65

———— deification of,   *Garth* 145

———— whether ever in Italy?   *Dry.* 5 : 228

Æneid, design of,   *Prior* 2 : 93

———— part of first translated,   *Pitt* 272

Æneis of Virgil,   *Dry.* 5 : 312

Æolia, a floating isle,   *Pope od.* 3 : 351

    where sons their sisters wed,   *Pope od.* 3 : 353

           Æolia,

Æolia, native region of storms, *Pitt* 275

Æolus, sovereign of the winds, *Pitt* 275

——— gives prosperous winds, *Pope od.* 3: 251

——— binds the adverse in bags, *Pope od.* 3: 251

——— tyrant of the wind, *Pope od.* 3: 251

——— harp of, *Thom.* 1: 212

———'s harp, ode on, *Thom.* 2: 192

Æsacus turned to a cormorant, *Dry.* 4: 69

Æschylus built a stage, *Rosc.* 269

——— devised a mask and theatre, *Dry.* 1: 278

——— first trod the stage, *Dry.* 2: 239

Æsculapius, birth of, *Add.* 128

Æther, stars and sun how sustained in, *Black.* 142

Ætherial soul, nor can death control, *Prior* 2: 16

Æthon, steed of state, *Dry.* 7: 8

Ætna described, *Add.* 14, 46

—— described, *Dry.* 6: 27

—— nurse of endless frost, *West* 195

—— the pillar'd prop of heaven, *West* 195

—— from whose caverns rise fountains of fire, *West* 195

—— abode of the Cyclops, *Dry.* 6: 214

—— torch of Sicily, *Watts* 70

—— unmelted snow on, *Wall.* 154

—— was then heard to roar, *Rowe L.* 73

Ætolia first threw off the yoke of kings, *Aken.* 168

——— to commerce and to arms devoted, *Aken.* 168

Affect not any thing in nature's spite, *Cng.* 144

Affectation fades the brightest form, *Young* 1: 148

——— faints into airs, and languishes with pride, *Pope* 1: 145

——— walks, for *graceful ease*, *Aken.* 346

Affectations

Affectations quite reverse the soul,   *Pope* 2 : 97

Affection is the chain of grateful minds,   *Hughes* 274

———— ties of, double all our joys,   *Aken.* 201

———— half disarms our pains,   *Aken.* 201

———— frail! train'd up by sense,   *Young* 3 : 92

Affections, born of earth, decay,   *Parn.* 105

Affidavit-customers, letting out ears to,   *Butl.* 2 : 107

Affliction is the good man's shining scene,   *Young* 3 : 15

———— purifies the mind,   *Sav.* 60

———— strong, gives the feeble force,   *Pope il.* 2 : 280

———— feel not in thy fears,   *Gay* 2 : 93

———— never pleads in vain,   *Pope od.* 3 : 204

Afflictions, soul to be great in,   *Yal.* 352

———— throw out virtues into practice,   *Add.* 284

———— mercies in disguise,   *Mall.* 270

———— lighter grow by chat,   *Gay* 2 : 175

———— to try our virtue, or for punishment,   *Pom.* 267

———— make us humble,   *Pom.* 267

———— and make us wise,   *Pom.* 267

———— of a friend,   *Watts* 211

Afflictive birch, cursed by idle youth, distils a liquor, *Phil.* 68

Agamemnon, king of men,   *Pope il.* 1, 69

———— king of kings,   *Pope il.* 1 : 71

———— tries what the Greeks may dare,   *Pope il.* 1. 70

———— majestically tall, like some proud bull,   *ib.* 86

———— his strength like Neptune, like Mars his mien, *ib.*

———— armed, leads to battle,   *Pope il.* 1 : 321

———— armour of, described,   *Pope il.* 1 : 322, seq.

———— bears all before him,   *Pope il.* 1 : 328

———— distinguishes himself as a general, *Pope il.* 1 : 136

Agamemnon

Agamemnon reviews the troops,   *Pope il.* 1 : 136

————— exhorts and reproves,   *Pope il.* 1 : 140

————— diftrefs of, on Achilles' refufal,   *Pope il.* 1 : 295

————— repairs to Neftor,   *Pope il.* 1 : 297

————— propofes to return to Greece,   *Pope il.* 1 : 266

————— ——— rich prefents for Achilles, *Pope il.* 1 : 270

————— ——— - to efcape by night,   *Pope il.* 2 : 44

————— entertains the chiefs,   *Pope il.* 1 : 83

————— death of,   *Pope od.* 3 : 88, 129

————— prologue to,   *Mall.* 176

Age has pains to footh,   *Young* 3 : 2

—— but taftes of pleafures,   *Dry.* 2 : 146

—— drops, like ripe fruit,   *Den.* 135

—— joys of,   *Den.* 142

—— effects of,   *Milt.* 2 : 103

—— miferies of,   *Den.* 113

—— impairs ftrength,   *Den.* 114

————— ——— underftanding,   *Den.* 119

—— weakens fenfe of pleafure,   *Den.* 125

—— the glory of, to wifh to die,   *Young* 2 : 118

Age, life's winter,   *Mall.* 158

—— alas ! who muft not yield to ?   *Pope il.* 2 : 313

—— herfelf, the foreft ill.   *Prior* 2 : 170

—— man wretched victim of,   *Prior* 2 : 171

—— advances venerably wife,   *Pope il.* 1 : 110

—— turns on all hands its difcerning eyes, *Pope il.* 1 : 110

—— fmooths our path to prudence,   *Young* 3 : 45

—— is ready to furmife,   *Pope od.* 4 : 63

—— on the verge of,   *Pope od.* 4 : 59.

—— fit to counfel or command,   *Rowe L.* 110.

Age is sacred,   *Pope od.* 4 : 220

—— steals the mimic forms and characters away, *Hughes* 209

—— bent me with his iron hand,   *Ham.* 210

—— benumbs my powers,   *Young* 2 : 83

—— steals on us unaware,   *Prior* 2 : 9

—— is twilight to the night of fate,   *Para.* 103

—— to sorrows oft the great betrays,   *Rowe L.* 330

—— regarded ever by the just and sage,   *Pope od.* 3 : 83

—— garrulous recounts the feats of youth,   *Thom.* 1 : 148

—— always narrative,   *Dry.* 7 : 119

—— Anacreontic,   *Cow.* 1 : 143

—— antiperistasis of,   *Cow.* 1 : 151

—— arts of,   *Den.* 112

—— on age improves,   *Collins* 275

Aged turn children,   *Cow.* 2 : 371

—— mendicant in tattered weeds,   *Pope od.* 4 : 80

Agenor makes a stand against Achilles,   *Pope il.* 2 : 258

—— rescued by Apollo,   *Pope il.* 2 : 258

Ages of the world described,   *Cong.* 22

—— of the world,   *Dry.* 3 : 301

Agesidamus of Locris gained victory at the caestus, *West* 179

Agib and Secander, the fugitives,   *Collins* 242

Agincourt strewed with Gallic corps,   *Add.* 11

—— has raised Henry's name,   *Hughes* 51

Agis, not the last of Spartan names,   *Pope* 1 : 208

Aglauros, story of,   *Add.* 135

Agriculture, origin of,   *Dry.* 5 : 99

—— tools of,   *Dry.* 5 : 100

—— seasons of,   *Dry.* 5 : 101

—— fair queen of arts,   *Thom.* 1 : 231

Agriculture,

Agriculture,   *Cow.* 2 : 297
———— pleafures of,   *Cow.* 2 : 298
———— utility of,   *Cow.* 2 : 296
———— neceffity of,   *Cow.* 2 : 299
———— innocence of,   *Cow.* 2 : 300
———— exhibits noble fcenes,   *Cow.* 2 : 301
———— antiquity of,   *Cow.* 2 : 302
———— with her fweet innocence we find,   *Thom.* 1 : 231
Agrigentum built,   *Cow.* 2 : 8
Agrippa held fcience vain,   *Butl.* 1 : 247
Ah willow, fong,   *Rowe L.* 65
Ajax, chofen by lot to combat Hector,   *Pope il.* 1 : 224
—— in all the toils of battle bred,   *Pope il.* 1 : 225
—— from Salamis drew his birth,   *Pope il.* 1 : 225
—— bulwark of the Grecian band,   *Pope il.* 1 : 225
—— fhield of, of feven-fold hides,   *Pope il.* 1 : 226
—— next in ftature, next in fame, to Peleus' fon,   *ib.* 2 : 148
—— tower-like,   *Pope il.* 2 : 316
—— himfelf a hoft,   *Pope il.* 1 : 115
—— alone withftands the Trojans,   *Pope il.* 1 : 343
—— retires flowly,   *Pope il.* 1 : 343
—— ftrikes Hector to the ground,   *Pope il.* 2 : 57
—— ftands the centre and the foul of all,   *Pope il.* 2 : 150
—— paragoned to none but Achilles,   *Fent.* 265
—— darling hope of all our hoft,   *Fent.* 268
—— in vain abfconded in a flower,   *Prior* 2 : 201
—— and Ulyffes, fpeeches of,   *Dry.* 4 : 102
—— death of,   *Dry.* 4 : 122
—— fullen ftalks away,   *Pope od.* 3 : 300
—— Oileus' valiant fon,   *Pope il.* 1 : 88

Ajax, fwift in purfuit, and active in the fight, *Pope il.* 1 : 88

—— in forty veffels cuts the liquid tide, *Pope il.* 1 : 88

——, Oïlean, in the race renowned, *Broome* 72

—— the lefs, fwifteft in the race, *Pope il.* 2 : 61

—— each, thunderbolts of war, *Pope il.* 1 : 242

Aikman, verfes on death of, *Thom.* 2 : 177

—— and fon, epitaph on, *Mall.* 157

—— —— —— dear to the wife and good, *Mall.* 157

Air, wifdom difcovered in, *Black.* 88

—— properties of, *Black.* 88

—— ufes of, *Black.* 88

—— vapours in, *Black.* 31

—— Air grafping at ! for what has earth befide ? *Young* 2 ; 66

Airy fhapes, once human bodies, *Dry.* 3 : 185

—— terrours fable every dream, *Pope od.* 4 : 164

Akenfide, pleafures of the imagination, *Aken.* 12—181

—— —— odes, 189—293

—— —— hymn to the Naiads, 299

—— —— infcriptions, 325—332

—— —— an epiftle to Curio, 333

—— —— Love, an elegy, 345

—— —— a Britifh philippic, 350

—— —— hymn to fcience, 356

—— —— ode for the winter-folftice, 361

A la mode, *Fent.* 276

Alafter, his youth and beauty plead in vain, *Pope il.* 2 : 231

—— —— unhappy boy ! no prayer avails, *Pope il.* 2 : 231

Albino, *A. Phil.* 306

—— —— his death we yearly mourn, *A. Phil.* 307

—— —— pledge of peaceful times, *A. Phil.* 308

Albino,

Albino, fair boaſt of this fair iſland, *A. Phil.* 308

———— the flowery turf lie light upon thy breaſt, *A. Phil.* 309

————lives, and will for ever live, *A. Phil.* 310

Albion ſhall hold the rightful ſcale, *Fent.* 199

———— briſtul ſeat of peace, *Phil.* 22

———— learn from others' mſeries to prize thy welfare, *Phil.* 22

———— rich queen of miſts and fogs, *Dyer* 35

———— happy, if thy ſons would know their happineſs, *Dye* 36

———— cliffs of, whitening to the view, *Tick.* 121

———— ſeveral places, famous for wool, *Dyer,* 70

Albula, ancient name of Tiber, *Dry.* 6 : 210

Alcaeus, Leſbian Patriot, *Aken.* 227

———— boldly ſung, *Swift* 2 : 317

———— for ſtrength renowned, *Fent.* 278

———— more ſublimely ſings, *Pope* 1 : 166

Alcides ſtooping, reſts on his club, *Pope* 1 : 205

———— Churchill of the ſkies, *Fent.* 206

Alcinous, Jove's delegate of empire, *Fent.* 265

———— entertains Ulyſſes with games, *Pope od.* 3 : 207

———— palace and gardens deſcribed, *Pope od.* 3 : 189

———— in a council, conveys Ulyſſes home, *Pope od.* 3 : 204

———— feaſts him, *Pope od.* 3 : 205

———— let fame be his; my country mine, *Pope od.* 3 : 193

Alcmena bore to Jove Alcides, *Fent.* 257

Aldrich, generous thoughts inſtils, *Phil.* 54

Ale, praiſe of, *Som.* 127

Alecto ſows ſeeds of diſcord, *Dry.* 6 : 182

Alexander, a proſperous robber, *Rowe L.* 434

———— the world too narrow for, *Butl.* 1 : 137

———— ſlighted beauties, *Milt.* 2 : 169

Alexander, feast of,	Dry. 2 : 274
———— feast of,	Hughes 174
Alexandria fired,	Rowe L. 457
Alexis,	{ Dry. 5 : 26
	{ Hughes 117
——— mourning muse of,	Cong. 5
Alfred the great,	Them. 2 : 105
——— father of the English name,	Aken. 215
——— ode on Masque of,	Mall. 192
Allan is now, what Homer was before,	Som. 219
All born to die,	A. Phil. 385
All-chearing Health, goddess rosy-fair,	Mall. 170
All-conquering Death, all victims to,	Pope il. 2 : 174
——— ———— gold exerts its power,	Gay 1 : 33
All-consuming care destroys the strength,	Pope od. 3 : 208
All cry and no wool,	Butl. 1 : 43
——— but little wool,	King 210
Allegorical expression, origin of,	Collins 302
———— imagery, what,	Collins 302
Allegories, long-spun fustiom grow,	Add. 35
Alley, pleasure of walking in,	Gay 1 : 120
——— not to be walked in by night,	Gay 1 : 136
Alliance with a tyrant race I hate,	Pope il. 1 : 282
All over love,	Cow. 1 : 253
All-seeing eye, at one regard,	Pope il. 2 : 159
All things below, uncertain stand,	Buck. 16
Alma,	Prior 2 : 31
——— in verse, in prose the mind,	Prior 2 : 32
——— can ne'er decay nor die,	Prior 2 : 39
all in all, throughout the body,	Prior 2 : 39
	Alma

Alma fits on her throne, the brain,	*Prior* 2 : 39
—— in either cafe fhe is extended,	*Prior* 2 : 34
—— upwards foars and down drops clay,	*Prior* 2 : 85
Almanac well-willer,	*But'.* 1 : 232
Almanara's fatal plain,	*Tick.* 135
Almanfor's rage, the people's not the writer's fin,	*Lanf.* 234
Almighty is the God of gods,	*Pope il.* 1 : 239
—— feat of,	*Cow.* 2 : 82
—— painter glows in every line,	*Som.* 225
—— Raphael's defign how mean compared,	*Som.* 225
—— and Titian's colouring,	*Som.* 225
Almighty power! our guide in counfel,	*Young* 3 : 231
—— and our ftrength in fight,	*Young* 3 : 231
—— at nature's helm on high,	*Young* 3 : 231
—— 'tis thine from death to free,	*Young* 3 : 232
Alms, vehicles of prayer,	*Dry.* 2 : 56
Alpha mark of approbation,	*Cow.* 1 : 54
—— and omega, firft and laft,	*Prior* 2 : 124
Alpheus, of rivers the pride,	*A. Phil.* 389
—— deck'd with olives flows,	*Weft* 136
—— mixes with Arethufa,	*Dry.* 6 : 33
—— unmixt, to his Sicilian river glides,	*Pope* 1 : 296
—— feeks, with pace, the lov'd Sicilian fhores,	*Hughes* 29
Alfop never but like Horace jokes,	*Pope* 1 : 233
Altar raifed to difeafe,	*Garth* 40
—— to love of French romances built,	*Pope* 1 : 133
Altis, facred grove of Olympic Jove,	*Weft* 219
Alva, fiery duke, Philip's fcourge of vengeance rofe,	*Hughes* 42
—— with flames of inquifition rofe from hell,	*Hughes* 42
Amaryllis,	*Dry.* 4 : 299

Amaryllis

Amaryllis, tears for,   *Cong.* 93

Amata inspired by Alecto opposes *Æneas,*   *Dry.* 6 : 173

———— diffuades Turnus from combat,   *Dry.* 7 : 49

———— hangs herself,   *Dry.* 7 : 76

Amazement chain'd the tongue,   *Pope od.* 4 : 172

Ambigue to compose,   *King* 214

Ambiguities, the laft excellence of a wit,   *Young* 1 : 74

Ambition, ever foaring high,   *Buck.* 89

———— gigantic phantom of the brain,   *A. Phil.* 358

———— curs'd, awakes the world to war and ruin, *Cong.* 61

———— fhall the guilty brothers fire,   *Gay* 1 : 330

———— and Thebes' embroil in war,   *Gay* 1 : 330

———— reftlefs,   *Ot.* 7.

———— proud has no bounds,   *Dry.* 3 : 127

———— knows no bounds,   *Rowe L.* 123

———— by mothers curft,   *Tick.* 103

———— to thee we owe all the great ills,   *Tick.* 102

———— favage Lord of an unpeopled land,   *Tick.* 103

———— fhuts the door againft content,   *Young* 2 : 122

———— weds a toil, a tempeft, in her ftead, *Young* 2 : 122

———— world-deftroying,   *Gay* 2 : 44

———— what havock it makes,   *Add.* 251

———— long has laid the fair creation wafte, *Hughes* 50

———— wild wings bold defire,   *Pope ed.* 3 : 119

———— fons of, mere children all,   *Sav.* 107

———— who hunt for toys,   *Sav.* 107

———— never gains its end,   *Gay* 2 : 186

———— found the vanity of column and buft, *Pope* 2 : 145

———— meannefs of,   *Cow.* 2 : 263

— mean, ignoble pride !   *Young* 3 : 226

Ambition

Ambition makes my little less,   Young 2 : 64

————— feeds on trath, and loaths a feast,   Young 1 : 103

————— fires ambition, ·   Young 2 : 96

————— charms, ev'n in age, ·   A. Phil. 333

————— should teach solitude,   Cow. 2 : 285

————— powerful source of good or ill !   Young 2 : 143

————— can destroy or save,   Pope 2 : 49

————— makes a patriot, as it makes a knave, Pope 2 : 49

————— truly great of virtuous praise,   Young 2 : 15

————— ends in public good, ·.   Cong. 4

————— avarice, two Demons,   Young 2 : 137

————— burn mankind,   Young 2 : 137

————— envy, faction's viperous brood,   West 312

————— and revenge have certain speed,   Prior 2 : 182

————'s aims, how endless,   Swift 2 : 195

Ambitious man, a slave,   Cow. 2 : 273

Ambrose Philips is preferr'd for wit, ·   Pope 3 : 204

Amiel, character of,   Dry. 1 : 155

Ammunition, to preach the faith with, ·   Butl. 2 : 74

Amoret, Waller to, ·   Wall. 60, 63

—————   Cong. 102

————— careless with artful care, ·   Cong. 102

Amorous old man, ·   Mall. 180

————— teazing ghost of the departed man, Mall. 180

Amphiaraus, skill'd in fate, and dark futurity,   Pope 1 : 306

————— immortal name !   Pope od. 4 : 56

Amphimachus and Naustes the Carians guide, Pope il. 1 : 102

————— the Vain, trick'd with gold,   Pope il. 1 : 102

Amphion strikes the lyre, behold a Thebes aspire, Pope 1 : 205

Amphitheatre described,   Dyer 12

   Amphitheatre,

Amphitheatre, barbarous use of,   Dyer 12

Amphius and Adrastus come from Apæsus,   Pope il. 1 : 100

———————————— rush to war and perish'd on the plain, ib. 100

Amri, character of,   Dry. 1 : 194

Amsanctus, a lake,   Dry. 6 : 183

Amuse, innocently to, is doing some service,   West 129

Amyntas, tears for,   Cong. 93

Amyntor and Theodora,   Mall. 235

———————— recovered from drowning,   Mall. 245

Anacreon, gay Anacreon, drunken priest,   Swift 2 : 317

———————— commended,   Cow. 1 : 151

———————— choaked by a grape-stone,   Cow. 1 : 153

———————— odes of,   Broome 162—176

———————— on his lute,   A. Phil. 396

———————— on women,   A. Phil. 396

———————— on love,   A. Phil. 397

———————— ode 3,   Higgons 56

———————— imitation of,   Buck. 42

———————— imitated,   Prior 1 : 83

———————— smiles and sings,   Aken. 226

———————— elegy on,   Cow. 1 : 150

Anacreontic,   Shen. 112

—————————————   Parn. 16, 19

—————————————   Som. 240

Anacreontics,   Cow. 1 : 139

Analogy, man's surest guide below,   Young 2 : 154

Analytic, skilled, in,   Buck. 1 : 7

Anana, pride of vegetable life,   Thom. 1 : 67

Anaphora. See Repetition.

           headlong steep of,   Dry. 1 : 213

                                                         Anarchy,

Anarchy, brought in by Puritans, — *Cow.* 1 : 352

Anaxagoras first afferted an eternal mind, *Black.* 6

———— condemned for irreligion, *Black* 6

Anceftors' difgrace, with virtuous acts efface, *Pope* 1 : 323

Anchifes prefages Iulus' greatnefs, *Dry.* 5 : 382

———— inftructs his fon, *Dry.* 6 : 145

———— fhews him a race of heroes, *Dry.* 147

———— dies, *Dry.* 6 : 33

Ancient-bards, fome catch raptures from, *Pitt* 351

———— fatire of Romans, what, *Dry.* 7 : 154

———— ways, ingulph'd, are feen no more, *Thom.* 2 : 22

———— words make a poem venerably great, *Smith* 194

Ancients, immortal heirs of univerfal praife, *Pope* 1 : 99

———— to borrow from by fair allufion, *Pitt* 371

———— employed much time on their works, *Pope* 1 : 7

———— explore with a watchful eye, *Pitt* 308

———— read and meditate, *Pitt* 368

———— their beft expreffions claim our care, *Pitt* 369

———— our ftyle beft form'd on them, *Pitt* 369

Ancilia, origin of, *Rowe L.* 397

Andromache, ftory of, *Dry.* 6 : 16

———— lamentation over Hector, *Cong.* 39

———— thy griefs 1 dread, *Pope il.* 1 : 210

———— Aëtion's wealthy heir, *Pope il.* 1 : 207

Andronicus, firft author of plays at Rome, *Dry.* 7 : 151

Angel fall'n, degenerates to a fiend, *Broome* 42

———— in the fun defcribed, *Milt.* 1 : 94

———— called Uriel, *Milt.* 1 : 94

———— deceived, *Milt.* 1 : 96

Angels cloathed with thickened air, *Cow.* 2 : 130

Angels

..... upon the lower faculties of sense,   *Milt.* 1 : 252

..... move swift as lightning,   *Cow.* 2 : 85

———— clad with eternal youth,   *Pom.* 351

——— song of,   *Watts* 103

—— proclaim Christ's birth,   *Milt.* 2 : 151

—— we rise, who mortals dy'd,   *Broome* 41

———— fall of,   *Milt.* 1 : 159, 161

———— food of,   *M lt.* 1 : 160

———— bad, their number,   *Milt.* 1 : 16, 22

———— erazed from book of life,   *Milt.* 1 : 17

Anger transforms manhood to beast,   *King* 327

——— pain of, punishes the fault,   *Pope od.* 4 : 91

——— how expressed,   *Waller* 77

——— mighty, what can it not do,   *Swift* 2 : 32

——— it makes the weak the strong pursue,   *Swift* 2 : 32

——— frantic, prone to wild extremes,   *Broome* 128

————— heaven blafphemes,   *Broome* 128

——— rush'd, his eyes on fire,   *Collins* 271

Angling,   *Som.* 154

Angry lovers mean not half they fay,   *Ham.* 211

Animalcule,   *Sav.* 132

Animals brought to Adam, to name,   *Milt.* 1 : 242

——— whipp'd tops,   *Butl.* 1 : 49

——— bandy'd balls,   *Butl.* 1 : 49

——— mercy to,   *Dyer* 57

Anna faid, let there be union,   *Phil.* 82

—— commanded, and Marlborough fought,   *Prior* 1 : 198

—— no brighter name adorns the lift of fame,   *Parn* 264

—— reftrains the rage of kings,   *Phil* 78

—— only fupports juftice oppreff'd,   *Phil.* 78

Anna

Anna fat arbitrefs of Europe's fate,   *Young* 3 : 153

—— filent, nor longer awful to be feen,   *Young* 3 : 152

Anne fhall rival great Eliza's reign,   *Hughes* 54

—— fhall fupply the Thunderer's place,   *Hughes* 54

Annals of a female day,   *Swift* 2 : 72

Annihilation, horrors of,   *Young* 2 : 195

Annus Mirabilis,   *Dry.* 1 : 61

Another-gates adventure,   *Butl.* 1 : 115

Anfon, voyage of,   *Dyer* 125

—— fuccefs againft the Spaniards,   *Dyer* 126

—— on death of lady,   *Mall.* 329

—— unwarp'd by folly, and by vice unftain'd, *Mall.* 331

Anfwer to a friend's queftion,   *Swift* 2 : 366

Ant,   *Watts* 364

—— teaches to provide againft want,   *Dry.* 7 : 268

—— and Fly,   *Som.* 265

Antaeus, ftory of,   *Rowe L.* 193

——, vanquifh'd by Hercules,   *Rowe L.* 194

Antalcidas gave up the Afiatic Greeks to Perfia, *Thom.* 2 : 50

Antenor propofes the reftitution of Helen,   *Pope il.* 1 : 231

Anti-chrift, a fiend's venom in an Angel's mien, *Pom.* 347

Anticlea, fhade of appears,   *Pope od.* 3 : 280

Antidote in female caprice in what it lies,   *Young* 1 : 132

Antilochus fent with the news of Patroclus, *Pope il.* 2 : 163

—— mourns the warriour, with a warriour's heart, *ib.* 170

—— the flaughter led,   *Pope il.* 1 : 144

—— by fwarthy Memnon flain,   *Pope od.* 3 : 113

—— a name not unrecorded in the rolls of fame, *ib.* 114

Ant.monial cups, their force to wine for ever impart, *Black.* 136

Antinous, the firft who by Ulyffes' arrow dy'd, *Pope od.* 4 : 252

Antinous, fon of Eupithes,   *Pope od.* 4 : 252

Antiope, daughter of Afopus,   *Fent.* 257

——— had Amphion and Zethus by Jove,   *Fent.* 257

Antipathies, devotion lies in,   *Butl.* 1 : 16

Antipathy mutual of plants,   *Cow.* 2 : 378

Antiquated words why revived,   ·   *Dry.* 7 : 94, 118

——— words fparingly to be ufed,   *Pitt.* 373

Antiftrophe, what,   ·   ·   *Cong.* 153

——— what,   *Weft* 117

Antonius, fpite of his age and eloquence, bled,   *Rowe L.* 88

Antony, to keep the fair, gave the world,   *Prior* 2 : 48

Anubis, dog, flatterer for his food,   *Prior* 2 : 160

Anxious jealoufy's corroding fmart,   *Prior* 1 : 242

Aonian train by the Medici reftor'd,   *Pitt* 314

Apathy let Stoics boaft,   *Pope* 2 : 45

Apelles, a painter of Co,   *Prior* 2 : 9

——— drawing Venus,   *Cow.* 1 : 164

——— firft brought Venus to our view,   *King* 325

Apennine, long-extended mountain,   *Rowe L.* 102

——— rich in the treafure of his watery ftores, *Rowe L.* 102

——— far as Hefperia's limits, runs his mighty mafs, *ib.* 103

Apes are ever walking upon two,   *Young* 1 : 93

——— like fools purfuing what nature has deny'd, *Young* 1 : 93

Apicius, two of that name,   *King* 228

——— of Lifter,   *King* 226

Apocryphal bigots,   *Butl.* 2 : 35

Apollo, far-fhooting king,   *Tick.* 181

——— making love,   *Tick.* 146

——— god of fweet fong and infpirer of lays,   *Tick.* 146

——— *eternal charms* his youthful cheeks diffufe, *Pitt* 201

                                                  Apollo,

Apollo, his tresses dropping with ambrosial dews, *Pitt* 201

———— pale death before him flies, *Pitt* 201

———— gave wit, to scandal prone, *Parn.* 7

———— animates the Trojans, *Pope il.* 1 : 146

———— and Daphne, *Hughes* 147, 217

———— Anacreon to, *Broome* 174

———— laurel, lyre and Delphic song belong to, *Broome* 175

———— hymn to, { *Broome* 199
{ *Swift* 2 : 243

———— to the Dean, *Swift* 1 : 183

———— edict of, *Swift* 2 : 367

———— out-witted, *Swift* 1 : 39

———— that sneaking, whey-fac'd god, *Prior* 1 : 34

———— of Belvidere, *Thom.* 2 : 86

————'s vengeance for his injur'd priest, *Pope il.* 1 : 41

Apollonius Rhodius, translations from, *West* 221

Apology, &c. *Swift* 2 : 355

———— for an unseasonable surprize, *Lanf.* 160

Apoplex of grief, *Dry.* 2 : 105

Apostate Angels their number, *Milt.* 1 : 164

Apostles, fishermen, *Milt.* 2 : 164

Apostrophe, address to inanimate things, *Pitt* 365

Apparel costly, let the fair one fly, *Cong.* 118

———— when more becoming, are less dear, *Cong.* 118

Apparition, a true story of, *Gay* 2 : 12

Appetite over-rules reason, *Milt.* 2 : 40

Appetites innocent, are nature's laws, *Buck.* 91

———— are tost from vice to vice, *Pope od.* 4 : 168

Appius consults the oracle of Delphos, *Rowe L.* 209

Applause, of all, be *fondest of your own*, *Young* 1 : 136

Applause,

Applause, not the ultimate end,   Dry. 9 : 313

———— the cares of dress impart,   Pope od. 3 : 170

Apple-grafts in crab-tree succeed well,   Phil. 43

Apple-husks to be laid at the roots of trees,   Phil. 64

Apples, different species of,   Phil. 49

Approbation strikes the string of joy,   Young 2 : 216

Apuleius, transformation of,   Garth 138

April awakes the blossoms and the breathing flowers, Hughes 247

———— new creates the fragrant year,   Hughes 247

———— poetry, what,   Dry. 7 : 132

Aqueducts described,   Dyer 16

———— musically falling,   Dyer 16

Arabella Fermor, leaving London,   P. urn. 287

Arabia, void of fountain, void of rain,   Broome 17

———— aromatic breathes,   Thom. 2 : 65

Arabian prophet, ignorance enthrones by law,   Pope 3 : 179

Arachne, story of,   Gay 1 : 333

———— durst with Pallas in her art contend,   Gay 1 : 333

Araminta, an elegy,   Gay 1 : 247

Arbitrary sway, poison to the Prince's mind,   Prior 2 : 190

———— O savage lust,   Hughes 50

———— insatiate fury,   Hughes 50

Arbour described,   Dry. 3 : 169, seq.

Arbuthnot knows his art, but not his trade,   Swift 1 : 149

Arbutus,   Mils. 3 : 112

Arcadia, kingdom of Shepherds,   Dyer 48

———— now under tyranny,   Dyer 48

Arcadian bands unite in sixty sail,   Pope il. 1 : 91

Architecture, orders of,   Thom. 2 : 48

Arctic continent, view of,   Mall. 205, seq.

  Arctophylax,

Aristophylax, ancestor of Orsin,　Ext. 1 : 56
Ardalio, a player, become a Christian,　Watts 125
Arden, Waller,　84
Ardenna's groves shall boast an Addison,　Som. 176
Areïthous in battle bore an iron mace,　Pope il. 1 : 222
Areopagus, supreme court of judicature,　Them. 2 : 40
Arete, Alcinous' queen,　Pope od. 3 : 187
—— the public wonder and public love,　Pope od. 3 : 188
—— in virtue rich, in blessing others, blest,　Pope od. 3 : 188
Argives in fourscore barks plow the watery way,　Pope il. 1 : 90
—— strip the heroes slain,　Pope il. 2 : 149
Argo, sailing of,　West 223
—— poetic ship,　Cow. 1 : 168
Argos, the fair, for warlike steeds renown'd,　Pope il. 1 : 197
—— thinks on, and dies,　Dry. 6 : 307
Argument none, like matter of fact,　Butl. 1 : 230
Arguments force of, depend on conciseness,　Pope 2 : 26
—— in mood and figure,　Butl. 1 : 147
Argus, eyes of, transplanted to peacock's train,　Dry. 3 : 319
—— the dog, Ulysses knew,　Pope od. 4 : 102
—— and dies with joy,　Pope od. 4 : 104
Argyle, shakes alike the senate and the field,　Pope 2 : 209
Argyripa, built by Diomede,　Dry. 7 : 14
Ariadne sav'd the brave Theseus,　Broome 157
—— and with Theseus fled,　Broome 157
—— now shines a star on high,　Broome 157
Ariadne's clue,　Gay 1 : 114
Ariconium (Hereford) swallowed,　Phil. 39, 40
Ariel, chief of the Sylphs and Sylphids,　Pope 1 : 135
Arion's harp be mine,　Young 1 : 189
. Ariosto

Ariosto without just design, *Dry.* 7 : 115

———— observes no unity of action, *Dry.* 7 : 115

———— style of, luxuriant, *Dry.* 7 : 115

———— adventures, without compass of nature, *Dry.* 7 : 115

Aristaeus, story of, *Dry.* 5 : 190

Aristides, banish'd for being just, *Som.* 170

Aristophanes, too vicious and prophane, *Swift* 1 : 165

Aristotle first gave Poets laws, *Pope* 1 : 118

———— and Machiavel compared, *Cow.* 2 : 255

———— scheme of, *Black.* 159

———— owns no choice, *Black.* 161

———— no artist's hand, *Black.* 161

———— determines all motion from fate, *Black.* 161

———— art, without an artist, maintains, *Black.* 171

Ark of covenant, *Milt.* 2 : 127

—— captured, *Cow.* 2 : 174

—— of Noah, *Milt.* 2 : 109

—— Noah and his sons enter into, *Milt.* 2 : 109

Armies and fleets alone ne'er won the day, *Young* 1 : 255

———— disarmed of aid from him, by whom the feeble stand, *ib.*

Arms alone, the conqueror's due, *Pope il.* 2 : 274

———— for love of arms, inclined to, *Rowe L.* 94

———— law of, bars venomed shot, *Butl.* 1 : 221

———— repel all, who with arms invade, *Cong.* 130

———— by Vulcan are bestow'd, *Pope il.* 2 : 195

———— worthy Achilles, fit to grace a God, *Pope il.* 2 : 195

———— of matchless art, confess the hand divine, *Pope il.* 2 : 196

———— which the father of the fire bestow'd, *Pope il.* 2 : 208

———— forg'd on th' eternal anvil of the gods, *Pope il.* 2 : 208

———— my new-modelled, *Butl.* 1 : 208

Arno,

Arno, the river, which runs by Florence, *Aken.* 90

—— the fertile plain, *Thom.* 2 : 90

Arod, character of, *Dry.* 1 : 178, seq.

Arqueänaffa of Colophos, *Hughes* 183

Array'd in flesh, he foon shall fee that vestment fade, *West* 212

—— at last to earth, the end of all, returned, *West* 212

Arranging an army and feast, equal skill requisite, *King* 185

Arrogance, a crime, *Broome* 13

Arse, to hang, *Butl.* 1 : 127

Arsie-versie fighting, *Butl.* 1 : 130

Arsinoe claims the throne of Egypt, *Rowe L.* 458

—— puts Achillas to death, *Rowe L.* 458

Art, rules of, unhappy to be tied up to, *Butl.* 2 : 243

—— Nature's hand-maid, *Dry.* 1 : 87

—— taught by Nature, *Milt.* 2 : 173

—— may err, but Nature cannot miss, *Dry.* 3 : 154

—— none can equal Nature, *Som.* 274

—— subdues the strong, *Pope od.* 3 : 215

—— supplies, where strength may fail, *Prior* 1 : 145

—— disguised, for Nature to appear, *Dry.* 2 : 128

—— affists, yet must that Art be hid, *Cong.* 120

—— need of, why should your lovers know, *Cong.* 121

—— chief pride of, still to cover Art, *Pitt* 341

—— not diffembled, difgraces, *King* 314

—— to fet off meanest things, *King* 214

—— tir'd without fuccefs, *Dry.* 1 : 304

—— reflected images to Art, *Pope* 2 : 146

—— laft and greateft, that to blot, *Pope* 2 : 228

—— is to pleafe or inform, *Tal.* 378

—— to make and *keep man happy, not to admire*, *Pope* 2 : 203

Art

Art shall be theirs to varnish an offence,   *Pope* 1 : 249

—— after Art goes out, and all is night,   *Pope* 3 : 263

—— and learning cultivate the mind,   *West* 175

——————————— and make the seeds of genius quicker grow, *ib.*

—— and toil give nature value,   *Dyer* 63

—— is vain to move desire,   *Hughes* 145, 227

—— helps a face,   *Cong.* 116

—— of love,
   { *Dry.* 4 : 203
   Tal. 408
   Cong. 111
   King 253

Artemis, the quiver'd huntress,   *Pope il.* 2 : 253

———— queen of woods,   *Pope il.* 2 : 253

———— thy sex's tyrant, with a tiger's heart, *Pope il.* 2 : 233

Artemisia, her voice theatrically loud,   *Pope* 1 : 352

Arteries, structure of,   *Black.* 188

Artful tongue can feign,   *Gay* 1 : 250

Arthur, power of his shield,   *Wall.* 39

———— round table of,   *Butl.* 1 · 22

———— twelve knights of,   *Dry.* 3 : 185

———— knights of, not of round, but gaming-table, *Mall.* 313

———————— fling away time, health, fame,   *Mall.* 313

Articles, which true ? the old, or Burnet's new ? *Pom.* 341

Artificers of death bleed by their own art,   *Dry.* 1 : 159

Arts useful,   *Black.* 95

—— to public virtue handmaids serv'd,   *Thom.* 2 : 47

—— the rich traffic of the soul,   *Young* 3 : 251

—— the secret spoils of peace,   *Dry.* 2 : 95

—— nursed in Greece,   *Dry.* 2 : 127

—— have their empires, their rise and fall,   *Fen.* 239

Arts

Arts polish, to deprave, .   *Mall.* 235

—— procuring wealth,   *Dyer* 99

—— in vain elude impending fate,   *Parn.* 48

—— versed in all, of wily womankind,   *Pope od.* 4 : 240

Aruns, kills Camilla,   *Dry.* 7 : 41

—— killed by Opis,   *Dry.* 43

—— a Tuscan prophet,   *Rowe L.* 75

—— presaging veins and fibres well he knew,   *Rowe L.* 75

Asaph, praise of,   *Dry.* 1 : 194

Albestos found in Euboea,   *Dyer* 70

Ascanius, second hope of Rome,   *Dry.* 7 : 55

Ascarides, two brothers described,   *Garth* 46

Ascaris, speech of,   *Garth* 52

Ashes, lend pomp to, and be vain in show,   *Broome* 124

Asia, birth-place of proud Monarchy,   *West* 260

—— soft climate, form'd to please,   *Rowe L.* 345

Asius Hyrtacides from Practius comes,   *Pope il* 1 : 100

Ask thyself, if all be well within,   *Aken.* 341

Asophicus, victor in the Olympic games,   *West* 186

—— whose speed the wreath for Orchomen obtain'd, *ib.* 188

Aspen leaves, confess the gentlest breeze,   *Gay* 1 : 4

Ass, nightingale of Brutes,   *Swift* 2 : 283

—— should like an Ass be treated,   *Gay* 2 : 170

—— intones to Ass,   *Pope* 3 : 149

Asses, arrogance of,   *Gay* 1 : 111

Ass's zaggs, more fit for the sheers,   *Swift* 2 : 298

Asted, ode in the Park at,   *Hughes* 245

Asteris, a small, but verdant isle,   *Pope od.* 3 : 142

—— with an ample port,   *Pope od.* 3 : 142

Astolfo's voyage, *additional stanzas to,*   *Lytt.* 90

Afton, Sir Willoughby, character of,   *Yal.* 430

——— pompous edifice,   *Yal.* 439

——— juft the proportions, and ftructure bold,   *Yal.* 439

——— great in thyfelf, but in thy founder more,   *Yal.* 439

——— the place, that gave his anceftors a name,   *Yal.* 439

Aftoreth, queen of heaven,   *Milt.* 1 : 19

——— called Aftarte,   *Milt.* 1 : 19

Aftraea, eldeft born of Jove,   *Mall.* 288

——— fick of violence and fraud to heaven fhe flew, *Mall.* 288

——— driven from earth to heaven,   *Wall.* 51

——— how loofely treads the ftage,   *Pope* 2 : 229

Aftronomy, old fyftem of, perplex'd   *Black.* 79

——————————— rear'd with little art,   *Black.* 80

——————————— new, a wifer fcheme,   *Black.* 80

——————————— Tychonic,   *Black.* 80

Aftyanax, the hope of Troy,   *Pope il.* 1 : 206

——— fair as the ftar, that gilds the morn, *Pope il.* 1 : 207

——— fcar'd at the dazling helm and nodding creft, *ib.* 211

Até, Jove's dread daughter,   *Pope il.* 2 : 198

—— fated to infeft the race of mortals,   *Pope il.* 2 : 198

—— prints her footfteps on the heads of men, *Pope il.* 2 : 198

—— inflicting inextricable woes,   *Pope il.* 2 : 198

—— ordain'd with men's contentious race to dwell, *ib.* 2 : 199

Athalia, ambition of,   *Cow.* 2 : 257

Atheift-wretch, all heaven defies,   *Pope il.* 2 : 227

——————— but fhudders, when the thunder flies, *ib.* 2 : 227

——— miftake of,   *Watts* 65

Atheifts, fuch as deny the being of a God,   *Black.* 8

——— fuch as deny his perfections,   *Black.* 8

——— Atheifts in a gown, a fcandal,   *Young* 3 : 202

       Athena,

Athena, War's triumphant maid, *Pope od.* 3 : 90

Athenian fowl, what, and how called, *Pope* 3 : 242

Athenian Society, ode to, *Swift* 1 : 9

———— great unknown and far-exalted men, *Swift* 1 : 11

Athens, with opening streets and shining *Pope od.* 3 : 188

———— sends full fifty ships, *Pope il.* 1 : 89

———— hive of science, *Thom.* 2 : 40

———— between Ilyssus and Cephissus glow'd, *ib.* 2 : 39

———— there a quick, refin'd and humane people *ib.* 2 : 40

———— where free, social life, where order reigns, *ib.* 2 : 40

———— there heroes, sages, wits, shone thick as stars, *ib.* 2 : 42

———— eye of Greece, *Milt.* 2 : 209

———— the pride of Greece, *Thom.* 1 : 168

———— taught the world sciences and arts, *Buck.* 116

———— plague of, *Sprat* 174

———— dismantled by Sparta, *Thom.* 2 : 50

———— restored by Conon, *Thom.* 2 : 50

———— rising near the Pole, *Pope* 1 : 83

A-tilt, to set one's heart, *Butl.* 1 : 194

Atlas described, *Dry.* 6 : 48

——— props the golden spheres, *Broome* 146

——— shook the heavens he bore, *Pope* 1 : 281

——— the minister of state, *Swift* 1 : 68

Atmosphere, sphere of Atoms, *Butl.* 2 : 200

Atoms, how attained their figure and bulk, *Black.* 143

———— why formed they not a rude mass, *Black.* 144

———— deflection of, unaccountable, *Black.* 128

———————— attempted to be explain'd, *Black.* 139

———————————— without directing mind, *Black.* 129

———— impossibility of forming the world by, *Black.* 138

Atoms, why they ſtop in their flight, *Black.* 139

———— dance round the centre, *Prior* 1 : 38

Atoſſa ſcarce once herſelf, by turns all womankind, *Pope* 2 : 109

Attaints ſpiritual, degraded by, *Butl.* 2 : 6

Attellane ſables, what, *Dry.* 7 : 153

Attention what, is now paid to fame or virtue? *Aken.* 351

Atterbury, burying Buckingham, *Prior* 2 : 256

Attornies, hue and cry after, *Swift* 2 : 145

Attraction, a thing unknown, *Black.* 84

Avarice of, *Cow.* 2 : 349

———— ſpecies of, *Cow.* 2 : 349

———— much wanting to, *Cow.* 2 : 350

———— a ſpecies of madneſs, *Cow.* 2 : 351

———— of the Puritans, *Cow.* 1 : 350

———— changed to luxury, *Cow.* 2 : 369

———— that ne'er can reſt, *Gay* 2 : 44

———— inſatiate, no bounds for, *Rowe L.* 409

———— with inſatiate jaws, the boſom tears, *Gay* 2 : 152

———— a collection of all vice, *Som.* 388

———— conſents to ſtarve for gold, *Rowe L.* 165

———— with abundance poor, *King* 375

———— hydropic thirſt, *King* 376

———— triplets on, *Butl.* 2 : 349

———— rarely taints the tuneful mind, *Pope* 2 : 224

———— the worſt is that of ſenſe, *Pope* 1 : 115

Aventinus deſcribed, *Dry.* 6 : 187

Averni, who from Ilium came, *Rowe L.* 67

Avernus deſcribed, *Dry.* 6 : 124

Averſion may be changed to complacency, *Aken.* 86

Aufidus the meeting ocean braves, *Rowe L.* 102

Augury

Augury may lye,   *Rowe L.* 77

Augufta, fair capital of liberty,   *Cong.* 160

———— proud town, nobleft fcene,   *Tick.* 122

———— o'er Thames her fpires their luftre fhed,   *Tick.* 122

———— queen of cities,   *Hughes* 156

———— condole my lofs and weep Devonia's fate, *Hughes* 156

Auguftus, amufement of,   *Caw.* 2 : 341

———— crimes of,   *Dry.* 7 : 188

Aura, come, allay this heat,   *Cong.* 138

——— raifes the jealoufy of Procris,   *Cong.* 139

Aurelius, the Hermit,   *Mall.* 237

Aurora, daughter of the dawn,   *Pope il.* 1 : 239

———— rofe from Tithonus' bed,   *Broome* 107

———— to proclaim the day to gods and men,   *Broome* 107

Aufonius, cento of,   *Dry.* 7 : 145

Auftrian eagle,   *Step.* 264

Author to write all he ought, not all he can,   *Dry.* 3 : 35

———— in the condition of a culprit,   *Prior* 2 : 91

———— upon himfelf,   *Swift* 1 : 93

———— verfes to,   *Mall.* 293

———— epitaph of,   *Gay* 1 : 281

Authority intoxicates,   *Butl.* 2 : 329

Authors, like coins, grow dear as they grow old, *Pope* 2 : 215

———— are partial to their wit,   *Pope* 1 : 91

———— blind to their own defects,   *Dry.* 7 : 314

———— why all this fcrawl and fcribbling fore, *Thom.* 1 : 216

———— ye lofe the prefent, to gain the future age, *ib.* 1 : 216

Autumn, with lavifh ftores, fpreads Nature's lap, *Hughes* 192

———— cries in,   *Gay* 1 : 126

———— a paftoral,   *Pope* 1 : 36

D 3

Autumn,   *Thom.* 1 : 106

———— crown'd with the fickle and wheaten fheaf, *ib.* 1 : 106

Awakening nature hears the new-creating word, *Thom.* 1 : 189

———————————— and ftarts to life,   *Thom.* 1 : 189

Ax of juftice ill-matched with fword of war,   *Rowe L.* 222

Axius, that leaves the diftant Amydon,   *Pope il.* 1 : 101

Axylus, a friend to human race,   *Pope il.* 1 : 191

Ay and no, a tale,   *Swift* 2 : 366

Aye and no,   *Gay* : 196

———— quick as Caefar, wins the day,   *Gay* 2 : 197

Ayes be in courts denial meant,   *Gay* 2 : 197

Ayfcough, verfes to,   *Lytt.* 25

Azazel, ftandard-bearer,   *Milt.* 1 : 23

Azure fky, fpread like an ample curtain,   *Prior* 2 : 117

B

Babel, tower of, built,   *Milt.* 2 : 120

Baboon and the poultry,   *Gay* 2 : 127

Babylon like a deluge rufhes on,   *Broome* 19

———— firft yielded to his arms,   *Hughes* 289

———— where now ?   *Hughes* 278

———— curfe of,   *Yald.* 365

———— for ever defolate,   *Yald.* 368

————'s proud walls rais'd by Semiramis,   *Hughes* 58

Babylonifh captivity, return from,   *Cow.* 2 : 128

———————— dialect,   *Butl.* 1 : 9

Bacchus,   *Parn.* 94

———— birth of,   *Add.* 154

———— triumphant,   *Som.* 349

———— barbarous diffonance of,   *Milt.* 1 : 208

Back, tranfpierc'd with a difhoneft wound, *Pope il.* 2 : 26

                                                       Bacon,

Bacon, wifeſt, brighteſt, meaneſt of mankind,   *Pope* 2 : 79
———— opens the way to philoſophy,   *Cow.* 1 : 216
———— by experiment and obſervation,   *Cow.* 1 : 217
———— world owes its knowledge to,   *Dry.* 2 : 122
———— led forth true philoſophy,   *Thom.* 1 : 96
———— Roger, a conjurer deemed,   *Butl.* 1 : 231
———— trembling for his brazen head,   *Pope* 3 : 180
————'s noddle of braſs,   *Butl.* 1 : 174
Bad in works cannot be defended,   *Pope* 1 : 11
——— grows better, which we well ſuſtain,   *Dry.* 3 : 136
——— ſervants wound their maſter's fame,   *Gay* 2 : 144
——— or good, as in or out of mode,   *Butl.* 2 : 247
Bagdat, populous and great,   *Thom.* 1 : 213
———— court of Caliphs old,   *Thom.* 1 : 213
Bag-pipe, muſic of the Highlanders,   *Som.* 102
———— deſcribed,   *Phil.* 75
Bagſhot heath, where gameſters oft repair their loſs, *Gay* 1 : 166
Baia, gentle ſeat,   *Add.* 42
Baiae, ſoft receſs,   *Dry.* 7 : 232
Bait, choice of proper,   *Gay* 1 : 7
Balaam under the power of avarice,   *Cow.* 2 : 102
———— inſpired,   *Milt.* 2 : 159
Balcarres, death of,   *Cow.* 1 : 170
———— praiſe,   *Cow.* 1 : 172
Bald Batchelor,   *Som.* 288
Bald-pated Welſhman and the Fly,   *Som.* 263
Ballad, pride of ancient time,   *Dry.* 1 : 273

Ballad,   { *Shen.*   173
                                               { *Swift* 2 : 214
                                               { *Som.*   247

Ballad-fingers to be guarded againſt, *Gay* 1 : 134

———————— aid the labours of the diving hand, *Gay* 1 : 134

Bally Spellin, ballad on, *Swift* 2 : 332

———————— anſwer to, *Swift* 2 : 335

Baniau tree, whoſe ſhoot, bending to earth, takes root, *Fiek.* 133

Bankers, run upon, *Swift* 1 : 189

Bankrupt, none ever found a fair-one kind, *Garth* 33

Banſtead downs, fit for ſheep, *Dyer* 31

Baptiſm, inſtitution of, *Milt.* 2 : 134

Bar, bulky volumes of, *Yal.* 442

———— undoes as faſt as war, *Butl.* 2 : 225

Barbacan, a watch-tower once, *Dry.* 2 : 111

Barbarians, fierce in arms, *Pope od.* 3 : 224

———————— irruption of, *Fent.* 238

Barbarous hands, what will they not for hire, *Gay* 2 : 172

Bard, *Gray* 351

———— was blind, that ſung Achilles' rage, *Hughes* 197

———— he ſung and begg'd, *Hughes* 197

———— ſings the wooden horſe, *Pope od.* 3 : 221

———— not fond of flattery, nor unpleas'd with praiſe, *ib.* 220

Bards, who ſo fond of fame, as youthful, *Pope* 1 : 225

———— ſome, enjoy the viſions of the Nine, *Pitt* 352

———— here they are to call-in reaſon and judgment, *Pitt* 352

———— let judgment calm the tempeſt of their mind, *Pitt* 352

Bare virtue could not live on praiſe, *Swift* 1 : 108

Bargain, *Cow.* 1 : 255

Bark, life of trees lies in, *Butl.* 2 : 281

———— a feather on the towering wave, *Young* 1 : 190

Barks made of oſiers, lin'd with ſkins, *Rowe L.* 167

Barley-mow and the dunghill, *Gay* 2 : 90

Barnacles

Barnacles turn Soland geese,   *Butl.* 2 : 37

Barn-elms,   *Hughes* 67

Barometer, defcription of,   *Add.* 78

Barons durft by arms reftrain their fovereign's pride, *Yal.* 439

———— permitted to alienate their lands,   *Thom.* 2 : 110

Barren grounds fir'd to fruitfulnefs,   *Dry.* 3 : 260

Barrennefs, a reproach,   *Milt.* 3 : 19

Barriers to fight at,   *Butl.* 2 : 279

Barrifter, a man in a ruff,   *Cow.* 1 : 77

Barzillai, character of,   *Dry.* 1 : 152

· Bafe have Lords,   *Thom.* 2 : 73

—— venal, will be bought,   *Thom.* 2 : 73

Bafenefs, it is not, to be poor,   *Dry.* 3 : 233

Bafilifk, teeth, fting and eye balls, all are death,   *King* 299

Bafkets, homely ruftic geer,   *Dyer* 64

———— woven of the flexile willow,   *Dyer* 64

Baffet-table, eclogue,   *Pope* 2 : 340

Baftard,   *Sav.* 84

———— born to himfelf,   *Sav.* 84

——— in freedom fofter'd, and by fortune fed,   *Sav.* 84

———— nature's unbounded fon,   *Sav.* 84

Baftile, to imprifon hands,   *Butl.* 1 : 98

Bafting, no blemifh,   *Butl.* 1 : 163

Bafto gain'd but one trump,   *Pope* 1 : 139

Batavian fleets defraud us of the finny fwarms, *Thom.* 1 : 137

Batavians fierce, whom hoarfe rattlings animate, *Rowe L.* 67

Bathing, defcribed,   *Thom.* 1 : 86

—— benefits of,   *Thom.* 1 : 86

—— in the river,   *Cow.* 1 : 320

Batrachomyomachia,   *Parn.* 37

Batter'd Beau, none so hideous,   *Som.* 296

Battle described,   { *Pope il.* 1 : 144
     Pope il. 1 : 324
     Pope il. 1 : 241
     Parn.   47

Battle imag'd by the roaring man,   *Pitt* 362

—— order of, at Pharsalia,   *Rowe L.* 298

—— of Gods and Titans,   *Broome* 143

—— of the sexes, to Author of,   *Pitt* 228

—— of Angels described,   *Milt.* 1 : 180, seq.

Battles won on the French,   *Cow.* 1 : 325

Battus transformed,   *Add.* 134

Bavaria laid waste by fire and sword,   *Add.* 59

Bavaroy, by whom worn,   *Gay* 1 : 103

Baucis and Philemon,   { *Dry.* 4 : 160
     Swift 1 : 48

Bawds residentiary,   *Butl.* 2 : 103

Bays, hide his baldness with,   *Broome* 101

Beacons flaming, signal of invasive war,   *Gay* 1 : 15

Beads drop useless thro' the zealot's hand,   *Tick.* 127

Bear, whelp'd without form,   *Butl.* 1 : 148

Bear, hide of sold, before caught,   *Wall.* 72

Bear our evils, wet or dry,   *Prior* 2 : 87

Bear-baiting,   *Butl.* 1 : 35

———— Antichristian,   *Butl.* 1 : 41

Beard, what,   *Butl.* 2 : 214

—— to jeer to one's,   *Butl.* 2 : 266

—— in cut and dye like a tile,   *Butl.* 1 : 18

—— monastic,   *Butl.* 1 : 18

—— to stand as long as monarchy,   *Butl.* 1 : 19

     Beard,

Beard, to pull the devil by,   *Butl.* 1 : 110

Bears have no tails,   *Butl.* 1 : 257

Beaſt, duteous to man,   *Milt.* 2 : 20

—— without language,   *Milt.* 2 : 21

—— in aid of man, and man of beaſt,   *Pope* 2 : 55

—— number of,   *Butl.* 2 : 43

Beaſts, formed,   *Milt.* 1 : 222, 223

———— of the elder houſe,   *Butl.* 1 : 67

———— prey to our luxury,   *Cow.* 2 : 112

———— neceſſity of deſtroying ſome,   *Som.* 69

——————————— preſerving others,   *Som.* 69

—— confeſſion of, to the prieſt,   *Swift* 2 : 282

—— urg'd by us, their fellow beaſts purſue,   *Pope* 1 : 62

—— and learn of man each other to undo,   *Pope* 1 : 62

—— kill for hunger, man for pay,   *Gay* 2 : 46

—— can like, but not diſtinguiſh,   *Dry.* 3 : 261

Beau, what,   *Dry.* 7 : 339

—— compared to Phaëton,   *Gay* 1 : 129

—— reply of,   *Swift* 2 : 70

Beavers killed for their ſtones,   *Butl.* 1 : 48

Beauclerk, Lord Aubrey, epitaph on,   *Young* 1 : 237

Beaufort, of kingly rights, aſſerter,   *Phil.* 55

—— addreſs to,   *King* 387

Beauties and Bards have pride,   *Gay* 2 : 108

——————————— with both all rivals are decry'd, *Gay* 2 : 108

Beautiful young nymph, going to bed,   *Swift* 2 : 230

—— looks are rul'd by fickle minds,   *Prior* 1 : 224

Beauty what? a flower that fades,   *Gay* 2 : 192

—— is Nature's coin,   *Milt.* 3 : 147

——————— brag,   *Milt.* 3 : 147.

Beauty,

Beauty,   *Cow.* 1 : 282

——— Anacreontic,   *Cow.* 1 : 141

——— is but a spell,   *Fent.* 301

——— a riddle,   *Prior* 1 : 121

——— Pandora's box of good and harm,   *Prior* 1 : 121

——— blew the flames, that ruin'd Troy,   *Prior* 1 : 121

——— progress of,   { *Swift* 1 : 195
                                                         { *Lanf.* 1 : 136

——— by no complection is defin'd,   *Lanf.* 138

——— is of all colours, and to none confin'd,   *Larf.* 133

——— not meant to vex, but please,   *Lanf.* 162

——— should be kind, as well as charm,   { *Lanf.* 163
                                                         { *Hughes* 171

——— to thee we owe gay wit and moving eloquence,   *ib.*

——— from thee painters derive their skill,   *Hughes* 172

——— to thee the poet tunes his lays,   *Hughes* 172

——— dies, while love is frowning,   *Hughes* 173

——— power of,   *Broome* 163

——— to conquer, dreadful in its charms,   *Broome* 163

——— conquers rudest minds,   *Wall.* 26

——— cynosure of neighbouring eyes,   *Milt.* 3 : 103

——— captives all,   *Dry.* 2 : 124

——— to draw true, shews a master's hand,   *Dry.* 2 : 127

——— joined with virtue, powerful,   *Dry.* 3 : 141

——— softly binds the chain,   *Hughes* 112

——— powerful glance of,   *Milt.* 1 : 249

——— draws us with a single hair,   *Pope* 1 : 133

——— unchaste, is beauty in disgrace,   *Pope od.* 3 : 215

——— perfect, but of guilty fame,   *Lanf.* 155

——— what cruel destiny waits on,   *Lanf.* 155

                                                         Beauty,

Beauty, fatal to the owners, Dry. 7 : 296

——— undone by beauty, Cow. 1 : 58

——— what hourly nonsense haunts, Gay 2 : 41

——— fantastic, Buck. 52

——— admir'd by weak minds, Milt. 2 : 170

——— the wise man's passion, the vain man's toast, Pope 1 : 151

——— to write in praise of, hard task, Cong. 57

——— tho' injurious, has charms, Milt. 3 : 40

——— like wit, to judges should be shewn, Lytt. 17

——— proper sphere, the town, the court, Lytt. 17

——— let rest serene and ever pleas'd, King 328

——— withers like a shrivel'd flower, Gay 1 : 229

——— fair flower ! soon fades away, Som. 241

——— flower of, quickly lost its pride, Prior 1 : 127

——— faded has no second spring, A. Phil. 299

——— ah ! how frail, how vain, Lanf. 181

——— a frail thing, Prior 1 : 268

——— borne swift away upon the wings of Time, Prior 1 : 71

——— like a shadow flies, Wall. 79

——— but a transient good at best, Gay 1 : 39

——— like flowers, it withers, Gay 1 : 39

——— who trusts to, trusts the fading rose, Gay 1 : 42

——— frail flower, that every season fears, Pope 2 : 334

——— but a varnish, Swift 2 : 227

——— which time and accidents will tarnish, Swift 2 : 227

——— and virtue seldom join'd, Duke 152

——— hard lot of, Lanf. 178

——— soon grows familiar, Add. 266

——— the gift of Gods, the sex's pride, Cong. 116

——— shall no more my passion move, Rowe L. 46

Beauty,

Beauty, employment of, *Sav.* 171

———— by conftraint poffeffing, *Hughes* 127

———— lifelefs charms without the heart, *Hughes* 127

———— and forrow refiftlefs, *Cow.* 2 : 91

———— and wit each other's aid require, *Hughes* 137

———— an Elegy to an old one, *Parn.* 63

———— receipt for, *Swift* 1 : 58

———— and Mufic, *Hughes* 37

———— true, is but virtue's face, *Young* 1 : 153

———— from order fprings, *King* 205

———— fource of pleafure, *Aken.* 121

———— in truth and good, *Aken.* 87

———— Beauty connefted with truth and good, *Aken.* 25, 126

———— different degrees of, *Aken.* 27, 28, 29

———— from variety, *Black.* 104

———— pleafure from, *Aken.* 22

——————— its final caufe, *Aken.* 23

———— different orders of, *Aken.* 129

———— connefted with true and good, *Aken.* 126

———— infinite and all-comprehending form of, *Aken.* 132

———— partial and artificial forms of, *Aken.* 133

———— origin and condufl of in man, *Aken.* 134

Bec, birth-day of, *Swift* 2 : 33

—— a New-years-gift for, *Swift* 1 : 289

Bed, how friendly is the fick man's *Hughes* 260

Bedford, to hear L'Epine, his dice forfakes, *Hughes* 162

———— level drain'd, *Dyer* 63

——————— erft a dreary pathlefs wafte, *Dyer* 63

Bedlam of love, *Pom.* 226, feq.

Bee, in a little bulk a mighty foul appears, *Gay* 1 : 4

Beelzebub,

Beelzebub, speech of,   *Milt.* 1 : 45, 46

———— character of,   *Milt.* 1 : 45, 46

———— proposes to explore the new world,   *Milt.* 1 : 47

———— counsel of, adopted,   *Milt.* 1 : 48

———————— undertaken by Satan,   *Milt.* 1 : 49, 50

———————— proclaimed,   *Milt.* 1 : 52

———— reply to Satan,   *Milt.* 1 : 9, 14

Beer, by thunder turn'd to vinegar,   *Butl.* 1 : 52

Bees, the busy nation, cling to the bud and suck   *Thom.* 1 : 20

—— station proper for,   *Dry.* 5 : 175

—— house in hives, in trees or ground,   *Dry.* 5 : 177

—— when they begin to gather honey,   *Dry.* 5 : 177

—— to call home, when they swarm,   *Dry.* 5 : 178

—— battle of,   *Dry.* 5 : 178

—— nature of,   *Dry.* 5 : 182

—— government of,   *Dry.* 5 : 185

—— how to take their honey,   *Dry.* 5 : 185

—— diseases of,   *Dry.* 5 : 187

———————— cure of,   *Dry.* 5 : 188

—— smoked,   *Thom.* 1 : 146

—— ingratefully used,   *Thom.* 1 : 146

Beetle wheels his droning flight,   *Gray* 337

Beeves, at his touch, at once to jelly turn,   *Pope* 3 : 254

Beggar sings before the thief,   *Dry.* 3 : 204

———— verses for,   *Mall.* 296

Beginning, none without an end,   *Buck.* 16

Behemoth described,   *Milt.* 1 : 221

———————— in plaited mail, rears his head,   *Thom.* 1 : 67

Being, vast chain, which leaves no void,   *Pope* 2 : 37

Belgic states arose,   *Thom.* 2 : 112

                                       Belial,

Belial, the moſt diſſolute ſpirit,   *Milt.* 2 : 168

———— deſcribed,   *Milt.* 1 : 21, 38, 39

———— ſons of,   *Milt.* 1 : 21, 38, 39

———— ſpeech of,   *Milt.* 1 : 39, 40, 41

Believe, and ſhew the reaſon of a man,   *Young* 2 : 87

———— and look with triumph on the tomb,   *Young* 2 : 87

Belinda,   *Lanſ.* 191

———— at the Bath,   *Broome* 60

———— ſmil'd, and all the world was gay,   *Pope* 1 : 134

———— verſes to,   *Broome* 20, 22

Belles mechanic, elegantly dreſt,   *Swift* 1 : 70

Bellona's prieſts, a frantic train,   *Rowe L.* 74

———— with yells the coming woes foretel,   *Rowe L.* 74

Belly, ſeat of Alma's empire,   *Prior* 2 : 74

Beloved, the faireſt and the only,   *Watts* 135

———— in peace and feared in arms,   *Ald.* 9

———— by all, not vainly popular,   *Pom.* 220

Benaiah, character of,   *Dry.* 1 : 188

Bending Ulyſſes' bow propoſed to the ſuitors, *Pope od.* 4 : 179

———— as the condition of winning   *ib.* 4 : 179

———— attempted in vain by all, *Pope od.* 4 : 184, ſeq.

Bendiſh, Henry, verſes to,   *Watts* 229

———— verſes to Mrs. B.   *Watts* 216

Beneficence to ſhed, celeſtial office,   *Dyer* 30

Benevolence graft on charities,   *Pope* 2 : 60

———— fair ! of generous minds,   *Aken.* 43

Ben-Jochanan, character of,   *Dry.* 1 : 172

Benſon, Bp. manners with candour given,   *Pope* 2 : 298

———— [Auditor], titles writ on poets' tombs, *Pope* 3 : 204

Bentley, that awful Ariſtarch,   *Pope* 3 : 231

Bentley, plow'd his front with many a deep remark, *Pope* 3 : 231

———— made Horace dull, and humbled Milton's strains, *ib.* 231

———— flashing with his desperate hook, *Pope* 2 : 219

Berkeley executes his King's commands, *Add.* 14

———— Bishop, had every virtue under heaven, *Pope* 2 : 298

Bermuda walled with rocks, *Wall.* 68

Best may be defy'd with mean reproaches, *Pope il.* 2 : 221

—— may slip, and the most cautious fall, *Pom.* 226

—— guilty by mistake, *Buck.* 114

—— all is, that highest wisdom ordains, *Milt.* 3 : 65

—— whatever heaven ordains, *Pope od.* 4 : 19

—— is not without allay, *Som.* 357

—— friends must part, *Som.* 293

—— of things, beyond their measure cloy, *Pope il.* 2 : 29

—— things corrupted, are the worst, *Den.* 108

Better the day of death, than day of birth, *Sav.* 111

———— borne to the mighty dead, *Sav.* 113

———— husband makes the wife the worse, *Dry.* 7 : 262

Bettefworth, verfes on, *Swift* 2 : 299

Betty the Grizette, *Swift* 2 : 191

—— queen of wit and beauty, *Swift* 2 : 191

—— spotted over like a leopard, *Swift* 2 : 191

—— wit of, set of phrases cut and dry, *Swift* 2 : 191

Bezaliel, character of, *Dry.* 1 : 192

Bibo and Charon, *Prior* 2 : 241

Bigot's rage, what magic can assuage, *Lanf.* 142

Bill of rights, *Thom.* 2 : 119

Billet-doux, its matter passionate, yet true, *Prior* 1 : 108

Billingsgate, there tongues that never cease, *Pope* 1 : 345

Binding fillets others *more become,* *Cong.* 118

Bion-ftile forfake,   *P, ior* 2 : 203

Birds, formation of,   *Milt.* 1 : 221

———— couple and build their nefts,   *Thom.* 1 : 25

———— patience of the female in brooding,   *Thom.* 1 : 25

———— affection of, in feeding their young,   *Thom.* 1 : 26

———— young feathered take their flight,   *Thom.* 1 : 27

———— and parental love diffolves,   *Thom.* 1 : 28

———— vagrants of air, unforeboding ftray,   *Pope od.* 3 : 68

———— charm filence with their lays,   *Dyer* 130

———— choirifters of love,   *Dry.* 3 : 243

———— on the language of,   *Shen.* 21

———— nor ftores nor granaries belong,   *Thom.* 2 : 182

———— yet with unfparing bounty fed,   *Thom.* 2 : 182

———— of paffage,   *Thom.* 1 : 134, feq.

———— of paffage flocking to St. Kilda,   *Mall.* 240

———— and beafts of prey to field of battle hafte, *Rowe L.* 326

Birks of Ender-may, fong,   *Mall.* 158

Birth is nothing, but our death begun,   *Young* 2 : 115

———— advantages of,   *Shen.* 43

Birth-day, verfes on,   *Pope* 2 : 354

———————— at three years old,   *Broome* 92

———————— on my own,   *Prior* 2 : 12

———————— of the Queen,   *Fent.* 320

———————— fong, directions to make,   *Swift* 2 : 134

Bifcay, working bay of,   *Dry.* 1 : 89

Bifhopricks are held in fee,   *Swift* 2 : 346

B;4   · · down,   *Butl.* 1 : 69

                                                          King 208

                         3adding train,   *Pitt* 215

            d revel on the Thracian plain,   *Pitt* 215

                                                          Bitches,

Bitches, fable of,	*Swift* 1 : 150
Bite, what,	*Swift* 1 : 123
Bitter and the sweet unmingled came,	*Rowe L.* 361
Bitters restore the taste, cloy'd with sweets,	*Cong.* 134
Black, to mourn in,	*Butl.* 2 : 199
Black despair succeeds brown study,	*Cong.* 172
Blakbourn, verses to,	*Watts* 186
Blackmore, verses under picture of,	*Gay* 1 : 296
—————— his Creation,	*Black.* 39
Blame is easy, to commend is bold,	*Buck.* 94
Blank oblivion, and untimely grave,	*Pope od.* 3 : 136
Blazing star, beacon of war,	*Butl.* 1 : 51
Bleeding marks of grace,	*Cow.* 1 : 187
Blenheim,	*Phil.* 9
—————— once a vulgar name,	{ *Tick.* 101 { *Lytt.* 19
—————— proud monument of British fame,	*Lytt.* 19
—————— sacred to her Leader's name,	*Lytt.* 20
—————— that auspicious field of Gaul's defeat,	*Lytt.* 20
—————— battle of,	*Add.* 62
Blessed alone who ne'er was born,	*Prior* 2 : 173
Blessing great in wish, in possession disappointing,	*Swift* 2 : 45
Blessings, when cheap or certain we despise,	*Lans.* 289
—————— wound, when discretion's lost,	*Young* 3 : 246
Blest would you be, despise low joys,	*Pope* 2 : 206
Blind to the future, to the present blind,	*Broome* 154
—— to ourselves, adopt each vice,	*Pope* 2 : 5
Blindness to the future kindly given,	*Pope* 2 : 32
—————— complaint of,	{ *Milt.* 1 : 74 { *Milt.* 3 : 10
Bliss, the *first*, the *greatest*, is in virtue to excel,	*West* 201

Bliss,

Bliss, the second, praise of doing well,   *West* 20?

—— fortune here below can give no richer meed,   *West* 201.

—— which Christian schemes alone ensure,   *Young* 2 : 56

—— without the sting receive,   *Prior* 2 : 155.

—— sublunary bliss ! proud words and vain,   *Young* 3 : 10.

—— that changeth with the moon,   *Prior* 1, : 228

—— of man is, not to act beyond mankind,   *Pope* 2. : 36

Blissful vision, each shares in, as he can bear, . *Dry.* 2 : 183

Blockhead is a slow worm,   *Pope* 2. : 348.

Blockheads, with reason, wicked wits abhor,   *Pope* 3 : 188.

Blood, its circle discover'd,   *Cow.* 1, : 175

—— welled out from wound,   .   *Dry.* 6 : 309.

—— of beasts typical of Christ,   *Milt.* 2 : 129

—— abstinence from,   *Dry.* 4. : 137.

—— was nothing without groats,   *Mall.* 328

—— none so loud as that of civil war,   *Cow.* 1 : 106

—— and forefathers are not our own,   *Lans.* 208.

Blood-stain'd Exile, ever doom'd to roam,   *Pope od.* 4 : 57

Blossom'd beans, Arabia cannot boast a fuller gale, *Thom.* 1 : 20.

Blount, epistle to,   *Pope* 2 : 335

Blown-up veal,   *Butl* 1, : 89.

Blows, to rain a storm of,   *Butl* 1 : 180.

Blunt honest Heroes, what easy tools !   *Smith* 159.

Blush, that spurious virtue in a maid,   *Swift* 1 : 106

Boadicia boasts of Orinda,   , .   *Cow.* 1 : 168.

Boar, Arabian method of hunting,   *Som.* 58, seq.

—— bled by boar, and goat by goat lay slain,   *Pope od.* 3 : 72

Boaster enormous, doom'd to vaunt in vain,   *Pope il.* 2. : 37

Boasters of liberty, fast bound in chains,   *Young* 2 : 203

Boasting is but an art, our fears to blind,   *Pope il.* 2 : 275

                                                    Boasting,

Boasting and with false terror sink another's mind, *Pope il.* 2 : 275

Boat, the bear in,   *Gay* 2 : 137

Boccace, author of the octave rhyme,   *Dry.* 3 : 15

Bodies to their proper centre move,   *Aken.* 44

Body, anagram of the world,   *Butl.* 1 : 300

—— how acts on mind,   *Garth* 21

—— does not its investing weed exceed ? *Thom.* 2 : 182

—— only I give o'er to death,   *Prior* 2 : 16

—— formation of man's a standing wonder, *Black.* 200

Bœotia sends full fifty ships,   *Pope il.* 1 : 87

Bœotian fields, that ill-omen'd plain,   *Pope* 1 : 288

——— where brothers were by brothers slain, *Pope* 1 : 288

Boileau, letter to,   *Prior* 1 : 188

——— like a vulture flies,   *Prior* 1 : 85

——— makes Louis take the wall of Jove, *Prior* 1 : 85

——— translation from,   *Hughes* 241

——— a Horace and a Juvenal,   *Dry.* 7 : 114

——— still in right of Horace sways, *Pope* 1 : 121

——— joined both the Roman satirists, *Young* 1 : 73

——— supported genius with a sage's care, *Pope* 2 : 18

——— fancy and sense to form his line conspire, *Pope* 2 : 19

——— strong in sense, and sharp in wit, *Lytt.* 28

——— from the ancients, like the ancients writ, *Lytt.* 28

Bold, a way will find or make,   *King* 356

—— without rudeness,   *Pom.* 290

—— in mischief be, to get honours, *Dry.* 7 : 225

Bolton, Dutchess of,   *Garth* 107

Bomb bears magazines of Death, *Broome* 49

—— glowing orb darts horrour, *Broome* 50

—— mows a thousand lives,   *Broome* 50

E 3.   Bombast,

Bombaſt, crying ſin, *Cow.* 1 : 132

Bombay, trade to, *Dyer* 115

Bonduca brandiſh'd high the Britiſh ſpear, *Prior* 1 : 230

———— bold, ſwift flew her arrows, *Broome* 135

Book and bell, to curſe with, *Dry.* 3 : 208

Book-learned wife, a great plague, *Dry.* 7 : 270

Books, ends of, *Den.* 91

———— and the world to be conjoined, *Butl.* 2 : 284

———— perfection in, to be plain and brief, *Butl.* 2 : 346

———— as affected are as men, *Gay* 2 : 27

———— are furniture, *Young* 1 : 89

Book-worm, *Parn.* 66

———————— ravening beaſt of prey, *Parn.* 66

Booming billows cloſed above my head, *Pope od.* 3 : 182

Booty, to perjure pro and con, *Butl.* 2 : 131

Borees, Tom was beſt at, *Swift* 2 : 92

Born to try the lot of man, to ſuffer and to die, *Pope od.* 3 : 85

Bottle, buried, *Swift* 1 : 253, 254

Boulter by name, is no Bolter of wit, *Swift* 2 : 366

Bounce, epiſtle to Fop, *Gay* 1 : 203

———— tho' no ſpaniel, am a friend, *Gay* 1 : 203

Bounds of good and evil to diſcern, *Dry.* 7 : 348

Bounty, like the ſun, ſpreads her ray, *Pope* 2 : 187

Bouts rimés, *Swift* 2 : 143

Bow, two ſtrings to, *Butl.* 1 : 274

———— in a cloud, ſign of peace, *Milt.* 2 : 114

———— etherial, a ſhowery priſm, *Thom.* 1 : 10

———— every hue unfolds from red to violet, *Thom.* 1 : 10

Bowel-hankerings for rule, *Butl.* 2 : 17

Bowels ſtony, how melt in thoſe, who never pity felt, *Swift* 2 : 263

        Bower,

Bower, description of,   *Milt.* 1 : 124

Bowing to the rising sun,   *Cow.* 2 : 170

Bowl temper'd with drugs, to assuage rage,   *Pope od.* 3 : 115

———————————— so friendly to the joys of life, *ib.*

Bowling-green,   { *Add.* 92
                                      { *Som.* 197

Bowls with weighty lead infus'd,   *Som.* 198

——— drive on with speed,   *Som.* 198

Bow-string fatal,   *Wall.* 156

Bowyer-god, who durst defy,   *Pope od.* 3 : 211

Boxing-match,   *Dry.* 6 : 88

Boyle, in wisdom found divine content,   *Lytt.* 26

——— whose pious search the Creator sought,   *Thom.* 1 : 97

Boyne, already sung in strains that ne'er shall die, *Hughes* 30

——— run thick with gore,   *Add.* 9

——— shall raise his laurel'd head,   *Prior* 1 : 175

Brabantia, clad with fields and crown'd with towers, *ib.* 260

Bradbury, his verses to Countess of Dorset,   *Prior* 1 : 41

——— verses to,   *Watts* 179

Bradshaw's bloody ghost,   *Cow.* 1 : 181

Brain, specious head without,   *Prior* 1 : 282

Brake, to thrid,   *Dry.* 3 : 72

Branch shall arise from Jesse's root,   *Pope* 1 : 48

Brandenburg, to Author of Memoirs of,   *Aken.* 287

Brave inspires with ardour,   *Pope il.* 1 : 136

——— ill befits, with words to combat,   *Pope il.* 2 : 124

——— asks no omen, but his country's cause,   *Pope il.* 1 : 366

——— to himself a Deity,   *Garth* 61

——— none but, deserves the fair,   *Hughes* 174

——— true courage never fails,   *Som.* 50

Brave doom'd to bear the gripes of poverty, *Pope od.* 4 : 122

———————————— and ftings of care, *Pope od.* 4 : 122

——— fire the brave, *Broome* 75.

——— live glorious, or lamented die, { *Pope il.* 1 : 173 / *Pope il.* 2 : 87.

——— o'erpower'd by numbers, but brave in vain, *Pope od.* 4 : 74.

——— love mercy, and delight to fave, *Gay* 2 : 30.

——— pafs many perils, *Dyer* 66

——— prevent misfortune, *Pope od.* 4 : 84

——— upon ignoble terms, difdain to fave, *Pom.* 286.

——— to conquer and to fave, *Wall.* 177

——— to perifh by a noble fall, *Pom.* 238.

——— man, triumphant in diftrefs, *Som.* 171.

——— men love the brave, *Pope il.* 1 : 164.

——— minds, howe'er at war, are fecret friends, *Tick.* 100

——————— their generous difcord with the battle ends, *ib.* 130

Bravely-patient to no fortune yields, *Pope od.* 4 : 102.

——————— on rolling oceans, and in fighting fields, *ib.* 102

Brazen age, *Dry.* 3 : 302.

Bread, that decaying man with ftrength fupplies, *Pope od.* 3 : 72

——— all-fuftaining, *Pope il.* 1 : 261

——— life-fuftaining, *Pope od.* 3 : 152

——— and wine, outward figns, *Dry.* 2 : 22

Breaking, citizens thrive by, *Butl.* 2 : 91.

Breath fweeter than the ripen'd hay, *Gay* 1 : 58.

——— by far excell'd the breathing cows, *Gay* 1 : 59.

Brede of divers colours, *Wall.* 133.

Breech, honour lodged in, *Butl.* 1 : 263

Breeches, women fight for, *Butl.* 1 : 215

Breeze to cheer, *Black.* 127

Brentford,

Brentford, tedious town,   Gay 1 : 165

———— for dirty streets, white-legg'd chickens known, ib.

———— a town of mud,   Thom. 1 : 251

Brentford-fight,   Cow. 1 : 334

Brettle, ode to be performed by,   Shen. 193

Brevity good,   Butl. 1 : 34

Briareus, monster Titan, with a hundred hands, Pope il. 1 : 54

Bribe-eaters, who,   Cow. 2 : 306

Bribes confefs a wicked cause,   Gay 2 : 161

———— have blinded common sense,   Gay 2 : 158

———— foiled reason, truth, and eloquence,   Gay 2 : 158

Bridges, supplement to character of,   Hughes 271

Bridget Jones,   Sav. 174

Bright Vision,   Watts 254

Brillante, apology to,   Sav. 137

Brimmers, provocatives of lust,   Dry. 7 : 266

Briseis' heavenly charms he seiz'd,   Pope il. 1 : 54

———— like the blooming rose,   Pope il. 2 : 203

———— radiant, as the queen of love,   Pope il. 2 : 205

Bristol, in a dark bottom sunk,   Sav. 192

———— praise, fawn, profefs, be all things but sincere, Sav. 192

Britain, sea-girt,   Wall. 35

———— a poem,   Thom. 2 : 81

———— panegyric on,   { Thom. 1 : 93
                                                 { Thom. 2 : 132

———— bid reign the miftrefs of the deep,   Thom. 1 : 137

———— betwixt the nations hold the scale,   Prior 1 : 174

———— mixt government,   Thom. 2 : 108

———————————— mutual, checking and supporting, ib.

———— Palladium of,   King 379

E

Britain,

Britain, chofen port of trade,   *Gay* 2 : 153

———— may luxury ne'er thy fons invade,   *Gay* 2 : 153

———— liberty received by,   *Thom.* 2 : 94

———— commerce of,   *Thom.* 2 : 95

———— abandon'd by the Romans,   *Thom.* 2 : 103

———— parted from the Continent,   *Thom.* 2 : 96

———— charitable inftitutions,   *Thom.* 2 : 97

———— land of light,   *Thom.* 2 : 98

———— rational and free,   *Thom.* 2 : 99

———— Celtic origin of,   *Thom.* 102

———— that word is an alarm,   *Young* 1 : 251

———— warms the blood,   *Young* 1 : 251

———— awakes the foul,   *Young* 1 : 251

———— be Britain ftill,   *Young* 1 : 252

———— Nature's anointed emprefs of the deep, *Young* 1 : 253

———— nurfe of merchants,   *Young* 1 : 253

———— of Gallic lilies eterna blaft !   *Young* 1 : 253

———— terror of Armadas !   *Young* 1 : 253

———— cut from the Continent, th t world of flaves, *ib.* 253

———— dedicated long to liberty,   *Young* 1 : 253

———— her foe moft fatal, Vice,   *Young* 1 : 253

———— care to watch o'er Europe's f te,   *Add.* 45

———— holds in balance each ftate,   *Add.* 45

———— guardian of the Continent,   *Add.* 52

———— 'tis thy own William next appea s,   *Hughes* 47

———— fee the accomplifh'd glory of thy race in him, *ib.* 47

———— fam'd for bright victorious eyes,   *ib.* 93

———— thy bleffing know,   *Young* 3 : 283

———— its end fulfill, fource adore,   *Young* 3 : 283

———— as pert as France, as grave as Spai ,   *Gay* 2 : 98

Britain, infamous for suicide,   *Young* 2 : 106

———— nurse of fools, to stock the Continent,   *Young* 1 : 101

———— ships export an annual fleece,   *Prior* 1 : 179

———— see ! sunk in lucre's sordid charms,   *Pope* 2 : 123

Britannia, fairest island of the sea,   *Hughes* 116

———— beauty's palm is thine confest,   *Hughes* 117

———— a Venus born from Ocean's bed,   *Cong.* 23

———— wields the trident of the main,   *Cong.* 23

———— rise, awake from iron sleep,   *Cong.* 24

———— again thy fortunes smile,   *Cong.* 24

———— noblest of the Ocean's isles,   *Rowe* 17

———— who dost amidst thy waters reign,   *Rowe* 17

———— wipe thy dusty brow,   *Fent.* 204

———— put the Bourbon laurels on,   *Fent.* 204

———— guiltless of civil rage, extend thy name,   *Fent.* 205

———— holds rival kings in equal scales,   *Tick.* 103

———— her sons, fam'd alike in arms, alike in arts, *Tick.* 104

———— the Ocean's stately queen,   *Tick.* 104

———— a poem,   *Thom.* 2 : 1

———— Rediviva,   *Dry.* 2 : 97

———— prologue to Masque of,   *Mall.* 338

British enchanters,   *Lans.* 239

———— prologue to,   *Lans.* 217

———— epilogue for,   *Lans.* 218

———— fair, far be the spirit of the chace from, *Thom.* 1 : 125

———— navy waves her double cross,   *Phil.* 83

———— peers grace the coats their fathers won,   *Add.* 15

———— Philippic,   *Aken.* 350

———— princes,   { *Wall.* 179   *Butl.* 2 : 197

British

British round, plainnefs its excellence,   Dry. 1 : 273.

———— failor, exultation of,   Young 3 : 226.

———————— prayer before engagement,   Young 230

Britons on foreign fields dare their fate,   Fent. 203

———— in war unknowing to retreat,   Fent. 203

———— cry, let us live free, or let us die,   Lanf. 284.

———— never like the fame thing long,   Mall. 175

———— driven to Wales,   Cow. 1 : 337

———— a hardy race,   Yal. 401

———— language of, unmix'd,   Yal. 402.

———— manners of, pure,   Yal. 402.

Britton, lines under print of,   Prior 2 : 262.

Broghill commended,   Cow. 1 : 163

Broom, nag of a Lapland hag,   Butl. 1 : 288

Broome, preface to his poems,   7

———— Habbakkuk, chap. iii, paraphrafe of,   15

———— to Belinda,   20, 22

———— Job, chap. 38, 39, paraphrafe of part of,   23

———— melancholy,   29.

———— Daphnis and Lycidas,   32.

———— firft ode of Horace,   38

———— epiftle to Fenton,   45

———— dialogue between a Lady and looking-glafs,   45

———— feat of war in Flanders,   47

———— to Charles, Lord Cornwallis,   56.

———— the Rofe-bud,   59

———— Belinda at the Bath,   60.

———— the coy,   61

———— to Elizabeth Townfhend,   64.

———— to Mr. Pope,   64, 115

Broome, part of tenth Iliad translated,   68

————— a pastoral,   84

————— poverty and poetry,   88

————— to a Lady, playing with a snake,   90

————— to a Lady of thirty,   91

————— on a Gentleman's birth-day,   92

————— Ecclesiasticus, chap. xliii. paraphrased,   95

————— conclusion of an epilogue,   101

————— the parting,   101

————— on a flower, given by Belinda,   102

————— story of Talus,   105

————— eleventh book of Iliad,   107

————— to Mrs. M——,   111

————— prologue to Fenton's Mariamne,   113

————— Maynard imitated,   114

————— on a mischievous woman,   116

————— the coquette,   118

————— widow and virgin-sisters,   119

————— on death of Fenton,   121

————— poem on death,   126

————— courage in love,   132

————— the complaint,   134

————— battle of Gods and Titans, &c.   143

————— love of Jason and Medea,   150

————— epistola ad amicum, &c.   158

————— sixteen odes of Anacreon,   162—176

Brother with brother in unnatural strife,   Tick. 156

Brother-protestants and fellow-christians, verses on, Swift 2:298

Brothers, with all the rage of their race possess'd, Pope 1:283

————— wake the furies within their breast. Pope 1:283

Brothers,

Brothers, their tortur'd minds envy tears,   *Pope* 1 : 234

———— who reprimand, firſt mend their own faults, *Gay* 2 : 11

———— epilogue to,   *Mall.* 175

Brown, clad all in,   *Swift* 2 : 94

———— beauty will like hollies laſt,   *Gay* 1 : 69

———— John, eſſay on ſatire,   *Pope* 2 : 3

Bruin deſcribed,   *Butl.* 1 : 57

————— quarter'd on his paws,   *Butl.* 1 : 58

Brunduſium, a Dictaean people hold,   *Rowe L.* 112

——————— a ſafe harbour yields,   *Rowe L.* 113

Brunſwick's glory with the world ſhall laſt,   *Som.* 236

Brutal coachman doom'd to a hackney-horſe,   *Gay* 1 : 119

———— mate, who cheriſhes, ſhall mourn the folly, *Gay* 2 : 114

———— ſoldier's rude, rapacious hand,   *Rowe L.* 322

Brutes, inferior family of heaven,   *Dry.* 2 : 16

Brutus, haughty Tarquin's dread,   *Rowe L.* 284

———— the proud Tarquins chac'd,   *Thom.* 2 : 59

———— ode on,   { *Buck.*   81
                          { *Cow.* 2 : 34

———— braveſt man of Rome,   *Cow.* 2 : 268

———— ſtabs his friend,   *Buck.* 114

———— deſponding, dubious of the right,   *Dyer* 11

———— prologue to,   *Buck.* 106

———— choruſes to,   *Buck.* 106

Brydges, firſt garter'd knight,   *Phil.* 53

——————— author of Chandos' ſtem,   *Phil.* 53

Bubble breaking, and a fable told, emblems of life, *Prior* 2 : 185

Buchanan, lines of, paraphraſed,   *Sav.* 170

Bucket-play 'twixt Whigs and Tories,   *Swift* 1 : 136

——————— ups and downs,   *Swift* 1 : 136

          Buckhurſt,

Buckhurst, for pointed satire,   Roch. 338
——— playing with a cat,   Prior 1 : 42
Buckingham, Villers duke of, his character,   Duke 91, 92
——— procures Clarendon's fall,   Duke 93
——— rov'd wild, the public jest,   Pitt 281
——— now some innholder's, now a monarch's guest,   ib.
——— his life and politics of every shape,   Pitt 282
——— this hour a Roman, and the next an ape, ib. 282
——— death of,   Wall. 21
——— Sheffield duke of, testimonies of Authors to,   5
——— poems of,   11
——— on love,   20
——— elegy,   24
——— letter from sea,   25
——— loves slavery,   26
——— the dream,   27
——— accused of being too sensual,   28
——— the Warning,   29
——— to Amoretta,   30
——— the Venture,   31
——— inconstancy excused,   32
——— Despair,   33
——— apprehension of losing what he gained,   35
——— the reconcilement,   36
——— to a coquette,   38
——— the relapse,   39
——— the recovery,   40
——— the convert,   41
——— the picture,   42
——— on Don Alonzo killed,   44
                                         Buckingham,

Buckingham, the furprize,   44
———— a dialogue,   46
———— one who died, difcovering her kindnefs,   47
———— Lucinda's death,   48
———— a lady retiring to a monaftry,   49
———— the vifion,   51
———— Helen to Paris,   57
———— ftory of Orpheus,   66
———— effay on poetry,   69
———— ode on Brutus,   81
———— mifcellanies,   88
———— the rapture,   88
———— Hobbes and his writings,   94
———— death of Purcell,   97
———— lofs of an only fon,   99
———— Pope and his poems,   100
———— ftanzas,   101
———— election of a Laureat,   103
———— on the times,   106
———— on Duke of York,   108
———— on the Deity,   110
———— prologue to Julius Cæfar,   111
———— chorufes in Julius Cæfar,   112
———— prologue to Marcus Brutus,   116
———— chorufes to Brutus,   118
———— reformed the tafte,   Fent. 236
———— Dutchefs of, verfes on,   Cow. 1 : 78
Bud,   Wall. 92
——— firft-born of fpring,   Thom. 1 : 21
Badge doctors of the Stoic fur,   Milt. 3: 146
                                                          Bull

Bull and mastiff,   *Gay* 2 : 43

Bulls, battle of,   *Dry.* 5 : 156

Bully cannot sleep, without a brawl,   *Dry.* 7 : 247

———— insolence of, to be corrected,   *Gay* 1 : 113

Bombastus, Paracelsus,   *Butl.* 2 : 246

Burgess for Bramber is no place to die in,   *Rowe* 29

Burlesque, two species of,   *Som.* 91

Burlington, epistle to,   *Gay* 1 : 165

Burnet (Tho.)   *Add.* 96

———— Bp. set on fire in his closet,   *Parn.* 278

———— scorch'd by a flaming speech on moderation, *Parn.* 278

Burning a dull poem,   *Swift* 2 : 111

———— several poems of Ovid, Martial, &c.   *Watts* 114

Buskin'd bards shall wisely rage,   *Tick.* 113

Busy indolent,   *Som.* 395

Butchers, always foremost in the hangman's train, *Gay* 1 : 112

Butler, Hudibras,   1 : 3

———— fragments of,   2 : 273

———— on an hypocritical Non-conformist,   2 : 286

———— on modern critics,   2 : 296

———— ode on Deval,   2 : 301

———— ballad on parliament,   2 : 309

———— ballad in two parts,   2 : 311, 314

———— miscellaneous thoughts,   2 : 318

———— triplets on avarice,   2 : 349

———— to his mistress,   2 : 350

———— on a club of sots,   2 : 350

———— description of Holland,   2 : 350

———— consummate master,   *Prior* 2 : 49

———— buffooning grave of,   *Dry.* 1 : 264

Butler speaks Scarron's low phrase,　　　　*Smith* 191

Butter not to be ate with eggs in shell,　　　　*King* 181

Butterflies, the beaux,　　　　*Mall.* 317

Butterfly, what youthful bride can equal her array, *Thom.* 1: 202

———— and snail,　　　　*Gay* 2: 71

———— but a caterpillar dreſt,　　　　*Gay* 2: 72

Buyers are bid beware,　　　　*Butl.* 1: 180

Buzzard, called hawk by courtesy,　　　　*Dry.* 2: 90

Bye-words, epitaph of,　　　　*Gay* 1: 281

C

Cabinet-deſigns of fate, to anticipate,　　　　*Butl.* 1: 224

Cable wrought of Byblos' reed,　　　　*Pope ed.* 4: 193

Cabled ſtone, uſed for anchor,　　　　*Dyer* 65

Cackling ſhews the gooſe is poor,　　　　*Swift* 1: 199

Cacus, deſcribed,　　　　*Dry.* 6: 204

———— quelled by Hercules,　　　　*Wall.* 25

———— ſlain by Hercules,　　　　*Dry.* 6: 207

Cadenus and Vaneſſa,　　　　*Swift* 1: 101

———— old in politics and wit,　　　　*Swift* 1: 118

———— of half mankind the dread and hate,　　　　*Swift* 1: 118

———— Vaneſſa much eſteem'd his wit,　　　　*Swift* 1: 118

———— underſtood not what was love,　　　　*Swift* 1: 119

———— his grief and ſhame,　　　　*Swift* 1: 126

———— could ſcarce oppoſe Vaneſſa's ſlame,　　　　*Swift* 1: 126

Cadet trembles, when Jehovah ſpeaks,　　　　*Pitt* 239

Cadmus, ſtory of,　　　　*Add.* 144

———— founded an empire in Boeotian ſields,　　　　*Pope* 1: 288

———— my verſe inſpire,　　　　*Tick.* 222

———— who the firſt materials brought,　　　　*Tick.* 222

　　　　　　　　Cadogan,

Cadogan, on the death of the Earl of,   *Tick.* 196

———— laſt of captains, to the grave deſcends,   *Tick.* 196

Cælia to Damon,   *Broome* 134

——— an ode to,   *Pitt* 227

——— and Dorinda,   *Duke* 175

——— ſoliloquy of,   *Duke* 176

——— her dreſſing-room,   *Swift* 2 : 218

Cæſar form'd for perils hard and great,   *Rowe L.* 218

——— addreſs to his mutinous ſoldiers,   *Rowe L.* 219

——— made dictator,   *Rowe L.* 222

——— bold ambition prompts,   *Rowe L.* 49

——— had a valour, which no ſucceſs could fate, *Rowe L.* 50

——— is all things in himſelf alone,   *Rowe L.* 126

——— never patient long in peace,   *Rowe L.* 114

——— to nothing leſs than all aſpires,   *Rowe L.* 115

——— for deſtruction eager burns,   *Rowe L.* 104

——— abhorring law, he chuſes to offend,   *Rowe L.* 104

——— bluſhes to be thought his country's friend, *Rowe L.* 104

——— finds no enemy, but Rome,   *Rowe L.* 112

——— diſdains to brook a rival power,   *Rowe L.* 115

——— a malefactor, not a foe, we ſeek,   *Rowe L.* 108

——— tranſports part of his army to Epirus,   *Rowe L.* 223

——— ventures to Brunduſium to tranſport the reſt, *Rowe L.* 228

——— undaunted in a ſtorm,   *Rowe L.* 231

——— marches to Theſſaly,   *Rowe L.* 262

——— took not more pleaſure to ſubmit, than ſave, *Pom.* 278

——— ſpeech to his army,   *Rowe L.* 299

——— behaviour after the victory,   *Rowe L.* 322, 324

——— refuſes burial to the ſlain,   *Rowe L.* 324

——— driven from the field by ſtench of ſlain, *Row: L.* 325

Cæſar

Cæfar goes in purfuit of Pompey,   *Rowe L.* 423

—— views the ruins of Troy,   *Rowe L.* 424

—— offers incenfe, and pays his vows at Troy, *Rowe L.* 425

—— fets fail for Egypt,   *Rowe L.* 426

—— on his arrival prefented with Pompey's head, *Rowe L.* 426

—— receives the head with feign'd abhorrence, *Rowe L.* 428

—— comes to Alexandria,   *Rowe L.* 433

—— views the tomb of Alexander,   *Rowe L.* 434

—— enquires about the hiftory of Egypt,   *Rowe L.* 441

—— when the Nile rifes,   *Rowe L.* 442

—— befieged by Achillas,   *Rowe L.* 454

—— fires the fhips,   *Rowe L.* 457

—— leaps into the fea, and fwims to his fleet, *Rowe L.* 460

—— efcapes amidft a thoufand javelins,   *Rowe L.* 460

—— by the gods was crown'd,   *Rowe L.* 49

—— ambition of,   *Cow.* 2 : 266

—— enthrals Rome,   *Cow.* 2 : 35

—— remarkable for difpatch,   *Cow.* 2 : 375

—— wont the lucky hour to chufe,   *Hughes* 310

—— took his fudden flight,   *Hughes* 310

—— raptur'd with the charm of rule,   *Dyer* 10

—— mingles lawlefs love with lawlefs arms, *Hughes* 290

—— grac'd with both Minervas,   *Pope* 1 : 208

—— ignobly vain, and impotently great,   *Pope* 1 : 161

Cæftus, gloves of death,   *Pope il.* 2 : 315

Cafres, land of Hottentots,   *Dyer* 112

Cajeta, Æneas' nurfe,   *Dry.* 6 : 156

Cain, envy of,   *Cow.* 2 : 256

Calamities are friends,   *Young* 2 : 101

Calamity, by thought refin'd, infpirits and adorns,   *Sav.* 7

         Calchas,

Calchas, things paft, prefent, and to come, defcries, *Tick.* 166

———— fuch wifdom Phœbus gave,   *Tick.* 166

———— augur of ills,   *Tick.* 168

Calendars muft all yield to Cæfar's,   *Hughes* 295

Calenture, what,   *Swift* 1 : 201

Caligula, manner of fighting,   *Butl.* 2 : 95

Califto, ftory of,   *Add.* 122

Callicoes come from weeds,   *Swift* 1 : 213

Callimachus, firft hymn of,   *Prior* 2 : 17

———— fecond hymn of,   *Prior* 2 : 22

———— hymn to Jupiter,   *Pitt* 195

———— hymn to Apollo,   *Pitt* 199

Calliope, daughter of Memory,   *Cong.* 158

Calm, feeking in a reftlefs world,   *Watts* 114

—— reftored,   *Dry.* 5 : 318

—— peace returns, and fruitful plenty is reftor'd, *Hughes* 21

Calumny, blafting ftorms of,   *A. Phil.* 305

———— unkind, as hail it falls,   *A. Phil.* 305

———— can the greateft merit wound,   *Swift* 1 : 209

Calypfo, ifland of, defcribed,   *Pope od.* 3 : 147, feq.

———— dreadful in her charms,   *Pope od.* 3 : 196

Cam, contribute to our woe,   *Fent.* 210

—— and bid thy ftream in plaintive murmurs flow, *Fent.* 210

Cambray, on approaching congrefs of, 1721,   *Pitt* 265

———— virtuous flave of Louis and of Rome,   *Lytt.* 26

———— whofe maxims warm the patriot breaft, *Gay* 1 : 179

Cambria, long to fame well known,   *Hughes* 232

Cambyfes, mad with luft of power,   *Hughes* 300

———— to promis'd fpoils a numerous army led, *Hughes* 300

———— *exhaufted he return'd, nor faw great* Nilus' head, ib.

Camel, inured to thirſt,   *Milt.* 2 : 154

———— patient of thirſt and toil,   *Thom.* 1 : 76

———— ſon of the Deſart,   *Thom.* 1 : 76

Cameleon,   *Prior* 1 : 198

———— emblem of the flattering hoſt,   *Gay* 2 : 32

———— like thoſe I flatter'd, feed on air,   *Gay* 2 : 33

Cameleons thrive on air,   *Lanſ.* 152

Camera obſcura,   *Gay* 1 : 35

Camilla, daughter of Metabus,   *Dry.* 7 : 29

———— preſerved from her foes,   *Dry.* 7 : 29

———— education of,   *Dry.* 7 : 30

———— armour of,   *Dry.* 7 : 34

———— a warrior-dame, famous for ſpeed,   *Dry.* 6 : 193

———— like a falcon,   *Dry.* 7 : 37

———— Volſcian Amazon,   *Dry.* 7 : 24

———— killed by Aruns,   *Dry.* 7 : 41

———— ſhines bright in Virgil's lines,   *Hughes* 79

———— love of ſpoils her female boſom fir'd,   *Gay* 1 : 38

Camiſado of ſurplices,   *Butl.* 2 : 21

Camlet affected by rain,   *Gay* 1 : 102

Campus Martius, exerciſes of,   *Dyer* 17

Campaign,   *Add.* 51

———— an Iliad riſing out of one,   *Add.* 52

Camus, gentle, ſilver-winding ſtream,   *Dyer* 63

Canace to Macareus,   *Dry.* 4 : 177

Canals, too lifeleſs ſhow,   *A. Phil.* 33

———— nor to the eye, nor to the ear, they flow,   *A. Phil.* 33

———— made by the French,   *Dyer* 102

Candid to all, but to himſelf ſevere,   *Smith* 196

Candle, elegy to,   *Cong.* 109

Candle,

Candle, like thine, my flames to my deftruction turn, *Cong.* 110

————— riddle on,   *Swift* 1 : 328

Candour, temper'd mirth,   *Thom.* 2 : 172

————— and innocence dwell with youth, *Rowe L.* 349

Cane, rich juices from,   *Rowe L.* 132

———— convenience of,   *Gay* 1 : 103

———— abufe of,   *Gay* 1 : 103

Canibals, who make mankind their prey,   *Som.* 327

Canidia, epithalamium of,   *Som.* 250

Cannæ, fatal plain,   *Rowe L.* 84

Cannon clears the cloudy air,   *Rowe* 29

————— riddle on,   *Swift* 1 : 327

Cannons mark'd, whom they were bid to fpare, *Prior* 1 : 100

Cantata, what,   *Hughes* 113

—————   *Hughes* 153

—————   *Hughes* 116, 126, 129, 131, 136, 139, 140, 147

—————   *Prior* 1 : 263

Cantharides, to fire the lazy blood,   *Pope* 1 : 239

Canticles, an oriental eclogue,   *Collins* 289

Cape of Good Hope,   *Dyer* 113

Caperdewfie, heels freed from,   *Butl.* 1 : 185

Capers prompt the tafte of luxury,   *Dyer* 107

Capitol, fite of,   *Milt.* 2 : 202

————— defcribed,   *Dyer* 13

Caprice, the daughter of Succefs,   *Young* 1 : 158

Captive trumpeter,   *Som.* 262

Caracalla, bath of,   *Dyer* 18

Caravans from Ruffia to China,   *Dyer* 119

Carberiæ rupes,   *Swift* 1 : 267

Carbery rocks by *Dunkin,*   *Swift* 1 : 268

Carcafe

Carcase has furrow'd thy mind, worn-out with age, Gay 1: 335
Cards, we know, are Pluto's books,   Swift 2: 195
———— to ease the pain of coward thought,   Prior 2: 84
Care, a thoughtful being, long and spare,   Parn. 69
———— in vain we seek to fly,   Gay, 2: 84
———— pursues every where,   Ot. 73
———— tosses on his iron bed,   Broome 128
———— or, musing, fastens on the ground his eye, Broome 128
———— divine oblivion of low-thoughted,   Pope 1: 193
———— forgetting, or striving to forget,   Cong. 148
———— will kill a cat,   Swift 2: 33
———— unseal'd his eyes,   Pope od. 4: 47
———— our country claims our utmost,   Buck. 83
Careless something, that all art exceeds,   King 274
Cares, daughters of meagre Avarice,   King 369
———— all creatures feek their several,   Gay 2: 189
———— how anxious and vain !   Dry. 7: 310
Caricatura, what,   West 115
Carinae, a street now in ruins,   Dyer 19
Carleton, elegy on Lord,   Gov. 1: 64
Carlisle,   Wall. 36, 37
Carmel, spicy root of,   Mall. 239
Carmen Seculare,   Prior 1: 161
Carrion is the quarry of a crow,   Mall. 162
Cart, antique theatre,   Buth 2: 208
Carter (Mr.),   King 421
———— (Mrs.) on reading her poems,   Dyer 84
Carteret,   A. Phil. 346
———— just and benign and elegant,   A. Phil. 346
———— Miss, in the small-pox,   A. Phil. 368
                                             Carteret,

Carteret, Georgiana,   A. Phil. 369

Cartesians, from foes to emptiness,   Fent. 227

Carthage, rise of,   Dry. 5 : 329

———— a Tyrian colony,   Pitt 273

———— rich, brave, and practis'd in the arts of war, Pitt 273

———— Rome's great rival, now no more,   Hughes 278

Carus described,   Garth 53

Cascade described,   Thom. 1 : 63

Case stated,   Prior 2 : 259

Cashel Archbishop of, verses on,   Swift 2 : 299

Casian mountains' far distinguish'd height,   Rowe L. 350

Cassandra, never believed,   Dry. 5 : 362

———— laments over Hector,   Cong. 38

Cassimere now fam'd for glossy fleeces,   Dyer 69

———— Paradise of India,   Dyer 69

Cassiona and Peter,   Swift 2 : 226

Castle of indolence, situation,   Thom. 1 : 200

———— furniture of,   Thom. 1 : 211

———— inhabitants of,   Thom. D : 210

———— employment of,   Thom. 211

Castlemain,   Dry. 2 : 123

Castlennok, little house at,   Swift D : 62

Castling foals,   Butl. 1 : 209

Castor curbs the steed,   Pope od. 3 : 289

Casuistry, in lawn,   Pope 3 : 218

Cat, ode on death of,   Gray 328

—— what is averse to fish ?   Gray 329

—— has nine lives,   Butl. 2 : 76

—— and Puss, repartees between,   Butl. 2 : 192

Catalans, great in your sufferings,   A. Phil. 339

Catchpole

Catchpole, fullen of afpect,   *Phil.* 5

———— lays on ill-fated debtor his ample hand,   *Phil.* 5

———— conveys him to fome enchanted caftle,   *Phil.* 5

Caterpillar, the fpring's voracious peft,   *Gay* 2 : 173

Caterwauling brethren,   *Butl.* 1 : 79

Catiline, hopocrify of,   *Cow.* 2 : 264

———— diffoluteness and rapacity,   *Cow.* 2 : 265

Cato gathers the fcatter'd remains of Pharfalia,   *Rowe L.* 372

—— tranfports them to Cyrene,   *Rowe L.* 372

—— reprefles a defertion,   *Rowe L.* 386

—— fpeech to encourage the foldiers,   *Rowe L.* 391

—— fets an example of bearing toil,   *Rowe L.* 403

—— was always laft in Cato's care,   *Rowe L.* 101

—— the vanquifhed owned,   *Rowe L.* 49

—— who could conquer, could forgive,   *Rowe L.* 387

—— fhall open to himfelf a paffage,   *Add.* 331

—— like Mount Atlas, ftands unmov'd,   *Add.* 293

—— rifes fuperior, and looks down on Cæfar,   *Add.* 294

—— difdains a life which Cæfar offers,   *Add.* 277

—— by Pompey courted and by Cæfar fear'd,   *Pitt* 393

—— for Rome and Liberty he liv'd and dy'd,   *Pitt* 393

—— bold flights, th' extravagance of virtue,   *Add.* 289

—— laft good man of Rome,   *Pope* 1 : 161

—— on Addifon's tragedy of,   { *Young* 1 : 234
    Tick. 117
    Hughes 195
    A. Phil. 372

—— fent to a Lady,   *Hughes* 198

—— prologue to,   *Pope* 1 : 160

—— epilogue to,   *Garth* 120

Cato,

Cato, speech of, to Labienus, *Lytt.* 96

—— his voice we hear, asserting Virtue's cause, *Hughes* 196

Cattle, management of, *Dry.* 5 : 147

—— and corn were all the gold and silver, *Buck.* 90

Catullus, ode of, *Cow.* 1 : 176

—— on Lesbia, *Swift* 1 : 98

Caucasus, view of, *Mall.* 207

—— crown'd with everlasting snow, *Broome* 135

Cavendish, praise of, *Cow.* 1 : 341

—— Harley, with Waller's poems, *Fent.* 327

Cavil in debate ruins public business, *Butl.* 2 : 11

Cause of liberty betray, *Rowe L.* 318

—— final, of the different dispositions, *Aken.* 118

Cautious Alice, *Prior* 2 : 252

Cease to know, what known will violate thy peace, *Pope od.* 3 : 127

—— to live, or cease to love, *Pope* 1 : 180

Cebrion, lawless offspring of Priam's bed, *Pope il.* 2 : 129

Cecilia, { *Dry.* 2 : 203
{ *Yal.* 386

—— inventress of the vocal frame, *Hughes* 180

—— added length to solemn sounds *Hughes* 180

—— drew an angel down, *Hughes* 180

—— more than all the Muses skill'd, *Cong.* 63

—— to her Maker's praise confin'd the sound, { *Pope* 1 : 77
{ *Pope* 1 : 81

Cedar, prince of trees, *Wall.* 69

—— supreme of trees, and mistress of the wood, *Prior* 2 : 130

Celaeno, prophecy of, *Dry.* 6 : 13

Celia singing, *Lanf.* 197, 201, 202

—— to Damon, *Prior* 1 : 70

Celia.

Celia. See Cælia.

Celtiberians draw their descent from Gaul, *Rowe L.* 160

Cenotaph to Agamemnon's name, *Pope od.* 3 : 131

Censure, *Swift* 2 : 47

Censures fall on dull pretenders, *Garth* 65

Centaurs spilt their drunken souls, *Phil.* 77

Cerberus, mastiff of the triple head, *Swift* 2 : 224

——— porter of hell, *Dry.* 6 : 131

Cercopians, transformation of, *Garth* 125

Cerdon described, *Butl.* 1 : 64, 65

Ceres, a cornucopia fill'd her weaker hand, *Hughes* 19

Cerrial oak, chaplets of, *Dry.* 3 : 174

Ceylon, deemed to be Ophir, *Dyer* 161

Ceyx and Alcyone, *Dry.* 4 : 51

——— is it thus, O dearer than my life ! *Dry.* 4 : 67

——— thus, thus return'st thou to thy longing wife, *Dry.* 4 : 67

Chace, *Som.* 13

——— sport of kings, *Som.* 14

——— image of war, *Som.* 14

——— time of, *Gay* 1 : 11

——— grey-hound, used in, *Gay* 1 : 11

——— described, *Gay* 1 : 14

Chain, which holds heaven and earth and main, *Pope il.* 1 : 240

——— holds on, and where it ends, unknown, *Pope* 2 : 56

Chains of pleasure and of pride we wear, *Young* 2 : 91

Chair, made of Drake's ship, *Cow.* 1 : 167

Chair-curule, what, *Butl.* 1 : 216

Chairs prejudicial to health, *Gay* 1 : 103

Chamber-practice is not like the bar, *Dry.* 2 : 269

Champions for virtue, who for virtue bled, *Broome* 125

Champions

Champions triumphant o'er the world, o'er fin and death, *ib.* 126

Chance could not arrange a world, *Black.* 125

———— an idol, inert and blind, *Black.* 126

———— no efficient caufe, *Black.* 146

———— vain theory of, *Fent.* 240

———— direction, which thou canft not fee, *Pope* 2 : 39

Change, *Cow.* 1 : 236

———— charms of, *Roch.* 283

———— all things in perpetual, *Dry.* 4 : 147

———— of mind with change of fortune, *Gay* 2 : 149

Change-alley, a gulf, where thoufands fell, *Swift* 1 : 205

Changes produced on the fall, *Milt.* 2 : 67, 68

———— in ftates under providence, *Cow.* 2 : 236

Chaos, what, *Dry.* 3 : 297

———— heaven with earth confufed, *Wall.* 53

———— unformed mafs of matter, *Aken.* 315

———— defcribed, *Milt.* 1 : 65

———— Satan fteers his courfe through, *Milt.* 1 : 66

———— how all things blended lay, *Weft* 221

———— addrefs to Satan, *Milt.* 1 : 68

———— directs his courfe, *Milt.* 1 : 68

———— a way paved by fin and death, *Milt.* 1 : 69

———— feat of, *Garth* 81

Character, *Sav.* 180

———— a man that makes, makes foes, *Young* 3 : 190

———— to be preferved, *Rofc.* 264

———— depends on our years, *Rofc.* 265

———— the poet to preferve, *Dry.* 1 : 279

———— unity of, *Pope od.* 3 : 30

———— perfect to make, vulgar error, *Buck.* 77

Character perfect, a faultless monster,   *Buck.* 77

Chariot of paternal deity,   *Milt.* 1 : 198

———— race, described,   *Dry.* 5 : 150

Charity, that pure etherial ray,   *Tal.* 446

———— into our breasts by heaven itself convey'd,   *Tal.* 446

———— is next heaven,   *Dry.* 2 : 179

———— a well-meaning guide,   *Dry.* 1 : 252

———— of words ne'er allows to idle thought,   *Pom.* 250

———— paraphrase on 1 Cor. xiii.   *Prior* 2 : 27

———— without, Faith were vain,   *Prior* 2 : 28

———— decent, modest, easy, kind,   *Prior* 2 : 28

———— not soon provoked, she easily forgives,   *Prior* 2 : 28

———— soft peace she brings,   *Prior* 2 : 28

———— not bound by time, nor subject to decay,   *Prior* 2 : 28

———— shall still survive,   *Prior* 2 : 29

———— most practised by walkers,   *Gay* 1 : 126

———— where given with judgment,   *Gay* 1 : 126

———— not to be delay'd,   *Gay* 1 : 126

———— diffus'd to human race,   *Hughes* 272

———— in imparted pleasures seeks its own,   ·   *Hughes* 173

Charlemain, twelve peers of,   *Dry.* 3 : 185

Charles I. on a picture of,   *Tick.* 138

———— the good, the great,   *Tick.* 138

———— spoil'd of empire by unhallow'd hands,   *Tick.* 138

———— best of kings, to fall by inglorious hands, *Phil.* 78

———— too high notions of prerogative,   *Thom.* 2 : 114

Charles II. character of,   { *Dry.* 1 : 115
                                                 { *Duke*   120
                                                 { *Hal.*   215
                                                 { *Ot.*   6, 7

Charles II. happiness of his reign,   *Hal.* 217

———— satire on age,   *Butl.* 2 : 229

Charleton,   *Dry.* 2 : 121

Charms are sweet, but charms are frail,   *Broome* 60

———— swift as the short-liv'd flower they flie,   *Broome* 60

———— strike the sight, but merit wins the soul,   *Pope* 1 : 151

———— possession of a day,   *Broome* 46

———— age or sickness soon or late disarms,   *Pope* 2 : 337

———— are nonsense,   *Roch.* 342

———— that from virtue flow,   *Yal.* 446

———— are heighten'd by religion,   *Yal.* 446

———— of sense in sparkling wit we find,   *Yal.* 441

———— in melody are found,   *Rowe* 67

———— of nature supplied by wit,   *Pope* 1 : 166

———— the world has false, but flattering,   *Watts* 45

Charon, described,   *Dry.* 6 : 126

———— who ferried over by,   *Dry.* 6 : 127

Charters of corporations seiz'd,   *Thom.* 2 : 117.

Charybdis described,   *Pope od.* 3 : 311.

Chaste Florimel,   *Prior* 2 : 254.

———— no epithet to suit with fair,   *Dry.* 7 : 297.

———— your thoughts, your expression clean,   *Hughes* 80

Chastity, in Saturn's reign,   *Dry.* 7 : 252

———— sun-clad, power of,   *Milt.* 3 : 148.

———— clads in complete steel,   *Milt.* 3 : 136

———— a wise, suspicious maid,   *Collins* 235.

———— denies to raise the blush,   *Pope od.* 3 : 178

Chaucer, a merry bard,   *Add.* 34

———— first polished English verse,   *Dry.* 3 : 16.

———— lame in his verse,   *Dry.* 3 : 27.

Chaucer,

Chaucer, like the morning ftar,   *Den.* 54

————— in his old ftyle has a modern grace,   *Dry.* 1 : 274

————— had all that beauty could infpire,   *Fent.* 240

————— borrows his fubjects from Boccace,   *Dry.* 3 : 23

————— comprifes the characters of his age,   *Dry.* 3 : 31

————— foul of, tranfpos'd into Spenfer,   *Dry.* 3 : 14

————— inclined to Wickliff's opinions,   *Dry.* 3 : 29

————— lives in younger Spenfer's ftrains,   *Smith* 194

————— Tale, in the manner of,   *Fent.* 295

————— imitated,   *Pope* 1 : 343

————— infcription for ftatue of,   *Aken.* 326

Chaulieu, prieft of pleafure,   *Aken.* 266

Chearfulnefs, a nymph of healthieft hue,   *Collins* 272

Cheat, in being cheated, pleafure of,   *Butl.* 1 : 223

Cheats of fenfe will all our learning fhare,   *Pom.* 338

Cheerfulnefs, hymn to,   *Aken.* 201

————— fhine thro' the cloud of care,   *Aken.* 202

————— Virtue's friend,   *Aken.* 202

————— fair guardian of domeftic life,   *Aken.* 203

————— kind banifher of homebred ftrife,   *Aken.* 203

————— thine was Homer's ancient might,   *Aken.* 204

————— Horace calls thy fportive choir,   *Aken.* 205

Cheefes, offspring of the pail,   *Parn.* 39

Chemos, where worfhiped,   *Milt.* 1 : 18

————— called Peor,   *Milt.* 1 : 18

————— god of luft,   *Milt.* 1 : 19

Cheronaea, battle, overthrow of Greece,   *Thom.* 2 : 51

Cherubim, defcribed,   *Milt.* 1 : 198

Chefs, game of,   *Den.* 77

Chevy-chafe, what woeful wars befel,   *Gay* 1 : 90

Chicane, in furs,   *Pope* 3 : 218

Chickens counted, ere hatched,   *Butl.* 1 : 258

Chief, who guides, ill fits indolent repose,   *Pope il.* 1 : 68

—— elate in thought, he facks untaken Troy, *Pope il.* 1 : 68

—— of domestic knights and errant,   *Butl.* 1 : 5

Child, complaint of,   *Watts* 352

Childhood shows the man,   *Milt.* 2 : 208

—————— through the round of age returns,   *Prior* 2 : 163

Children in the wood,   *Gay* 1 : 89

—————— their corpse Robin-red-breast strew'd,   *Gay* 1 : 89

Chimaera, a mingled monster,   *Pope il.* 1 : 198

China, trade to,   *Dyer* 118

—— fertility of,   *Dyer* 118

—— ladies, with little feet and winking eyes,   *Gay* 1 : 40

Chine, the honour of the feast,   ,   *Pope od.* 4 : 89

—— an honorary part,   *Pope od.* 3 : 210

Chinese lie-in for their ladies,   *Butl.* 1 : 298

Chiron, fire of pharmacy,   *Pope il.* 1 : 353

—————— the Shovel of a former age,   *Young* 3 : 275

Chloe,   *Lanf.* 189

—— like morning fair,   .   *Lanf.* 189

——·— and common as the air,   ˝   *Lanf.* 189

Chloreus, priest of Cybele,   *Dry.* 7 : 39

——·— armour of,   *Dry.* 7. 39

Chloris,   *Wall.* 184

—————— and Hylas,   *Wall.* 116

—————— of Amphion's stem, had Neftor by Neleus, *Fent.* 257

Choafpes, drink of kings alone,   *Milt.* 2 : 192

Choice,   { *Pom.* 215
                                 { *Dyer* 140

Choice alone can blefs,   *Som.* 281

———— of friends fhews our good or evil name,   *Gay* 2 : 69

———— of good and ill permitted,   *Dry.* 2 : 245

———— of heaven fafer than our own,   *Young* 3 : 113

Choral lays, fweet tribute, paid by the Mufe to virtue, *Weft* 214

Choroebus, fam'd for virtue, as for arms,   *Pope* 1 : 316

Chorus to fupply want of action,   *Rofc.* 267

———— of Seneca's Thyaftes imitated,   *Lanf.* 186

———— of Athenians to Brutus,   *Pope* 1 : 82

———— of youths and virgins,   *Pope* 1 : 83

Chrift, nativity of,   *Watts* 51

——— feed of the woman,   *Milt.* 2 : 139

——— is God and man,   *Dry.* 1 : 255

——— the morning-ftar,   *Milt.* 2 : 153

——— fafted forty days,   *Milt.* 2 : 153

——— baptized,   *Milt.* 2 : 144

——— proclaimed fon of God,   *Milt.* 2 : 144, 146

——— flight to Egypt,   *Milt.* 2 : 165

——— laid in a manger,   *Milt.* 2 : 165

——— expofed to Satan's temptations,   *Milt.* 2 : 148, 149

——— tempted with kingdoms,   *Milt.* 2 : 191

——— unfhaken in temptation,   *Milt.* 2 : 215

——— pronounced fon of God,   *Milt.* 2 : 218

——— proof againft temptation,   *Milt.* 2 : 219

——— fet on the pinacle of temple,   *Milt.* 2 : 219

——— tempted to throw himfelf down,   *Milt.* 2 : 119

——— an over-match for Satan,   *Milt.* 2 : 201

——— fecond Adam,   *Milt.* 2 : 98

——— kingdom of, extenfive,   *Milt.* 2 : 206

——— no end of his kingdom,   *Milt.* 2 : 151

Chrift,

Chrift, heir of both worlds,   *Milt.* 2 : 222

———— queller of Satan,   *Milt.* 2 : 222

———— dying, rifing, and reigning,   *Watts* 100

———— led the monfter, Death, in chains,   *Watts* 100

———— love of fhould inflame our,   *Cow.* 1 : 157

———— paffion of,   { *Cow.* 1 : 155
                                            { *Pitt*   . 219

———— judge of quick and dead,   *Milt.* 2 : 134

———— blood of, cancels our debt,   *Rofc.* 251

———————— our balfam,   *Den.* 93

———— love to, prefent or abfent,   *Watts* 148

———— abfence of,   *Watts* 149

———— defcent to earth defired,   *Watts* 151.

———— afcending to in heaven,   *Watts* 152

———— longing for his return,   *Watts* 154

———— converfe with,   *Watts* 144

———— defiring to love,   *Watts* 132

———— fight of,   *Watts* 139

Chriftian, the higheft ftile of man,   *Young* 2 : 88

————————machinery, whether weaker than Heathen, *Dry.* 7 : 120

———————— triumph,   *Young* 2 : 62

———————— poet, ridiculous in a Pagan drefs,   *Black.* 26

Chriftianity increafed by oppreffion,   *Butl.* 2 : 12

Chriftians fewed in bear-fkins,   *Butl.* 1 : 41

Chriftmas, the joyous period of the year,   *Gay* 1 : 126

Chromis led the Myfian train,   *Pope il.* 1 : 102

Chromius praifed,   *Cow.* 2 : 16

———————— victor in the Nemean games,   *Weft* 202

Chronicle,   *Cow.* 1 : 125

Chryfeis to her fire was fent,   *Pope il.* 1 : 54

Chryfeis,

Chryseis, give to these arms again,   *Pope il.* 1 : 38

Church, my garden,   *Parn.* 208

———— nor raise, a rival to the state,   *Lytt.* 27

———— a den of thieves, what makes,   *Butl.* 1 : 318

———— increased by Martyrs' blood,   *Butl.* 2 : 293

———— power of, to persuade,   *Dry.* 2 : 25

———— to meet good company at,   *Broome* 120

Church-monuments foretel the weather,   *Gay* 1 : 107

Church-yard, elegy in,   *Gray* 337

Chyle, formation of,   *Black.* 193

———— progress of, to the heart,   *Black.* 195

Cibberian forehead, leaving shame no room,   *Pope* 3 : 253

Cicero, fond of fame,   *Dry.* 7 : 107

Ciceroni, who,   *West* 278

Ciconians, Ulysses' adventure among,   *Pope od.* 3 : 228

Cimmeria described,   *Pope od.* 3 : 277

Cimmerians, darkling dwell,   *Fent.* 248

Cinder-picking fair,   *Swift* 2 : 87

Cinga rolls his rapid waves,   *Rowe L.* 161

Cinyras and Myrrha,   *Dry.* 4 : 37

Cippus, story of,   *Garth* 152

Circassia, ever fam'd for pure and happy loves,   *Collins* 244

———— boasts the fairest of the fair,   *Collins* 244

Circe, daughter of the sun,   *Dry.* 6 : 157

———— changes men to beasts,   *Dry.* 6 : 157

———— foretels Ulysses' future fate,   *Pope od.* 3 : 308

———— advises to avoid the Sirens' song,   *Pope od.* 3 : 309

———— Scylla and Charybdis,   *Pope od.* 3 : 309

———— enchantments of,   *Garth* 130

———— island of,   *Pope od.* 3 : 256

Circe transforming to hogs,   *Pope od.* 3 : 26

Circius' loud blaft is heard to roar,   *Rowe L.* 66

Circulation difcovered by Harvey,   *Garth* 88

Circumcifion appointed,   *Cow.* 2 : 113

Circle, riddle on,   *Swift* 1 : 319

Circles to fquare, and cubes to double,   *Prior* 2 : 79

———————— give exceffive trouble,   *Prior* 2 : 79

Cithæron's top falutes the fky,   *Pope* 1 : 283

Cities built,   *Milt.* 2 : 106

Cits know to fin, as well as fot,   *Mall.* 306

—— who prefer a guinea to mankind,   *Young* 1 : 86

City-fhower defcribed,   *Swift* 1 : 60

Civil dudgeon grew high,   *Butl.* 1 : 3

Civil life fecured by children and a wife,   *Butl.* 1 : 301

Civil war,   *Cow.* 1 : 324

—— wars deny bays to the brow,   *Cow.* 1 : 105

———————— of York and Lancafter,   *Gray* 356

———————— white rofe and red,   *Gray* 357

———————— curft,   *Dry.* 1 : 127

———————— fierce,   *Butl.* 2 : 255

Civility to Walkers,   *Gay* 1 : 112

Claremont,   *Garth* 92

Clarendon, character of,   *Duke* 85

———————— had law and fenfe,   *Dry.* 2 : 202

Clarinda,   *Lanf.* 192

Clark, Nicholas, verfes to,   *Watts* 209

Clark, elegy on Richard,   *Cow.* 1 : 65

Claffic ground, to tread on,   *Add.* 40

—— learning loft on claffic ground,   *Pope* 3 : 239

Claudian combines repugnant ideas,   *Add.* 190

G 3   *Claudian*

Claudian couches mean thoughts in high words,   *Add.* 180

————— his old man of Verona,   *Cow* 2 : 365

Clausus, author of the Claudian race,   *Dry.* 6 : 189

Cleanthes, hymn of,   *West* 232

Clelia to Urania,   *Walsh* 338

Clemency makes power rever'd,   *Prior* 1 : 169

Clement's church, pass of dangerous,   *Gay* 1 : 132

Cleomenes, prologue to,   *Prior* 1 : 74

Cleone, epilogue to,   *Sben.* 195

Cleopatra flies to Cæsar,   *Rowe L.* 436

————— complains of her brother's injustice,   *Rowe L.* 437

————— prostitutes herself to Cæsar,   *Rowe L.* 438

————— hopes to become Cæsar's consort,   *Rowe L.* 439

————— entertains Cæsar with grandeur,   *Rowe L.* 440

————— the fate and fury of the Roman race,   *Hughes* 289

Cleora,   *Lans.* 193

Clergy covetous,   *Ot.* 8

Clergymen praise Classics more than holy writ,   *Swift* 2 : 14

Clever Tom Clinch going to be hanged,   *Swift* 2 : 50

Clifford was fierce and brave,   *Dry.* 2 : 202

Climate, defects of,   *Dyer* 34

————— English, vindicated,   *Dyer* 34

Clinches defiling a land,   *Cow.* 1 : 131

Clitumnus, smooth,   *Add.* 41

Cloacina, goddess of common sewers,   *Gay* 1 : 115

————— goddess bright,   *Swift* 2 : 178

Cloe,   *Prior* 1 : 275

—— hunting,   *Prior* 1 : 107

—— jealous,   *Prior* 1 : 126

————— answer to,   *Prior* 1 : 128

Cloe jealous, better anfwer,   *Prior* 1 : 129

Cloe weeping,   *Prior* 1 : 103

Cloris,   *Wall.* 96

Cloth, to cut the coat according to,   *Dry.* 3 : 139

Cloud, fimile for a woman,   *Swift* 2 : 320

———— turns with every wind,   *Swift* 2 : 320

———— frightens with its thunder,   *Swift* 2 : 320

———— weeps, tears womens' rain,   *Swift* 2 : 320

———— roams, women never at home,   *Swift* 2 : 320

———— builds caftles in the air, as women do,   *Swift* 2 : 320

———— delights in change, as ladies,   *Swift* 2 : 321

———— every woman is,   *Swift* 2 : 322

Cloud-compelling Jove,   *Wall.* 15

Cloud-condenfing, as the weft-wind blows,   *Pope il.* 1 : 37

Cloud-difpelling winds,   *Dry.* 3 : 309

Cloud and pillar of fire,   *Milt.* 2 : 126

Clouds fall in fhowers, to wake the flowers,   *Broome* 167

———— reduced to no art,   *Wall.* 88

———— we grafp at, and beat the air,   *Prior* 2 : 127

Clowns are to polifh'd manners blind,   *Gay* 2 : 81

Coaches dangerous in fnowy weather,   *Gay* 1 : 122

———— ftops of, defcribed,   *Gay* 1 : 133

Coafting, the firft navigation,   *Dry.* 1 : 87

Coat for winter,   *Gay* 1 : 102

Cobham, letter to,   *Cong.* 146

———— in nature learned and humanely wife,   *Ham.* 227

Cock defcribed,   *Dry.* 3 : 140, feq.

——— and fox,   *Dry.* 3 : 139

Cock-a-hoop with victory,   *Butl.* 1 : 101

Cocks proclaim'd the crimfon dawn of day,   *Parn.* 46

Cocytus,

Cocytus, lamentable waters,   *Pope od.* 3 : 271

Codrus fhould·expeƈt a Juvenal,   *Garth* 65

Coena dubia, what,   *Dry.* 7 : 132

Coffee makes the politician wife,   *Pope* 1 : 141

Cohefion inexplicable,   *Black.* 44.

Coins hardened by allay,   *Butl.* 2 : 30

Colchefter, news from,   *Den.* 67

Colchis improv'd the fleece,   *Dyer* 64

Cold feet are pointed to the door,   *Pope il.* 2 : 202

—— iron, danger of meddling with,   *Butl.* 1 : 100

Coldnefs,   *Cow.* 1 : 279

Cole, whofe dark ftreams his flowery iflands lave, *Pope* 1 : 71

Colemira,   *Shen.* 163

Colin, complaint of,   *Rowe* 51

—— thy hopes are in vain,   *Rowe* 52

—— reply to,   *Rowe* 53

—— fong of,   -   *Shen.* 50

—— and Lucy,   *Tick.* 191

Collar, verfes on,   *Hughes* 204

College for experimental philofophy,   *Cow.* 2 : 388

College-joke, to cure the dumps,   *Swift* 2 : 227

Collins's eclogues,   233—242

—— odes,   245—270,

—— epiftle to Hanmer,   274, 321

—— dirge in Cymbeline,   280, 321

—— on death of Thomfon,   281.

—— verfes on a paper with bride-cake,   283

—— general obfervations on the Oriental eclogues, 285—295.

—— on his odes,   298—319

Colocynthus, harangue of,   *Garth* 44

Colon

Colon described, — Butl. 1 : 66; Garth 31

Colonies, advantages of our American, — Dyer 122.

——— Grecian, — Thom. 2 : 57.

—————— spread liberty, — Thom. 57.

Colossus stood near Rhodes acrofs the raging flood, — Tick. 110

——— his stride an hour's sail, — Tick. 110.

Colour, wear what best becomes, — Cong. 119.

——— no complexion all alike can bear, — Cong. 119.

Colours mellow to shade and ripen into light, — Pitt 209

——— are but phantoms of the day, — Hughes 271.

——— with that they're born, with that they fade away, — ib.

Colt's tooth to have, — King 356.

Columbus difcovers America, — Cow. 2 : 30

Combat, folemn conditions of, — Pope il. 1 : 117

——— lifts of difpos'd, — Pope il. 1 : 118.

——— of Hudibras and Talgol, — Butl. 1 : 83, 84.

——— of Ralph and Colon, — Butl. 1 : 84, 85.

——— of Crowdero and Hudibras, — Butl. 1 : 89.

Come, Lord Jefus, — Watts 157

Comedy loves an humble verfe, — Rofc. 263.

——— fometimes raifes its voice, — Rofc. 263.

——— abufe of, — Dry. 1 : 286, feq.

——— expofed follies of men, — Dry. 1 : 287.

——— reflects fpots or graces, — Wall. 105

Comets, what, — Dry. 1 : 64

——— God's beacons, — Cow. 2 : 143

——— heralds of woe, — Broome 27

——— wild omens to the vulgar, fcience to the wife, — Sav. 38

——— fhook their fatal hair, — Rome L. 72

Comets

Comets forewarn'd the Theban war, *Pope il.* 1 : 141

———— their paths various, *Mall.* 225

———— march with lawless horrour bright, . *Prior* 1 : 180

Comforter sent, *Milt.* 2 : 135

Comforts of a friend, . *Watts* 212

Commands are no constraints, . *Milt.* 3 : 53

Commendation, nine-pence, *Butl.* 1 : 27

Commentators each dark passage shun, *Young* 1 : 161

——————— and hold their farthing candle to the sun, *ib.* 161

——————— in Homer view, more than he knew, *Swift* 2 : 303

——————— partiality of, *Dry.* 7 : 164

Commerce, wealthy goddess, . *Gay* 1 : 164

———— child of Liberty and Peace, *Sav.* 16.

———— brings riches, . *Young* 3 : 246

———— gives arts as well as gain, *Young* 3 : 251

———— learning, virtue, gold, . *Young* 3 : 251

———— spread through every land, *Pitt* 266

———— brings India home, *Pitt* 266

———— mix'd mankind, *Rowe L.* 130

———— ancient channels of, *Dyer* 110

Common crime one common fate requires, . *Pope od.* 4 : 209

———— fame, nothing so false, *Roch.* 318

———— forms were not design'd, . *Swift* 1 : 121

———— directors to a noble mind, *Swift* 1 : 121

Common-sewers foretell the weather, *Gay* 1 : 107

Common-wealth sounds like a common whore, *Dry.* 2 : 251

Common wit supposes common sense, *Dry.* 2 : 159

Commoner of love, without a wife, . *Fent.* 289

Commons house of, first appointed, *Thom.* 2 : 107

Communion is an inward feast, *Parn.* 197

Commutual

Commutual death, the fate of war,   *Pope il.* 1 : 242

Companions in woe yield no relief,   *Milt.* 2 : 156

Company, he who loves not his own, is wretched, *Cow.* 2 : 290.

———— like all, except your own,   *Pitt* 285

Comparison,   *Shen.* 146

———— just, what,   *Butl.* 1 : 43

———— and complaint,   *Watts* 94

Comparisons are odious,   *Swift* 2 : 328

Compassion checks my spleen,   *Parn.* 99

———— swells our grief,   *Young* 1 : 60

———— ill-judged, dangerous,   *Ot.* 4

Competence is vital to content,   *Young* 2 : 147

Competency yields happiness,   *Cow.* 2 : 357

Complaint,
{
  Cow. 1 : 199
  Young 2 : 3
  Broome 134.
  Aken. 289
  Watts 209

———— advantage of the first,   *Butl.* 2 : 101

Complexion, how soon fades,   *Cong.* 115

Compost to dung the ground,   *Dry.* 3 : 148

Compotation dire prolong'd, reason quits her empire, *Phil.* 76

Comus,   *Milt.* 3 : 121

———— son of Bacchus and Circe,   *Milt.* 3 : 139

Concealment,   *Cow.* 1 : 285

———— artful ill becomes the brave,   *Pope od.* 3 : 223

Conceit, a glittering thought,   *Pope* 1 : 103

———— all glares alike,   *Pope* 1 : 104

Conceits, misty sons of Night,   *Parn.* 105

Concertion of design, in works of God,   *Young* 3 : 49

    Conciseness

Concifenefs pleafes every gueft in verfe,   *Weft* 200.

Concord, heavenly-born, foul of the world,   *Tick.* 157

———— life of the world and fafety of mankind, *Rowe L.* 170.

———— who the warring elements doft bind, *Rowe L.* 170

———— come, and bolt the iron-gates of war, *Pitt* 266

———— before whofe balm Rage drops his fteel, *Collins* 261

Confeffion and pardon,   *Watts* 89

Confidence fupplies all worth,   *Butl.* 2 : 304

Conflagration of the world,   *Milt.* 2 : 115

———————— and judgment,   *Pom.* 327

Conformity divine, man created to,   *Milt.* 2 : 105

Confucius ftood fuperior and alone,   *Pope* 1 : 206

Confufion of tongues,   *Milt.* 2 : 121

Congreve, poems of,   3

———— epiftle to Halifax,   3

———— mourning mufe of Alexis,   5

———— to the king,   13

———— birth of the Mufe,   20

———— on Mrs. Hunt finging,   29

———— Priam's lamentation,   33

———— lamentations of Hecuba, &c.   37

———— paraphrafe on Horace,   44

———— ftanzas in imitation of Horace,   45

———— imitation of Horace,   48

———— fong,   51

———— the reconciliation,   52

———— abfence,   53

———— fong,   53

———— fong in dialogue,   54

———— fong,   55

Congreve,

Congreve, the petition, 55

———— song, 56

———— song, 56

———— verses occasioned by a lady's writing, 57

———— epigram on Mrs. Hunt, 57

———— song, 58

———— hymn to harmony, 58

———— verses to the memory of Gethin, 64

———— epitaph on the Huntingdons, 65

———— to Dryden on his Persius, 66

———— eleventh satire of Juvenal, 68

———— prologue to Queen Mary, 81

———— epilogue at the opening the theatre, 83

———— prologue to Pyrrhus, 84

———— epilogue to Oroonoko, 85

———— prologue to Husband his own cuckold, 87

———— prologue to A very good wife, 89

———— prologue to the Court, 91

———— tears of Amaryllis for Amyntas, 93

———— to Cynthia, 99

———— Amoret, 102

———— Lesbia, 103

———— Doris, 103

———— to sleep, elegy, 106

———— to Kneller, 108

———— to a candle, elegy, 109

———— Ovid's third book of love, 111

———— of pleasing, 142

———— letter to Cobham, 146

———— on Miss Temple, 149

Congreve.

Congreve, Pindaric ode, 15ɛ

———— to Godolphin, 164

———— an impoſſible thing, 169

———— peaſant in ſearch of his heifer, 176

———— Homer's hymn to Venus, { 177
Dry. 2 : 137

———— harmonious, Add. 38

———— fancy's unexhauſted ſtore, Add. 38

Conjugal love, no greater bliſs, Milt. 2 : 12

Conquer, who believe they can, Dry. 6 : 82

Conquering people to themſelves a prey, Thom. 2 : 71

Conqueror greateſt, lord of his appetites, Lanſ. 188

———— introduced the chace, Som. 16

Conquerors, illuſtrious by triumph, Butl. 1 : 94

———— cruel ſpoilers, Ot. 15

———— foes of peace and ſcourges of mankind, Pope od. 4 : 26

Conqueſt, right of Cow. 2 : 230

———— is heaven's gift, Cow. 2 : 123

———— deſtruction of mankind, Broome 55

———— its laurels flouriſh, but in human woe, Broome 55

———— is thy flight, Pope od. 3 : 312

———— ceaſe, and ſlavery be no more, Pope 1 : 74

Conſcience, court of, Butl. 1 : 201

———— God's umpire, Milt. 1 : 79

———— wakes deſpair, Milt. 1 : 102

———— condemns or acquits, Dry. 1 : 251

———— upbraiding, is the fiend that haunts, Hughes 265

———— teſt of every mind, Dry. 7 : 310

———— well informed is ever the ſame, Dry. 2 : 79

———— more than friendſhip ſway'd, Smith 196

Conſcience,

Conscience, of guilt is prophecy of pain, *Young* 2 : 184

———— makes the guilty squeak, *Gay* 2 : 123

———— interest ill-disguised, *Dry.* 2 : 103

———— should have vacation, *Butl.* 1 : 201

———— stretchers, who, *Butl.* 2 : 108

Conscientious frauds, *Butl.* 2 : 87

Conscious honour supplies peace of mind, *Som.* 169

———— merit, justly bold, *Dry.* 2 : 55

Consent makes the act one's own, *Butl.* 1 : 206

Consequences imputed, if not necessary, unfair, *Black.* 6

Consolation, *Young* 3 : 1

———— cancels the complaint, *Young* 3 : 18

———— lost on the afflicted, *Milt.* 3 : 29

———— source of from above, *Milt.* 3 : 29

Consolations, what heights of, crown my song, *Young* 3 : 81

Conspiracies no sooner form'd than executed, *Add.* 255

Constable, to outrun, *Butl.* 1 : 151

Constancy, like a rock, *Dry.* 6 : 184

———— is built on manly minds, *Rowe L.* 341

———— true, no time, no power can move, *Gay* 2 : 226

Constant, *Cow.* 1 : 302

———— to keep the purposed end in view, *Rowe L.* 101

———— minds by grief are try'd, *Prior* 1 : 79

Constantine, on his paintings, *Hughes* 249

Constraint turns pleasure into pain, *Som.* 281

Consumption, a flattering disease, *Dry.* 5 : 224

Contemplation, sedate compeer of night, *Thom.* 1 : 160

Contempt of order, manners profligate, *West* 312

———— symptoms of a diseas'd and bloated state, *ib.* 312

Contending nations won and lost the day, *Pope il* 2 : 179

Content,

Content, happiness of, — *Den.* 8

———— a cordial in keenest grief, — *Pom.* 268

———— from noise and courts retires, — *Sav.* 8

———— on a life well-spent, — *Swift* 2 : 2

———— O sweetness of, seraphic joy ! — *Lanf.* 186

———— nothing wanting, nothing can destroy, — *Lanf.* 186

———— who finds, finds happiness, — *Gay* 2 : 150

———— is wealth, — *Dry.* 3 : 203

———— the style below, — *Young* 3 : 107

———— is joy and virtue too, — *Young* 3 : 107

———— dame of the ruddy cheek, — *Parn.* 60

———— of spirit must from science flow, — *Prior* 2 : 103

———— is all the gods can give, — *Som.* 260

———— with ease, — *Broome* 53

———— of mind, the poor man's wealth, — *Dry.* 2 : 51

———— that lives to reason, — *Mall.* 236

———— bear thy lot, — *Prior* 2 : 17

———— thyself to be obscurely good, — *Add.* 328

———— to live, content to die, unknown, — *A. Phil.* 334

Contented Shepherd, — *Rowe* 63

———— every thing charms, — *Dyer* 143

Contentedly he slept, as cheaply as he din'd, — *Cong.* 74

Contention, with superior sway, to wave, — *Pope il.* 2 : 312

———— shun, sure source of woe, — *Pope il.* 1 : 276

Contentment, — *Rowe* 49

———— where not too little, or too much gives peace, — *ib.* 49

———— hymn to, — *Parn* 78

———— lovely, lasting peace of mind, — *Parn* 78

———— sweet delight of human kind, — *Parn* 78

———— surest friend, — *Thom.* 2 : 135

Contentment,

Contentment, laugh'd with peace,   *Parn.* 144

Conteft hard, not for fame, but life,   *Pope il.* 2 : 179

—— with force, brutifh,   *Milt.* 1 : 177

Contefts mighty rife from trivial things,   *Pope* 1 : 127

Contingency, page of ftrong,   *Dry.* 1 : 315

Converfation,   *Prior* 2 : 225

—————— is but carving,   *Swift* 2 : 21

Converfe, by gay lively fenfe infpir'd,   *Thom.* 1 : 63

—— when moral wifdom fhines,   *Thom.* 1 : 63

—— of the wife and good, as free, as joyous, *Thom.* 2 : 171

—— breathing mix'd improvement with delight, *id.* 2 : 171

Converfion by fire and fword,   *Butl.* 2 : 295

Convert, love of,   *Parn.* 253

—————— furpaffes the lover and the parent, *Parn.* 254

—————— a torch of love divine,   *Parn.* 254

Conviction breathes conviction,   *Thom.* 2 : 169

Cook, art of, whether natural or acquired,   *King* 221

—— muft pleafe by cleanlinefs,   *King* 224

Cookery, art of,   *King* 203

—— extent of,   *Shen.* 171

Cooks, Homer's heroes,   *King* 210

Cook-maid, the turnfpit and the ox,   *Gay* 2 : 186

Cooper, work for,   *Gay* 2 : 4

Cooper's hill,   *Den.* 7

—————— eternal wreaths fhall grow,   *Pope* 1 : 67

Coquet,   { *Som.* 238 { *Hughes* 122

——— faireft tyrant of the plain,   *Hughes* 122

——— laugh'd at her adoring fwain,   *Hughes* 122

Coquette,   *Broome* 118

Coquette mother and daughter,   Gay 1: 261

Coquettes, in fylphs, aloft repair,   Pope 1: 129

Corah, character of,   Dry. 1: 146, feq.

Cordus expoſtulates with the gods,   Rowe L. 365

———— rehearfes his military exploits,   Rowe L. 366

———— execrates Egypt, the fatal land,   Rowe L. 366

———— pictures to himſelf the removal of the aſhes,   ib. 367

———— burns Pompey's body,   Rowe L. 363

———— erects a monument for Pompey,   Rowe L. 365

———— writes an inſcription,   Rowe L. 365

Corinna,   { Lanſ. 190
                                                 { Swift 1: 79

Corinthian order, rife of,   Dyer 14

Coriolanus, prologue to,   Lytt. 101

Corkſcrew, riddle on,   Swift 1: 311

Cormorants, that croud the court,   Pope M. 4: 170

———— nor human right, nor wrath divine revere, id. 4: 170

Corneille, with Lucan's fpirit fir'd,   Collins 277

———— with Shakefpeare's force and fire,   Lytt. 28

Cornelia, paſſion of, on the death of Pompey,   Rowe L. 373

———— communicates Pompey's laſt commands, Rowe L. 375

———— gives herſelf up to grief,   Rowe L. 375

———— performs the laſt rites to Pompey,   Rowe L. 380

———— faints at the fight of Pompey,   Rowe L. 332

Cornifh fquire, prologue to,   Garrb 117

Cornutus, character of,   Dry. 7: 175

———— praife of,   Dry. 7: 346

Cornwall, verſes on [by Mr. Duncombe],   Lytt. 88

———— fav'd his leader's life, but loſt his own, Lytt. 89

Cornwallis, verſes to Lord,   Broome 56

                                                 Cornwallis,

Cornwallis, great, without the vices of the great, *Broome* 56

Coromandel, coast of, *Dyer* 116

———— trade to, *Dyer* 116

Coronet, this commoner's head akes for, *Prior* 1 : 153

Coronis, story of, *Add.* 128

Corruption of nature tempts to ambition, *Cow.* 2 : 221

———————— transmitted, *Milt.* 2 : 72

————— bane of freedom, *Thom.* 2 : 51

————— mortal bane of freedom, *Aken.* 213

————— o'er court, o'er senate spread, *Aken.* 213

————— undermining hand of, *Thom.* 2 : 120

————— of the times, *Rosc.* 255

————— like a flood, shall deluge all, *Pope* 2 : 123

————— dark like fate, saps a state, *Pope* 2 : 13

————— sways mankind, *Gay* 2 : 158

————— barr'd by staying from vain travel, *West* 260

————— in a distant soil, strongly assays the youthful, *ib.* 261

————— spreads contagion o'er the land, *Gay* 2 : 151

————— deep, eats our soul away, *Thom.* 2 : 176

————— dash, in her proud career, *Aken.* 345

————— her slaves be taught, that Vice was born to fear, *ib.*

————— dragg'd at length to her fate, *Aken.* 333

Corydon, *Hughes* 121

Cost on graves is merely thrown away, *Pope* 1 : 265

Cotton, growth of every sultry clime, *Dyer* 71

Couch plain, and only rich his mind, *Cong.* 74

Covenant to espouse, *Butl.* 1 : 324

Coventry, Lady Anne, *Som.* 224

Covetous man, a Tantalus, *Cow.* 2 : 354

————— a slave, *Cow.* 2 : 273

INDEX.

Covetous man, folly of,   *Cow.* 2 : 273
Council it befeems to fpeak,   .   *Pope il.* 2 : 124
Counfel,   .   *Cow.* 1 : 257, 307
Counfels of Almighty mind, feek not to find,   *Pope il.* 1 : 60
Countenance, to fcrew,   *Butl.* 1 : 271
Country, love of, chief end of life,   *Phil.* 54
———— was his deareft mother,   *Swift* 2 : 288
———— love of, zealous and blind,   *Weft* 260
———————— and fond, as is the love of womankind, *ib.* 260
———— pleafure of,   *Milt.* 2 : 18
———— view of,   *Shen.* 59
———— dogs love nobler fport,   *Gay* 1 : 203
———————— and fcorn the pranks of dogs at court, *Gay* 1 : 203
Country-life,   { *Cow.* 2/1 : 324
                  { *Swift* . : 219
———————— happinefs of,   { *Thom.* 1 : 148
                        { *Dry.* 2 : 144
———————— praife of,   *Dry.* 5 : 138
Countryman and Jupiter,   *Gay* 2 : 148
Country-moufe,   *Cow.* 2 : 317
———— parfon, happy life of,   *Pope* 1 : 354
———— walk, how fair a face nature wears in,   *Dyer* 129
———— workhoufes propofed,   *Dyer* 89
Courage length of life denies,   *Pope il.* 1 : 208
———— from hearts, and not from numbers grows, *Dry.* 1 : 73
———— with virtue over-rul'd,   *Add.* 55
———— in deceiving fhown,   *Aken.* 346
———— by an impious caufe is curft,   *Rowe L.* 252
———— difhonour'd to the Bravo's trade,   *Thom.* 2 : 84
'rfe, the defperateft, is wifeft,   *Butl.* 1 : 269

Courfe

Courfe of nature is the art of God, *Young* 3 : 44

Court, fplendor of, all a cheat, *A. Phil.* 335

────── deceitful lottery of, *Cow.* 1 : 202

────── refines the language of the plain, *Gay* 1 : 163

────── affords much food for fatire, *Young* 1 : 83

────── it abounds in lords, . *Young* 1 : 83

────── prologue to, *Cong.* 91

Courtefy oft found in lowly fheds, *Milt.* 3 : 132

Courtier muft be fupple, full of guile, *A. Phil.* 334

────── any ape furpaffes, *Swift* 2 : 143

────── in malice and grimaces, *Swift* 2 : 148

Courtier-trick, to ferve himfelf and forget his friend, *Prior* 2 : 2

────── and Proteus, *Gay* 2 : 86

────── of reptile race, *Gay* 2 : 87

────── practifes the frauds of every fhape, *Gay* 2 : 87

────── never forc'd to leave his lyes, *Gay* 2 : 88

Courtiers, who moft promife, are the leaft fincere, *Gay* 2 : 260

────── are difciplin'd to cheat, *Gay* 2 : 262

────── rife upon their mafters' fall, *Swift* 2 : 42

Courtly fycophants, caitifs vile, *Weft* 269

Courts, fneaking tribe of flattery, . *Dyer* 131

────── that infalubrious foil to peace, *Young* 2 : 247

────── flattery and falfehood flourifh, *Prior* 2 : 211

────── paffion does with intereft barter, *Prior* 2 : 212

────── Hymen holds by Mammon's charter, *Prior* 2 : 212

Coward, no force, no firmnefs fhows, . *Pope il.* 2 : 15

────── his colour comes and goes, *Pope il.* 2 : 15

────── a bloodlefs image of defpair, *Pope il.* 2 : 15

────── driven headlong on by fear, *Rowe L.* 292

──────'s weapon never hurts the brave, , *Pope il.* 1 : 337

Cowardice

Cowardice alone is lofs of fame,   *Dry.* 3 : 124

Cowards, moft men are,   *Recb.* 324

———— call for death,   *Hughes* 61

———— good counfel loft on,   *Dry.* 2 : 70

———— arts of mean expedients try,   *Dry.* 2 : 84

———— their own misfortunes frame,   *Rowe L.* 70

———— by their own feigning fancies betray'd, *Rowe L.* 70

———— are cruel,   *Gay* 2 : 30

———— never tread the paths of dangerous fame, *Weft* 141

Cowley, elegia dedicatoria,   1 : 3

———— preface to edition of 1656,   1 : 7

———— juvenile poems,   1 : 25

———— to Bifhop of Lincoln,   1 : 27, 112

———— preface to juvenile poems,   1 : 28

———— to the reader,   1 : 30

———— Conftantia and Philautus,   1 : 31, 47

———— echo,   1 : 35

———— fong,   1 : 37

———— letter,   1 : 46

———— fong,   1 : 49

———— Pyramus and Thifbe,   1 : 54

———— Sylva,   1 : 64

———— Carleton, elegy on,   1 : 64

———— Clarke, elegy on,   1 : 65

———— dream of Elyfium,   1 : 67

———— on the king's return,   1 : 70

———— vote,   1 : 73

———— poetical revenge,   1 : 76

———— to Dutchefs of Buckingham,   1 : 78

———— to his godfather,   1 : 79

Cowley on Littleton's death,   I : 81

———— on the Bleſſed Virgin,   I : 83

———— on poetry,   I : 86

———— pleaſant poverty preferable to diſcontented riches, I : 87

———— to his miſtreſs,   I : 89

———— on incertainty of fortune,   I : 90

———— in praiſe of the preſent,   I : 91

———— on ſhortneſs of life,   I : 92

———— on an invitation to Cambridge,   I : 93

———— motto,   I : 95

———— on wit,   I : 97

———— to Lord Falkland,   I : 99

———— on death of Sir Wootton,   I : 101

———— on death of Jordan,   I : 102

———— on his majeſty's return,   I : 104

———— on death of Vandyke,   I : 107

———— on Prometheus, ill-painted,   I : 108

———— ode inviting to drink,   I : 109

———— friendſhip in abſence,   I : 110

———— to a lady, who made poſies for rings,   I : 114

———— prologue to Guardian,   I : 116

———— epilogue to Guardian,   I : 117

———— death of William Hervey,   I : 117

———— imitation of Horace,   I : 123

———————————— Martial,   I : 124

———— the chronicle,   I : 125

———— to Davenant,   I : 129

———— verſes ſent to Jerſey,   I : 130

———— tree of knowledge,   I : 132

———— on reaſon,   I : 134

Cowley

Cowley on Crashaw,   1 : 136

———— Anacreontics,   1 : 139

———— elegy on Anacreon,   1 : 150

———— occasional verses,   1 : 155

———— Christ's passion,   1 : 155

———— on Orinda,   1 : 158

———— on Lord Broghill,   1 : 161

———— to Oxford,   1 : 164

———— on the chair made of Drake's ship,   1 : 167

———— on the death of the Earl of Balcarres,   1 : 170

———— on Dr. Harvey,   1 : 173

———— ode from Catullus,   1 : 176

———— on the Restoration,   1 : 179

———— on the queen,   1 : 195

———— complaint,   1 : 199

———— on Tuke's tragi-comedy,   1 : 205

———— on Philips' death,   1 : 206

———— hymn to light,   1 : 210

———— to Royal Society,   1 : 214

———— on Drake's chair,   1 : 220

———— prologue to Cutter of Colman-street,   1 : 221

———— the mistress,   1 : 223

———— thraldom,   1 : 225

———— the given love,   1 : 226

———— Spring,   1 : 229

———— writing in lemon-juice,   1 : 231

———— inconstancy,   1 : 233

———— not fair,   1 : 234

———— Platonic love,   1 : 235

———— the change,   1 : 236

Cowley clad all in white,   1 : 237
———— leaving me, loving many,.   1 : 238
———— my heart difcovered,   1 : 229
———— anfwer to Platonics,,   .   1 : 240
———— vain love,   1 : 241
———— the foul,   I : 243, 271
———— the paffions,.   1 : 246
———— wifdom,   1 : 247
———— the defpair,.   1 : 248
———— the wifh,   1 : 249
———— my diet,   1 : 251
———— the thief,.   .   1 : 252
———— all over love,.   1 : 253
———— love and life,.   1 : 254
———— the bargain,   1 : 255
———— the long life,   3 : 256
———— counfel,.   1 : 257, 307
———— refolved to be loved,.   1 : 259
———— difcovery,   1 : 261
———— againft fruition,   1 : 262
———— love undifcovered,.   1 : 263
———— the given heart,   .   1 : 264
———— the prophet,   1 : 265
———— the refolution,.   3 : 266
———— called Inconftant,.   1 : 267
———— the welcome,   3 : 267
———— the heart fled again,.   1 : 269
———— women's fuperftition,   1 : 270
———— the foul,   1 : 271
———— echo,   1 : 272
                                                             Cowley

Cowley, the rich rival,   1 : 273

———— againſt hope,   1 : 274

———— for hope,   1 : 275

———— love's ingratitude,   1 : 277

———— the frailty,   1 : 278

———— coldneſs,   1 : 279

———— enjoyment,   1 : 279

———— ſleep,   1 : 281

———— beauty,   1 : 282

———— the parting,   1 : 283

———— my picture,   1 : 284

———— the concealment,   1 : 285

———— the monopoly,   1 : 286

———— the diſtance,   1 : 287

———— the increaſe,   1 : 288

———— love's inviſibility,   1 : 289

———— looking on and diſcourſing with miſtreſs,   1 : 289

———— reſolved to love,   1 : 290

———— my fate,   1 : 292

———— heart-breaking,   1 : 293

———— the uſurpation,   1 : 294

———— maiden-head,   1 : 295

———— impoſſibilities,   1 : 297

———— ſilence,   1 : 298

———— the diſſembler,   1 : 299

———— the inconſtant,   1 : 300

———— the conſtant,   1 : 302

———— her name,   1 : 303

———— weeping,   1 : 304

———— diſcretion,   1 : 305

                  Cowley,

Cowley, the waiting-maid,   1 : 306
———— the cure,   1 : 308
———— the feparation,   1 : 308
———— the tree,   1 : 309
———— unbelief,   1 : 310
———— the gazers,   1 : 311
———— the incurable,   1 : 312
———— honour,   1 : 313
———— the innocent-ill,   1 : 314
———— dialogue,   1 : 316
———— verfes loft on a wager,   1 : 318
———— bathing in the river,   1 : 320
———— love given over,   1 : 321
———— poem on the late civil-war,   1 : 323
———— Puritan and Papift,   1 : 343
———— character of a holy fifter,   1 : 353
———— force of love,   1 : 354
———— on power of love,   1 : 356
———— pindaric odes,   2 : 3
———— Olympic ode,   2 : 7
———— Nemean ode,   2 : 15
———— praife of Pindar,   2 : 20
———— the refurrection,   2 : 22
———— the Mufe,   2 : 25
———— to Hobbes,   2 : 28
———— deftiny,   2 : 31
———— Brutus,   2 : 34
———— to Dr. Scarborough,   2 : 37
———— life and fame,   2 : 41
———— the extafy,   2 : 43
                                           Cowley,

Cowley, to the New Year, 2 : 46
——— life, 2 : 49
——— Ifaiah, chap. xxxiv. 2 : 51
——— plagues of Egypt, 2 : 54
——— Davideis, 2 : 70
——— on Cromwell's government, 2 : 209
——— effays, 2 : 261
——— ode on liberty, 2 : 261, 279
——— tranflations from Martial, 2 : 277
——— of folitude, 2 : 284
——— of obfcurity, 2 : 291
——— of agriculture, 2 : 297
——— paraphrafe of Horace, 2 : 321
——— country-life, 2 : 324
——— the garden, 2 : 326
——— of greatnefs, 2 : 337
——— of avarice, 2 : 349
——— paraphrafe on Horace, 2 : 355
——— dangers of an honeft man, 2 : 358
——— Claudian's old man of Verona, 2 : 265
——— fhortnefs of life, 2 : 366
——— uncertainty of riches, 2 : 366
——— danger of procraftination, 2 : 372
——— of myfelf, 2 : 377
——— wifh of, 2 : 379
——— prompted to poetry how, 2 : 380
——— epitaphium auctoris, 2 : 387
——— on experimental philofophy, 2 : 388
——— tranflation of his epitaph, Add. 68
——— a mighty genius, Add. 35

Cowley,

Cowley, o'er-run with wit,   *Add.* 35

———— fits deep-mouth'd Pindar to his lyre,   *Add.* 35

———— admirer of mixt wit,   *Add.* 165

———— affectation of,   *Dry.* 7 : 106

———— his moral pleafes, not his pointed wit, *Pope* 2 : 217

———— imitated,   *Pope* 1 : 347

———— irregular in his ftanzas,   *Cong.* 156

———— on death of,   *Den.* 54

Cowper, lord Chancellor, ode to,   { *Hugbes* 237 *A. Phil.* 354

———— fupport of friendlefs right,   *A. Phil.* 357

———— lips with thymy language fweet,   *A. Phil.* 357

———— the robe of Juftice wore,   *A. Phil.* 359

Coxcomb, made by induftry and art,   *Roch.* 311

Coxcombs, an ever empty race,   *Gay* 2 : 62

———— to all but coxcombs are a jeft,   *Gay* 2 : 69

———— prating, kindle wrath, comtempt or hate, *Gay* 2 : 110

———— blind to real merit,   *Gay* 2 : 169

———— in vicious frolics fancy fpirit,   *Gay* 2 : 169

———— are of all ranks and kinds,   *Gay* 2 : 138

———— vanity befots them all,   *Gay* 2 : 138

Coy, an ode,   *Broome* 61

Cradle-hymn,   *Watts* 368

Cradle and the tomb fo nigh,   *Prior* 2 : 183

Craft of woman-kind would you encreafe,   *Cong.* 111

Craggs, epiftle to,   { *Pope* 2 : 331 *A. Phil.* 340

———— will be afham'd of,   *Pope* 1 : 357

———— for candour known,   *A. Phil.* 340

———— ftatefman, yet friend to truth,   *Pope* 2 : 146

         Craggs,

Cragg, ennobled by himself, by all approv'd,   *Pope i* : 147

————— and prais'd, unenvy'd, by the Muse he lov'd, *ib.* 2 : 147

————— in death to Addison succeeds,   *Tick.* 190

————— swift after him thy social spirit flies,   *Tick.* 191

Cranes to pigmy nations bring wounds and death, *Pope il.* 1 : 105

Crashaw, death of,   *Cow.* 1 : 136

Create, Gods and Poets only can,   *Pitt* 228

Created-good, illusive all,   *Mall.* 226

Creation, of love divine the child,   *Young* 3 : 104

Creation, sang,   *Milt.* 1 : 227, 228

————— all very good,   *Milt.* 1 : 225

————— is one vast exchange,   *Young* 3 : 265

————— ends, one link dissolved,   *Watt.* 21

Creator proved from view of animals,   *Black.* 205

——————————— their sensations,   *Black.* 207, seq.

——————————— their instincts,   *Black.* 207

——————————— from the intellectual world,   *Black.* 208

————— hymn to,   *Black.* 216

————— of the world, ode to,   *Hughes* 189

————— praises of, the most ancient use of poetry, *Hughes* 188

————— spoke, and light arose,   *Hughes* 190

————— taught time to try his infant wings,   *Hughes* 190

————— present at once in all, and by no place confin'd, *id.* 190

————— without beginning, without end,   *Hughes* 190

————— his hand unseen divides to all their food,   *Hughes* 191

————— and the whole world of life sustains,   *Hughes* 191

————— all in all,   *Som.* 221

————— remember your,   *Watts* 71

————— and creatures,   *Watts* 50

Creatures execute God's word, vengeance or the law, *Watts* 42

Creatures,

Creatures, scourges of our Maker's rod,   *Watts* 43
———— Hazard of loving.   *Watts* 131
Crecy's fight eternal honours won,   *Hughes* 51
Creech, on his translation of Lucretius,   *Wall.* 180
Credit raise not by another's blush,   *King* 301
Crescent to lay low,   *Wall.* 199
Cressy was lost by kickshaws and soup-meagre,   *Fent.* 333
———— swam in blood,   *Add.* 11
Cressy.   See Crecy.
Cretans, through mere completion lie,   *Pitt* 195
Crete, queen of isles,   *Broome* 105
———— chalky cliffs,   *Pope od.* 4 : 34
———— ancient home of law,   *Aken.* 176
Creusa missing,   *Dry.* 5 : 384
———— foretels future fate of Æneas,   *Dry.* 5 : 384
Cries, now awake the dead,   *Mall.* 192
———— of the town,   *Gay* 1 : 125
Crimes, but permitted, not decreed,   *Dry.* 3 : 272
———— expiate less with greater,   *But.* 1 : 193
———— lead to crimes,   *Mall.* 177
———— there are ills to come for,   *Dyer* 112
Crimson, discoverer of,   *Dyer,* 77
———— blush,   *Dry.* 7 : 49
Critic, office of,   *Broome* 8
———— abuse of the office of,   *Broome* 8
———— partial, who,   *Broome* 10
———— envious and malicious,   *Broome* 10
———————— Tartars in learning,   *Broome* 11
———— eye, that microscope of wit,   *Pope* 3 : 234
———— learning flourish'd most in France,   *Pope* 1 : 121
Critical

Critical moment,   *Prior* 1 : 271

Criticifm, effay on,   *Pope* 1 : 91

———— the Mufes' handmaid,   *Pope* 1 : 95

———— denotes difpraife,   *Broome* 11

———— modefty effential to true,   *Broome* 12

———— to be circumfcribed by Candour,   *Broome* 13

———— verbal,   *Mall.* 159

Critics, fate of,   *Gay* 1 : 146

———— what muft be their morals,   *Pope* 1 : 114

———— on verfe, as fquibs, on triumphs wait,   *Young* 1 : 99

———— are partial to their judgment,   *Pope* 1 : 91

———— like curs, feed on fcraps,   *Pitt* 389

———— taught by the Thracian dog to fnarl,   *Pitt* 389

———— cull the weeds for the flowers,   *Garth* 50

———— foes to the tribe whence they trace their clan,   *Fent.* 315

———— on modern plays,   *Butl.* 2 : 207

———— regulate our theatres,   *Dry.* 2 : 249

Crocodile, whofe fell tears enfnare,   *Thom.* 2 : 101

Crocodile's eye, hieroglyphic for the morning,   *Young* 1 : 231

———— vulnerable in the belly,   *Butl.* 2 : 306

Croft, journey of,   *Den.* 40

Cromwell defcribed,   *Cow.* 1 : 336

———— government of,   *Cow.* 2 : 209

———— funeral folemnity,   *Cow.* 2 : 210

———— an extraordinary man,   *Cow.* 2 : 215

———— tramples on king and parliament,   *Cow.* 2 : 216

———— fets up a protectorfhip,   *Cow.* 2 : 116

———— wickednefs of,   *Cow.* 2 : 218

———— fuppreffed juftice, if againft him,   *Cow.* 2 : 249

———— changes the nature of things,   *Cow.* 2 : 250

Cromwell,

Cromwell, executions frequent under,   Cow. 2 : 251

———— sold men to slavery,   Cow. 2 : 251

———— breaks through Magna Charta,   Cow, 2 : 252

———— noted for diligence and dissimulation,   Cow 2 : 245

———— government of,   Cow. 2 : 245

———— a common deceiver,   Cow. 2 : 241

———— great boldness of,   Cow. 2 : 243

———— personal courage,   Cow, 2 : 244

———— absolute in power,   Cow. 2 : 228

———— a thief and robber,   Cow. 2 : 232

———— no usurper more execrable than,   Cow. 2 : 233

———— alters the constitution,   Cow. 2 : 234

———— the jest and sport of fortune,   Cow. 2 : 253

———— uncontrolable,   Cow. 2 : 253

———— death of, more fortunate than his life,   Cow. 2 : 254

———— damn'd to everlasting fame,   Pope 2 : 79

———— on death of,   Dry. 1 : 13

———— carried off in a tempest,   Cow. 1 : 181

———— left the commonwealth in debt,   Cow. 2 : 247

————(Richard) blameless character,   Cow. 2 : 254

Crosier o'er the sword prevails,   Tick. 98

Cross, touch'd by, we live,   Young 2 : 85

—— to exalt,   Wall. 199

Cross-grain'd freak, to have,   Butl. 1 : 112

Croud, a hurrying, heartless train,   Rowe L. 70

—— parted by a coach,   Gay 1 : 135

Crow, to pull,   Butl. 1 : 207

——'s feet round his eyes,   Swift 2 : 210

Crowd are clouds that tack with the wind,   Dry. 2 : 245

—— a sea, tossed by every wind,   Duke 90

Crowdero, a fiddler,   Butl. 1 : 51
————— for leg had deputy of oak,   Butl. 1 : 33
————— led in triumph and imprisoned,   Butl. 1 : 96, 97
Crowds run to extremes,   Dry. 1 : 212
Crown, a pageant,   Lanf. 181
————— a wreath of thorns,   Milt. 2 : 178
————— learn not to flatter, nor insult,   Lytt. 27
————— on stealing one,   Swift 1 : 355
Crowns, a noble gem in, to pardon,   Butl. 2 : 116
————— below skill and courage wore,   Tick. 128
Crows to shoot, is powder flung away,   Gay 1 : 183
——— flee from smell of powder,   Butl. 1 : 121
——— and ravens croaking, ominous,   Butl. 1 : 250
Crucifixion, by Angelo,   Young 1 : 233
Cruel heart ill suits a manly mind,   Pope il. 1 : 285
——— mistress makes a froward wife,   King 323
——— gift, epilogue,   Rowe 35
Cruelty, made a sport,   Butl. 2 : 194
————— to hate remorseless succeeds,   Tham. 2 : 196
————— and lust,   Pom. 275
————— and mother, shall they stand so near, Sov. 39
Crusades, banditti saints,   Tham. 2 : 84
Crystal with quick scents revives the modish spleen, Gay 1 : 23
Cuckolds hear the last,   Dry. 1 : 299
Cuckoo sends her unison of woe,   Sov. 98
Cuckow, ode to,   Akin. 255
————— rustic herald of the spring,   Akin. 255
Cuddy,   A. Phil. 318
Cudgel-playing,   Som. 149
Cudgels to cross,   Butl. 2 : 5
                                                               Culture

Culture of the heart is man's science,   Young 3 : 63
Comæ, temple of, described,   Dry. 6 : 114
Cunning over-reached,   Milt. 2 : 201
Cunning-woman is a knavish fool,   Lytt. 41
Cupid, God of soft desire,   Hughes 178
—— wounds hearts, and leaves them to a woman, Gay 1 : 41
—— bow-bending,   Dry. 2 : 157
—— review of,   Hughes 73
—— in ambush,   Prior 2 : 29
—— turned ploughman,   Prior 2 : 248
—————— stroller,   Prior 2 : 248
—— mistaken,   Prior 1 : 111
—— and Ganymede,   Prior 1 : 108
—— and Hymen,   { Math. 184 / Fent. 222
—————— gods of love and marriage,   Math. 184
—— and Plutus,   Sheh. 194
—— Hymen and Plutus,   Gay 2 : 49
—— and Scarlati,   Hughes 128
——, his promise,   Prior 2 : 260
Cupids ride the Lion of the deep,   Pope 3 : 239
Cur, was ever one so curs'd?   Gay 2 : 288
—— the horse and shepherd's dog,   Gay 2 : 109
—— and mastiff,   Gay 2 : 74
Curate, complaint of hard duty,   Swift 1 : 99
Cure, far worse than the disease,   { Crw. 1 : 308 / Buck. 119
Cureless ill with patience to bear,   Dry. 3 : 63
Curfew, knell of parting day,   Gray 337
—— bell,   Thom. 2 : 106

Curio,

Curio, a speaker turbulent and bold,   *Rowe L.* 58

———— barter'd liberty for gold,   *Rowe L.* 202

———— falls in Afric,   *Rowe L.* 201

———— what avail thy popular arts,   *Rowe L.* 201

———— thy restless mind, that shook thy country, *Rowe L.* 201

———— thou the first victim of thy war,   *Rowe L.* 201

———— epistle to,   *Aken.* 333

———— ode to,   *Aken.* 212

———— by infamy the mindful dæmon sway'd,   *Aken.* 216

Curiosity, a mighty traveller,   *West* 264

————— makes pilgrims,   *Cow.* 1 : 169

————— a crime, which in the sex needs no excuse, *Swift* 1 : 11

Curll, from the blanket, flies high in air,   *Pope* 3 : 141

Curls on curls, the head is built before,   *Dry.* 7 : 273

Curse hangs over the blasphemer's head,   *A. Phil.* 383

———— of curses is our curse to love,   *Young* 3 : 2

———— of kings, for subjects to be poor,   *Rowe L.* 128

Cursed with blessings,   *Cong.* 40

Curship opposed to worship,   *Butl.* 1 : 90

Custard blasphemed,   *Butl.* 1 : 17

Custom, power of,   { *Butl.* 2 : 267 { *West*   299

———— how vast his influence; how wide his sway! *West* 312

———— exemplified in the Spartan youth,   *West* 300

———— o'erawes the faint and timorous mind,   *West* 312

———— is a law,   *Lanf.* 205

———— the world's great idol, we adore,   *Pom.* 341

———— makes current in the man follies of the child, *Fent.* 227

———— conquers fear and shame,   *Gay* 2 : 52

Cutts, verses to Lord John,   *Watts* 113

             Cyclops,

Cyclops, one-eyed brothers,   *Add.* 50

———— host of Giants,   *Add.* 50

———— habitation and character of,   *Dry.* 6 : 29

———— character of,   *Pope od.* 3 : 231

———— a lawless nation of gigantic foes,   *Pope od.* 3 : 169

———— rude and unconscious of a stranger's right, *ib.* 3 : 233

———— of Euripides,   *Dry.* 7 : 143

———— of Theocritus,   *Duke* 99

Cyenus transformed,   *Add.* 120

Cyder,   *Phil.* 33

——— bottled,   *Phil.* 72

——— improved,   *Phil.* 72

——— new, wash sorrow from the soul,   *Gay* 1 : 79

Cyder-land unstain'd with guilt,   *Phil.* 78

———————— obsequious still to thrones,   *Phil.* 78

Cyder-mill,   *Phil.* 63

Cyllarus and Hylonome, loves and death of,   *Dry.* 4 : 92

Cymbeline, dirge in,   *Collins* 280

Cymon and Iphigenia,   *Dry.* 3 : 256

Cynarctomachy,   *Butl.* 1 : 39

Cynthia shines at noon of night,   *Hughes* 66

——— elegy,   *Cong.* 99

——— ode to,   *Shen.* 147

Cypress by the noble mourner worn,   *Rowe L.* 142

Cyprus to Love's goddess dear,   *Rowe L.* 349

Cyrene, built under the Auspices of a crow,   *Pitt* 202

———— Carnean feast annually kept at,   *Pitt* 203

D

Dab at Taw,   *Som.* 297

Dad and Mam, names too common,   *Dry.* 2 : 262

Dædalus

Dædalus built the temple at Cumæ,   *Dry.* 6 : 113

Dagger, dead-do'ng blade!   *Som.* 339

Dagon, god of Philiftins,   *Milt.* 1 : 20, 21

———— worfhiping of,   *Butl.* 1 : 42

D'Aiguillon, invitation to Duohefs,   *Lytt.* 86

Dalila, Samfon's fnare,   *Milt.* 3 : 14

———— gains on Samfon to reveal his fecret,   *Milt.* 3 : 15

Damagetus, nor will I pafs unfung, thy fire,   *Weft* 172

———————— the friend of juftice and of truth,   *Weft* 172

Damafcus, prologue to fiege of,   *Mall.* 173

Damafk'd meads yield flowers ufeful in potables,   *Phil.* 68

Dame lofes pity, who loft her fhame,   *Dry.* 7 : 298

——— religion, fought for,   *Butl.* 1 : 4

Dames, who native beauty want,   *Prior* 2 : 60

———— uglier look, the more they paint,   *Prior* 2 : 60

Damme, cries another,   *Gay* 2 : 24

Damned, place of,   *Swift* 2 : 245

Damocles like all great men,   *Cow.* 2 : 348

Damon, an eclogue,   *Walfh* 348

———— and Alexis,   *Duke* 174

———— and Cupid,   *Gay* 1 : 258

———— and Daphne, an eclogue,   *Walfh* 343

———— and Delia, epiftle to,   { *Lytt.* 47 / *Sav.* 152

———— a bookifh mind with pedantry unfraught,   *Sav.* 152

Damps of oblivion fhed on the filial dulnefs,   *Dry.* 2 : 114

Damfels cull the fnowy fleece, or twift the purpled *Pope* od. 3 : 171

Dan Jackfon, his picture,   *Swift* 1 : 233, 234, 235

———————— defence of,   *Swift* 1 : 236

Danomg, a ceremony of religion,   *Cow.* 2 : 303

Dane,

Dine, fiery-treſſed,   Collins 260
Danger, what mortal eye can fix'd beholds,   Collins 247
———— not aſſay'd, no praiſe gain'd,   Prior 1 : 235
———— ſerves to enhance the prize,   Add. 54
———— waits on all untimely joy,   Pope od. 4 : 187
———— lies in death's uncertainty,   Young 2 : 120
Dangers ſtrow the paths the mighty tread,   Rowe L. 215
———— preſſing, cowards will grow bold,   Lanſ. 253
———— that might the bold affright,   Rowe L. 168
Dahgling and loyalty,   Butl. 2 : 32
Dante began to poliſh Italian,   Dry. 3 : 16
Danube, vaſt and deep, ſupreme of rivers,   Phil. 16
———— French, puſh'd into,   Phil. 16
———— reſcued, and the empire ſav'd,   Prior 1 : 189
Daphne,   { Lanſ. 157
         { Swift 2 : 196
———— and Apollo,   Prior 2 : 241
———— changed to a laurel,   Dry. 3 : 318
———— viſit of,   Shen. 129
Daphnis,   Dry. 5 : 43
———— and Chloe,   Gay 1 : 258
———— and Lycidas,   Broome 32
Darent, ſtain'd with Daniſh blood,   Pope 1 : 71
Dares, a prieſt, rich without a fault,   Pope il. 1 : 151
Daring love, for the danger's ſake,   Rowe L. 392
———— zeal with cool debate is join'd,   Pope od. 4 : 170
Darius flies, young Ammon urges on,   Prior 1 : 53
Darkening error from deep to depth fallen,   Dyer 10
Darkling grope, not knowing we are blind,   Prior 2 : 126
Darkneſs, what,   Milt. 2 : 214

I 4.

Darkneſs,

Darkness, one of the Egyptian plagues,   *Cow.* 2 : 63

———— hymn to,   *Yal.* 355

———— things appear alike in,   *Yal.* 357

———— pavilion of God,   *Tal.* 358

———— guilt's inevitable doom,   *Young* 3 : 71

Dart, swift to perform heaven's will,   *Pope il.* 2 : 59

Date short is, prescrib'd to mortal man,   *Pope il.* 2 : 117

———— whose bounds were fix'd, before his race began, *ib.* 117

Date short, of all-flagitious power,   , *Lauf.* 298

Davenant, too aspiring, miscarries,   { *Dry.* 1 : 265
                                                 { *Wall.* 109

Daughters of men,   . *Milt.* 2 : 105

David, character of,   { *Dry.* 1 : 136
                                                 { *Parn.* 154

———— whose harp devotion in a rapture strung,   *Parn.* 154

———— from the flock, advanced to the throne,   *Parn.* 163

———— renowned for music and poetry,   . *Buck.* 97

———— the monarch after God's own mind,   *Pope* 1 : 259

———— his life a scene of danger and a state of war, *Prior* 2 : 180

———— feigns madness,   *Cow.* 2 : 134

———— resort to at Adullam,   *Cow.* 2 : 135

———— encounters Goliah,   *Cow.* 2 : 151

———— lamentation over Saul and Jonathan,   *Som.* 204

Davideis,   *Cow.* 2 : 70

Day, each breathes his, then sinks into his clay, *Gay* 2 : 192

———— each steals me from myself away,   *Broome* 164

———— after day brings truth to light,   *A. Phil.* 381

———— each has its unguarded hour,   *Gay* 1 : 209

———— one abstemious, to grief and anguish,   *Pope il.* 2 : 206

———— of death, shall pronounce on all our days, *Young* 3 : 142

Day

Day of death, absolve them or condemn,   *Young* 2 : 142
Day decreed by fates, yet come it will,   *Pope il.* 17 : 210
—— of judgment,   *Rosc.* 249
Days to curtail,   *Butl.* 1 : 122
—— to number teach,   *Pitt* 244
—— good or bad for scenting,   *Som.* 26
Dead, how sacred !   *Young* 2 : 49
—— to insult, is cruel and unjust,   *Pope od.* 4 : 212
—— fate and their crime have sunk them to the dust, *ib.* 212
—— alone find true repose,   *Mall.* 333
—— sin and sorrow are no more,   *Mall.* 333
—— are the best acquaintance,   *Swift* 2 : 29
—— will ne'er complain,   *Garth* 65
—— the lumber of the world,   *Roch.* 331
—— and for ever lost, Patroclus lies,   *Pope il.* 2 : 314
—— friend, character of,   *Mall.* 205
—— as a door-nail,   *Gay* 1 : 271
—— horse, the venison of the prescient brood,   *Gay* 2 : 193
—— lift at, to help out,   *Butl.* 1 : 110
Dean [Swift], his manner of living,   *Swift* 2 : 361
—— panegyric on,   *Swift* 2 : 165
—— long privileg'd to rail,   *Swift* 2 : 113
—— letter to, when in England,   *Swift* 2 : 28
—— on-birth-day of,   *Swift* 2 : 371
—— verses on his birth-day,   *Swift* 2 : 340
—— and Duke,   *Swift* 2 : 343
—— epilogue by,   *Swift* 1 : 214
Dearest friends, they say, must part,   *Swift* 2 : 263
Dears, of all her, she never slander'd one,   *Pope* 2 : 112
Dearth of words a woman need not fear,   *Young* 1 : 119

Death,

122

Death,

⸺ one of the guards of Hell, described,
⸺ described,
⸺ nothing but, can cure a broken heart,
⸺ what? blood only stopp'd interrupted breath,
⸺ motion, end of, which with life began,
⸺ only shews us what we knew was near,
⸺ what? an end of all our tumults here,
⸺ equal lot of poverty and state,
⸺ none but the dead do know,
⸺ wishing for, and yet afraid to die,
⸺ no mortal can repel,
⸺ ourselves and all our works we owe,
⸺ true portrait of, who can take?
⸺ the tyrant never sat,
⸺ sin-born,
⸺ son of Sin,
⸺ begot by Satan on Sin,
⸺ irresistible,
⸺ description of,
⸺ Sin's wages, Grace's now,
⸺ endless misery,
⸺ by sin,
⸺ to life is crown or shame,
⸺ like sleep,
⸺ nature shrinks at,
⸺ kinds of,
⸺ to the good, gate of life,
⸺ thou pleasing end of human woe,

{ Lans. 180
{ Wash. 317
Milt. 1 : 57
Buck. 12
Buck. 14
Prinr 2 : 183
Prior 2 : 183
Prior 2 : 183
Pom. 282
Pom. 282
Pom. 320
Pom. 320
Pom. 324
Hughes 209
Young 2 : 131
Young 2 : 131
Milt. 2 : 65
Mil. 2 : 53
Milt. 1 : 60, 61
Milt. 1 : 62
Milt. 1 : 57
Dry. 1 : 9
Milt. 2 : 72
Milt. 2 : 87
Milt. 3 : 60
Milt. 2 : 133
Milt. 2 : 100
Milt. 2 : 100, 101
Milt. 2 : 138
Rowe L. 19
Deatl

Death, thou cure for life, thou greatest good below, *Rowe L.* 192

———— still may'st thou fly the coward and the slave, *ib.* 192

———— and thy soft slumbers only bless the brave, . *ib.* 192

———— thoughts of, terrify, - *Den.* 134

———— to be wished, or despised, *Den.* 134

———— a port from tempest, *Den.* 136

———— that frightful sound, *Dry.* 1 : 305

———— passage from an inn, *Den.* 141

———— the passage to heaven, . *Wall.* 40

———— our appointed goal, . *Pitt* 244

———— fear of, none happy under, *Black.* 122

———— religion, thy force alone disarms, . *Black.* 124

———— thought of, indulge, *Young* 2 : 53

———— slain by her patient victor, *Prior* 1 : 22

———— thought of, sole victor of its dread, *Young* 3 : 81

———— kills not the buds of virtue, they spread, *Thom.* 1 : 63

———— you only prove, what dust we doat on, . *Pope* 1 : 194

———— double of man, *Young* 2 : 206

———— certain, time uncertain, - *Den.* 137

———— the dark, irremeable way, *Pope il.* 2 : 205

———— stands ardent on the edge of war, *Pope il.* 2 : 214

———— inevitable descends on all, *Pom.* 324

———— what makes it sweet, are certain hopes of bliss, *ib.* 324

———— inexorable, *Cow.* 1 : 66

———— unavoidable, { *Cow.* 1 : 154, { *Ching.* 46

———————— if heaven decree, *Dry.* 7 : 50

———— strips us of all, *Cong.* 47

———— gives scope to the heir to riot, *Cong.* 47

———— only is the lot, which none can miss, *Pope od.* 3 : 90

Death, that cup the beſt muſt taſte, *Pope od.* 3 : 90

———— a deſtroyer of quotidian prey, *Young* 2 : 115

———— his, my youth, my noon-tide his, *Young* 2 : 115

———— be your theme, in every place and hour, *Young* 2 : 115

———— that mighty hunter, earths them all, *Young* 2 : 65

———— ſtill frowns, guilt points the tyrant's ſpear, *Young* 2 : 67

———— a fate which all muſt try, *Pope il.* 2 : 84

———— to be expected, but not feared, *Prior* 2 : 94

———— will not always wait upon command, *Rowe L.* 85

———— nor aw'd by foreſight, nor miſled by chance, *Prior* 1 : 184

———— directs his ebon lance, *Prior* 1 : 184

———— inſults of, the wiſe defy, *Garth* 45

———— fools, through inſenſibility, *Garth* 45

———— what the guilty fear, *Garth* 45

———————— the pious crave, *Garth* 45

———— ſought by the wretch, *Garth* 45

———— vanquiſh'd by the brave, *Garth* 45

———— though a tyrant, offers liberty, *Garth* 45

———— an iron ſlumber, *Dry.* 1 : 300

———— iron reign of, *Dry.* 3 : 128

———— iron hand of, *Smith* 113

———— ſure lot of every mortal excellence, *Broome* 95

———— call it ſoft tranſition, *Young* 2 : 58

———— but entombs the body, *Young* 2 : 58

———— age and diſeaſe its harbingers, *Young* 2 : 59

———— friend of human woes, *Mall.* 296

———— a glad relief from grief, *Dry.* 3 : 136

———— not call untimely, what heaven decreed, *Dry.* 3 : 137

———— the balm of miſeries, *Milt.* 3 : 28

———— the opium of pain, *Milt.* 3 : 28

Death,

Death, that opiate of the foul, Pope 2 : 108
——— the gift moſt welcome to woe, Gay 1 : 320
——— ends all pain, Milt. 3 : 26
——— the wretch's laſt relief, Pope 1 : 243
——— cure of the miſer's wiſh, and coward's fear, Prior 2 : 183
——— anger dread not, but expect his power, Prior 2 : 184
——— in time of miſery, delays, Pom. 228
——— is a path, that muſt be trod, Parn. 77
——— a port of calm, a ſtate of eaſe, Parn. 77
——— ſad refuge from the ſtorms of fate, Gray 346
——— to the wretched is an end of care, Lanſ. 294
——— is free, that laſt relief, Rowe L. 240
——— comes opportunely like a friend, Rowe L. 357
——— to ſet me free from fortune's power, Rowe L. 352
——— ſets all free, Milt. 3 : 59
——— a ſure retreat from infamy, Garth 75
——— thou cure of all our idle ſtrife, Broome 131
——— wiſh of the juſt, and refuge of th' oppreſt, Broome 131
——— the great arrear all muſt pay, Broome 44
——— unworthy of our fears, Rowe L. 122
——— to chooſe, diſtinguiſhes the brave, Rowe L. 187
——— is only certain oracle, Lytt. 97
——— the curtain drops, and ſhuts the ſcene of woe, Hughes 281
——— leads to life and to the bleſt abode, Black. 124
——— the wretch's laſt relief, Dry. 3 : 69
——— man's make encloſes its ſure ſeeds, Young 2 : 33
——— ſure fate of every mortal, Pope od. 4 : 5
——— knocks, we hear, and yet we will not hear, Young 2 : 112
——— ſtill draws nearer, never ſeeming near, Pope 2 : 57
——— haſtes amain, Broome 165
Death,

Death, ill-exchang'd for bondage,   *Pope ed.* 4 : 168

———— quite breaks the spring, and motion ends,   *Young* 3 : 74

———— opens to our eyes all science,   *Som.* 244

———— makes the good man in a moment wife,   *Som.* 244

———— is what we should disdain,   *Prior* 1 : 148

———— despised for fame,   *Buck.* 98

———— flies from grief,   *Lanf.* 162

———— how beautiful, when earn'd by virtue,   *Add.* 325

———— pangs of, gentler than despair,   *Fent.* 283

———— cave of,   *Garth* 81

———— court of,   *Gay* 2 : 110

———— prospect of,   *Pom.* 319

———— temple of,   *Buck.* 11

———— vale of,   *Buck.* 11

———— guardians of the temple of,   *Buck.* 12

———— we seek and shun,   *Young* 2 : 25

———— the great teacher wait,   *Pope* 2 : 32

———— is beyond the goddess Fortune's power,   *Rowe L.* 325

———— pursues the coward as he flies,   *Swift* 1 : 152

———— solemn thoughts of,   *Watts* 338

———— black fear of, that saddens all,   *Pope* 2 : 256

———— unwinds the labyrinths of fate,   *Young* 2 : 135

———— and straightens its inextricable maze,   *Young* 2 : 135

———— great proprietor of all,   *Young* 3 : 10

———— the deep, the bitter draught,   *Pope od.* 4 : 197

———— wraps all in shades,   *Pope od.* 4 : 198

———— nor beauty can arrest, nor music charm,   *A. Phil.* 315

———— dissolv'd the marriage-knot,   *Prior* 2 : 205

———— shall mix the fame of every field,   *Rowe L.* 284

  — demands a tear,   *Mall.* 243

Death

Death, ghastly with pale suffusion,   *Mall.* 244

——— makes us all a name,   *Dry.* 7 : 353

——— strikes the sexton no farther than his fees, *Gay* 2 : 193

——— a night-piece on,   *Parn.* 75

——— a poem on,   *Broome* 126

——— a thousand ways lead to,   *Broome* 126

——— unaw'd by power, beggars and kings alike to it, *ib.* 127

——— the great birth-right of mankind,   *Thom.* 2 : 180

——— the bark, that wafts us to the shore,   *Thom.* 2 : 180

——— marks in blood her way,   *Broome* 49

——— and Daphne,   *Swift* 2 : 192

——— should get young deathlings,   *Swift* 2 : 193

——— faculty, his humble friends,   *Swift* 2 : 194

——— majesty of terrors,   *Swift* 2 : 193

——— of Roman soldiers by serpents,   *Rowe L.* 411

——— and eternity,   *Watts* 60

——— and life by woman,   *Cow.* 1 : 84

——— of a relation, verses on,   *Watts* 290

——— untimely of an acquaintance,   *Shen.* 16

——— I have heard myself to,   *Young* 3 : 189

——— a pleasant road, that leads to fame,   *Lanf.* 184

———'s harbingers lie latent in the draught,   *Prior* 2 : 134

Death-charged pistols,   *Butl.* 1 : 50

Deaths stand, like Mercuries, in every way,   *Young* 2 : 163

——— ten thousand, better than stain honour,   *Add.* 265

Deathless laurel, the victor's due,   *Dry.* 3 : 185

——— we were, from repetition of reprieve,   *Young* 2 : 111

——— far from it, such are already dead,   *Young* 2 : 111

——— their hearts are bury'd, the world their grave, *ib.*

Debate destroys dispatch,   *Den.* 90

                                                 Deborah,

Deborah,   *Parn.* 135

————— woman born to fame,   *Parn.* 133

————— rofe a mother of the land,   *Parn.* 139

Decay of parts we all muft feel,   *Pope* 2 : 289

Deceiving the world, what,   *Cow.* 2 : 292

Deceit, whofe confcious eye ne'er looks direct,   *Thom.* 2 : 62

December warns to annual jollities,   *Phil.* 75

Decencies, content to dwell for ever, in,   *Pope* 2 : 111

Decency, celeftial maid,   *Swift* 1 : 240

————— defcend from heaven to Beauty's aid, *Swift* 2 : 240

————— 'tis thou muft fan the lover's fire,   *Swift* 2 : 240

————— of mind, fo lovely in the fex,   *Swift* 1 : 106

————— want of, want of fenfe,   *Rofc.* 217

Decent boldnefs ever meets with friends,   *Pope od.* 3 : 187

————————— and even a ftranger recommends, *ib.* 3 : 187

————— competence we fully tafte,   .   *Young* 1 : 147

Decimation under Cromwell,   *Cow.* 2 : 248

Decree of God, madnefs to queftion,   *Dry.* 1 : 312

————— not neceffitating,   *Milt.* 2 : 46

————— vain the fearch to find,   *Tick.* 184

————— immutable, no force can fhake,   *Pope il.* 1 : 61

Dedication is a wooden leg,   *Young* 1 : 113

Deed moral, or well-natured, exceeds other defert, *Buck.* 101

Deeds, though mute, fpeak loud,   *Milt.* 3 : 15

————— alone our counfel muft commend,   *Pope od.* 3 : 139

————— above the nerve of mortal arm,   *Milt.* 3 : 28

————— to pray by,   *Dry.* 2 : 179

————— muft decide our fate,   *Pope il.* 2 : 227

————— beft, how wanting in their weight !   *Young* 2 : 132

————— feats made victories,   *Butl.* 2 : 92

                                                     Defencelefs

Defenceless virtue meets with fate unkind,   *King* 308

Defender of the faith,   *Cow.* 1 : 182

———————————— Henry VIII,   *Den.* 12

Deformity in manners and in face,   *King* 304

Degenerate bees,   *Gay* 2 : 163

——————— world, that courts the yoke,   *Add.* 252

Degree, confiftent with liberty,   *Milt.* 1 : 165

Deification of Claudius, Varronian fatire,   *Dry.* 7 : 162

Deiotarus follicited to beg fupplies of Parthia,   *Rowe L.* 338

Deift, felf-deceived,   *Dry.* 1 : 246

Deity, on,   *Buck.* 110

——— with all perfection crown'd,   *Prior* 2 : 115

——— 'tis hard to ftrive againft,   *Prior* 2 : 23

De la Motte, dialogue from,   *Hughes* 165

Delany, epiftle to Carteret,   *Swift* 2 : 112

————— news from Parnaffus,   *Swift* 1 : 186

————— poem by,   *Swift* 1 : 216

————— reply of,   *Swift* 1 : 241

————— villa of,   *Swift* 1 : 264

————— on the libels againft him,   *Swift* 2 : 128

————— to George-Nim-Dan-Dean,   *Swift* 1 : 229

————— verfes by, to Swift,   *Swift* 2 : 280

————— and Carteret, libel on,   *Swift* 2 : 128

————— to,   *Swift* 1 : 159

Delay, danger of,   *Watts* 341

Delays to jealous minds a torment prove,   *A. Phil* 377

Delia, an eclogue,   *Walfh* 354

——— epiftle to,   *Pom.* 253

——— young, fickle, fair, a levity inborn,   *Sav.* 153

——— adjur'd to pity,   *Ham.* 213

Delia in the country,   *Ham.* 214

—— she breathes in woods the fragrant air,   *Ham.* 214

—— despair of possessing,   *Ham.* 216

—— lost,   *Ham.* 217

—— married to,   *Ham.* 221

—— with her I scorn the idle breath of praise,   *Ham.* 223

—— alone can please, and never tire,   *Ham.* 224

—— on birth-day of,   *Ham.* 218

—— virgin-fears her nicer tongue restrain,   *Ham.* 219

—— verses to,   *Ham.* 220, 225

—— to,   *Shen.* 72

Delight beyond the bliss of dreams,   *Milt.* 3 : 149

Delphian oracle dumb,   *Dry.* 7 : 275

Delirious faction bellowing loud, Liberty,   *Thom.* 2 : 140

Deluge, brought on the earth,   *Milt.* 2 : 110, 112

—— abated,   *Milt.* 2 : 113

—— began to fall, that mighty ebb, never to flow, *Swift* 1 : 9

—— mankind retrieved after,   { *Dry.* 3 : 309
                                                     { *Dry.* 3 : 315

—— would enlarge the king's domain,   *Wall.* 23

—— and conflagration, ministers of vengeance, *Young* 3 : 6

Delville, verses on one of the windows of,   *Swift* 1 : 266

Delusion, world given up to,   *Milt.* 2 : 158

Demar, elegy on,   *Swift* 1 : 179

Democritus and Heraclitus,   *Prior* 2 : 12

—— laughs at the follies of men,   *Dry.* 7 : 284

Demodocus, bard of fame, taught by the gods, *Pope ed.* 3 : 204

—— the loves of Mars and Cytherea sings, *ib.* 3 : 213

Demogorgon, tyrant of Fairies,   *Dry.* 3 : 183

—— places dispossessed,   *Milt.* 2 : 222

6   Demosthenes

Demosthenes used pebbles, to help his speech,   *Butl.* 1 : 10

Demosthenic strength, weight of sense,   *King* 386

Denham, poems of,   7

————— Cooper's hill,   7

————— destruction of Troy,   20

————— on Stafford,   39

————— on Lord Croft's journey,   40

————— on Killigrew and Murrey,   43

————— to Mennis,   44

————— epigram,   47

————— to five Members of House of Commons,   62

————— Western wonder,   64, 65

————— news from Colchester,   67

————— on Cowley's death,   54

————— speech against peace,   58

————— song,   70

————— on Fletcher,   71

————— to Fanshaw,   72

————— a dialogue,   74

————— on game of chess,   77

————— on Dido's passion,   78

————— of prudence,   87

————— of justice,   97

————— progress of learning,   102

————— old age,   110

————— remembered, as long as Cooper's hill,   *Add.* 38

Dennis, a pindaric ode,   *Dry.* 2 : 297

————— who long had warr'd with modern Huns, *Pope* 2 : 347

Deptford, navy-building town,   *Pope* 1 : 346

Derision, that tongue of gall,   *Sav.* 43

Derisive taunts spread from guest to guest,   *Pope od.* 3 : 73

Dermot and Sheelah,   *Swift* 2 : 64

Description, to avoid trivial accidents in,   *Dry.* 1 : 284

———————— held the place of sense,   *Pope* 2 : 155

Descriptions foul, offensive,   *Rosc.* 218

———————— lively and affecting,   *Pitt* 349

Desert, to rise on firm basis of,   *Add.* 53

Desire and possession,   *Swift* 2 : 45

——— not in Nature's power to quench,   *King* 266

——— our own to have, most formidable fate,   *Young* 3 : 113

——— to reign, scorns the reversion of a throne, *Pope* 1 : 284

——— of conquest, sways the giddy maid,   *Gay* 1 : 335

Desires prove our ruin,   *Dry.* 7 : 282

Despair,   *Cow.* 1 : 248

——— no vulture like,   *Lanf.* 222

——— worst of miseries,   *Pom.* 271

——— black child of Guilt,   *Fent.* 294

——— sullen sounds his grief beguil'd,   *Collins* 271

——— grim-visag'd,   *Gray* 332

——— mounts light, alternate hopes prevail, *Pope od.* 4 : 170

——— when nigh, delays are fatal,   *Pom.* 247

——— seek for counsel in,   *Rowe L.* 340

——— the last and best defence,   *Buth* 2 : 34

——— gives courage to the weak,   *Som.* 65

——— of life, the means of saving shows,   *Dry.* 5 : 466

Despairing lover,   { *Dry.* 4 : 308

                      { *Walsh* 333

——————— shepherd,   *Prior* 1 : 45

Desperate cures for desperate ills,   *Dry.* 2 : 90

——————— villain, steel'd by his crimes, dares, *Hughes* 302

                                 Dessert

Deffert graces all the feaft,   King 212
Deftiny,   Cow. 2 : 31
————— extenfive fway,   Cow. 2 + 32
————— pathlefs,   Dry. 1 : 94
————— whatever is, is done by,   Dry. 3 : 63
————— forms in caufes firft, what is to be,   Dry. 3 : 76
————— in the planets,   Butl 1 : 32
Deftruction, grim with blood,   Phil. 19
——————— like a vulture, hovers nigh,   Hughs 279
——————— prefages of, to a realm,   Hal. 227
Detraction from her prefence flies,   Hughes 232
Devil, the firft rebel,   Butl. 2 : 325
————— tempts, then betrays,   Butl. 2 : 31
————— name him, and he's always near,   Prior 1 : 139
————— out-witted,   Sav. 335
Devon, hail native land !   Gay 1 : 170
Devonfhire, to the Duke of,   Prior 1 : 280
Devotion and the Mufe,   Watts 127
——————— when luke-warm, is undevout,   Young 2 : 84
——————— did her time divide,   Young 3 : 151
——————— advanced by perfecution,   Butl. 2 : 76
——————— by promotion,   Butl. 2 : 70
——————— to the public, glorious flame,   Thom. 2 : 138
——————— moral gravitation,   Thom. 2 : 139
Dew, tranfparent beauties of the dawn,   Hughes 211
Dews, filver-footed,   Mall. 239
Diagoras the Rhodian, victor at the caftus,   Weft 168
Dialogue,   { Cow. 1 : 316
                                                       { Pope 1 : 357
——————— an art now almoft loft,   Buck. 76

Dialogue.

Dialogue, which the old Grecians knew,   *Buck.* 76

———— in allusion to Horace,   *Swift* 2 : 109

———— between a poet and his servant,   *Pitt* 281

Diamond rings felonious hands adorn,   *Cong.* 128

Dian, quiver'd, sister of the Day,   *Pope il.* 2 : 216

Diana, temple of,   *Dry.* 3 : 97

——— lady of the leaf,   *Dry.* 3 : 184

Diasenna, harangue of,   *Garth* 42

Dice have banished all taste,   *Mall.* 297

——— riddle on a pair of,   *Swift* 1 : 328

Dick, a maggot,   *Swift* 2 : 93

——— variety of,   *Swift* 2 : 95

Diction, only the colouring,   *D y.* 3 : 20

Didius, vile usurer, bought the empire,   *Dyer* 25

Dido, story of,   *Dry.* 5 : 328

——— passion of,   *Dry.* 6 : 35

——— prepares a hunting match,   *Dry.* 6 : 41

——— by a storm driven to a cave with Æneas,   *Dry.* 6 : 44

——— contrives her own death,   *Dry.* 6 : 67

——— to Æneas,   *Dry.* 4 : 193

Die, to die is to be free,   *Lansf.* 291

——— betimes, die innocent,   *Pom.* 284

——— is but the surest way to live,   *Broome* 129

——— as we do, we must remain,   *Pom.* 326

——— the dastard first, who dreads to die,   *Pope il.* 1 : 81

——— or conquer, are the terms of war,   *Pope il.* 2 : 146

——— of nothing, but a rage to live,   *Pope* 2 : 109

Dies novissima,   *Pom.* 344

Diet,   *Cow.* 1 : 251

Difficulties prove a soul great,   *Dry.* 1 : 314

    Digestion,

Digestion, instruments of,   Black. 193

Dignity of dress adorns the great,   Pope od. 3 : 171

———— of mien, to awe,   Pope od. 3 : 203

Dingley and Brent,   Swift 1 : 290

Dioclesian, Salonian garden of,   Cow. 2 : 336

Diogenes, a coiner,   Butl. 2 : 275

———— paltry tub of,   Butl. 1 : 137

Diomed, the force of, Tydeus' son,   Pope il. 1 : 185

———— opposes the return to Greece,   Pope il. 1 : 267

———— seconded by Nestor,   Pope il. 1 : 267

———— wounded by Paris,   Pope il. 1 : 337

———— wounded by Pandarus,   Pope il. 1 : 155

———— cured by Minerva,   Pope il. 1 : 156

———— enabled to discern gods from mortals, Pope il. 1 : 156

———— kills Pandarus,   Pope il. 1 : 163

———— wounds Venus,   Pope il. 1 : 165

———— greatly distinguishes himself,   Pope il. 1 : 151

———— like a sweeping torrent,   Pope il. 1 : 155

———— undertakes to go as spy,   Pope il. 1 : 303

———— accompanied by Ulysses,   Pope il. 1 : 304

———— chides Venus,   Pope il. 1 : 165

———— and Glaucus, interview,   Pope il. 1 : 147

———————————— exchange armour, Pope il. 1 : 202

Diomede refuses to engage in the war,   Dry. 7 : 15

———— recounts the miseries of war,   Dry. 7 : 14

Diomedes, adventures of,   Garth 137

Dione, a pastoral tragedy,   Gay 2 : 207

———— prologue for,   Gay 1 : 275

Dionysius, Homer's thoughts refines,   Pope 1 : 119

Diores, leader of the Epian race,   Pope il. 1 : 148

Diores, in vain his valour, and illustrious line, *Pope il.* 1 : 147

Diræ, daughters of night, *Dry.* 7 : 88

Dire is the omen, when the valiant fear, *Rowe L.* 304

Dirce's fountain blush'd with Grecian blood, *Pope* 1 : 276

Directors build castles in the seas, *Swift* 2 : 208

———— promises but wind, *Swift* 1 : 208

Dirge, *Gay* 1 : 79

Disappointment *Shen.* 159

———————— of a promised hour, *Young* 2 : 34

———————— and relief, *Watts* 196

Disarray, the tumult of the fight, *Pope il.* 2 : 41

Discarded toast, *Som.* 241

Discontent, universal, *Cow.* 2 : 352

———————— a proof of immortality, *Young* 2 : 164

———————— incurable consumption of our peace, *Young* 2 : 164

Discontented and unquiet, *Watts* 240

Discord, soliloquy of, *Garth* 64

———— nurse of War, *King* 368

———— dire sister of the Slaughtering Power, *Pope il.* 1 : 143

———— small at her birth, but rising every hour, *ib.* 1 : 143

———— red with blood, *Broome* 107

———— dire parent of tremendous woes, *Broome* 109

———— waits upon divided power, *Pope* 1 : 284

———— lust of, fires thy soul, *Pope* 1 : 295

———— in patriot form, debauches us, *Dry.* 1 : 297

———— periwigg'd with snakes, *Swift* 2 : 350

———— harmony not understood, *Pope* 2 : 32

Discords make the sweetest airs, *But.* 1 : 305

Discovery, { *Cow.* 1 : 261
{ *Lans.* 166

Difcovery, Swift 1 : 59
Mall. 294

Difcourfe, the medicine of the mind, Pope il. 2 : 80
———— the banquet of the mind, Pope od. 3 : 116
———— banquet of the mind, Dry. 3 : 181
———— fenfations and inftructive, Yal. 444
Difcretion ! Cow. 1 : 305
———— thou wert ne'er a friend to Love, Swift 1 : 131
———— moderate your coft, King 113
———— be thy guide, Lanf 150
———— covers what it would blame, King 306
———— all virtue in, Duke 115
Difdain, Watts 245
———— provokes difdain, Lanf. 289
Difdainful look reveals feeds of hatred, King 328
Difeafe, defcribed, Garth 56
———— prayer to, Garth 40
———— Death's dark agent to luxuriant Eafe, Sav. 40
Difeafes, feat of, Garth 83
———— conquered, Cow. 2 : 38
———— incident to cattle, Dry. 5 : 167
Difguife, 'tis great, 'tis manly, to difdain, Young 2 : 225
Difh, to lay in, Butl. 1 : 108
Difhes few encreafe the appetite, King 217
Difheveled locks graceful are to fome, Geng. 118
Difhonour, worfe than death, Pope od. 4 : 74
Difintereftnefs defcribed, Shen. 28
Difobedience, reward of, Milt. 1 : 203
———— Adam cautioned againft, Milt. 1 : 203, 208
———— effects of, Milt. 2 : 3
Difpenfary,

Difpenfary, building of, *Garth* 19, 23

Difpofitions, variety of, *Aken.* 15

———————— final caufe of, *Aken.* 16

Difputants like knights-errant, *Butl.* 2 : 278

Difputation, to run in debt, by, *Butl.* 1 : 8

Difpute about religion feldom accompanies practice, *Young* 2 : 127

Difputes, in wrangling fpend the day, *Den.* 92

Diffembler, *Cow.* 1 : 299

Diffenfions, like fmall ftreams, firft begin, *Garth* 44

Diftaff, fpinning-wheel, and loom, far are caft, *Thom.* 1 : 229

Diftance, *Cow.* 1 : 287

———————— immenfe ! between the gods and man, *Pope il.* 1 : 169

Diftinction nice, to fplit a cafe, *Butl.* 1 : 201

Diftinctions overftrained, *Butl.* 2 : 277

———————— of this life are quite cutaneous, *Young* 2 : 228

———————— none on the dead await, *Broome* 44

Diftrefs muft afk, and gratefully receive, *King* 274

Diftreffes induftry infpire, *Sav.* 61

Diftruftful fenfe with modeft caution fpeaks, *Pope* 1 : 117

Dittany defcribed, *Dry.* 7 : 67

Ditties to troll, *Butl.* 1 : 211

Ditty, *Gay* 1 : 62

Diverfions profeft, prefent us with a fhroud, *Young* 3 : 3

———————— talk of death, like garlands o'er a grave, *Young* 3 : 4

Divine attributes, *Pom.* 297

———————— love, { *Wall.* 205
{ *Parn.* 262

———————— fweet affections flow from, *Parn.* 262

———————— above the joys of fenfe, *Parn.* 262

———————— O, extreme of fweet defire, *Parn.* 263

Divine

Divine nature, properties, divided into persons,   *Pope od.* 3 : 2

———— poesy,   .   .   *Wall.* 223

———— poetry,   .   *Hughes* 81

Divines, who change with the changing scene,   *Swift* 1 : 90

Divinity Supreme, Author of Nature,   *West* 232

———— paramount to all, by all obey'd,   .   *West* 233

———— supreme, unbounded, universal Lord,   *West* 233

———— in thick darkness mak'st thy dread abode,   *West* 233

———— without a Νοῦς,   *Pope* 3 : 234

Division cease, and nations join in leagues of peace, *Pope* 1 : 118

Divorce, the public brand of shameful life,   .   *Parn.* 12

Doctor, incomparable soporific,   *Thom.* 2 : 183

———— sweet, sleeky, dear, pacific soul,   *Thom.* 2 : 183

———— around you the consenting audience sleeps, *Thom.* 2 : 183

Doctors differ,   .   *Prior* 2 : 255

Doctrine, to be judged of by analogy,   *Dry.* 1 : 255

Dodder'd oaks divide,   *Pope od.* 4 : 167

Doeg, character of,   *Dry.* 1 : 174

Dog, description of a good sort,   *Tick.* 143

——— choice of, for the female,   *Som.* 70

——— will be patient, struck with a bone,   *Swift* 2 : 329

——— and bear,   *Som.* 268

——— and the fox,   *Gay* 2 : 119

——— and shadow,   *Swift* 1 : 209

——— and thief,   *Swift* 2 : 15

Dogs, management of,   *Dry.* 5 : 165

——— snarl about a bone,   *Butl.* 2 : 5

——— symptoms of their madness,   *Som.* 75, seq.

——— heal their wounds by licking,   *Butl.* 2 : 82

Dog-bolt fortune,   .   *Butl.* 1 : 156

Dog-ftar's unpropitious ray,   Pope 3 : 215
Dog-trick, Fortune shews,   Butl. 1 : 100
Dog-trot to ride,   Butl. 1 : 217
D'Oily ftuffs ufelefs in winter,   Gay 1 : 102
Dole dealed among foes,   . Milt. 3 : 58
Dolon undertakes to be a fcout,   Pope il. 1 : 307
——— fwift of foot, and matchlefs in the race,   Pope il. 1 : 307
——— tells the fituation of the Trojans,   Pope il. 1 : 311
——— flain,   . Pope il. 1 : 312
Domeftic-manners,   Akm. 290
——— peace, that port, to which the wife are bound, Wefl 283
Domingo, mifcarriage at,   Cow. 2 : 247
Dominion's limits fixed by its end,   Akm. 340
Domitilla, verfes on,   Swift 2 : 143
Donavert taken,   Add. 58
Donne, fatires of,   Pope 2 : 260
——— has falt, but no numbers,   Dry. 7 : 205
——— affects metaphyfics,   Dry. 6 : 206
——— in honeft vengeance rofe,   Pope 2 : 17
——— third fatire of,   Parn 99
Doom, man's dark and uncertain,   Rowe L. 287
——— no hoftile hand can antedate,   Pope il. 2 : 212
——— eternal, unconquerable,   Dry. 2 : 302
Dorcheſter, border'd by meads and waſh'd by brooks, Gay 1 : 168
——— fit for fheep,   Dyer 32
Doric, adapted for paftoral,   Pope 1 : 22
Dorian, fam'd for Thamyris' difgrace,   Pope il. 1 : 92
Doris,   Gang. 105
Dormoufe, fattened by fleep,   King 237
Dorothy Sydney's picture,   Wall. 46

                                                      Dorſet,

Dorfet, poems of, 184
———— to Edward Howard, 187
———— to Sir Thomas St. Serf, 190
———— epilogue to Tartuffe, 891
———————— to Every man in his humour, 193
———— fong by, 195
———— on Countefs of Dorchefter, 198
———— on knotting, 199
———— antiquated coquet, 201
———— fong by, 204, 205, 206, 207
———— epiftle to, from Copenhagen, A. Phil. 335
———— character of, Dry. 1 : 118
Dotard, his mind to every fenfe is loft, Pope od. 4 : 175
———————— to reafon blind, Pope od. 4 : 175
Double-load of toils and years ! Broome 74
Doubt, boundlefs fea of, Roch. 319
———— a greater evil than defpair, Den. 17
———— refolved by intereft, Butl. 1 : 207
Doubtful, are the only wife, where difficulty lies; Buck. 115
Dove, Prior 1 : 113
———— fent out, returns, Milt. 2 : 113
Dover, country about, fit for fheep, Dyer 31
———— tremendous cliff of, Dyer 31
Down-hall, Prior 2 : 213
Drake, on a chair made out of his fhip, Corn 1 : 167, 220
———— who made thee miftrefs of the deep, Thom. 1 : 94
———— Sir Henry Francis, ode to, Aken. 223
Drances, foe to Turnus, Dry. 7 : 7
———— character of, Dry. 7 : 19
Drapier, the nation-faving paper, Swift 2 : 184
Drapier's

... ...	*Swift* 2 : 160
... ...	*Swift* 2 : 161
... ...	*Swift* 2 : 161
... ... thought,	*Broome* 165
... ...	*Hom.* 161
Dreadfulli... on wheels with local joys	*Rat.* 213
Dream,	*Roff.* 244
... ... imitation,	*Fent.* 325
... ... from dream,	*But..* 2 : 193
... ... a court of coblers, and a mob of kings,	*Pitt* 203
... ... illusive hovers o'er Atrides' head,	*Pope il.* 1 : 67
... ... in unusuary form, like Nestor,	*Pope il.* 1 : 69
Dreams,	{ *King* 414 }{ *Swift* 1 : 292 }
——— nature,	*Step.* 264
——— what,	*Swift* 1 : 292
——— our waking thoughts pursue,	*Dry.* 2 : 156
——— from repletion,	*Dry.* 3 : 143
——— rheum, choler aduft,	*Dry.* 3 : 144
——— come from God,	*Dry.* 3 : 146
——— vain illusions of the mind,	*Pope od.* 3 : 285
——— interludes of fancy,	*Dry.* 3 : 150
——— a mob of coblers, and a court of kings,	*Dry.* 3 : 150
——— not always vain,	*Dry.* 3 : 151
——— often prophefies,	*Dry.* 3 : 152
——— defcend from Jove,	*Tick.* 166
——— foretel, as learned men have fhown,	*Pope* 1 : 265
——— gild the glowing fceues of fancy,	*Fent.* 282
Drefs, propriety therein to be obferved,	*Gay* 1 : 105
Dreffing-room,	*Swift* 2 : 218

Driblet of a day, juft to pay,   *Dry.* 1 : 313
Drink, 'twas rage, 'twas noife,   *Prior* 2 : 133
Drinking, Anacreontic,   *Cow.* 1 : 140
Drinking-glaffes, verfes on,   *Lanf.* 228
Drones o'er dying tapers fnore,   *Garth* 25
Drooping arts revive by encouragement,   *Dry.* 1 : 310
———— fpirit with bold words repair,   *Pope od.* 3 : 242
Dropfy pale, with fallow face,   *Swift* 2 : 175
Drowned perfon recovered by friction,   *Mall.* 245
Drowning reckon'd an accurfed death,   *Dry.* 5 : 243
Drubs, to confute with,   *Butl.* 2 : 88
Drudgery and knowledge, of kin,   *Butl.* 2 : 235
———— of prayer, left to tatter'd crape,   *Garth* 24
Drugget-filk, improper in cold weather,   *Gay* 1 : 102
Druids, character of,   *Garth* 97
———— opinions of,   *Garth* 98
———— doctrines of,   *Fent.* 239
———— taught, that death but fhifts the fcene, *Thom.* 2 : 102
———— borrowed, to pay in the other world,   *Butl.* 1 : 260
———— who fingular religion love,   *Rowe L.* 68
———— teach other bodies in new worlds to find, *Rowe L.* 68
———— thrice happy, who the fear of death defpife, *Rowe L.* 68
Drumgold, verfes to,   *Lytt.* 86
Drums dreadful mufic of the war,   *Broome* 48
Drummers, improper at a wedding,   *Gay* 1 : 111
Drunk as a piper all day long,   *Gay* 1 : 270
Drunken metamorphofis,   *Parn.* 94
Drunkennefs, fatire on,   *Butl.* 2 : 249
Drury-lane, the Paphos of the town,   *Tick.* 129
———— dangerous to virtue,   *Gay* 1 : 141
                                                        Drufi,

Drusi, popular in faction's cause,   Rowe L. 284
Dryden, poems of,   1 : 9
———— on death of Haftings,   1 : 9
———— on death of Cromwell,   1 : 13
———— on the Reftoration,   1 : 19
———— to his Majefty,   1 : 30
———— to Hyde,   1 : 35
———— fatire on Dutch,   1 : 40
———— to Dutchefs of York,   1 : 42
———— annus mirabilis,   1 : 61
———— effay on fatire,   1 : 112
———— Abfalom and Achitophel,   1 : 125
———— the medal,   1 : 209
———— Tarquin and Tullia,   1 : 220
———— fuum cuique,   1 : 225
———— Religio Laici,   1 : 244
———— art of poetry,   1 : 260
———— Threnodia Auguftalis,   1 : 298
———— Veni Creator Spiritus,   1 : 316
———— the foliloquy,   1 : 318
———— Hind and Panther,   2 : 8
———— Britannia Rediviva,   2 : 97
———— Mac-Fleckno,   2 : 109
———— epiftles of,   2 : 117
———— elegies and epitaphs,   2 : 161
———— fongs and odes,   2 : 201
———— St. Cecilia,   2 : 203
———— Alexander's feaft,   2 : 214
———— fecular mafque,   2 : 220
———— prologues and epilogues,   2 : 227

Dryden,

Dryden, verses to,   *Dry.* 2 : 289
———— preface to fables,   3 : 13
———— unimpaired by years,   3 : 17
———— profe and verfe equally familiar to,   3 : 17
———— tales from Chaucer,   3 : 49
———————— from Boccace,   3 : 215
———— tranflations from Metamorphofes,   *id.* 3 : 281 | 4 : 1
———— concerning his tranflations,   4 : 277
———————— from Ovid's epiftles,   4 : 161
———————————————— art of love,   4 : 203
———————— from Homer,   4 : 237
———————— from Theocritus,   4 : 299
———————— from Lucretius,   4 : 315
———————— from Horace,   4 : 323
———————— from Virgil,   5 : 21 | 6 : 1 | 7 : 1
———————— from Juvenal,   7 : 221
———————— from Perfius,   7 : 308
———— on his tranflation of Perfius,   *Cong.* 66
———— old in rhyme, charming ev'n in years,   *Add.* 5
———— affords fweeteft numbers and fitteft words,   *Add.* 38
———— wears all dreffes and charms in all,   *Add.* 38
———— has numbers,   *Hal.* 231
———— perfected rhyme,   *Prior* 2 : 96
———— taught to join the varying verfe,   *Pope* 2 : 228
———— pride, malice, folly, rofe againft,   *Pope* 1 : 110
———— fhall be, what Chaucer is,   *Pope* 1 : 110
———— ill-fated, extremes of wit and meannefs join, *ib.* 2 : 11
———— foul of harmony,   *Lanf.* 203
———— oft in rhyme his weaknefs hides,   *Smith* 195
Dryope, fable of,   *Pope* 1 : 327

Dryope changed to the lotos,	*Pope* 1 : 329
Dub fallen, of drums,	*Butl.* 1 . 211
Duck and drake, what,	*Butl.* 1 : 234
Duel, anacreontic,	.*Cow.* 1 : 142
Duke, poems of,	·83
—— to Cælia,	·104
—— to the Queen,	:106
—— on Abſalom and Achitophel,	111
—— an epithalamium,	112
—— on marriage of Prince George,	116
—— on death of Chaıles II.	119
—— prologue to Lee's Brutus,	123
—— to Creech,	126
—— ſong by,	134
—— to Waller,	·133
—— to Dickenſon,	137
—— to Dryden,	138
—— to diſbanded officers,	·177
——'to a Roman Catholic,	·178
—— to Otway,	179
Duke upon duke, a ballad,	·*Gay* 2 : 198
Dukes of Venice wed the Adriatic,	*Butl.* 1 : 216
Dulichium, crown'd with fruitful ſtores,	·*Pope* od. 4 : 35
——————— land of plenty,	*Pope* od. 4 : 84
——————— bleſt with every grain,	*Pope* od. 4 : 84
Dull is the jeſter, when the joke's unkind,	*Young* 1 : 91
—— lad, with travel finiſhes the fool,	*Gay* 2 : 54
—— and venal, a new world to mould,	*Pope* 3 : 216
Dulneſs, daughter of Chaos and eternal Night,	*Pope* 3 : 79
———— born a goddeſs, never dies,	*Pope* 3 : 80

Dulneſs,

Dulness, hatches a new Saturnian age of lead,   *Pope* 3 : 81
———— supporters of,   *Pope* 3 : 83
.———— cloud-compelling queen,   *Pope* 3 : 85
———— is sacred in a sound Divine,   *Pope* 3 : 162
———— all, when the fancy's bad,   *Buck.* 70
———— nor less a sin than drunkenness,   *Som.* 245
———— a misfortune,   *Broome* 13
———— ever must be regular,   *Lytt.* 18
———— ever loves a joke,   *Pope* 3 : 127
———— is ever apt to magnify,   *Pope* 1 : 107
———— gives her page the word,   *Pope* 3 : 218
Dom-founding, a recreation,   *Dry.* 2 : 274
Dumps,   *Gay* 1 : 66
Dun, horrible monster,   *Phil.* 4
———— entrench'd with many a frown,   *Phil.* 5
Dunce, subtle doctor,   *Beth.* 1 : 12
Dunciad,   *Pope* 3 : 73
Dunkirk taken under Cromwell,   *Cow.* 2 : 247
———— sold,   *Thom.* 2 : 117
Dunmow-bacon, few marry'd fowl do peck,   *Prior* 2 : 205
Dupe to party, child and man the same,   *Pope* 3 : 250
Durance of chain, and banishment of God,   *Prior* 2 : 121
Duration, thy, a moment, foolish man !   *Prior* 2 : 120
D'Urfey, bard of wondrous meed,   *Gay* 1 : 67
Durselley, Prior to, on Milton,   1 : 42
Dust (in) vanquish'd and the victor lie,   *Pope il.* 1 : 148
———— shall pride devour,   *Saw.* 76
———— form'd us all, the king, the beggar is the same,   *Gay* 2 : 192
Dustman offensive,   *Gay* 1 : 112
Dutch, satire on,   *Dry.* 1 : 40

Dutch, victory obtained over,	*Wall.* 185
——— boors akin to Sooterkins,	*Butl.* 2 : 10
——— commentators, character of,	*Dry.* 3 : 291
——— maxim to save money,	*King* 217
——— proverb,	*Prior* 1 : 142
——— war,	*Dry.* 1 : 61
Duty, sum of, be humble and be just,	*Prior* 2 : 195
——— to God and our neighbour,	*Watts* 357
——— wide opens to receive distress,	*Sav.* 14
Duval, ode on,	*Butl.* 2 : 301
Dwarf-pye, what,	*King* 183
Dwarfs, marriage of,	*Wall.* 85
Dyer, Grongar hill,	1
——— ruins of Rome,	7
——— the fleece,	29
——— the country walk,	129
——— the enquiry,	134
——— epistle to a famous painter,	135
——— to Aaron Hill,	137
——— the choice,	140
——— to Mr. Savage,	142
——— an epistle to a friend in town,	143
——— Clio to Mr. Dyer,	144
——— epistle to,	*Sav.* 161
——— verses to,	*Sav.* 127
Dying, what,	*Garth* 45
——— Christian to his soul,	*Pope* 1 : 86
——— kid,	*Shen.* 115
——— of cloth,	*Dyer* 87
——— French, excel in,	*Dyer* 88
	Dying,

Dying materials, few in England, *Dyer* 78

———————— neceffity of importing, *Dyer* 78

Dyrrhachium, fituation of, *Rowe L.* 245

———————— near it, Cæfar and Pompey encamp, *ib.* 245

E

Each man is man, and all our fex is one, *Prior* 1 : 237

Eagle defcribed, *Young* 1 : 218

———— fwifteft and ftrongeft of th' aerial race, *Pope il.* 2 : 244

———— fovereign of the plumy race, *Pope il.* 2 : 340

———— called Percnos by the gods, *Pope il.* 2 : 340

———— tries her young againft the fun, *Rowe L.* 421

———— prepares her young to bear the fun, *Yal.* 436

———— affeffor of Jove's throne, *Pitt* 198

———— flies, charged with his thunder, *Pitt* 198

———— full dexter, aufpicious fight, *Pope od.* 4 : 53

———— and affembly of animals, *Gay* 2 : 35

———— employed in falconry, *Som.* 145

Eagle-eyed to another's faults, *Dry.* 7 : 339

Eagle-radiance to the faded eye, *Fent.* 290

Eagles caft their bills, *King* 310

———— try their young againft the fun, *Butl.* 2 : 230

Eaglet fafely dares the fun, *Dry.* 2 : 101

Eager love denies the leaft delay, *Pope il.* 2 : 52

Eagre, rode o'er the tide, *Dry.* 1 : 302

Early piety, examples of, *Watts* 342

———— religion, advantages of, *Watts* 340

Ears, labels to the foul, *Butl.* 2 : 234

———— refute the cenfure of our eyes, *Pope il.* 1 : 114

Earth

Earth formed,   *Milt.* 1 : 216

------ and water feparated,   *Milt.* 1 : 217

------ brings forth plants and trees,   *Milt.* 1 : 217

------ a punctual fpot,   *Milt.* 1 : 232

------ fpeck of, O how fmall,   *Mall.* 216

------------------ creation,   *Young* 1 : 25

------ but an atom,   *Watts* 115

------ fpinning on her axle,   *Milt.* 1 : 236

------ well-fhower'd, is deep enrich'd,   *Thom.* 1 : 9

------ grows daily on the yielding main,   *Rowe L.* 388

------ no perfection to be found on,   *Cong.* 65

------ where pleafure fcarce can pleafe,   *Broome* 122

------ the Bedlam of the Univerfe,   *Young* 3 : 61

------ where reafon runs mad,   *Young* 3 : 61

------ Aceldama, a field of blood,   *Young* 2 : 133

------ this vaft toy-fhop,   *Broome* 31

------ a nurfery for heaven,   *Butl.* 2 : 220

------ from, all came, to Earth muft all return,   *Prior* 2 : 171

------ fhadow of heaven,   *Milt.* 1 : 158

------ fon of,   *Dry.* 7 : 362

------ fcum and fon of,   *Butl.* 2 : 61

------ and heaven,   *Watts* 44

------'s proud tyrants low in afhes laid,   *Pope Il.* 1 : 139

Earth-born Lycon may afcend a throne,   *Smith* 108

Earthquakes, caufes of,   *Garth* 80

------------ figns and caufes of,   *Mall.* 208

------------ horrors of,   *Mall.* 209

------------ effects of,   *Mall.* 210, 211, 212

------------ convulfions of the ground,   *Dry.* 2 : 105

------------ convulfive, the land in pieces tear,   *Hughes* 280

                                                       Earthquakes

Earthquakes rend the cleaving ground, *Broome* 49

Ease in writing flows from art, not chance, *Pope* 2 : 248

—— voluptuous, child of Wealth, *Swift* 2 : 175

Easy ear deceives, and is deceived, *Den.* 94

Eastern boldness, false opinion of, *Young* 1 : 231

Eat to live, *Garth* 96

Ecclesiasticus, chap. xliii, *Broome* 95

Echerus, worst of mortals, worst of kings, *Pope* od. 4 : 190

———— monster of a king, *Pope* od. 4 : 121

———— fiercest of the tyrant-kind, *Pope* od. 4 : 120

Echo, *Cow.* 1 : 272

—— queen of parley, *Milt.* 3 : 129

—— resounds, *Butl.* 1 : 107

—— transformation of, *Add.* 158

—— riddle on, *Swift* 1 : 323

Ecstasy, ode, *Hughes* 277

Eddystone light-house, *Gay* 1 : 143

Eden, delicious spot, *Milt.* 2 : 17

—— river of, *Milt.* 1 : 108, 109

—— the vicinage of heaven, *Pom.* 257

—— groves of, live in description, *Pope* 1 : 57

Edgar cemented all contending powers, *Phil.* 79

—— pacific monarch, *Phil.* 79

—— impos'd a tribute of wolves on Wales, *Som.* 48

—— chac'd the growling wolf, *Dyer* 70

Edgbaston, ecl.o at, *Shen.* 311

Edge sharpest, of death or life, to stand on, *Pope* il. 1 : 301

Edge-hill fight, *Cow.* 1 : 331

Education, *West* 281

———— parent of science, *W.A* 281

L 4

Education goodly difcipline, from heaven fprung, *Wef.* 281

—————— want every virtue grows, *Wef.* 263

—————— brings Genius to light, *Som.* 376

—————— can the Genius raife, *Lytt.* 76

—————— forms the common mind, *Pope* 2 : 100

—————— ill ufed by, *Dry.* 2 : 65

—————— more than Truth prevails, *Pitt.* 342

—————— modern arts of, *Butl.* 2 : 269

Edward, laws of, *Thom.* 2 : 106

—————— third, his right with-held, awakens vengeance, *Phil.* 80

—————————— with golden iris, his fhield embofs'd, *Phil.* 81

—————— firft in civil fame, *Aken.* 215

—————— fcourge of France, *Gray* 355

—————— black prince, fable warrior, *Gray* 355

—————— dreadful with his fable fhield, *Prior* 1 : 257

Edwards, Thomas, ode to, *Aken.* 274

Edwin and Emma, *Mall.* 323

Effect, muft prefuppofe a caufe, *Prior* 2 : 115

—————————————— a fource, a deity, *Prior* 2 : 115

Effects to find, while caufes lie conceal'd, *Dyer* 77

—————— are to their caufes chain'd, *Rowe L.* 276

—————— reveal the caufe, *Para.* 168

Effeminacy yokes man a flave, *Milt.* 3 : 20

Egbert united the Saxon kingdoms, *Thom.* 2 : 104

Egg, the vulgar boil, the learned roaft, *Pope* 2 : 243

—— roafted, better than boiled, *King* 180

—— one vaft, produces human race, *Pope* 3 : 197

—— fmall worlds, *King* 297

—— frefh or addle, *Butl.* 1 : 214

Egypt, the place of Pompey's retreat, *Rowe L.* 349

Egypt,

Egypt, want of rain supplied by the Nile,   *Black.* 92

———— plagues of,   *Cow.* 2 ∗ 54

Egypt, slothful nation, disused to toil,   *Rowe L.* 353

———— conceal'd her learning in emblems,   *Black.* 173

———— fanatic,   *Milt.* 1 : 21

———— mysterious, rank nursery of superstitions, *West* 260

———— Gods of,   *Black.* 120

———— tyrants of,   *Thom.* 2 : 37

Egyptian years, lunar months,   *King* 173

Egyptians worship'd dogs,   *Butl.* 1 : 40

Elbow-chair, address to,   *Som.* 226

———————— my dear companion and faithful friend, *Som.* 226

Eld, weight of, who may sustain,   *A. Phil.* 302

Eldership of right to assist,   *Dry.* 3 : 65

———————— on truth's delightful side,   *Parn.* 102

Eleanor of Bretagne,   *Shen.* 69

———————— of Castile, character of,   *Gray* 357

Eleazar, lamentation of,   *Pom.* 312

Election, but a market vile,   *Thom.* 2 : 134

———————— sons of Anstis, by,   *Prior* 2 : 258

Elective kingdom, conditions of,   *Dry.* 5 : 226

Elector Palatine abandon'd,   *Thom.* 2 : 113

Elegance of mind, be that your ornament,   *Lytt.* 40

Elegies,   *Shen.* 13

———————— designed for grief,   *Rosc.* 262

———————— and Epitaphs,   *Dry.* 2 : 161

Elegy,   *Lytt.* 94

———————— what,   *Shen.* 4

———————— occasions of,   *Shen.* 4

———————— end and use of,   *Shen.* 5

Elegy, etymology of,   Shen. 3

—— notion of,   Shen. 4

—— origin of,   Shen. 4

—— deviation from its origin,   Shen. 5

—— ftyle of,   Shen. 6

—— metre proper for,   Shen. 7

—— in moving numbers flows,   Gay 1 : 213

—— loves a mournful ftile,   Dry. 1 : 270

—— of fweet and folemn voice,   Buck. 72

—— defpairing love complains in,   Buck. 72

Elements of Ariftotle, earth, water, air, and fire,   Black. 168

—— four,   Dry. 4 : 145

Eleonora,   Dry. 2 : 176

Elephant, wifeft of Brutes,   Thom. 1 : 68

—— with gentle might endow'd,   Thom. 1 : 68

—— pride of kings,   Thom. 1 : 68

—— and bookfeller,   Gay 2 : 45

—— for parts and fenfe renown'd,   Gay 2 : 45

—— in the moon,   Butl. 2 : 147, 166

Elf, the devil's valet,   Butl. 1 : 287

Eli, venerably great in filver'd age,   Parn. 146

—— and his fons flain,   Cow. 2 : 174

Eliab, character of,   Dry. 1 : 194

Elijah fafting,   Milt. 2 : 155

—— fed by ravens,   Milt. 2 : 172

—— rapt,   Cow. 2 : 44

Elis in forty fhips moves under Meges,   Pope il. 1 : 92

—— courfer-breeding plain,   Pope od. 4 : 191

Eliza, hymn to,   Lytt. 82

—— boldly wife, and fortunately great,   Prior 1 : 248

Elizabeth,

Elizabeth, her lion-port, awe-commanding face, _Gray_ 358
——————— ballad alluding to, _Shen._ 91
Elmerick, prologue to, _Ham._ 228
——————— epilogue to, _Lytt._ 102
Elms, be facred ftill to beauty and to love, _Hughes_ 68
Eloifa to Abelard, _Pope_ 1 : 163
Eloquence, upon her tongue perfuafion, _Parn._ 276
——————— decent action dwells upon her hand, _Parn._ 276
——————— power of, _Milt._ 2 : 210
——————— fatal to the owners, _Dry._ 7 : 288
——————— of female tears, _Broome_ 135
——————— of Menelaus and Ulyffes, _Pope il._ 1 : 114
Elpenor, nor much for fenfe, nor courage, fam'd, _Pope od._ 3 : 273
——————— begs for funeral rites, _Pope od._ 3 : 280
——————— fepulchral honours paid to, _Pope od._ 3 : 307
Elyfium, _Parn._ 279
——————— dream of, _Cow._ 1 : 67
——————— defcribed, { _Cow._ 1 : 68
{ _Dry._ 6 : 142
——————— pleafures of, _Dry._ 6 : 142
Embaffies, hollow compliments and lies, _Milt._ 2 : 205
Embaffy to Achilles unfuccefsful, _Pope il._ 1 : 298
Eminence makes Envy rife, _Swift_ 2 : 129
Emma and the Nutbrown Maid were one, _Prior_ 1 : 220
Emmet, _Watts_ 364
Empedocles, philofopher and juggler, _Butl._ 2 : 275
Empire, only power in truft, _Dry._ 1 : 139
——————— on Virtue's rock unfhaken ftands, _Young_ 1 : 254
——————— funs of, _Wall._ 153
——————— a feather for a fool, _Young_ 3 : 136

Empire

Empire and Love' the vision of a day,   *Young* 1 : 50
Empty heads confute with empty sound,   *Pope* 3 : 253
——— found from solid sense to know,   *Pom.* 251
Empyreal forms gash'd, easily unite,   *Tick.* 212
Emulate (to) a generous warmth implies,   *Young* 3 : 212
Emulation turns to envy,   *Swift* 2 : 257
Encampment, where pitched,   *Butl.* 2 : 94
Enchantment,   { *Ot.*   24
                                          { *Lanf.* 169
Encouragement makes Science spread,   *Gay* 1 : 180
Encrease and multiply, was Heaven's command, *Pope* 1 : 255
Engines to destroy foxes,   *Pom.* 54
——————————— and other wild beasts,   *Pom.* 56
England, scene of changes,   *Dry.* 2 : 246
——— to the country-gentlemen of,   *Aken.* 277
English, apter to improve than invent,   *Dry.* 3 : 23
——— not incapable of harmony,   *Hughes* 113
——— language and poetry improved,   *Dry.* 7 : 94
——— purity of, began in Chaucer,   *Dry.* 3 : 22
——— numbers in their nonage,   *Dry.* 3 : 28
——— beauty,   ..   *Hughes* 116
——— padlock,   .   *Prior* 1 : 134
——— plains blush with pomaceous harvests,   *Phil.* 63
——— poets,   *Add.* 34
——— poets imitated,   *Pope* 1': 343, feq.
——— prosody, none extant,   *Dry.* 7 : 215
——— shepherds, advantages of,   *Dyer* 46
——— compared with those of colder or hotter climes, *Dyer* 46
——— verse,   *Wall.* 171
Enigmas,   ' *Prior* 2 : 257
                                                           Enjoyment,

Enjoyment,   { Cow. 1 : 279
                                              { Yal.   363
——————— cloys the appetite,   Yal. 364
Ennius fancies Homer's foul transfufed to him, Dry. 7 : 156
——— firft author of Roman fatire,   Dry. 7 : 156
——— infpir'd with wine, his heroes fung,   Pitt 387
——— fixt the verdant crown on his own head,   Pitt 312
——— reviving lives in Maro's page,   Smith 194
Enoch tranflated,   Milt. 2 : 108
Enquiry,   Dyer 134
Entail of death, nothing can cut off,   Pom. 322
Entertainment, to be adapted to company,   King 216
Envy, abode of,   Garth 27
——— defcribed,   Garth 22
——— companions of,   Garth 29
——— effects of,   Garth 29
——— direft fiend of hell,   Cow. 2 : 76
——— fheds her baleful influence into men,   Cow. 2 : 77
——— her effects on Saul,   Cow. 2 : 79
——— effaces all obligations,   Cow. 2 : 171
——— baffles the greateft charms,   Cow. 2 : 88
——— fharpens cunning,   Duke 91
——— withers at another's joy,   Thom. 1 : 13
——— hates that excellence it cannot reach,   Thom. 1 : 13
——— with mifery refides,   Dry. 1 : 39
——— joy and revenge of ruin'd pride,   Dry. 1 : 39
——— a canker-worm,   Swift 2 : 100
——— fees her fmile, and dies,   Hughes 232
——— fpitting cat, foe to peace,   Pope 1 : 345
——— will merit, as its fhade purfue,   Pope 1 : 110

Envy,

Envy, but like a shadow, proves the substance true, *Pope* 1 : 110

—— a sharper spur than pay, *Gay* 2 : 47

—— is blind, *Gay* 2 : 187

—— never dwells in noble hearts, *Dry.* 3 : 124

—— defames, as Harpies devour the food they first *Swift* 2 : 201

—— ill becomes the human mind, *West* 205

—— its guilt pity, and its rage despise, *Young* 3 : 161

—— strove with evil deeds to conquer good, *West* 154

—— waits, that lover of the dead, *Tick.* 196

—— wears a mean malignant face, *Young* 3 : 212

—— pursues alone the brave and wise, *Sav.* 19

—— stings our darling passion, pride, *Sav.* 20

—— reigns and lives among the dead, *Pitt* 212

—— never conquer'd, but by death, *Pope* 2 : 214

—— breaks, and merit shines, *Gay* 2 : 78

—— ill-judging and verbose, *Prior* 2 : 27

—— is emulation in the learn'd or brave, *Pope* 2 : 48

Envious mind each blemish strikes, *Gay* 2 : 49

——————— blind to all apparent beauties, *Gay* 2 : 49

——————— wall, why destroy the lovers' hopes, *Hughes* 59

——————— why forbid the joy, *Hughes* 59

Epeans in four bands, of ten ships each, *Pope il.* 1 : 92

Epaminondas, first and best of men, *Thom.* 2 : 144

Epic poem, view of, *Pope od.* 3 : 1

———— what, *Pope od.* 3 : 3

———— action of, *Pope od.* 17

———— a full-length draught of life, *Dry.* 5 : 210

———— more for the manners, *Dry.* 213

———— principal parts in, *Dry.* 3 : 20

———— passions, *Pope od.* 3 : 28

Epic poem, manners of,   Pope od. 3 : 29
Epic requires a lofty ſtrain,   Dry. 1 : 281
——— narration of a great deſign,   Dry. 1 : 281
Epicaſte, ſheeny form of, woo'd by Oedipus her ſon,   Fent. 257
Epicure, Anacreontic,   Cow. 1 : 146
Epicurean philoſophy,   Dry. 5 : 51
——————— principles, no poem can be writ on,   Dry. 5 : 273
Epicurus, life in a garden,   Cow. 2 : 332
——————— Greece, thy everlaſting ſhame,   Black. 135
——————— who built by chance this mighty frame, Black. 135
——————— his glad eaſe,   Thom. 2 : 43
Epigram, a ſentence in a diſtich,   Dry. 1 : 272
——————— point of,   Dry. 1 : 272
——————— miniature of wit,   Yal. 375
——————— ſtrikes at folly in a ſingle line,   Gay 1 : 214
——————— on the buſts in Richmond Hermitage, Swift 2 : 278
——————— on a lady weeping at the tragedy of Cato,   Rowe 56
——————— on the humanity of the Prince of Wales,   Rowe 58
——————— extempore,   Prior 2 : 240
Epigrams on the intended hoſpital for ideots, &c. Swift 2 : 370
Epilogue, concluſion of,   Broome 101
Epiſodes, or under-actions, neceſſary,   Dry. 5 : 207
Epiſtle upon an Epiſtle,   Swift 2 : 116
Epiſtles,   { Dry. 2 : 117
                                         { A. Phil. 331
Epitaph, extempore,   Prior 2 : 13
——————— verſes making part of,   Lytt. 74
——————— on Lord Beauclerk,   Young 1 : 237
——————— on father, mother, and brother,   Pitt 296
——————— this laſt pledge from a brother and a ſon, Pitt 296
                                                          Epitaphs,

Epitaphs, *Pope* 2 : 356

Epithalamium of Helen and Menalaus, *Dry.* 4 : 304

———————— from Claudian, *Hughes* 138

Epithets thick laid, as varnish on a harlot, *Milt.* 2 : 212

Epode, what, *West* 117

Equal course, hard to steer, *Dry.* 1 : 221

——— government, makes king and people happy, *Wall.* 149

Equicola, character of, *Dry.* 6 : 191

Equipage, price of, *Shen.* 176

Equivocation, *Gay* 2 : 10

Erasmus stem'd the torrent of a barbarous age, *Pope* 1 : 120

——————— drove the monks, the holy Vandals, off the stage, *ib.* 120

——————— a passage in his Moria, *Prior.* 1 : 158

Eretria, of all Euboean cities queen, *Aken.* 168

Ergoteles, victor in the Olympic games, *West* 182

Erichtho, described, *Rowe L.* 271

——————— her cell, *Rowe L.* 277

——————— her magical composition, *Rowe L.* 278

——————— dreadful hoarseness of voice, *Rowe L.* 279

——————— prayer of, *Rowe L.* 279

Eridanus, prince of streams, *Rowe L.* 102

——————— king of floods, *Add.* 41

Eriphyle, for gold betray'd her lord, *Fent.* 259

Eris, sounds the loud Orthian song, *Pope Il.* 1 : 321

Eros and Anteros on either side, *Dry.* 3 : 138

Err, is human, to forgive divine, *Pope* 1 : 112

Err by use, go wrong by rules, *Prior* 2 : 84

Erratic throngs their Saviour's blood deny, *Pom.* 346

Erring twice, none, in love and war, *Pom.* 224

Error best evinced by its own arms, *Milt.* 2 : 209

Error's

Error's mazy grove we roam,   *Fent.* 215

Errors removed will smooth the way to truth,   *Pom.* 342

———— seize the wise,   *Pope od.* 4 : 225

Erymedusa, nurse of Nausicaa,   *Pope od.* 3 : 185

———————— tender second to a mother's cares, *Pope od.* 3 : 185

Esher, enchanting vale,   *Thom.* 1 : 92

Espousal,   *Gay* 1 : 238

Essay on Man,   *Pope* 2 : 27

———————— to the Author of,   *Som.* 225

———————— Satire,   *Pope* 2 : 2

Essays Moral,   *Pope* 2 : 95, seq.

———— in verse and prose,   *Cow.* 2 : 261

Essential One, and co-eternal Three,   *Pom.* 333

Estates have wings, and hang in Fortune's power, *Pope* 2 : 252

———— swallowed at a meal,   *Dry.* 7 : 228

Esté, of ancient Stock,   *Lanf.* 126

Esteem is virtue's right alone,   *Gay* 2 : 128

———— seldom does so much good, as ill-will harm, *Pope* 1 : 6

Eteocles, fortune the crown decrees,   *Pope* 1 : 286

———— pleased to behold unbounded power thy own, *ib.* 287

Eternal, whose nod controls the world,   *Pope il.* 2 : 70

———— being to undergo eternal punishment,   *Milk.* 1 : 10

Eternal burnings who can bear?   *Pom.* 335

———— life is nature's ardent wish,   *Young* 2 : 207

———— matter never wears,   *Dry.* 3 : 134

Eternity! thou pleasing, dreadful thought!   *Add.* 329

———— is all instant,   *Wall.* 180

———— has neither past nor future,   *Wall.* 180

———— infathomable sea!   *Watts* 61

———— deeps without a shore,   *Watts* 61

Eternity, boundless realms of vast,   *Pom.* 282

———— thought on,   *Gay* 1 : 279

———— divine, thou endless thought,   *Gay* 1 : 279

———— whate'er endears, is mercy,   *Young* 3 : 129

———— endears, what most imbitters Time,   *Young* 3 : 130

———— a boundless space, which Time can never run, *Cong.* 45

———— launching into,   *Watts* 117

————'s regard we give to Time,   *Young* 2 : 57

Etherege, Dryden to,   2 : 131

———— a sheer original,   *Roch.* 337

———— and Sedley deserved applause,   *Fent.* 236

Eton-college, distant prospect of,   *Gray* 330

———— founded by Henry VI,   *Gray* 330

Evander welcomes Æneas,   *Dry.* 6 : 202

———— sends Pallas his son,   *Dry.* 6 : 218

———— mourns over Pallas,   *Dry.* 7 : 9

———— comforted by the prospect of Turnus' death, *ib.* 7 : 10

———— feast of, revived,   *Cong.* 72

Evasions uncover crimes more,   *Milt.* 3 : 35

Euboea sends the Abantes in forty ships,   *Pope il.* 1 : 88

Eve taken out of Adam,   *Milt.* 1 : 115

— relates her thoughts of herself,   *Milt.* 1 : 116

— daughter of God and man,   *Milt.* 2 : 12

— describes Adam,   *Milt.* 1 : 117

— submission to Adam,   *Milt.* 1 : 122

— professes her happiness in Adam,   *Milt.* 1 : 123

— charms of,   *Milt.* 2 : 16, 18

— troublesome dream of,   *Milt.* 1 : 140

— tempted to eat the forbidden fruit,   *Milt.* 1 : 141

———— and become a Goddess,   *Milt.* 1 : 141

Eve staggered by sophistry,　　　　　*Milt.* 2 : 29

—— plucked the fruit, and eat,　　　　*Milt.* 2 : 29

—— sudden change of,　　　　　　　*Milt.* 2 : 29

—— resolves to make Adam share in her sin,　*Milt.* 2 : 30

—— prevails on him to eat,　　　　　*Milt.* 2 : 26

—— thought herself a Goddess,　　　　*Milt.* 2 : 29, 36

—— reason of, disturbed,　　　　　　*Milt.* 2 : 30

—— intoxicated by eating forbidden fruit,　*Milt.* 2 : 31, 32

—— sin of, affects all nature,　　　　*Milt.* 2 : 29

—— charges the serpent with her sin,　　*Milt.* 2 : 50.

—— her fickle taste transgress'd the law,　*Gay* 2 : 186

——————— entail'd the curse on man,　*Gay* 2 : 186

—— her regret on quitting Paradise,　　*Milt.* 2 : 94.

Evelyn,　　　　　　　　　　　　　　· *Wall.* 112

Evening described,
{ *Thom.* 1 : 90, 100.
　Gay 1 : 132
　Mall. 202

—————— hymn for,　　　　　*Parn.* 246

—————— ode to,　　　　　　, *Collins* 264

—————— song,　　　　　　*Watts* 353

—————— of the Lord's day,　　*Watts* 355.

—————— philomel, to bid the sun farewel,　*Coug.* 5

Evening-star, love's harbinger,　　　*Milt.* 2 : 104

—————————— ode to,　　*Akin* 233

Event deceives our most sanguine views,　*West* 184

—————— and veils in sudden grief the smiling ray,　*West* 184

Everlasting yawns confess the penalties of idleness, *Pope* 3 : 241.

Every Dog shall have his day,　　　*Som.* 301.

Evesham, vale of,　　　　　　　*Som.* 96

—————— seat of Hobbinol,　　*Som.*

Euge

Eugene, a name to every Briton dear,   *Rowe* 21

—— Aufonia's weeping ftates to free,   *Fent.* 205

—— fwift on th' imperial eagle flies,   *Fent.* 205

—— fhook the Turcheftan throne,   *Phil.* 11

Evil, offspring of Satan,   *Milt.* 1 : 182

—— redounds on the author,   *Milt.* 1 : 209

—— recoils back on itfelf,   *Milt.* 3 : 142

—— unapproved leaves no fpot,   *Milt.* 1 : 143

—— expected, worfe than felt,   *Milt.* 2 : 190

—— who flights, finds it leaft,   *Prior* 2 : 208

—— company,   *Watts* 349

—— news ride poft,   *Milt.* 3 : 58

—— tongue, what wounds forer,   *A. Phil.* 305

—— fpirits their amufements,   *Milt.* 1 : 52, 53

———— expofed to extremes of heat and cold, *M lt.* 1 : 55

Evils we cannot fhun, we muft endure,   *Lanf.* 175

—— natural, are moral goods,   *Young* 3 : 14

—— paft, the melancholy joy,   *Pope od* 4 : 61

Eulogy give Death,   *Young* 2 : 52

Eumæus, fwineherd to Ulyffes,   *Pope od.* 4 : 24

———— habitation, defcribed,   *Pope od.* 4 : 23

Eumelus, whom Alcefte bore, in ten fhips embark'd, *Pope il.* 1 : 96

———— mares of, were foremoft in the chace,   *Pope il.* 1 : 98

Euphemus leads the Ciconians,   *Pope il.* 1 : 101

Euphrates rolls a mighty torrent, black with mud,   *Pitt* 204

Euphrofyne, goddefs of Mirth,   *Sav.* 88

———— all life, all bloom,   *Sav.* 88

———— of Youth and Fancy born,   *Sav.* 88

———— the gentle queen of Smiles,   *Aken.* 47

———— eternal youth o'er all her form,   *Aken.* 48

           Evremont,

Evremont, renown'd for wit and dirt, *Pitt* 281

———— changes his living oftener than his shirt, *Pitt* 281

Euripides, Pella's bard, there torn by dogs, *Collins* 245

———— soft Pity's priest, *West* 132

———— who melts in useful woes the bleeding breast, *id.* 132

———— translation from, *Hughes* 259

Europa, rape of, *Add.* 140

Europe recovered from ignorance, *Den.* 107

———— shall her great deliverer own, *Hughes* 20

———— freed, and France repell'd, *Prior* 1 : 168

———— midland part of, *Mall.* 208

———— he saw, and Europe saw him too, *Pope* 3 : 238

Euryclea informs Penalope of Ulysses' return, *Pope od.* 4 : 219

——————————— and death of the suitors, *id.* 219

Eurypylus in forty barks commands, *Pope il.* 1 : 96

Eusden thirsts no more for sack or praise, *Pope* 3 : 114

Example is a lesson, that all can read, *West* 314

———— draws, where precept fails, *Prior* 2 : 203

———— must reclaim a graceless age, *Garth* 103

———— strikes all human hearts, *Young* 3 : 73

———— bad, more, *Young* 3 : 73

———— imperious Dictator, *Butl.* 2 : 232

———— reconciles contrarieties, *Butl.* 2 : 232

———— let it not sway thee, *Rowe* 4

———— sad, and theme of future song, *Pope il.* 1 : 206

Examples great are but vain, *Swift* 1 : 115

———— where ignorance begets disdain, *Swift* 1 : 115

Exauns of Saints, *Butl.* 2 : 34

Excess decays the body, and impairs the mind, *Buck* 91

Excessive sorrow is exceeding dry, *Gay* 1 : 85

M 3

Exclufion, bill of,　　　　　　　　　　　　Dry. 1 : 186

Excurfion,　　　　　　　　　　　　　　Mall. 295

Exercife, Health's mountain-fifter,　　　　　Parn. 59

———— fweats ill humours out,　　　　　Dry. 3 : 140

———— fome zeft for eafe,　　　　　　Thom. 1 : 205

Exeter, Countefs of, playing on the lute,　　Prior 1 : 28

Exodiarii, what,　　　　　　　　　　　Dry. 7 : 154

Exorbitances fit for Bedlam,　　　　　　　Butl. 1 : 76

Expectance of a blifs delay'd breeds anxious doubt, Parn. 202

Expectation endears a bleffing,　　　　　Wall. 119

Expended Deity on human weal !　　　　　Young 2 : 69

Experience, flow guide, but fure,　　　　Thom. 2 : 82

———— difcovers qualities of things,　　Phil. 44

———— lies in the hoary head,　　　　Gay 1 : 334

———— lay on plain, foundations low,　　Pope 3 : 248

———— attains to fomething prophetic,　Milt. 3 : 112

———— firft, and then truft,　　　　　King 421

Experienc'd Time, tutor of nations,　　　Aken. 282

Experiment make precept found by,　　　Prior 1 : 178

Experimental philofophy how advanced,　　Cow. 2 : 388

Expoftulation,　　　　　　　　　　　Gay 1 : 280

Expreffion obfcene fhows infected breaft,　Dry. 1 : 293

Expreffive filence mufe his praife,　　　Thom. 1 : 194

Extacy,　　　　　　　　　　　　　Parn. 258

———— to rife from earth and vifit heaven,　Parn. 259

———— ftrange enjoyment of a blifs within,　Parn. 259

———— from the world refin'd,　　　　Parn. 259

———— all is excefs of joy,　　　　　Parn. 260

Extafy,　　　　　　　　　　　　　Cow. 2 : 43

Extremes are fhort, of ill and good,　　　Dry. 3 : 221

　　　　　　　　　　　　　　　　　Extremes

Extremes in nature equal good produce,   *Pope* 2 : 124
————— man, concur to general use,   *Pope* 2 : 124
————— men run to,   *Den.* 12
Eye, an archer,   *Gow.* 1 : 144
———— with seeing cloy'd,   *Prior* 2 : 132
———— to catch, is to convince the mind,   *Garth* 53
Eyes as black as jet,   *Gay* 1 : 271
———— the language of the soul explain,   *Gay* 1 : 248
———— sealed in lasting night,   *Dry.* 6 : 305
———— everlasting slumber seals,   *Pope il.* 2 : 26
———— enforce prayers, soft beauty pleads,   *Hughes* 292
———— unfriended of repose,   *Pope od.* 4 : 162

F

Fable distinguished into its species,   *Pope il.* 1 : 4
———— probable, what,   *Pope il.* 1 : 4
———— allegorical, what,   *Pope il.* 1 : 6
———— marvellous, what,   *Pope il.* 1 : 6
———— unity of,   *Pope od.* 3 : 16
———— alone can crown the Poet's brow,   *Som.* 235
———— in it all things hold discourse,   *Gay* 2 : 196
Fabii fell on Cremera's bank,   *Thom.* 2 : 62
Fabius, in council flow, saved his country,   *Wall.* 169
Fabricius, scorner of all-conquering gold,   *Thom.* 1 : 170
Face busy, never-meaning,   *Swift* 2 : 83
———— counterfeit and brass,   *Butl.* 1 : 273
Faction embroils the world,   *Gay* 1 : 2
Factions like a rapid torrent,   *Dry.* 7 : 17
———— of the Gods in Homer and Virgil,   *Pitt* 347
Factious souls, wearied into peace,   *Dry.* 1 : 30

Facts

Facts only known to man,   *Den.* 109

Faggot,   *Swift* 1 : 96

———— applied to denote the benefit of concord; *Swift* 1 : 96

Faint heart ne'er won fair lady,   *King* 356

Fair have nails as well as eyes,   *Tick.* 129

—— inconstant,   *Rowe* 68

—— nun,   *Fent.* 227

—— traveller,   *Hughes* 126

—— kept on the Thames,   *Gay* 1 : 123

Fairbone, epitaph on,   *Dry.* 2 : 196

Fair-dealing, as the plainest, is the best, *Mall.* 165

Fairer mind inclos'd in a fair frame,   *Rowe* 47

Fairfax, wildly bold,   *Aken.* 261

Fairings various of the country maid,   *Gay* 1 : 89

Fair weather, signs of,   *Gay* 1 : 106

Fairwell peace and injur'd laws,   *Rowe L.* 55

Fairy show,   *Dry.* 3 : 172

———— tale,   *Parn.* 21

Faith speaks aloud, distinct,   *Young* 2 : 86

—— removes the mountain, death's terror, *Young* 2 : 86

—— disarms destruction,   *Young* 2 : 86

—— to live by, beyond Time's bound,   *Mall.* 238

—— test of a Christian,   *Dry.* 1 : 315

—— is not Reason's labour, but repose, *Young* 2 : 211

—— for Reason's light, will give her perspective, *Prior* 1 : 23

—— needful truths of, few and plain,   *Dry.* 1 : 259

—— can govern Death,   *Watts* 117

—— and hope shall die,   *Prior* 2 : 29

—— lost in certainty,   *Prior* 2 : 29

——— the daughter of the skies,   *Fent.* 321

                     Faith

Faith lost in certainty, — Dry. 3 : 128

—— implicit blind Ignaro leads, — Parn. 101

—— enormous, of many made for one, — Pope 2 : 64

—— by Death approv'd, — Rowe L. 191

—— uncommon to the changing Greeks, — Rowe L. 135

—— of men vanish'd like the smoke, — Pope il. 1 : 80

—— none due to the wicked, — Butl. 1 : 199

Faithful tongue for no bribe betrays, — Gay 2 : 247

Faithless, fay, will he not care for you, — Thom. 2 : 182

—— heart, how despicably small! — Young 3 : 47

——————— fill'd and foul'd with self, — Young 3 : 47

—— men with constant care avoid, — Cong. 129

Falcon, swiftest racer of the liquid skies, — Pope il. 2 : 269

Falkland, verses to, — Cow. 1 : 99

—— commended, — Cow. 1 : 100

—— Waller to, — Wall. 80

Fall, — Wall. 91

Fallen Angel, a fallen wit, — Young 3 : 207

False greatness, — Watts 175

—— friends, deadliest foes, — Dry. 2 : 84

—— historians, a satire on, — Sav. 175

——————— scandals from, spot the worst, — Sav. 175

—— joy pursue, and suffer real woe, — Prior 2 : 102

—— liberty, what, — Dry. 7 : 349

—— praises are the whoredoms of the pen, — Young 3 : 160

——————— which prostitute fair fame to worthless men, ib. 160

——————— profanation of celestial fire, — ib. 160

—— rules, prankt in Reason's garb, — Milt. 3 : 148

—— sex, is caught with lies, — Broome 47

—— woman, arts of, — Milt. 3 : 32

False woman, a bosom snake,   Milt. 3 : 32

Falsehood, child of Hell,   West 268

———— is folly,   Pope ed. 4 : 202

———— does poison on your praise diffuse,   Prior 1 : 54

———— best repaid with neglect,   Aken. 198

———— of sacred Truth usurps the name,   Prior 2 : 224

———— smiles in thy lips, and flatters in thy eyes, Smith 117

———— and Fraud shoot up in every soil,   Add. 323

———————— the product of all climes,   Add. 323

————'s brood, vice and deceitful pleasure,   Aken. 114

Fame, what ? but the getting of a name,   Swift 1 : 34

——— what ? a passing blaze,   Pope 2 : 206

——— a reversion after death,   Swift 1 : 8

——— is a reversion,   Young 1 : 114

——— a breath,   Prior 1 : 160

——— the breath of fools,   Lans. 184

——— bait of flattering knaves,   Lans. 184

——— but common breath,   Broome 31

——— is a bubble,   Young 1 : 115

——— the world's debt to deeds of high degree,   Young 1 : 116

——— but if you pay yourself ; the world is free, Young 1 : 116

——— a cameleon,   Butl. 1 : 156

——— carries truth, oft lies,   Butl. 1 : 156

——— tattling gossip,   Butl. 1 : 157

——— but empty breath,   Prior 1 : 48

——— is a breath, and men are dust,   Young 1 : 6

——— life's phantom,   Young 1 : 173

——— a fancy'd life in other's breath,   Pope 2 : 78

——— is foreign, but of true desert,   Pope 2 : 78

——— is a public mistress,   Young 3 : 189

Fame, with which in just proportion Envy grows, *Young* 3: 196

—— fondness for, is avarice for air, *Young* 2: 91

—— eternal voice in future days, *Pope od.* 4: 198

—— described, { *Dry.* 6: 44
{ *Pope* 1: 213

—— Muses, her virgin handmaids, *Pope* 1: 213

—— good and bad, alike fond of, *Pope* 1: 214

—— is all we must expect below, *Pope* 1: 215

—— whose exalted size extends to skies, *Cong.* 14

—— a thousand tongues the monster bears, *Cong.* 14

—————— waking eyes, *Cong.* 14

—————— ever open ears, *Cong.* 14

—— house of, *Dry.* 4: 75

—— temple of, *Pope* 1: 201

—— decays not more by envy, than excess of praise, *id.* 1: 203

—— the messenger of Jove, *Pope il.* 1: 71

—— that delights around the world to stray, *Pope* 1: 323

—— the babbler, *Tick.* 147

—— double-mouthed, *Milt.* 3: 39

—— her whisper has, as well as trumpet, *Young* 2: 230

—— Falsehood cloaths in Truth's disguise, *Gay* 1: 318

—— and swells her little bulk with growing lies, *Gay* 1: 318

—— officious, new terror still supplies, *Rowe L.* 69

—— messenger of ill, *Rowe L.* 69

—— the last infirmity of noble minds, *Milt.* 3: 161

—— fatal love of, *Add.* 54

—— only destructive to the brave and great, *Add.* 57

—— chace of, destruction to the multitude, *Dry.* 7: 289

—— voice of, how partial ! *Prior* 1: 197

—— calls up calumny and spite, *Gay* 2: 77

Fame,

Fame, our second life, now is lost,   *Pope* 1 : 110

—— romantic increases,   *Pope* 1 : 207

—— sweetest music to an honest ear,   *Pope* 2 : 186

—— mouldering monuments of, delude vain hopes, *Hughes* 193

—— 'tis all the dead can have, shall live,   *Pope il.* 2 : 117

—— rouses the dead,   *Cow.* 1 : 95

—— when young, malice pursues,   *Buck.* 95

—— men toil for, which no man lives to find,   *Buck.* 95

—— emulation breeds in virtuous breast,   *West.* 262

—— then farewell,   *Tick.* 197

—— unfaithful promiser of good,   *Tick.* 197

—— and censure, link'd together,   *Swift* 2 : 129

—— and fortune, both are made of prose,   *Young* 1 : 96

—— power and wealth allure,   *Fent.* 310

——————— for which ease and innocence resign'd, *Fent.* 310

—— wealth and honour, what are you to love, *Pope* 1 : 185

—— deserving, but still shunning,   *Mall.* 292

—— our rival's hurts creates,   *Prior* 2 : 38

—— Marlborough and Alexander vie for,   *Lytt.* 21

—— of cripple slain, but lame,   *Butl.* 1 : 94

—— sought through infamy,   *Milt.* 1 : 186

Famine described,   *Rowe L.* 250

—— address to,   *King* 340

—— a resistless foe,   *Rowe L.* 182

—— on war and pestilence attends,   *Rowe L.* 165

Fanatic rage,   *Cow.* 1 : 335

Fan, a poem,   *Gay* 1 : 19

—— shades the face, or bids cool Zephyrs play, *Gay* 1 : 29

—— that graceful toy,   *Gay* 1 : 19

—— described,   *Gay* 1 : 24

Fan, waving, fupply the fceptre's place,   *Gay* 1 : 29

——— adorn'd with Loves and Graces,   *Gay* 1 : 29

————————— or fome chafte ftory from the pencil flow, *ib.* 30

——— of the Author's defign,   *Pope* 1 : 347

——— this toy, in Delia's hand, is fatal,   *Pope* 1 : 347

Fancy,   *Lanf.* 198

——— defcribed,   *M.lt.* 1 : 142

——— oft awake, while reafon fleeps,   *Mall.* 250

——— mocks with mimic fhews,   *Mall.* 250

——— apt to fave,   *Milt.* 1 : 237

——— wild and pathlefs ways will chufe,   *Cong.* 13

——— queen of the foul,   *Ot.* 62

——— reafon over-rules,   *Lanf.* 159

——— is but mad, without judgment,   *Buck.* 70

——— is the feather of the pen,   *Buck.* 70

——— whofe trade it is to make the fineft fool, *Young* 3 : 139

——— who lives to, ne'er can be rich,   *Young* 2 : 147

——— tipt the candle's flame with blue,   *Gay* 2 : 14

——— finks beneath a weight of woe,   *Pope* 1 : 179

——— firft, and then affert,   *Prior* 2 : 68

Fanfhaw,   *Den.* 72

Farce, what dear delight to Britons yields,   *Pope* 2 : 200

——— ever the tafte of mobs, but now of lords, *Pope* 2 : 200

Farewel the female heaven, the female hell,   *Aken.* 348

——— a glad, to the God of Love,   *Aken.* 348

Farewell,   *Watts* 109

——— — thou mighty mole-hill, Earth,   *Watts* 109

Farmer, uncertain all his toil,   *Phil.* 62

Farmer's wife and the raven,   *Gay* 2 : 93

Farquhar, what pert low dialogue he wrote,   *Pope* 2 : 229

J   Farrier's

Farrier's shop described,   Gay 1 : 109
Fart, let in the House of Commons,   Prior 2 : 242
Fashion to fix, impossible,   King 206
Fashionable world, rank coward to !   Young 3 : 67
Fast and loose, play at,   Butl. 2 : 26
Fatal ambition ! that deludes mankind,   Rowe 13
—— curiosity,   Tick. 147
—— friendship, to Author of,   Hughes 79
Fatal love,   Prior 2 : 242
—— seeds luxurious vices sow,   Rowe L. 51
—— sisters,   Gray 362
Fatalists, wild scheme of,   Black. 158
Fate,   Crew. 1 : 292
—— an equivocal term,   Black. 156
—— it may signify the connection of cause and effect, ib. 156
—— —————— something absolutely necessary,   ib. 156
—— the universal system of causes,   Akins. 325
—— fixed laws of,   Fint. 252
—— book of, hid from creatures,   Pope 2 : 31
—— its great ends by slow degrees attains,   Prior 1 : 59
—— bounds of, unpassable,   Dry. 7 : 73
—— had been charm'd, had Fate an ear,   Hughes 55
—— each irrevocable word,   Pope 1 : 291
—— superior to Jupiter,   Dry. 5 : 245
—— has wove the thread of life,   Pope od. 3 : 193
—— foredoom'd, that waited from my birth,   Pope il. 2 : 292
—— ———— has sever'd me from the sons of earth, Pope il. 2 : 292
—— gives the wound, and man is born to bear, Pope il. 2 : 329
—— colour of, changed,   Pope od. 4 : 33
—— different of men, makes the world chance,   King 368

                                                      Fate

Fate spin thy future with a whiter clue,   *Pope od.* 4 : 169

———— and a milder aspect shew,   *Pope od.* 4 : 169

———— men steered by,   *Butl.* 1 : 44

————'hath in various stations rank'd mankind,   *West* 143

———— reserv'd him to perform its doom,   *Rowe L.* 86

———— furnishes out life's stage with war and strife, *Hughes* 281

———— allows no solitude to kings,   *A. Phil.* 341

———— rarely on the valiant frowns,   *Pom.* 233

———— propitious once and kind, then welcome, *Pope il.* 2 : 276

———— nobler to be envied, than to be pitied,   *West* 200

———— to infamy and hatred dooms Sicilia's tyrant,   *West* 201

———— ill-news wing'd with,   *Dry.* 1 : 299

Fates of men are in the hands of Jove,   *Pope od.* 4 : 30

———— can never change their first decree,   *Fent.* 213

———— alike deny, the dead to live, or fairy forms to die, *Tick.* 216

Father and Jupiter,   *Gay* 2 : 96

———— shines full in the filial frame,   *Pope od.* 3 : 111

———— his port, his features, and his shape the same, *id.* 3 : 111

———— of life, teach me what is good,   *Thom.* 1 : 160

————————————— thyself,   *Thom.* 1 : 160

———————— feed me with never-fading bliss, *Thom.* 1 : 161

Father Francis, prayer of,   *West* 318

Fathers, our first, most tender care,   *Pope il.* 2 : 99

———— were cowards, and begot us slaves,   *Rowe L.* 318

Faulchion in a plow-share end,   *Pope* 1 : 51

Fault should move pity, not mirth,   *Swift* 2 : 17

Faultless piece, never was, nor is, nor e'er shall be, *Pope* 1 : 102

Faults seek the dark,   *King* 263

———— of raging love, her virtues all her own,   *Smith* 188

———— in your person or your face correct,   *Cong.* 122

Faults

Faults in other men we fpy,   *Gay* 2 : 94

Favour, too great is fafely plac'd on none,   *Buck.* 89

Favourite has no friend,   *Gray* 329

Favours come from caprice, not from choice,   *Young* 1 : 103

———— unexpected doubly pleafe,   *Cong.* 148

Fawning cringe be far,   *Phil.* 58

Fawns, a prey to every favage,   *Pope il.* 2 : 78

Fear, ode to,   *Collins* 247

——— thy hurried ftep, thy haggard eye,   *Collins* 247

——— back recoil'd,   *Collins* 271

——— freezes minds,   *Dry.* 3 : 208

——— is an ague,   *Butl.* 1 : 117

——— pale comrade of inglorious flight,   *Pope il.* 1 : 265

——— and Flight, yoke Mars's chariot,   *Pope il.* 2 : 69

——— fpring of our actions,   *Roch.* 324

——— its effects on men,   *Butl.* 2 : 80, 81

——— gives fwallows wings,   *Cow.* 1 : 60

——— no human fate exempt from,   *Wall.* 71

——— falfe alarms of, felf-delufion,   *Milt.* 3 : 134

——— does greater feats than courage,   *Butl.* 1 : 312

——— in public councils, betrays like treafon,   *Add.* 276

——— does half the work of lying fame,   *Rowe L.* 70

——— buries fear, and ills on ills attend,   *Young* 1 : 55

——— of death lefs bafe than fear of life,   *Young* 2 : 106

————————— for ever lie entomb'd,   *Young* 2 : 83

——— worfhiping with,   *Watts* 39

Fearful with reproaches fire,   *Pope il.* 1 : 136

————— and the brave, all fink alike,   *Pope il.* 1 : 212

Fearlefs lover wants no beam of light,   *Ham.* 212

————— belongs to Venus, and can never ftray,   *Ham.* 212

         Fears

Fears to be laid on Providence, *Milt.* 2 : 165

—— ne'er move the daring and the wife, *Pom.* 233

—— to outrun, *Butl.* 1 : 116

—— and doubts, to jealoufy will turn, *Cong.* 102

Feaft, if not beft, 'tis naught, *King* 219

—— of death! the feafters doom'd to bleed! *Pope od.* 4 : 176

Feaftful-mirth, be this white hour affign'd, *Pope od.* 3 : 116

Feafts for friends and not for cooks, *Cong.* 86

Feather'd-death, a dart, *Dry.* 6 : 260

Feeble-age will all thy nerves difarm, *Gay* 1 : 280

Felicities of labour learn, *Dyer* 30

Felicity in what placed, *Milt.* 2 : 211

—— is, ill firmly to fupport, good fully tafte, *Young* 2 : 240

—— fincere, none can boaft, *Dry.* 3 : 129

—— above, *Watts* 46

Female drefs, inconftant equipage, *Gay* 1 : 26

—————— a maze of fafhions, *Gay* 1 : 27

—— fears, fubmit to female fires, *Pope* 1 : 177

—— faults, what, *Milt.* 3 : 33

—— guide, to be avoided, *Gay* 1 : 114

—— walkers, what neceffary for, *Gay* 1 : 108

—— phaeton, *Prior* 2 : 228

—— pleafure, to be great, *Gay* 2 : 261

—— floven, is an odious fight, *Young* 1 : 145

Fenton, on death of, *Broome* 121

—— early loft, *Broome* 122

—— ftrong were thy thoughts, *Broome* 122

—— to mortals' empty fame, a foe, *Broome* 123

—— epiftle to, *Broome* 40

—— poems of, *Fent.* 197

Fenton, ode to the sun,   *Fent.* 197

———— Florelio,   207

———— an ode,   214

———— part of 14th of Isaiah,   218

———— verses on the union,   220

———— Cupid and Hymen,   222

———— Olivia,   224

———— to a lady before her glass,   225

———— to the same, reading art of love,   226

———— the fair Nun,   227

———— epistle to Southern,   233

———— letter to knight of sable shield,   243

———— eleventh Odyssey,   247

———— Widow's Wile,   272

———— Alamode,   277

———— Sappho to Phaon,   277

———— Phaon to Sappho,   286

———— a tale in Chaucer's manner,   295

———— to Pope,   299

———— platonic spell,   . 300

———— Marullus to Neæra,   302

———— kisses,   303, 304

———— epistle to Lambard,   306

———— to the queen,   320

———— ode to Gower,   322

———— the dream,   325

———— to lady Cavendish Harley,   327

———— prologue to Spartan dame,   332

Fern springs up,   *Dry.* 7 : 341

——— seeds of, imperceptibly small,   *Black.* 137

    Fescennine,

Fescennine verses, what,   *Dry.* 7 : 147

· Festivals, double reason of,   *Dry.* 7 : 138

——————- mixture of devotion and debauchery,   *Dry.* 7 : 139

Fever argues better than a Clarke,   *Young* 1 : 109

Fevers lash on lingering destiny,   *Fent.* 214

. Few follow Wisdom or her rules,   *Gay* 2 : 101

——— are the distinguish'd great,   *Rowe L.* 220

. ——- can write, and fewer can reward,   *Dry.* 3 : 98

——— know to ask, or decently receive,   *Broome* 57

——— fewer still, know how to give,   *Broome* 57

· Fibres may err,   *Rowe L.* 77

. Fickle ear soon glutted with the sound,   *Prior* 2 : 132

————- sex, who change constant lover for the new, *ib.* 1 : 218

————- Fortune's play,   *Tick.* 210

——————————- a slave, a chief in one revolving day, *ib.* 210

Fiction decks the truth with spurious rays,   *Add.* 67

Fictions improbable in Homer and Virgil,   *P. w* 346

Fiddle, engine of vile noise,   .   *Butl.* 1 : 77

——— of the town, to be made,   *Roch.* 306

Fiddling, Arcadians famous for,   *B. tl.* 2 : 150

Fidelity no where to be found,   *C w.* 2 : 364

——— but a jest,   *Buck.* 107

Field and river can supply mankind,   *Rowe L.* 181

——— of combat fits the young and bold,   *Pope il.* 1 : 139

——— of glory is a field for all,   *Pope* 3 : 127

——— of battle is this mortal life,   *Young* 2 : 256

Fields are full of eyes,   *Lr..* 3 : 78

Field-sports,   *Som.* 145

Fiend commences with the child,   *Fent.* 214

——— none so cruel, as a reasoning brute,   *Pom.* 258

Fiends.

Fiends, dogs of Orcus, *Broome* 106

Fifteen is full as mortal as threefcore, *Young* 1 : 143

Fifth monarchy to reftore, *Butl.* 2 : 68

Fight, horror of, defcribed, *Rowe L.* 317

——— a fiery deluge nam'd, *Pitt* 362

——— hung long in equal fcale, *Phil.* 14

——— at fea, *Wall.* 141

Figure in language, fprung from neceffity, *Pitt* 364

———, to fupply its fcantinefs, *Pitt* 364

Figures, art's needlefs varnifh, *Buck.* 76

——— are but paint upon a beauteous face, *Buck.* 76

——— in defcriptions only claim a place, *Buck.* 76

——— in the picture feem to live, *Gay* 1 : 336

Figulus exclaims, the ftars are in confufion hurl'd, *Rowe L.* 78

Fine arts, the quinteffence of all, *Thom.* 1 : 232

——— growth of labouring time, *Thom.* 1 : 232

Fingers, long before we'd forks, *King* 303

Finite cannot grafp infinity, *Dry.* 2 : 11

——— every nature but his own, *Young* 2 : 76

——— mind, incapable of grafping Nature's fyftem, *Black.* 84

Fire, air, earth, &c. praife the Lord, *Watts* 107

——— water, woman, are man's ruin, *Prior* 1 : 142

——— the precious gold refines, *Broome* 21

——— and fulphur, cure of noxious fumes, *Pope od.* 4 : 214

——— purge the blood-polluted rooms, *ib.* 4 : 214

——— defcription of one, *Gay* 1 : 144

——— of London, { *Ot.* 37 / *Dry.* 1 : 96

——— duration of, *Dry.* 1 : 107

——— of love, the more conceal'd, the fiercer rag'd, *Hughes* 58

Fish, production of,   Mil.

—— mute as,   Som.

—— to marinate,   King

—— to taste of the sea,

—— mighty, feed on the small,

Fishmonger's stall described,

Five ladies' answer to the beau,

—— senses, riddle on,   Swift

Flail, no fence against,   Swift

—— of sense,

Flame, shall waste this earth and sea,   Rowe

Flames, on guilty towns, exert Heaven's wrath,   Pope

—— and fire, the vain disguise of love,   Thom.

—— or else a fleeting passion prove,   Thom.

—— the frantic fury of the veins,   Thom.

Flaminius proclaims liberty to Greece,   Thom.

Flanders, seat of war, poem on,   Prior 47

—— where luxurious plenty reigns,   Prior 47

Flanders, towers lie monuments of rage,   *Broome* 47

Flandria, by plenty, made the home of war,   *Prior* 1 : 260

————— long the field of deftructive war,   *Hughes* 17

Flatterer, an earwig grows,   *Pope* 2 : 349

Flatterers, to beware of,   *Dry.* 3 : 166

Flattery, fmooth infinuating bane,   *F. nt.* 315

————— her fulfom arts footh our pride,   *F. nt.* 316

————— pleafing bane,   *Broome* 43

————— in perfumes it kills,   *Broome* 43

————— not eafily diftinguifhed,   *King* 222

————— oft like friendfhip fhows,   *Den.* 94

————— never feems abfurd,   *Gay* 2 : 59

————— curft affaffin,   *Weft* 273

————— is the food of fools,   *Swift* 1 : 126

————— is the nurfe of crimes,   *Gay* 2 : 29

————— betrays,   *Den.* 97

————— conquers truth,   *Prior* 1 : 224

————— proud fall by,   *Dry.* 3 : 155

————— is a fhocking vice,   *Gay* 2 : 190

————— can it footh the dull cold ear of death,   *Gray* 338

Flavia,   { *Waller* 90
            { *Lanf.* 198

————— epiftle to,   *Rowe* 24

————— gardens of, efcape a flood,   *Lanf.* 212

Flaws in the beft,   *Young* 2 : 63

Flax, Batavia yields,   *Dyer* 71

Fleece,   *Dyer* 30

Fleeces of Arcadia, Attica, and Theffaly,   *Dyer* 68

————— none in torrid zone,   *Dyer* 38

Flefh is grafs,   *Butl.* 1 : 66

                                        Fleet,

Fleet, involv'd in fire and smoke,   *Pope il.* 2 : 110

—— refcued by Patroclus' arm,   *Pope il.* 2 : 110

—— haunt of the Mufes,   *Pope* 3 : 168

—— ditch, king of dykes,   *Pope* 3 : 153

Fleetwood Shepheard, epiſtles to,   *Prior* 1 : 33, 35

Fleetwood, (C. and S.) verfes to,   *Watt.* 184

Fletcher, praife of, in eafy dialogue,   *Dry.* 2 : 138

—————— on his plays,   *Wall.* 106

—————— had all from nature,   *Den.* 55

—————— the Smiles and Graces own his ſtrain, *Collins* 276

—————— and Beaumont, like radiant twins,   *F. m* 235

Flies,   *Prior* 1 : 202

—— an eclogue,   *Pa n.* 61

—— faireſt fruit attract,   *Swift* 2 : 119

Flight, their worſt death,   *Thom.* 2 : 63

Flights,   *Gay* 1 : 86

—— drunkards require fonorous lays,   *Gay* 1 : 86

Flints, feeds of latent fire from,   *Dry.* 3 : 181

Flirt and Phil.   *Shen.* 161

Floods bury towns beneath their tide,   *Hughes* 289

Flora, goddeſs of the youthful year,   *Hughes* 119

Florelio, a paſtoral,   *Fent.* 207

—— the grace and grief of every Britiſh fwain, *Fent.* 208

Floriana, a paſtoral,   *Duke* 107

Flour, the ſtrength of wheat,   *Pope od.* 3 : 75

—— the growth and ſtrength of man,   *Pope od.* 4 : 155

Flower, verfes on,   *Broome* 1 : 2

—— lovely offspring of the May,   *Broome* 1 : 2

—— ſhort-liv'd beauty of an hour,   *Broome* 1 : 3

—— painted by Varelſt,   *Prior* 2 : 8

Flowet-

Flower-book, verses in,   *Shen.* 111

——— lady of, short-lived,   *Dry.* 3 : 185

——— and leaf,   *Dry.* 3 : 167

Flowered carpet, verses on,   *Pitt* 291

——————— wrought by Pallas' pupils,   *Pitt* 291

Flowers, aromatic souls of,   *Pope* 1 : 66

——— their sunny robes resign,   *Thom.* 1 : 140

——— present of to a lady,   *Tick.* 154

——— too soon, these fleeting charms decay,   *Tick.* 154

——— of joy soon fall, soon seeds of hatred shoot, *Prior* 1 : 74

Floyd, Mrs. Biddy, on,   *Swift* 1 : 38

Fly for fishing,   *Gay* 1 : 7

— materials for,   *Gay* 1 : 7

— the proper for each season,   *Gay* 1 : 8

— ye profane, the God, the God appears,   *Pitt* 199

— like rats from finking ship,   *Swift* 2 : 377

— to fight again,   *Butl.* 2 : 91

Flying fowls and creeping things praise the Lord, *Watts* 93

Foe, drawn up and drilled,   *Butl.* 1 : 116

— he makes, who makes a jest,   *Gay* 2 : 109

— to God, was ne'er true friend to man,   *Young* 2 : 236

— to man, was never friend to God,   *Lytt.* 27

Fogs described,   *Thom.* 1 : 130, seq.

Follies men act, which poets toil to write,   *Dry.* 2 : 282

——— are miscall'd crimes of fate,   *Pope od.* 3 : 40

Folly, my son, has still a friend at court,   *Pope* 3 : 116

——— the proper quarry of Horace,   *Dry.* 7 : 182

——— more extravagant, as it grows old,   *Butl.* 1 : 269

——— of prying into futurity,   *Cow.* 2 : 48

——— vexatious to the wife,   *Cow.* 2 : 362

                                                                        Folly

Folly broods o'er grief,   *Prior* 2 : 159

—— one ebb and flow of, all my life,   *Pope* 2 : 201

—— relentless steels thy breast,   *Pope od.* 3 : 106

—— obdurate to reject the stranger-guest,   *Pope od.* 3 : 106

—— of believing nothing or all,   *Dry.* 1 : 129

—— suffering more from, than from fate,   *Young* 2 : 219

—— and pride, sister-twins of sloth,   *Fent.* 318

Fond of the power, but fonder of the prize,   *Pope il.* 1 : 42

—— man acquires wants, which nature never knew, *Tick.* 230

—————— prone to ambition, to example blind,   *Tick.* 220

Fondness lost on woman's pride,   *King* 296

Fontinella to Florinda,   *Swift* 1 : 322

Fool, who meets, must find conceit,   *Gay* 2 : 85

—— at forty, is a fool indeed,   *Young* 1 : 96

—— ! from thyself thou canst not fly,   *Hughes* 104

———————— source of all thy care,   *Hughes* 104

—— lies hid in inconsistencies,   *Pope* 2 : 97

—— of fate, thy manufacture, man,   *Pope od.* 4 : 169

—— or knave, that wears a title, lyes,   *Young* 1 : 82

—— and knave, 'tis glorious to offend,   *Young* 1 : 105

———————— none so busy,   *Dry.* 1 : 215

—— is nauseous, but a coward worse,   *Dry.* 3 : 143

—— that loves and hates, more fool to own it,   *Smith* 97

—— none smarts so little as,   *Pope* 2 : 152

—— with fool, is barbarous civil war,   *Pope* 3 : 188

Foolish praise is satire on the fair,   *Hughes* 94

Fools admire, but men of sense approve,   *Pope* 1 : 107

—— always buz about the great,   *Som.* 264

—— create themselves new appetites,   *Young* 1 : 124

—— in derision follow fools,   *Gay* 2 : 101

                                                           Fools

Fools are the game, which knaves pursue,   *Gay* 2 : 172

—— are vain, when fools admire,   *Gay* 2 : 63

—— are infolent and vain,   *Swift* 1 : 147

—— doubly fools, endeavouring to be wife,   *Dry.* 2 : 90

—— make attempts beyond their skill,   *Cong.* 71

—— known by looking wife,   *Butl.* 1 : 271

—— whom love or verfe undo,   *Rowe* 24

—— may our fcorn, not envy raife,   *Gay* 2 : 107

—— are ftubborn,   *Butl.* 2 : 30

—— only choofe wretches for their friends,   *Rowe L.* 353

—— wicked at their own coft,   *Roch.* 313

—— ftay to feel, and are wife too late,   *Pope il.* 2 : 138

Foot-ball defcribed,   *Gay* 1 : 123

Foot-man very arrogant,   *Gay* 1 : 137

Footmen Lords and Dukes can act,   *Swift* 2 : 149

Foot races,   *Dry.* 6 : 86

Footftool earth, canopy the fkies,   *Pope* 2 : 34

Fop, defcribed,   *Gay* 1 : 113

—— outweighs in female fcales,   *Young* 1 : 131

—— can dance and make a leg,   *Gay* 1 : 203

—— can fetch and carry, cringe and beg,   *Gay* 1 : 203

Fopland, the greateft part of this ifle,   *Hal.* 239

Fops, who,   *Dry.* 1 : 114

—— fly, never fix'd, but fugitives in love,   *Cong.* 128

—— if once wrong, will needs be always fo,   *Pope* 1 : 114

Forbid, that want fhould fink me to a lye,   *Pope od.* 3 : 197

Force greater than command,   *Butl.* 2 : 118

—— to a generous mind unpleafing,   *Milt.* 2 : 179

—— is of brutes,   *Dry.* 3 : 124

—— in the lion dwells,   *Den.* 99

Force

Force how vain ! Love ne'er can be compell'd,   *Gay* 2 : 211.

—— first made conqueft,   *Pope* 2 : 64

—— to prove, is only mine, the event is love's,   *Pope il.* 2 : 156.

Forcers of confcience,   *Milt.* 3 : 168

Ford, birth-day verfes on,   *Swift* 1 : 276

Forecaft fails againft ill-luck,   *A. Phil.* 303.

Foreign countries, declining to vifit,   *Shen.* 37.

Forefight, to neceffitate the will by,   *Dry.* 3 : 83.

Forefkins, a dowry by David,   *Cow.* 2 : 165.

Forfeit pay of their haughty lord,   *Pope il.* 2 : 100.

Forget what we beftow, befpeaks a noble mind,   *Cong.* 105.

Forgetfulnefs of death, furpaffing fault,   *Young* 2 : 111.

Form, joined with virtue, rare,   *Dry.* 7 : 297.

Formalifts, cold-hearted, frozen,   *Young* 2 : 83.

—————— pronounce the witty mad,   *Pitt* 402.

Forms decay,   *Dry.* 3 : 134

—— have their affigned time,   *Dry.* 3 : 134

—— of matter, all diffolving, die,   *Rowe L.* 325

—— loft in Nature's blending bofom lie,   *Rowe L.* 325

—— that perifh, other forms fupply,   *Pope* 2 : 55

—— lovely, dignify the foul's abode,   *Yal.* 441

Forfaken, yet hoping,   *Watts* 161

Fortefcue, Mifs Lucy, verfes to,   *Lytt.* 55

———————————— with Hammond's Elegies,   *Lytt.* 55

Fortitude affumes the patient mind,   *Sav.* 22.

Fortunate complaint,   *Pom.* 242

—————— Iflands defcribed,   { *Cow.* 2 : 12.
                               { *Garth* 60

Fortune,   *Prior* 2 : 252

—— defcribed,   *Garth* 69.

Fortune,

Fortune, incertainty of,   *Cow.* 1 : 98

———— fickle,   *Butl.* 1 : 118

———— goodyſhip of,   *Butl.* 1 : 119

———— addreſs to,   *Sben.* 30

———— Author's compared with others' diſtreſs,   *Sben.* 56

———— fair, like all thy treacherous kind,   *Pope* 1 : 243

———— faithleſs ſtill, and wavering as the wind, *Pope* 1 : 243

———— gives us birth,   *Pope il.* 2 : 222

———— entruſt to powers above,   *Dry.* 7 : 299

———— an unrelenting foe to love,   *Thom.* 2 : 187

———— buſy to join the gentle to the rude,   *Thom.* 2 : 188

———— is the common miſtreſs of us all,   *Hughes* 304

———— can depreſs or advance,   *Dry.* 3 : 234

———— never worſhiped by the wiſe,   *Dry.* 7 : 300

———— is ador'd by fools alone,   *Som.* 302

———— the wiſe man always makes his own,   *Som.* 302

———— leads a wild-gooſe chace,   *Som.* 305

———— mocks with a ſmiling face,   *Den.* 96

———— none is ſincerely bleſt,   *Mall.* 329

———— what can ſhe give beyond content ?   *Gay* 2 : 149

———— befriends the bold,   *Dry.* 6 : 283

———— fights on Cæſar's ſide,   *Hughes* 309

———— favours, ſtill the fair are kind,   *Pope* 1 : 237

———— nor courted ſmiles, nor ſunk beneath her frown, *Yal.* 445

———— puſh not by ill means,   *King* 301

———— ſmiles of never bleſt the bad,   *Young* 2 : 247

———— frowns of, never rob innocence of joys, *Young* 2 : 247

———— all aſk, and aſk no more,   *Gay* 2 : 50

———— we moſt unjuſtly partial call,   *Lanſ.* 184

———— and cowardice ſucceed,   *Butl.* 1 : 45

Fortune in a string, — Dry. 7 : 234

Fortune-hunter, — Som. 296

Forty days, and Nineveh shall fall, — Parn. 226

Foster, character of, — Sav. 147

———— a priest from avarice and ambition free, — Sav. 148

———— whose heart and tongue benevolence inspires, Sav. 148

Fought, but swore, they ne'er could hate, — Tick. 158

Foundling, a nameless issue, — Dry. 7 : 277

Fountain, plan of, — Prior 1 : 198

———— of light, thou first and best, — Mall. 253

———— from human search ineffably remov'd, — ib. 253

Fountains and rivers, rise of, — Thom. 1 : 132

Four Matadores, and lose Codille, — Swift 2 : 72

Fowling described, — Thom. 1 : 119

Fox described, — Dry. 3 : 143

—— pursuit of, — Dry. 3 : 163

—— cunning of, — Som. 53

—— escapes by feigning death, — Butl. 1 : 265

—— retains all his father's wiles, — West 181

—— at the point of death, — Gay 2 : 79

—— a line of thieves from son to son, — Gay 2 : 80

—— like a pick-pocket, — Gay 1 : 134

Foxes weigh the geese they carry, — Butl. 1 : 297

———— false deluding teachers, — Parn. 201

Fox-hunting, — { Som. 48
{ Thom. 1 : 122

Fragment, — { Mall. 180
{ Hughes 199
{ Hughes 137
{ Pope 1 : 358

Fragments,

Fragments, *Butl.* 2 : 273

Frail is the boasted attribute of wife, *Pope od.* 3 : 118

—— author dies before the man, *Pitt* 371

———————— his fame is more contracted than his span, *Pitt* 371

—— thoughts dally with false surmise, *Milt.* 3 : 164

Frailties are his children's spots, *Parn.* 123

Frailty, *Cow.* 1 : 278

—— not unusual to woman, *Dry.* 3 : 226

France, land of levity, land of guilt, *Young* 2 : 158

—— staple of new modes, *Butl.* 2 : 303

—— on universal sway intent, *Prior* 1 : 258

—— is she the standard of your skill ? *Aken.* 251

—— to Philips, as to Churchill, bends, *Smith* 191

Frantic flights are like a madman's dream, *Lanf.* 233

———————— like castles built in air, *Lanf.* 233

———————— heroes and gods to different sides divide, *ib.* 233

Fraud various, virtue one, *King* 276

—— should with fraud be paid, *Cong.* 130

—— what he got by, is lost by stocks, *Swift* 2 : 343

—— in the fox, *Dem.* 99

Fray described, *Som.* 108, feq.

Frazer (Dr.) verses to, *Mall.* 171

Free, the brave, wife, honest man alone, *Pitt* 284

—— proof to grandeur, pride and pelf, *Pitt* 284

—— and (greater still) is master of himself, *Pitt* 284

—— in every turn of fortune still the same, *Pitt* 284

—— from malice, live obscure, *Gay* 1 : 182

—— liberty, *Butl.* 1 : 40

—— philosophy, *Watts* 191

Freeborn spirit no force can constrain, *Dry.* 2 : 107

Freedom,

Freedom, *Young* 200
————— no obedience without, *Milt.* 1 : 76
————— decreed to rational creatures, *Milt.* 1 : 77
————— abuse of, their sin, *Milt.* 1 : 77
————— birth-right of all thinking kind, *Milt.* 258
————— reason's great charter, *Milt.* 258
————— man's right divine, *Milt.* 258
————— sovereign boon of heaven, *Milt.* 183
————— great charter, with our being given, *Milt.* 183
————— gives eloquence, *Young* 3 : 260
————— gives gain, *Young* 3 : 260
————— is more dear than life, *Pope* 1 : 358
————— is the only treasure, *Lanf.* 283
————— seek in the arms of death, *Pom.* 318
————— great citizen of Albion, *Aken.* 211
————— thee, heroic valour still attends, *Aken.* 211
————— prerogative of English subject, *Dry.* 1 : 303
————— without, peace a dull slavery, *Dry.* 1 : 308
————— laughs, the fruitful fields abound, *Rowe* 19
————— blessings equally on all bestows, *Swift* 2 : 11
————— maintained, not restrained by Law, *Butl.* 2 : 344
————— to princes is a chain, *Wall.* 170
————— our pain, *Dry.* 1 : 162
————— a word false patriots use, *Dry.* 1 : 221
————— and arts together fall, *Pope* 1 : 83
Freeman, who, *Gau.* 2 : 275
————— his right to speak his thoughts, *Pope il.* 1 : 365
Freemen how happy, slaves how wretched! *Thom.* 2 : 145
Free-will happiness by, *Dry.* 2 : 745
French, better critics, as they are worse poets, *Dry.* 3 : 235
French

French deal in foups and hautgouts, *King* 217

——— with happy follies rife above their fate, *Lytt.* 28

——— the jeft and envy of each wifer ftate, *Lytt.* 28

——— vain in want, in bondage bleft, *Lytt.* 27

——— tho' plunder'd, gay; induftrious, tho' oppreft, *Lytt.* 27

Frenchmen, fo many cooks, *King* 171

——————— all, of *petit-maitre* kind, *Gay* 1 : 179

——————— monkeys in action, perroquets in talk, *Gay* 1 : 172

——————— can a king of, lie! *Mall.* 309

French fong imitated, *Prior* 2 : 259

——— fong, paraphrafe on, *Som.* 229

——— ftage, different from the Englifh, *Dry.* 7 : 103

——— tranflators, *Rofc.* 214

——— verfes, imitation of, *Parn.* 73

Frequent debauch to habitude prevails, *Prior* 2 : 159

Friday, *Gay* 1 : 79

——— how to know, *Gay* 1 : 125

Friend, *Sav.* 157

——— deep is felt, when felt in grief, *Sav.* 158

——— of truth, the friend of human race, *Sav.* 160

——— to, *Wall.* 120

——— a letter to, *Hugbes* 98

——— epiftle to, *Dyer* 143

——— to, *Sben.* 179

——— Swift to, 1 : 209

——— ode on death of, *Hugbes* 55

——— ! every facred name in one, *Pope od.* 4 : 204

——— foes how weak ! oppos'd againft, *Pope od.* 4 : 205

——— abfent or dead, be dear, *Pope* 2 : 329

——— is facred, *Pope od.* 3 : 211

Friend,

Friend, base-ro, to his own interest blind, *Pope od.* 3 : 211

——— who bore a brother's part, *Pope od.* 3 : 224

——— claim'd by merit, not by blood, the heart, *Pope od.* 3 : 224

——— by long hereditary claim, *Pope od.* 4 : 54

——— equal in toils, and in years the same, *Pope od.* 4 54

——— greatest blessing heaven can send, *Lanf.* 302

——— gladness and anguish to share, *Phil.* 57

——— rarely find, who depend on many, *Gay* 2 : 116

——— affects to speak, as Terence spoke, *Pope* 3 : 233

——— to aid, without a bye designing end, *Parn.* 251

——— rules to walk with, *Gay* 1 : 135

——— chuse out the virtuous man, *Rowe* 2

——— estranged, *Shen.* 35

——— under affliction, *Pom.* 265

——— best physic of the mind, *Som.* 254

——— other self, distinguish'd but by face, *Som.* 245

——— the best elixir, *Som.* 194

——— comforts of, *Watts* 212

——— in rags I lov'd, *Som.* 227

——— pretended, worse than open foe, *Gay* 2 : 59

——— under a long indisposition, *Ham.* 209

——— at Court, invitation to, *Pitt* 397

——— and benefactor always bind, *Lanf.* 250

——— to human kind, *Thom.* 2 : 173

Friendly apology for a Justice, *Swift* 2 : 330

Friends, two bodies with one soul inspir'd, *Pope il.* 2 : 108

——— the sun-shine of the soul, *Thom.* 2 : 172

——— neglected, when ends are got, *Swift* 2 : 41

——— modern, one serves the other's ends, *Prior* 2 : 54

——— use for your private ends, *Gay* 2 : 53

Friends, often how counterfeit a coin,   *Milt.* 3 : 13

———— rife of, what more offends ?   *Mall.* 309

Friendfhip, thou charmer of the mind,   *Watts* 170

———— raife an altar to,   *Hughes* 68

———— ftrict the union of,   *Hughes* 69

———— joys or forrows not divided,   *Hughes* 70

———— in one comprifes two fouls,   *Rofc.* 239

———— infpires one foul,   *Dry.* 3 : 65

———— forms an union in the mind,   *Swift* 2 : 164

———— is like the fun's eternal rays,   *Gay* 2 : 263

———— ftill is giving, and ftill burns the fame, *Gay* 2 : 263

———— no cold medium knows,   *Pope il.* 1 : 289

———— burns with one love, with one refentment glows, *ib.*

———— blifs of, to mix minds,   *Dry.* 2 : 184

———— 'tis facrilege to touch, what belongs to, *Buck.* 84

———— nobleft quality and greateft good,   *Buck.* 85

———— by fweet reproof is fhown,   *Gay* 2 : 29

———— ftrongeft yields to pride,   *Swift* 2 : 257

———— at beft a trade,   *Cow.* 2 : 107

———— of Jonathan and David,   *Cow.* 2 : 104

———— of Pirithous and Thefeus,   *Dry.* 3 : 67

———— between Sachariffa and Amoret,   *Wall.* 62

———— againft love,   *Den.* 50

———— in abfence,   *Cow.* 1 : 110

Friendfhips of the world, confederacies in vice, *Add.* 296

———————————— or leagues of pleafure, *Add.* 296

Frieze, defects of,   *Gay* 1 : 102

Frog's choice,   *Som.* 276

Frogs, one of the plagues of Egypt,   *Cow.* 2 : 58

———— that have the foul to die,   *Parn.* 43

Frogs, armour of,   *Para.* 44

—— and mice, battle of,   *Para.* 37

—— attacked by mice,   *Butl.* 2 : 94

Frost,   *Thom.* 1 : 177

—— binds the ocean,   *Thom.* 1 : 185

—— various effects of,   *Black.* 75

—— an episode of the great one,   *Gay* 1 : 123

Froths swell and sink,   *Butl.* 2 : 49

Frowzy pores, that taint the air,   *Dry.* 2 : 288

Frozen Zone, where Winter plants her throne,   *Rowe L.* 165

Frugal plenty should my table spread,   *Pom.* 216

Fruition, against,   *Cow.* 1 : 261

—— dulls,   *Wall.* 118

—— ceas'd, by its own force destroy'd,   *Prior* 2 : 159

—— creates joy,   *Dry.* 1 : 32

Fruits and blossoms on the same tree,   *Wall.* 70

Fruit-women, &c. verses for,   *Swift* 2 : 362

Fulhams, to have at command,   *Butl.* 2 : 238

—— of poetic fiction,   *Butl.* 1 : 178

Fulling-mill, described,   *Dyer* 86

Fulvia,   { *Lanf.* 200
         { *Sav.* 164

—— a slave to will,   *Sav.* 164

—— her darling passions, scandal and quadrille,   *Sav.* 164

—— her deeds, a satire on herself alone,   *Sav.* 164

—— wife of Anthony, was ugly,   *Hughes* 184

Fond of words and images prepare,   *Pit* 308

Funeral,   *Gay* 1 : 233

—— contemplation of,   *Gay* 1 : 139

—— games for Patroclus,   *Pope il.* 2 : 300

Funeral

Funeral hymn,   *Mall.* 338

------ pile deſcribed,   *Dry.* 3 : 132

------ piles prepared,   *Dry.* 7 : 8

------ thrice ſurrounded,   *Dry.* 7 : 11

------ for thoſe who fell at Pharſalia,   *Rowe L.* 380

Furmetary,   *King* 337

------ attack on,   *King* 345

Fartheſt way about, neareſt home,   *Butl.* 1 : 163

Fury will deform the fineſt face,   *Cong.* 131

------ of a patient man, beware,   *Dry.* 1 : 159

------ popular, how blind ! how perverſe !   *Som.* 113

Fuſca, the gipſy deſcribed,   *Som.* 130

------ falls,   *Som.* 134

Fuſtian, not poetry, but proſe run mad,   *Pope* 2 : 156

Future, of the preſent is the ſoul,   *Young* 2 : 184

------ when fear'd, life is no longer wiſh'd,   *Young* 2 : 207

------ we miſtake, view'd through hope's deluding glaſs, *Dyer* 5 t.

------ ſtate proved,   *Black.* 204 t

------ mighty raptures of,   *Pom.* 253

Futurity for ever future !   *Young* 2 : 148

------ prying into, folly of,   *Cow.* 2 : 48

------ 's impervious gloom no wiſdom can pierce,   *Weſt* 184

G

Gabriel, next in proweſs to Michael,   *Milt.* 1 : 174

Gain, oh, thirſt of !   *Gay* 2 : 15

------ ſavage thirſt,   *Thom.* 1 : 202

------ hard-hearted, baniſh'd Aſtræa,   *Thom.* 1 : 202

------ thirſt of, oft turn'd to rage and madneſs,   *Weſt* 215

Gain, life, soul, and heaven of men,   *Gay* 2 : 77

—— rule of faith in all profeſſions,   *Butl.* 2 : 69

—— Diana of the Epheſians,   *Butl.* 2 : 69

—— no miſtake in,   *Garth* 37

Gait, nor ſhew too nice, nor too robuſt,   *Cong.* 124

Galanthis, transformation of,   *Gay* 1 : 326

—— ſtrong-limb'd, red-hair'd,   *Gay* 1 : 327

Galatea,   *Wall.* 100

—— an eclogue,   *Walſh* 345

Gales of Fortune various blow,   *Weſt* 178

—— to-day tempeſtuous, and to-morrow fair,   *Weſt* 178

Gallantry of Pilgrims kiſſes,   *Butl.* 2 : 49

Gallia taught to yield,   *Prior* 1 : 243

—— depreſt beneath the will of one,   *Thom.* 2 : 146

Gallic monarch aimed at univerſal ſway,   *Phil.* 9

—— ſtood like an oak ſecure, till Churchill roſe, *Phil.* 10

—— ſhips confined in port,   *Add.* 12

Gallows, riddle on,   *Swift* 1 : 326

Gallus,   *Dry.* 5 : 72

Game, quarrels and brawls ariſe,   *Cong.* 126

Gameſter, chariot of,   *Gay* 1 : 105

—— prologue to,   *Rowe* 32

Gameſters for patrimonies play,   *Dry.* 7 : 226

—— tear their loſing-cards,   *Butl.* 2 : 90

—— loſing, all the gods defy,   *Cong.* 126

Gaming, ſatire on,   *Butl.* 2 : 236

Gaming, love of, is the worſt of ills,   *Young* 1 : 153

—— a vain devotion to the mode,   *Young* 1 : 155

—— the torrent ſweeps all womankind along, *Young* 1 : 155

Ganderetta ſtrips for the race,   *Som.* 130

Ganderetta,

Ganderetta, her fpeed,   *Som.* 134

———— her bill of fare,   *Som.* 126

Ganges rolls his facred wave,   *Thom.* 1 : 68

———— the limit to Alexander's arms,   *Rowe L.* 132

Ganymedes, cup-bearer to Jove,   *Duke* 149

Garden,   *Cow.* 2 : 320

———— pleafures of,   *Cow.* 2 : 329

———— here mankind fell, and hence muft rife again, *Swift* 1 : 7

———— verfes on,   *Lanf.* 156

———— an emblem of the fair,   *Lanf.* 156

———— a thought in,   *Hughes* 149

———— where all is filent, all is fweet,   *Hughes* 149

Gardener and the dog,   *Gay* 2 : 132

Garden-plot,   *King* 430

Garland,   *Prior* 1 : 124

Garter, order of inftituted,   *Den.* 10

———— knights of, their number,   *Dry.* 3 : 185

Garth, the Difpenfary,   19

———— Claremont,   92

———— to lady Louifa Lenos,   104

———— to earl of Burlington,   105

———— to dutchefs of Bolton,   107

———— to duke of Marlborough,   108

———— to lord Godolphin,   109

———— on Q. Anne's ftatue,   110

———— on the new confpiracy,   111

———— on the King of Spain,   112

———— on Kit Cat Club,   113

———— prologue for Tamerlane,   115

———————— at mufic-meeting,   116

Garth prologue to Cornish squire, 117
———— at opening the Queen's theatre, 118
——— epilogue to Cato, 120
——— translations of the Metamorphoses, 122—154
——— soliloquy from the Italian, 155
——— epigrams, 156, 157
——— Anacreontic epistle to Gay, 156 | Gay 1 : 208
——— the best christian, though he know it not, Pope 1 : 355
Gate of heaven described, Milt. 1 : 90
——————— prospect of world from, Milt. 1 : 91
Gaudy fiction, seduces oft the human-heart, West 137
——— pride, corrupts the lavish age, Gay 1 : 105
Gaul intent on universal sway, Fent. 220
——— sunk the thought of universal reign, Parn. 264
——— and but escap'd the chains she meant to give, Parn. 264
Gauls take Rome, Dry. 6 : 225
Gaulstown-house, Swift 1 : 218.
Gay, to be, read thy Bible, Young 2 : 239
——— hope, by fancy fed, less pleasing when possest, Gray 332
——— life, Broome 168
——— queen of pleasure, thee the dance attends, West 192
——————— the jocund strains her listening feet inspire, ib. 192
——— youth ill suits the stern heroic part, Pope od. 3 : 72
GAY, rural sports, Gay 1 : 1
——— fan, 1 : 19
——— shepherd's week, 1 : 45—98
——— prologue to Bolingbroke, 1 : 51
——— loves all mankind, flatters none, Pope 1 : 356
——— dies unpension'd, Pope 3 : 205
——— transcrib'd what Phœbus sung, Garth 156

O 4

Gay, epiſtle to,   Swift 2 : 247
——— Trivia,   Gay 1 : 99
——— epiſtle to a lady,   1 : 157, 210
————————— to Earl of Burlington,   1 : 163
————————— to William Pulteney,   1 : 169
————————— to Paul Methuen,   1 : 178
————————— to Henrietta Dutcheſs of Marlborough,   1 : 182
————————— to Pope,   1 : 185
————————— to Thomas Snow,   1 : 193
————————— Mary Gulliver to Captain Gulliver,   1 : 196
————————— Bounce to Fop,   1 : 201
————————— to Lowndes,   1 : 205
————————— to a young lady,   1 : 208
————————— on a Miſcellany,   1 : 213
————————— to Earl of Oxford,   1 : 217
——— eclogue, birth of the Squire,   1 : 219
————————— the toilette,   1 : 224
————————— the tea-table,   1 : 228
————————— the funeral,   1 : 233
            the eſpouſal,   1 : 238
——— elegy, Panthea,   1 : 243
————— Araminta,   1 : 247
————————— on a lap-dog,   1 : 251
——— William's farewel to Suſan,   1 : 253
——— ballad from the What-d'ye call it,   1 : 255
——— lady's lamentation,   1 : 256
——— Damon and Cupid,   1 : 258
——— Daphnis and Chloe,   1 : 259
——— coquette mother and daughter,   1 : 261
——— Molly Mog,   1 : 263
                                                          Gay,

Gay, ballad,   Gay 1 : 265
———— on quadrille,   1 : 267
——— new song of new families,   1 : 270
——— Newgate's garland,   1 : 273
——— prologue to Dione,   1 : 275
——— contemplation on night,   1 : 277
——— thought on eternity,   1 : 279
——— epigrammatical expostulation,   1 : 280
——— epitaph of bye-words,   1 : 281
——— my own epitaph,   1 : 281
——— motto for Mutius Scaevola,   1 : 281
——— wine,   1 : 282
——— lamentation, a pastoral,   1 : 292
——— to Quinbus Flestrin,   1 : 295
——— verses to put under Blackmore's picture,   1 : 296
——— receipt for stewing veal,   1 : 298
——— Acis and Galatea,   1 : 300
——— story of Achelous and Hercules,   1 : 311
——— death of Nessus,   1 : 316
——— death of Hercules,   1 : 318
——— transformation of Lychas,   1 : 322
——— apotheosis of Hercules,   1 : 324
——— transformation of Galanthis,   1 : 326
       Iolau restor'd to youth,   1 : 329
——— prophecy of Themis,   1 : 330
——— debate of the gods,   1 : 331
——— story of Arachne,   1 : 333
——— answe o the Sompner's prologue,   2 : 1
——— work for cooper,   2 : 4
——— the equivocation,   2 : 10
                                                     Gay,

Gay, true story of an apparition, *Gay* 2 : 12

—— the mad dog, 2 : 17

—— the Quidnuncki's, 2 : 23

—— shepherd and philosopher, 2 : 25

—— the lion, the tiger, and the traveller, 2 : 29

—— the spaniel and camelion, 2 : 32

—— the mother, the nurse, and the fairy, 2 : 33

—— the eagle and the assembly of animals, 2 : 35

—— the wild boar and the ram, 2 : 37

—— the miser and Plutus, 2 : 38

—— the lion, the fox, and the geese, 2 : 40

—— the lady and the wasp, 2 : 41

—— the bull and the mastiff, 2 : 43

—— the elephant and the bookseller, 2 : 45

—— the peacock, the turkey, and the goose, 2 : 47

—— Cupid, Hymen, and Plutus, 2 : 49

—— the tame stag, 2 : 51

—— the monkey, who had seen the world, 2 : 52

—— the philosopher and the pheasants, 2 : 54

—— the pin and the needle, 2 : 56

—— the shepherd's dog and the wolf, 2 : 58

—— the painter, who pleased nobody, &c. 2 : 59

—— the lion and the cub, 2 : 61

—— the old hen and the cock, 2 : 63

—— the rat-catcher and cats, 2 : 65

—— the goat without a beard, 2 : 67

—— the old woman and her cats, 2 : 69

—— the butterfly and the snail, 2 : 71

—— the scold and the parrot, 2 : 72

—— the cur and the mastiff, 2 : 74

Gay, the fick man and the angel,   Gay 2 : 75
—— the Perfian, the fun, and the cloud,   2 : 77
—— the fox at the point of death,   2 : 79
—— the fetting dog and the partridge,   2 : 81
—— the univerfal apparition,   2 : 82
—— the two owls and the fparrow,   2 : 84
—— the courtier and Proteus,   2 : 86
—— the maftiffs,   2 : 88
—— the barley-mow and the dunghill,   2 : 90
—— Pythagoras and the countryman,   2 : 91
—— the farmer's wife and the raven,   2 : 93
—— the turkey and the ant,   2 : 94
—— the father and Jupiter,   2 : 96
—— the two monkeys,   2 : 97
—— the owl and the farmer,   2 : 100
—— the jugglers,   2 : 101
—— the council of horfes,   2 : 104
—— the hound and the huntfman,   2 : 106
—— the poet and the rofe,   2 : 107
—— the cur, the horfe, and fhepherd's dog,   2 : 109
—— the court of Death,   2 : 110
—— the gardener and the hog,   2 : 112
—— the man and the flea,   2 : 114
—— the hare and many friends,   2 : 116
—— the dog and the fox,   2 : 119
—— the vulture, the fparrow, &c.   2 : 123
—— the baboon and the poultry,   2 : 127
—— the ant in office,   2 : 132
—— the bear in a boat,   2 : 137
—— the fquire and his cur,   2 : 142

Gay,

Gay, countryman and Jupiter, — Gay 2 : 148

—— the man, the cat, the dog and fly, — 2 : 153

—— the jackal, leopard, and other beasts, — 2 : 158

—— the degenerate bees, — 2 : 163

—— the pack-horse and the carrier, — 2 : 166

—— Pan and Fortune, — 2 : 170

—— Plutus, Cupid, and Time, — 2 : 174

—— the owl, the swan, the cock, &c. — 2 : 180

—— the cook-maid, turnspit, and ox, — 2 : 186

—— the raven, the sexton, and earthworm, — 2 : 190

—— aye and no, — 2 : 196

—— duke upon duke, — 2 : 198

—— Dione, a pastoral tragedy, — 2 : 207

Gazers, — Cow. 1 : 311

Gebenna lifts high her hoary head: — Rowe L. 67

Geese, warders of the capitol, — Bath 1 : 253

—— nations save, — Young 1 : 108

General doom all must obey, — Prior 2 : 200

Generation equivocal, none, — Black. 182

—————— parents, only instruments in, — Black. 184

Generous Conqueror, prologue to, — Lansf. 210

—————— soul, approaching to divine, — Sav. 7

—————— victors softest pity know, — Hughes 95

Genius, hard to distinguish from inclination, — Pope 1 : 4

—————— cannot be forc'd, — Som. 298

—————— must be born, never taught, — Dry. 2 : 139

—————— soul of poetry, — Buck. 69

—————— and Art, Ambition's boasted wings, — Young 2 : 138

—————— to cheat, — Dry. 7 : 363

Gentile world, a mystic Israel grown, — Parn. 129

Gentlemen,

Gentleman,   *Sav.* 146

————— the social manners, and the heart humane, *Sav.* 146

————— a nature ever great and never vain, *Sav.* 146

————— reason by narrow principles uncheck'd, *Sav.* 146

————— slave to no party, bigot to no sect, *Sav.* 146

————— knowledge of various life, of learning too, *Sav.* 146

————— an humble, though an elevated mind, *Sav.* 146

————— who married his cast mistress, *Sam.* 246

Gentle sleep, in thy embrace all sorrow dies, *Gay.* 1 : 345

Geneva, situate on the Leman lake, *Thom.* 2 : 92

Genoa, described, *Thom.* 2 : 90

Genuine birth on female truth relies, *Pope od.* 3 : 48

George-Nim-Dan-Dean, verses to and from, *Swift* 1 : 224, *seq.*

Georgia, culture of silk in, *Dyer* 123

Georgic, what, *Add.* 201, 202

————— of Virgil, most finished piece of antiquity, *Add.* 212

————— fourth, *Add.* 17

————— Muse, sallies of, please, *Smith* 192

Georgics, essay on, *Add.* 200

————— of Virgil, *Dry.* 5 : 91

German prince, proud of pedigree, is poor of purse, *Pope* 2 : 207

Geron, Hobbinol, Lanquet, *A. Phil.* 322

Gethin, verses to memory of, *Cong.* 64

Ghosts, by saucer eye-balls known, *Gay* 2 : 12

Giant of the hundred hands, *Tick.* 178

————— Briareus named above, Ægeon here, *Tick.* 178

Giant-ills of earth are dwarf'd by grace, *Young* 3 : 136

Giants, origin of, *Mik.* 2 : 108

————— tower-like warriors, *Broome* 143

————— rear an hundred arms, *Broome* 143

Giants;

Giants, war of,	Feht. 258
	Dry. 3 : 304
Giantſhip creſt-fallen,	Milt. 3 : 48
Gibeah, lewdneſs of,	Cow. 3 : 173
Gibſon, verſes to,	Watts 173
Gideon's Miracle,	Cow. 1 : 201
Gift void, who gives what's not his own,	Lanſ. 209
—— what avails to fools,	Pope od. 3 : 252
—— we like, when we the giver prize,	Buck. 59
—— acceptable to Heaven,	Dry. 7 : 325
—— of induſtry, is all that embelliſhes life,	Thom. 1 : 111
Gifted brethren,	Butl. 1 : 139
—— phraſes,	Butl. 2 : 36
Gifts, plagiary ſhifts,	Butl. 1 : 149
—— can conquer every ſoul but thine,	Pope il. 1 : 290
—— ſcorned, where givers are deſpiſed,	Dry. 2 : 54
Gilboa, laſt ſad ſcene of Iſrael's tragedy,	Som. 204
—— no fattening dews be on thy lawns diſtill'd,	Som. 204
—— no kindly ſhowers refreſh,	Som. 204
—— accurs'd by men, and hateful to the ſkies,	Som. 104
Girdle, on,	Wall. 87
Given heart,	Cow. 1 : 264
Glad poverty, an honeſt thing,	Dry. 3 : 203
Gladiator fighting,	Thom. 2 : 86
—— dying,	Thom 2 : 86
Glands, what,	Black. 188, 196
Glaſier, ſkill at foot-ball,	Gay 1 : 123
Glaſs, the ice of fire,	Butl. 1 : 296
Glaſs-blowing,	Phil. 72
Glaſſes, that revelation to the fight,	Young 3 : 54

Glaucus

Glaucus and Scylla, story of,   *Rowe* 86

——— new to the sea, and late receiv'd a god,   *Rowe* 86

——— ends in a fish's wreathy tail below,   *Rowe* 86

——— transformation of,   *Rowe* 88

——— and Sarpedon lead the Lycians,   *Pope il.* 1 : 102

Globe, general prospect of,   *Mall.* 207

Globes, their weight, self-balanc'd, bear,   *Hughes* 281

Glocester, character of,   *Ot.* 6

Glories of the dusty plain,   *Pope il.* 2 : 7

Glorious acts more glorious acts inspire,   *Pope il.* 1 : 172

——— morn is come,   *Thom.* 1 : 189

——— second birth of heaven and earth,   *Thom.* 1 : 189

Glory, what,   *Milt.* 2 : 184, 185

——— true, what,   *Milt.* 2 : 185, 187

——— how obtained,   *Milt.* 2 : 186

——— God made all things for his,   *Milt.* 2 : 186

——— man has no claim to,   *Milt.* 2 : 187

——— what,   *Wall.* 220

——— love of,   *Pope* 2 : 4

——— excitement to great actions,   *Milt.* 2 : 184

——— we rise in, as we sink in pride,   *Young* 2 : 230

——— cannot be in a tyrant's race,   *Rowe* 11

——— who pants for, finds but short repose,   *Pope* 2 : 230

——— a breath revives, or a breath overthrows,   *Pope* 2 : 230

——— tasks of, painful are and hard,   *Lanf.* 247

——— no pitch of, free from grave,   *Wall.* 146

——— in her death compleat,   *Prior* 1 : 82

——— ode on a Sermon against,   *Aken.* 238

——— to the Father, &c.   *Watts* 359

Glover, verses to, on his Leonidas,   *Lytt.* 98

       Glover,

Glover, liberty and virtue claim thy song,   *Lytt.* 98

Glumdalclitch, lamentation of,   *Gay* 1 : 292

Glutted market makes provisions cheap,   *Pope* 1 : 264

Gluttons in murder, wanton to destroy,   *Lanf.* 247

Gluttony, sure men are cursed for,   *Gay* 2 : 95

Gnomes, dæmons of earth mischievous,   *Pope* 1 : 126

Goat distill'd her milk for Jupiter,   *Pitt* 197

—— expires with feebler cries,   *Pope il.* 2 : 290.

—— without a beard,   *Gay* 2 : 67

Goats, management of,   *Dry.* 5 : 161

Goblet described,   *Pope* 1 : 311

—— I drain, and then 'tis sweet to rave,   *Broome* 166

God demonstrated from the creation,   *Black.* 40

———————— from final causes,   *Black.* 41

—— only known to himself,   *Watts* 109

—— sacred One, almighty Three,   *Watts* 110

—— described,   *Mall.* 198

—— incomprehensible and infinite,   *Prior* 1 : 20

—— perfections of, unfounded depth,   *Mall.* 226

—— could not be, could we conceive him,   *Young* 3 : 29

—— alone can comprehend a God,   *Young* 3 : 29

—— unity of,   *Pom.* 297

—— eternity,   *Pom.* 297

—— power,   *Pom.* 298

—— wisdom,   *Pom.* 301

—— providence,   *Pom.* 302

—— omnipresence,   *Pom.* 304

—— immutability,   *Pom.* 306

—— justice,   *Pom.* 307

—— goodness,   *Pom.* 309

God,

God, not a neceffary caufe, but freely acting, *Black.* 159

—— acts to one end, but by various laws, *Pope* 2 : 55

———— not by partial, but by general laws, *Pope* 2 : 34

———— by arbitrary laws, *Black.* 103

———— frames creatures diftinguifh'd in perfection, *Black.* 103

—— whofe broad eye, future and paft joins to prefent, *Young* 3 : 75

—— all-knowing, all-unknown, *Young* 3 : 75

—— caufe uncaufed, fole root of nature, *Young* 3 : 75

—— father of this immeafurable mafs of matters, *Young* 3 : 75

———————— fpirits, *Young* 3 : 75

———————— immortality to man, *Young* 3 : 77

—— triune, unutterable, unconceived, *Young* 3 : 78

—— with one almighty call rais'd the world, *Broome* 24

—— is light, { *Thom.* 1 : 49 *Milt.* 1 : 73

—— in uncreated light, deep invefted, dwells, *Thom.* 1 : 49

—— eternal caufe, fupport and end of things, *Thom.* 1 : 50

—— all-feeing, *Watts* 337

—— folemn thoughts of, *Watts* 338

—— fhade and light the fame to, *Pitt* 248

—— lead in the way that leads to thee, *Pitt* 249

—— guards my life, and fhields me from my foes, *Pitt* 250

—— fees and moves all, himfelf unmov'd, unfeen, *Broome* 100

—— prefent, by providential care, *Young* 3 : 121

—— fupreme, the regifters of fate expanded lie to, *Pope od.* 4 : 164

—— omnifcient, *Milt.* 2 : 45

—— wife and juft in all things, *Milt.* 2 : 45

—— fupreme in might, fublime in majefty, *Pope od.* 3 : 145

—— ideas of, exemplars of all things, *Aken.* 115

—— perfect in himfelf, *Milt.* 1 : 245

God, omnipresence of,   *Milt.* 2 : 96

—— makes this world his care,   *Parn.* 221

—— supreme and all-sufficient,   *Watts* 96

—— is all,   *Watts* 96

—— his age, one eternal now,   *Watts* 97

—— of thunder,   *Watts* 101

—— ways of, just,   { *Milt.* 2 : 66 / *Milt.* 3 : 17

———————— vindicate to man,   *Pope* 2 : 29

—— absolute dominion of,   *Watts* 85

—— his favour is my life,   *Watts* 87

—— was still the first, and still the last,   *Parn.* 143

—— thy days beyond duration run,   *Pitt* 243

—— swears, I live for ever and for ever,   *Parn.* 127

—— gives death or life,   *Parn.* 127

—— majesty of, in the conquest of Canaan,   *Parn.* 239

—— be for ever in my view,   *Parn.* 247

—— with a single thought can grasp creation,   *Young* 3 : 68

—— to whom, for mercy the vile may fly,   *Young* 3 : 69

—— the source of all power,   *Cow.* 2 : 229

—— his voice controls the raging sea,   *Pitt* 239

—— when he speaks, the mountains fly,   *Pitt* 239

—— his mighty voice divides the fire,   *Pitt* 239

—— reigns o'er all,   *Pitt* 240

—— bids, what reason bids,   *Young* 2 : 241

—— is nought, but reason infinite,   *Young* 3 : 249

—— in grandeur, and our world on fire,   *Young* 3 : 8

—— exalted above all praise,   *Watts* 162

—— will of, is fate,   *Milt.* 1 : 213

—— acts of, immediate,   *Milt.* 1 : 213

God creates good out of evil, *Milt.* 1 : 213

—— dominion and decrees of, *Watts* 47

—— glorious, *Watts* 53

—— hand most just, rewarding or afflicting, *Mall.* 262

—— who strength from weakness can draw, *Mall.* 265

—— bids the din of war to cease, *Pitt* 242

—— alone fill my heart, *Pope* 1 : 190

—— living source of beauteous and sublime, *Aken.* 132

———————— of intellectual day, *Aken.* 147

—— descended to dispense the law, *Parn.* 114

—— address to his son, *Milt.* 1 : 75, 76, 77

—— prescience of man's fall, *Milt.* 1 : 76, 77

—— pleas'd and bless'd with him alone, *Parn.* 80

—— render'd up his son to redeem his foe, *Pitt* 219

—— no access to, without a mediator, *Milt.* 2 : 127

—— alone can save, *Parn.* 107

—— triumphant in his wondrous ways, *Parn.* 108

—— love of, to man, *Wall.* 207

——————— in creation, *Wall.* 208

——————— in redemption, *Wall.* 209

——————— power of, *Wall.* 211

——————— to reform mankind, *Wall.* 211, 212

——————— to be kept in memory, *Wall.* 215

—— fear of, what, *Wall.* 217

—— of seasons sing, *Thom.* 1 : 194

—— is ever present, *Thom.* 1 : 194

—— from seeming evil still ed c'ng good, *Thom.* 1 : 194

—— and better thence again in infinite progression, *Thom.* 1 : 194

—— of harvest how good, *Thom.* 1 : 112

—— who pours abundance over flowing fields, *Thom.* 1 : 112

God never wants a voice to speak his will,   *Rowe L.* 402

—— raises fit instruments to execute his will,   *Cow.* 2 : 172

—— presence of, worth dying,   *Watts* 153

—— taking his name in vain,   *Watts* 347

—— image of, destroyed by sin,   *Milt.* 2 : 102

—— in the nature of each, founds its bliss,   *Pope* 2 : 59

—— and nature, only are the same,   *Pope* 2 : 98

—— my trust in dangers, and my shield in fight,   *Parn.* 171

—— 'tis he that treads our great opposers down,   *Parn.* 173

—— thy strength is armour,   *Parn.* 173

—— only to be served,   *Milt.* 2 : 207

—— punishes to spare,   *Parn.* 227

—— repose in, shunning mad despair,   *Parn.* 227

—— such as Lucretius drew, without a thought,   *Pope* 3 : 249

—— regardless of our merit or default,   *Pope* 3 : 249

—— his judgments against sinners,   *Cow.* 2 : 53

—— in externals cannot place content,   *Pope* 2 : 71

—— bright evidence reveals,   *Pope il.* 2 : 6

—— of the silver bow, avenge thy servant,   *Pope il.* 1 : 39

—— fierce as he mov'd his silver shafts resound,   *Pope il.* 1 : 39

Goddess shrin'd in every tree,   *Pope* 1 : 332

Godhead, incarnate,   *Pom.* 337

Godlike, an attempt the world to mend,   *Young* 1 : 105

———— happiness to give,   *Swift* 2 : 115

Godliness, mere ware,   *Butl.* 1 : 142

Godolphin, earl of,   *Garth* 109

———— ode to,   *Cong.* 164

———— wife and just,   *Phil.* 10

———— to Garth,   *Garth* 157

Gods preposterous, of fear and ignorance,   *Dyer* 10

                                                     Gods,

Gods, 'tis impious to contend with,   *Pitt* 200

—— first pay thy humble homage to,   *Rowe* 2

—— who revere, the gods will bless,   *Pope il.* 1 : 46

—— say of, nought unseemly, nought profane,   *West* 137

—— turn, to various ends; the various talents of, *Pope od.* 4 : 31

—— dispose the lot of man,   *Pope od.* 3 : 308

—— with ease, frail man depress or raise,   *Pope od.* 4 : 78

—— exalt the lowly, or the proud debase,   *Pope od.* 4 : 78

—— the weak enlighten and the wise confound, *Pope od.* 4 : 219

—— depress or raise,   *Pope od.* 219

—— best know, what's for our good,   *King* 354

—— thank for whate'er happens,   *King* 353

—— command me to forgive the past,   *Pope il.* 1 : 50

—— live like, though we die like men,   *Pom.* 323

—— have searching eyes,   *Parn.* 41

—— avenge the dead,   *Pope od.* 3 : 280

—— nor bread of man sustains,   *Pope il.* 1 : 165

—— as we are by Homer told,   *Swift* 1 : 110

—— can in celestial language scold,   *Swift* 1 : 110

—— debate of,   *Gay* 1 : 331

—— Jove spoke, their tumults cease,   *Gay* 1 : 331

—— that make, shall keep the worthy friends, *Pope il.* 1 : 141

—— as well as men mistaken,   *Prior* 1 : 87

Gold, Anacreontic,   *Cow.* 1 : 145

—— power of,   *Cow.* 2 : 356

—— first in lustre and esteem,   *West* 135

—— decks the treasures of the proud,   *West* 135

—— what art thou, but shining earth ?   *Broome* 31

—— pledge of wealth,   *Dyer* 106

—— spur of activity to good or ill,   *Dyer* 106

Gold, for some to heap, and some to throw away, *Pope* 2 : 118

—— beſtows, what nature wants, *Pope* 2 : 119

—— great ſource of human cares, *Hughes* 91

—— baniſh'd honour from the mind, *Gay* 2 : 38

—— abus'd by avarice and pride, *Gay* 2 : 39

—— in virtuous hands it bleſſes, *Gay* 2 : 39

—— is the allay to human kind, *Buck.* 90

—— tempts friends to part, or foes to join, *Buck.* 90

—— the greateſt vigilance beguiles, *Cong.* 136

—— hazard happineſs for, *Broome* 38

—— how few ſubdue thirſt of, *Broome* 42

—— defiles with frequent touch, *Swift* 1 : 74

—— nothing fouls the hands ſo much, *Swift* 1 : 74

—— bribes a ſenate, and the land's betray'd, *Pope* 2 : 119

—— if ſecret ſap, heroes may fight, and patriots rave in vain, *ib.*

—— drags the ſlaviſh world in chains, *Swift* 1 : 158

—— ah cruel thirſt ! *Young* 1 : 193

—— rage of, diſdains a ſhore, *Young* 1 : 194

—— pleaſure buys, *Young* 1 : 194

—— ſordid love of, *Rowe L.* 126

—— unkingly thirſt of, *Thom.* 2 : 146

—— ſacred hunger of, *Dry.* 3 : 147

—— the greateſt God, *Dry.* 7 : 227

—— we worſhip, though we pray to heaven, *Cong.* 75

—— attractive gold ! *Som.* 320

—— to thee each ſtubborn virtue bends, *Som.* 320

—— thy zealots ranſack ſea and land, *Som.* 321

—— reſtleſs diſturber of mankind, *Som.* 330

—— canſt thou give health, or peace of mind, *Som.* 330

—— corruption, luxury, and envy, miſchiefs of, *Weſt* 259

Gold imp'd by thee, can compass hardest things, *Pope* 2 : 120

—— ill-perfuading, *Pope od.* 3 : 128

—— o'erturns the even scale of life, *Ham.* 220

—— makes a patrician of a slave, *Garth* 32

—— can make an avaricious coward bold, *Fent.* 290

—— what female can despise ? *Gray* 329

—— not all that glisters, *Gray* 329

—— all is not, that glisters, *Som.* 357

—— is all the view in marriage, · *Gay* 2 : 50

—— no deed discolour'd with guilt of, ·· *Fent.* 331

—— riddle on, . *Swift* 1 : 307

—— and silver, betray simple manners, *Dry.* 7 : 266

Golden age, *Dry.* 3 : 301

———————— restored, *Walsh* 361

———————— is but a dream, · *Cong.* 149

Golden-age of the Latin ended in *Ovid*, · *Dry.* 3 : 22

Golden ass of Apuleius, Varronian Satire, *Dry.* 7 : 162

—— fleece carried off by Phryxus, *Dyer* 64

———————— recovered by Jason, *Dyer* 67

———— mean, ever keep, *Rowe* 5

———————— bear your fortune in, *Pitt* 396

———————— unchanging to pursue, · *Rowe L.* 305

———————— prudence confines to, *Den.* 96

———————— beyond there's nought of health or pleasure, *Phil.* 76

———— present caught Atalanta's eyes, · *Gay* 1 : 22

Goldfinch described, *Dry.* 3 : 170

Goliah slain by David, *Cow.* 2 : 133, 153

Gondibert, verses on, *Cow.* 1 : 129

———— formal style of, *Dry.* 1 : 291

Good unexpected, evils unforeseen, appear in turn, *Dry.* 7 : 23

Good, that alone, which centres in God's will,   *Prior* 2 : 194

—— in works will defend itself,   *Pope* 1 : 15

—— is mixed with ill,   *A. Phil.* 366

—— much more safe than evil deed,   *Pope od.* 4 : 211

—— done, returns with interest to the generous mind, *Som.* 284

—— the only true and real, is seated in the mind, *Gay* 2 : 295

—— lot of,   *Milt* 2 : 185

—— suffers, while the bad prevails,   *Pope od.* 3 : 176

—— live an unlaborious life,   *A. Phil.* 393

—— be, as well as seem,   *Hughes* 262

—— dare to be,   *Parn.* 90

—— seek to be, but aim not to be great,   *Lytt.* 41

—— be, let heaven answer for the rest,   *Young* 2 : 248

—— none perfect, to be found,   *Ot.* 73

—— blended with bad, the common stroke have felt, *Pitt* 263

—— actions maintained with good,   *Dry.* 1 : 33

—— dinner, brother to a good poem,   *King* 187

—— head more useful than a heart,   *Cong.* 84

Good-breeding, truth is disapproved without,   *Pope* 1 : 114

————————— is the blossom of good-sense,   *Young* 1 : 133

Good-conscience, a port landlock'd,   *Dry.* 5 : 88

Good-fame, the shadow of virtue,   *Cow.* 2 : 295

Good-humour only teaches charms to last,   *Pope* 2 : 337

————————— ever to good sense ally'd,   *Hughes* 273

————————— verses on,   *Lytt.* 89

————————— magic power can make ev'n folly please, *ib.* 89

Good man, in the city cant,   *Som.* 316

————— cash not morals make,   *Som.* 316

Good-nature is beneficence and candour,   *Dry.* 7 : 103

————————— and good-sense must ever join,   *Pope* 1 : 112

Good news bait,   *Milt.* 3 : 58
—— old caufe, what,   *Butl.* 2 : 7
—— parfon,   *Dry.* 3 : 207
—— refolutions,   *Watts* 365
—— fenfe, the gift of heaven,   *Pope* 2 : 138
———— and tho' no fcience, fairly worth the Seven, *ib.* 138.
———— and fomething previous ev'n to tafte,   *ib.* 138
———— of every art the foul,   *ib.* 138
———— is of all ages,   *Dry.* 7 : 112
———— defac'd by falfe learning,   *Pope* 1 : 92
—— and great, no monarch can beftow,   *Mall.* 329
Goode, half malice and half whim,   *Pope* 3 : 185
Goodnefs in excefs, a fin,   *Hal.* 218
———— only is above laws,   *Dry.* 1 : 28
———— is greatnefs in its utmoft height,   *Young* 3 : 171
———— prevails, when beauty fails,   *King* 321
———— in him alone, who only is but one,   *Pope* 1 : 250
Goofe, clofe-grazer,   *Phil.* 37
—— in death contracts his talons,   *Butl.* 1 : 119
—— can hardly tell how to cry Bo to,   *Swift* 2 : 158
Gordian knot to cut,   *Wall.* 148
———— to unty,   *Wall.* 148
Gorges and lady Meath, epitaph on,   *Swift* 2 : 96
Gorgonius, Hockleian hero, character of,   *Som.* 117
———— foiled by young Hobbinol,   *Som.* 120
———— falls on Twangdillo,   *Som.* 121
Gofpel, fuccefs of,   *Milt.* 2 : 136
—— tainted by fuperftition,   *Milt.* 2 : 136
Goffiping defcribed,   *Som.* 127
Goths and Vandals, as the breach of waters, whelm all, *Dyer* 26
Government,

Government, origin of,　　　　　　　　　　　　*Milt.* 2 : 122

———————— forms of, let fools conteft,　　　　*Pope* 2 : 66

———————— whate'er is beft adminifter'd, is beft, *Pope* 2 : 66

———————— called the helm,　　　　　　　　*Butl.* 2 : 75

Gouge (Thomas) elegy on,　　　　　　　　　*Watts* 312

Gould, verfes to,　　　　　　　　　　　　　*Watts* 171

Gout, a lift of feveral fimples, ufed for,　　　*Weft* 249

——— drop of anguifh,　　　　　　　　　　*Weft* 251

——— impracticable maid,　　　　　　　　　*Weft* 251 .

——— thy cramps our limbs diftort,　　　　　*Weft* 252

——— thy knots our joints invade,　　　　　*Weft* 252

——— O mighty conquerefs of human kind,　*Weft* 257

——— nor mov'd by pity, nor by drugs fubdued, *Weft-*257

——— triumphs of,　　　　　　　　　　　　*Weft* 237

——— horrid name, detefted by the gods,　　*Weft* 243

——— rueful gout,　　　　　　　　　　　　*Weft* 243

——— excludes leffer pains,　　　　　　　　*Butl.* 2 : 79

——— lordly, wrapt up in fur,　　　　　　　*Swift* 2 : 175

——— afk, what torment is in guilt,　　　　*Young* 2 : 242

Gower, ode to,　　　　　　　　　　　　　　*Fent.* 322

Gracchi, fond of mifchief-making laws,　　　*Rowe L.* 284

Grace divine, the pledge of joy,　　　　　　*Parn.* 250

———————————— of full joy, portion as a fon, *Parn.* 250

Grace condefcending,　　　　　　　　　　　*Watts* 87

——— fhining,　　　　　　　　　　　　　　*Watts* 146

——— impart, ftill in the right to ftay,　　*Pope* 2 : 88

——— founded in dominion,　　　　　　　　*Butl.* 1 : 144

——— introduced by fin,　　　　　　　　　*Butl.* 2 : 57

——— phyfiognomy of,　　　　　　　　　　*Butl.* 1 : 143

——— before and after meat,　　-　　.　　*Swift* 2 : 286

Grace,

Grace at table is a fong, *Pope* 2 : 223

—— manner, and decorum, fet off actions, *Prior* 1 : 143

—— peculiar to fmall things, *Yal.* 375

Grace-cup, what, *King* 213

Graces, fplendor ye, and fame confer, *Weft* 187

—— to you, all owe their power of pleafing, *Hughes* 267

—— are Kildare, *Lanf.* 145

Gradation, nature's facred law, *Young* 3 : 66

—— juft, thofe fubjected to thofe, *Pope* 2 : 37

Grafting, art of, *Cow.* 2 : 335

Grafton and chief juftice, a caufe between, *Lanf.* 204

Grain different for different foils, *Dry.* 5 : 95

—— to argue againft, *Butl.* 1 : 207

Granadoes rain, difploding murderous bowels, *Phil.* 14

Granaries defcribed, *Dyer* 16

Grand morality is love of thee, *Young* 2 : 88

—— queftion, *Swift* 2 : 152

—— world, vices of, *Caew.* 2 : 306

Grandeur, a fplendid curfe, *Pitt* 396

—— none above the reach of woe, *Pom.* 266

—— affectation of, *Cow.* 2 : 338

—— date of tranfitory, *Som.* 167

—— relieved by meaner occupations, *Cow.* 2 : 340

—— deny me, but goodnefs grant, *Broome* 41

—— to defpife, is not in woman, *Gay* 2 : 267

Grandios, all men in fome degree are, *Cow.* 2 : 339

Grant, ill-tim'd, makes the favour lefs, *King* 2 71

Granville had Waller's lute, *Fent.* 240

—— Dryden to, 2 : 140

Granville, town of, bombarded, *Lanf.* 210

Grapes,

Grapes,   *Broome* 164.

Grapes luxuriant cheer the foul with wine,   *Parn.* 167

Grafshopper, Anacreontic,   *Cow.* 1 : 148

Grafshoppers, a bloodlefs race, with feeble voice, *Pope il.* 1 : 111

Gratitude, but rare at beft,   *Buck.* 107

Gratius tranflated,   *Wall.* 110

Grave, mute as,   *Cow.* 1 : 119

—— how little from, we claim,   *Pope* 2 : 334

—— fets bounds to fublunary blifs,   *Young* 3 : 171

—— pregnant with life, as fruitful wombs,   *Broome* 21

—— refigns us to our fecond birth,   *Broome* 21

—— where blended lie th' oppreffor and opprefs'd, *Pope* 2 : 70

—— where the wicked ceafe their crimes,   *Pitt* 254

—— where blended fleep the coward and the brave, *Pitt* 254

—— claims no lefs the fearful than the brave, *Pope il.* 1 : 370

—— from ftorm the fafe refort,   *Young* 3 : 143

—— feat of peace, manfion of repofe,   *Young* 1 : 212

—— fafe in, and free among the dead,   *Prior* 2 : 183

—— none prince or beggar there,   *Ot.* 12

—— beyond, ftupendous regions lie,   *Pom.* 282

Grave owl, can never face the fun,   *Gay* 1 : 88

——————— as fwains obferve, detefts the light,   *Gay* 1 : 88

Gravitation, univerfal law,   *Mall.* 221

——————— difcovered by Newton,   *Mall.* 221

Gravity inexplicable,   *Black.* 43

Gray, ode on a diftant profpect of Eaton College,   330

—— hymn to adverfity,   335

—— elegy in a country church-yard,   337

—— the epitaph,   341

—— progrefs of poefy,   343

        Gray,

Gray, the bard, 351

—— the fatal sisters, 360

—— the descent of Odin, 365

—— the triumphs of Owen, 369

—— ode on the spring, 385

—————— death of a favourite cat, 388

Great, pompous misery of being, *Broome* 52

—— all affect to be, *Dry.* 7 : 287

—— many would be, few good, *Dry.* 7 : 289

—— debase their eminence to brutal sense, *West* 306

—— to wild passions resign'd, *West* 306

—— in you the health and sickness of the commonweal, *ib.* 313

—— person little as his mind, *Pitt* 287

—— without pride, and amiably good, *Fent.* 331

—— must be good, *Mall.* 290

—— only, by doing good, *Hughes* 275

—————— who can himself command, *Lanf.* 187

—————— whose guard is innocence, *Lanf.* 187

—————— guide is reason, *Lanf.* 187

—— must suffer, and good must mourn, *Mall.* 329

—— acts prove treason to princes, *Cow.* 2 : 120

Great-Britain, reason of the name, *Cow.* 2 : 146

—————— queen, guardian of mankind, *Lanf.* 320

Great day! for which all other days were made, *Young* 3 : 8

—————— of consummation, *Young* 3 : 9

—————— nature's renovation, *Young* 3 : 10

—————— lock'd from created beings in darkness, *Young* 3 : 10

—————— in which time falls on his own scythe, *Young* 3 : 11

—— fortune, great servitude, *Cow.* 2 : 268

—— guilt knew never joy at heart, *Gay* 2 : 150

Great objects make great minds, *Young* 3 : 37

—— rogues enjoy their state, *Gay* 2 : 92

—— souls by instinct to each other turn, *Add.* 55

—— wits to madness near allied, *Dry.* 1 : 130

Greatest souls to goodness only bow, *Prior* 1 : 75

Greatly wise to talk with our past hours, *Young* 2 : 32

Greatness, *Cow.* 2 : 337

———— by what actions grows, *Lanf.* 183

———— pleasure from, *Aken.* 17

———— final cause of, *Aken.* 18

———— nearer viewed, ceases to charm, *Cow.* 2 : 381

———— embarrassment of, *Cow.* 2 : 270, 271

———— insatiable, *Cow.* 2 : 344

———— a creature of fancy, *Cow.* 2 : 346

———— genuine, shuns the being great, *Sav.* 34

Grecian plans reform Britannia's stage, *Tick.* 113

Greece, hail Nature's utmost boast, *Thom.* 2 : 38

—— a country rich and gay, *Thom.* 2 : 38

—— second part of liberty, *Thom.* 2 : 35

—— one comedian, *Dry.* 7 : 237

—— slave and tutoress of protecting Rome, *Lytt.* 25

—— affords a train of lovely dames, *Pope od.* 3 : 69

—— fam'd for steeds, for beauty more, *Pope il.* 1 : 116

———— beauties, *Lanf.* 137

—— the land of lovely dames, *Pope il.* 1 : 284

—— has beauteous dames on every shore, *Pope od.* 4 : 188

—— in her native fortitude elate, *Pope il.* 2 : 149

—— honours not with solemn fasts the dead, *Pope il.* 2 : 202

—— shone in genius, science, and in arts, *Thom.* 2 : 140

—— improv'd or found arts and sciences, *Black.* 173

4

Greece, sapient nurse of finer arts, *Thom.* 2 : 43

———— heroic song was thine, *Thom.* 2 : 44

———— thy workmen left ev'n Nature's self behind, *ib.* 2 : 45

———— orators, with factious breath infested, *ib.* 2 : 50

———— happy in compound words, *Pitt* 373

Greek has a natural greatness, *Add.* 200

———— most adapted for an heroic poem, *Add.* 200

———— epigram, imitated, *Prior* 2 : 245

Greeks pour forth, like swarms of driving bees, *Pope il.* 1 : 70

———— beneath their steps groans the ground, *Pope il.* 1 : 71

———— as numerous as embodied cranes, *Pope il.* 1 : 85

———— thick as in spring the flowers, *Pope il.* 1 : 85

———— or as insects play, *Pope il.* 1 : 85

———— march silent, breathing rage, *Pope il.* 1 : 105

———— raise a bulwark to protect their fleet, *Pope il.* 1 : 234

———— pursued to their ships, *Pope il.* 1 : 375

———— carry off the body of Patroclus, *Pope il.* 2 : 178

Green, smiling Nature's universal robe, *Thom.* 1 : 6

———— the Prophet's sacred hue, *Tick.* 211

———— old age, unconscious of decays, *Pope il.* 2 : 320

———— years, old proverbs cross, *A. Phil.* 304

Greenhithe, verses written in a window at, *Hughes* 161

Greenwich-park, *Hughes* 93

———————— is now the Cyprian grove, *Hughes* 93

Grenville, verses to, *Ham.* 226

———— polite with honesty, and learn'd with ease, *Ham.* 226

———— epitaph on, *Lytt.* 88

———— unrepining for his country dy'd, *Lytt.* 88

Greve, place of execution at Paris, *Prior* 1 : 273

Grey, tho' our heads, our thoughts and aims are green, *Young* 2 : 112

Grey

Grey mare, the better horfe,   { *Butl.* 1 : 215 / *Prior* 1 : 272

Grief, heart-chilled,   *Fent.* 255

——— if whelm'd in pleafures, finds relief,   *A. Phil.* 390

——— deftroy, what time a while would fpare,   *Pope od.* 3 : 75

——— furfeit in,   *Milt.* 3 : 59

——— is wrought to frenzy,   *Smith* 98

——— forgets to groan, and loves to weep,   *Pope* 1 : 193

——— date of, not to be foreftalled,   *Milt.* 3 : 134

——— repeating, but renews,   *Prior* 2 : 209

Griefs, I wake to all, I left behind,   *Pope* 1 : 191

——— how fwift, remedies how flow,   *Prior* 2 : 141

Grimace, ftage debauch'd with lewd,   *Dry.* 2 : 254

Grimalkin, to thoughtlefs mice fure ruin,   *Phil.* 5

Griper, Senna,   *Garth* 40

Grongar, a hill in S. Wales,   *Dyer* 132

——— profpect from,   *Dyer* 132

Grongar hill,   *Dyer* 1

——— in whofe moffy cells fweet quiet dwells,   *Dyer* 1

——— profpect from,   *Dyer* 2

Grofted of Lincoln, a conjurer deemed,   *Butl.* 1 : 231

Giotto, infcription for,   *Aken.* 325

Grove, meditation in,   *Watts* 134

——— the haunt of meditation,   *Thom.* 1 : 61

——— where ancient bards felt infpiring breath,   *Thom.* 1 : 61

Grout, a Danifh difh,   *King* 182

Grown young,   *Broome* 173

Grub, enemy to the apple,   *Phil.* 48

Grubftreet, thy ftage fhall ftand,   *Pope* 3 : 203

——— verfe-writers, advice to,   *Swift* 2 : 16

Grubstreet verse-writers, poets ragged and forlorn, *Swift* 2 : 16

Gualterus Danistonus imitated, *Prior* 2 : 16

Guardian laws, despotic power restrain, *Gay* 1 : 179

———— angels, whether to be used as machines, *Dry.* 7 124

Guardian-prudence guides the youthful flame, *Lytt.* 76

Gudgeons to swallow, ere caught, *Butl.* 1 : 258

Guilt, a hell within, *Milt.* 2 : 18

———— infeebles, *Milt.* 2 : 19

———— follows guilt, *Aken.* 208

———— sits painful on each heaving breast, *Rowe L.* 323

———— only startles at the name of guilt, *Young* 1 : 264

———— eye of, can sharply penetrate, *Prior* 1 : 51

———— is eternal, without end the woe, *Hughes* 193

———— is doom'd to sink in infamy, *Pope* 2 : 21

———— would bring to shame, *Gay* 2 : 132

———— a heavy load, *Watts* 43

———— advanc'd with time, *Prior* 2 : 178

———— brought-on the deluge, *Prior* 2 : 178

———— to midnight caves shall shrink away, *Hughes* 194

———— equal, gives equality of state, *Rowe L.* 217

———— he knows none, who knows no sin, *Swift* 2 : 105

———— how removed, *Dry.* 6 : 147

———— wip'd off by the Redeemer's blood, *Pem.* 336

———— chills my zeal, *Young* 2 : 83

Guiltless suffers most, who least offends, *Som.* 113

Guilty and guiltless find an equal fate, *Pope il.* 2 : 70

———— without fears, *Pope od.* 4 : 26

———— presents win the greedy fair, *Ham.* 206

———— spirits feel eternal pain, *Pope* 1 : 278

Guilty-great, nor basely servile, court, *Lytt.* 27

Gulfs unvoyageable,   *Fent.* 258

Gulph of all poffeffions,   *Swift* 1 : 313

Guinea-gold firft procured,   *Dry.* 1 : 99

Guinea, trade to,   *Dyer* 111

———— gold-duft of,   *Dyer* 112

———— once from a patriot's cloak dropping, fpoke, *Pope* 2 : 119

———— and told, old Cato is as great a rogue as you, *ib.* 119

Guinea-droppers,   *Gay* 1 : 140

Gun ufed in fowling,   *Gay* 1 : 13

———— as certain as,   *Butl.* 1 : 100

Guneus, in twenty fail, the Perrhæbians led,   *Pope il.* 1 : 97

Gun-powder, invention of Satan,   *Milt.* 1 : 189

Guns contrived in hell,   *Milt.* 1 : 190

———— overcharged, recoil,   *Butl.* 1 : 272

Gunfton (Thomas), verfes to,   *Watts* 245

———————— poem on death of,   *Watts* 294

Guts, thofe worft of duns,   *Som.* 354

———— fit for mufic or for pudden,   *Butl.* 1 : 52

Gygæ, fields, where Hyllus' waves are roll'd, *Pope il.* 2 : 228

———— and Hermus fwell with tides of gold,   *Pope il.* 2 : 228

H

Habakkuk,   *Parn.* 236

———— complains of labour fpent in vain,   *Parn.* 236

———— foretels the Jewifh captivity,   *Parn.* 237

———— the deftruction of Babylon,   *Parn.* 237

———— rejoices in God, all earthly comforts fled, *Parn.* 241

———— chap. iii, paraphrafed,   *Broome* 15

Haberdafher of fmall wares in politics,   *Butl.* 2 : 28

Hæmus' hills with fnows eternal crown'd,   *Pope il.* 2 : 49

                              Hagley,

Hagley, infcriptions at,   *Lytt.* 103, feq.

Hail, one of the plagues of Egypt,   *Cow.* 2 : 62

—— fellow, well met,   *Swift* 2 : 63

Hair, harveft of the head,   *Milt.* 3 : 41

—— may gain or lofe a grace,   *Cong.* 117

—— and much become or mifbecome a face,   *Cong.* 117

—— pledge of unviolated vow,   *Milt.* 3 : 45

—— offered to the dead,   *Pope il.* 2 : 294

Hairlefs head, ungraceful as upverdant mead,   *Cong.* 122

Halcyon,   *Sben.* 132

—————— peace, a fmiling afpect wears,   *Sav.* 128

Hale, uprooting hills with moft ftupendous,   *Cong.* 17

Hales, irrefragable doctor,   *Butl.* 1 : 11

Halefus comes to aid Turnus,   *Dry.* 6 : 190

Half more than the whole,   *Cow.* 2 : 306

Half-honeft, very much a knave,   *Roch.* 341

Half wits and beaux, ravenous birds of prey,   *Cong.* 85

Halifax, poems by,   *Hal.* 215

—————— on death of Charles II,   215

—————— ode on marriage of prince George,   220

—————— man of honour,   224

—————— to Dorfet,   229

—————— on lady Sunderland's picture,   237

—————— verfes on Kit Cat Club,   237

—————— on countefs of,   239

—————— on Orpheus,   240

—————— earl of,   *Som.* 235

—————— name for ever dear to Phœbus,   *Som.* 235

—————— patron of verfe,   *A. Phil.* 338

—————— thy name fhall through ages rife in fame, *A. Phil.* 350

Halifax, Addison to,   *Add.* 40

————— epistle to,   *Cong.* 3

Hall (William), ode to, with Chaulieu's Works,   *Aken.* 265

Hallelujah universal,   *Watts* 63

Hallelujahs rise, the chorus of eternal skies,   *Parn.* 106

Halstead, lines on a column in church of,   *Prior* 2 : 30

Halt in sheep, what, and how cured,   *Dyer* 39

Halting vengeance overtakes at last,   *Dry.* 1 : 219

Halves gives by, who hesitates to give,   *Broome* 57

Ham, servant of servants,   *Milt.* 2 : 122

Hamilton, baron of,   *Swift* 2 : 152

Hammond, elegy on Neæra,   *Ham.* 205

————————— unable to satisfy her avarice,   207

————————— upbraids Neæra's avarice,   208

————————— to his friend,   209

————————— the lover,   211

————————— adjures Delia to pity him,   ·   213

————————— on Delia in the country,   214

————————— despairs of possessing Delia,   216.

————————— has lost Delia,   217

————————— on Delia's birth-day,   218

————————— against lovers going to war,   219

————————— to Delia,   220, 225

————————— married to Delia,   221

————————— to Mr. George Grenville,   226

————————— prologue to Lillo's Elmeric,   228

Hands, use of,   *Gay* 1 : 146

————— guiltless, heart defil'd,   *Smith* 102

Handy-blows, come to,   *Buth.* 1 : 118

Hanging goes by destiny,   *Buth.* 2 : 106

                    Hanmer,

Hanmer, epiftle to Sir Thomas,   *Collins* 274

————— thofe fibyl leaves by thee difpos'd,   *Collins* 279

Hannah,   *Parn.* 146

————— reproach'd for barren,   *Parn.* 146

Hannes, Addifon to,   *Add.* 93

Hans Carvel,   *Prior* 1 : 137

————— towns of Germany,   *Thom.* 2 : 92

Happieft tafte not happinefs fincere,   *Pope il.* 2 : 349

————— but find the draught dafh'd with care, *Pope il.* 2 : 349

Happinefs is but opinion,   *Prior* 1 : 156

————— fphere of action,   *Roch.* 322

————— ingredients of,   *Cow.* 2 : 384

————— way to,   *Parn.* 252

————— Jefus is the way,   *Parn.* 252

————— fpring of,   *Parn.* 252

————— in this life,   *Parn.* 257

————— the world but promifes, and can't perform, *Parn.* 258

————— only in God,   *Parn.* 258

————— unbounded as his power, lafting as his love, *Pom.* 334

————— and a created being is able to receive,   *Pom.* 337

————— the beft fame,   *Cow.* 2 : 13

————— few can find,   *Dry.* 3 : 70

————— good confcience, and a foul refign'd,   *Pom.* 267

————— the right ufe of poffeffion,   *King* 376

————— is only to be found in content,   *Som.* 334

————— each want of, fupply'd by hope,   *Pope* 2 : 52

————— to no rank confin'd,   *Gay* 2 : 153

————— dwells in every honeft mind,   *Gay* 2 : 153

————— of truly eftimating life,   *Ot.* 12

————— our being's end and aim,   *Pope* 2 : 69

Happinefs.

Happiness, for which we bear to live, or dare to die, *Pope* 2 : 69

———— those call it pleasure, and contentment these, *ib.* 70

———— is the same in subject, or in king, *ib.* 71

———— thou empty name ! *Broome* 31

———— art thou bought by gold or fame, *Broome* 31

———— cause of our care, and error of our mind, *Prior* 2 : 102

———— is near allied to love, *Lytt.* 33

———— not allotted poets, *Cow.* 1 : 203

———— to wait for, in female smiles, *Ak.n.* 347

———— to barter for state, *Prior* 1 : 132

———— and true philosophy are social, *Thom.* 1 : 151

Happy none, till his end, *Dry.* 7 : 295

——-- what man is, till he knows his end ? *Pope od.* 4 : 236

——-- always, he that's just, *Pom.* 272

——-- be, and learn content, *Gay* 2 : 36

——-- nor imitate th' ambition of mankind, *Gay* 2 : 36

——-- seldom heed th' unhappy's pain, *Sav.* 110

——-- only are the truly great, *Young* 1 : 147

——-- to be, learn to please, *Prior* 2 : 138

——-- he ! who without rigour saves, *Thom.* 1 : 236

——-- how they ! who wake no more, *Young* 3 : 3

——-- counsels flow from sober feasts, *Pope il.* 1 : 268

——-- disappointment, *Som.* 365

——-- frailty, *Watts* 115

Happy-life, *Broome* 162

——-- lunatic, *Som.* 403

Happy man, { *Watts* 232
{ *Parn.* 249
{ *Thom.* 2 : 184

———— who, *Cow.* 2 : 276

Happy

Happy man, who, taking up his cross, follows Jesus, *Pain.* 249

———— none, without the mind, *Thom.* 2 : 184

——— the man, from vain desires free, *Lanf.* 185

——— swain, *A. Phil.* 329

Harbingers of vice, ignorance, ease, and wanton play, *West* 297

Hard to gain, much harder to enjoy, *Young* 3 : 247

Hardest fate ! to fall by shew of friendship, *Phil.* 35

Hardinge (Caleb), ode to, *Aken.* 236

Hardships many, many fall by ease, *Prior* 1 : 185

Hardwicke, letter to, *Lytt.* 81

———————— law's oracle, the nation's pride, *Lytt.* 82

Hardy soldier, *Watts* 213

Hare and many friends, *Gay* 2 : 116

——— afraid to keep or leave her form, *Prior* 1 : 5

——— her change of seats or forms, *Som.* 29

——— Dirge of, *Som.* 38

Hare-hunting described, *Som.* 32

Harlequin, a Punch below, *Swift* 2 : 150

——————— plot discovered by, *Swift* 1 : 270

Harley, on his marriage, *Swift* 1 : 146

———— wounded by Guiscard, *Prior* 2 : 2

———— lady Elizabeth, Prior to, 2 : 8

Harm precedes not sin, *Milt.* 2 : 14

——— against his will, man receives none, *Milt.* 2 : 14

Harma, where Apollo's prophet fell, *Pope il.* 1 : 87

Harmony from discord, *Den.* 14

———— hymn to, *Cong.* 58

———— confusion heard thy voice, and fled, *Cong.* 59

———— gave birth to heaven and earth, *Cong.* 59

———— springs from order, union, *Pope* 2 : 65

Harmony, the univerſe moves by, *Roch.* 283

———— mutual love, *Roch.* 287

———— force of, to turn and ſanctify the ſoul, *Prior* 1 : 28

———— attuning all the paſſions into love, *Thom.* 1 : 40

———— can chace grief and gloom, *Hughes* 143

———— how thou our cares allayeſt, *Hughes* 120

———— how ſoftly ſteal'ſt our eaſy hours away, *Hughes* 122

———— in love, is Nature's voice, *King* 263

———— in wedded pair, grateful, *Milt.* 1 : 252

Harms, from doubtful, we run to certain, *Rowe L.* 71

Harpies deſcribed, *Dry.* 6 : 11

———— place of abode, *Dry.* 6 : 12

———— invulnerable, *Dry.* 6 : 12

———— dogs of Jove, *Weſt* 231

———— purſued by the ſons of Boreas, *Weſt* 230

Harps attun'd to moral airs, *Fent.* 307

Harry's vice is not much talking, *Swift* 2 : 189

Hartley moneyleſs, but not very dirtleſs, *Swift* 2 : 328

———— had many a grubbing, *Swift* 2 : 329

Hartopp (John), verſes to, *Watts* 243, 243

Harveſt, beſt portion of the various year, *Phil.* 63

Harvey, Cowley on, 1 : 173

———— diſcovers the circulation, *Black.* 192

Haſte makes waſte, *Butl.* 1 : 146

Haſtings, battle of, *Thom.* 2 : 105

———— death of, *Dry.* 1 : 9

Haſſan, the camel-driver, *Collins* 236

Hate, engender'd by ſuſpicious fears, *Pope* 1 : 284

———— and rancour, rang'd at will, *Rowe L.* 89

Hated by fools, and fools to hate, *Swift* 2 : 133

Hated

Hated by fools, be that my motto and my fate, *Swift* 2 : 133

Haughty Gaul in ten campaigns o'er thrown, *Tick.* 99

———————— on glory past reflects with secret pain, *Tick.* 99

———————— on mines exhausted, and on millions slain, *ib.* 99

Hawk described, *Young* 1 : 218

Hawker, when crying newt, *Gay* 1 : 111

Hawking, *Som.* 145

Hay-making, *Thom.* 1 : 55

Haywood, verses to, *Sav.* 135

Head is clear, because the heart is cool, *Young* 2 : 252

——— can art or genius guide, *Akin.* 342

——— where truth and freedom from the heart are fled, *ib.* 342

——— to give for the washing, *Butl.* 1 : 109

Heads many, wiser still than one, *Pope* 1 : 230

——— without name, the common rout, *Milt.* 3 : 29

Health, *Parn.* 58

——— country goddess, *Parn.* 59

——— described, *Garth* 77

——— ode to, *Shen.* 98

——— salt of life, *Cow.* 2 : 333

——— is the vital principle of bliss, *Thom.* 1 : 243

——— consists in temperance alone, *Pope* 2 : 72

——— fails, and years increase, *Prior* 1 : 154

——— the monarch's bliss, the beggar's wealth, *Mall.* 181

——— seasoning of all good below, *Mall.* 181

——— is riches to the poor, *Fent.* 274

——— suppress'd by wine's continued force, *Prior* 2 : 134

——— that prince of earthly treasures, *West* 167

——— keeps an Atheist in the dark, *Young* 1 : 109

——— of body, and content of mind, *Dry.* 7 : 300

Health

Health acquired by walking,   *Gay* 1 : 103
———— ſtrengthens mirth,   *Sav.* 90
———— oblivion pour of life-confuming pain,   *Weſt* 197
Healths drinking,   *Wall.* 81
Heaps on heaps, a monument of dead,   *Pope il.* 2 : 116
Heart, cauſe of the circulation,   *Black.* 188
———— out of,   *Butl.* 1 : 106
———— deſcending to their breeches,   *Prior* 2 : 46
—————————— muſt give ſtomach cruel twitches, *id.* 2 : 46
———— what takes, muſt merit our eſteem,   *id.* 2 : 133
———— to melt at others woe,   *Pope od.* 4 : 126
———— to glow for others good,   *Pope od.* 4 : 126
Heart-breaking,   *Cow.* 1 : 293
———— deteſting, what the ear allows,   *Pope od.* 3 : 45
———— diſcovered,   *Cow.* 1 : 239
———— fled again,   *Cow.* 1 : 269
———— generous, repairs a ſlanderous tongue,   *Pope od.* 3 : 217
———— given away,   *Watts* 133
———— impervious,   *Cow.* 1 : 174
Hearts tangled in amorous nets,   *Milt.* 2 : 168
———— are ty'd with threads of gold,   *Fent.* 273
———— found as any bell or roach,   *Gay* 1 : 271
Heat, with thirſt and languor in his train,   *Mall.* 182
Heaven has gods,   *Parn.* 41
———— magnificence of,   *Mall.* 215
———— region mild of peace,   *Pope od.* 3 : 170
———— full joy, eternity of eaſe,   *Pope od.* 3 : 170
———— no happineſs to the wicked,   *Milt.* 2 : 157
———— the book of God,   *Milt.* 1 : 233
———— fabric of, left to men's diſputes,   *Milt.* 1 : 233
                                                              Heaven

Heaven speaks the Maker's magnificence,   *Milt.* 1 : 234

————— is won by violence of song,   *Pope* 2 : 226

————— hopes on,   *Add.* 52

————— discharges all its watery stores,   *Gay* 2 : 13

————— and beauty's honour, 'tis they can give,   *King* 274

————— and earth, two magnets,   *Dry.* 2 : 65

————— and hell,   *Watts* 339

————— like a top,   *Butl.* 1 : 256

————— disposes all,   [*Pope il.* 1 : 118

————— ways dark and intricate,   *Add.* 253

————— counsels of the wise, belong to,   *Rowe* 8

————— purposes of, how deep,   *Mall.* 210

————— will of, unerring, wisest, justest, best,   *Mall.* 211

————— deep wisdom to the fool supplies,   *Pitt* 403

————— but oft infatuates and confounds the wise,   *Pitt* 403

————— to gracious ends directs the storm,   *Thom.* 2 : 115

————— punishes the bad,   *Dry.* 1 : 126

————— proves the just,   *Dry.* 1 : 126

————— protects the just,   *Pope od.* 4 : 113

————— never will forsake the virtuous,   *Gay* 2 : 247

————— most chastises, whom he likes,   *Pom.* 268

————— chastises, what best it loves,   *Pope* 1 : 236

————— when it afflicts, 'tis mine to hearken and adore, *Mall.* 271

————— wounds to heal,   *Young* 3 : 93

————— its frowns are friends,   *Young* 3 : 93

————— its strokes severe most kind,   *Young* 3 : 93

————— rules, and gods there are above,   *Pope od.* 4 : 248

————— alone confers success in war,   *Pope il.* 2 : 229

————— shews a thrift in his œconomy,   *Dry.* 2 : 178

————— forms each on other to depend,   *Pope* 2 : 51

Heaven

Heaven has wove the thread of life with pain, *Pope od.* 4: 73

———— juſt are the ways of, *Pope od.* 3: 224

———— the woes of man proceed from, *Pope od.* 3: 224

———— all good proceeds from, *Cong.* 166

———— wills it, and my hour is nigh, *Pope il.* 2: 275

———— purſues, we ſhun the ſtroke in vain, *Gay* 1: 36

———— alone knows events of actions and fates, *Pope ed.* 4: 207

———— itſelf points out an hereafter, *Add.* 329

———— look to, be blind to all below, *Prior* 1: 23

———— ſells all pleaſure, *Young* 2: 239

———— its gifts not all at once beſtows, *Pope il.* 1: 139

———— theſe years with wiſdom crowns, with action thoſe, *ib.*

———— offended, and a prieſt profan'd, *Pope il.* 1: 41

———— will revenge, and gods there are, *Pope od.* 4: ●

———— 's revenge is ſlow, *Pope il.* 1: 133

———— 's Swiſs, who fight for any god or man, *Pope* 3: 363

Heavenly charms prefer to proffer'd gold, *Pope il.* 1: 41

———— country, breathing towards, *Watts* 124

Heaven-taught poet charms the ear, *Pope od.* 4: 111

———————————— ſuſpending ſorrow, *Pope od.* 4: 111

Hebe, goddeſs ever young, *Swift* 2: 234

Hector, favourite of the ſkies, *Broome* 69

———— ſad reverſe of woes await, *Broome* 72

———— the whole ſupport of Troy, *A. Phil.* 394

———— to combat born, and bred amidſt alarms, *Pope il.* 1: 226

———— carries Paris's challenge to Menelaus, *Pope il.* 1: 109

———— prefers a prayer for his ſon, *Pope il.* 1: 211

———— guardian of the Trojan ſtate, *Pope il.* 1: 217

———— challenges the Greeks, *Pope il.* 1: 219

———— mighty man of war, *Pope il.* 1: 220

Hector,

Hector, challenge of, accepted by nine,   *Pope il.* 1 : 283

———— throwing a stone, bursts open one of the gates, *ib.* 375

———— heads his native bands,   *Pope il.* 1 : 109

———— arrests Patroclus with a mortal wound, *Pope il.* 2 : 132

———— at whose feet he dying lies,   *Pope il.* 2 : 132

———— flies, Patroclus shakes his lance,   *Pope il.* 2 : 114

———— that slew Achilles, in his friend,   *Pope il.* 2 : 229

———— rescued by Apollo,   *Pope il.* 2 : 230

———— the defence of Troy,   *Pope il.* 2 : 281

———— thy parents pride and joy,   *Pope il.* 2 : 281

———— wretched husband of a wretched wife, *Pope il.* 2 : 283

———— returning, makes a great slaughter,   *Pope il.* 1 : 334

———— opposed by Ulysses and Diomed,   *Pope il.* 1 : 334

———— comes against Ajax,   *Pope il.* 1 : 343

———— swift as whirl-wind, drives the foe,   *Pope il.* 1 : 179

———— terror of the Greeks, that man of men, *Pope il.* 1 : 254

———— fury of the field,   *Pope il.* 1 : 251

———— like Gorgon wither'd all their host,   *Pope il.* 1 : 253

———— when he rag'd, resistless; when he stopt, unmov'd, *ib.* 2 : 9

———— prepares the Trojans for battle,   *Pope il.* 1 : 323

———— warned to quit the field,   *Pope il.* 1 : 329

———— wields Achilles' arms,   *Pope il.* 2 : 155

———— spear of, described,   *Pope il.* 1 : 259

———— resolv'd Achilles' force to dare,   *Pope il.* 2 : 264

———— in vain diffuaded by his parents,   *Pope il.* 2 : 264

———— pursued by Achilles thrice round Troy, *Pope il.* 2 : 270

———— to his fears resign'd,   *Pope il.* 2 : 270

———— how chang'd, who like Jove of late, *Pope il.* 2 : 278

———— is dead, and Ilion is no more,   *Pope il.* 2 : 279

———— dragg'd thrice round Patroclus' tomb, *Pope il.* 2 : 328

Hector,

Hector, his body preserv'd incorrupt, *Pope il.* 2 : 328

———— ranfom of, *Pope il.* 2 : 351

'———— dead, lamentations over, $\begin{cases} \textit{Pope il. } 2:356 \\ \textit{Cong.} \quad\; 37 \end{cases}$

———— funeral of, *Pope il.* 2 : 360

———————— pile of, *Cong.* 43

———— and Andromache parting, *Dry.* 4 : 267

Hecuba, lamentation over Hector, *Cong.* 41

Heels degraded of their fpurs, *Butl.* 2 : 125

Heifer, peafant in fearch of, *Cong.* 176

———— when ftuck aloft her tail, forbodes a fhower, *Gay* 1 : 56

Height of blifs, but height of charity, .. *Pope* 2 : 82

Heir urges heir, like wave impelling wave, *Pope* 2 : 253

Helen for ten whole years engag'd the world in arms, *Pitt* 272

———— invited to view the combat, *Pope il.* 1 : 111

———— her affection for her hufband and country revives, *ib.* 111

———— her beauty commended, *Pope il.* 1 : 112

———— points out to Priam the principal Greeks, *Pope il.* 1 : 112

———— fcorn'd the champion, but the man fhe lov'd, *Pope il.* 1 : 121

———— mix'd a mirth-infpiring bowl, *Pope od.* 3 : 115

———— lamentation over Hector, *Cong.* 42

———— to Paris, from Ovid, $\begin{cases} \textit{Dry. } 4:183 \\ \textit{Buck.} \quad\; 57 \end{cases}$

Helena ftolen by Thefeus, *Duke* 147

Helenus, ftory of, *Dry.* 6 : 15

———— prophecy of, *Dry.* 6 : 18

———— difpenfing fate, *Pope il.* 2 : 35

Heliacal rifing, what, *Dry.* 5 : 270

Hell endlefs as its pains, *Cow.* 2 : 74

———— defcribed, *Milt.* 1 : 7, 11

              Hell

Hell defcribed,   *Dry.* 6 : 129

—— gate of, defcribed,   *Milt.* 1 : 56

—— portals nine of,   *Gray* 366

—— place of evil,   *Milt.* 1 : 182

—— houfe of woe and pain,   *Milt.* 1 : 202

—— the woes, the horrours, and the laws,   *Pope od.* 3 : 286

—— different objects in,   *Dry.* 6 : 132

—— had been, had there been no God,   *Young* 3 : 68

—— landing apes in,   *Walfb* 337

Hellanodic, judge of the games,   *Weft* 155

Hellefpont fatal to love,   *Dyer* 66

Helon, character of,   *Dry.* 1 : 194

Helfham, epiftle to,   *Swift* 2 : 274

—————— anfwer,   *Swift* 2 : 276

Helter-fkelter,   *Swift* 2 : 145

Hemp, to beat,   *Butl.* 1 : 237

—— forg'd on wooden anvils,   *Butl.* 1 : 286

—— to depart in,   *Butl.* 1 : 275

Henchman to a knight,   *Dry.* 3 : 176

Heniochi of Sparta's valiant breed,   *Rowe L.* 134

————— fkilful to rein the fiery fteed,   *Rowe L.* 134

Henley feem'd a prieft in drink,   *Pope* 3 : 168

————— embrown'd with bronze, lo ftands,   *Pope* 3 : 191

————— decent prieft, where monkeys were the gods, *id.* 3 : 193

————— tuning his voice and balancing his hands, *Pope* 3 : 91

————— preacher at once, and zany of thy age,   *Pope* 3 : 93

————— verfes at an inn,   *Shen.* 183

Henrietta Cavendifh-Holles Harley, verfes to,   *Prior* 2 : 220

————— Cavendifh-Holles, her character,   *Hughes* 204

————— duchefs of Marlborough, epiftle to,   *Gay* 1 : 184

Henry

INDEX.

Henry VI. prologue to,   *Sav.* 131

———— good than great,   *Sav.* 131

———— of Richmond removes deftructive difcord,   *Phil.* 82

———————— unites by wife alliance Fergus' line, *Phil.* 82

———— VIII. fhook off papal yoke,   *Thom.* 2 : 111

———— Naffau alone can match his brother's deeds, *Hughes* 44

———— none fiercer did purfue the flying foe,   *Hughes* 44

———— liv'd to compleat the great republic,   *Hughes* 45

———— and Emma,   *Prior* 1 : 218

Heraclitus weeps the crimes of men,   *Dry.* 7 : 283

Herald lark falutes the morn,   *Milt.* 2 : 172

Heralds, minifters of Gods and men,   *Tick.* 176

———— facred minifters of men and gods,   *Pope il.* 1 : 51

———— facred minifters of earth and heaven, *Pope il.* 1 : 228

———— moons, all crefcents,   *Butl.* 1 : 170

Herbs o'er all the deep-green earth fpring,   *Thom.* 1 : 11

———— beyond the power of Botanifts to number, *Thom.* 1 : 11

———— their virtues who can declare!   *Thom.* 1 : 11

Hercules, a babe, kills two ferpents,   *Cow.* 2 : 19

———— death of,   *Gay* 1 : 318

———— apotheofis of,   *Gay* 1 : 334

———— now a fhadowy form,   *Pope od.* 3 : 302

———— a towering fpectre of gigantic mould,   *ib.* 3 : 301

———— labours of,   *Dry.* 6 : 208

———— no labours too hard for,   *Garth* 52

———— judgment of,   *Shen.* 197

———— abides affociate with gods,   *Fent.* 271

———— of Farnefe,   *Thom.* 2 : 85

Hereford, encomium of,   *Phil.* 51, 52

———— women of,   *Phil.* 56

                                                     Hermaphroditus,

Hermaphroditus, story of,　　　　　　　　　Add. 174

Hermes, described,　　　　　　　　　　　Dry. 6 : 47

———— in his attire,　　　　　　　　Pope il. 2 : 341

———— conducts Priam to Achilles,　　Pope il. 2 : 345

———— mediates between gods and men,　Pope il. 2 : 343

———— accoutred as the messenger of the gods, Pope od. 3 : 147

———— god of the golden wand,　　　Pope od. 3 : 148

————— the charming rod,　　　Pope od. 3 : 151

———— patron of industry and manual arts,　Pope od. 4 : 58

———— of profitable arts the fire,　　Pope il. 2 : 214

———— gave the pilfering temper of a wife,　Parn. 7

Hermetic powder for wounds,　　　　　　Butl. 1 : 56

Hermione, the fairest of her kind,　　Pope od. 3 : 105

———— resembling Venus in attractive state, Pope od. 3 : 105

Hermit,　　　　　　　　　　　　　　{ Parn. 81
　　　　　　　　　　　　　　　　　{ Mall. 235

Hermaphrodite, meer poetical,　　　　　Dry. 2 : 279

Hern-hawking, described,　　　　　　　Som. 148

Hero, character of,　　　　　　　　　Pope od. 3 : 29

———— how differs from the brute,　　Add. 263

———— mind, unchangeable and free,　　Som. 165

———— how vain, without the merit, is the name, Pope il. 2 : 142

———— self-conquer'd, inured to quell his rage, Pope od. 4 : 100

———— scorns despair,　　　　　　Pope od. 4 : 74

———— school of morality, of,　　　　Watts 198

————'s headless trunk besmear'd with gore,　Rowe L. 80

Herod, savage on a throne,　　　　　Broome 113

Heroes find a task to tame the monster vice,　Hughes 48

———— fight for glory, not for prize,　Lanf. 146

———— from heroes rise,　　　　　Pope od. 3 : 71

Heroes like, they bore, but felt like men, *Pope il.* 2 : 448

———— in heaven's peculiar mold are caft, *Dry.* 1 : 413

———— in fearch of fame, the world embroil, *Eanf.* 130

———— made by flaughter, *Butl.* 1 : 60

———— of the nibbling race, *Parn.* 39

———— good-eating expedient for, *Som.* 125

———— and kings now are but a name, *Broome* 129

Heroic poem, utmoft ftretch of human fenfe, *Buck.* 80

——————— but two produced, *Buck.* 80

——————— forms the mind by example, *Dry.* 5 : 207

——————— grave, majeftic, and fublime, *Dry.* 5 : 208

——————— poetry, why the greateft work, *Dry.* 7 : 134

——————— antiquity of, *Dry.* 7 : 134

——————— virtue, from Tyrtaeus, *Hughes* 124

Herring, dead as, *Butl.* 1 : 266

Herfilia, affumption of, *Garth* 150

Hervey (William), on death of, *Cow.* 1 : 117

———— commended, *Cow.* 1 : 120

———— verfes to lord, *Lytt.* 37

———— favourite of Venus and the tuneful Nine, *Lytt.* 37

Hefiod, *Parn.* 5

———— contemporary with Homer, *Cow.* 2 : 306

———— tranflation from, *King* 426

———— had more of the hufbandman than poet, *Add.* 206

———— defcriptions of, are nature in her fimplicity, *Add.* 207

———— precepts of, clog his poem, *Add.* 208

Hezekiah, *Parn.* 228

———— who cleanfed the temple, *Parn.* 228

———— lies fick, his death pronounc'd, *Parn.* 229

———— reftor'd to health, on his prayer, *Parn.* 230

           Hezekiah,

Hezekiah, his life extended to fifteen years, *Parn.* 480

Hiarba, slighted by Dido, *Dry.* 6 : 45

Hibernia, how soon thy arms regain'd, *Hughes* 52

Hiccius Doctius, to play, *Butl.* 2 : 102

Hierarchy, double tyrants, *Thom.* 2 : 85

Hiero of Syracuse victor in the Pythian games, *West* 190

———— by Pythian heralds were his praises sung, *West* 196

———— plucks every virtue's fairest flower, *West* 136

Higden, Dryden to, 2 : 136

Higgons, *Wall.* 113

———— on Mrs. *Wall.* 201

High, exposed to storms, *Den.* 15

———— bliss is only for a higher state, *Thom.* 2 : 181

———— desert embraces fair renown, *Young* 3 : 163

———— stations tumult, but not bliss create, *Young* 1 : 85

———— worth is elevated place, *Young* 2 : 141

Hill (Aaron), verses to, *Sav.* 130, 140

———— on his Gideon, *Dyer* 137

Himself, let each man know, *King* 301

Hind and Panther, *Dry.* 2 : 8

Hip, *Som.* 193

———— who pines for sunshine, *Som.* 193

Hippolytus, story of, *Dry.* 6 : 192

———— son of the Amazon Camilla, *Smith* 96

———— his courage charms the man, *Smith* 96

———— his form the woman, *Smith* 96

———— obstinately good, *Smith* 110

Hippomolgians, fam'd for justice and longevity, *Pope il.* 2 : 3

———— from milk innoxious seek their food, *ib.* 2 : 3

Hippothous and Pyleus from Larissa come, *Pope il.* 1 : 101

Hirelings!

Hirelings ! your venal conscience I despise,   Gay 2 : 162

Historian's annals, acts of worthy men,   Gay 1 : 206

History, far-looking sage,   Mall. 172

Hoadly, for a period of a mile,   Pope 2 : 273

Hobbes, Cowley to,   2 : 28

———— and his writings,   Buck. 94

———— Atheistic opinions of,   Black. 117

Hobbinol, a burlesque,   Som. 95

———— on the pride and luxury of middling sort,   Som. 94

———— described,   Som. 97

———— young, character of,   Som. 98

———— bred up with Ganderetta,   Som. 98

———— Ganderetta king and queen of May,   Som. 99

———— lays the prize at Ganderetta's fret,   Som. 134

———— mutual triumph of,   Som. 135

———— dragg'd to prison,   Som. 139

———— triumphant,   Som. 125

Hockly i'th' hole,   Butl. 1 : 137

Hockstet seen, tumultuous passions roll,   Tick. 102

Holland, description of,   Butl. 2 : 350

———— streets of, described,   Gay 1 : 104

———— on leaving,   Aken. 209

———— where Mountain Zephyr never blew,   Aken. 209

———— countess,   Cow. 1 : 159

Holy-sister, character of,   Cow. 1 : 353

——— spirit, hail, supremely kind,   Parn. 156

———— raise my voice, and in my numbers shine, id. 157

——— wars, scenes of blood,   Butl. 2 : 295

Home, the resort of joy, of peace, and plenty, Thom. 1 : 109

———— of a wise man, all countries,   Butl. 2 : 63

                                                Homely

Homely features, to keep home,   *Milt.* 3 : 147

Homer, Sol's first-born,   *Cow.* 1 : 69

———— adamant compos'd his throne,   *Pope* 1 : 209

———— father of verse,   *Pope* 1 : 209

———— parent of song,   *Thom.* 1 : 171

———— princely bard !   *Swift* 2 : 317

———— matchless in his art,   *Dry.* 1 : 285

———— shines supreme in distant majesty,   *Pitt* 311

———— nodded oftener o'er the glass,   *Pitt* 387

———— repetitions in,   *Pitt* 346

———— too talkative and digressive,   *Dry.* 3 : 294

———— violent, impetuous, and full of fire,   *Dry.* 3 : 19

———— had the greatest invention,   *Pope il.* 1 : 1

———— poetical fire,   *Pope il.* 1 : 3

———— variety of distinct characters,   *Pope il.* 1 : 7

———— sublimity of sentiment,   *Pope il.* 1 : 9

———— father of poetical diction,   *Pope il.* 1 : 11

———— affects compound epithets,   *Pope il.* 1 : 11

———— versification harmonious,   *Pope il.* 1 : 12

———— similes like pictures,   *Pope il.* 1 : 17

———— praised for keeping a good table,   *Som.* 125

———— hymn of, to Venus,   *Cong.* 177

———— first Iliad, translated,   *Dry.* 4 : 237

———— imitation of,   *Yal.* 399

———— translations from,   *Dry.* 4 : 238

———— be your study and delight,   *Pope* 1 : 96

———— and Nature are the same,   *Pope* 1 : 97

———— own'd with pride he was in Britain born,   *Pitt* 272

Homicide of names,   *Dry.* 2 : 61

Homicides of Warwick-lane,   *Garth* 27

Homely,

Homily, in each deed,   Cow. 1 : 80

Honeſt man, ſimple of heart,   Phil. 58

———— ſtudious of virtue,   Phil. 59

———— is the nobleſt work of God,   Pope 2 : 78

Honeſty conſiſts in meaning well,   Rowe L. 402

———— way to,   Den. 89

———— plain is her look,   Hughes 206

———— juſt alike to friends and foes,   Hughes 206

———— thrice beauteous !   Lanſ. 184

———— is often in the wrong,   Rowe L. 351

———— when ſtubborn rules her zealots puſh,   Rowe L. 351

Honiton, where lace induſtrious laſſes weave,   Gay 1 : 169

Honour,   Cow. 1 : 313

———— a fragment,   Prior 2 : 256

———— honeſt fame,   Prior 2 : 256

———— plac'd in probity alone,   Garth 96

———— from good deeds alone,   Cow. 1 : 75

———— of adamantine proof,   Thom. 2 : 169

———— is the informing ſpirit of the ſoul,   Swift 1 : 175

———— anſwers faith in things divine,   Swift 1 : 175

———— comprehends all the virtues,   Swift 1 : 176

———— what it is not,   Swift 1 : 176

———— as my life, I prize,   Gay 2 : 122

———— is of man,   Dry. 3 : 124

———— made ſincere,   Mall. 192

———— man of ſtrict, undaunted,   Hal. 224

———— ſpark of celeſtial fire,   Hal. 225

———— treaſure of a generous breaſt,   Hal. 225

———— fair, godlike acts inſpires,   Hughes 205

———— the more obſtructed, ſtronger ſhines,   Sav. 29

     Honour

Honour on yourself depends,   *Gay* 2 : 168.

———— noble confidence,   *Roch.* 291.

———— ye gods! or let me gain or give,   *Pope ih.* 2 : 181.

———— like glassy bubble,   *Butl.* 1 : 203.

———— is but a word,   *Butl.* 1 : 204.

———— is an airy bubble,   *Hughes* 177

———— the hero's tyrant,   *Garth* 46

———— lives on air,   *Garth.* 47

———— an idle name,   *Gru.* 2 : 100

———— barter for estate,   *Prior* 1 : 155

———— hurt, is wont to rage,   *Butl.* 1 : 163.

———— lost, it is a relief to die,   *Garth.* 75.

———— is a lease for lives,   *Butl.* 1 : 138.

———— truckle-bed of,   *Butl.* 1 : 138.

———— and shame from no condition rise,   *Pope* 2 : 76.

———— like a widow won,   *Butl* 1 : 46.

———— is a sacred tie,   *Add.* 291.

———— aids and strengthens virtue,   *Add.* 291.

———— imitates her actions, where she is not,   *Add.* 291.

Honour's the noblest chace,   *Lanf.* 256

———— temple, door through virtue,   *Butl.* 1 : 133

Honours make the face of virtue fair,   *Young* 3 : 162

———— if true, from seeds of merit grow,   *Sav.* 162

———— of the butt and laurel,   *Pope* 3 : 100

———— soaring to, like Icarus fate,   *Cow.* 1 : 50

Hook or crook, to carry by,   *Butl.* 2 : 47

Hope,   *Shen.* 154

———— against,   *Cow.* 1 : 274

———— for,   *Cow.* 1 : 275

———— the last thing that in us dies,   *Buck.* 19

Hope, fond inmate of the human mind,   *Weft* 215

——— kindlieft inmate of youthful breaft,   *Aken.* 127

——— th' unhappy's laft referve,   *Som.* 65

——— frefh-blooming, daughter of the fky,   *Pope* 1 : 193

——— revives my foul,   *Parn.* 225

——— conceived from defpair,   *Milt.* 1 : 199

——— tempts belief,   *Milt.* 3 : 58

——— kind flatterer,   *Sav.* 100

——— the glad ray, glanc'd from eternal good,   *Thom.* 2 : 23

——— that life enlivens, and exalts its power,   *Thom.* 2 : 23

——— is but the dream of thofe that wake,   *Prior* 2 : 169

——— béguiling,   *Hughes* 171

——— like the moon and ocean fmiling,   *Hughes* 171

——— deferr'd has made me fick,   *Parn.* 199

——— fair-ey'd,   *Parn.* 227

——— enchanted fmil'd,   *Collins* 271

——— high-minded,   *Thom.* 2 : 61

——— immortal, that fole anchor,   *Young* 2 : 221

——— travels through, nor quits us when we die,   *Pope* 2 : 52

——— fuftains the human heart,   *Mall.* 276

——— loft in joy,   *Prior* 2 : 29

——— in darknefs,   *Watts* 155

——— may fome boundlefs future blifs embrace,   *Hughes* 195

——— but what, or when, or how, or where, mazes all, *id.* 195

——— falfe,   *Wall.* 67

——— enlarges the profpect,   *Yal.* 364

——— relieves the miferable mind,   *Rowe L.* 82

——— how vain, and how vexatious thought,   *Prior* 2 : 183

——— too long, with vain delufion fled,   *Pope od.* 2 : 46

——— in love,   *Lytt.* 6

Hope,

Hope, in that word, peace and transport are return'd, *Lyt.* 8.

—— and jealousy in love, *Cow.* 1 : 59.

Hopes of an unknown state, |*Black.* 219.

—— are vain, that haughty mind imparts, *Pope il.* 2 : 37.

—— frail air, *Som.* 107

—— joys are vain, *Prior* 2 : 175

—— deceiv'd, from war's inconstant turns, *Rowe* 14

—— of vengeance triumph'd over love, *Tick.* 210.

—— numbers lost by, *Butl.* 3 : 336.

—— and fears give conscience all her power, *Young* 2 : 202.

—— and fears void of reason, *Dry.* 7 : 281

Hopton commended, *Cow.* 1 : 338

Horace, pedigree of and education, *Dry.* 7 : 175

—— style of, adapted to his subject, *Dry.* 7 : 176.

—— includes all the rules of morality, *Dry.* 7 : 181

———————————— and of conversation, *Dry.* 7 : 181.

—— delicacy of his turns, *Dry* 7 : 177

—— choice of words, *Dry.* 7 : 177.

—— more general in his instructions, *Dry.* 7 : 181

—— smil'd reproof, *Fent.* 307

—— and tickled with his sting, *Fent.* 307.

—— sportive caught the generous fire, *Pope* 2 : 16.

—— improves satire, *Dry.* 7 : 159.

—— the best master in laughing satire, *Young* 1 : 73

—— laughed at follies, { *Dry.* 1 : 273
{ *Dry.* 7 : 318
{ *Dry.* 7 : 182

—— salt of, insipid, *Dry.* 7 : 183

—— in his Satires a philosopher and critic, *Dry.* 5 : 81

—— wanting in pointedness of thought, *Dry.* 7 : 105.

Horace,

Horace, a court-satirist,   Dry. 7 : 195

———— excells in the comical satire,   Dry. 7 : 198

———— his the curious happiness of wit,   Mall. 164

———— best of masters, and examples too,   Buck. 72

———— that curious speaker,   Prior 2 : 43

———— writ as wild or sober maggots bit,   Prior 2 : 45

———— talks us into sense,   Pope 1 : 118

———— judg'd with coolness, though he sung with fire, ib. 119

———— touched the Lesbian lyre,   Fent. 238

———— happy, tun'd th' Ausonian lyre,   Pope 1 : 211

———— prizes his liberty,   Conv. 2 : 272

———— prefers his manor to a court,   Conv. 2 : 309

———— praise of a country life,   Conv. 2 : 315

———— advice to,   King 418

———— and Virgil, wit and learning shine,   Pom. 215

———— Book i. Ode i.   Broome 38

———— Book i. Ode v.   Milt. 3 : 166

———— Book i. Ode xii.   Pitt 229

———— Book i. Ode ii.   Pitt 231

———— Book i. Ode xix. paraphrased,   Cong. 44

———— Book ii. Ode xiv. imitated,   Cong. 45

———— Book i. Ode ix. imitated,   Cong. 48

———— Book i. Ode xiv.   Swift 2 : 4

———— Book i. Ode xxii.   Hughes 99

———— Book ii. Ode xvi.   Hughes 102

———— an allusion to, Book i. Ode xxii.   Hughes 212

———— Book ii. Ode i.   Swift 1 : 135

———— Book ii. Ode iii. paraphrased,   Pitt 261

———— Book iv. Ode iii.   Pitt 263

———— Book ii. Ode iv. imitated,   Rowe 39

Horace, Book iii. Ode xxi. imitated,   Rowe 441
—— Book iv. Ode ix.   Swift 1 : 158
—— Book iv. Ode ix. imitated,   Som. 180
—— Book ii. Ode iv.   Duke 95
—— Book ii. Ode viii.   Duke 96
—— Book iii. Ode ix.   Duke 97
—— Book iii. Ode ii.   Swift 1 : 152
—— Book iii. Ode iii.   Hughes 88
—— Book iv. Ode i. to Venus,   Rowe 45
—— Book i. Epistle iv. imitated,   Rowe 47
—— Book iv. Ode iv.   Lytt. 75
—— Book iv. Ode xix. imitated,   Swift 2 : 316
—— Epode vii.   Duke 125
—— imitated,   Cow. 1 : 123
—— ode, in imitation of,   Prior 1 : 49
—— translation from,   Hughes 203
—— imitation of,   Fall. 394
—— part of Book i. Sat. vi.   Swift 2 : 337
—— Epistle x. translated,   Som. 254
—— epistle of imitated,   King 198
—— Book i. Epistle iv. imitated,   Pitt 392
—— Book i. Epistle iv. imitated,   Pope 2 : 370
—— Book i. Epistle v.   Swift 1 : 140
—— Book i. Epistle 7.   Swift 1 : 84
—— Book ii. Sat. vi.   Swift 1 : 89
—— Book i. Epistle x. imitated,   Pitt 394
—— Book i. Epistle xviii. imitated,   Pitt 399
—— Book ii. Epistle xix. imitated,   Pitt 387
—— imitation of,   Walsh 358
—— imitations of,   Pope 2 : 170

Horace,

Horace, imitations of,   Pope 2 : 304

———— translation from,   Add. 100

———— translations from,   Dry. 4 : 323

Horn, riddle on,   Swift 1 : 310

Horn-book, in praise of,   Tick. 221

———— perfect centre of concordancy,   Tick. 223

———— ancient book, most venerable code,   Tick. 223

———— learning's first cradle,   Tick. 223

———— in all tongues the same,   Tick. 222

Hornet vengeful, foul all o'er,   Pope il. 2 : 158

———— bold son of air and heat,   Pope il. 2 : 158

Horoscope, described, and consulted,   Garth 33

———— faints away,   Garth 36

———— restored by Squirt,   Garth 36

Horror, tyrant of the throbbing breast,   Gray 359

Horse described,   Young 1 : 219

——— snuffs the battle from afar,   Broome 28

——— demands the fight, and rushes on the foe,   Broome 29

——— that, nobly wild, neighs on the hills,   Smith 97

——— fed on man's flesh,   Butl. 1 : 66

——— and the olive,   Parn. 97

Horses clad in mail,   Milt. 2 : 195

——— like Parthians,   Gay 1 : 121

——— breeding of,   Dry. 5 : 151

——— council of,   Gay 2 : 104

——— pride of man is our reproach,   Gay 2 : 104

——— we share the toil, and share the grain,   Gay 2 : 106

Horseshoe, each threshold's guard,   Gay 2 : 70

Horse-vaulter,   Pope il 2 : 92

Horte (Josiah), verses to,   Watts 265

Hosanna,

Hosanna, Watts 357
Hospirable gift bestow, Pope od. 34 237
————— 'tis what the happy to th' unhappy owe, id. ib. 3 : 237
————— 'tis what the gods require, Pope il. 3 : 237
Host, to count without, Butl. 1 : 101
Hottentots with guts and tripe deck them, Prior 2 : 63
Houghton, Swift 1 : 181
Hound, in scent and speed unrival'd, Som. 17
————— breathing death, Som. 17
————— and huntsman, Gay 2 : 106
Hounds, choice of, Som. 22
————— fit for chacing the otter, or stag, Som. 23
————— sizing of, Som. 22
————— seek out their own physic, Som. 20
————— season for breeding of, Som. 69
————— diseases of, Som. 74
————— sagacious power of, Dry. 2 : 28
Hour of death, in vain do mortals seek to know, A. Phil. 391
Hour-glass, carnal, Butl. 1 : 139
Hours guard the gates of heaven, Pope il. 1 : 182
————— mis-spent in trifling visits, Hughes 79
House blown-up, described, Gay 1 : 145
Houses on London-bridge, Cow. 2 : 197
Howard (Hon. Edward), Butler to, Butl. 2 : 197
————————————— Waller to, Wall. 179
————————————— Denham to, Den. 143
————————————— Sprat to, Sprat 162
————————————— Dorset to, Dorf. 187
Howard (Sir Robert), Dryden to, Dry. 2 : 117
Howard, Prior to, Prior 1 : 104

. Howe

Howe (John), verfes to,   *Watts* 294

—————— lady, lines written in her Ovid,   *Prior* 12 : 263

Hudibras,   *Butl.* 1 : 3

—————— gifted,   *Butl.* 1 : 17

—————— beard,   *Butl.* 1 : 18

—————— outward form of,   *Butl.* 1 : 18

—————— doublet and breeches of,   *Butl.* 1 : 20

—————— carried vittle in his hofe,   *Butl.* 1 : 21

—————— fword of,   *Butl.* 1 : 22

—————— dagger of,   *Butl.* 1 : 23

—————— holfters of,   *Butl.* 1 : 24

—————— horfe of, defcribed,   *Butl.* 1 : 24

—————— faddle of,   *Butl.* 1 : 24

—————— fpur of,   *Butl.* 1 : 25

—————— fquire of,   *Butl.* 1 : 26

—————— compared to Sir Samuel Luke,   *Butl.* 1 : 45

—————— thrown on bear from horfe,   *Butl.* 1 : 85

—————— laid in ftocks,   *Butl.* 1 : 135, 137

—————— cheered with ends of verfe,   *Butl.* 1 : 137

—————— fayings of philofophers, *Butl.* 1 : 157

—————— to his lady,   *Butl.* 2 : 111

—————— to Sidrophel,   *Butl.* 1 : 268

—————— 's elegy,   *Butl.* 2 : 352

—————— 's epitaph,   *Butl.* 2 : 357

—————— imitated,   *Hughes* 184

—————— and Milton reconcil'd,   *Som.* 230

—————— a Varronian fatire,   *Dry.* 7 : 208

Hue and cry,   *Hughes* 254

—————— of heaven purfue the guilty,   *Dry.* 3 : 148

Hues on hues, expreffion cannot paint,   *Thom.* 1 : 22

Hugger-mugger, to lurk in,   Book I 110

Hughes, poems of,   27

————— triumph of peace,   27

————— recommendatory poems on,   3

————— court of Neptune,   23

————— house of Naffau,   37

————— ode on the death of a friend,   55

————— Anacreon, ode 3,   56

————— Pyramus and Thifbe,   58

————— triumph of love,   63

————— the picture,   65

————— Barn elms,   67

————— Phœbe and Afteria,   68

————— fongs,   82, 106, 127, 181

————— to Octavia indifpofed,   72

————— beauty and mufic,   73

————— Cupid's review,   73

————— to a lady playing on the organ,   76

————— fonnet,   76

————— to a painter,   77

————— to the Author of fatal Friendſhip,   79

————— on divine poetry,   81

————— on a peacock,   83

————— on Lucinda's tea-table,   85

————— the march,   86

————— lines written in a lady's prayer-book,   87

————— on the fpring,   87

————— Horace, Book iii. Ode iii,   88

————— Greenwich Park,   93

————— to Molinda,   96

Hughes,

Hughes, letter to a friend in the country, . _Hughes_ 98

———— Horace, Book i. Ode xxii. 99

———— Book i. Ode xvi. 102

———— birth of the rose, 106

———— praises of heroic virtue, 124

———— under the print of Tom Britton, 125

———— Cantatas, 111, 126, 129, 136, 139, 153, 170

———— Cupid and Scarlati, 128

———— Paftora, 131

———— a pastoral mask, 132

———— fragments, 137, 199

———— Claudianus, 138

———— the soldier in love, 140

———— ode in praise of music, 142

———— Apollo and Daphne 147, 215

———— thought in a garden, 149

———— a wish, 151

———— an ode, 155

———— an epilogue, 160

———— lines written on a window at Greenhithe, 161

———— the toasters, 162

———— Tofts and Margaretta, 162

———— the wandering beauty, 163

———— dialogue, 164

———— Venus and Adonis, 168

———— beauty, an ode, 171

———— Myra, 173

———— Alexander's feast, 174

———— translations from Perfian verfes, 182

———— on Arqueanaffa of Colophos, 183

Hughes,

Hughes, on Fulvia, wife of Anthony,   *Hughes* 184

———— Hudibras imitated,   184

———— ode to the Creator of the world,   187

———— to Mr. Addison,   195

———— Advice to Mr. Pope,   197

———— to the memory of Milton,   198

———— to a lady,   198

———— Serenata,   200

———— Horatius,   203

———— on a collar for happy Gill,   204

———— character of lady Henrietta Cavendish Holles, 204

———— truth, honour, honesty,   205

———— hymn,   206

———— a monumental ode,   208

———— allusion to Horace, Book i. Ode xxii.   212

———— ode for the birth-day of the princess of Wales, 229

———— letter to lord chancellor Cowper,   235

———— ode to lord chancellor Cowper,   237

———— what is man,   239

———— Boileau,   240

———— image of pleasure,   244

———— ode in the park at Afted,   245

———— to Mr. Conftantine, on his painting,   249

———— to Urania,   250

———— fupplement to Milton's Il penferofo,   253

———— the hue and cry,   254

———— the patriot,   256

———— fcene in Oreftes,   258

———— on birth-day of lord chancellor Parker,   266

———— 14th Olympic of Pindar,   267

Hughes, the morning apparition,   *Hughes* 269

———— the fupplement,   271

———— the ecftacy,   276

———— 10th Book of Lucan's Pharfália,   285

Human good depends on human will,   *Dry.* 1 : 133

——— hope by crofs event deftroy'd,   *Prior* 2 :: 163

——— joys are feldom lafting,   *Fent.* 229

Human-kind, vain, fantaftic race !   *Swift* 2 : 257

————— thy various follies, who can trace, *Swift* 2 : 257

————— to learn the moral end of,   *Dry.* 7 : 331

——— life,   *Yal.* 359

——— mind, is wrapt in error,   *Weft* 173

——— blifs, is ever infecure,   *Wieft* 173

——— pride, with confutation ne'er comply'd, *Gay* 2 : 194

——— race, fons of forrow,   *Mall.* 274

————— heirs of tranfmitted labour,   *Mall.* 274

——— fcience, is uncertain guefs,   *Prior* 2 : 126

——— ftate, precarious terms of,   *Pitt* 215

——— things, fubject to decay,   *Dry.* 2 : 109

————— frail eftate of,   *Dry.* 1 : 312

——— virtue, from the Gods proceeds,   *Weft* 196

——— wifdom, to divine, is folly,   *Den.* 109

Humanity dwells with love,   *Mall.* 249

——— on piety is built,   *Young* 2 : 237

——— in him, feiz'd eternal youth,   *Young* 2 : 72

——— feiz'd in our name,   *Young* 2 : 72

Humble enquiry,   *Watts* 54

——— heart, the refidence of God,   *Young* 2 : 229

————— God's other feat,   *Young* 3 : 134

Humbled groan beneath the hand of Jove, *Pope od.* 3 : 238

Humbled all, and lead, ye great, the way,   *Pope od.* 3 : 67

Humblest victor, and the kindest king,   *Prior* 1 : 170

Hum-drum, to stand still,   *Butl.* 1 : 104

Humility, with charms serene, forbids vain pomp,   *Hughes* 275

Humour, undefinable,   *Swift* 1 : 159

———— is odd, grotesque, and wild,   *Swift* 1 : 159

———— gives delight,   *Swift* 1 : 159

———— known to Britain's isle alone,   *Collins* 269

———— the dull rogue's last shift,   *Young* 3 : 206

———— folly-painting,   *Thom.* 1 : 174

———— dominating makes dreams,   *Dry.* 3 : 144

———— is all,   *Buck.* 78

———— and fashions change each day,   *King* 312

———— and riches rarely meet,   *Fent.* 301

Humours different in different minds,   *Dry.* 1 : 288

Hundreds smart in Timon and in Balaam,   *Pope* 2 : 172

Hunger, address to,   *King* 142

———— sure attendant upon want,   *Phil.* 3

———— parent of arts,   *Som.* 341

———— life's enemy,   *Milt.* 2 : 173

———— is insolent, and will be fed,   *Pope od.* 3 : 195

———— pale, wastes the manly strength,   *Pope od.* 3 : 320

———— a seasoning,   *King* 220

———— will break through walls of stone,   *Fent.* 275

Hungry to supply with food,   *Pope od.* 4 : 74

———— multitudes obey no law,   *Rowe L.* 123

Hunt (Mrs. Arabella), singing,   *Cong.* 29

Hunting described,   *Thom.* 1 : 120

———— formed heroes for war,   *Som.* 4

———— conducive to health,   *Som.* 7

Hunting, sport of the brave and bold,   *Som.* 377

————— fragment of a poem on,   *Tick.* 140

————— Asiatic manner,   *Som.* 38

Hunting-song,   *Som.* 252

Huntingdon, epitaph on,   *Cong.* 65

————— ode to Francis earl of,   *Aken.* 239

————— descended from Edward III, *Aken.* 296

Hurricane described,   *Thom.* 1 : 77

Husband and wife,   *Prior* 2 : 222

————— his own cuckold, prologue to,   *Cong.* 87

Hushai, character of,   *Dry.* 1 : 155

Hyde, lord chancellor, to,   *Dry.* 1 : 35

————— lady Catharine,   *Prior* 2 : 228

————————— Venus is,   *Lanf.* 145

————————— in the small-pox,   *Lanf.* 147

————————— sitting for her picture,   *Lanf.* 155

Hyde-park for pleasure and for beauty fam'd,   *Hughes* 74

Hydropsy, soft-swoln and pale,   *Thom.* 1 : 224

Hyena, fellest of the fell,   *Thom.* 1 : 75

Hymen, source of every social tye,   *Pope* 1 : 84

Hymen's blessings last for ever,   *Hughes* 135

Hymettus, a mountain near Athens,   *Thom.* 2 : 39

Hymn, $\begin{cases} Hughes & 206 \\ Thom. & 1 : 191 \end{cases}$

————— to Father and Son,   *Milt.* 1 : 83, 84, 85

Hyperbole the bounds of truth exceeds,   *Pitt* 365

Hyperboles come short of self-conceit,   *Gay* 2 : 59

————————— daring, yet by rules control'd,   *Lanf.* 232

Hypochondria, moping here did sit,   *Thom.* 1 : 224

————————— mother of Spleen,   *Thom.* 1 : 224

Hypochondria,

Hypochondria, her humour ever wavering, *Thom.* 1 : 274.

Hypocrisy cloaths words and looks with innocence, *Gay* 2 : 267

———————— with frown severe, *Swift* 2 : 75

———————— we join to pride, *Prior* 2 : 84

———————— visible to God alone, *Milt.* 1 : 96

———————— soft-smiling and demure, *Dry.* 3 : 95

———————— of wickedness, *Butl.* 2 : 231

———————— the Saints' bell, *Butl.* 1 : 316

———————— succeeded by licentiousness, *Butl.* 2 : 230

———————— propagates a church, *Butl.* 2 : 330

Hypocrite, in pension with his conscience, *Butl.* 2 : 288

Hypocritical Non-conformist, *Butl.* 2 : 286

I.

I, the little hero of each tale, *Young* 1 : 81

Jabberers, dialects of, *Butl.* 2 : 10

Jabesh-Gilead, distress of, *Cow.* 2 : 185

———————— delivered by Saul, *Cow.* 2 : 186

Jack, the skilful bowler's guide, *Som.* 198

Jackal, leopard, and other beasts, *Gay* 2 : 158

Jacob goes down to Egypt, *Milt.* 2 : 124

———— his posterity enthraled, *Milt.* 2 : 124

———————— delivered therefrom, *Milt.* 2 : 124

Jacob (Giles), the scourge of Grammar, *Pope* 3 : 183

———— blunderbuss of law, *Pope* 3 : 183

Jael, inhospitable guile of, *Milt.* 3 : 40

Jail-delivery, set free by, *Butl.* 1 : 183

I am that I am, *Prior* 1 : 19

I am, thy name, existence all thy own, *Young* 3 : 54

Jamaica,

Jamaica conquered under Cromwell,   *Cow.* 2 : 246

Iambics appropriated to stage,   *Rosc.* 262

James, heaven's favourite, first Britannic king,   *Phil.* 82

James I. lost his people's love,   *Thom.* 2 : 113

James II. character of,   { *Dry.* 1 : 182 / *Duke* 122

———————— bigot king,   *Thom.* 2 : 118

Jane Shore, epilogue to,   *Pope* 1 : 162

January and May,   *Pope* 1 : 227

Iapis, the physician,   *Dry.* 7 : 66

Jargon of the schools is but noisy nonsense,   *Pom.* 340

————————— confounds, not enlightens,   *Pom.* 340

Jason leads to Colchos magic land,   *West* 227

———— author of unutterable woes,   *Broome* 156

———— Hasard, motto for,   *Swift* 1 : 164

Jaundiced eye, all looks yellow to,   *Pope* 1 : 114

Iberia, how sunk among the nations now,   *Rowe* 9

———— bold in defence of liberty she stood,   *Rowe* 9

Icarus' fate, like soaring to honours,   *Cow.* 1 : 51

Icelos, what,   *Dry.* 4 : 63

Ichneumon clears the teeth of crocodile,   *King* 173

Ichor, blood of gods,   *Pope il.* 1 : 168

Ida, fount-full hill,   *Pope il.* 2 : 221

———— fair nurse of fountains and of game,   *Pope il.* 1 : 241

———— mother of savages,   *Pope il.* 2 : 51

———— resounding with a hundred rills,   *Pope il.* 2 : 51

———— water'd with descending floods,   *Pope il.* 2 : 294

———— yields wood for Patroclus' pyre,   *Pope il.* 2 : 294

Ideas in the divine mind,   *Aken.* 15

———————— origin of every pleasing quality,   *Aken.* 15

Ideas,

Ideas, clad in honest prose, I prize,   *Fent.* 308

Idleness, lewd nurse of villains,   *Thom.* 2 : 152

———— ill consequences of,   *Dyer* 89

———— and mischief,   *Watts* 348

———— reproach of,   *Dry.* 7 : 327

Idol is nothing in the world,   *Cow.* 2 : 246

Idolatry, origin of,   *Milt.* 2 : 123

———— put down,   *Cow.* 2 : 126

Idomen, lance-fam'd of Crete,   *Pope il.* 2 : 12

Idomeneus in eighty-ships commands the Cretans, *Pope il.* 1 : 93

Jealous, waspish, wrong-head, rhyming race,   *Pope* 2 : 246

———— men on their own crimes reflect,   *Pope* 1 : 247

———— learn from thence their ladies to suspect, *ib.* 1 : 247

———— you, not your wife unkind,   *Pope* 1 : 254

———— of air, to air I yield my breath,   *Cong.* 140

Jealousy,   { *Swift* 1 : 264
                      { *Walsh* 383

———— cure of,   *Walsh* 316

———— force of,   *Yald.* 389

———— power of,   *Milt* 3 : 33

———— love raised to extreme,   *Roch.* 293

———— rage of, fires the soul,   *Dry.* 3 : 71

———— inly gnaws the secret heart,   *Gray* 332

———— jaundice in the lover's eye,   *Lanf.* 223

———— the jaundice of the soul,   *Dry.* 2 : 55

———— the lover's hell,   *Milt.* 1 : 154

———— of other ills the worst,   *Lanf.* 174

———— molests the joys of love,   *Lytt.* 10

———— blasts all love's paradise,   *Thom.* 1 : 39

———— to nought was fix'd,   *Collins* 272

Jealoufy, cruel as death,   *Broome* 138

———— infatiate as the grave,   *Broome* 138

———— from excefs of love,   *King* 334

———— a grincam of the mind,   *Butl.* 1 : 298

———— and hope in love,   *Cow.* 1 : 59

———— fatal to Athens and Sparta,   *Thom.* 2 : 50

Jebufites, inhabitants of Jebus,   *Dry.* 1 : 128

———— religion of,   *Dry.* 1 : 129

Jemmy Dawfon,   *Shen.* 149

Jericho, city of palms,   *Milt.* 2 : 168

Ierne, renown'd for valour, policy, and arts,   *Swift* 2 : 7

———————— for knowledge human and divine, *Swift* 2 : 10

Jervas, epiftle to,   *Pope* 2 : 332

Jerufalem deftroyed,   *Cow.* 2 : 127

Jeft, teem'd with many a dead-born,   *Pope od.* 4 : 172

———— in fcorn hits home,   *Roch.* 337

Jefting fuits ill with pain,   *Dry.* 3 : 64

———————— with faith broken,   *Dry.* 3 : 64

———————— with friendfhip betray'd,   *Dry.* 3 : 64

Jefu, Lord of life,   *Parn.* 248

———— change my fenfe of forrow for fin to joy,   *Parn.* 248

———— what needs my blood, fince thine will do ?   *Parn.* 249

———— thy death reftores my foul to life,   *Parn.* 249

———— thy forrow proves the cure of mine,   *Parn.* 249

———— Lord of mercy, Lord of love,   *Parn.* 250

Jefuits, founded by a foldier,   *Butl.* 2 : 74

———— write, who never lye,   *Prior* 2 : 63

Jefus, the only Saviour,   *Watts* 97

———— to thy wounds I fly,   *Watts* 111

———— wafh away my fin,   *Watts* 111

Jew

Jew of Venice, epilogue to,   Lanf. 216
Jewels, condenfed flame,-   Cow. 1 : 213
Jews, character of,   Dry 1 : 126
———— a murmuring generation,-   Dry. 1 : 173
———— who bow to fome myfterious name,   Rowe L. 111
Ignoble fpirits by revenge are known,   Pom. 278
Ignorance, characters of,   Butl. 2 : 322
———————— makes men admire,.   Cong. 54
———————— devotion,   Butl. 1 : 113.
———————— devotion's dam,.   Den. 106
———————— overfpreads Europe,   Den. 106
———————— where blifs,.'tis folly to be wife, .   Gray 334
———————— our comfort flows from,   Prior 1 : 47
———————— and Vice in concert foul agree,   Thom. 2 : 165
Jig, Dick could neatly dance,   Swift 2 : 92
Jilts rul'd the ftate,   Pope 1 : 113
Ilerda crown'd the fummit of a mountain, .   Rowe L. 161
Iliad, defign of, .   Prior 2 : 93
—— fable of,   Pope od. 3 : 3
—— action of, .   Pope od. 3 : 18
—— firft book of,   Tick. 165
—— part of tenth tranflated,.   Broome 68
—— eleventh, part of tranflated, .   Broome. 107
Ilion, city of many-languag'd men,   Pope il. 2 : 225
———— warr'd nine years, fell the tenth, .   Pope od. 4 : 32
Ill, who thinks of fhould feel it firft, .   King 275
—— great is human force and wit in,   Cong. 15
—— with good attemper'd,   Aken. 193
—— partial, is univerfal good,   Pope 2 : 73
—— the gay fports with troubled hearts agree, Pope od. 3 : 208

I.. choice enfures ill fate,   Toung 3 : 68
—— cuftoms rife to habits,   Dry. 4 : 156
—— habits become exalted vice,   Dry. 4 : 156
—— nat re, like an ancient maid,   Pope 1 : 145
—— news goes faft,   Prior 1 : 109
Ills difcreetly yield to, and patiently endure,   Som. 276
—— we wifh for, when we wifh to live,   Toung 3 : 15
—— many, to ftricteft juftice belong,   Rowe L. 351
—— forefeen, the prefent blifs deftroy,   Prior 1 : 71
—— all built on life, that fundamental ill,   Prior 2 : 173
—— no degree of, for all are worft,   Pem. 281
—— deferving fhun, and learn to bear,   Som. 21
—— from our paffions flow,   Lytt. 38
Il Penferofo,   Milt. 3 : 106
——————— of Milton, fupplement to,   Hughes 253
Ilva renowned for fteel,   Dry. 6 : 278
Ilyffus, a river running to the Eaft of Athens,   Aken. 89
—— weeps her filent fchools,   Dyer 12
Images, that raife blufhes, be flightly touch'd,   Pitt 356
—— as Æneas and Dido may repair to the fame cave, ib. 356
Imagination, creative power,   Mall. 195
—— excurfive traveller,   Mall. 205
—— plies her dangerous art,   Pope 2 : 47
—— wit, fpirit, faculties, make it worfe, Pope 2 : 47
—— law of,   .   Aken. 72
—— well-form'd, advantages of,   Aken. 81
—— blends and divides images,   Aken. 74
—— infinitely varies,   Aken. 74
—— pleafure from,   Aken. 75
—— influence on morals,   Aken. 82, 95
                                                                 Imagination,

Imagination, pleasures of, _Aken._ 13
———— whence refult pleafures of, _Aken._ 17
———— fource of the imitative arts, _Aken._ 17
———— fine idea of, _Aken._ 16
———— connected with the moral faculty, _Aken._ 30
———— arts of, proftituted, _Aken._ 35
———— reunion of, under liberty, _Aken._ 36
———— conjoined with philofophy, _Aken._ 37
———— heightened by fenfe, _Aken._ 37
———— pleafures of depend on the difpofition, _Aken._ 37
Imitation, _Garth_ 156
———— what, _King_ 249
———— differs from copying, _Dry._ 5 : 271
———— of French, fatire on, _Butl._ 2 : 244
Immoderate grief, _Yald._ 351
———— valour fwells into a fault, _Add._ 276
Immortal fame is virtue's food, _King_ 274
Immortality defcribed, _Young_ 2 : 132
———— alone, the foul can comfort, _Young_ 2 : 149
———— a fubject the moft interefting, _Young_ 2 : 158
———— renders our prefent ftate intelligible, _Young_ 2 : 180
———— proved from man's paffions and powers, _id._ 2 : 165
———— from progrefs of reafon, _Young_ 2 : 165
———— from fear of death, _Young_ 2 : 166
———— from the nature of hope, _Young_ 2 : 166
———— from the nature of virtue, _Young_ 2 : 166
———— from love and knowledge, _Young_ 2 : 171
———— from the order of creation, _Young_ 2 : 172
———— from the nature of ambition, _id._ 2 : 174
———— from avarice, _Young_ 2 : 178
Immortality

Immortality proved from pleasure,   *Young* 2 : 179

Impatience makes thy tongue offend,   *Pope il.* 2 : 35

———————— makes our wishes earnest grow,   *Pom.* 280

————— blames and loaths a tedious feast,   *West* 200

Impenitent alone excluded from mercy,   *Milt.* 1 : 79

Imperfection call, what thou fancy'st such,   *Pope* 2 : 33

Impertinence, the scurvy of mankind,   *Swift* 1 : 11

———————— more than enough, is but,   *Pom.* 219

———————— round beauty swarms,   *Gay* 2 : 41

Impiety vexatious to the pious,   *Cow.* 2 : 362

Impious, self-judg'd, abandon'd, overcome,   *Hughes* 194

————— sigh, a long eternity of pain,   *Hughes* 194

————— tost in an ocean of desire without a shore,   *id.* 194

————— man! whose anger is his guide,   *Pope il.* 2 : 46

————— who glories in unutterable pride, *Pope il.* 2 : 46

————— world, contriv'd for knaves and fools,   *Lanf.* 284

Implicit faith, a virtue made,   *Pom.* 342

Impossibilities,   *Cow.* 1 : 297

Imposthumate with pride,   *Pope od.* 4 : 172

Impostors, when known, are undone,   *Butl.* 1 : 273

Impotence of faith! doubt you the gods,   *Pope od.* 4 : 163

Impromptu on a lady,   *Mall.* 178

Impudence, with front of brass,   *Swift* 2 : 75

———————— what no lawyer never lack'd,   *Swift* 1 : 102

———————— a fair pretence to all things,   *Butl.* 1 : 273

———————— to all things has pretence,   *Butl.* 2 : 319

Inanimate things, resemblance to properties of the,   *Brr.* 71

Inauguration of King William,   *Addi.* 69

lascivious rather than her brother wed,   *Hughes* 303

Inclination, how vain, when reason bears the sway, *Hughes* 223

                                                 Inclination

Inclination to learn without capacity, a drudgery, *Butl.* 2 : 269

Incomprehensible Three-One, *Fent.* 216

———————— the Infinite Unknown, *Watts* 59, 60

Inconstancy, *Cow.* 1 : 233

———————— bewailing my own, *Watts* 159

Inconstant, called, *Cow.* 1 : 267, 300

———————— a blacker fate than unfortunate, *Buck.* 26

———————— epilogue to, *Rowe* 30

Increase, *Cow.* 1 : 288

Incurable, { *Cow.* 1 : 312
{ *Prior* 2 : 252

Incurious Bencher, *Som.* 392

Indecency, as men, offends our pride, *Young* 1 : 74

———————— and taste, as judges, *Young* 1 : 74

Indefeasible hereditary right, *Thom.* 2 : 113

Independence, heaven's next best gift, *Thom.* 2 : 135

———————— life of life, *Thom.* 2 : 135

Independents, what, *Butl.* 2 : 8

Index-learning holds the eel of science by the tail, *Pope* 3 : 113

Indian fig, embowering endless, *Thom.* 1 : 66

Indian-muck to run at all, *Dry.* 2 : 93

——— ode, *King* 419

——— philosopher, *Watts* 230

Indifference affected, *Aken.* 198

———————— come, and heal my breast, *Lytt.* 13

———————— clad in wisdom's guise, *Swift* 2 : 263

———————— all fortitude of mind supplies, *Swift* 2 : 263

Indifferent poet worse than a bad, *Dry.* 7 : 107

Individuals die, ordained, *Dry.* 3 : 135

Indolence, ode to, *Shen.* 97

Indolence,

Indolence, that foul-enfeebling wizard,   *Thom.* 1 : 234

———— falfe enchanter,   *Thom.* 1 : 225

———— addrefs to the world,   *Thom.* 1 : 202

———— fteeps forrows in oblivion,   *Thom.* 1 : 203

———— o'erflows the heart with milky blood, *Thom.* 1 : 204

———— unknits the joints, and finews melts, *Thom.* 1 : 206

———— caftle of,   *Thom.* 1 : 199

———— nought around, but images of reft,   *Thom.* 1 : 200

———— clogs the mind,   *Gay* 2 : 177

Indulgence is fo human frailty due,   *Som.* 219

———— fuites with a noble mind,   *King* 288

Induftry, good effects of,   *Dyer* 90, 92

———— rough power,   *Thom.* 1 : 108

———— whom labour, fweat, and pain attend, *Thom.* 1 : 108

———— fupplies nature,   *But.* 2 : 262

———— fupports us all,   *Gay* 2 : 155

———— the various wants of man redreffes, *Gay* 2 : 155

———— inftance of, in the Romans,   *Young* 3 : 243

———— a full exertion of our powers,   *Young* 3 : 243

———— itfelf fubmits to death,   *Gay* 1 : 124

Inexorable death fhall level all,   *Pope* 2 : 253

Infallibility, where lodged,   *Dry.* 2 : 30

Infamy, dark as the grave, and fpacious as the fky, *Aken.* 342

———— the Dæmon o'er her vaffals reigns,   *Aken.* 343

———— of dead for benefit of living,   *Cow.* 2 : 220

Infected feems, all that th' infected fpy,   *Pope* 1 : 114

Infernal rivers defcribed,   *Mil.* 1 : 54

Infidel reclaimed,   *Young* 2 : 127

Infidels fet at odds heaven's attributes,   *Young* 2 : 70

———— with one excellence another wound,   *Young* 2 : 70

Infidels are Satan's hypocrites,   *Young* 2 : 207

Infinite names, how infinite they be,   *Watts* 88.

———— thy essence is a vast abyss,   *Watts* 88

Infinity, finite cannot reach,   *Dry.* 1 : 245

Infirmity, sad sister of Decay,   *Young* 3 : 87

Informers' words take not on trust,   *Gay* 2 : 75

Ingenuity, foul contrivances called,   *Buck.* 106

Ingenuous mind, sorrow of,   *Shen.* 74

Ingraffing, methods of,   *Dry.* 5 : 120

Ingratitude, the lot of worthiest deeds,   *Milt.* 3 : 16

———— a vice peculiar to man,   *Gay* 2 : 55

Inhabitants numerous and industrious, source of wealth, *Dyer* 99

Injured virtue, care of heaven,   *Yal.* 386

Injuries put up rather than resent,   *Pom.* 220

Injurious minds just answers but provoke,   *Pope od.* 4 : 107

Injustice fears truth,   *Den.* 99

Ink, riddle on,   *Swift* 1 : 320

Innocence betray'd with visard'd falsehood,   *Milt.* 3 : 146

———— no support, in the court of Scandal,   *Swift* 2 : 47

———— adamantine armour,   *Hughes* 100

———— no sense of danger can disturb,   *Hughes* 100

———— a defence only for patience,   *Butl.* 2 · 327

Innocent keep me, make others great,   *Lans.* 188

———— within, is arm'd without,   *Pope* 2 : 197

———— be this thy wall of brass,   *Pope* 2 : 197

———— ill,   *Cow.* 1 : 314

———— play,   *Watts* 362

Inordinate-affections, hell,   *Dry.* 5 : 89

Inquietudes love always brings,   *Pom.* 224

Inquisitive bridegroom,   *Som.* 346

Insatiable

Insatiable priest,   *Prior* 2 : 258

Inscription to memory of a justice,   *Shen.* 177

———— for Swift's monument, 1765,   *Swift* 2 : 378

———— epigram occasioned by it,   *Swift* 2 : 378

———— on the trophies of two victories,   *Akm.* 293

Inscriptions,
         Akm. 325—333
         Lut. 103, 104
         Shen. 297

Insect,   *Yal.* 374

Insects, the wandering nation of a summer's day,   *Pope* 1 : 85

———— hosts of a day, or nations of an hour,   *Pitt* 397

———— one of the plagues of Egypt,   *Cw.* 2 : 59

———— a feeble race, yet oft the sons of vengeance,   *Thom.* 1 : 7

———— destroyed by smoke,   .   *Thom.* 1 : 7

———————— by dust of pungent pepper,   *Thom.* 1 : 8

———————— drowned by water,   *Thom.* 1 : 8

Insheath'd the martial sword, he hung on high,   *Hughes* 20

Insolence ! indecently to rail without offence, *Pope od.* 4 : 117

Instalment,   *Young* 3 : 159

Instinct is complete,   *Young* 2 : 165

———— in animals, how sure !   *Dyer* 41

———— power of, in brutes,   *Som.* 28

———— in the roe-buck and hare,   *Som.* 28, 29

———— varies in different animals,   *Pope* 2 : 37

———— 'twixt that and reason, what a nice barrier, *Pope* 2 : 37

———— honest, comes a volunteer,   *Pope* 2 : 58

———— sure never to o'ershoot, but just to hit,   *Pope* 2 : 58

———— and reason, how can we divide,   *Prior* 2 : 109

 ferable wrong cries to the gods,   *Pope od.* 3 : 63

 " suits a prudent mind,   *Pope il.* 2 : 143

             Intellect,

Intellect, that sovereign power, *Young* 2 : 145

———— which sense and fancy summon to the bar, *id.* 2 : 145

———— forms art and science, *id.* 2 : 145

Intellectual rickets, what, *Butl.* 2 : 284

Intelligible world, what, *Butl.* 1 : 232

Intemperance, as a courted guest, destroys, *Gay* 2 : 112

———— Toil's scoffing foe, *Dyer* 89

Intemperate rage a wordy war began, *Pope od.* 3 : 54

Interest perverts the mind, *Gay* 2 : 158

———— a sly seducer, *Dry.* 2 : 66

———— a jaundice in the sight, *Dry.* 3 : 233

———— that waves on party-colour'd wings, *Pope* 3 : 253

———— and as she turns, the colours fall or rise, *Pope* 3 : 253

Internecine war, *Butl.* 1 : 40

Interrogations contribute much to sublime, *Young* 1 : 226

Intolerable woes the impious soul infest, *West* 152

Intuition, quick as, he snatch'd the truth, *Thom.* 2 : 168

Invective, the underwood of Satire, *Dry.* 7 : 145

Invention, the first virtue of an Epic poet, *Dry.* 3 : 20

———— distinguishes genius, *Pope il.* 1 : 1

———— to increase, search the Greeks, *Pitt* 357

Inventions, owing mostly to chance, *Butl.* 2 : 349

———— at first mean, *Butl.* 2 : 262

Invidious, *Shen.* 175

Invincible armada defeated, *Cow.* 1 : 326

Invious ways to prove, *Butl.* 1 : 114

Invitation extempore to Oxford, *Prior* 2 : 4

Invitation to drink, *Cow.* 1 : 109

Inundation described, *Thom.* 1 : 118

Inward man and outward, at odds, *Butl.* 1 : 193

Io turned to a heifer,   Dry. 3,: 323

Joan cudgels Ned,   Swift 1 : 280

Job, perseverance of,   Milt. 2 : 148

— paraphrase of part of,   Young 1 : 211

— happy state,   Young 1 : 211

— misfortunes of,   Young 1 : 211

— Author of,   Young 1 : 225

— chap. iii. of,   Pitt 252

— curs'd his birth,   Pitt 252

— heir of affliction, and son of woe,   Pitt 254

— chap. xxv. paraphrased,   Pitt 225

— part of, paraphrased,   Broome 23

John, Christ's harbinger,   Milt. 2 : 145

— baptism of,   Milt. 2 : 145

Iolaus, restor'd to youth,   Gay 1 : 329

Jonah,   Parn. 220

— would'st thou fly thy God ?   Parn. 220

— sleeper, rise and pray,   Parn. 221

— Lot falls on,   Parn. 221

— sign of the son of man,   Parn. 226

Jonas, character of,   Dry. 1 : 144

Jonathan described,   Cow. 2 : 187

— compared to an eagle,   Crw. 2 : 189

— kills king of Ammonites,   Cow. 2 : 190

— condemned to die,   Cow. 2 : 205

— saved by the people,   Cow. 2 : 207

— friendship for David,   Cow. 2 : 155

— my friend, my brother,   Som. 206

— each youthful charm bloom'd on thy face,   Som. 206

— how wonderful his love !   Som. 206

                                                         Jonathan

Jonathan defeats the Philiftins, *Cow.* 2 : 194, 198

Jones (Mrs.), epitaph on, *Sav.* 182

—— a neighbour's woe or welfare was her own, *Sav.* 182

Ionian waves truft rather than woman's rage, *Smith* 116

Ionic fchool, founded by Thales, *Black.* 10

—— divided into fects, *Black.* 10

Jonfon, *Wall.* 104

—— nature loft in art, *Collins* 276

—— pleafed by ftrength of judgment, *Dry.* 2 : 138

—— affected a monopoly of his learning, *Dry.* 7 : 103

—— fparing in his panegyric of Shakfpeare, *Dry.* 7 : 105

—— debafed his plays with farce, *Dry.* 1 : 288

—— art predominates in, *Den.* 55

Jordan, death of, *Cow.* 1 : 102

—— commended, *Cow.* 1 : 103

Jotham, character of, *Dry.* 1 : 155

Jothran, character of, *Dry.* 188

Jove, what theme more proper to be fung, *Pitt* 195

—— give wealth and virtue, and indulge our prayers, *Pitt* 199

—— the great, eternal king, *Pitt* 199

—— royal, province is the care of kings, *Pitt* 198

—— who fo good ? *Pope il.* 2 : 339

—— firft and greateft, *Pope il.* 2 : 339

—— all-good, all-wife, and all-furviving, *Pope il.* 2 : 204

—— high will of, o'er-ruling all, *Pope il.* 2 : 204

—— unchang'd, immortal, fupremely bleft, *Pope od.* 3 : 108

—— the ftrong withers, and confounds the bold, *Pope il.* 2 : 143

—— at whofe nod, empires rife or fall, *Pope il.* 1 : 266

—— at whofe command, empires rife or fall, *Pope il.* 1 : 72

—— refiftlefs Lord of all, *Pope il.* 1 : 72

from, whose long extent is set and set, Psal 230

——— father's sceptre is vengeant, Psal 231

——— gives the wanderer on his way, Pope od. 3 : 192

——— both the stranger and the poor, Pope od. 4 : 25

——— whom mercy's works delight, Pope od. 4 : 33

——— kindly for the stranger on his way, Pope od. 3 : 198

——— to whom the stranger's cause belongs, Brodne 157

——— fire of the distress'd, Pope il. 1 : 248

——— Panomphæan, Pope il. 1 : 249

——— power above all powers, Pope od. 4 : 4

——— ever-wakeful eyes of, Pope il. 1 : 67

——— his teeming head brought Wit's fair goddess, Swift 2 : 132

——— for after-birth, a footer kin, the critic vermin, id. 2 : 132

——— all-wife disposer of the fates of men, Pope il. 2 : 83

——— cuts short the views of poor, designing man, id. 182

——— guides each arrow, by what hand soever thrown, ib. 160

——— himself It has on the past no power, Pope il. 2 : 43

——— tempers the fates of human race, Pope od. 3 : 116

——— desires alternate our good or ill, Pope od. 3 : 116

——— the fates restrain, Gay 1 : 331

——— thou endues the soul with worth, Pope il. 2 : 222

——— lover of power and might, Pope il. 2 : 222

——— all honour courage gives or takes away, Pope il. 2 : 222

——— have er god, or wretchedness banished exercised mind, id. 33

——— after its done care use, Gay 2 : 33

——— you have to meet your use, Gay 2 : 33

——— have redeem the wretched life, Pope 2 : 250

——— on love I go haven, Pope 2 : 250

——— whenever a daughter gift, Pope 2 : 322

——— such with love or the way, Swift 3 : 324

Joy, none shall last, by fate's decree,   *Gay* 1 : 324

—— sweet-healing, smarts of evils destroys,   *A. Phil.* 390

——— innocent of thought,   *Pope* 3 : 197

——— the bubble, still laughs in Folly's cup,   *Pope* 2 : 83

——— latter end is woe,   *Dry.* 3 : 155

——— unbottom'd in reflection, cannot stand,   *Young* 2 : 140

——— the daughter of Severity,   *Young* 2 : 140

——— not for the future lose the present,   *Hughes* 243

——— still sought, can never be attain'd,   *Prior* 2 : 102

——— extatic trial,   *Collins* 173

——— by minutes, but by years we mourn,   *Pom.* 209

——— or curse, not present good or ill,   *Pope* 2 : 55

————————— but views of better or of worse, *Pope* 2 : 5

——— discord and jars are,   *Tick.* 1, 4

——— to my heart, my wishes are my own,   *Aken.* 348

Joyful to live, not unwilling to die,   *Prior* 2 : 214

————————— yet not afraid to die,   *Prior* 1 : 110

Joys below how frail !   *Som.* 366

———— dazzling meteors, flash and show,   *Som.* 366

——— present, sweeter for past pain,   *Lansd.* 10

——— ever young, unmix'd with pain or fear, *Pope od.* 3 : 190

——— fill the wide circle of th' eternal year, *Pope od.* 3 : 190

——— highest here, small cordials to support in pain, *Young* 2 : 132

——— there, beyond conception, as desert,   *Young* 2 : 134

——— how short a space endure,   *Pope* 1 : 243

——— how great, how soon they fled,   *Prior* 1 : 16

——— how insincere all,   *Dry.* 1 : 96

——— in length of wishes lost,   *Pope* 1 : 300

——— fading bought with lasting woes,   *Milt.* 2 : 69

——— of friendship, poetry, and love,   *Hughes* 99

T 3   Joys

Joys and woes from God's own hand defcend, *Pope od.* 4 : 39

Iphis and Ianthe, *Dry.* 4 : 24

—— and Anaxarete, ftory of, *Garth* 146

Ire pernicious, learn betimes to curb, *Pope il.* 1 : 288

Iris, goddefs of the fhowery bow, *Pope il.* 2 : 71

—— meffenger of Jove, *Pope il.* 2 : 71

—— the various-colour'd maid, *Pope il.* 1 : 255

Irifh bifhops, *Swift* 2 : 253

—— club, *Swift* 2 : 207

—— feaft, defcription of, *Swift* 1 : 192

Iron age, *Dry.* 4 : 303

—— fleep, *Dry.* 7 : 62

Iron-fleet of arrowy fhower, *Gray* 362

Irony, the meaning contrary to the words, *Pitt* 366

Irrefolution, what like, *Dry.* 6 : 196

Irus infults Ulyffes, *Pope od.* 4 : 117

—— worfted by Ulyffes, *Pope od.* 4 : 121

Ifaac, facrifice of, *Cow.* 2 : 114

Ifabel, fhe-wolf of France, *Gray* 354

Ifabella, playing on the lute, *Wall.* 83

Ifaiah, chap. xxxiv. *Cow.* 2 : 51

—— paraphrafed, c. xiv. *Fent.* 218

Ifara winding through many a mead, *Rowe L.* 65

Ifhban, character of, *Dry.* 1 : 170

Ifis and her hufband Tame, *Prior* 1 : 219

Ifmenus leaves Bœotia's plain, *Weft* 223

Ifraelites reject God's reign, *Cow.* 2 : 192

Iffachar, ears of the tribe of, *Butl.* 1 : 269

Italian, aptnefs and facility of, for notes, *Hughes* 112

Italians, authors of falfe glittering poetry, *Dry.* 1 : 262

Italic

Italic school, founded by Pythagoras, *Black.* 12

Italy, praise of, *Dry.* 5 : 123

—— ancient and modern, compared, *Thom.* 2 : 17

—— proud oppression reigns, *Add.* 44

Ithaca, brown with pendent woods, *Pope od.* 3 : 84

Ithacians under Eupithes rise against Ulysses, *Pope od.* 4 : 252

Juba, extent of his kingdom, *Rowe L.* 196

—— defeats Curio, *Rowe L.* 201

Jubal, author of music, *Yal.* 388

Jubilee, a spiritual fair, *Butl.* 2 : 343

Judas, character of, *Dry.* 1 : 171

—— gone to his own place, *Swift* 2 : 246

Judea weeps beneath her palm, *Pope* 2 : 145

Judge, qualities of, *Mall.* 290

—— will read with the spirit, the author writ, *Pope* 1 : 101

—— of ill, is still the lord of grace, *Parn.* 227

Judges brib'd, betray the righteous cause, *Pope il.* 2 : 114

Judgment, inconstancy of, *Pope* 1 : 108

—————— betwixt sense and nonsense changing, *Pope* 1 : 108

—————— giving law to fancy strong, *Young* 3 : 224

—————— keeps fancy in awe, *Den.* 56

—————— an overpoise to imagination, *Dry.* 5 : 81

—————— weak, and passion strong, *Swift* 2 : 188

—————— tally to wit, *Butl.* 2 : 26

—————— ground of writing well, *Rosc.* 270

—————— day of, { *Watts* 102 { *Swift* 2 : 339

—————— for, sons of men prepare, *Young* 1 : 25

Judgments divine, *Watts* 42

Juggler, sleight of, less understood, more admired, *Butl.* 1 : 223

Jugglers,

Jugglers,   *Gay* 2 : 101

———— to be avoided,   *Gay* 1 : 121

———— on superstition palm'd for saints,   *Sav.* 175

Juice that may try thy feeble feet,   *Phil.* 35

Julia dead, kindred-ties were broke,   *Rowe L.* 48

Julian, Dryden to,   *Dry.* 2 : 157

Julius Cæsar, prologue to,   *Buck.* 111

———— choruses in,   *Buck.* 112

Iülus, head of, in a lambent flame,   *Dry.* 5 : 381

June, cry of,   *Gay* 1 : 125

Juno, white-arm'd goddess,   *Pope il.* 2 : 68

——— Jove's sister-wife, and empress of the gods,   *Pitt* 274

——— heaven's awful empress,   *Pope il.* 1 : 254

——— headstrong and imperious still,   *Pope il.* 1 : 255

——— impotent of rage,   *Pope il.* 1 : 258

———————— of passion,   *Pope il.* 1 : 128

——— consort of the thundering Jove,   *Pope il.* 1 : 130

——— car of, described,   *Pope il.* 1 : 180

——— opposes Æneas' match,   *Dry.* 6 : 170

——— rouses Alecto to revenge her,   *Dry.* 6 : 172

Juno's hate to Thebes,   *Pope* 1 : 274

Jupiter threatens with Tartarus any god aiding either side, *ib.* 239

——— in golden scales explored the fate of Greece and Troy, 242

——— calls a council,   *Dry.* 6 : 269

——— forbids joining either party,   *Dry.* 6 : 269

——— Ammon, temple of,   *Rowe L.* 399

Juries packt,   *Butl.* 1 : 203

Just, name of, to prefer to great,   *Lanf.* 130

——— deceit opposed to unjust force,   *Cow.* 2 : 90

——— education forms the man,   *Gay* 2 : 181

4

Juſt or unjuſt, alike ſeem miſerable,   *Milt.* 3 : 39

—— to give applauſe where 'tis deſerv'd,   *Add.* 323

Juſtice, Denham of,   *Den.* 97

—————— queen of Virtues,   *Prior* 2 : 226

—————— is blind,   *Den.* 100

—————— ſword-bearer of,   *Butl.* 1 : 81

—————— painted blind,   *Butl.* 2 : 107

—————— deaf to perſuaſion,   *Lanſ.* 208

—————— to temptation blind,   *Lanſ.* 208

—————— loves truth,   *Den.* 99

—————— a ſtronger guard than laws,   *Lanſ.* 130

—————— fled,   *Dry.* 7 : 253

—————— winking at crimes,   *Butl.* 1 : 99

—————— ſhall triumph o'er oppreſſive rage,   *Fent.* 220

—————— ſuſpends her courſe,   *Rowe L.* 81

—————— is always ſure, though ſlow,   *Som.* 369

—————— o'er thy word and deed preſide,   *Rowe* 3

—————— gives way to force,   *Add.* 322

—————— rage and ſlaughter yield,   *Rowe L.* 170

—————— thrives moſt, when lawyers moſt repine,   *Sav.* 98

—————— and freedom on his conqueſts wait,   *Prior* 1 : 57

—————— makes the fine,   *Dry.* 1 : 248

Juſtification by faith,   *Milt.* 2 : 129

Juſts deſcribed,   *Dry.* 3 : 176

Juturna, ſiſter of Turnus,   *Dry.* 7 : 53

—————— made a Nais,   *Dry.* 7 : 53

—————— forewarn'd of Turnus' fate,   *Dry.* 7 : 54

—————— grieves for him,   *Dry.* 7 : 54

—————— laments Turnus,   *Dry.* 7 : 89

Juvenal, a noble fire appears in,   *Dry.* 1 : 274

Juvenal, more ardent eloquence inflames,   *Pope* 2 : 17

————— his numbers aw'd corrupted Rome,   *Pope* 2 : 17

————— swept audacious greatness to its doom,   *Pope* 2 : 17

————— is too luxuriant,   *Dry.* 7 : 183

————— thoughts of, elevated,   *Dry.* 7 : 183

————— expression sonorous and noble,   *Dry.* 7 : 183

————— verse more numerous,   *Dry.* 7 : 183

————— the greater poet in satire,   *Dry.* 7 : 186

————— is ever in a passion,   *Young* 1 : 73

————— lashes great vices,   *Dry.* 7 : 192

————— difficulty of chusing a meaning in,   *Dry.* 7 : 197

————— excels in the tragical satire,   *Dry.* 7 : 198

————— more limited in his instructions,   *Dry.* 7 : 181

————— sentences of, instructive,   *Dry.* 7 : 181

————— exhorts to particular virtues,   *Dry.* 7 : 182

————— of a vigorous wit,   *Dry.* 7 : 183

————— invective against the fair sex,   *Dry.* 7 : 249

————— Satire i.   *Dry.* 7 : 220

————— Satire iii.   *Dry.* 7 : 231

————— Satire v.   *Duke* 164

————— Satire vi.   *Dry.* 7 : 249

————— Satire x.   *Dry.* 7 : 281

————— Satire xi.   *Cong.* 68

————— Satire xvi.   *Dry.* 7 : 301

————— invective on the army,   *Dry.* 7 : 301

K

Keepers, who shall keep,   *Dry.* 7 : 267

Keil, the astronomer, epitaph on,   *Pitt* 304

————— who while on earth had rang'd the skies,   *Pitt* 304

Keil, now he enjoys thofe realms he could explore, *Pitt* 304

Kennel, fituation of, *Som.* 18

————— to be kept from offenfive fmells, *Som.* 19

————— to be open and airy, *Som.* 19

————— near water, *Som.* 19

————— near cool fhades, *Som.* 19

Kennet fwift, for filver eels renown'd, *Pope* 1 : 75

Kenfington Garden, *Tick.* 200

————————————— lov'd feat of royal Oberon, *Tick.* 202

————————————— facred to Britannia's monarch, *Tick.* 217

Kevan Bayl's new ballad, *Swift* 2 : 296

Keynton field, *Cow.* 1 : 340

Kidderminfter poetry, *Shen.* 169

Kids, young believers, *Parn.* 197

Kilda (St.) character of inhabitants, *Mall.* 232, 235

————— fituation of, *Mall.* 235

Killegrew, Waller to, *Wall.* 175

————— and Murrey, *Den.* 43

Kind, not in words alone, *Pope od.* 4 : 55

Kindnefs, charms of, *Roch.* 302

King, letters of, *King* 169, 226

——— art of cookery, 203

——— love, 253

——— ode of Malherbe, 336

——— furmetary, 337

——— Mully of Mountown, 347

——— Orpheus and Euridice, 352

——— Rufinus, 367

——— Britain's Palladium, 379

——— Mifcellany Poems, 388

King.

King, laſt billet, *King*	389
—— to Beaufort,	387
—— imitation of Petrarch,	390
—— Mad Lover,	393
—— Soldier's Wedding,	394
—— Old Cheeſe,	395
—— the Skillet,	397
—— Fiſherman,	399
—— Caſe of Conſcience,	401
—— the Conſtable,	402
—— Little Mouths,	403
—— Hold faſt below,	405
—— Beggar Woman,	406
—— the Veſtry,	408
—— the Monarch,	410
—— Juſt as you pleaſe,	412
—— Dreams,	414
—— art of making puddings,	415
—— to Carter,	421
—— advice to Horace,	418
—— Indian ode,	419
—— experience firſt, and then truſt,	421
—— Nero,	422
—— Ulyſſes and Tireſias,	424
—— Taſſo, tranſlation from,	425
—— Heſiod, tranſlation from,	426
—— Thame and Iſis,	426
—— Laughter how expreſſed,	426
—— Stumbling-block,	427
—— Garden-plot,	430
	King

King derived his wit from wine,   *Pitt* 387

King eternal and divine,   *Pitt* 235

—— whose power controls the war,   *Pitt* 238

—— infants' tongue shall speak thy praise,   *Pitt* 238

—— is to be good and just,   *Gay* 1 : 179

—— in mind !   *Pope od.* 3 : 292

—— a part of government,   *Dry.* 1 : 158

—— an earthly god,   *Prior* 2 : 161

—— a man condemn'd to bear the nation's care, *Prior* 2 : 175

—— nurs'd in flattery, and estrang'd from truth, *Prior* 2 : 175

—— how best formed,   *Milt.* 2 : 213

—— office of, in what consists,   *Milt.* 2 : 178

—— a Briton, who can govern well,   *Young* 3 : 155

—— who fittest to be,   *Cow.* 2 : 235

—— power of, employ'd against himself,   *Hal.* 228

—— can he bear a rival in his sway?   *Pope il.* 1 : 50

—— proclaim'd by horse-neigh,   *Butl.* 1 : 53

—— less illustrious than a saint,   *Broome* 41

—— his power of doing good,   *Sen.* 287

—— Waller to, on return,   *Wall.* 146, 196

—— verses to,   *Lans.* 129, 130

King William, on death of,   *A. Phil* 331

—— ode to,   { *Prior* 1 : 76
                              { *Young* 1 : 169

—— on return of, 1720,   *Pitt* 221

King's birth-day, song for,   *Rowe* 76

———————— 1718, ode for,   *Rowe* 82

Kingdom, on virtue alone can stand,   *Thom.* 2 : 134

—————— to a ship compare,   *Swift* 1 : 38

Kings can do no wrong,   *Dry.* 1 : 213 | 2 : 94

I N D E X

Kings blessing are bless'd,   *Som.* 287

—— long harden'd in the regal trade,   *Rowe L.* 349

—— by interest and by craft alone are sway'd, *Rowe L.* 349

—— be just, and sovereign power preside,   *Pope il.* 1 : 49

—— but play their part,   *Dry.* 3 : 129

—— officers in trust,   *Dry.* 1 : 151

—— and empires, for broken faith punish'd,   *Fent.* 289

—— minion-rid,   *Thom.* 2 : 108

—— are allow'd to feign the gout,   *Prior* 1 : 89

—— fight for kingdoms,   *Dry.* 3 : 87

—— by giving, give themselves away,   *Den.* 19

—— make subjects bold by oppression,   *Den.* 19

—— cannot reign, unless their subjects give, *Dry.* 2 : 156

—— subject to the Gods alone,   *Pope il.* 1 : 45

—— draw lustre from the robe of state, *Pope od.* 3 : 171

—— too tame, despicably good,   *Dry.* 2 : 104

Kit-Cat-Club, verses on,   *Garth* 113

Kitchen, handmaid to physic,   *King* 227

Kishon, river of renown,   *Parn.* 141

Kisses, translation,   *Fent.* 303

Knack of trades, living on the spoil,   *Dry.* 1 : 215

Knave, what is he without his tools,   *Gay* 2 : 125

—— the more, the more a fool,   *Pope* 2 : 78

—— and fool are their own libellers,   *Pope* 2 : 8

—— or fool should perish in each line,   *Young* 1 : 81

—— is a knave in every state,   *Pope* 2 : 163

—— is a fool,   *Young* 1 : 194

Knaves would starve, if fools agreed,   *Som* 275

—— my scorn, and coxcombs are my sport,   *Som.* 226

—— and fools are near of kin,   *Butl.* 2 : 10

         Kneller,

Kneller, Addison to,   *Add.* 212
—— — to,   *Cong.* 108
———— nature and art alike contend in,   *Cong.* 108
. ———— Dryden to,   *Dry.* 2 : 151
———— Tickell to,   *Tick.* 194
———— thee nature taught, nor art deny'd her aid, *Tick.* 195
———— live and die the monarch of thy art,   *Tick.* 195
———— only shews, what Celia was,   *Prior* 1 : 72
———— judgment and genius concur in,   *Cong.* 109
Knight, girt with sword and spur,   *Butl.* 1 : 80
———— of arts and industry,   *Thom.* 1 : 227
———————— atchievements,   *Thom.* 1 : 228
———————— settles in Britain,   *Thom.* 1 : 231
———— of the sable shield, letter to,   *Fent.* 243
Knights of the post,   *Butl.* 1 : 31
Knight-errant, character of,   *Dry.* 5 : 239
———————— neither eat nor drink,   *Butl.* 1 : 21
Knitting-blossoms harden into fruit,   *Broome* 33
Knives always sever love,   *Gay* 1 : 65
Knobs, that grow on married brow,   *Butl.* 1 : 179
Knotted law, caught in, as in nets,   *Butl.* 1 : 224
Knotty points, which all discuss,   *Prior* 2 : 79
———————— but few can clear,   *Prior* 2 : 79
Know thyself, a rule from heaven sent,   *Cong.* 71
——— thy vain self,   *Pope il.* 1 : 177
——— we never can ourselves,   *Gay* 2 : 26
Knowledge,   *Prior* 2 : 101
———————— is as t ed,   *Milt.* 1 : 211
———————— is ourselves to know,   *Pope* 2 : 84
———————— true, hard   *Cong.* 64

Knowledge

Knowledge forbid, dangerous to purfue,   *Pom.* 271
——— may grieve, but fear diftracts the heart, *Pope od.* 4 : 228
——— how many griefs flow from ?   *Akin.* 236
——— but mere remembrance,   *Swift* 1 : 2
——— taught us, like Spaniards, to be proud and poor, *ib.* 3
——— aggravates a fault,   *Prior* 2 : 155
——— bought too high,   *Butl.* 2 : 270
——— defire of, natural,   *Butl.* 2 : 271
——— to grow above,   *Butl.* 2 : 235

END OF VOL. LVII.

John Dickinson

1786

I N D E X

TO THE

ENGLISH POETS.

VOLUME II.

Vol. LVIII.

INDEX

TO THE

ENGLISH POETS.

VOLUME THE SECOND.

L O N D O N;

PRINTED BY J. NICHOLS;

FOR C. BATHURST, J. BUCKLAND, W. STRAHAN, J. RIVING-
TON AND SONS, T. DAVIES, T. PAYNE, L. DAVIS, W. OWEN,
B. WHITE, S. CROWDER, T. CASLON, T. LONGMAN,
B. LAW, E. AND C. DILLY, J. DODSLEY, J. WILKIE,
J. ROBSON, J. JOHNSON, T. LOWNDES, T. BECKET,
G. ROBINSON, T. CADELL, J. NICHOLS, F. NEW-
BERY, T. EVANS, J. RIDLEY, R. BALDWIN,
G. NICOL, LEIGH AND SOTHEBY, J. BEW,
M. CONANT, J. MURRAY, W. FOX, J. BOWEN.

MDCCLXXX.

Brad. R. R 2
Gift
Albert Greene
1-15-1935

I N D E X

TO THE

ENGLISH POETS.

N. B. When the poet is in one volume only, the number de-
notes the page: when in more volumes than one, the first
number, separated by a colon, denotes the volume; the
second, the page of that volume.

L

LABOUR, great reason for,   *Thom.* 1 : 199

———— without it, loose life, unruly passions come, *ib.* 199

————————————— and diseases pale,   *ib.* 199

—————————— is the price of rest,   *A. Phil.* 367

—————————— must have rest at last,   *Pope* 1 : 240

—————————— and art will every aim atchieve, *Dyer* 63

Labours, first to the gods commend,   *Rowe* 6

Labyrinth of joy and woe, this world,   *Aken.* 162

———————— dark of human hearts,   *Young* 2 : 223

Lacedæmon, fam'd for the dance,   *Pope od.* 4 : 47

Lachæa, an isle oppos'd to the Cyclopean coast, *Pope od.* 3 : 231

———————— uninhabited, untill'd, unfown,   *Pope od.* 3 : 232

Lacteals receive the chyle,   *Black.* 194

Ladies, like variegated tulips, show,   *Pope* 2 : 107

———— fine by defect, and delicately weak,   *Pope* 2 : 107

Ladies, their happy spots the nice admirer take, *Pope* 2 : 107

———— with shame and decency at war, *Mall.* 312

———— into vice intrepid rush, *Mall.* 312

———— advice to, *Som.* 240

———— hardship upon, *Swift* 2 : 291

———— new simile for, by Sheridan, *Swift* 2 : 319

Ladle, *Prior* 1 : 148

Lady, to a fair, *Wall.* 125

———— Prior to, *Prior* 1 : 67

———— who made posies for rings, *Cow.* 1 : 114

———— in retirement, *Wall.* 103

———— who offers her looking-glass to Venus, *Prior* 1 : 126

———— singing, *Rowe* 67

———— sitting at her glass, *Fent* 225

———— reading art of love, *Fent* 226

———— who made a present of a silver pen, *Som.* 195

———— complaining of the Dean's stay in England, *Swift* 2 : 27

———— answer of, to Hudibras, *Butl.* 2 : 125

———— strange riddle of, *Butl.* 1 : 112

———— fond of fortune-telling, *Prior* 2 : 244

———— advice to, *Lytt.* 39

———— sincerity to bear, your merit, *Lytt.* 40

———— buried in marriage, *Shen.* 162

———— epistle to, *Gay* 1 : 159 210

———— China is the passion of her soul, *Gay* 1 : 210

———— epistle from, to a gentleman, *Tick.* 127

———— verses to, before marriage, *Tick.* 218

———— form'd by nature, and refin'd by art, *Tick.* 218

———— of quality, to, *Shen.* 101

———— who wanted heroic verses to be written on her, *Swift* 2 : 17.

Lady to, with paterns of flowers,   *Shen.* 108

—— and looking-glaſs, dialogue,   *Broome* 45

—— and waſp,   *Gay* 2 : 41

Lady's lamentation, ·   *Gay* 1 : 256

———————— and complaint, ·   *Swift* 2 : 60

—— looking-glaſs,   *Prior* 1 : 62

—— prayer-book, verſes in,   *Hughes* 87

Laertes kills Eupithes in battle,   *Pope od.* 4 : 255

—— faints at diſcovering Ulyſſes,   *Pope od.* 4 : 248

—— ſon of Arceſius,   *Pope od.* 4 : 255

Lahor, now fam'd for wool,   *Dyer* 69

—— Roe firſt open'd trade to,   *Dyer* 69

Laius' blood ſhed by the murdering ſon,   *Pope* 1 : 293

—— his bed violated,   *Pope* 1 : 293

Lake-reſounding frogs,   *Parn.* 39

L'Allegro,   *Milt.* 3 : 101

Lamb, renown'd for cutting corns,   *Swift* 2 : 294

Lambard, epiſtle to,   *Fent.* 306

Lambent dulneſs play'd around his face,   *Dry.* 2 : 113

Lambs, caſtration of,   *Dyer* 42

—— new-fallen, care of,   *Dyer* 44

—— with wolves ſhall graze the mead,   *Pope* 1 : 52

Lamentations to be ſhort and conciſe,   *Add.* 197

Lamenting or lamented, all our lot,   *Young* 2 : 31

Lamp, inſcription on,   *Prior* 2 : 196

—— of day is quench'd beneath the deep,   *Pope od.* 3 : 95

Lances into ſcythes ſhall bend,   *Pope* 1 : 51

Land none, but yields advantage,   *Phil.* 37

—— rejoicing, and a people bleſt,   *Pope od.* 3 : 227

Landau falls,   *Add.* 65

Lands of singing or of dancing slaves,   Pope 3 : 239
Landskip,   Shen. 118
Language to be well observed,   Dry. 1 : 266
————— pure, gives profit and delight,   Dry. 1 : 266
————— changing forbids immortality,   Wall. 171
Languages patch'd and py-ball'd,   Butl. 1 : 9
————— curse of Babylon,   Butl. 2 : 268
Lansdowne, poems of,   Lans. 125
————— verses by, at twelve years,   128
————— to the king,   129, 130
————— to Waller,   131
————— to Waller's memory,   132
————— on the queen's picture,   134
————— on the queen,   135
————— love,   135
————— progress of beauty,   136
————— on lady Hyde,   147, 155, 159, 161
————— to Myra,   148, 212
————— in praise of Myra,   153
————— verses in a garden,   156
————— to Daphne,   157
————— to a learned lady,   157
————— Thyrsis and Delia,   158
————— Apology,   160
————— Discovery,   166
————— Enchantment,   169
————— Vision,   175
————— Death,   180
————— verses by a lady,   182
————— answered,   183

Lansdowne, an imitation,   *Lanf.* 186
——————— Chloe,   189
——————— Corinna,   190
——————— Belinda,   191
——————— Clarinda,   192
——————— Cleora,   193
——————— Macro,   196
——————— Phyllis drinking,   196
——————— Celia,   197, 201
——————— Flavia,   198, 212
——————— Love,   198
——————— Women,   198
——————— Fancy,   198
——————— Liberality,   199
——————— verfes in Clarinda's prayer-book,   200
——————— Fulvia,   200
——————— to Dryden,   203
——————— on a caufe in the Houfe of Lords,   204
——————— on burning Granville,   210
——————— to Garth,   211
——————— verfes in a novel,   213
——————— Prologue,   213, 217, 220
——————— Epilogue,   215, 216, 218
——————— Peleus and Thetis,   221
——————— verfes on Hare,   228
——————— verfes on Bolton,   228
——————— Latin infcription,   229
——————— morning hymn,   229
——————— effay on unnatural flights,   231
——————— character of Wycherley,   235.

Lansdowne, Muse's last dying song,   237

———— verses to princess royal,   238

———— British enchanters,   243

———— epistle to,   *Young* 3 : 167

Lanx Satura, what,   *Dry.* 7 : 147

Laocoon, story of,   *Dry.* 5 : 359

———— and his two sons,   *Thom.* 2 : 87

Lap-dog, elegy on,   *Gay* 1 : 251

———— poor Shock is now no more,   *Gay* 1 : 251

Lapithæ and Centaurs, fray of,   *Dry.* 4 : 83

Lapland witches sell bottled air,   *Butl.* 1 : 202

Laplanders, character of,   *Thom.* 1 : 182

Lark, messenger of day,   *Dry.* 3 : 77

—— upsprings, shrill-voiced,   *Thom.* 1 : 23

—— the messenger of morn,   *Thom.* 1 : 23

—— he mounted sings,   *Thom.* 1 : 23

—— to dare with a hobby,   *Som.* 153

Lash and lashing smile, ill befits a lofty style,   *Swift* 2 : 22

Last day,   *Young* 1 : 7

—— epiphany,   *Pom.* 344

—— judgment,   *Rowe* 50

Late, who lies down, as late will rise,   *A. Phil.* 317

Latian blood the Punic ghosts atone,   *Rowe L.* 44

———— kings, line of,   *Garth* 142

———— line continued,   *Garth* 148

Latin poems,   { *Milt.* 3 : 229 / *Add.* 69 / *Smith* 200

Latins, defeat of,   *Dry.* 7 : 44

Latinus king of Latium,   *Dry.* 6 : 159

  Latinus,

Latinus, palace of described, .   *Dry.* 6 : 164

——— favourably receives the Trojans,   *Dry.* 6 : 168

——— fends prefents to Æneas,   *Dry.* 6 : 169

——— offers his daughter,   *Dry.* 6 : 169

——— calls a council for peace,   *Dry.* 7 : 13

Latium, reafon of the name,   *Dry.* 6 : 210

——— ancient people of, defcribed, .   *Dry.* 6 : 209

———prudent in peace,   *Prior* 1 : 162

Latium's language flourifh'd from wealth of Greece, *Pitt* 372

Latrant race, trace the genius of,   *Tick.* 141

——————— in powers diftinct excel,   *Tick.* 141

——————— in fight, or fwiftnefs, or fagacious fmell, *Tick.* 141

——————— learn well their lineage,   *Tick.* 142

Lava defcribed,   *Mall.* 214

Laugh or fpoils a face or mends,   *Cong.* 123

——— and grow wife,   *Swift* 2 : 26

Laughing, reforming by, not by ftorming,   *Swift* 2 : 25

Laughter, how expreffed,   *King* 426

——————— is pride or emptinefs,   *Young* 2 : 238

——————— portentous fign of grief approaching, *Young* 2 : 238

——————— unextinguifh'd, fhakes the fkies, { *Pope il.* 1 : 63 / *Pope od.* 3 : 215

——————— rude, like to burft,   *Swift* 2 : 75

Laureat, that is no poet,   *Swift* 2 : 160

Laurel, wet with foldiers' blood and widows' tears, *Prior* 2 : 176

Laurels, from living foes,   *Butl.* 1 : 94

Laurentum, reafon of the name,   *Dry.* 6 : 159

——————— fired,   *Dry.* 7 : 78

Laufus, character of,   *Dry.* 6 : 187

——— death of,   *Dry.* 6 : 309

Law, what,   *Butl.* 2 : 97

—— has neither eyes nor ears,   *Lanf.* 208

—— given at Sinai,   *Milt.* 2 : 126

—— speaks all despair,   *Watts* 97

—— fulfilled by obedience and suffering,   *Milt.* 2 : 132

—— nailed to the crofs,   *Milt.* 2 : 133

—— use of,   *Milt.* 2 : 129

—— maintains, not reftrains freedom,   *Butl.* 2 : 344

—— abufed to ftrife,   *Ot.* 8

—— nothing certain in, but expence,   *Butl.* 2 : 109

—— fubfifts by power,   *Dry.* 1 : 185

—— and gofpel,   *Watts* 113

Lawes, Waller to,   *Wall.* 108

Lawlefs foldiers know their guilt,   *Tick.* 159

Laws inexplicable guide the moral world,   *Mall.* 227

—— have no paffion of their own,   *Butl.* 2 : 116

—— have no force, till broken,   *Butl.* 1 : 200

—— guide, but cannot reign,   *Cow.* 2 : 179

—— mifconftrued, doubtful iffue of,   *Prior* 2 : 172

—— appear obfcure and intricate,   *Yal.* 442

—— perplex'd with comments,   *Yal* 442

—— weather-gage of,   *Butl.* 2 : 109

—— in war are dumb,   *Rowe L.* 58

—— of council bid the tongue be bold,   *Pope il.* 1 : 266

Law-fuits I'd fhun, as lions' dens,   *Pom.* 220

Lawyer, with periods long, in terms abftrufe,   *Swift* 2 : 106

—— what pains he takes to be prolix,   *Swift* 2 : 106

—— a thoufand lines to ftand for fix !   *Swift* 2 : 106

—— of common fenfe without a word in !   *Swift* 2 : 106

—— the ftatefman feem'd in part,   *Gay* 2 : 152

Lawyer, and bore similitude of heart,   *Gay* 2 : 152

———— scepticism is your profession,   *Gay* 2 : 120

———— you hold there's doubt in all expression, *Gay* 2 : 120

Lawyers arts of,   *Butl.* 1 : 54

———— can with ease twist words as they please, *Gay* 2 : 119

———— like the Swiss,   *Butl.* 2 : 98

———— fees to such excess are run,   *Young* 1 : 101

———— their clients are redressed, till undone, *Young* 1 : 101

Lazy, morrow like to-day,   *Dry.* 7 : 348

Leaf, like Sibyl's, shall scatter to and fro our fates, *Pope* 2 : 120

———— pregnant with thousands, flits unseen,   *Pope* 2 : 120

———— sells a king, or buys a queen,   *Pope* 2 : 120

League of France,   *Butl.* 1 : 76

Leap-frog, to play at,   *Butl.* 1 : 168

Learn to live well,   *Pope* 2 : 257

———————— that you may die so,   *Den.* 91

Learn well to know, how much need not be known, *Young* 2 : 115

Learned, full of inward pride,   *Gay* 2 : 97

———— the fops of outward show deride,   *Gay* 2 : 97

———— yet well-bred,   *Pope* 1 : 117

———— themselves, we book-worms name,   *Pope* 2 : 349

———— young lady, Lansdowne to,   *Lans.* 157

Learning is but to know the sense of predecessors, *Pope* 1 : 8

———— on abuse of,   *Butl.* 2 : 265

———— on imperfection of,   *Butl.* 2 : 265

———— dear-bought purchase of the trading mind, *Pom.* 342

———— progress of,   *Den.* 102

———— passed from Chaldea to Egypt,   *Den.* 102

———————— from Egypt to Greece,   *Den.* 103

———————— from Greece to Italy,   *Den.* 104

Learning,

Lewis XIV. by oppreſſion great,   *Som.* 182

———— for oppreſſion born,   *Smith* 208

———— in his turn ſhall mourn,   *Smith* 208

———— ceaſe to plague mankind,   *Add.* 13

Leyden, the Belgian Muſe's ſober ſeat,   *Aken.* 209

Liars we can never truſt,   *Watts* 343

Libation deſtin'd to the powers divine,   *Pope od.* 4 : 52

Libel, vindication of,   *Swift* 2 : 328

Libellers, free from wit, as from morality,   *Dry.* 7 : 109

Libels, a ſatire againſt,   *Ot.* 25

Liberality,   *Lanſ.* 199

Libertine, ironical conceſſions to,   *Black.* 202

———— muſt come to an accqunt,   *Black.* 204

Liberty, ode on,   *Cow.* 2 : 279

———— birds emblem of,   *Cow.* 2 : 280

———— happineſs of,   *Cow.* 2 : 281

———— bound only by conſcience,   *Cow.* 2 : 282

———— what,   *Cow.* 2 : 261

———— ode to,   *Collins* 256

———— hail, nymph, ador'd by Britain, hail,   *Collins* 258

———— Britannia's goddeſs,   *Pope* 2 : 61

———— genius of,   *Sav.* 167

———— whoſe charge is Albion's iſle,   *Sav.* 167

———— profuſe of bliſs !   *Add.* 44

———— crowns Britannia's iſle,   *Add.* 45

———— that great prerogative of human kind,   *Weſt* 279

———— love of, given with life,   *Dry.* 3 : 86

———— the nobleſt wealth,   *Pitt* 396

———— light of life, ſun of human kind,   *Thom.* 2 : 10

———— a poem,   *Thom.* 2 : 17

                           Liberty,

Liberty, shield of mankind, against pride and lust, *Thom.* 2 : 28

——— hail, glorious theme ! *Thom.* 2 : 29

——— that houshold godhead, *Aken.* 218

——— her cause snatch from fantastic demagogues, *ib.* 218

——— parent of happiness, *Dyer* 14

——— inestimable good ! *Dyer* 15

——— parent of arts, *Dyer* 15

——— consistent with order, *Milt.* 1 : 165

——— the noblest feast, *Som.* 272

——— how sweet, *Lansf.* 284

——— a-day, an hour of, worth eternity in bonds, *Add.* 276

——— was all his cry, *Swift* 2 : 269

——— for her he stood prepar'd to die, *Swift* 2 : 269

——— begets desire of more, *Dry.* 2 : 26

——— lost, where kings prevail, *Rowe L.* 128

——— in Devonia's loss, bewail a friend, *Hughes* 158

——— or Cæsar, be the word, *Rowe L.* 320

——— the false fair-seeming patriot's boast, *Thom.* 2 : 140

——— had lost the power to please, *Rowe L.* 52

——— betray'd, and banish'd justice, fly to him, *Hughes* 32

——— of conscience, what, *Butl.* 1 : 318, 319

——— of conscience granted, *Dry.* 2 : 95

——— lost, since the fall, *Milt.* 2 : 122

——— in what consists, *Milt.* 2 : 122

——— and love, *Som.* 279

Libya, deserts of, *Rowe L.* 394

——— abounding in serpents, *Rowe L.* 404

Licence did all the dregs of bold Socinus drain, *Pope* 1 : 113

Licence, to run bold lengths, but never to run mad, *Pitt* 293

Licences, use of by Ancients, *Pope* 1 : 98

Lichas,

Lichas, transformation of, — Gay 1: 322

—— hurl'd into the main, — Gay 1: 323

—— transform'd to stone, — Gay 1: 323

Lie in verse or prose the same, — Pope 2: 163

—— and truth contending for the way, — Pope 1: 225

Life, — Cow. 2: 49

—— a dream, — Cow. 2: 50

—— a well-ordered poem, — Cow. 2: 283

—— is war, — Young 2: 19

—— novelty of, how short, — Shen. 32

—— what art thou! — Broome 130

—— a breath, a single gasp puffs away, — Broome 130

—— a short-liv'd flower, — Broome 130

—— a stream, that silently but swiftly glides, — Broome 130

—— thy name is woe, — Broome 131

—— a waking dream, — Prior 2: 102

—— is a measur'd race, — Hughes 125

—— frail offspring of a day, — Broome 30

—— puff'd with one short gasp away, — Broome 30

—— swift as short-liv'd flower, dies, — Broome 30

—— springs, blooms, fades, it dies, — Broome 30

—— uncertain, — Don. 134

—— to be neither loved, nor hated, — Milt. 2: 103

—— length of, permitted to heaven, — Milt. 2: 103

—— how short, — Lans. 181

—— a span, — Lans. 181

—— not to be bought with gold, — Pope il. 1: 282

—— at best is pain, — Prior 1: 148

—— is a farce, the world a jest, — Swift 2: 149

—— but an instant now, — Cong. 49

Life,

Life, bitter draught,   *Pitt* 243

—— well expofed for public good,   *Milt.* 3 : 63

—— is long, that anfwers life's great end,   *Young* 2 : 117

—— we think long and fhort,   *Young* 2 : 25

—— a night of dread and mifery,   *Som.* 327

—— lying vanities of,   *Thom.* 1 : 160

—— vexation, difappointment, and remorfe,   *Thom.* 1 : 160

—— one fcene of toil, of fuffering, and of fate,   *Thom.* 1 : 165

—— is a fpan,   *Som.* 398

—— a fcene of rapine, want, and woe,   *Thom.* 1 : 230

—— negleft of the end of, to get the means,   *Walfh* 332

—— entombs the foul,   *Young* 2 : 58

—— is a debtor to the grave,   *Young* 2 : 59

—— lives beyond the grave,   *Young* 2 : 60

—— born from death, rolls the vaft mafs,   *Young* 2 : 153

—— no fingle atom once in, loft,   *Young* 2 : 153

—— title to more woe,   *Young* 2 : 131

—— never fincerely bleft,   *Dry.* 1 : 126

—— a miracle,   *Young* 2 : 210

—— party-colour'd, half pleafure, half care,   *Prior* 2 : 14

—— is carried down the rolling years,   *Parn.* 116

—— worth of, to know,   *Ot.* 20

—— beft exchange of, for praife,   *Dry.* 7 : 49

—— is but one common care,   *Prior* 2 : 174

—— with freedom, or a death with fame,   *Buck.* 119

—— has no value as an end, but means,   *Young* 2 : 57

—— had no charms, when Rome and glory call'd,   *Thom.* 2 : 63

—— does it not its nourifhment exceed ?   *Thom.* 2 : 182

—— to the laft, like harden'd felons, lyes,   *Young* 2 : 217

—— along the cool fequefter'd vale, to keep the way, *Gray* 339

Life,

Life, to steal from, by slow degrees, *Broome* 52

―― to the dark grave retiring as to rest, *Broome* 52

―― each step of, I speed to mingle with the dead, *Broome* 164

―― of wanderings is the greatest woe, *Pope od.* 4 : 59

―― is to be free, *Add.* 281

―― grows insipid, when liberty is gone, *Add.* 281

―― all covet, yet call it pain, *Prior* 1 : 156

―― and fame, *Cow.* 2 : 41

―― or death is equal, *Young* 2 : 67

―― death and immortality, *Young* 2 : 3

―― give me but, and make that life most wretched, *Smith* 181

―― ne'er unbent, were but a life of woe, *Parn.* 277

―― in fame be thine, O Swift, *Parn.* 278

――'s idle business at one gasp is o'er, *Pope* 1 : 159

Liffy's stinking tide at Dublin, *Swift* 1 : 274

Light, hymn to, *Cow.* 1 : 210

―― fairest of beings, *Mall.* 218

―― source of colours, *Mall.* 218

―― swiftness of, *Mall.* 220

―― velocity of, *Black.* 79

―― and eye, mutually adapted, *Black.* 79

―― of all material beings best, *Thom.* 1 : 46

―― Nature's resplendent robe, *Thom.* 1 : 46

―― truth's emblem, *Parn.* 195

―― created, *Milt.* 1 : 215

―― male and female, *Milt.* 1 : 236

―― God dwells in, *Milt.* 1 : 73

Lightning gilds the unrelenting storm, *Garth* 30

Ligurian, born to cheat, *Dry.* 7 : 36

Lillies, a spotless race, *Parn.* 211

Lily,

Lily, neither toils nor ſpins, *Thom.* 2 : 182

—— yet what king ſo ſhining, or queen ſo fair, *Thom.* 2 : 182

Limbo of vanity deſcribed, *Milt.* 1 : 88, 89

Limbs, how act ſummons of the will, *Garth* 22

Lime-hounds, their uſe, *Pom.* 23

Lincoln, biſhop of, on his enlargement, *Cow.* 1 : 112

Lines written in an Ovid, *Prior* 1 : 264

—— form'd to inſtruct and pleaſe, *Broome* 124

—— poliſhed as marble, ſhall as marble laſt, *Wall.* 200

Lingones, rich in many-colour'd arms, *Rowe L.* 65

Link whate'er you ſtrike from Nature's chain, breaks *Pope* 2 : 38

Linkman truſt not along the lonely wall, *Gay* 1 : 136

Linnets, little ſportlings of the ſpring, *Swift* 2 : 365

Lion deſcribed, *Young* 1 : 220

—— retreat of, *Dry.* 7 : 46

—— and cub, *Gay* 2 : 61

—— fox and geeſe, *Gay* 2 : 40

—— tiger and traveller, *Gay* 2 : 29

—— his ſkin lengthen'd by the fox's tail, *Prior* 1 : 145

Liquoriſh mouth muſt have a lecherous tail, *Pope* 1 : 262

Liſetta, queſtion to, *Prior* 1 : 123

—— reply of, *Prior* 1 : 123

Liſt prepared for combat, *Dry.* 7 : 52

Liſter, Apicius of, *King* 226

Little-creatures enterprize the moſt, *Gay* 1 : 293

Little learning is a dangerous thing, *Pope* 1 : 100

—— ſouls on little ſhifts rely, *Dry.* 2 : 84

—— villains ſubmit to fate, *Garth* 19

Littleneſs of ſoul betray'd, by nations laid in blood, *Young* 2 : 141

—————— is in approach to woe, *Young* 3 : 48

Littleton, elegy on,   *Cow.* 1 : 81

Live and enjoy the providence of heaven,   *Pope od.* 3 : 257

—— is but to wake to daily cares,   *Gay* 2 : 282

'—— and journey through a tedious vale of tears, *Gay* 2 : 282

Live-o'er paſt times,   *Broome* 53

—— with glory, or with glory die,   *Pope il.* 2 : 17

—— diſeas'd with life, and dread to die,   *Fent.* 311

—— tenacious of the golden mean,   *Fent.* 309

—— while thou liveſt,   *Dry.* 7 : 353

—— as thou may'ſt learn to die,   *Sav.* 81

—— and die is all we have to do,   { *Den.*   91
                                         { *Pope* 2 : 159

Lively faith will bear aloft the mind,   *Dry.* 2 : 87

————— and leave the luggage of good works behind, *ib.* 87

Living-dead to join dead-living to,   *Dry.* 2 : 280

Living, Lord, the living only praiſe,   *Parn.* 233

—— manner of the Dean's,   *Swift* 2 : 361

Lob's-pound, thrown into,   *Butl.* 1 : 133

Lobbin,   *A. Phil.* 297

Lock, rape of,   *Pope* 1 : 127

—— the glittering ſheers diſſever,   *Pope* 1 : 143

—— that time would ſpare, from ſteel receives its date, *ib.* 144

—— this ſacred lock, my hand ſhall ever wear, *Pope* 1 : 149

—— which never more ſhall join its parted hair, *Pope* 1 : 149

—— reſtore, the vaulted roofs rebound,   *Pope* 1 : 154

—— loſt on earth, mounted to the lunar ſphere, *Pope* 1 : 154

—— chang'd to a ſtar, to quick poetic eyes,   *Pope* 1 : 155

—— which adds new glory to the ſhining ſphere, *Pope* 1 : 155

—— the Muſe ſhall conſecrate to fame,   *Pope* 1 : 156

Locke, retired from buſineſs,   *Watts* 168

Locke, on his fickness, to Shute,   *Watts* 169

———— on Annotations of,   *Watts* 202

Lockman, the fame with Æfop,   *King* 185

Locks contain a nation's ftrength,   *Milt.* 3 : 57

———— curl'd or uncurl'd, will turn to grey,   *Pope* 1 : 151

Locrians, fkilled at the bow and fling,   *Pope il.* 2 : 32

Locuft fpreads famine o'er the land,   . *Gay* 2 : 173

Loddon flow, with verdant alders crown'd,   *Pope* 1 : 71

Logic is no friend to love,   *Prior* 2 : 206

———— great critic, in,   *Butl.* 1 : 7

Logicians refuted,   *Swift* 2 : 147

Loiterers ever-liftlefs,   *Pope* 3 : 241

———————— that attend no caufe, no truft, no duty and no friend, *ib.*

Lombard fchool,   *Thom.* 2 : 89

London, the nation, not metropolis,   *Roch.* 332

———— calls, get money, money ftill,   *Pope* 2 : 196

———— fire of, $\begin{cases} Dry. & 1:96 \\ Butl. & 2:229 \end{cases}$

———— plague in,   *Butl.* 2 : 229

———— port of,   *Dyer* 103

———— rebuilt,   *Dry.* 1 : 110

———— art of walking ftreets,   *Gay* 1 : 101

———— farewel to,   *Pope* 1 : 355

———— and Briftol,   *Sáv.* 191

———— thy manly fons of liberal mind,   *Sav.* 191

Long life,   *Cow.* 1 : 256

Longevity abfurd! more life, more wealth, it cries, *Young* 2 : 112

———————— more wherefore, when relifh fails, *Young* 2 : 112

Longinus, all the Nine infpire,   *Pope* 1 : 119

———————— with warmth gives fentence, yet always juft, *ib.* 119

Longinus

Longinus is, himself, that great sublime he draws, *Pope* 1 : 120

———— read the poet with a poet's flame, *Pitt* 389

Longitude uncertain, in spite of Whiston, *Prior* 2 : 80

Look before you leap, *Butl.* 1 : 207

Looking-glass, use of, *Som.* 374

Looking upward, *Watts* 99

Looks, emblems of thoughts, *Yal.* 384

———— the language of the mind, *Garth* 96

———— speak love, *Gay* 1 : 249

———— at variance with our thoughts, *Add.* 262

———— are lyes, *Smith* 117

———— fraught with wiles, for openness of heart, *Aken.* 346

———— are snares, *Lanf.* 196

Loom described, *Dyer* 85

———— variety of, *Dyer* 86

———— labours of, preferable, *Dyer* 93

———— hardens the constitution, *Dyer* 95

Loose desire for love mistaken, *Prior* 1 : 236

———— love, what ? a transient gust, *Pope* 1 : 84

———— a wandering, self-consuming fire, *Pope* 1 : 84

Looseness of manners improved to intellectual impiety, *Black.* 15

Lord, prayer of, *Wall.* 229, 230

———— most righteous and most holy too, *Parn.* 123

———— that kills, the Lord that makes alive, *Parn.* 149

———— by sickness brings to gaping graves, *Parn.* 150

———— by health restoring, from sickness saves, *Parn.* 150

———— makes the poor, by keeping back his store, *Parn.* 150

———— the rich, by blessing them with more, *Parn.* 150

———— the beggar from off the dunghill takes, *Parn.* 150

to mix with princes in a rank supreme, *Parn.* 150

Lord commands in war,   *Pitt* 257

—— hangs out and guides the balance of the fight, *Pitt* 257

—— o'erthrew the courser and the car,   *Pitt* 258

—— sunk Pharaoh's pride, and o'erwhelm'd his war, *Pitt* 258

—— Jacob bought at vast expence of wonders,   *Pitt* 260

—— led through the dark recesses of the floods,   *Pitt* 260

—— thy throne shall stand, when Time shall cease, *Pitt* 260

—— of heaven, is there equal to ?   *Pope il.* 2 : 78

—— not birth, but money makes,   *Dry.* 7 : 227

Lords are lordliest in their wine,   *Milt.* 3 : 54

Loretto, chapel of,   *Cow.* 1 : 137

Losers must have leave to speak,   *Mall.* 304

Losing game play'd with conduct,   *Dry.* 1 : 303

Loss of virility, loss of beard,   *Butl.* 1 : 180

—— of empire comes with length of days,   *Rowe L.* 330

Lost good name is ne'er retriev'd,   *Gay* 2 : 80

Lot retires to Sodom,   *Cow.* 2 : 140

—— wife of, turned to stone,   *Cow.* 2 : 141

—— of man below is labour,   *Pope il.* 1 : 297

Lotophagi,   *Pope od.* 3 : 230

———— not prone to ill, nor strange to stranger, *id.* 230

———— they eat and drink, and nature gives the feast, *ib.* 230

Lotos, effects of,   *Pope od.* 3 : 230

—— whose fruits in colours vie with Tyrian dye, *Pope* 1 : 328

Lots of fight drawn,   *Pope il.* 1 : 118

London, men of, possessed,   *Butl.* 1 : 229

Love,   { *Swift* 1 : 135 { *Lans.* 135

—— to dissembled joys invites vain men,   *Lans.* 135

—— nature of,   *Cow.* 2 : 105

C 3.   Love,

Love, ode on,	{ *Aken.* 220
	{ *Buck.* 20
—— refines mankind,	*Buck.* 20
—— makes all embraces chaste,	*Buck.* 21
—— Nature's Hymen,	*Buck.* 21
—— power of,	*Buck.* 22
—— falt of life,	*Buck.* 23
—— hymn to,	*Milt.* 1 : 126
—— poem,	*Swift* 2 : 52
—— is chaste defire,	*Thom.* 1 : 114
—— delights to pleafe,	*Gay* 1 : 239
—— the boundlefs influence of,	*Buck.* 92
—— apology for,	*Wall.* 121
—— power of,	*Cow.* 1 : 224
—— progrefs of,	{ *Swift* 1 : 153
	{ *Lytt.* 3
—— uncertainty in,	*Lytt.* 3
—— every care feem'd trifling now but,	*Lytt.* 4
—— that trouble of the heart,	*Lytt.* 4
—— where friendfhip full-exerts her power,	*Thom.* 1 : 40
—— nought but love can anfwer,	*Thom.* 1 : 41
—— fympathy of foul,	*Thom.* 1 : 41
—— fomething than beauty dearer,	*Thom.* 1 : 41
—— kindnefs and conftancy, the only pillars of,	*Prior* 1 : 32
—— is not in our power,	*Gay* 2 : 216
—— is feated in the foul, and never dies,	*Gay* 2 : 226
—— is innocence,	*Gay* 2 : 242
—— refolved to,	*Cow.* 1 : 290
—— his enchanting fnare beware,	*Aken.* 220
—— unbends the force of thought,	*Aken.* 220
	Love

Love will rule alone, *Pom.* 244

―― and fuffer no copartner in his throne, . *Pom.* 244

―― no partnerfhip allows, . *Prior* 1 : 238

―― no cure will have, *A. Phil.* 297

―― whofe miferies delight, *Thom.* 1 : 39

―― a life of fever'd rapture, or of cruel care, . *Thom.* 1 : 40

―― fole king of pleafures, *Weft* 276

―― confifts in paffion, *Milt.* 1 : 251

―― refines the thoughts, *Milt.* 1 : 251

―― has its feat in reafon, *Milt.* 1 : 251

―― empire of, unequalled, . *Wall.* 29

―― was liberty, and nature law, . *Pope* 2 : 62

―― undifcovered, *Cow.* 1 : 263

――the moft generous paffion, *Roch.* 307

―― fofteft refuge of innocence, . *Roch.* 307

―― cordial drop in our cup, . *Roch.* 307

―― cherifh'd with hope, grows, . *Prior* 2 : 138

―― longings with defpair, *Cow.* 1 : 242

―― a canker-worm, *Mall.* 153

―― ftrongeft tie of nature, *Lanf.* 283

―― but ill agrees with kingly pride, . *Add.* 141

―― throws darts at random, *Wall.* 41

――difarmed, *Prior* 1 : 105

―― by love repaid, blifs of angels, . *Mall.* 248

―― ingenious, . *Dry.* 3 : 217

―― is foft joy and gentle ftrife, . *Prior* 2 : 200

―― a fire celeftial, chafte, refin'd, . *Swift* 1 : 102

―― tyrant-god, ftings and racks, *Broome* 151

―― is a fummer flower, that dies, *Lanf.* 190

―― is eagle-ey'd, *Hughes* 58

Love

Love gives courage,   *Hughes* 60

—— is a sacred voluntary fire,   *Gay* 2 : 252

—— gold never bought that pure, that chaste desire, *id.* 2 : 252

—— is beyond the price of gold,   *Gay* 2 : 178

—— hath every bliss in store,   *Gay* 2 : 179

—— 'tis friendship, 'tis something more,   *Gay* 2 : 179

—— not to know, is not to live,   *Gay* 2 : 179

—— is begot by fancy,   *Lanf.* 198

—— bred by ignorance,   *Lanf.* 198

—— by expectation fed,   *Lanf.* 198

—— lost in the moment 'tis possost,   *Lanf.* 198

—— and hate are fancy all,   *Lanf.* 198

—— all, in powerful fancy lies,   *Lanf.* 198

—— triumphant over reason,   *Pom.* 221

—— fatal labyrinth, where fools are lost,   *Pom.* 222

—— inquietudes always brings,   *Pom.* 224

—— its joys fleeting dreams,   *Roch.* 282

—— its woes severe extremes,   *Roch.* 282

—— give me back my heart again,   *Lanf.* 180

—— with justice or with mercy reign,   *Lanf.* 180

—— sincere resents the smallest scorn,   *Pom.* 246

—— force of,   *Dry.* 5 : 157

—— fights for love alone,   *Dry.* 3 : 87

—— haughty pride far from,   *King* 291

—— augment in just degrees,   *King* 291

—— not to be reason'd down,   *Add.* 253

—— 'tis second life,   *Add.* 254

—— world, born to,   *Prior* 1 : 264

—— Be   f described,   *Pom.* 226,

—   at,   *Butl.* 1 : 166

Love can with speech inspire a mute,   *Swift* I : 125

—— taught Vanessa to dispute,   *Swift* I : 125

—— why do we one passion call, .   *Swift* I : 127

—— 'tis a compound of them all, .   *Swift* I : 127

—— has eloquence beyond the schools,   *King* 274

—— force of,   *Cow.* I : 354

—— universal sway of,   *Cow.* I · 355

—— power of,   *Cow.* I : 356

—— our wills control'd in, .   *Wall.* 61

—— bears different sway o'er different ages,   *King* 329

—— that tyrant-god, that restless conqueror,   *Prior* I : 73

—— sublimes,   *Dry.* 3 : 208

—— well-meaning, has wrought much woe,   *Milt.* 3 : 34

—— is a jest, and vows are wind,   *Prior* I : 133

—— is strong as death,   *Parn.* 217

—— alike imperious, vainly check'd alike,   *Parn.* 217

—— no chilling floods can slack,   *Parn.* 217

—— wealth of nations, too small a price for,   *Parn.* 218

—— a lambent flame about the breast,   *Dry.* 2 : 165

—— Cupid bathing in Diana's stream, .   *Dry.* 2 : 165

—— raptures of refining, . .   *Thom.* 1 : 19

—— first invented verse, ,   *Dry.* 3 : 257

—— made the coward bold,   *Dry.* 3 : 257

—— exalts the mind,   *Dry.* 3 : 257

—— teaches good-manners,   *Dry.* 3 : 262

—— like ambition, dies as 'tis enjoy'd,   *Lans.* 289

—— by doubt provok'd,   *Lans.* 289

—— by certainty destroy'd,   *Lans.* 289

—— is a subject to himself alone,   *Lans.* 254

—— knows no other empire but his own, . .   *Lans.* 254

Love is blind, *Gay* 1 : 60, 68

—— all busy-head destroys, *Gay* 1 : 62

—— blinds the wise, *Dry.* 3 : 88

—— gives eye-sight to the blind, *Dry.* 3 : 88

—— is love's reward, *Dry.* 3 : 88

—— is always blind, *Pope* 1 : 235

—— a blind and foolish passion, *Add.* 270

—— though blind, yet artful, *Cow.* 1 : 56

—— imparts a style, more excellent than art, *King* 323

—— skill of, like the art of war, *King* 324

—— monarch passion of the mind, *Pom.* 249

—— rais'd on beauty, will like that decay, *Pope* 2 : 337

—— never thinks of rich and poor, *Swift* 1 : 155

—— a burglarer, *Butl.* 1 : 170

—— a fire, *Butl.* 1 : 171

—— returns, and pride gives way, *Lanf.* 298

—— be the business of our life, *Pope il.* 1 : 123

—— sweet vicissitude of, *Som.* 292

—— power of, *Dry.* 3 : 224

—— hard to cure, *Duke* 99

—— fond, inglorious toil, *Pom.* 231

—— temple of, *Pom.* 238, 239

—— a malady, without a cure, *Dry.* 3 : 79

—— endures no tie, *Dry.* 3 : 81

—— bears no rival, *Dry.* 3 : 81

—— what misery attends on, *Pom.* 229

—— proud usuper of reason's throne, *Pom.* 229

—— a poignard hung but by a single thread, *Pom.* 229

—— banquets kill or surfeit all that eat, *Pom.* 230

—— fire of Fate, *Aken.* 301

Love

Love elder than Chaos,   *Aken.* 301

—— a paſſion nurſt with ſtrong deſires,   *Dry.* 3 : 65

—— no law made for,   *Dry.* 3 : 65

—— not in our choice, but in our fate,   *Dry.* 3 : 66

—— Nature's ſanction, and her firſt decree,   *Dry.* 3 : 66

—— leads to heaven,   *Milt.* 1 : 252

—— roſy red, hue of,   *Milt.* 1 : 252

—— without, no happineſs,   *Milt.* 1 : 252

—— of God, to obey,   *Milt.* 1 : 252

—— ſtronger than death,   *Watts* 138

—— the only ſweet of life,   *Pope od.* 3 : 150

—— ſtudied as an art,   *Butl.* 2 : 128

—— ruins none, men themſelves deſtroy,   *Pom.* 236

—— and luſt eſſentially divide,   *Pom.* 236

—— hath wings,   *Cow.* 1 : 94

—— common link of creation,   *Dry.* 3 : 134

—— in ſucceſſion,   *Cow.* 1 : 126

—— given over,   *Cow.* 1 : 321

—— train of,   *Cow.* 2 : 106

—— wild-gooſe chace,   *Walſh* 340

—— arrows of, ſhot at rovers,   *Butl.* 1 : 306

—— courage in,   *Broome* 132

—— an hero in, as in wars,   *Broome* 133

—— that's naked, ſtill is love in arms,   *Parn.* 31

—— raptures of, more taking in dreams,   *Butl.* 2 : 193

—— well-choſen, never dies,   *Waller* 68

—— 'tis joy or ſorrow, peace or ſtrife,   *Prior* 2 : 137

—— like death, makes all diſtinction void,   *Prior* 2 : 137

—— his ſorrows, as his joys, are true,   *Prior* 2 : 209

—— o'ercomes the beſt,   *Buck.* 58

Love like falconers, *Wall.* 90

—— flavery of, *Buck.* 26

—— pair'd the birds, *Parn.* 17

—— contributes to its own deceit, *Buck.* 64

—— an ague reverft, *Butl.* 1 : 296

—— deceives the beft of womankind, *Pope od.* 4 : 62

—— can the wife beguile, *Buck.* 87

—— makes the feeble ftrong, *Ot.* 55

—— the world's prefervative, *Butl.* 2 : 114

—— controls the power of fate, *Butl.* 2 : 115

—— confounds fenfe of right and wrong, *Dry.* 3 : 127

—— ftrong has no bounds, *Dry.* 3 : 127

—— produces care, *Dry.* 2 : 39

—— rooted out, again will never grow, *Swift* 2 : 65

—— is it for wealth or power or title bought ? *Gay* 2 : 248

—— free fervice, *Mil.* 1 : 157

—— immenfe, inviolably juft, *Young* 2 : 69

—— an elegy, *Aken.* 345

—— too long hath reafon left her throne to, *Aken.* 345

—— feldom haunts the breaft, where learning lies, *Pope* 1 : 267

—— of fame, *Young* 1 : 77

————— univerfal paffion, *Young* 1 : 77

————— hurl'd Empedocles down Ætna, *Young* 1 : 80

————— made Alexander weep, *Young* 1 : 80

—— of praife reigns more or lefs in every heart, *Young* 1 : 79

————— nor ends with life, adorns our hearfe, *id.* 1 : 79

—— of genuine fame with virtue ever join'd, *Young* 2 : 163

—— of gold, jaundice of the foul, *Cow.* 2 : 247

—— of gold ! thou meaneft of amours, *Young* 2 : 74

—— finks to foftnefs all our tragic rage, *Tick.* 117

Love

Love debas'd our manhood,   *Tick.* 117
—— triumph of,   *Hughes* 63
—— ingenious to deſtroy,   *Hughes* 63
—— all ſhall ſubmit to,   *Hughes* 64
—— thy preſence does reach the heart,   *Hughes* 65
—— the fair diſtribute,   *Lanſ.* 162
—— darting eyes,   *Milt.* 3 : 147
——'s inviſibility,   *Cow.* 1 : 289
—— hardeſt hearts are melted by,   *Lanſ* 170
—— only wakes,   *Lanſ.* 171
—— in deſerts bred, by cruel tigers nurſt,   *Lanſ.* 171
—— ſwifter than time,   *Wall.* 79
—— to what odd whims inveigles men !   *Pitt* 267
—— with vocal art informs the lyre,   *Fent.* 327
—— to worthy deeds, in all great ſouls the ſame,   *Hughes* 42
—— or fear, form'd ſocieties,   *Pope* 2 : 62
—— ſubmit to friendſhip's laws,   *Prior* 1 · 66
—— to a friend unſucceſsful in,   *Aken.* 195
—— dangerous of ſeeming friends,   *Prior* 2 : 168
—— almighty reigns, death of death,   *Young* 3 : 80
———————— that cordial of deſpair,   *Young* 3 : 80
—— on a croſs and a throne,   *Watt.* 142
—— divine in evils to diſcern,   *Young* 3 : 89
———————— firſt leſſon which we want,   *Young* 3 · 69
———————— lateſt, which we learn,   *Young* 3 : 89
—— and love only, is the loan for love,   *Young* 2 : 38
—— crowns, arms, and triumphs, what to,   *Pitt* 208
—— exceſſive deceives,   *Cong.* 139
—— all it fears, too eaſily believes,   *Cong.* 139
—— of honourable deeds,   *Pope il.* 1 : 49

Love

Love, intrigues of,   *Butl.* 2 : 120

—— forrow and joy alternate in,   *Smith* 146

—— fweet the blifs, diftracting the pain,   *Smith* 146

—— elegies,   *Ham.* 205

—— of Jafon and Medea,   *Broome* 150

—— and defpair, like twins,   *Lanf.* 152

—— and friendfhip,   *Prior* 1 : 64

———————————— compared,   *Shen.* 20

—— and honour,   *Shen.* 273

—— and life,   *Cow.* 1 : 254

——————— are for a day,   *Prior* 1 : 205

—— and money to burn for,   *Butl.* 1 : 274

—— and mufic,   *Shen.* 144

——————— melt their fouls away,   *Thom.* 2 : 23

—— and fhame, fuch inconfiftent things,   *Pope* 1 : 173

—— and wifdom are at ftrife,   *Prior* 2 : 155

—— and worfe ambition conquer,   *Prior* 2 : 85

—— between brothers and fifters,   *Watts* 345

—— of learning fhall be fame,   *Mall.* 301

—— nothing more averfe to, than pride,   *King* 328

—— as hot as pepper'd brandy,   *King* 366

—— paffions, like parables,   *Butl.* 1 : 171

—— powder, philtres of,   *Butl.* 2 : 116

Love-quarrels oft end in concord,   *Milt.* 3 : 40

Love-fong,   *Swift* 2 : 292

Love's a fierce, involuntary flame,   *Gay* 1 : 236

—— ingratitude,   *Cow.* 1 : 277

—— ftolen pleafures, infincere,   *Hughes* 135

Love for love, epilogue,   *Rowe* 33

Lovelinefs, when unadorn'd, is moft adorn'd, *Thom.* 1 : 113

Lovely

Lovely continue, if you'll be beloved, *King* 286

Lover cannot harm, *A. Phil.* 299

—— interview of, *Ham.* 211

—— pendent on a willow-tree, *Phil.* 6

—— flave to his miftrefs, *Butl.* 2 : 118

—— lofe, with pride, in the man, *Aken.* 350

—— various changes of his ftate, *Lytt.* 3

—— and friend, names facred, *Mall.* 256

——'s anger, *Prior* 1 : 118

——'s fires, how fiercely burn, *Pope* 1 : 179

—— hell of, what, *Dry.* 3 : 92

——.leap of, *Fent.* 283

Lovers, complaints of, eafe their pain, *Dry.* 2 : 55

—— converfe by the eye, *Butl.* 2 : 115

—— change their mood, *Dry.* 3 : 78

—— going to war difapprov'd, *Ham.* 219

—— and minifters are feldom true, *Lytt.* 40

—— ftate, what pleagues attend ? *Aken.* 346

—— hearts not their own, *Butl.* 1 : 242

—— and the glafs alike deceive, · *Gay* 1 : 37

Loves be mindful of, and live, *Pope* 1 : 172

Loving an object never feen, *Walfh* 339

—— at firft fight, { *Lanf.* 151 { *Wall.* 97

Louis, as patron of arts, not inferior to Auguftus, *Dry.* 7 : 114

——' feather, that fhone fo like a ftar, *Prior* 1 : 93

—— knows Verfailles its proper ftation, *Prior* 1 : 95

Louifa to Strephon, *Swift* 1 : 316

Low-conceit, a ftall the palace of the fteed, *Pitt* 367

—————— calling grafs the treffes of Rhæa's head, *Pitt* 367

Low

Low fortune preferable to high,   Cow. 2 : 343

Lowther, verses to Mrs.   Tick. 153

————— loveliest of the loveliest race,   Tick. 153

Lownds, epistle to,   Gay 1 : 205

Loyola's all-aping sons,   Young 1 : 248

————— whose name, from Jesus, and hearts from hell, ib. 252

Lucan, part of the fourth book,   Tick. 156

————— wanting in design and subject,   Dry. 7 : 115

————— too full of heat and affectation,   Dry. 7 : 115

————— translation of 10th book,   Hughes 286

————— family of,   Rowe L. 6

————— place of nativity,   Rowe L. 6

————— education,   Rowe L. 7

————— his Pharsalia an invective,   Rowe L. 7

————— rhetoric his favourite study,   Rowe L. 8

————— reckoned among the rhetoricians,   Rowe L. 8

————— advanced by Nero to honours,   Rowe L. 9

————— marriage of,   Rowe L. 9

————— disputes the prize of eloquence with Nero, Rowe L. 11

————— death, manner of,   Rowe L. 13

————— died young,   Rowe L. 14

————— character of,   Rowe L. 39

————— burial of,   Rowe L. 39

————— style, character of,   Rowe L. 36

————— writings of,   Rowe L. 15

————— his character of Cæsar unjust,   Rowe L. 22

————— Pharsalia,   Rowe L. 41

Lucian indiscriminately laughs,   Young 1 : 74

————— betraying poverty of wit,   Young 1 : 74

————— postponing virtue to a jest,   Young 1 : 77

                     Lucian,

Lucian, dialogues of, Varronian satires,   *Dry.* 7 : 162

Lucifer, palace of,   *Milt.* 1 : 164

Lucilius, a Roman satirist,   *Dry.* 7 : 156

———— lashed the town,   *Dry.* 7 : 192

———————— the city,   *Dry.* 7 : 318

———— first exposed vice,   *Dry.* 1 : 273

———— neglected style, numbers and purity,   *Dry.* 7 : 185

Lucinda, tea-table of,   *Hughes* 85

Lucius, epilogue to,   *Prior* 1 : 2ᵐ8

Lucre, sacred thirst of gold,   *Young* 3 : 201

Lucretius, translations from,   *Dry.* 4 : 315

———— sets to view the principles of things,   *Pitt* 312

———— transplants epicurism to Rome,   *Black.* 66

———— ascribes every evil to religion,   *Black.* 66

———— tuneful sophist,   *Black.* 99

———— holds the world, a casual concourse,   *Black.* 100

———— because unable to account for its faults, *id.* 100

———— objections of, answered,   *id.* 101

———— all is chance,   *Prior* 2 : 36

———— members first, and then their use, *Prior* 2 : 36

———— translated,   *Wall.* 112

Lucy Sidney,   *Wall.* 59

Luez, a bone in the rump,   *Butl.* 2 : 76

Luke-warm patriots, sober conduct is a virtue in,   *Add.* 281

Lumber of a land, swept to the war,   *Pope il.* 1 : 75

Lumber (Hugh), epitaph on,   *Som.* 192

Lungs, structure and use of,   *Black.* 191

Lust, short blessings bought with long remorse,   *Sav.* 39

———— seed of bitter thought,   *Sav.* 39

——— strongest vice of woman,   *Dry.* 7 : 251

Luft, confequences of,   *Cow.* 2 : 173

—— well refin'd, is gentle love,   *Pope* 2 : 48

—— and love, deceitful all and vain,   *Prior* 2 : 163

—— and reafon only foes,   *Pom.* 236

Lute is fit for love,   *Fent.* 327

—— fong for,   *Som.* 237

Luther misjoins the body with the bread,   *Dry.* 2 : 32

Lutrin, a Varronian fatire,   *Dry.* 7 : 210

Luxe of coftly pride I try'd,   *Prior* 2 : 130

Luxury, called magnificence,   *Milt.* 2 : 204

—— befots the nobleft mind,   *Weft* 266

—— with Charles reftor'd,   *Pope* 2 : 221

—— whole patrimonies fweeps,   *Pope od.* 4 : 109

—— mother of Vice, rapacious, cruel,   *Thom.* 2 : 69

—— from the conquer'd Eaft came that plague, *Thom.* 2 : 69

—— hence virtue flacken'd into floth,   *Thom.* 2 : 70

—— which commerce pours,   *Aken.* 218

—— foft Syren,   *Mall.* 235

—— fheds unheeded bane,   *Dyer* 24

—— wealth's bane,   *King* 369

—— confumes the guilty ftore,   *Lytt* 98

—— and bids the villain be a flave for more,   *Lytt.* 98

—— ranfacks fea, earth, and air,   *Gay* 1 : 138

—— fatal victor of mankind,   *Pope* 2 : 17

—— thou foft, but fure deceit,   *Buck.* 90

—— rife of the mean, and ruin of the great,   *Buck.* 90

—— bane of empires, and the change of ftates,   *Buck.* 90

—— of the mind, works of immortal wit,   *Pitt* 288

Lyceum, fchool of Ariftotle,   *Aken.* 89

Lycidas,   *Milt.* 3 : 159

                   Lycidas

Lycidas and Moeris,   *Dry.* 5 : 67

Lycon, an eclogue,   *Walsh.* 351

Lycurgus, the lawgiver, brought Homer into Greece, *Aken.* 293

Lying, against,   *Watts* 343

———— a faint-like virtue,   *Butl.* 1 : 195

Lyre, invention of Mercury,   *Cong.* 159

———— the joy of youth, and the relief of age,   *Tal.* 443

———— is drown'd in the deep organ's sound,   *Cing.* 63

Lyric poetry, on,   *Young* 1 : 177

———————— ode on,   *Aken.* 226

Lyrics, what properly,   *Hughes* 113

Lyttelton, progress of love,   3—14

———— soliloquy of beauty in the country,   17

———— Blenheim,   19

———— to Dr. Ayscough,   25

———— to Poyntz,   30

———— verses under Poyntz's picture,   33

———— epistle to Pope,   34

———— to lord Hervey,   37

———— advice to a lady,   39

———— song,   44, 45, 52

———— Damon and Delia,   47

———— ode, in imitation of Pastor Fido,   49

———— parts of an elegy of Tibullus,   50

———— verses to Mrs. Greville,   53

———— epigram,   54

———— to Mr. West,   54

———— to Miss Lucy Fortescue,   55—61

———— Horace, Book iv. Ode iv.   75

———— Virtue and Fame.   79

D 2

Lyttelton, lord Hardwicke to,   80
———— letter to lord Hardwicke,   81
———— hymn to Eliza,   82
———— on reading Miss Carter's poems,   84
———— Mount Edgecumbe,   85
———— invitation,   86
———— to colonel Drumgold,   86
———— epitaph on captain Grenville,   88
———————— on captain Cornwall [not Lyttelton's],   88
———— on good-humour,   89
———— additional stanzas to Astolfo's voyage,   90
———— to a young lady,   93
———— elegy,   94
———— inscription for a bust of lady Suffolk,   95
———— Sulpicia to Cerinthus,   96
———— Cato's speech to Labienus,   96
———— to Glover, on his Leonidas,   98
———— to William Pitt,   100
———— prologue to Thomson's Coriolanus,   101
———— epilogue to Lillo's Elmerick,   102
———— inscriptions at Hagley,   103, 104

M

Macareus, adventures of,   *Garth* 129
Maccabeus, prowess of,   *Milt.* 2 : 188
Macar   character,   *Pope* 2 : 347
Mac-Fleckno,   *Dry.* 2 : 109
Machaon cures Menelaus of his wound,   *Pope il.* 1 : 135
———— wounded,   *Pope il.* 1 : 342
                                          Machaon,

Machaon carried off by Neftor,   *Pope il.* 1 : 342
——— a wife phyfician, is more than armies,   *id.* 1 : 342
——— panegyric on,   *Garth* 70
Machiavel gave his name to Old Nick,   *Butl.* 1 : 319
Machinery, what,   { *Pope* 1 : 125
                  { *Pope od.* 3 : 32
——— marvellous, probable, and moral, *Pope od.* 3 : 36
Machines in poetry, ufe of,   *Dry.* 5 : 273
Mackenzie, verfes to Dr.   *Som.* 187
Macrinus, birth-day of,   *Dry.* 7 : 321
Macro,   *Lanf.* 196
Mad-dog,   *Gay* 2 : 77
——— has a worm in his tongue,   *Butl.* 2 : 299
Madmen, worft of, is a faint run mad,   *Pope* 2 : 305
——— fight for applaufe,   *Dry.* 3 : 87
Madnefs of hoarding,   *Cow.* 2 : 18
——— in dogs, two forts,   *Som.* 75, 76
——— effects of,   *Som.* 77
——— burning recommended in,   *Som.* 78
Madrigal moves foft paffions,   *Dry.* 1 : 273
Mæcenas,   *Rowe* 57
——— a knight of ancient Tufcan race,   *Rowe* 57
Magazine of hail and fnows,   *Young* 1 : 215
——— funds of vengeance for the day of war, *Young* 1 : 215
Maggots turn to flies,   *Butl.* 2 : 52
Magi beget fons on their mothers,   *Butl.* 2 : 4
Magic, power of,   *Rowe L.* 271
Magna Charta figned,   *Thom.* 2 : 107
——— held in contempt,   *Cow.* 2 : 252
Magnanimity, great things to fcorn,   *Young* 2 : 247

Magnano deſcribed,   *Butl.* 1 : 60, 61

Magnetiſm inexplicable,   *Black.* 47

Magnificence of old with virtue could reſide, *Pope od.* 3 : 49

Mahomet Ali Beg,   *Som.* 375

———— the Turk's patriarch,   *Butl.* 2 : 294

———— fond of a ſhoulder of mutton,   *King* 186

———— poiſoned by one,   *King* 186

————'s tomb, 'twixt earth and heaven,   *Prior* 2 : 55

Maid, crown'd with willow die,   *Gay* 1 : 78

——— unaſk'd may own a well-plac'd flame,   *Lytt.* 42

——— not loving firſt, but loving wrong, is ſhame, *Lytt.* 42

——— unmatch'd in manners as in face,   *Pope il.* 1 : 42

——— ſkill'd in each art, crown'd with every grace, *id.* 1 : 42

Maidenhead,   *Cow.* 1 : 295

Maids, before they're aſk'd, can they refuſe,   *Prior* 2 : 37

——— few, that now on merit ſmile,   *Ham.* 207

Majeſty, verſes to her,   *Watts* 164

———'s return,   *Cow.* 1 : 104

——— derives a grace from ſtate,   *Pope od.* 3 : 170

——— gives its proud trappings o'er,   *Rowe L.* 339

——— and ſeeks for ſafety from the poor,   *Rowe L.* 339

Mail, compact and firm with many a jointed ſcale, *Pope il.* 2 : 86

Majority of voices rules in ſenates, ſo in ſchools, *Prior* 2 : 71

Main, a world of wonders in thyſelf,   *Them.* 1 : 192

——— is Britain's reign,   *Young* 1 : 189

——— rain, ſnow, the plunder of,   *Young* 1 : 192

Maintenon, Scarron's leaving,   *Rowe* 39

Maker's praiſe, ſuch was the ſacred art,   *Hughes* 81

Maladies, that lead to Death's grim cave,   *Phil.* 76

——— joint-racking gout,   *Phil.* 76

    Maladies,

Maladies, inteſtine ſtone,   *Phil.* 77
————— pining Atrophy,   *Phil.* 77
————— dropſy all-a-float,   *Phil.* 77
Malherbe, ode of,   *King* 336
Malice, queen of far-ſpread lies,   *Ot.* 40
————— always judging worſt,   *Swift* 2 : 75
————— the mother of vindictive rage,   *Sav.* 73
————— prone the virtuous to defame,   *Pope od.* 3 : 180
————— to muſic forc'd to yield,   *Prior* 1 : 29
————— the beſt way to baulk,   *Swift* 2 : 47
————— vanquiſh'd heightens Virtue's praiſe,   *Prior* 1 : 229
Malignant, a term of reproach,   *Cow.* 2 : 258
Mall, king plays in,   *Wall.* 152
Mallet, William and Margaret,   *Mall.* 153
————— epitaph on Aikman and ſon,   157
————— on a young lady,   157
————— ſong to a Scotch tune,   158, 342
————— verbal criticiſm,   159
————— verſes to the prince of Orange,   168
————— on Dr. Frazer's rebuilding, &c.   171
————— prologue to the Siege of Damaſcus,   173
————— epilogue to The Brothers,   175
————— prologue to Agamemnon,   176
————— impromptu on a lady, &c.   178
————— epigram,   191
————— a ſimile in Prior,   179
————— on an amorous old man,   180
————— on J. H.   180
————— a fragment,   180
————— Cupid and Hymen,   184

Mallet, an ode in the mask of Alfred, _Mall._ 192

———— the excursion, 295

———— Amintor and Theodora, . 235

———— to the duke of Marlborough, . .. 283

———— truth in rhyme, . 287

———— to the author of the preceding, 293

———— the discovery, . .. 294

———— verses for a beggar, 296

———— the reward, . . . 297

———— Tyburn, .. 302

———— Zephyr, 315

———— Edwin and Emma, 323

———— on death of lady Anson, 329

———— funeral hymn, 332

———— to Myra, 334

———— a winter's day, 335

———— prologue to Mask of Britannia, 338

———— inscription for a picture, 340

———— to Thomson, on his Winter, 341

Malvern, ridge of hills near Worcester, _Dyer_ 33

Mammon, speech of, _Milt._ 1 : 42, 43

———— advises peace, _Milt._ 1 : 44

Man created in image of God, _Milt._ 1 : 224

——- to rule over the earth, · _Milt._ 1 : 224

———— male and female, _Milt._ 1 : 224

——- to abstain from tree of knowledge, _Milt._ 1 : 225

——- not good for, to be alone, : · . _Milt._ 1 : 246

——- falls asleep, _Milt._ 1 : 246

——- rib taken, to form woman, _Milt._ 1 : 246

——- never to depart from his power over woman, _Milt._ 3 : 42

Man may err,   Dry. 2 : 29
—— deceivable and vain,   Milt. 3 : 18
—— folly of, in accusing God,   Milt. 2 : 70
—— fellow-servant of angels,   Milt. 1 : 238
—— charge of angels,   Milt. 2 : 8
—— world created for,   Milt. 2 : 8
—— favourite of heaven,   Milt. 2 : 9
—— false to himself, ere others to him,   Milt. 3 : 34
—— sole cause of his misery,   Milt. 3 : 19
—— not immutable,   Milt. 1 : 156
—— Satan's purposed prey,   Milt. 2 : 17
—— banished Paradise,   Milt. 2 : 88
—— dust, and thither to return,   Milt. 2 : 91
—— saved of grace,   Milt. 1 : 79
—— powers of, renewed,   Milt. 1 : 79
—— what,   Hughes 239
—— creature of a day,   Hughes 239
—— how frail,   Prior 2 : 147
—— by himself insensibly betray'd,   Prior 2 : 147
—— from beast, by words, is known,   Pope 3 : 227
—— first vegetative, then feels and reasons last, Dry. 3 : 136
—— rich of three souls,   Dry. 3 : 136
—— and lives all three to waste,   Dry. 3 : 136
—— exhibits life and growth of plants, sense of beast, Prior 2 : 167
—— born to lament, to labour, and to die,   Prior 2 : 169
—— thy fabric's like a well-form'd state,   Sav. 40
—— his frame discovers art,   Black. 185
—— a nice machine,   Parn. 73
—— by nature form'd to fail,   Parn. 73
—— abridgment of the world,   Crw. 2 : 99
                                                  Man,

Man, what,   *Pope il.* 2 : 255
——— calamitous by birth,   *Pope il.* 2 : 253
——— feeble race, what ills await?   *Gray* 346
———! vifion of a moment,   *Young* 1 : 217
——— dream of a dream,   *Young* 1 : 217
——— is not made to queftion, but adore,   *Young* 1 : 224
——— the gilded vanity,   *Parn.* 119
——— that riddle !   .   .   *Young* 3 : 128
——— born for infinite,   *Young* 3 : 128
——— thine is redemption,   *Young* 2 : 77
——— double fon of heaven, the made and the re-made, *id.* 1 : 78
——— know thyfelf,   *Young* 2 : 78
——— muft fatisfy for man,   .   .   .   *Milt.* 1 : 83
——— muft die for juftice,   .   *Milt.* 1 : 80
——— of vile and humble birth, .   .   ʻ   *Pitt* 250
——— fhort-liv'd fovereign of the world below,   *Pitt* 257
——— like his Maker, faw that all was right, .   *Pope* 2 : 63
——— reftoration of, envied by Satan,   *Milt.* 2 : 156·
——— how vain and unwife,   *Dry.* 1 : 121
——— by nature form'd for all mankind,   *Aken.* 43
——— in fociety, born for public good,   *Dyer* 74
——— a rugged wight, worft of brutes,   *Thom.* 1 : 230
——— on his own kind he ruthlefs prey'd,   *Thom.* 1 : 230
——— ftrongeft ftill the weakeft over-ran,   *Thom.* 1 : 230
——— perverfe and lawlefs,   *Fent.* 216
——— fearchlefs providence would found, .   *Fent.* 216
——— vainly wicked, thinks he's wife,   *Fent.* 216
——— probationer of happinefs,   *Fent.* 217·
——— is to man all kind of beafts,   *Cow.* 2 : 359·
——— differs more from man, than from beaft,   *Roch.* 326·
                                                    Man,

Man, theme of the poet,   *Wall.* 110

—— is a very worm by birth,   *Pope* 2 : 349

—— heaven's pride, when upright,   *Tick.* 96

—— deprav'd, heaven's fcorn,   *Tick.* 96

— - turning from his God, brings endlefs night,   *Young* 3 : 68

—— the fport of fortune, then the morfel of defpair, *id.* 3 : 70

—— alone, life's ruder trials wait,   *Rowe L.* 332

—— outcaft of nature, wretched thrall,   *Thom.* 1 : 202

—— prey of death,   *Aken.* 141

—— a mortal, preordain'd to death,   *Pope il.* 2 : 271

—— allegory on,   *Parn.* 69

—— is born to bear,   *Pope il.* 2 : 349

—— only vaunts his force, and vaunts in vain, *Pope il.* 2 : 138

—— how thoughtlefs,   *Rofc.* 222

—— how active in his own trepan,   *Rofc.* 222

—— proud of vain wifdom,   *Hughes* 239

—— heir of thy father's vice,   *Hughes* 239

—— propagated folly,   *Hughes* 239

—— fated to be curft,   *Pope il.* 2 : 266

—— to right inflexibly inclin'd, refts fecure,   *Hughes* 88

—— in merit humble, in pretenfions high,   *Buck.* 110

—— and all his ways are vain,   *Swift* 2 : 147

—— boafted Lord of nature, weak and erring,   *Swift* 2 : 147

—— led by folly, combats nature,   *Swift* 2 : 300

—— awakes to cares, with the dawn,   *Brooke* 152

—— the moft conceited creature,   *Gay* 2 : 115

—— of blood be doom'd to bleed,   *Pope od.* 3 : 41

—— no one is pleafed with what he has,   *Cong.* 142

————— difpleafed with what he is,   *Cong.* 142

—— perverfe, againft nature ftrives,   *Cong.* 143

Man, vain man, in folly only wife,   *Pope* 2 : 4

—— only from himfelf can fuffer wrong,   *A. Phil.* 335

—— who fuffers, loudly may complain,   *Pope il.* 1 : 43

—— is practis'd in difguife,   *Gay* 2 : 26

—— who ftudies nature's laws,   *Gay* 2 : 28

—— maxims draws from certain truth,   *Gay* 2 : 28

—— what a miracle to man,   *Young* 2 : 6

—— though a fool, yet God is wife,   *Pope* 2 : 53

——'s of a jealous and miftaking mind,   *Pope od.* 4 : 198

—— turn'd on man, a fiercer favage,   *Pope* 2 : 61

—— be dumb, when heaven afflicts,   *Pope od.* 4 : 122

—— effay on,   *Pope* 2 : 29

—— is as perfect as he ought,   *Pope* 2 : 31

—— his knowledge meafur'd to his ftate,   *Pope* 2 : 31

—— his time a moment, and a point his fpan,   *Pope* 2 : 31

—— never is, but always to be bleft,   *Pope* 2 : 32

—— the proper ftudy of mankind,   *Pope* 2 : 41

—— chaos of thought and paffion,   *Pope* 2 : 41

—— Lord of all, yet a prey to all,   *Pope* 2 : 41

—— glory, jeft, and riddle of the world,   *Pope* 2 : 41

—— moft vain, of all that breathes,   *Pope od.* 4 : 122

—— calamitous by birth,   *Pope od.* 4 : 122

—— untaught to bear, 'gainft heaven rebels,   *Pope od.* 4 : 122

—— changeful, as his blifs or woe,   *Pope od.* 4 : 122

—— too high, when profperous,   *Pope od.* 4 : 122

—— when diftreft too low,   *Pope od.* 4 : 122

—— let him not be proud, but firm of mind,   *Pope od.* 4 : 122

—— his crimes forgive, forgive his virtues too,   *Young* 3 : 79

—— on frail, unknowing, man relies,   *Pope od.* 4 : 163

—— fcene of, a mighty maze,   *Pope* 2 : 29

                                           Man,

Man, a wild, where weeds and flowers shoot,   *Pope* 2 : 29

—— views the world with partial eyes,   *Gay* 2 : 151

—- to man a prey,   *Gay* 2 : 46

—— is now become the lion of the plain,   *Thom.* 1 : 15

—— how rash to plunge in ill,   *Dry.* 1 : 213

—— tyrant of the sex,   *Dry.* 3 : 107

—— lowly servant, but a lofty mate,   *Dry.* 3 : 107

—— loves knowledge,   *Aken.* 38

———————— above the blandishments of sense, *Aken.* 38

—— cheats himself,   *Garth* 37

—— hates realities,   *Garth* 38

—— hugs the cheat,   *Garth* 38

—— how blind, how thoughtless of his fate,   *Pitt* 215

—— all his systems, but conjectures are,   *Gay* 1 : 278

—— though dead, retains part of himself,   *Pope il.* 2 : 293

—— th' immortal mind remains,   *Pope il.* 2 : 293

—— form subsists without the body's aid,   *Pope il.* 2 : 293

—— aërial semblance, and an empty shade,   *Pope il.* 2 : 293

—— is a self-survivor every year,   *Young* 2 : 115

—— like a stream, is in perpetual flow,   *Young* 2 : 115

—— while growing, life is in decrease,   *Young* 2 : 115

—— half-dead before he dies,   *Broome* 174

—— how weak thy fabric,   *Sav.* 13

—— is born to die,   *Pope od.* 4 : 86

—— by vain passions sway'd,   *Broome* 42

—— proud of his reason, by his will betray'd,   *Broome* 42

—— blindly wanders in pursuit of vice,   *Broome* 43

—— perversely fond to stray,   *Broome* 43

—— whose eye has swept th' unbounded scheme? *Thom.* 1 : 54

—— flutters on from vanity to vice,   *Thom.* 1 : 55

Man alone betrays man,   *Rxb.* 323

—— oppreſt, dependant, yet a man,   *Pope od.* 4 : 25

—— ſlave to the inſolence of youthful lords,   *Pope od.* 4 : 25

—— haughty man, is of obdurate kind,   *Broome* 156

—— though bold, is not a match for heaven,   *Weſt* 258

—— decays, when man contends with ſtorms, *Pope od.* 3 : 208

—— diſſembling man, worſt ill, that curſt our ſex, *Broome* 138

—— ſatire on,   *Butl.* 2 : 220

—— of animals the worſt,   *Gay* 2 : 55

—— what ? perhaps the tyrant of a day,   *Gay* 2 : 192

—— greatly lives, who greatly dies,   *Young* 2 : 229

—— hard of heart to man,   *Young* 2 : 50

—— to man the ſoreſt, ſureſt ill,   *Young* 2 : 50

—— of half that live, the butcher and the tomb, *Pope* 3 : 60

—— is the tale of narrative old time,   *Young* 2 : 217

———— ſad tale,   *Young* 2 : 217

—— of wealth is dubb'd a man of worth,   *Pope* 2 : 207

—— it is not in, the fix'd decree to move,   *Pope il.* 1 : 245

—— courage breathes in man,   *Pope il.* 2 : 91

—— has his autumn,   *Sprat* 175

—— of the world anſwered,   *Young* 2 : 213

————————— proud of that inglorious ſtyle, *Young* 2 : 213

—— ſtill enquiring, ſtill miſtaken,   *Prior* 1 : 22

—— lines ſtudies, and fictitious circles draws, *Prior* 1 : 21

—— child of reaſon,   *Thom.* 2 : 76

—— of ſenſe can artifice diſdain,   *Young* 1 : 93

—— nothing more weak, calamitous and blind, *Pope il.* 2 : 154

—— a miſerable race !   *Pope il.* 2 : 154

—— ſtarting from his couch, ſhall ſleep no more, *Young* 3 : 8

——·· *is blind,*   *Thom.* 2 : 115

Man, what, at enmity with truth ?   *Aken.* 261

—— is born to bear,   *Pope od.* 3 : 176

—— in ftature, ftill a boy in heart,   *Pope od.* 4 : 125

—— who dares think one thing and another tell, *Pope il.* 1 : 278

—— is dead, who for the body lives,   *Young* 2 : 242

—— unfullied with a crime,   *Pitt* 231

—— his folid virtue is his helm,   *Pitt* 232

—— fhould lead the chorus of this lower world, *Thom.* 1 : 86

—— to make man,   *Young* 2 : 133

—— fo great, fo mean,   *Young* 2 : 144

—— buys difappointment with his pain,   *Broome* 58

—— who pardons, difappoints his foe,   *Young* 1 : 91

—— in the moon, what,   *Butl.* 1 : 233

—— and the flea,   *Gay* 2 : 114

—— the cat, the dog, and the fly,   *Gay* 2 : 153

——'s to fight, but heaven's to give fuccefs, *Pope il.* 1 : 205

——'s joys are joys of conqueft, not of peace, *Young* 1 : 12

——'s woe from woman,   *Milt.* 2 : 106

Manhood joined with Deity,   *Cow.* 1 : 84

———— of nine taylors,   *Butl.* 1 : 48

Manillio forc'd captive trumps to yield,   *Pope* 1 : 139

Manly form without a manly mind,   *Pope il.* 2 : 142

—— fhame forbids inglorious flight,   *Pope il.* 2 : 91

—— virtue,   *Swift* 1 : 300

Mankind, fabulous rife of,   *Black.* 177

———— fpontaneous birth of,   *Black.* 178

———— gave not themfelves being,   *Black.* 184

———————————— why difcontinued,   *Black.* 181

———— true origin of,   *Black.* 183

———— calamities of,   *Black.* 150

Mankind,

Mankind, their state requires there should be a God, *Black.* 151

———— how much a nothing, *Swift* 1 : 15

———— rough-hewn by nature, *Butl.* 2 : 133

———— polished by art, *Butl.* 2 : 133

———— but a rabble, *Butl.* 2 : 348

———— news and politics divide, *Gay* 1 : 2

———— a certain change of joy and sorrow find, *Prior* 1 : 27

———— alike require the grace of heaven, *Pope od.* 3 : 83

———— all born to want, a miserable race, *Pope od.* 3 : 83

———— perverse charge their guilt on the gods, *Pope od.* 3 : 40

———— assembled for Pharsalia's day, *Rowe L.* 135

Manna falling, lies in tender grass, *Parn.* 114

Manners make the man, *Som.* 219

———— the basis of the public peace, *Young* 1 : 257

———— example stamps them on the multitude, *Young* 1 : 257

———— white, unblemish'd, now are found no more, *Thom.* 1 : 12

———— pure, from affectation free, *Fent.* 309

———— with fortunes turn, *Pope* 2 : 101

———— should like our countenance be, *King* 327

———— poetically good, *Dry.* 5 : 213

———— take a tincture from our own, *Pope* 2 : 96

———— an ode, *Collins* 267

———— to be learned from life, *Collins* 268

Manoah, father of Samson, *Milt.* 3 : 18

Mansion lies, high o'er the rolling heavens, *Pope* 1 : 290

———— whence gods survey earth, air, and sea, *Pope* 1 : 290

———— here sacred Silence reigns, and Peace, *Pope* 1 : 290

Mantling blood glow'd in his cheeks, *Smith* 114

Mantua, reason of the name, *Dry.* 6 : 279

Mantuan, great without pride, in modest majesty, *Pope* 1 : 210

Manufactures

Manufactures exported, *Dyer* 105

———— roads and rivers, for, *Dyer* 100

Many, flaw all over, *Young* 2 : 63

Marcellus, short-lived, *Dry.* 6 : 154

Marcley-hill removed, *Phil.* 36

Margaret of Anjou, character of, *Gray* 356

———— Cavendish Harley, lady, letters to, *Prior* 2 : 262

Margites, a satire, *Dry.* 7 : 155

Mariamne, prologue to, *Broome* 113

———— meets misfortune, glorious in disgrace, *Broome* 114

Marii fierce, with human gore embrued, *Rowe L.* 284

Marine Society, *Mall.* 302

———— Tyburn's fatal foe, *Mall.* 305

Mariners transformed to dolphins, *Add.* 167

Marius had various turns of good and bad, *Rowe L.* 89

——— slaughter-loving, *Rowe L.* 109

——— an end of exile only sought, *Rowe L.* 93

Mark, betrays the lover's heart, *Broome* 173

Market-hill, revolution at, *Swift* 2 : 179

Marlborough, duke of, *Garth* 108

———— ode to, *Som.* 163

———— best deserving chief, *Som.* 166

———— turned for the camp or court, *Add.* 65

———— sacred to verse, and sure of fame, *Prior* 1 : 190

——— compared to Midas, *Swift* 1 : 73

———— embarking for Ostend, *Som.* 168

———— prudence and fortitude guard, *Rowe* 16

———— his labours liberty cheer'd, *Rowe* 16

———— came, defeated Gallia fled, *Gay* 1 : 185

———— whose laurels shall never fade, *Gay* 1 : 186

Marlborough bore his shatter'd foes to Danube's shore, *Smith* 207

———— calmness of, in action,   *Add.* 65

———— like an angel directing a storm,   *Add.* 63

———— bears the force of armies in his name,   *Add.* 65

Marmaridans, that match'd the wind,   *Rowe L.* 196

Maro, humble tenement of,   *Dyer* 20

——— dwelt on the Esculian mount,   *Dyer* 20

Marriage, progress of,   *Swift* 2 : 208

———— the happiest bond, when hearts agree,   *Lanf.* 305

———— vows render more than friends,   *King* 296

———— honour of,   *Mih.* 1 : 126

———— a vow,   *Butl.* 2 : 130

———— satire on,   *Butl.* 2 : 253

———— grown a money-league,   *Swift* 1 : 101

———— is but a money-job at best,   *Gay* 2 : 178

———— no heaven in,   *Butl.* 1 : 293

———— a bargain at a venture,   *Butl.* 1 : 294

———— of earl of ———,   *Pom.* 296

Marriages were made in heaven,   *Swift* 1 : 155

Married, quarrels of, recruits of love,   *Butl.* 1 : 305

Marrow-puddings to pamper with,   *Butl.* 1 : 218

Marry in good time, or not at all,   *Som.* 296

——— who will, our sex is to be sold,   *Pope* 1 : 260

Mars fiery-helm'd,   *Pope il.* 2 : 214

——— the homicide,   *Pope il.* 1 : 185

——— rash, furious blind, from these to those he flies, *id.* 1 : 185

——— wounded, bellows with pain,   *Pope il.* 1 : 186

——— wide destroyer of the race of man,   *Pope il.* 2 : 15

——— attendants of,   *Dry.* 7 : 63

——— is our common Lord, alike to all,   *Pope il.* 2 : 181

Mars now lords it o'er the heavens alone,   *Rowe L.* 79
——— to kindle with military sounds,   *Dry.* 3 : 164
———'cur'd by Pæon of his wound,   *Pope il.* 1 : 188
——— rallies the Trojans,   *Pope il.* 1 : 170
——— the warrior's god,   *Dry.* 3 : 104
——— rules the realm of love,   *Dry.* 3 : 105
——— sways Thracia's winter coast,   *Dry.* 3 : 109
——— temple of,   *Dry.* 3 : 93
Martial imitated,   *Cow.* 1 : 124
——— to Cirinus,   *Watts* 265
Martyrs' blood, seed of Church,   *Cow.* 1 : 185
Marullus to Neæra,   *Fent.* 302
Mary, second Eve,   *Milt.* 1 : 152
——— overshadowed by the Holy Ghost,   *Milt.* 2 : 147
——— princess of Orange,   *Wall.* 166
——————————— death of,   *Roch.* 333
——— queen, described,   *Step.* 260
——— a name to grief for ever sacred as to fame, *Prior* 1 : 165
Mary Scot, song,   *Mall.* 340
Mary the cook-maid's letter,   *Swift* 1 : 286
Mary Gulliver to captain Gulliver,   *Gay* 1 : 198
Marygold, a riddle,   *Gay* 1 : 60
Masquerades, on the,   *Pitt* 223
——————— refine upon the sin of whoring,   *Pitt* 224
——————— the modish evil,   *Pitt* 224
——————— one promiscuous whim,   *Pitt* 224
Massic grape, pregnant of racy juice,   *Phil.* 61
Massilia clogg'd Cæsar's rapid conquest,   *Rowe L.* 139
——— th' approaching slavery retards,   *Rowe L.* 139
Master of himself, has none else,   *Cow.* 2 : 278

                                                           Master,

Master, sworn to none, of no sect,   *Pope* 2 : 195

———— of the seven-fold face,   *Pope* 3 : 109

Master's commands resistless,   *Milt.* 3 : 54

Master-jest to break,   *Butl.* 2 : 47

Master-passion swallows up the rest,   *Pope* 2 : 46

———————— the mind's disease,   *Pope* 2 : 47

Master-strokes the nobler passions move,   *Lytt.* 103

Master-talent missing, we err without redress,   *Fent.* 312

Mastiffs,   *Gay* 2 : 88

Match implies likeness and equality,   *Butl.* 1 : 179

Matches, few happy,   *Watts* 217

————— 'tis friendship makes the bondage sweet,   *Watts* 219

Mate to kill, what beast was e'er accomplice,   *Fent.* 263

Mathesis, running round the circle, finds it square,   *Pope* 3 : 219

Matrimonial state, feigned love and real hate,   *Fent.* 272

Matrimony goes by destiny,   *Butl.* 1 : 185 | 2 : 106

Matter, mutual action of,   *Black.* 84

———— no necessary being,   *Black.* 98

———— immortal ! and shall spirit die ?   *Young* 2 : 153

Matthew, paraphrase on a part of,   *Thom.* 2 : 181

Maudlin whigs deplore their Cato's fate,   *Rowe* 56

Maurice and Henry, thunder-bolts of war,   *Hughes* 44

————— first resign'd to fate,   *Hughes* 45

————— far exceeds his father's fame,   *Hughes* 44

————— skill'd, camps, sieges, battles, to ordain,   *Hughes* 44

Maximins rant in rhyme,   *Fent.* 236

Maxims are drawn from notions,   *Pope* 2 : 95

May, her vigils kept,   *Dry.* 3 : 61

——— to dance about,   *Dry.* 3 : 185

——— faithless April of,   *Cow.* 1 : 124

                                                            May,

May, merry month,   *Hughes* 66

May-games,   *Som.* 100

May-morning,   *Milt.* 3 : 97

Maynard imitated,   *Broome* 117

Mayor, pageants borne before,   *Butl.* 2 : 311

Maze, dark, poor mortals tread,   *Buck.* 118

Me, me, he cry'd, turn all your swords on me, *Dry.* 6 : 250

—— give sweet content on foot,   *Gay* 1 : 131

—— wrapt in my virtue, and a good surtout, *Gay* 1 : 131

Mean lies between excess and famine,   *Pope* 2 : 183

—— like showery bow, proud with beauties not his own, *Fent.* 217

Meanest Briton scorns the highest slave,   *Add.* 61

Meanings lewd and double entendres,   *Swift* 2 : 75

Meanness accompanies riches,   *Cow.* 1 : 50

Means have no merit, if our end amiss, *Young* 2 : 139

—— to gain, and then to lose the end,   *Buck.* 89

Meats sweetest, soonest cloy,   *Prior* 2 : 205

Medal,   *Dry.* 1 : 209

—— inscription on,   *Lans.* 229

—— faithful to its charge of fame,   *Pope* 2 : 145

—— thro' climes and ages bears each form and name, *ib.* 145

Medea, a new edition of old Æson gave,   *Pope* 3 : 224

—— wakes, a prey to love,   *Broome* 151

—— be fam'd for guilt,   *Broome* 152

Mediocrities never enrich,   *Cow.* 2 : 255

Meditate my doom, to crown their joy, *Pope od.* 3 : 50

Mediterranean, view of,   *Dyer* 107

Medon, skill'd in song,   *Pope od.* 4 : 80

—— the herald spar'd at Telemachus' request, *Pope od.* 4 : 210

Medlar-fruit, delicious in decay,   *Phil.* 7

E 3   [Medlars,

Medlars, from the haw-thorn,   Phil. 44

Medusa, seat of,   Rowe L. 405.

———— look of, killing,   Rowe L. 406.

———— slain by Perseus,   Rowe L. 406

———— curl'd with snaky locks,   Fent. 272

Megara, of Creon's race, spous'd by Alcides,   Fent. 257

Meek-honour, female shame,   Aken. 290

———— whither from Albion dost thou fly ? Aken. 290

———— once the fame of Albion's daughters, Aken. 290

———— Beauty's only friend,   Aken. 290

Meekness, lovely virtue,   Parn. 108

Melancholy, an ode,   Broome 29

———— hide me in thy pensive train,   Broome 29

———— blissful mourner, wisely sad,   Broome 29

———— hail ! sage and holy !   Milt. 3 : 106.

———— death-like silence, and dread repose, Pope 1 : 188.

———— gloomy presence darkens all the scene, id. 1 : 188.

———— sat retired,   Collins 272

———— a kindly mood of,   Dyer 19

———— how deep thy diapason,   Dyer 20

———— mark'd him for her own,   Gray 341

Melanthius, lopp'd piece-meal,   Pope od. 4 : 214.

Meleager and Atalanta,   Dry 4 : 1

———— slays the ravaging boar,   Pope il. 1 : 287

Melesigenes, name of Homer,   Milt. 2 : 209

Meliboeus,   Dry. 5 : 55

Melody, 'tis Love creates,   Thom. 1 : 24

———— the voice of Love,   Thom. 1 : 24

Memnon, though stone, was counted vocal,   Prior 1 : 37

———— statue of musical,   Lansf. 127

                                                      Memory,

Memory, ode to,   Shen. 89
————— thou foul of joy and pain,   Sav. 86
————— actor of our paffions o'er again,   Sav. 86
————— want of, curfe of wit,   Lanf. 219
Men, progeny of God,   Milt. 1 : 156
——— all fons of God,   Milt. 2 : 218
——— race of, like leaves on trees,   Pope il. 1 : 197
——— they fall fuccoffive, and fuccoffive rife,   Pope il. 1 : 197
——— a fhort-liv'd race,   A. Phil. 384
——— creatures of a day,   Cow. 2 : 367
——— invite ruin on themfelves,   Milt. 3 : 63
——— but bubbles on the ftream of time,   Young 1 : 96
——— we various ruling paffions find in,   Pope 2 : 113
——— of different inclinations,   Dry. 7 : 359
——— different purfuits of,   Dry. 7 : 347
——— ways of, fo mutable,   Milt. 3 : 54
——— like beafts, each other's prey,   Dry. 1 : 161
——— once ignorant, are flaves,   Pope 1 : 83
——— whom lying vanities enfnare, forfake thy mercy, Parn. 225
——— of the world, the terræ-filial breed,   Young 2 : 222
——— doating on heaps of yellow duft,   Buck. 89
——— for that defpifing honour and eafe,   Buck. 89
——— homage pay to men,   Young 2 : 74
——— and turn their back on thee,   Young 2 : 74
——— forge the patents, that create them fots, Young 1 : 100
——— may live fools, but fools they cannot die, Young 2 : 90
——— would be angels, angels would be gods,   Pope 2 : 34
——— may be read, as well as books,   Pope 2 : 95
——— faithlefs men, make the fex their prey, Pope od. 4 : 226
——— blind to their own errors,   Gay 2 : 94

E 4

Men judge of happiness and woe by outward show,   Gay 2 : 97
—— who liv'd and dy'd without a name,   Swift 1 : 20
—— are the chief heroes in the lift of fame,   Swift 1 : 20
—— prove with child, as fancy works,   Pope 1 : 146
—— vain flaves of interest and of pride,   Thom. 2 : 191
—— whose bosoms tender pity warms,   Pope od. 3 : 224
—— be in action, as in name,   Pope il. 2 : 144
—— whose vice but makes them scandalously great, Parn. 164
—— are all mad,   Gay 2 : 21
—— and when the briny cure they try'd,   Gay 2 : 21
—— some part still kept above the tide,   Gay 2 : 21
—— mistake their talents,   Swift 2 : 289
—— beasts may degenerate into,   Swift 2 : 289
—— have ever been the same,   Cong. 149
—— only feel the smart, but not the vice,   Pope 2 : 250
—— oft are false,   Cong. 113
—— have four legs by nature,   Butl. 1 : 181
—— are all dedication-proof,   Gay 1 : 181
—— and gods with gifts are pleased,   Cong. 136
—— and women made for each other,   Butl. 2 : 133
—— young and old, praise the Lord,   Watts 92
Menam, nightly shines with infect-lamps,   Thom. 1 : 72
Mendicant, a truly vagrant.   Pope il. 4 : 117
Menelaus, in fifty ships leads the Spartans,   Pope il. 1 : 90
—— a chief once thought, no terror of the field, ib. 159
—— accepts Paris's challenge,   Pope il. 1 : 109
—— magnificence of his palace,   Pope od. 3 : 108
Menœtheus no chief like thee,   Pope il. 1 : 80
Menippean satire what,   Pope il. — : 120
Mennis, Denham to,   Jon. 44
                                                 Watts

Mental eye, paft, prefent, future, can defcry,   *Weft* 227

Mentes, monarch of the Taphian land,   *Pope od.* 3 : 43

———— whofe form Minerva takes,   *Pope od.* 3 : 43

Mentor, Ulyffes' faithful friend,   *Pope od.* 3 : 69

Merab, promifed to David,   *Cow.* 2 : 156

———— defpifes David,   *Cow.* 2 : 156

Mercenary war, flave of gold,   *Rowe L.* 452

———————— thy courage bought and fold, *Rowe L.* 452

Merchant,   *Young* 3 : 239

———— is no inglorious name,   *Young* 3 : 265

———— with purple monarch vies,   *Young* 3 : 265

———— accomplifh'd, is an accomplifh'd man, *Young* 3 : 266

Mercury defcribed,   *Pope* 1 : 299

———— god of gain,   *Dry.* 3 : 150

———— with filver tongue,   *Swift* 2 : 234

———— conveys the fuitors' fouls to the fhades, *Pope od.* 4 : 235

———— wand, that feals in, or chaces fleep, *Pope od.* 4 : 235

———— and Cupid,   *Prior* 1 : 119

Mercy, ode to,   *Collins* 255

———— gentleft of fky-born forms,   *Collins* 255

———— how fwift its aid,   *Parn.* 136

———— to forgive,   *Dry.* 2 : 17

———— heaven's firft attribute,   *Mall.* 296

———— embracing man and brute,   *Mall.* 296

———— attribute of heaven,   *Ot.* 4

———— decreed fallen man,   *Milt.* 1 : 77

———— heavenly born,   *Som.* 67

———— thou beft prerogative of power,   *Som.* 67

———— fweeteft act divine,   *Parn.* 118

———— melts the finner,   *Dry.* 3 : 208

                                           Mercy

Mercy I to others shew, that mercy shew to me,   Pope 2 : 88
———— quits the score,   Dry. 1 : 248
———— works of, a part of rest,   Dry. 2 : 180
———— the brightest virtue of the mind,   Pom. 286
———— sways the brave,   Pope od. 4 : 120
———— and justice, virtues that adorn a king,   Parn. 163
———— what, can the zealot's heart assuage,   Young 1 : 56
Merion, burning with a hero's rage,   Pope il. 2 : 147
Merit, a mark, at which disgrace is thrown,   Sav. 60
———— was a crime,   Som. 171
———— obscure shall raise its head,   Som. 376
———— can it hope success in woman's eyes,   Gay 2 : 215
———— chiefly plac'd in judgment, wit, and taste,   Swift 1 : 111
———— wanting, no favour, no praise, will avail,   Pope 1 : 11
———— we are bound to give applause,   Bush. 94
———— who conscious of, shuns the praise,   Hughes 276
———— distress'd impartial heaven relieves,   Pope 1 : 321
Merlin, prophecy of,   Swift 1 : 58
———— discovers the Cambrian mines,   Yal. 405
Meroe, where shadow both way falls,   Milt. 2 : 203
———— fruitful to a sooty race,   Hughes 302
———— and proud of ebon woods,   Hughes 305
Meroz came not in the field prepar'd,   Parn. 142
Merry Andrew,   Prior 1 : 200
———— poetaster,   Garth 157
Mesappus described,   Dry. 6 : 189
Methy hayes prepares,   Rowe L. 184
Messapus, sea-born,   Dry. 7 : 74
Messiah, a sacred eclogue,   Pope 1 : 47
———— promise of,   Milt. 2 : 189
                                                   Messiah

Meffiah anointed king,   *Milt.* 1 : 161
———— born to fuffering, penury, and fcorn,   *Sav.* 22
———— returned victorious,   *Milt.* 1 : 202
———— enfign of,   *Milt.* 1 : 199
———— Solomon, his church the bride,   *Parn.* 204
Meftles and Antiphus the Mæonians head,   *Pope il.* 1 : 102
Metals difcovered,   *Milt.* 2 : 104
———— how formed,   *Yal.* 403
Metamorphofes, tranflations of,   *Garth* 122
————————— notes on,   *Add.* 179
Metaphor, what,   *Dry.* 5 : 264
————————— bard diverfifies fong by,   *Pitt* 363
Metaphoric meat and drink is to underftand and think *Swift* 2 : 21
Metaphorical terms, unfitting philofophy,   *Black.* 3
————————————— ufed by Cicero,   *Black.* 3
Metaphors, tranfparent veils,   *Lanf.* 232
————————— cover, and not hide,   *Lanf.* 232
Metaurus, red with Punic blood,   *Rowe L.* 102
Meteors, now in various forms appear,   *Rowe L.* 72
Methuen, epiftle to,   *Gay* 1 : 180
———— of fincereft mind,   *Gay* 189
Mezentius, character of,   *Dry.* 6 : 187, 217
————————— flies to Turnus,   *Dry.* 6 : 217
————————— impiety of,   *Dry.* 6 : 312
————————— killed,   *Dry.* 6 : 314
————————— fpoils of, a trophy,   *Dry.* 7 : 1
Mezeray's hiftory, lines written in,   *Prior* 1 : 155
Mice, arm'd for battle,   *Parn.* 42
———— Erle Robert's, in Chaucer's ftyle,   *Prior* 2 : 5
Michael, prince of celeftial armies,   *Milt.* 1 : 174
                                                           Michael,

Michael, fword of,   *Milt.* 1 : 180, 185

Michal, character of,   *Dry.* 1 : 162

———— in love with David,   *Cow.* 2 : 158

Microfcope, difcoveries by,   *Phil.* 45

Microfcopes enlarge our knowledge,   *Cow.* 1 : 219

Midas, fable of,   *Swift* 1 : 71

———— ears of,   *Dry.* 3 : 193

Middle ftate, who keeps, knows how to live, .   *Pope* 2 : 184

Midnight riot, fpreads illufive joys,   *Sav.* 40

————————— fortune, health, and dearer time deftroys, *id.* 40

Midwife-time, a ffifts at all events,   *Dry.* 3 : 95

Might, called heroic virtue,   . *Milt.* 2 : 108

Mighty fled, purfued by ftronger might,   *Pope il.* 2 : 270

————— Hector purfued by Achilles,   *Pope il.* 2 : 270.

————————————— thrice round the Trojan wall, *ib.* 270

————————— to his fears refign'd,   *Pope il.* 2 : 270.

————— hearts are held in flender chains, .   *Pope* 1 : 133

Mildnefs has a force divine,   ,   *King* 288

Milky way, innumerable ftars,   *Mall.* 223

Milo-like, furveys his arms and hands, .   *Pope* 3 : 154

Milonides, mafter of the ring,   *Som.* 102

————— proclaims the prizes,   *Som.* 103 .

Milton, Paradife Loft,   *Milt.* 1 : 5 .

——————— Regained,   2 : 143

———— Samfon Agoniftes,   3 : 7 .

———— occafional poems,   3 : 71 .

———— Chrift's nativity,   .   3 : 79

———— the paffion,   3 : 89

———— on time,   3 : 93

———— May-morning,   3 : 97

                                                     Milton,

Milton, on Shakspeare,   *Milt.* 3 : 98

———— L'Allegro,   3 : 101

———— Penseroso,   3 : 106

———— Arcades,   3 : 112

———— Comus,   3 : 121

———— Lycidas,   3 : 159

———— Latin poems,   3 : 229

———— imitated,   *Add.* 46

———— memory of,   *Hughes* 198

———— lot blended good with ill,   *Hughes* 198

———— strength of his sacred lines,   *Ham.* 225

———— happily copied Homer,   *Dry.* 7 : 117

———— rhyme not his talent,   *Dry.* 7 : 118

———— unfetter'd in numbers,   *Add.* 36

———— spurns mortality,   *Add.* 36

———— sets th' almighty thunderer in arms,   *Add.* 36

———— describes the gay scenes of Paradise,   *Add.* 36

———— varnishes o'er the guilt of rebels,   *Add.* 36

———— and Butler in thy Muse combine,   *Smith* 192

Mimickry of *deep yet clear,*   *Swift* 2 : 369

Minc'd pies quarrel with,   *Butl.* 1 : 17

Mind, power of abstracting,   *Black.* 210

———— separating,   *Black.* 210

———— uniting ideas,   *Black.* 211

———— reasoning,   *Black.* 211

———— in invention,   *Black.* 213

———— freedom of choice,   *Black.* 216

———— controlling appetite,   *Black.* 214

———— operations of, in works of imagination,   *Aken.* 72

———— artist at creating self-alarms,   *Young* 2 : 131

        Mind,

Mind, rich in expedients for inquietude, *Young* 1 : 132

———— contains sources of new, beauteous, and sublime, *Aken.* 29

———— sagacious, sees the train of consequences rise, *West* 205

———— nauseates what she can't believe, *Tick.* 119

———— to brace to dignity of thought, *Broome* 93

———— humble as osiers, bending to the wind, *Cong.* 8

———— true nobility is of the, *Dry.* 3 : 254

———— to be happy, must be great, *Young* 3 : 47

———— from envy free, to charity inclin'd, *Pope od.* 4 : 107

———— not to be laid by the heels, *Butl.* 1 : 137

Minds of men, different dispositions of, *Aken.* 116

Mineral-waters, salutariness of, *Aken.* 307

Minerva, armour of, described, *Pope il.* 1 : 181

———— breaks the truce, *Pope il.* 1 : 131

———— persuades Pandarus to aim at Menelaus, *Pope il.* 1 : 131

———— fires the Grecians, *Pope il.* 1 : 147

———— in form of Mentes, tutors Telemachus, *Pope od.* 3 : 43

———— sees the misrule of the suitor-train, *Pope od.* 3 : 43

———— introduced by Telemachus, *Pope od.* 3 : 44

———— entertained, *Pope od.* 3 : 45

———— takes Mentor's form, *Pope od.* 3 : 71

———— helps him to a ship, *Pope od.* 3 : 70

———— vanishes in the form of an eagle, *Pope od.* 3 : 96

———— breathes within her breast, *Pope od.* 3 : 95

———— train'd to twirl the spindle, *Parn.* 7

Mines, contents of, *Garth* 79

———— verses on those of Sir Carbery Price, *Yal.* 400

———— of Wales, how discovered, *Yal.* 405

———— that whirl'd battalions to the skies, *Tick.* 101

Minister of state, *Swift* 1 : 68

Ministers

Ministers bleſt with prudence, great the profit,   Pope il. 2 · 92

———— may thirſt for gain,   Gay 2 : 334

Minos, the rigid arbiter of right,   Som. 259

———— absolves the juſt, the guilty dooms,   Pope od. 7 : 302

Minſtrelſy, by ſtring or wine,   Butl 1 · 52

Minute philoſophers, who!   Den. 342

Minute, none in a lover's fears,   King 297

Minyas breeds the fourth ſtream,   Hughes 367

Miracle, an alarm, to wake the world,   Young 3 : 43

Miracles, appeal to ſenſe,   Dry. 2 : 32

Miranda,   Hughes 122

———————— thine, the ———— ———— of memory,   Hughes 124

———————— verſes it,   Lov. 344

———————— leaving the ————,   Som. 278

Mirmilla, ſaved again,   Garth 50

———————— ———— ———,   Garth 49

———————— ſoliloquy of,   Garth 62

Mirror, ———— ———, —,   Som. 49

Mirrors ———— ———,   Wat 36

Mirth inſpires ————,   Lov. 97

———— exalts a ————,   Parn. 29

———— ſober'd ————,   Tom 2 : 178

Miſcellanea,   Yom 2 : 204

Miſcellania,   Yom 2 : 227 / Lov. 18

Miſcellany ————,   Som. 503

———————— of ———— ————,   Gay 2 : 223

———————— ———— ———— ————,   Gay 2 : 223

———————— ———— ———— ————,   Sop. 2 : 223

Miſers ———— ———— ———— ————,   Som. 192

————   ————

Misenus, fate of,   *Dry.* 6 : 121, 123

————— honoured with funeral rites,   *Dry.* 6 : 123

————— gives name to a cape,   *Dry.* 6 : 124

Miser, speech of,   { *Wall.* 104   *Som.* 257

————— starves, to raise a son,   *Buck.* 107

————— must make up his plum,   *Prior* 1 : 153

————— though wealthy, he no wealth enjoys,   *Sav.* 40

————— unfriended lives, and unlamented dies,   *Sav.* 40

————— epitaph on,   *Swift* 1 : 181

————— and Plutus,   *Gay* 2 : 38

————— his breast, a troubled ocean, ne'er at rest, *Gay* 2 : 151

————— his fear anticipates disgrace,   *Gay* 2 : 151

Miseries feel, before they come,   *Rowe L.* 81

————— that groan for the grave's shelter, *Young* 3 : 73

Misers brood o'er their stores of gold,   *Smith* 166

————— are muck-worms,   *Pope* 2 : 349

Misery, can words avail?   *Pope od.* 3 : 325

————— Death's harbinger,   *Milt.* 2 : 3

————— even to Gods is sacred,   *Pope od.* 3 : 164

————— often points the path to bliss,   *Sav.* 35

Misfortune serves to make us wise,   *Gay* 2 : 52

Misfortunes heighten happiness,   *Cow.* 1 : 188

————— borne with courage, please heaven, *Cow.* 1 : 190

————— harden virtue,   *Cow.* 1 : 189

————— travel in a train,   *Young* 1 : 55

————— oft in life form one chain,   *Young* 1 : 55

Miss M. H. with Pope's works,   *Sav.* 154

————— life of loveliness, thou soul of joy !   *Sav.* 155

Misselto, produced on the oak,   *Garth* 97

5   Mistress,

Miftrefs, Anacreon to,   *Broome* 16g

———— or Love-verfes,   *Cow.* 1 : 223

———— looking on and talking with,   *Cow.* 1 : 28g

Mithras, to whofe beams the Perfian bows,   *Pops* 1 : 326

———— whofe head the blaze of light adorns,   *Pope* 1 : 326

Mitio, verfes to,   *Watts* 24g

Mityleniant, their invitation refufed by Pompey, *Rowe L.* 334

Mnestheus, author of Maximian line,   *Dry.* 7 : 53

Moab defcribed,   *Cota.* 2 : 137

———— affords a retreat to David's parents,   *Cow.* 2 : 138

Mobs to be avoided,   *Gay* 1 : 134

Moderate man, wifh of,   *Cow.* 2 : 27g

Modern courfe to India,   *Dyer* 110

———— critics,   *Batl.* 2 : 196

———— Grecians degenerate,   *Batl.* 2 : 222

———— lady, journal of,   *Swift* 2 : 71

———— Latin, can bear no criticifm,   *Dry.* 5 : 18

———— faint,   *Prior* 2 : 243

———— wits, mounted on the old, fee far,   *Batl.* 1 : 50

Modes, extremity of, imitated by fools,   *Dry.* 2 : 119

Modeft dulnefs preferable to learned arrogance, *Broome* 13

Modefty, lead the train of virtue,   *Collins* 235

———— adorns our looks,   *Prior* 2 : 213

———— ne'er was fo great a dearth of,   *Cong.* 72

Mohocks, a fet of modern rakes,   *Gay* 1 : 143

———— flafh our fons with bloody knives,   *Gay* 1 : 180

Mole, that hides his diving flood,   *Pope* 1 : 71

Moliere, firft of Comic wits,   *Lytt.* 28

———— by keen, but decent fatire, fkill'd to pleafe, *Lytt.* 28

———— with morals mirth uniting, ftrength with eafe, *id.* 28

Moliere, chastis'd and regular,   Thom. 2 : 197
Molinda,   Hughes 96
Molly Mog,   Gay 1 : 263
———————— fair maid of the Inn,   Gay 1 : 263
Moloch described,   Milt. 1 : 18, 36
————— where worshiped,   Milt. 1 : 36
————— speech of,   Milt. 1 : 136
————— cloven to the waist,   Milt. 1 : 185
Moly, effects of,   Pope od. 3 : 263
————— described,   Pope od. 3 : 263
Moment, thy duration, foolish man,   Prior 2 : 220
Momus, a buffoon above,   Swift 2 : 150
————— with a noisy laugh forestalls his joke, Gay 1 : 32
Monarch founds his greatness on his subjects' love, Prior 1 : 187
————— be the scourge of God,   Pope od. 3 : 145
————— crush the nations with an iron rod,   Pope od. 3 : 145
————— when in mouldering urn he lies,   West 201
————— his fame in lively characters remains, West 201
Monarchs by the gods are plung'd in woe,   Pope od. 4 : 169
————— rule by God appointed,   Prior 2 : 83
————— by indulgence undone,   Dry. 1 : 161
————— what petty motives rule,   Swift 1 : 5
Monarch's praise, his country's parent,   Tick. 105
Monasteries suppress'd,   Thom. 2 : 111
Monday,   Gay 1 : 55
Mopsa shall mourn her sinking fane,   Rowe L. 64
Money, mankind fall down before,   Butl. 2 : 65
————— the last reason of kings,   Butl. 2 : 65
————— brings honour, friends, and realms,   Milt. 2 : 177
————— power of, in love,   Butl. 2 : 129
                                               . Money,

Money, the life-blood of the nation,   *Swift* 1 : 189

————— circulation, its motion and its heat maintains, *ib.* 189

————— impudent, and prevails,   *Dry.* 7 : 297

————— tempts to every distant mart,   *Collins* 237

————— mythologic sense of love,   *Butl.* 1 : 171

Money-jobbers fatten by a nation's spoils,   *Mall.* 312

Monk, Zerubbabel,   *Cow.* 1 : 193

Monkey who had seen the world,   *Gay* 2 : 52

Monks finish'd what the Goths began,   *Pope* 1 : 120

Monmouth, on his Bentivoglio,   *Wall.* 174

————— duke of,   *Wall.* 176

Monody,   *Lytt.* 63

Monopolies,   *Thom.* 1 : 114

Monopoly,   *Cow.* 1 : 286

Monster ! mix'd of insolence and fear,   *Pope il.* 1 : 47

————— dog in forehead, but in heart a deer, *Pope il.* 1 : 47

————— scourge of thy people, violent and base, *Pope il.* 1 : 47

————— sent in Jove's anger on a slavish race, *Pope il.* 1 : 47

Montague, for wit, for humour, and judgment famed, *Add.* 38

————— negligently graceful,   *Add.* 38

————— best of patrons and of poets too, *Hughes* 23

————— Prior to,   *Prior* 1 : 46

Montaigne's Essays, lines written in,   *Prior* 1 : 278

Montpelier, church at, demolish'd,   *Watts* 126

Monument of mortal hands, how short a period, *Pope il.* 1 : 357

————— for Prior,   *Prior* 2 : 14

Monumental ode,   *Hughes* 208

Monuments decay, frail mansions of the dead, *Hughes* 208

————— like men, submit to fate,   *Pope* 1 : 144

Mood and figure wise, a pest,   *Dry.* 7 : 290

Moon changes still, another, yet the same,   *Broome* 96

————— queen of the gay attendants of the night,   *Broome* 97

————— changeful, intends the tides,   *Hughes* 196

————— swells ocean into tides,   *Mall.* 219

————— drinking borrowed light,   *Dry.* 3 : 98

————— refulgent lamp of night,   *Pope il.* 1 : 262

————— o'er heaven's azure spreads her light,   *Pope il.* 262

————— distributes fainter day,   *Prior* 2 : 118

————— various her beams, and changeable her face, *id.* 2 : 158

————— empress of the night,   *Pitt* 235

————— fair queen of Silence,   *Watts* 74

————— sea and land in,   *Butl.* 1 : 256

————— not made of green cheese,   *Butl.* 1 : 238

————— elephants in,   *Butl.* 2 : 152

————— dismounted from her sphere,   *Butl.* 1 : 245

————— and stars, heaven's golden alphabet,   *Young* 3 : 57

————— riddle on,   *Swift* 1 : 319

Moony troops of the Solymean sultan,   *Phil.* 28

Moore, to,   *Pope* 2 : 349

————— in memory of the reverend Mr.   *Som.* 191

————— of humble birth, but of more humble mind, *Som.* 191

————— obliging to the rich, a father to the poor,   *Som.* 191

Moral death, that ties me to the world!   *Young* 2 : 114

————— essays,   *Pope* 2 : 95

————— evidence shall quite decay,   *Pope* 3 : 248

————— grandeur makes the mighty man,   *Young* 2 : 157

————— knowledge, poesy was queen of,   *Dry.* 2 : 118

————— pieces,   *Shen.* 197

Morality added to Philosophy and Divinity,   *Pope od.* 3 : 2

————— forms the Epic poem,   *Pope od.* 3 : 2

                                  Morality

Morality unawares expires,   *Pope* 3 : 264

———— will guide the wise and good,   *Buck.* 95

Morals practise, and be poor,   *Gay* 2 : 148

Morbleu ! cries one,   *Gay* 2 : 24

Mordanto fills the trump of fame,   *Swift* 1 : 36

———— his body active as his mind,   *Swift* 1 : 37

———— in senates bold, and fierce in war, *Swift* 1 : 37

———— heroic actions early bred in,   *Swift* 1 : 37

Morell to Thomson,   *Thom.* 1 : 252

Morgan and Mandevile could prate no more,   *Pope* 3 : 166

Moriah rears his summit nearer to the skies, *Pitt* 260

Morn, rosy-finger'd,   *Pope od.* 4 : 3

———— described,   { *Milt.* 1 : 173
                                            { *Mall.* 196

———— gay daughter of the Air,   *Mall.* 196

———— mother of Dews,   *Thom.* 1 : 45

Morning, description of,   *Swift* 1 : 59

———— described,   *Gay* 1 : 111

———— pledge of day,   *Yal.* 353

———— a glorious, but short-liv'd state,   *Yal.* 355

———— brightest offspring of light,   *Yal.* 355

———— apparition,   *Hughes* 269

———— dreams foreshow,   *Dry.* 3 : 146

———— lark, to welcome day,   *Cong.* 5

———— of the Lord's day,   *Watts* 354

———— hymn for,   *Parn.* 243

———— song,   *Watts* 352

Morpheus, the player God,   *Dry.* 4 : 64

———— raises a world of gayer tinct and grace, *Thom.* 1 : 213

Mortal, more than, that never err'd at all, *Pom.* 225

Mortal, think, what it is to die,   *Parn.* 76

———— blifs, not lafting,   *Dry.* 3 : 57

————— how frail, how flight,   *Lytt.* 74

———— joy, a fhade,   *Sav.* 32

———— pleafures, all in a moment fade,   *Gay* 1 : 251

———— man, why burn with fury, that never dies, *Pope il.* 2 : 197

————— a wretch of humble birth,   *Pope il.* 1 : 169

———— a fhort-liv'd reptile in the duft of earth, *Pope il.* 1 : 169

———— pride, fhort is the reign,   *Som.* 135

———— fchemes how frail!   *Som.* 200

—————— built on fand,   *Som.* 200

Mortality, gayeft fcenes fpeak man's,   *Young* 3 : 3

Mortals, blind in fate,   *Dry.* 6 : 293

———— to their future fate blind,   *Rowe L.* 82

———— fhort of fight!   *Young* 1 : 54

———— boaft of prowefs not their own,   *Pope il.* 2 : 137

———— vainly glitter in the fphere of change,   *Parn.* 119

———— mif-judging, felf-deceiv'd,   *Som.* 97

———— fprung from, with immortals ceafe to vie, *Tick.* 211

———— fooner or late, all know the grave,   *Rowe L.* 187

Morton, to lady,   *Wall.* 123

Mofes, majeftically mild, ferenely good,   *Parn.* 106, 108

———— his wand become a ferpent,   *Cow.* 2 : 56

———— with wants and hardfhips muft engage, *Prior* 2 : 180

———— plots and rebellions muft difturb his age, *Prior* 2 : 180

———— forbid to tread the promis'd land he faw, *Prior* 2 : 180

———— fong of, paraphrafed,   *Pitt* 257

———— fafting,   *Mil.* 2 : 154

———— type of Chrift,   *Mil.* 2 : 117

———— death of,   *Watts* 153

                                                Mofes

Moses by Michael Angelo,   Thom. 2 : 88

Most hands dispatch,   Butl. 2.: 19

Mother, yet no mother,   Sav. 84

———— unenslav'd to nature's narrow laws,   Sav. 84

———— of soul severe,   Sav. 87

———— nurse and fairy,   Gay 2 : 33

———— was ever who'd give her booby for another,   id. 2 : 34

———— bled in the son's defence,   Pope il. 1 : 166

Motion inexplicable without God,   Black. 52

———— direction of, inexplicable,   Black. 53

———— and its cause, not the same,   Black. 130

———— must a power to move suppose,   Black. 131

———— involuntary in the body,   Black. 198

———— voluntary,   Black. 198

Motive dignifies the scar,   Pope od. 4 : 109

Motives, like weights, prevail,   Prior 2 : 55

Motteux, Dryden to,   Dry. 2 : 142

Mount Edgecumbe,   Lytt. 85

Mountain in labour of a mouse,   Butl. 2 : 159

Mountains, use of,   Black. 55

———— lift their green heads to the sky,   Thom. 1 : 4

———— overwhelm the rebel angels,   Milt. 1 : 194

———— what are they in a lover's way ?   Parn. 200

Mountown, panegyric on,   King 347

Mourning-piece,   Watts 250

Mouth to water, with longings,   Butl. 1 : 114

———— padlock for,   Sim. 369

Mouths, without hands,   Dry. 3 : 269

Mulberries change hue,   Cow. 1 : 61

———— of snowy hue,   Hughes 59

Mulberries

Mulberries turned red by Pyramus's blood, *Hughes* 61

Mules, fecurely flow, *Pope il.* 2 : 293

———— a ftrong laborious race, *Pope od.* 5 : 133

Mulgrave, character of, *Dry.* 1 : 118

———— effay on fatire, *Dry.* 1 : 112

Mullinix and Timothy, dialogue between, *Swift* 2 : 81

Mully of Mountown, *King* 347

———— defcribed, *King* 350

———— death of, *King* 351

Multitude always in wrong; *Rofe.* 219

———————— way of, *Watts* 192

Mum, quoth Echo, *Butl.* 1 : 108

Mundungus, ill-perfuming fcent, *Phil.* 4

———————— trucks for viler rhymes, *Pope* 3 : 108

Murder may pafs unpunifhed for a time, *Dry.* 3 : 148

———— fitted to the rules of Art, *Tick.* 102

Murderer dies for public good, *Gay* 2 : 92

Murex, difcovery of, *Dyer* 77

Murmur, diftruft make us wretched, God is juft, *Gay* 2 : 186

Murmurs rifing ftay, nor dare arraign the wife Difpofer, *Lytt.* 73

Murrain among the cattle in Egypt, *Cow.* 2 : 60

———————— in hogs and fheep, *Butl.* 1 : 227

Murdoch, verfes to, *Thom.* 2 : 181

Mufcovites have mow'd their chins, *Gay* 2 : 68

Mufe, goddefs of numbers, and of thoughts fublime, *Hughes* 39

———— whofe fong can fix heroic acts, *Hughes* 39

———— ode to, *Aken.* 218

———— harmonious maid, *Aken.* 218

———— o'er Time and Fame, unbounded power has, *Cong.* 28

———— by Heaven infpir'd, *Hughes* 81

Mufe,

Muse, the heathen Nine her absence can't supply, *Hughes* 82

———— tun'd to pious notes the Psalmist's lyre, *Hughes* 82

———— fill'd Isaiah's breast with more than Pindar's fire, *id.* 82

———— ne'er inspires against conviction, *Swift* 2 : 131

———— though she delights in fiction, *Swift* 2 : 131

———— none proof against a golden shower, *Garth* 93

———— the Bard inspires, exalts his mind, *Pope od.* 3 : 220

———— indulgent loves th' harmonious kind, *Pope od.* 3 : 220

———— power of, *Cow.* 2 : 25, 26

———— birth of, *Cong.* 20

———— and Time set forth with equal pace, *Cong.* 20

———— and Time to all eternity contend, *Cong.* 20

———— from Jove derive thy song, *Cong.* 21

———— imp of Jove, *Thom.* 1 : 209

———— sacred should its product be, *Wall.* 224

———— invoked, *Butl.* 1 : 33

———— if e'er I please, to thee I owe my honours, *Pitt* 265

———— despising gain, strung not for gold her lyre, *West* 217

———— but suffers now far other principles to hold, *West* 218

———————— that man is worthless without gold, *West* 218

———— foe of flattery, *Cow.* 1 : 194

———— last dying song of, *Lansf.* 237

Muses are virgins, till they portions get, *Broome* 88

———— shine in trifles, like our ladies, *Broome* 89

———— Nine, daughters of Jove, *Pope il.* 1 : 86

———— ever young, *Dry.* 1 : 311

———— fly from Tyrants and from Priests, *Lytt.* 34

———— daughters of reason and of liberty, *Lytt.* 34

———— taught civil life, *Wall.* 174

———— thron'd above the starry frame, *Pope il.* 2 : 103

Muses

Mufes write for glory, not for gold,   *Young* 3 : 179

——— conducted by their fquire Apollo, .   *Swift* 2 : 234

Mufic, ode in praife of,   *Hughes* 142

——— her foft, affuafive voice applies, .   *Pope* 1 : 78

——— in cares, exalts the foul,   *Pope* 1 : 78

——— warriors fires with animated founds, .   *Pope* 1 : 78

——— conquers death,   *Pope* 1 : 80

——— can foften pain to eafe,   *Pope* 1 : 81

——— improve our joys below, .   *Pope* 1 : 81

——— antedate the blifs above,   *Pope* 1 : 81

——— has charms alone for peaceful minds, .   *Pope* 1 : 165

——— exalts man's nature,   *Buck.* 98

——— infpires elevated thoughts, or kind defires, .   *Buck.* 98

——— bloffom of delight,   *A. Phil.* 380

——— fphere-defcended maid, .   *Collins* 273

——— devote to virtue, fancy, art, .   *Collins* 274

——— power of,   { *Dry.* 2 : 214
    Buck. 66
    Add. 32
    King 322
    Hughes 174

——— native voice of undiffembled joy, .   *Thm.* 1 : 45

——— an univerfal good,   *Yal.* 387

——— refembles poetry, .   *Pope* 1 : 97

——— can tame the furious beaft,   *Prior* 2 : 132

——— lulls the daughters of neceffity,   *Milt.* 3 : 115

——— can raife and quell paffion, .   *Dry.* 2 : 204

——— fhall untune the fky, .   *Dry.* 2 : 205

——— its influence on rage,   *Cow.* 2 : 85

——— charms defpair, .   *Lanf.* 262

    Mufic

Music softens every care,   Lansf. 262
——— gives life to verses,   Wall. 108
——— every passion yields to thee,   Hughes 117
——— is the voice of love,   Hughes 118
——— was herald of the peace,   Hughes 145
——— proclaim'd the Saviour's birth,   Hughes 145
——— must again call the nations under ground,   Hughes 146
——— alone can calm the troubled mind,   Cong. 60
——— has learn'd the discords of the state,   Hughes 162
——— and concerts jar with Whig and Tory hate,   Hughes 162
——— first invented,   Milt. 2 : 103
——— the banquet's most refin'd delight,   Pope od. 4 : 194
——— of the spheres,   Butl. 1 : 197
——— phantastical conceits of writers on,   West 119
Music-meeting, prologue to,   Garth 116
Musk-apple commended,   Phil. 50
Mustapha, prologue to,   Thom. 2 : 195
Musters false, bane of war,   Dry. 3 : 119
Mutable fair,   Wall. 87
Mutiny against Cæsar,   Rowe L. 215
——— quelled,   Rowe L. 221
Mutius Scævola, motto for,   Gay 1 : 281
Mutual reverence, mutual warmth, inspire,   Pope il. 2 : 87
Mycene in a hundred ships sends her powers,   Pope il. 1 : 90
——— under Agamemnon, king of men,   Pope il. 1 : 90
Myco, Argol,   A. Phil. 311
Myra, praise of,   Lansf. 153
——— singing,   Lansf. 161
——— in her riding habit,   Lansf. 161
——— seems the God of love,   Lansf. 161
                                                               Myra,

Myra,   { Hughes 173
         { Mall. 334

—— sweetness her's, and unaffected ease,   Mall. 335

—— Lansdowne to,   Lanf. 148

—— song to,   Lanf. 180, 212

—— parrot of,   Lanf. 164

—— at a review,   Lanf. 167

Myself, Cowley of,   Cow. 2 : 377

—— my love, my life, renounce,   Pope 1 : 189

Mysteries, like the sun, are plain, but dazzling too, Parn. 103

—— confistent with reason,   Cow. 1 : 135

—— rest on heaven's authority,   Dry. 2 : 12

Mysterious love inexplicable,   Cow. 1 : 156

Mystery see! to mathematics fly,   Pope 3 : 264

Mystic dreams descend from Jove,   Pope il. 1 : 40

Mystic string, that makes the knight companion, Prior 1 : 176

N

Naiads, nymphs presiding over fountains,   Aken. 299

—— hymn to,   Aken. 300

—— daughters of Tethys,   Aken. 301

—— giving motion to the air,   Aken. 301

—— nourishing vegetables,   Aken. 302

—— rendering rivers navigable,   Aken. 303

—— contributing to commerce,   Aken. 303

—— to maritime power,   Aken. 304

—— influencing health,   Aken. 305, 307

—— inspiring poets,   Aken. 308

Nail not work, that will not drive,   Som. 302

Nails, Chinese wear long,   King 175

                           Naked,

d, from th' inclement sky to cloath,   *Pope od.* 4 : 74

;   *Cow.* 1 : 303

– by birth alone, descends,   *Gay* 2 : 168

– a mortal immortality,   *Young* 2 : 137

s distinctive, from the natal hour,   *Pope od.* 3 : 223

ir, on the taking of,   *Prior* 1 : 49

— ballad on taking,   *Prior* 1 : 85

— on taking,   *Cong.* 13

— the prize and mistress of the war,   *Cong.* 15

— whose widen'd gates a conquest owns,   *Hughes* 34

y of the Vale,   *Shen.* 94

s, future fate of,   *Gay* 1 : 145

ing, taken,   *Butl.* 1 : 116

tumultuous in his course,   *Add.* 42

ssus, story of,   *Add.* 166

—– foolish youth, admires himself,   *Gay* 1 : 39

olfact a plot,   *Butl.* 1 : 39

tion to be short and lively,   *Dry.* 1 : 284

nones, nation of, described,   *Rowe L.* 395

u, character of,   *Garth* 89

— house of,   *Hughes* 37

— race of, heroes and patriots,   *Hal.* 230

— born to subdue tyrants,   *Hal.* 230

— great deliverer, wise, and bold,   *Aken.* 260

— designed to curb oppressors,   *Add.* 10

— the world's great patriot,   *Add.* 11

— conquests freedom to the world afford,   *Add.* 12

n happy, and an happy king,   *Pope od.* 3 : 177

– stands sure fixt on virtue,   *Pope od.* 4 : 5

– bless'd, who Jehovah know,   *Pitt* 252

Nations,

5

Nations, manners of, not to confound, *Dry.* 7 : 215

————— bleed, when bigotry prevails, *Sav.* 95

————— of slaves, with tyranny debas'd, *Add.* 54

————— corrupt, enslaved, *Milt.* 3 : 16

————— many-languag'd, *Pope od.* 3 : 94

————— set free may bless his name, *Prior* 1 : 91

————— as bodies, punish'd here, *Young* 1 : 262

Native islanders alone their care, *Pope od.* 3 : 186

————— hateful he, who breathes a foreign air, *Pope od.* 3 : 186

————— isle, fair freedom's happiest seat, *Lytt.* 29

Nativity of Christ, *Cow.* 2 : 129

————— Christ's, *Milt.* 3 : 79

Natura naturata, *Den.* 46

Nature, different meaning of, *Black.* 112

————— works of, marks of wisdom in, *Black.* 114

————— we are Adam's sons by, *Prior* 2 : 258

————— teach me to subdue, *Pope* 1 : 189

————— deprav'd, abundance does pursue, *Black.* 123

————— her first and pure demands are few, *Black.* 123

————— scale of, *Milt.* 1 : 154

————— inexplicable without God, *Black.* 48

————— knowledge of, imperfect, *Prior* 2 : 103

————— lies in shade of night, *Garth* 20

————— dædal hand of, *Phil.* 56

————— various in her frame, *Dry.* 7 : 347

————— wonders in, *Black.* 103

————— how various! *Young* 3 : 247

————— art divine, *Young* 3 : 248

————— has nothing made in vain, *Gay* 1 : 256

————— made nothing in vain, *Rosc.* 314

Nature led through, to Nature's God,   *Pope* 3 : 248

———— works of, design and judgment in,   *Black.* 164

———— has wise ends in view,   *Black.* 167

———— with foresight works, and designs pursues, *Black.* 167

———— all o'er is consecrated ground,   *Young* 3 : 64

———— sending incense to the throne,   *Young* 3 : 65

———— delights in progress from worse to better, *Young* 3 : 67

———— to follow, is by rules to write,   *Som.* 218

———— she led the way, and taught the Stagyrite, *Som.* 218

———— to follow, and regard his end,   *Pope* 1 : 67

———— follow, and resemble God,   *Young* 2 : 241

———— who can paint like?   *Thom.* 1 : 19

———— can Imagination boast hues like her's, *Thom.* 1 : 19

———— or mix them with that matchless skill, *Thom.* 1 : 19

———— sing, and Nature's God,   *Thom.* 1 : 62

———— to each allots his proper sphere,   *Cong.* 143

———— good cateress,   *Milt.* 3 : 148

———— provides each animal its foe,   *Swift* 2 : 132

———— taught art,   *Milt.* 2 : 173

———— to copy, is the task of art,   *Pitt* 353

———— from her the characters are trac'd, *Pitt* 353

———— to all things fix'd the limits fit,   *Pope* 1 : 93

———— at once the source and end, and test of art, *Pope* 1 : 94

———— does the puppy's eyelid close,   *Gay* 1 : 89

———— till the sun has nine times set and rose, *Gay* 1 : 89

———— is frugal, and her wants are few,   *Young* 1 : 123

———— frugal, little needs,   *Pope od.* 4 : 64

——————— needs but daily bread and wine, *Pope od.* 4 : 64

———— affects variety,   *Butl.* 2 : 146

———— jealous maze of,   *Aken.* 39

Nature,

Nature, ever-changing birth of the immutable, *Young* 2 : 152

———— all change, no death, *Young* 2 : 152

———— emblem of man, who passes, not expires, *Young* 2 : 153

———— swarms with life, *Thom.* 1 : 53

———— in various moulds has beauty cast, *Gay* 2 : 240

———— and form'd the feature for each taste, *Gay* 2 : 240

———— herself appears improv'd by art, *Gay* 1 : 340

———— is but art, unknown to thee, *Pope* 2 : 39

———— smiles not alike on all, *Fent.* 312

———— disjoins the beauteous and prophane, *Young* 1 : 153

———— the poet's object, *Lanf.* 235

———— only the true laurel gives, *Gay* 1 : 267

———— the best mistress, *King* 172

———— gifts of improv'd by art, *Phil.* 33

———— on all the power of bliss bestows, *King* 376

———— breaks through all disguise, *Lanf.* 192

———— alone can love inspire, *Hughes* 148, 227

———— still speaks in woman's eyes, *Gay* 1 : 260

———— in spite of art prevails, *Som.* 346

———— lives by toil, *Dyer* 82

———— state of, was the reign of God, *Pope* 2 : 60

———— through the world the war declar'd, *Rowe L.* 81

———— our society adores, where Tindal dictates, *Pope* 3 : 249

———— smiles, will only Delia frown? *Lytt.* 8

———— fainting, *Watts* 146

———— is a friend to truth, *Young* 2 : 85

———— preaches to mankind, *Young* 2 : 86

———— and grace confess the Infinite Unknown, *Watts* 50

———— and skill, two tops of Parnassus, *Den.* 72

Natures generous purify their clay, *Yal.* 441

Natures known by abſtracts, *Butl.* 1 : 11

Naval crown binds to his brow, *Rowe L.* 158

—— games, *Dry.* 6 : 78

Naval-ſtandard, the dire Spaniard's bane, *Aken.* 250

Navel, whether Adam and Eve had, *Butl.* 1 : 14

Navigation makes one city of the univerſe, *Dry.* 1 : 88

Nœæra, on falling in love with, *Ham.* 205

—— covetous temper of, *Ham.* 207, 208

Neat in ſmall fortune is plenty, *King* 209

Neceſſity, gigantic power, *Aken.* 148

—— abſolute, what, *Black.* 152, 154

—— hypothetical, in the world, *Black.* 155

———— adapting means to ends, *Black.* 155

—— to make a virtue of, {*Dry.* 3 : 136
{*King* 358

—— demands our daily bread, *Pope od.* 3 : 195

—— and Chance approach not God, *Milt.* 1 : 212

Nectar, ſweet refection of the gods, *Pope il.* 2 : 207

—— of refreſhing ſtreams, *Smith* 100

Neda, nurſe of Jupiter, *Pitt* 196

Neglect, ſtudied art, *Roſc.* 224

Negligence, a ſort of, deemed as excellence, *King* 313

Nell and John, *Prior* 2 : 241

Nelly, ballad on, *Gay* 1 : 265

Nemean ode, *Crw.* 2 : 15

—— odes, *Weſt* 202

Nepenthe, fountain of, *Thom.* 1 : 208

———— cauſes ſweet oblivion of vile care, *Thom.* 1 : 208

Neptune, court of, *Hughes* 23

—— earth-ſhaking power, *Pope il.* 2 : 56

Neptune, shaker of the earth,   *Pope od.* 4 : 8

———— whose earthquakes rock the ground,   *Pope od.* 4 : 9

———— changes the Phæacian ship to a rock,   *Pope od.* 4 : 9

———— chides the winds,   *Pitt* 279

———— in form of Calchas, encourages the Greeks, *Pope il.* 2 : 5

———— opposes Ulysses' return,   *Pope od.* 3 : 42

Nereus, prophecy of, imitated,   *Tick.* 124

Neritus the clouds divides,   *Pope od.* 4 : 16

Nero, amusement of,   { *King* 422 } { *Cow.* 2 : 341 }

———— thou hast slain thy mother,   *Prior* 1 : 111

Nerves, how fashioned,   *Garth* 21

———— rise and progress of,   *Black.* 197

———— use of,   *Black.* 197

———— organs of sensation,   *Prior* 2 : 33, 34

Nervii, oft rebelling, oft subdued,   *Rowe L.* 67

Nessus, death of,   *Gay* 1 : 316

Nestor, in ninety sail conducts his host,   *Pope il.* 1 : 91

———— experienc'd, in persuasion skill'd,   *Pope il.* 1 : 48

———— two ages o'er his native realm reign'd, *Pope il.* 1 : 48

———— his tongue dropp'd honey,   *Tick.* 173

———— lived three ages o'er,   *Tick.* 173

———— through three ages shin'd,   *Pope od.* 3 : 91

———— benevolent, as wise,   *Pope od.* 3 : 96

———— full of days,   { *Pope od.* 3 : 91 } { *Pope il.* 2 : 314 }

———— narrative of old man,   *Pope od.* 3 : 83

———— grace and glory of the Grecian name, *Pope od.* 3 : 84

———— proposes an embassy to Achilles,   *Pope il.* 1 : 270

———— names the persons for the embassy,   *Pope il.* 1 : 272

Nestor,

Nestor, sage protector of the Greeks,   *Pope il.* 1 : 297

———— old in arms, disdain'd the peace of age, *Pope il.* 1 : 297

———— with inspiring eloquence commands, *Pope il.* 1 : 138

———— master of the martial art,   *Pope il.* 1 : 139

———— grace and glory of th' Achaian name, *Pope il.* 2 : 42

———— rescued by Diomed,   *Pope il.* 1 : 243

———— sacrifices to Minerva,   *Pope od.* 3 : 99

Net of woe, twisted by the Sisters three,   *Thom.* 1 : 235, 239

Nevil, great to settle or dethrone,   *Prior* 1 : 259

Neuter, pleas'd to stand, while the world's at war, *Rowe L.* 82

New conspiracy,   *Garth* 111

Newgate, on a printer sent to,   *Swift* 2 : 339

Newgate's garland,   *Gay* 1 : 273

New-laid eggs preserv'd in hay,   *Gay* 1 : 77

New-light, creature of fancy,   *Butl.* 2 : 287

New-market fame, pride in,   *Pope* 2 : 98

—————————'s glory rose, as Britain's fell, *Pope* 2 : 225

New passions new opinions excite,   *Garth* 38

———— similes, a new song of,   *Gay* 1 : 270

———— song,   *Swift* 1 : 74, 193

News travel with increase from mouth to mouth, *Pope* 1 : 224

Newton, poem to memory of,   *Thom.* 2 : 157

———— all-piercing sage,   *Thom.* 2 : 157

———— all-intellectual eye,   *Thom.* 2 : 158

———— by gravitation and projection saw the whole revolve, *ib.*

———— fix'd the wandering queen of night,   *Thom.* 2 : 158

————————— her influence on the main,   *Thom.* 2 : 158

———— pursued the comet thro' her long curve, *Thom.* 2 : 159

———— freed the heavens from whirling vortices, *Thom.* 2 : 159

———— untwisted the shining robe of light,   *Thom.* 2 : 160

Newton,

. . . . know ledge, *Thom.* 2 : 161

. . . . ivinely good, *Thom.* 2 : 162

. . . . *Thom.* 2 : 163

. . . . *Thom.* 1 : 97

. . . . , . . . each'd before, *Saw.* 99

. . . . . Dryden's stile repeat, *Prior* 1 : 191

. . . . . ky to, *Cow.* 2 : 46

. . . . . . creating its evils, *Cow.* 2 : 47

. . . 16, 1717, ode for, *Rowe* 71, 98

. . . help to make one old, *Swift* 2 : 39

. . . . who breaks windows with half-pence, *Gay* 1 : 143

. . . and Valentini, *Rowe* 30

{ *Milt.* 1 : 121

Butl. 1 : 319

. . . ght, defcription of,   { *King* 361

Thom. 1 : 101

Mall. 203

——— Day's elder-born ! *Young* 3 : 19

——— opes the noblest fcenes, *Young* 3 : 25

——— confort of Chaos, *Milt.* 1 : 67

——— eldeft of things, *Milt.* 1 : 67

——— daughters of, *Dry.* 7 : 83

——— contemplation on, *Gay* 1 : 277

——— Sabbath of mankind, *Butl.* 1 : 320

——— is Virtue's immemorial friend, *Young* 2 : 97

——— friend to our woe, and parent of our fears, *Prior* 2 : 117

——— defcen ling, intercepts the way, *Pope od.* 4 : 54

——— rufh'd o'er the fhaded landfcape, *Pope od.* 3 : 101

——— fpeads her ebon curtains round, *Pom.* 349

——— fevenfold winding jet her temples bound, *Pom.* 349

Nightingale,

Nightingale, beft poet of the grove,   *Thom.* 2 : 190

Night-piece,   { *Wall.*   126
   Pope 1 : 301, 308
   Mall.   203

Night-thoughts,   *Young* 2 : 3

Night-walker reclaim'd,   *Som.* 352

Night-warbler glads with melodious woe,   *Broome* 32

Nile fupplies want of rain,   *Wall.* 33

—— Egypt places her only truft in,   *Rowe L.* 349

—— time of rifing,   *Rowe L.* 444

—— continuance of its overflowing,   *Rowe L.* 444

—— caufes of its overflowing,   *Rowe L.* 444

—— fpring of, unknown,   *Rowe L.* 447

—— divided at Meroe,   *Rowe L.* 448

—— provokes his ftreams, when the dog-ftar beams,   *Hughes* 297

—— joining the Red Sea,   *Dyer* 101

—— rich king of floods,   *Thom.* 1 : 71

Nimble-footed minutes ceas'd to run,   *Broome* 18

Nimmers, to difcover,   *Butl.* 1 : 264

Nimrod, a mighty hunter,   *Milt.* 2 : 120

—— firft made war on beafts,   *Som.* 15

—— the lion's trophies wore,   *Tick.* 145

—— the bloody chace began,   *Pope* 2 : 59

—— a mighty hunter, and his prey was man,   *Pope* 2 : 59

Nimrods, meditating prey on human kind,   *Sav.* 49

Nine, ye tuneful daughters of Almighty Jove,   *Pitt* 331

—— your prieft and bard with rage divine infpire,   *Pitt* 331

—— worthies, who,   *Dry.* 3 : 185

Nineveh believes, and God forgives,   *Parn.* 226

Ninus fhone there, founder of the Perfi.n name;   *Pope* 1 : 206

Ninus's

Ninus's tomb, Pyramus and Thisbe to meet there, *Hughes* 59

Niobe stands her own sad monument of woe, *Pitt* 200

Nireus in three ships sought the Trojan shore, *Pope il.* 1 : 94

———— loveliest youth of all the Greeks, *Pope il.* 1 : 94

Nisus and Euryalus, character of, *Dry.* 6 : 238

——————————— recall Æneas, *Dry.* 6 : 241

——————————— friendship of, *Dry.* 6 : 250

——————————— slain by Volscens, *Dry.* 6 : 250

Noah, preacher of righteousness, *Milt.* 2 : 109

——— builds the ark, *Milt.* 2 : 109

——— head of a new stock, *Milt.* 2 : 119

——— stood exempt from general doom, *Prior* 2 : 179

——— three sons, future hopes of earth, *Prior* 2 : 179

——— plants a vine, *Butl.* 2 : 253

Noailles, epigram to, *Prior* 1 : 268

Nobility of blood, fallacious good, *Dry.* 3 : 201

Noble mind disdains not to repent, *Pope il.* 2 : 72

Nobles look backward, and so lose the race, *Young* 1 : 81

Noblest minds, can such anger dwell? *Phil.* 81

Nod, the great, the certain sign of Jove propitious, *Tick.* 183

——— Olympus trembled at, *Tick.* 183

——— that seals his word, the sanction of the God, *Pope il.* 2 : 145

——— that ratifies the will divine, *Pope il.* 1 : 60

——— the faithful, fix'd, irrevocable sign, *Pope il.* 1 : 60

——— the stamp of Fate, and sanction of the God, *Pope il.* 1 : 60

Nokes, verses to, *Watts* 170

Nomenclators among Romans, *Butl.* 2 : 272

Nominal, profound, in, *Butl.* 1 : 13

No wine, like Fabius, by delay, *Gay* 2 : 197

Noes in bishops give consent, *Gay* 2 : 197

Noman

Noman is my name, *Pope od.* 3 : 241

None judge fo wrong, as thofe who think amifs, *Pope* 1 : 254

None defcends into himfelf, *Dry.* 7 : 339

Non-entity, gave birth to all, from, *Pom.* 337

Non-exiftence, the only refuge of the bad, *Young* 2 : 159

Non-juror, prologue to, *Rowe* 37

Nonpareil, *Prior* 2 : 253

Non-refiftance trims between a rebel and a king, *Dry.* 2 : 75

Nonfenfe, what, *Butl.* 2 : 280

———— gargled in an eunuch's throat, *Fent.* 333

———— mending into doubtful meaning, *Mall.* 162

Noon defcribed, { *Mall.* 199 { *Thom.* 1 : 58

——— hymn for, *Pain.* 245

Noon-tide in our lives there is, *Swift* 1 : 19

———— which ftill the fooner it arrives, *Swift* 1 : 19

———— fo much fooner comes the long and gloomy night, *ib.*

Noric blade, beft-temper'd fteel, *Phil.* 13

Normanton, in Rutlandfhire, fit for fheep, *Dyer* 31

North, great nurfe of Goths, of Alans, and of Huns, *Pope* 3 : 179

———— brings her undaunted warriors forth, *Rowe L.* 345

———— ftubborn of foul, and fteady in the field, *Rowe L.* 345

Northern gales awake, *Pain.* 207

———— lights defcribed, *Thom.* 1 : 144

Northumberland, Waller to, *Wall.* 42

Notbrowne Mayde, ballad of, *Prior* 1 : 205

Nothing, great negative, *Roch.* 328, 329

———— inftances in, *Roch.* 330

———— defolate abyfs, *Thom.* 1 : 55

———— can be brought from nothing, *Dry.* 7 : 332

G 4.

Nothing

Nothing can be turned to magic,   Dry. 5 : 332
———— is destroyed,   Dry. 4 : 146
———— stands alone,   Pope 2 : 56
———— by itself was made,   Prior 2 : 122
———— meaner than a wretch of state,   Young 1 : 147
———— human foreign was to him,   Thom. 2 : 173
———— pleases the difficult,   Mil. 2 : 206
Nothingness in deed and name,   Eael. 1 : 93
Notions are drawn from guess,   Pope 2 : 95
Noons never fair,   Young 3 : 261
Nouveaux Interêts des Princes, lines written in,   Prior 1 : 156
Novel, verses written in,   Lanf. 213
Novelty, pleasure from,   Aken. 20
———— final cause of,   Aken. 21
———— loses its charms by repetition,   Aken. 85
———— man can be true to,   Cong. 83
Nought is vain, which gratitude inspires,   Thom. 2 : 176
———— treads so silent as the foot of time,   Young 1 : 134
Nugent, earl, epistle to, by Dunkin,   Swift 2 : 374
Numa, king of Rome,   Dry. 4 : 133
———— taught religion,   Dry. 4 : 157
———— soften'd Rome's rapacious sons,   Thom. 1 : 170
———— the rites of strict religion knew,   Prior 1 : 163
Number and cadence unknown to old writers,   Dry. 1 : 264
Numbers, power of,   Wall. 33
———— smooth or rough, are right or wrong,   Pope 1 : 105
———— more sweet than woman,   Cowl. 1 : 160
———— like music, can ev'n grief control,   Gay 1 : 184
Numidia, mother of the yellow brood,   Hughes 101
———— where the stern lion shakes his mane,   Hughes 101
                                                         Nuptial

Nuptial song,   *Thom.* 2 : 189
Nuptials of form, of interest, or of state,   *Lanf.* 249
———— of a friend,   *Prior* 2 : 245
Nutrition carried on,   *Black.* 196
Nye, beard of,   *Butl.* 2 : 214
Nymphs, yielding minds,   *Pope* 1 : 129
———— Æneas' ships changed to,   *Dry.* 6 : 235

O

Oak, age of,   *Dry.* 3 : 135
Oaks, fair Albion's best defence,   *Watts* 84
Oath to make, what,   *Butl.* 2 : 106
—— breaking of, saint-like virtue,   *Butl.* 1 : 195
—— supplies the vacancy of sense,   *Young* 1 : 132
Oaths to pin on the sleeve,   *Butl.* 1 : 291
—— not to be taken literally,   *Butl.* 2 : 113
—— are but words,   *Butl.* 1 : 194
—— tests of true and false,   *Butl.* 1 : 282
Ob and Sollers, paltry,   *Butl.* 2 : 59
Obedience, best,   *Milt.* 2 : 137
———— happiness,   *Milt.* 1 : 156
———— entire happiness,   *Milt.* 1 : 197
Obelisks, mark'd with dark Egyptian lore,   *Thom.* 2 : 25
Oberon, a subtle spright,   *Tick.* 211
Object may deceive, by being new,   *King* 328
—— alter'd, the desire the same,   *Prior* 1 : 238
Objects, different of different minds,   *Aken.* 89
———— great and exalted, our admiration,   *Aken.* 84
Obscenity vile, no pardon should find,   *Pope* 1 : 113
———— with dulness, shameful,   *Pope* 1 : 113
                                                     Obscenity,

Obscenity, in the fat age of pleasure sprung the weed, *Pope* i :119.

Obscure, shunning courts or name,   *Dyer* 141

Obscurement palpable,   *Pom.* 349

Obscurity, happiness of,   *Cow.* 2 : 291, 293

Obstinacy stiff in the wrong,   *Birk* 2 : 30

Occasion, bald behind,   *Cow.* 1 : 58

———— calls, 'tis fatal to delay,   *Rowe L.* 58

Occasional poems,   *Milt.* 71

Ocean, an ode,   *Young* 1 : 187

———— field of commerce and big war,   *Young* 1 : 188

———— where wonders dwell,   *Young* 1 : 188

———— where terrors swell,   *Young* 1 : 188

———— womb of riches and the grave,   *Young* 3 : 259

———— Death's capital,   *Young* 2 : 219

———— and Tethys, parents of the gods,   *Pope il.* 2 : 52

Octavia indisposed,   *Hughes* 72

Ocyrrhoë transformed,   *Add.* 132

Odds of combat lie on valour's side,   *Pope il.* 2 : 87

Ode,   { *Prior*   1 : 98
                   { *Fent.*   214
                   { *Thom.* 2 : 178, 190

———— for music,   *Hughes* 155

———— reason of the motions in singing,   *Cong.* 153

———— kept strictly to the same measure,   *Cong.* 153

——— the oldest kind of poetry,   *Young* 1 : 179

———— its thoughts uncommon and moral,   *Young* 1 : 179

——— its numbers full, easy, and harmonious, *Young* 1 : 179

——— its expression, of a curious felicity,   *Young* 1 : 179

———— its conduct rapturous and immethodical, *Young* 1 : 179

——— its subject sublime,   *Young* 1 : 180

                                  Ode,

Ode, end, and effence of, is harmony,.   *Cong.* 156·

---- is bold in its flight,   *Dry.* 1 : 270·

---- fhows her art by a brave diforder,.   *Dry.* 1 : 291·

---- the moft fpirited kind of poetry,   *Young* 3 : 238·

---- gift of friendfhip, and the pledge of fame,   *Weft* 171·

---- thee and thy Rhodes, Diagoras, to fing,.   *Weft* 172·

---- for 1705,   *Smith* 207·

---- written in 1739,.   *Shen.* 113·

Odes, &   { *Shen.* 79·
         A. Phil. 348·
         Aken. 189—193·

---- notes on,.   *Aken.* 293·

---- a higher flight and happier force,.   *Buck.* 73·

---- the poet here muft be infpir'd indeed,.   *Buck.* 73·

---- accompanied with dancing,   *Weft* 117·

---- whofe numbers ratify the voice of fame,   *Weft* 180

---- and to illuftrious worth infure a **lafting name,** *Weft* 180

Od'n, defcent of,   *Gray* 365

Od us and Epiftrophus the Halizonians led,   *Pope il.* 1 : 101

Odyffey, a moral and political work,.   *Pope od.* 4 : 265

-------- the reverfe of the Iliad,   *Pope od.* 4 : 265

-------- fable of,   *Pope od.* 3 : 8·

-------- action of,.   *Pope od.* 3 : 20

-------- defign of,.   *Prior* 2 : 93

-------- fpecimen of a tranflation,   *Pitt* 403

-------- eleventh tranflated,.   *Fent.* 245

-------- the whole,.   *Pope od.* 3 : 39, & feq.

Oebalus, origin of,   *Dry.* 6 : 191·

Oeconomy,   *Shen.* 237·

Oedipus, trace from the difafter of his race,   *Pope* 1 : 274·

                                  Oedipus,

Oedipus, deprived of fight,   *Pope* 1 : 277
Offences, to mend by other men's,   *Den.* 95
Office, ant in,   *Gay* 2 : 132
Officious meffenger,   *Som.* 336
Og, character of,   *Dry.* 1 : 176
Oglios brought from Spain,   *King* 215
Ointments, all thy virtues, fweetly fmell,   *Para.* 207
'Old, if to be, were to be happy too,   *Den.* 132
—— have intereft always in their eye,   *Pope* 1 : 237
Old age, Denham on,   *Den.* 110
———— with all her difmal train,   *Watts* 73
———— inconvenience of,   *Dry.* 7 : 292
———— vaunting in fpeech, in action impotent,   *Weft* 240
Old dogs to make young,   *Butl.* 2 : 154
Oldfield, epiftle to,   *Sav.* 138
Old gentry,   *Prior* 2 : 257
'Old hay is equal to old gold,   *Swift* 1 : 72
Old hen and the cock,   *Gay* 2 : 63
Old man, relapfe of,   *Young* 3 : 215
Old-men, Time's offals,   *Dry.* 1 : 12
Old October reddens every nofe,   *Gay* 1 : 219
Old woman and her cats,   *Gay* 2 : 69
Old worn-out Vice fet down for Virtue fair,   *Young* 2 : 111
Olive and laurel, emblems of peace and liberty,   *Mall.* 282
Olive-trees, how dreffed,   *Dry.* 5 : 136
Oliver dead in a hurricane,   *Butl.* 2 : 14
Olivia,   *Fent.* 224
Olympic ode of Pindar,   *Cow.* 2 : 7
———— odes,   *Weft* 135
———— trophies, effect of,   *Cow.* 2 : 10
                                                   Olympus,

Olympus, crown'd with fleecy snow,   *Pope il.* 1 : 55

Ombre, playing at,   *Prior* 2 : 260

Omen'd voice, the meſſenger of Jove,   *Pope od.* 3 : 51

Omens preceding the battle of Pharſalia,   *Rowe L.* 295

On, city of the ſun,   *Aken.* 175

One againſt numbers too unequal,   *Butl.* 1 : 103

Once warn'd is well bewar'd,   *Dry.* 3 : 166

One reliev'd tranſcends a million ſlain,   *Young* 3 : 152

—— age the hero, one the poet breeds,   *Add.* 10

Onſlaught, to inveſt by,   *Butl.* 1 : 115

Opera, firſt Italians taught,   *Tick.* 115

——— enrich'd with ſongs, but innocent of thought, *ib.* 115

——— melodious trifles, and enervate ſtrains,   *Tick.* 115

Ophelia, urn of,   *Shen.* 18

Opiniators differ from other men,   *Butl.* 2 : 346

Opinion ſways reaſon,   *Butl.* 1 : 280

——— mazy tracts of,   *Aken.* 181

——— where mortals roam,   *Aken.* 181

——— great, gives effectual awe,   *Parn.* 134

Opinions on the waves of ignorance float,   *Pom.* 343

——— govern mankind,   *Butl.* 2 : 328

Oppoſition makes a hero great,   *Dry.* 2 : 99

Oppreſſion, ravag'd in the night of lawleſs power, *Hughes* 33

——— defeated, fly,   *Hughes* 33

——— richeſt plains reduced to fens,   *Thom.* 2 : 21

——— fail'd, and prevail'd the right,   *Rowe* 20

Oracle, origin of,   *Rowe L.* 208

—— from heart of oak,   *Butl.* 1 : 175

—— of ſieve and ſheers,   *Butl.* 1 : 244

Oracles ambiguous and dark,   *Milt.* 2 : 157

       Oracles

Chaos in scale,   { Mil.   2 : 158
                                             { ..... L. 207, 210

    ......,   Bal. 1 : 322

Creation of Adam and Eve,   Milt. 1 : 125, 144

Change, power of, nature of mankind,   Thom. 2 : 118

    this name, that tyrants dread,   Prior 1 : 53

    hears Belgia's liberty expiring,   Hughs. 43

    hears, and to her aid brings sprightly war, Hughes 43

    superior and serene amidst the stormy waves, Hughes 43

    fell by the vile hand of a bold ruffian, Hughes 43

    in his offspring doubly lives,   Hughes 44

    ....,   Mall. 168

    in youth, the Titus of mankind,   Mal. 169

    favourite of the ....,   Young 3 : 161

    with ...... and ..... in rival pomp,   Young 3 : 161

Change, ... both blossoms and fruit, ... 92

Charms, ...,   Bal. 2 : 282

    ....,   Mil. 2 : 223

    ....,   Prior 2 : 02

    with ....ited Greece, Thom. 2 : 52

    ....,   ... 523

    .... eloquence,   ... 523

    .... may learn,   Pult. 523

....,   Thom. 1 : ...

....,   Pit. . 24

    .. ..,   Phil. 25

.. ..le vessels,   Pope ... 1 : ...

... .,   Hill. 1 : ...

... ...,   Pope 1 : ...

... .,   Pit. 2 : ...

                                             &c.

Order, confiftent with liberty,   *Milt.* 1 : 165

Orellana, huge, defcends from Andes,   *Thom.* 1 : 72

———— monarch of mighty floods,   *Weft* 131

———— foaming from cliff to cliff,   *Weft* 131

Oreftes revenges Agamemnon's death,   *Pope od.* 3 : 89, 94

———— fir'd with great revenge, gain'd praife, *Pope od.* 3 : 52

———— caus'd blood to atone for blood,   *Pope od.* 3 : 52

Organ, lady playing on,   *Hughes* 76

Organs found fedately grave,   *Parn* 113

Orgueil, a mount in Jerfey,   *Cow.* 1 : 131

Oriental eclogues,   *Collins* 233

———————— obfervations on,   *Collins* 285

Orinda, ode on,   *Cow.* 1 : 158

———— excelling in wit and virtue,   *Cow.* 1 : 209

———— woman laureat,   *Cow.* 1 : 207

Ormond, the theme of every Oxford Mufe,   *Add.* 15

———— picture of,   *Prior* 1 : 69

Oronoque rolls a brown deluge,   *Thom.* 1 : 72

Oroonoko, epilogue to,   *Cong.* 85

Orphan, prologue to,   *Prior* 2 : 221

Orphans of the pen, what,   *Black.* 2 : 260

Orpheus could charm the trees,   *Pope* 1 : 346

———— here fings, trees moving to the found,   *Pope* 1 : 205

———— fings, the ghofts no more complain,   *Smith* 192

———— tamed men,   *Rofc.* 274

———— tranflation from Virgil,   *Buck.* 66

———— and Eurydice,   *King* 352

Orrery to Swift,   *Swift* 2 : 279

Orfin, defcribed,   *Butl.* 1 : 53, 57

———— nurfed by a bear,   *Butl.* 1 : 54

          Orthodoxy,

Orthodoxy, what, *Butl.* 1 : 317
Os Sacrum, what, *Butl.* 2 : 76
Ostiacs, misery of, *Dyer* 120
Ostrich, described, *Young* 1 : 217
Ostrogoths on Latium fall, *Pope* 3 : 179
O thou most Christian enemy to peace, *Young* 2 : 142
———— again in arms ! again provoking fate ! *Young* 2 : 142
Otter-chace, *Gay* 1 : 10
———— hunting, described, *Som.* 81
———— his dirge, *Som.* 84
Otway, Windsor-castle, 3
———— to Duke, *Ot.* 59
———— to Creech, 63
———— epilogue to duke of York, 66
———— to dutchess of York, 69
———— prologue to City heiress, 70
———— ode of Horace, 72
———— prologue to Constantine, 75
———— pastoral on death of Charles II. 77
———— fail'd to polish or refine, *Pope* 2 : 228
Ovation, what, *Butl.* 1 : 216
Ovid has sublime thoughts in plain words, *Add.* 180
——— ill commented, *Add.* 181
——— has something of the best and worst poets, *Add.* 182
——— abounds in turns, easy and natural, *Add.* 183
——— seems to confound the diurnal and annual motion, *ib.* 183
——— wit of, has something of the pun, *Add.* 184
——— mixes two repugnant ideas, *Add.* 189
——— copious in invention, *Add.* 192
——— knows not when he has said enough, *Add.* 196

Ovid has great infight into nature,   *Add.* 196

—— abounds in mixt wit,   *Add.* 195, 197

—— famous for paffionate fpeeches,   *Add.* 197

—— employs his invention more than his judgment, *ib.* 198

—— luxuriant,   *Dry.* 3 : 290

—— writ with wonderful facility,   *Dry.* 3 : 22

—— abounds in conceits,   *Dry.* 3 : 24

—— turn of words excels in,   *Dry.* 3 : 26

—— all the turns of Love's paffion knew,   *Pom.* 216

—— in whom ftrong Art with ftronger Nature joins, *Pom.* 216

—— thoughts fo tender, and exprefs'd fo well,   *Pom.* 216

—— too often addreffes the imagination,   *Ham.* 204

—— has the mafterfhip of Love,   *King* 307

—— exile chilled,   *Add.* 5

—— Art of Love,   { *Dry.* 4 : 203
                                                          Yal.   408
                                                          Cong.   111
                                                          King   253

—— Metamorphofes,   *Dry.* 3 : 297

—— Elegy v.   *Duke* 94

—— tranflations from,   *Add.* 105 | *Dry.* 3 : 297 | 4 : 1

Out-cant the Babylonian labourers,   *Butl.* 2 : 10

Out-houfes to our tombs, what,   *Butl.* 2 : 223

Outrage legal,   *Thom.* 1 : 150

—— enfnaring in the toils of law,   *Thom.* 1 : 150

—— fomenting difcord and perplexing right, *Thom.* 1 : 150

Outrag'd, ceafe that outrage to repel,   *Pope od.* 4 : 81

—— bear it, howe'er thy heart rebel,   *Pope od.* 4 : 81

Outward act is prompted from within,   *Prior* 1 : 325

—— acts defile not, without the heart,   *Milt.* 3 : 53

Outward shew, how false we judge by, *Gay* 2 : 85

Owen, triumphs of, *Gray* 369

—— fairest flower of Roderic's stem, *Gray* 369

Owl and farmer, *Gay* 2 : 100

—— the swan, the cock, the spider, &c. *Gay* 2 : 180

Owl-eyed race, whom virtue's lustre blinds, *Aken.* 335

Owls Athenian, sceptic, *Butl.* 1 : 253

Ox, laborious, of honest front, *Thom.* 1 : 60

—— bears the various labours of the year, *Gay* 2 : 189

—— think on, and learn content, *Gay* 2 : 189

—— bellowing falls, *Pope il.* 2 : 290

Oxen, management of, *Dry.* 5 : 156

Oxford, Learning's Pantheon, *Cow.* 1 : 164

———— Wit's galaxy, *Cow.* 1 : 165

———— encomium of, *Phil.* 54

———— prologue to University of, *Tick.* 136

———— extempore verses to, *Prior* 2 : 261

———— epistle to earl of, *Gay* 1 : 217

———— inscription for monument of countess of, *Pom.* 294

Oyster, contest about, *Som.* 274

P

Pacific Ocean, passage into, *Dyer* 124

Pack, over-numerous ceasure of, *Som.* 53

Packhorse and the carrier, *Gay* 2 : 166

Pacuvius, Roman Satirist, *Dry.* 7 : 156

Padders, who rob by sun-shine, *Dry.* 2 : 280

———'s face, falser than, *Butl.* 2 : 48

Paddy, character of the Intelligencer, *Swift* 2 : 99

Padua, with sighs, beholds her Livy burn, *Pope* 3 : 180

  Pageants

Pageants of a patriot's name, a foulness hid,   *Aken.* 334

Pain subdues all,   *Milt.* 1 : 188

—— overturns all patience,   *Milt.* 1 : 138

—— foil of pleasure,   *Butl.* 2 : 194

—— past, more dear than pleasure,   *Butl.* 2 : 194

—— Hate, Fear, and Grief, family of,   *Pope* 2 : 46

Pain'd sense alone frees us from Fancy's tyranny, *Young* 3 : 123

Paint, strange power of, creator art!   *Tick.* 155

Painter,   *Hughes* 77

—— epistle to,   *Dyer* 135

—— master of the loveliest art,   *Dyer* 135

—— who pleased none and every one,   *Gay* 2 : 59

—— drawing Dorinda,   *Pom.* 273

—— after finishing,   *Pom.* 275

—— instructions to,   *Wall.* 185

—— muse begin, boldly draw crouds of virtues, *Hughes* 252

Painting, origin of,   *Dry.* 2 : 152

—— revived by the Roman and Lombard schools, *id.* 2 : 153

—— and Poetry, sisters,   *Dry.* 2 : 154

—— on a lady's,   *Waller* 94

Painture, allied to poetry,   *Dry.* 2 : 161

Pair-royal made up by three knaves,   *Butl.* 2 : 310

Palæmon,   *Dry.* 5 : 31

Palamon and Arcite,   *Dry.* 3 : 51

Palanteum, founder of,   *Dry.* 6 : 1.

Palatine, prospect from Mount,   *Dy.*

—— library, Phœbus' letter'd dome,   *D.*

Paleness from too much or too little valour,   *Butl.*

Palinodia,   *W*

—— Horace, Book i. Ode xvi.   *Sw.*

H 2

Palinody,   *Butl* 2 : 195

Palinurus nodded at the helm,   *Pope* 3 : 254

———— slain,   *Dry.* 6 : 125

———— gives name to a place,   *Dry.* 6 : 130 .

Pallas, Tritonian maid,   *Rowe L.* 389

———— virgin armipotent,   *Broome* 77.

———— taught the texture of the loom,   *Pope od.* 4 : 164

———— first taught poetry and spinning,   *Swift* 1 : 215

———— discovers to Ulysses his country,   *Pope od.* 4 : 12

———— robb'd the many of their mind,   *Pope il.* 2 : 181

———— the worse advice to chuse, the better to refuse, *id.* 2 : 181

———— and Venus,   *Prior* 1 : 130

———— son of Evander,   *Dry.* 6 : 209

———— described,   *Dry.* 6 : 222

———— slain,   *Dry.* 6 : 292

Pall-mall celebrated,   *Gay* 1 : 120

Palm, amorous tree,   *Wall.* 53

Palmetto shoots like the tall pine,   *Gay* 1 : 19

———— leaves of, used as a fan,   *Gay* 1 : 20

Palmito, wine of,   *Waller* 69

Palms, speed by oppression,   *Cow.* 2 : 72

Pam mow'd down armies in the fights of Lu,   *Pope* 1 : 139

———— enigma on,   *Prior* 2 : 257

Pamphlet in Sir Bob's defence,   *Swift* 2 : 306

———— will never fail to bring in pence,   *Swift* 2 : 306

Pan, poet of the plain,   *Fent.* 326

···· to Moses lends his pagan horn,   *Pope* 3 : 180

———— and Fortune,   *Gay* 2 : 170

Pandarus leads those of Zeleia,   *Pope il.* 1 : 100

———— aims an arrow at Menelaus,   *Pope il.* 1 : 132

     Pandarus,

Pandarus, defcription of his bow,   *Pope il.* 1 : 131

———— wounds Menelaus,   *Pope il.* 1 : 132

Pandemonium, palace of Satan,   *Milt.* 1 : 28

————————— Mulciber, architect of,   *Milt.* 1 : 29

————————— council held in,   *Milt.* 1 : 31, 35

————————— feat of Lucifer,   *Milt.* 2 : 59

Pandora's box, a hundred ills, to vex mankind, *Prior* 2 : 210

Panegyric on Denham,   *Butl.* 2 : 203

Pantaloons, laws for,   *Butl.* 1 : 134

Panthea, an elegy,   *Gay* 1 : 243

———— felt Love's fecret fmart,   *Gay* 1 : 243

Pantheon defcribed,   *Dyer* 13

———— emblem of this our world,   *Dyer* 13

Panther, faireft of the fpotted kind,   *Dry.* 2 : 19

Papal dominion,   *Thom.* 2 : 111

Paper containing bride-cake, verfes on,   *Collins* 283

Paper-credit bleft ! laft and beft fupply,   *Pope* 2 : 119

———————— that lends corruption lighter wings to fly, *ib.* 119

Papift in philofophy,   *Prior* 2 : 74

Parables, a pleafing way to convey truth,   *Dry.* 3 : 166

Paradife, feat of,   *Butl.* 1 : 14

———— defcribed,   *Milt.* 1 : 105, 106, 108

———— guarded,   *Milt.* 2 : 89

———————— by Cherubim,   *Milt.* 2 : 140

———— gate of, to the Eaft,   *Milt.* 1 : 107

———— Loft,   *Milt.* 1 : 5

———— Regained,   *Milt.* 2 : 143, 221

———— of fools,   *Milt.* 1 : 89

Parallel,   *Prior* 2 : 243

Parallels all, are wrongs or blafphemy,   *Tick.* 132

Parafite

Pastime will eat and talk,   Kay 213
Passion, bought with blood,   Young 2:73
—— how sweet the sound!   War 56
—— and satisfaction,   War 120
Parent's joy, no expression can tell,   Buck 100
Parents, with lovely duty, how to,   Rowe 2
—— obedience to,   West 351
—— blind to their children,   Dry 3:225
—— and lovers, by nature fools,   Prior 2:83
Paris, build a fleet to ravish Helen,   Duke 145
—— dissuaded by Cassandra,   Duke 146
—— ill-fated, slave to woman kind,   Pope il. 2:35
—— as smooth of face, as fraudulent of mind,   id. 2:35
—— dar'd the bravest of the Greeks,   Pope il. 1:106
—— daunted at the sight of Menelaus,   Pope il. 1:106
—— upbraided by Hector,   Pope il. 1:107
—— stands reproved,   Pope il. 1:108
—— agrees to a single combat with Menelaus,   Pope il. 1:108
—— snatch'd away in a cloud by Venus,   Pope il. 1:120
—— a flaming brand to his country,   Buck. 64
—— pest of Troy, that ruin of our race,   Pope il. 1:203
—— wretch ill-fated, and thy country's foe!   Pope il. 1:204
—— like a pamper'd horse,   Pope il. 1:213
—— consents to restore the treasures, not Helen,   id. 1:231
—— proposal of, rejected,   Pope il. 1:233
—— to Helen,   Duke 140
—— foretold to be a burning torch,   Duke 143
—— made umpire of beauty,   Duke 144
—— judgment of,   Parn. 284
—— is false, Oenone is undone,   Gay 1:32
Parker,

Parker, chancellor, birth-day of,   *Hughes* 266
Parliament, ballad on,   *Butl.* 2 : 309
————— only support of Richard,   *Butl.* 2 : 17
————— drew up petitions to itself,   *Butl.* 1 : 74
————— or den of thieves,   *Swift* 2 : 305
Parody on Smedley's character,   *Swift* 2 : 101
————— on a song of the earl of Dorset,   *Shen.* 132
Parnell, Hesiod,   *Parn.* 5
————— rise of woman,   5
————— Song,   14, 15
————— Anacreontic,   16—19
————— Fairy Tale,   21
————— Vigil of Venus,   29
————— Battle of the frogs and mice,   37
————— to Mr. Pope,   54
————— part of the first Canto of the Rape of the Lock,   57
————— Health,   58
————— the Flies,   61
————— elegy to an old Beauty,   63
————— the Book-worm,   66
————— an allegory on Man,   69
————— an imitation of French verses,   73
————— a Night-piece on Death,   75
————— hymn to Contentment,   78
————— the Hermit,   81
————— Piety, or the Vision,   89
————— Bacchus,   94
————— the Horse and the Olive,   97
————— Donne's third Satire,   99
————— the gift of Poetry,   104

Parnell, Moses,   *Parn.* 106

——— Deborah,   133

——— Hannah,   146

——— David,   154

——— Solomon,   193

——— Jonah,   220

——— Hezekiah,   228

——— Habakkuk,   236

——— Hymn for morning,   243

——————— for noon,   245

——————— for evening,   246

——— the soul in sorrow,   248

——— the happy man,   249

——— the way to happiness,   252

——— the Convert's love,   253

——— a desire to praise,   255

——— on happiness in this life,   257

——— Extacy,   258

——— on divine love,   262

——— on Queen Anne's peace, 1712,   263

——— to Dr. Swift, on his birth-day,   275

——— on Bp. Burnet set on fire,   278

——— Elysium,   279

——— the judgement of Paris,   284

——— on Mrs. Fermor,   287

——— a Riddle,   288

——— verses on,   *Pope* 2 : 329

Parrot, henceforth be bird of love,   *Lanf.* 164

Parson, advice to,   *Swift* 2 : 289

——— case of,   *Swift* 2 : 290

Parthenope,

Parthenope, Naples,   *Aken.* 90

Parthia trembled at his proud alarms,   *Hughes* 289

Parthian, as he fled, he flew,   *Prior* 1 : 69

Parthians dreadful in flight, as in purfuit,   *Milt.* 2 : 193

———————— conquer by flight,   *Milt.* 2 : 194

———————— triumph'd o'er Craffus,   *Rowe L.* 342

———————— nurs'd in the hate and rivalfhip of Rome, *id.* 342

Partial evil, univerfal good,   *Pope* 2 : 39

Partial fame,   *Prior* 1 : 197

Partiality in judgement to be avoided,   *Pope* 1 : 107

Particles, to fill up gaps,   *Butl.* 2 : 201

Partie quarrée is quadrille,   *Gay* 1 : 268

Parties, felfifh, on oar vitals prey,   *Thom.* 2 : 176

———————— at parties bawl,   *Young* 3 : 189

———————— fcorns all, tho' by parties fought,   *Pitt* 393

———————— who greatly thinks, and truly fpeaks his tho't, *id.* 393

Parting,   *Cow.* 1 : 283

———————— a fong,   *Broome* 101

Partition, treaty of, begat a war,   *Prior* 2 : 226

Partition-wall, built till he comes,   *Parn.* 200

———————————— 'tis only then to fall,   *Parn.* 200

Partlet defcribed,   *Dry.* 3 : 141

Partners prone to cheat their public intereft,   *Butl.* 2 : 162

Partridge-hawking,   *Som.* 153

Partridge, elegy on,   *Swift* 1 : 54

——————— epitaph on,   *Swift* 1 : 57

Parts relate to whole,   *Pope* 2 : 55

——— various to various men affign'd,   *Weft* 205

——— all to perfection and to praife will lead,   *Weft* 205

——— paths purfued, as nature bids us tread,   *Weft* 205

                                                           Parts

Parts but expose the men, who virtue quit,   *Young* 3 : 207

Party, puzzling sons of,   *Thom.* 1 : 217

———— when raised, another set succeeds,   *Thom.* 1 : 217

———— and spleen have turn'd his brain,   *Swift* 2 : 184

Party-quarrels, who engages in, lifts an hired Bravo, *Gay* 1 : 181

Party-rage, that tyrant of our age,   *Mall.* 173

·Party-spirit sways the judgement,   *Pope* 1 : 109

Passage of the Red Sea,   *Milt.* 2 : 125

Passion, mazy tracts of, where mortals roam, ·   *Aken.* 181 ·

———— overturns reason,   *Cow.* 1 : 62

———— sooths every gust to peace,   *Thom.* 1 : 19

———— may oft the wisest heart surprize, ·   *West* 173

———— a blind usurper mounts the throne,   *Fent.* 314

———— casts a mist before the mind,   *Dry.* 3 : 87 ·

———— let not o'er sense prevail,   *Cong.* 138 ·

———— not excited, unless felt, ·   *Rosc.* 223 ·

———— feign'd, at no repulse is griev'd, ·   *Pom.* 246 ·

———— when feign'd and when sincere,   *Cong.* 129

———— billet-doux will shew,·   *Cong.* 129

———— stoop'd to common good,   *Thom.* 2 : 62·

———— rouzes the mind's whole·fabric,   *Aken.* 40

———— tender, administers delight,   *Aken.* 40

———— can depress or raise,   *Prior* 1 : 113

———— for this world, sole fountain of distress, *Young* 3 : 135 ·

———— of Christ,   .   *Pitt* 219

———— eternal king's unfathom'd love,·   *Pitt* 219

———— a mighty mystery,   { *Milt.* 3 : 89
    { ·*Pitt*   219

Passions,   .   *Cow.* 1 : 246 ·

———— modes of self-love,   *Pope* 2 : 45

    Passions,

Paffions, real good, or feeming, moves them all, *Pope* 2 : 45

———— good or ill, as ufed, *Young* 3 : 246

———— ufe of, *Aken.* 157

———— are the elements of life, *Pope* 2 : 35

———— tender, are the moft fevere, *Thom.* 2 : 181

———— grandeur of, *Young* 2 : 180

———— when in ferment, work out, *Swift* 1 : 32

———— as anger does in vermin, *Swift* 1 : 32

———— enflave, *Dry.* 7 : 352

———— darken reafon's light, *Swift* 2 : 36

———— our underftanding with darknefs fill, *Pom.* 339

———— and pervert the will, *Pom.* 339

———— vultures of the mind, *Gray* 332

———— raife ftormy ftrife, and trouble life, *Prior* 2 : 167

———— plebeians are, which faction raife, *Sav.* 40

———— rage, obftructed in their courfe, *Pope* 2 : 5

———— how frail, *Wall.* 144

———— an ode, *Collins* 270

———— to wind, delicate the art, *Tick.* 137

———— cloathed in a different drefs, *Dry.* 1 : 280

———— in various plants, *Phil.* 42

Paffive courage, gallant, *Butl.* 1 : 165

———— obedience, *Thom.* 2 : 113

————————— whence parties, Whig and Tory, *Thom.* 2 : 113

Paffover inftituted, *Cow.* 2 : 66

Paft life, ours no more, *Roch.* 296

Paft and future clofe to waking thought, *Parn.* 116

Pafton, epitaph on, *Dry.* 2 : 199

Paftor Fido, ode in imitation of, *Lytt.* 49

Paftora, *Hughes* 131

Paftoral,

Paftoral, origin of,   *Collins* 285

———— to be plain and humble,   *Dry.* 1 : 268

———— not flat and heavy,   *Dry.* 1 : 269

———— Virgil and Theocritus, guides in,   *Dry.* 1 : 269

———— difcourfe on,   *Pope* 1 : 17

———— probably, the moft ancient poetry,   *Pope* 1 : 17

———— reafon of the name,   *Pope* 1 : 18

———— what,   *Pope* 1 : 18

———— form of,   *Pope* 1 : 18

———— character of,   *Pope* 1 : 18

———— fhould have an air of piety,   *Pope* 1 : 19

———— numbers of, eafy and flowing,   *Pope* 1 : 20

———— not fo well exprefled as in Greek,   *Add.* 200

———— to the author of,   *Prior* 1 : 66

———— to the bifhop of Ely,   *Prior* 1 : 25

———— to a young lady,   *Broome* 84

———— ballad,   *Shen* 152

———— cantata,   *Hughes* 170

———— dialogue,   *Swift* 2 : 40, 64

———— eclogues,   *Walfh.* 343

———— mafk,   *Hughes* 132

———— ode,   *Shen.* 135

———— poems,   *A. Phil.* 297

Paftorals, on certain,   *Shen* 169

———— of Virgil,   *Dry.* 5 : 21

Paftorel, character of,   *Som.* 103

———— figure of,   *Som.* 104

———— foiled by Hobbinol,   *Som.* 106

Paftures fit for fleep,   *Dyer* 30

———— defects of,   *Dyer* 32

                                               Pate,

Pate, the duller block, *Butl.* 1 : 270

Paternal rule, first, *Milt.* 2 : 120

Path, in his blest life, I see, *Young* 2 : 71

Paths of glory lead but to the grave, *Gray* 338

———— of Gods, what mortal can survey, *Pope od.* 3 : 274

Patience, fortitude of, *Milt.* 2 : 4

————— truest fortitude, *Milt.* 3 : 29

————— trial of fortitude, *Milt.* 3 : 50

————— that baffled fortune's rage, *Thom.* 2 : 61

———— softens every sad extreme, *Sav.* 66

———— disarms disease of pain, *Sav.* 66

———— mocks slander's sting, *Sav.* 66

———— strips of terrors the terrific king, *Sav.* 66

———— smiling sees th' ingratitude of friends, *Sav.* 66

———— raises hope, and smiles away despair, *Sav.* 14

———— of toil and love of virtue fail, *Prior* 2 : 159

———— and resignation, pillars of peace, *Young* 2 : 248

Patrick's well, sudden drying up, *Swift* 2 : 7

Patriot, *Hughes* 256

———— nor brib'd by hopes, nor by mean fears control'd, *ib.* 256

———— proof alike against both foes and friends, *Hughes* 256

———— ne'er from the golden mean of virtue bends, *Hughes* 256

———— wisely fix'd, maintains the purpose of his mind, *id.* 256

———— but where, by these virtues known? *Hughes* 256

———— unsway'd by others passions or his own? *Hughes* 256

———— just to his prince, and to the publick true, *Hughes* 256

———— in all events, shuns each partial view, *Hughes* 256

———— is a dangerous post, *Swift* 2 : 186

———— the people's brave, *Dry.* 1 : 157

———— the politician's tool, *Dry.* 1 : 157

Patriot,

Patriot, of the moral world,   *Young* 1 : 254

———— like, ſtrut and frown,   *Swift* 1 : 138

Patriots of their own intereſt,   *Dry.* 5 : 224

———— for a place abandon fame,   *Garth* 42

———— ſupple, of the modern ſort,   *Swift* 2 : 6

———— turn with every gale that blows from court, *ib.* 2 : 6

Patroclus ſent to enquire about Machaon, *Pope il.* 1 : 345

———— adviſed to fight in Achilles' armour, *Pope il.* 1 : 352

———— requeſt of,   *Yald.* 396

———— go, in Achilles' arms,   *Pope il.* 2 : 102

———— lead forth my Myrmidons,   *Pope il.* 2 : 102

———— and conquer in my right,   *Pope il.* 2 : 102

———— touch not Hector, Hector is my due, *Pope il.* 2 : 102

———— puts on Achilles' armour,   *Pope il.* 2 : 104

———— Achilles' dearer part,   *Pope il.* 2 : 145

———— is now an empty name,   *Pope il.* 2 : 155

———— dead, his arms are Hector's right, *Pope il.* 2 : 170

———— lamented by Achilles,   *Pope il.* 2 : 170

———— of mildeſt manners, and the gentleſt heart, *id.* 2 : 162

———— in death a hero, as in life a friend, *Pope il.* 2 : 162

———— lov'd beyond myſelf, is ſlain,   *Pope il.* 2 : 172

———— dead, Achilles hates to live,   *Pope il.* 2 : 173

———— dead, whoever meets me dies,   *Pope il.* 2 : 239

———— gone, I ſtay but half behind,   *Pope il.* 2 : 109

———— hail ! bloody Hector ſtretch'd before thee, *id.* 2 : 290

———— funeral proceſſion of,   *Pope il.* 2 : 294

————————— pyre of,   *Pope il.* 2 : 296

———— funeral games for,   *Pope il.* 2 : 300

Pattens, invention of,   *Gay* 1 : 108

———— reaſon of the name,   *Gay* 1 : 110

                                        Paul

"Paul nor Swithin rule the clouds and wind, *Gay* 1 : 107

—— (St.) deduces the Creator from the creation, *Black.* 5

——————— that church proposed to be fold, *Cow.* 2 : 248

Paulo Purganti and his wife, *Prior* 1 : 142

Paulus, by Mr. Lindsay, *Swift* 2 : 103

—— answer to, *Swift* 2 : 103

Peace, ode to, *Collins* 266

—— come to grace thy Western isle, *Collins* 267

—— ode to, 1717, *Rowe* 80

—— fairest, sweetest daughter of the skies, *Rowe* 80

—— still voice of, *Cow.* 1 : 184

—— accent divine, *King* 385

—— O Virtue, peace is all thy own, *Pope* 2 : 72

—— first of human blessings, *Thom.* 2 : 5

—— thou source and soul of social life, *Thom.* 2 : 5

—— beneath which, Science her views enlarges, *Thom.* 2 : 5

—— harmony of, destroyed by war, *Cong.* 62

—— mild and galless dove, *Cow.* 1 : 180

—— that goodness bosoms ever, *Milt.* 3 : 134

—— how happy the man assign'd to, *Rows L.* 181

—— goodness ever shares, *Mall.* 250

—— goddess serene, in robes of spotless white, *Hughes* 53

—— art-nursing, *Thom.* 2 : 104

—— stretch thy reign from shore to shore, *Pope* 1 : 74

—— triumph of, *Hughes* 17

—— the blest land, and joys incessant crown, *Pope od.* 3 : 62

—— o'er the world her olive wand extends, *Pope* 1 : 48

—— how glorious in pains! *Young* 3 : 127

—— secured by succession, *Dry.* 1 : 213

—— the fruit of love, *Dry.* 1 : 317

Peace springs from an humble heart,   *Young* 2 : 227
——— the full portion of mankind below,   *Young* 2 : 123
——— wealth and liberty, that nobleft boon,   *Weft* 312
——————— are bleffings only to the wife and good, *Weft* 312
——— from the toils of war we value,   *King* 297
——— cannot dwell with hate or love,   *Prior* 1 : 155
——— my dear delight, not Fleury's more,   *Pope* 2 : 174
——— reftored,   *Add.* 72
——— is thy choice,   *Lanf.* 130
——— fpeech againft,   *Den.* 58
——— corrupts,   *Milt.* 2 : 111
——— waftes with luxury,   *Butl.* 2 : 224
——— with liberty bought,   *Rowe L.* 172
——— between Ulyffes and his fubjects,   *Pope od.* 4 : 255
——— concludes the Odyffey,   *Pope od.* 4 : 256
——— of 1712,   *Parn.* 263
——— mother of Plenty, daughter of the fkies,   *Parn.* 263
——— amongft thy train, foft eafe and pleafure, *Parn.* 264
——— reftores the comforts of a calm repofe,   *Parn.* 271
——— from itfelf its pleafures enjoys,   *Parn.* 98
——— articles of,   *Dry.* 7 : 55
——— broken by the Rutuli,   *Dry.* 7 : 60
——— profpect of,   *Tick.* 97
——— a gentler note I raife,   *Tick.* 97
——— and efteem is all that age can hope,   *Young* 2 : 113
——————— folly bars both,   *Young* 2 : 113
——————————— what ranker can be ?   *Young* 2 : 113
——— and Dunkirk, a ballad,   *Swift* 1 : 82
——— and plenty on thy word fhall wait,   *Prior* 1 : 241
Peaceful kings poife a martial people,   *Dry.* 1 : 63

Peacock

Peacock described,   *Young* 1 : 218

———— squalls with a hellish noise,   *Swift* 2 : 204

———— strains the discord of his throat,   *Fent.* 319

———— gay starry plumes his length of tail bedeck, *Fent.* 319

——— cut in vellum,   *Hughes* 83

———— spread his ample train, enrich'd with eyes, *Hughes* 84

———— turkey, and goose,   *Gay* 2 : 47

———— (Mary), on sudden death of,   *Watts* 281

Peasant sleeps, while cares awake a King,   *Broome* 44

Pedant,   *Prior* 2 : 251

Pedantry, a corn or wart,   *Butl.* 2 : 284

———— cannot for humour pass,   *Swift* 2 : 151

Pedants, what,   *Butl.* 2 : 283

Peer, to swear on gospel of his honour,   *Butl.* 1 : 197

——— must have rule and sway,   *Prior* 1 : 153

Peerage is a wither'd flower,   *Swift* 2 : 268

———— where titles give no right or power, *Swift* 2 : 268

Peg, to take one down,   *Butl.* 1 : 208

Peleus and Thetis,   *Lanf.* 221

Pelf, tyrant of fools, the wise man's slave,   *Som.* 259

——— that buys the sea, a tyrant o'er itself,   *Pope* 2 : 116

——— men of, but hate their neighbours as themselves, *id.* 2 : 121

——— equal fate betides the slave who digs it,   *id.* 2 : 122

————————————— and the slave that hides, *ib.*

Pell-mell, to come to blows,   *Butl.* 1 : 118

Peloponnesian war,   *Thom.* 2 : 50

Pelorus, part of Apennine,   *Rowe L.* 103

Pelusium, where Nile pours his ample tide, *Hughes* 289

Pen, riddle on,   *Swift* 1 : 300

Penal creeds, mischiefs of,   *Black.* 66

Penance in a paper lantern, *Butl.* 3 : 186

Pencil speaks an univerfal tongue, *Dry.* 2 : 155

Penelope, fkill'd in delays, and politickly flow, *Pitt* 337

———— pious frauds, of chafte, *Pitt* 272

———— eludes her fuitors, *Pope od.* 4 : 140

———— by night revers'd the labours of the day, *id.* 3 : 65

———— a wondrous monument of female wiles, *id.* 3 : 65

———— at length convinc'd, that Ulyffes is return'd, *id.* 4 :226

———— faints away, *Pope od.* 4 : 226

Penitence, how diftinguifh'd from love, *Pope* 1 : 189

Penitent pardoned, *Watts* 55

Penny, be fure to turn, *Dry.* 7 : 352

———— fav'd, a penny got, { *Som.* 389 *Thom.* 1 : 215

Pennyworth of thought, to pafs time, *Butl.* 1 : 225

Pens Hurft, at, *Wall.* 49, 58

Penfion of a prince's praife is great, *Dry.* 1 : 311

Penfioner, one more St. Stephen gains, *Pope* 2 : 133

Penthefilia, Amazon queen, *Dry.* 7 : 34

Pentheus, ftory of, *Add.* 165

———— death of, *Add.* 172

Penury, contempt, and care, the galling load of, *Pope od.* 4 : 169

People, what, *Milt.* 2 : 184

———— are a many-headed beaft, *Pope* 2 : 199

———— prone to forget the good, and blame the ill, *Prior* 2 : 168

———— dy'd for the king's offence, *Pope il.* 1 : 37

———— 's voice is, and is not, the voice of God, *Pope* 2 : 218

Peor, another name of Chemos, *Milt.* 1 : 18

Pepper-corn for rent, *Prior* 1 : 36

Perceptions, fource of knowledge, *Black.* 209

Perceptions, the matter of reflection,   *Black.* 210

Perfect, nothing in mankind,   *Dry.* 7 : 104

Perfection, degrees of, determin'd by the ends,   *Black.* 105

———————— none must hope to find,   *Pope* 1 : 233

———————— not to be expected in a work of man,   *Pope* 1 : 3

———————— all my soul endeavours at,   *Add.* 285

———————— truths not to be declared,   *Butl.* 1 : 96

Perfumes restored by a jakes,   *Garth* 53

Periods, how sweet, neither said nor sung,   *Pope* 3 : 192

Periphrasis, a pompous circle, and a crowd of words, *Pitt* 373

Perjurers lose their ears,   *Butl.* 2 : 112, 113

Perjur'd princes mighty woes await,   *Pope il.* 1 : 134

———————— mistress,   *Som.* 242

Perjuries, or chains or death avenge,   *Pope il.* 1 : 37

Perjury, a mere ceremony,   *Butl.* 1 : 197

———————— to deal with at pleasure,   *Butl.* 1 : 201

Pernicious flattery, bane of honest deeds,   *Prior* 2 : 125

Perpetuity of bliss, is bliss,   *Young* 2 : 9

Persecution mourn her broken wheel,   *Pope* 1 : 74

Perseus dreadful, with Minerva's shield,   *Pope* 1 : 205

Persia rising, frugal in extreme,   *Thom.* 2 : 37

———— thence revers'd into luxurious waste,   *Thom.* 2 : 37

———— trade to, precarious,   *Dyer* 114

Persian, the sun and the cloud,   *Gay* 2 : 77

———————— verses, translation from,   *Hughes* 182

Persius writes to noblemen,   *Dry.* 7 : 182

———— recommends the Stoic philosophy,   *Dry.* 7 : 183

———— grave,   *Dry.* 7 : 192

———— difficulty of finding a meaning in,   *Dry.* 7 : 197

———— in graver strains majestic wrote,   *Pope* 2 : 16

Persius,

Persius, in some things excellent,   *Dry.* 7 : 166

——— neither his numbers nor purity defensible, *Dry.* 7 : 166

——— diction hard,   *Dry.* 7 : 167

——— figures too bold, and metaphors strained, *Dry.* 7 : 167

——— reason of his obscurity,   *Dry.* 7 : 167

——— obscure, but full of sense,   *Dry.* 1 : 274

——— insulted over rather than exposed vice,   *Dry.* 7 : 168

——— broad and fulsom in some places,   *Dry.* 7 : 168

——— is below Horace,   *Dry.* 7 : 168

——— not a laughable writer,   *Dry.* 7 : 169

——— Scotinus,   *Dry.* 7 : 169

——— in what he most excelled,   *Dry.* 7 : 172

——— prologue of,   *Dry.* 7 : 308

——— first satire of,   *Dry.* 7 : 310

——— second satire, on prayers,   *Dry.* 7 : 321

——— third satire,   *Dry.* 7 : 327

——— fourth satire,   *Dry.* 7 : 337

——— fifth satire,   *Dry.* 7 : 345

——— sixth satire,   *Dry.* 7 : 357

Person spare, and expose the vice,   *Pope* 2 : 296

Persuasion, efficacy of,   *Milt.* 2 : 150

Pert infidelity is wit's cockade,   *Young* 2 : 209

Pestilence described,   { *Rowe L.* 249
                                      { *Thom.* 1 : 79

——— fiercest child of Nemesis,   *Thom.* 1 : 79

——— man is her destin'd prey,   *Thom.* 1 : 80

——— her rage the brutes escape,   *Thom.* 1 : 80

——— unpeoples cities, sweeps the plains,   *Hughes* 279

——— in open war, traverses mid-day air,   *Prior* 2 : 169

——— and scatters death, P   2 : 173

                                                       Prior

Peter, keys of, exchanged for Peter's sword,   Den. 106

——— (Czar), immortal, first of Monarchs,   Thom. 1 : 186

——— raised the Barbarian to the Man,   Thom. 1 : 186

Peterborow, earl of,   Swift 1 : 36

Peterborough, verses on,   Lanf. 125

Petersburg, mart of,   Dyer 110

Peter Waters, rogue of ministerial kind,   Swift 2 : 250

Pethox, the great,   Swift 1 : 283

Petition,   Cong. 55

——— of Mrs. Harris,   Swift 1 : 21

Petronius, greatest Roman wit,   Dry. 3 : 283

——— fancy and art please in,   Pope 1 : 119

Petticoat, rampant,   Butl. 1 : 213

Petty rogues submit to fate,   Gay 2 : 92

Phæacians, a proud unpolish'd race,   Pope od 3 : 180

——— boisterous as their seas,   Pope od. 3 : 186

——— ever to the stranger kind,   Pope od. 4 : 79

Phædra to Hippolytus,   Ot. 52

——— and Hippolytus,   Smith 95

——— prologue to,   Prior 1 : 267

Phædrus, fable from,   Prior 1 : 282

Phaeton, story of,   Add. 106

Phaleg, character of,   Dry. 1 : 172

Phanfy described,   Cow. 2 : 118

Phantasus, what,   Dry. 4 : 63

Phantom-nations of the dead,   Pope od. 3 : 271

Phaon to Sappho,   P. m. 286

——— rules unrival'd in my breast,   Pope 258

——— alone by Phaon must be lov'd,   Pope 1 : 167

——— gone, those shades delight no more,   Pope 1 : 170

Pharaoh, character of, _Dry._ 1 : 183

———— his influence on Jews, _Dry._ 1 : 184

———— and his host overwhelmed, _Milt._ 2 : 126

Pharian sceptre oft sway'd by the sex, _Hughes_ 291

Pharmaceutria, _Dry._ 5 : 60

Pharos of authority, _Butl._ 1 : 36

Pharsalia, battle of, _Rowe_ 310

———— gave Cæsar Rome, _Add._ 273

Pharsalia, an historical poem, _Rowe L._ 18, & seq.

Pheasant and the lark, _Swift_ 2 : 198

———————— answer to, _Swift_ 2 : 203

Pheasant's wing, bedropt with flakes of snow, _Fent._ 291

Phemius, skill'd in song, _Pope od._ 4 : 80

———— alone the hand of vengeance spar'd, _Pope od._ 4 : 209

———— the sweet, the heaven-instructed bard, _Pope od._ 4 : 209

———— self-taught he sung, _Pope od._ 2 : 210

Phenix, a secular bird of lives (see Phœnix), _Milt._ 3 : 64

Philibert, unmatch'd in fight, _Hughes_ 41

———— made Rome and Naples own his might, _Hughes_ 41

Philip, his haughty son, afraid of William, _Hughes_ 42

———— chose his father's favourite to depose, _Hughes_ 42

————'s son renown'd in bounty as in arms, _Prior_ 1 : 104

————'s mad son, the prosperous robber, _Hughes_ 187

———— gave curst example to ambition, _Hughes_ 188

———— o'er the fruitful East enlarg'd his sway, _Hughes_ 188

———— the wrath of heaven, a star of dire portent, _Hughes_ 188

Philips (Ambrose), pastoral poems, _A. Phil._ 297—322

——————— Lobbin, 297

——————— Thenot, Colinet, 301

——————— Albino, 306

Philips

Philips (Ambrose), Myco, Argol,   *A. Phil.* 311

———————— Cuddy,   318

———————— Geron, Hobbinol, Lanquet,   322

———————— the stray-nymph,   328

———————— the happy swain,   329

———————— epistle to a friend,   331

———————— from Holland,   333

———————— to Dorset,   335

———————— to lord Halifax,   338

———————— to James Craggs,   340

———————— to lord Carteret,   346

———————— Songs,   348, 349

———————— to Cuzzoni,   348, 349

———————— to the memory of Halifax,   350

———————— to Miss Carteret,   351, 368

———————— on the death of earl Cowper,   354

———————— to William Pulteney,   361

———————— to Miss Margaret Pulteney,   363

———————— to Miss Charlotte Pulteney,   364

———————— to Sir Robert Walpole,   365

———————— to Georgina, daughter to L. Carteret, 369

———————— epigram,   371

———————— on bad dancers [by Mr. Jeffreys], 371

———————— in answer to, What is thought? 371

———————— on Cato,   372

———————— on wit and wisdom,   372

———————— Epitaph,   373

———————— fable of Thule,   375

———————— first Olympionic of Pindar,   379

———————— second Olympionic,   388

I 4   Philips

Philips (Ambrose), firft Ode of Anacreon,   *A. Phil.* 396

———————————— fecond Ode, o.: Women,   396

———————————— third Ode, on Love,   397

———————————— hymn to Venus, from Sappho,   398

———————————— a fragment of Sappho,   400

Philips (Catharine), death,   *Cow.* 1 : 206

Philips (John), fplendid fhilling,   *Phil.* 3

——— Blenheim,   9

——— (St. John), ode to,   29

——— Cyder,   33

——— to memory of,   *Smith* 190

——— rattling coughs his heaving veffels tore,   *Smith* 190

——— pain much, but your affliction more,   *Smith* 190

——— thee defpairing Vaga mourns,   *Smith* 198

——— beft of fons, of brothers, and of friends,   *Smith* 196

——— Pindar's rage and Euclid's reafon join'd,   *Smith* 197

——— tho' learn'd, not vain ; humble, tho' admir'd,   *id.* 196

——— Pomona's bard,   *Thom.* 1 : 128

Philoctetes, in feven fhips fail'd from Lemnos, *Pope il.* 1 : 96

———————— fkill'd in the fcience of the dart and bow,   *ib.* 96

Philology, a turbid mafs of waters,   *Weft* 294

Philomel, charmer of the fhades,   *Fent.* 207

——————— forgetting Tereus, make my forrows thine, *Fent.* 208

——————— the poet of the Spring,   *Sav.* 106

——————— fober-fuited fongftrefs,   *Thom.* 1 : 69

——————— greets the rifing or the falling day,   *Broome* 85

——————— queen of the quire,   *Dry.* 3 : 168

——————— rural poet of the melody,   *Dry.* 3 : 171

Philomela, charm the fhades,   *Thom.* 1 : 193

————————————— and teach the Night his praife,   *ib.*

Philofopher

Philosopher and pheasants, — Gay 2 : 54

Philosophers go beyond their reach, — Butl 2 : 270

Philosophy, praise of, — Thom. 1 : 102

——————— work of, — Cow 2 : 360

——————— set free, — Cow. 1 : 215

——————— frees the world from superstition, — Cow. 1 : 216

——————— descended from heaven, — Milt. 2 : 210

——————— musical as Apollo's lute, — Milt. 3 : 137

——————— a medley of all ages, — Swift 1 : 17

——————— guides the passions, and amends the heart, Lytt. 16

——————— sublimes the thought, — Yal. 442

——————— runs into vain speculations, — Black. 96

——————— shrinks to her second cause, — Pope 3 : 264

——————— make thy friend, — Pope 2 : 196

——————— companion ever new, — Thom. 2 : 135

Phineus, story of, — West 225

——————— Agenor's son, — West 225

——————— plagued by the Harpies, — West 226

Phlegethon, a river of Hell, — Dry. 6 : 138

——————— loud torrents, — Pope od. 3 : 271

Phobeter, what, — Dry. 4 : 63

Phocians, in forty barks to Troy repair, — Pope il. 1 : 87

Phocion, the good, — Thom. 1 : 169

Phœbe and Asteria, — Hughes 68

Phœbus, praise of, — Pope 1 : 324

——————— the world's great eye, — Fent. 251

——————— silver-shafted, — Pope il. 2 : 216

——————— God of every healing art, — Pope il. 2 : 120

——————— the Minstrel-god, — Pope il. 2 : 329

——————— patron of the lyre, — Hughes 178

Phœbus,

Phœbus, fons of, never break their truft,   *Swift* 2 : 247

———— and Daphne, ftory of,   *Wall.* 54

———— and Paris fhall avenge my fate,   *Pope il.* 2 : 278

———— and ftretch thee here before this Scaean gate, *ib.* 278

Phœnicia, foil that arts and infant letters bore, *Pope* 3 : 179

———— firft for letters fam'd,   *Thom.* 2 : 37

Phœnicians firft knew the ufe of letters,   *Rowe L.* 131

———— the power of words by figures convey'd, *ib.* 131

Phœnix arifes from a maggot (fee Phenix),   *Butl.* 2 : 204

———— felf-born,   *Dry.* 4 : 153

———— age of, five centuries,   *Dry.* 4 : 153

———— defcription of,   *Tick.* 147

———— fairer in a purer flame,   *Tick.* 148

———— a god-like bird,   *Tick.* 149

———— contemns the power of fate,   *Tick.* 149

———— fire of himfelf, and of himfelf the fon, *Tick.* 149

———— new-born, ftarting from the flame,   *Tick.* 151

———— lays the relicks of himfelf on the fun's altar, *Tick.* 152

———— death thy deathlefs vigour fupplies,   *Tick.* 153

Pharbas, whom Hermes taught the arts of gain, *Pope il.* 2 : 60

Phorcis and Afcanius lead the Afcanians,   *Pope il.* 1 : 108

Phorcys, port of, defcribed,   *Pope od.* 4 : 16

Phryne,   *Pope* 1 : 353

———— obfcure by birth,   *Pope* 1 : 353

———— renown'd by crimes,   *Pope* 1 : 353

Phthia's realms no hoftile troops affail'd,   *Pope il.* 1 : 44

———— rich in her fruits, and martial race,   *Pope il.* 1 : 44

Phyllis,   { *Wall.*   41
                               { *Swift* 1 : 153

———— toy   *Som.* 234

                                               Phyllis,

Phyllis, resolution of, _Walsh_ 335

Phyllis's age, _Wall._ 42

Phyllising the fair, _Garth_ 24

Physic can but mend our crazy state, _Dry._ 3 : 125

——————— not create a new building, _Dry._ 3 : 125

—— drawn from the fields, in draughts of air, _Dry._ 2 : 148

—— a weak ally to Love, _Prior_ 2 : 232

—— of metaphysic begs defence, _Pope_ 3 : 264

Physician sage eludes the urn, _Prior_ 2 : 24

Physicians, made by debauch, _Dry._ 2 : 146

Physignathus I, from Peleus' race, _Parn._ 38

Physiology, old dog at, _Butl._ 1 : 231

——————— added to Divinity, _Pope od._ 3 : 1

Pick-purse at the bar or bench, _Swift_ 2 : 305

Picking epithets, and yoking rhyme, _Fent._ 308

Picture, { _Cow._ 1 : 284
         { _Hughes_ 65

—— inscription for, _Mall._ 340

—— verses on, _Broome_ 111

—— art, that grace to shadows gives, _Broome_ 111

—— on a lady's, _Tick._ 155

—— of a youth, _Wall._ 133

Picus and Canens, story of, _Garth_ 133

Piepowder court, _Butl._ 1 : 201

Piety, _Parn._ 89

—— first-born of Rationality, _Young_ 2 : 236

—— bright paths of, pursue, _Young_ 1 : 16

—— first of virtues, awful, yet serene, _Hughes_ 272

—— free from false zeal and superstition's fear, _Hughes_ 272

—— triumphant goddess, hail ! _Parn._ 145

Piety,

Piety, the foul's fecureſt guard,　　　　　*Pope* 1 : 319

——— thy guide,　　　　　　　　　*Lanſ.* 130

——— meaning of, among the Romans,　*Dry.* 5 : 234

——— predominant quality of Æneas,　*Dry.* 5 : 236

——— of men exceeded by brutes,　　　*Wall.* 75

——— conſiſts in pride,　　　　　　*Butl.* 1 : 144

Pig, how to roaſt,　　　　　　　　*King* 220

Pigeons billing,　　　　　　　　　*Swift* 2 : 234

——— eaſtern, carry letters,　　　　*Butl.* 1 : 156

Pigs ſee the wind,　　　　　　　　*Butl.* 2 : 53

Pigſney with, to ſhine on,　　　　　*Butl.* 1 : 175

Pikes, the tyrants of the watery plains,　*Pope* 2 : 63

——— diſpeoplers of the lake,　　　*Gay* 1 : 10

Pilgrim, a ſuffocating wind ſmites with death,　*Thom.* 1 : 76

——— buried in eddies of burning ſand,　*Thom.* 1 : 76

Pin and needle,　　　　　　　　　*Gay* 2 : 56

Pindar, man of Thebes,　　　　　　*Aken.* 228

——— majeſtic in the frown of years,　*Aken.* 228

——— praiſe of,　　　　　　　　*Cow.* 2 : 20

——— that eagle, mounts the ſkies,　*Prior* 1 : 85

——— like ſome furious prophet, rode,　*Pope* 1 : 210

——— odes of, very regular,　　　　*Cong.* 152

——— ſongs of triumph,　　　　　*Cong.* 152

——— conſiſted of three ſtanzas,　　*Cong.* 152

——— regular and connected,　　　*Weſt* 116

——— as natural as Anacreon,　　　*Young* 3 : 237

——— his digreſſions accounted for,　*Weſt* 121

——— his characteriſtical beauties,　*Weſt* 123

——— in his odes not a ſingle antitheſis,　*Weſt* 124

——— with deſultory fury borne along,　*Weſt* 127

　　　　　　　　　　　　　　　Pindar,

Pindar, rolls his impetuous, vaft, unfathomable fong, *Weft* 127

—— odes of, *Weft* 133

—— firft Olympionic, *A. Phil.* 379

—— fecond Olympionic, *A. Phil.* 388

—— tranflation of 14th Olympic, *Hughes* 267

—— his rage, without his fire, *Prior* 1 : 169

Pindaric, the moft fpirited kind of ode, *Young* 3 : 238

——— ode, *Cong.* 158

——— difcourfe on, *Cong.* 151

——— generally mifcalled, *Cong.* 151

——— odes, *Cow.* 2 : 3

Pindarics, now a bundle of rambling thoughts, *Cong.* 152

Pine, tafteful apple, *Phil.* 63

—— and penury, a meagre train, *Pope od.* 4 : 59

Pineal gland, feat of the foul, *Fent.* 227

Pink of puppies, *Young* 1 : 161

Pinners edg'd with Colbertcen, *Swift* 1 : 53

Pip, chickens languifh, *Butl.* 1 : 227

Pipkins tried by ringing, *Butl.* 1 : 143

Pirates, feeking others lives, venture their own, *Pope od.* 3 : 84

—— their power by murders gain, *Gay* 2 : 31

—— wear all falfe colours, *Butl.* 2 : 117

Pirithous' fame, lives there a chief to match, *Pope il.* 1 : 48

Pirus, the pride of Thrace, *Pope il.* 1 : 148

Pifa, fcene of Olympic games, *Thom.* 2 : 41

—— Jove's delight, *A. Phil.* 388

——'s honour'd games excel, *Weft* 136

—— where the fwift, the active, and the bold, contend, *id.* 142

Pifh, quoth Echo, *Butl.* 1 : 108

Pififtratus, with every art of pleafing and perfuading, *Hen* 163

P i f a r u s

Pififtratus enflav'd his country, *Aken.* 169

Pit, the many-headed monfter, *Pope* 2 : 230

—— a fenfelefs, worthlefs, and unhonour'd crowd, *Pope* 2 : 230

—— not always kind to fenfe, *Dry.* 2 : 134

—— nor juft to wit, *Dry.* 2 : 134

—— curs'd with the wrong fide of wit, *Buck.* 117

Pit-fall for the lion, *Som.* 56

———————— the elephant, *Som.* 56

Pitt (Chriftopher), poems of, *Pitt* 189

—— epiftle to Dr. Young, 189

—— on the approaching delivery of the princefs, &c. 193

—— firft hymn of Callimachus, 195

—— fecond hymn of Callimachus, 199

—— to Sir James Thornhill, 205

—— part of the fecond book of Statius, 211

—— on the death of a young gentleman, 218

—— Chrift's paffion, 219

—— on the king's return in 1720, 221

—— on the mafquerades, 223

—— on a fhadow, 225

—— to Cælia, playing on a lute, 227

—— to the Author of the Battle of the Sexes, 228

—— twelfth ode of the firft book of Horace, 229

—— the twenty-fecond ode of the firft book of Horace, 231

—— prologue for the ftrollers, 233

—— Pfalm viii. tranflated, 235

———————— xxiv. paraphrafed, 236

———————— xxix. 239

———————— xlvi. paraphrafed, 240

———————— xc. paraphrafed, 242

4

Pitt (Christopher), pſalm cxxxix. paraphraſed,   *Pitt* 245

———————— pſalm cxliv. paraphraſed,   *Pitt* 250

—— Job, chap. iii.   252

———————— xxv. paraphraſed,   255

—— ſong of Moſes,   257

—— third ode of the ſecond book of Horace,   261

——————— of the fourth book of Horace,   263

—— on the approaching congreſs of Cambray,   265

—— fable of young man and cat,   267

—— to Mr. Pope, on the tranſlation of Homer,   270

—— part of the firſt Æneid tranſlated,   272

—— on his Majeſty playing with a tiger,   280

—— dialogue between a Poet and his ſervant,   281

—— ode to John Pitt,   285, 288

—— on Mrs. Walker's poems,   290

—— verſes on a flower'd carpet,   291, 292

—— on the art of preaching,   293

—— an epitaph,   296

——————— on Dr. Keil,   304

—— a poem on the death of the earl of Stanhope,   297

—— Vida's Art of Poetry,   305

—— Horace, Book ii. Epiſtle xix.   387

—— poem to Mr. Spence,   389

—— imitation of Spenſer,   390

—— epiſtle to J. Pitt,   392

——————— to Mr. Spence,   394, 399

—— invitation to a friend at Court,   397

—— ſpecimen of a tranſlation of Odyſſey,   403

Pitt (William), verſes to,   *Lytt.* 100

—— thy country's early boaſt,   *Thom.* 1 : 141

Pitt (Will.), a Roman's virtue with a Courtier's ease, *Ham.* 217

Pity, ode to,   *Collins* 245

——— thou, the friend of man assign'd,   *Collins* 245

——— soonest runs in softest minds,   *Dy.* 3 : 87

——— mitigates the rising grief,   *Prior* 1 : 149

——— melts the soul to love,   *Hughes* 177

——— may at last be chang'd to love,   *Pom.* 245

——— tenderest part of love,   *Yal.* 377

——— human woe !   *Pope od.* 3 : 191

——— 'tis what the happy to th' unhappy owe, *Pope od.* 3 : 191

——— of a king, power of,   *Dry.* 1 : 101

Place and wealth, if possible, get with grace,   *Pope* 2 : 198

———————————— if not, by any means,   *Pope* 2 : 198

Placebo, mild his looks, and pleasing was his tone, *Pope* 2 : 232

Plagiaries, course of,   *Butl.* 2 : 100

———————— satire on,   *Butl.* 2 : 258

Plague came from Ethiopia,   *Sprat* 176

——— fell on Egypt,   *Sprat* 177

——— over-run Persia,   *Sprat* 178

——— seized Greece,   *Sprat* 178

——— attacked the Piræus,   *Sprat* 180

———————— then Athens,   *Sprat* 180

——— seized the head,   *Sprat* 182

———————— then breast,   *Sprat* 183

——— fell down to stomach,   *Sprat* 184

——— brought loss of memory,   *Sprat* 184

——— Physicians fell a prey to,   *Sprat* 185

——— dead of, lie untouched,   *Sprat* 188

——— of London,   { *Dry.* 1 : 105
                                                   { *Ot.*   37

                                                            Plague

Plague of cattle, described, *Dry.* 5 : 169

———— destroying, whom the sword would spare, *Pope il.* 1 : 43

———— none like reigning passions, *Watts* 81

Plain honest hearts suspect no cheat, *Buck.* 64

Plainness sets off sprightly wit, *Pope* 1 : 104

Plaintiff, eldest-hand, *Butl.* 2 : 102

Planet derives its house from earth, *Butl.* 1 : 254

Planets, inequal course of, *Black.* 81, 83

——— circle other suns, *Pope* 2 : 29

——— their course with different periods bound, *Prior* 2 : 118

——— dart furtive beams, and glory not their own, *id.* 2 : 118

——— how formed by Epicurus, *Black.* 141

——————— sustained in æther, inexplicable, *Black.* 142

Plantagenets and Tudors from the first William, *Prior* 1 : 164

——————— kindred rage destroy'd, *Thom.* 2 : 110

Plants, weapons against death, *Cow.* 2 : 334

Platæa famous for the victory over the Persians, *Aken.* 293

Plate sent to the Mint, to carry-on rebellion, *Butl.* 1 : 71

Platonic love, *Cow.* 1 : 235

——————— what, *Buck.* 45

——————— spell, *Tent.* 300

Platonics, answer to, *Cow.* 1 : 240

Plautus, more wit and humour in, than in Terence, *Swift* 1 : 165

Play, lust of, not regal income can defray, *Gay* 2 : 149

——— to drive out thinking, *Swift* 2 : 20

Player, the monarch of an hour, *Tick.* 136

Players, billet to, *Swift* 1 : 210

Playing the game of faces on each other, *Young* 2 : 225

——— on words inexcusable, *Add.* 194

Please, who can, is certain to persuade, *Prior* 2 : 145

Pleafe too little, and to love too much,   *Pom.* 247

Pleas'd to be pleas'd,   *Rowe* 25

———— to look forward, pleas'd to look behind,   *Pope* 2 : 256

———— woman, by not ftudying to pleafe,   *Lytt.* 12

Pleafing, epiftle of,   *Cong.* 142

———— frenzy,   *Broome* 165

———— hope to nourifh, and conquer anxious fear,   *Lytt.* 38

Pleafure,   *Prior* 2 : 129

———— an image of,   *Hughes* 244

———— falfe, as fair,   *Hughes* 244

———— how faithlefs are thy charms, how fhort thy ftay,   *ib.*

———— muft be dafh'd with pain,   *Watts* 45

———— rills of, never run fincere,   *Watts* 45

———— but a dream,   *Cow.* 1 : 70

———— empty phantom,   *Prior* 2 : 139

———— fource of, lies in our own breafts,   *Lytt.* 37

———— fprings from purity of heart,   *Young* 2 : 227

———— rage of, maddens every breaft,   *Thom.* 1 : 235

———— palls, if enjoy'd too long,   *Ot.* 55

———— dies, the grofs fruition cloys,   *Young* 1 : 194

———— to excefs, not good,   *Thom.* 1 : 220

———— elates, then finks the foul as low,   *Thom.* 1 : 220

———— declin'd, is luxury,   *Young* 3 : 271

———— enjoy'd, the tumult of an hour,   *Young* 3 : 271

———— is a toil, when conftantly purfued,   *Cong.* 81

———— is pain,   *Fail* 2 : 195

———— miftrefs of the world below,   *Young* 2 : 231

———— love of, pulfe of the world,   *Young* 2 : 238

———— imperial, her defpotic fway,   *Young* 2 : 232

———— true, is firm and folid as a rock,   *Young* 2 : 244

Pleasure false, slippery, and tossing as the wave, *Young* 2 : 244

———— or wrong or rightly understood,   *Pope* 2 : 45

———— greatest evil, or our greatest good,   *Pope* 2 : 45

———— Love, Hope, and Joy, smiling train of,   *Pope* 2 : 46

———— all taste of, flies with health,   *Gay* 2 : 83

———— of sense, fallacious,   *Milt.* 2 : 105

———— false, taken for love,   *Roch.* 293

———— after pain is sweet,   *Hughes* 176

———— to eye and palate makes cook complete,   *King* 218

———— over-pays the pain,   *Som.* 187

———— the sovereign bliss of human kind,   *Pope* 1 : 242

———— grows languid with restraint,   *Fent.* 223

———— rais'd in hope, forebodes success,   *Parn.* 104

———— calls with voice alluring,   *Hughes* 122

———————— for love,   *Aken.* 348

———— what we want, grant in fame,   *Pope* 1 : 219

———— may tempt, but virtue more should move,   *Buck.* 60

———— in observing the manners of men,   *Aken.* 61

———— of the blest, is doing well,   *King* 301

———— of a thing, that has art and difficulty,   *Cnng.* 156

———— the second, in the end of poetry,   *Dry.* 7 : 187

———— to be join'd with instruction,   *Dry.* 3 : 166

———— and pain, fasten'd by the tail,   *Swift* 2 : 129

———— and pride by nature mortal foes,   *Young* 2 : 92

Pleasures fantastical,   *Butl.* 2 : 223

———— known do seldom last,   *Rowe* 32

———— on levity's smooth surface flow,   *Prior* 2 : 155

———— are few, and fewer we enjoy,   *Young* 1 : 127

———— the sex, as children birds pursue,   *Pope* 2 : 114

———— from friendship,   *Rosc.* 239

Pleasures

Pleasures from knowledge,   *Rosc.* 239

——— of imagination, source of,   *Aken.* 119

Plenty walk in hand with peace,   *Parn.* 145

——— our disease,   *Dry.* 1 : 162

——— is a means, and joy her end,   *Young* 3 : 247

Plotian islands, why called Strophades,   *West* 231

Plotting-parlour, what,   *Aken* 296

Plough employ'd kings and heroes,   *Thom.* 1 : 5

——— in a field arable, noblest arms,   *Cow.* 2 : 302

Plumpers, dextrously draws,   *Swift* 2 : 230

——— that serve to fill her hollow jaws,   *Swift* 2 : 230

Plutus, Cupid, and Time,   *Gay* 2 : 174

Podalirius and Machaon in thirty sail command, *Pope il.* 1 : 96

——— divine professors of the Healing Arts, *ib.* 96

Podes with riches honour'd, and with courage blest, *ib.* 2 : 158

——— Hector's comrade, and his guest,   *Pope il.* 2 : 158

Poem,   *Pom.* 215

——— each has its perfection apart,   *Dry.* 1 : 273

——— though born in snow, it dy'd in flame,   *Swift* 2 : 112

Poems,   { *Fenton* 197 / *Prior* 2 : 1 / *Swift* 1 : 1

——— like pictures,   *Rosc.* 272

Poesy, progress of,   *Gray* 343

——— from Greece to Italy,   *Gray* 347

——— sullen cares and frantic passions bear thee,   *Gray* 344

——— from Italy to Albion,   *Gray* 349

——— thee the voice the dance obey,   *Gray* 345

——— its influence over the most uncivilized,   *Gray* 346

——— smooth enchantress of mankind,   *West* 137

Poesy,

Poefy, dry domains of,   *Young* 3 : 160

—— fource of pleafures ever new,   *A. Phil.* 381

—— feeds of, by Heaven alone are fown,   *Pope od.* 4 : 210

—— gift of, how prophaned,   *Dry.* 2 : 164

—— ordained for tongues of Angels,   *Dry.* 2 : 164

—— proftituted to vice and profanenefs,   *Watts* 13

—— the gift of heaven,   *Watts* 13

—— in early heathenifm devoted to religion,   *Watts* 14

—— debafed by the later Pagan poets,   *Watts* 14

—— perfected by Virgil,   *Cow.* 1 : 96

Poet, reafon of the name,   *Pitt* 349

—— a maker,   *Dry.* 5 : 258

—— complaint of,   *Ot.* 26, 73

—— to be tried by his peers,   *Butl.* 2 : 209

—— not bound to the rules of an hiftorian,   *Prior* 2 : 95

—— not to be hafty in his publication,   *Pitt* 380

—— to lofe the father in the Judge,   *Pitt* 381

—— to confult impartial friends,   *Pitt* 381

—— often to review his verfes,   *Pitt* 382

—— not to exceed in corrections,   *Pitt* 382

—— to examine his force,   *Rofc.* 216

—— to feek a congenial writer,   *Rofc.* 216

—— not to offend by wanton found,   *Rofc.* 217

—— what worthy regard,   *Cow.* 1 : 152

—— to inftruct and pleafe,   *Rofc.* 271

—— lines of, to be correct and few,   *Tal.* 375

—— fubject, moral and great,   *Rofc.* 217

—— to know, from the man of Rhymes,   *Pope* 2 : 232

—— ho who gives my breaft a thoufand pains,   *Pope* 2 : 232

—— can make me feel each paffion,   *Pope* 2 : 232

K 3

Poe

Poet enrage, compose, with more than magic art, *Pope* 2 : 232

——— with pity and with terror, tear my heart, *Pope* 2 : 232

——— corruption of, generation of a critic, *Dry.* 3 : 282

——— his power to immortalize, *Cow.* 2 : 22

——— shame to be a bad one, *Dry.* 7 : 130

——— owes his fortune to his wit, *Gay* 1 : 162

——— cares of, all terminate in fame, *King* 325

——— enly to translate a poet, *Dry.* 7 : 193

——— dependence of, *Sav.* 149

————————— to starve on hope, *Sav.* 151

——— and Dun, *Shen.* 182

——— and the Rose, *Gay* 2 : 107

Poetaster, dreaded and proscribed, *Rosc.* 276

Poetic clan, obnoxious to vanity, *Young* 1 : 178

——————— irritable, *Young* 1 : 178

——————— most ridiculous, *Young* 1 : 177

Poetical character, Ode on, *Collins* 251

——————— inspiration not to be forc'd, *Pitt* 350

Poet-laureat, election of, *Buck.* 103

Poetry, progress of, *Swift* 1 : 199

——— child of Joy, begot by Liberty, *Dry.* 1 : 274

——— born among Shepherds, *Cow.* 2 : 305

——— encomium on, *Rowe L.* 424

——— praise of, *Cow.* 1 : 86

——— use of, { *Wall.* 173
{ *Aken.* 207

——— softens the manners, *Dry.* 1 : 295

——— genuine province of, *Mall.* 234

——— conveys truth in the pleasanteft way, *Add.* 102

serious, admits no vulgar phrase, *Add.* 206

Poetry originally consecrated to God, Dry. 7 : 137

———— the language of the Gods, Pope od. 3 : 1

———— gift of, Parn. 104

———— inspired by heaven, Wall. 226, 227

———— prostitution of, { Milt. 2 : 212 / Garth 94

———— misapplied, C. w. 2 : 72

———— to be in a course of, Dry. 2 : 160

———— sacred, a tree of life, Lanf. 132

———— without morality, is but the blossom of a fruit tree, Shen. 11

———— admits no mean, Dry. 1 : 291

———— love of, Shen. 26

———— versification and numbers, pleasure of, Dry. 7 : 185

———— few good judges in, Dry. 1 : 292

———— to join the pleasant and useful, Dry. 1 : 293

———— not to corrupt the heart, Dry. 1 : 293

———————— be debased to gain, Dry. 1 : 294, 295

———— only writes to starve, Gay 1 : 105

———— Art of, Dry. 1 : 260

——————— Horace's, Rofc. 259

———— rhapsody on, Swift 2 : 300

———— vain to attempt, without genius, Dry. 1 : 260

———— Essay on, Buck. 69

———— at a loss to express mens's follies, Swift 1 : 15

———— true test of, an epistle to the Author of, Gay 1 : 207

———— and Music nearly allied, Hughes 113

———— and Painting, sisters, Dry. 2 : 154

——————————— two kindred arts, Ot. 18

Poets poor, Cow. 2 : 33

———— militant, Cow. 1 : 138

K 4

Poets starve, _Ot._ 76

—— live on fancy, and can feed on air; _Gay_ 1 : 196.

—— may have bread, as well as praise, _Parn._ 67

—— subject to envy, _Cow._ 1 : 162

—— first instructors, _Rosc._ 274.

—— without wit, _Dry._ 1 : 171

—— the first Divines, _Den._ 103

—— fables of, represent the Divine Nature, _Pope od._ 3 : 1

—— therefore called Divines, _Pope od._ 3 : 11

—— lords of infamy and praise, _Swift_ 1 : 172.

—— guardians of a state, _Rosc._ 225

—— clothe thoughts with language and numbers, _Aken._ 184.

—— inspir'd, write only for a name, _Cong._ 127

—— not of the head, but of the hand, _Dry._ 2 : 281

—— your toil all night, your labour all the day, _Pitt_ 323.

—— are not form'd in haste, _Dry._ 1 : 313

—— to rise, must fawn, _Gay_ 2 : 132

—— write half to profit, half to please, _Prior_ 2 : 44.

—— to instruct and please, _Dry._ 1 : 112

—— art and nature concur to form, _Rosc._ 274.

—— ever were a careless kind, _Collins_ 279

—— sleepless, to give their readers sleep, _Pope_ 3 : 86

—— covered with the lightest earth, _Dry._ 2 : 169.

—— must fall, like those they sung, _Pope_ 1 : 159

—— of Provence, strolling bards, _Aken._ 89

—— and Critics must from heaven derive their light, _Pope_ 1 : 91

Pointedness of thought wanting in Horace, _Dry._ 7 : 105.

Poison heals, in just proportion us'd, _Pope_ 2 : 127

Poland, crown of, venal twice an age, _Pope_ 2 : 123

Poles, victory of, over Osman, _Watts_ 221

Polhill,

Polhill (David); epiſtle to,   *Watts* 219

———————— verſes to,   *Watts* 235

Poliſh medal, favourite of the town,   *Dry.* 1 : 209

Politeſſe, all falſe pretence and hollow ſhow,   *Weſt* 266

Politician with many heads,   *Butl.* 2 : 24

Politicians thrive in broils of ſtate,   *Garth* 31

Politics like the cunning of a cheat,   *Butl.* 2 : 340

——— debas'd my mind,   *Swift* 2 : 90

Pollio,   *Dry.* 5 : 39

Pollux wields the deathful gauntlet,   *Pope od.* 3 : 289

Polycletus diſcovered proportions of the human body,   *Aken.* 88

Polydamas, ſkill'd to diſcern future by the paſt,   *Pope il.* 2 : 179

Polydore, youngeſt hope of Priam,   *Pope il.* 2 : 228

———————— whoſe feet for ſwiftneſs in the race ſurpaſt, *id.* 2 : 228

———————— with all his ſwiftneſs ſlain,   *Pope il.* 2 : 229

———————— ſtory of,   *Dry.* 6 : 4

Polynices, baniſh'd, roves,   *Pope* 1 : 299

——— bids the year with ſwifter motion run,   *Pope* 1 : 300

——————— ſon of Jocaſta and Oedipus,   *Pope* 1 : 322

Polypheme, a match for gods,   *Tick.* 173

Polyphemus deſcribed,   { *Add.* 49   *Dry.* 6 : 31

———————————— and his cave,   { *Pope od.* 3 : 240   *Add.* 48

——————— man of blood,   *Pope od.* 3 : 240

——————— deprived of ſight,   { *Add.* 49   *Dry.* 6 : 30

Polypoetes leads forty ſhips,   *Pope il.* 1 : 97

Pomfret, poems of,   *Pom.* 215

———— the Choice,   215

Pomfret, love triumphant over reason,   *Pom.* 221

———— Fortunate Complaint,   242

———— Strephon's love for Delia justified,   248

———— epistle to Delia,   253

———— pastoral essay on death of queen Mary,   258

———— to his friend under affliction,   265

———— to another under affliction,   269

———— to his friend inclined to marry,   272

———— to a painter, drawing Dorinda's picture, 273

———— to the painter, after finishing,   275

———— Cruelty and Lust,   275

———— on the marriage of earl of A.   290

———— inscription on monument of countess of Oxford, 294

———— divine attributes,   .297

———— Eleazar's lamentation,   312

———— prospect of death,   319

———— general conflagration,   327

———— reason,   338

———— last epiphany,   344

Pomona taught the trees to bear,   *Pope* 1 : 334

———————— graffing,   *Pope* 1 : 335

Pomp becomes the great,   *Pope od.* 3 : 170

Pompey, jealous glory burns within,   *Rowe L.* 49

———— on his former fortune much relied, *Rowe L.* 50

———— not proof against ambition, *Rowe L.* 98

———— once stil'd the great,   *Rowe L.* 118

———— how chang'd since sovereign of the main, *Rowe L.* 119

———— when fierce Pirates fled before thee, *Rowe L.* 119

———— sends his wife Cornelia to Lesbos, *Rowe L.* 238

———— the affecting manner in which he parts, *Rowe L.* 238

Pompey marches after Cæfar,   *Rowe* L. 263

———— his dream before the battle,   *Rowe* L. 287

———— urged to fight againft his mind,   *Rowe* L. 289, 292

———— his fpeech to his army,   *Rowe* L. 304

———— made Conful, yet a youth,   *Rowe* L. 283

———— propofes Parthia, whither to retreat,   *Rowe* L. 342

———— embarks for Afia,   *Rowe* L. 336

———— is joined by his fon and others,   *Rowe* L. 338

———— praifed by Cato,   *Rowe* L. 381

———— happy by falling with the falling ftate,   *Rowe* L. 382

———— freedom at leaft, he by dying gains,   *Rowe* L. 382

———— in the fall of thoufands, felt his own,   *Rowe* L. 318

———— befought the gods to pity poor mankind,   *Rowe* L. 318

———— neglects his advantage,   *Rowe* L. 261

———— flight after the battle,   *Rowe* L. 319, 329

———— fails for Lefbos,   *Rowe* L. 331

———— head of, fix'd on a fpear,   *Rowe* L. 359

———— body thrown into the fea,   *Rowe* L. 360

———— head embalmed,   *Rowe* L. 366

———— body burnt by Cordus,   *Rowe* L. 363

———— apotheofis of,   *Rowe* L. 370

———— lamented by his party,   *Rowe* L. 379

———— the elder, rage of, on his father's death, *Rowe* L. 378

———————— repreffed by Cato,   *Rowe* L. 379

Pomps are little more than dreams,   *Young* 1 : 53

Pontius and Pontia,   *Prior* 2 : 249

Poor, are they who know their wealth,   *Wall.* 119

——— dare to be,   *Dry.* 6 : 212

——— unbleft with greatnefs, and unvex'd with fear, *Rowe* L. 339

——— are only poor,   *Young* 1 : 147

Poor are the brethren of the bays,   Broome 88

—— pleasure to relieve,   Pope od. 4 : 60

—— ambitious to be fine,   Dry. 7 : 242

—— offender dies,   Den. 100

—— rogues run seldom mad,   Young 1 : 108

—— dreading the crime of being,   Broome 38

—— man's call is God's command,   Som. 187

Pope, preface,   Pope 1 : 3

—— discourse of Pastoral,   1 : 17

—— Spring,   1 : 25

—— Summer,   1 : 31

—— Autumn,   1 : 36

—— Winter,   1 : 40

—— Messiah,   1 : 47

—— Windsor Forest,   1 : 57

—— Cecilia's day,   1 : 77

—— two choruses to Brutus,   1 : 82

—— Ode on Solitude,   1 : 85

—— Dying Christian to his Soul,   1 : 86

—— Essay on Criticism,   1 : 91

—— Rape of the Lock,   1 : 127

—— Elegy on an unfortunate lady,   1 : 157

—— Prologue to Cato,   1 : 160

—— Epilogue to Jane Shore,   1 : 162

—— Sappho to Phaon,   1 : 164

—— Eloisa to Abelard,   1 : 183

—— Temple of Fame,   1 : 201

—— January and May,   1 : 227

—— Wife of Bath,   1 : 255

—— First Book of Thebais,   1 : 273

                                     Pope,

Pope, Fable of Dryope,   Pope 1 : 327

———— Vertumnus and Pomona,   1 : 334

———— Imitations of English Poets,   1 : 343

———— on a fan,   1 : 347

———— Phryne,   1 : 353

———— Farewell to London,   1 : 355

———— Dialogue,   1 : 357

———— Epigram on a dog's collar,   1 : 357

———————— on an invitation to court,   1 : 357

———— a fragment,   1 : 358

———— Essay on Man,   2 : 27

———— Universal Prayer,   2 : 87

———— Moral essay,   2 : 93

———— Satires and Epistles of Horace,   2 : 170

———— Donne's Satires,   2 : 260

———— Dialogues,   2 : 289

———— Imitations of Horace,   2 : 309

———— Miscellanies,   2 : 327

———— Epitaphs,   2 : 356

———— Dunciad,   3 : 73

———— preface,   ib. 1 : 1

———— Odyssey,   3 : 39

———— must be asham'd of Craggs,   Pope 1 : 357

———— thy fate to comment and translate,   Pope 3 : 206

———— advice to,   Hughes 197

———— epistle to,   Lytt. 34

———— verses to,   Lytt. 53

———— verses made to a simile of,   Rowe 58

———— verses on his works,   Broome 64

———— sure to survive, when time shall all whelm in dust, ib. 64

                           Pope,

Pope, to every theme responds thy various lay,   Broome 66

—— verses to,   Broome 115

—— epistle to,   Gay 1 : 187

—— with thee I've trod Sigæan ground,   Gay 1 : 187

—— from siege, from battle, and from storm return'd, id. 189

—— to Swift,   Swift 2 : 51

—— to Fenton,   Fent. 299

—— sparing-paper,   Swift 2 : 16

—— to,   Parn. 54

—— and his poems,   Buck. 100

—— epistles to,   Young 3 : 189, 200

—— the monarch of the tuneful train,   Sav. 19

—— on translation of Iliad,   Pitt 270

—— in thee the soul of Homer breathes,   Pitt 270

—— brought in, and naturaliz'd the bard,   Pitt 270

Pope of Rome, to know no more than,   Butl. 1 : 110

———— wears three crowns,   Butl. 2 : 37

Popery rose in dark ages,   Dry. 1 : 257

Popular sway runs to extremes,   Den. 19

———— and arbitrary reign, extremes,   Dry. 1 : 217

Porkers, choicest of the tusky kind,   Pope od. 4 : 167

———— all brawny-chin'd,   Pope od. 4 : 169

Portrait,   Swift 1 : 354

Porus, the bravest that ever fought,   Dyer 135

Possess our soul, and while we live, to live,   Dry. 3 : 137

Possessing all, covets more,   Pom. 320

Possession, and desire, his brother,   Swift 2 : 45

———— still at variance with each other, id. 2 : 45

———— in love,   Lytt. 14

Post of honour shall be mine,   Gay 2 : 126

   Post

f honour is a private ftation, when vice prevails, *Add.* 328

ior, riddle on,   *Swift* 1 : 308

umous reputation,   *Shen.* 15

nus brooding mifchief,   *Hughes* 302

—— deep in arts of mifchief read, *Rowe L.* 351

—— advifes to take Pompey's life, *Rowe L.* 351

—— Pompey's ghoft infpires new monfters in, *Hughes* 302

——. guilt, juftice demands doom on, *Hughes* 310

—— attempts to take off Cæfar, *Rowe L.* 449

—— difcovered, and put to death, *Rowe L.* 457

:y praife, and gold a crime,   *Hughes* 294

— alone was bafe,   *Gay* 2 : 165

— held the greateft vice,   *Prior* 1 : 199

— all men fly,   *Som.* 325

— her mob of friends fhe fees no more, *Som.* 325

— preferable to riches,   *Cow.* 1 : 87

— thou greateft good, but feldom underftood,*Rowe L.* 228

— fecurity thy narrow limits keeps, *Rowe L.* 228

— fafe thy cottages, and found thy fleeps, *Rowe L.* 228

— tranquil fhall lull to reft,   *Lytt.* 50

— ftood fmiling in my fight, *Pope od.* 4 : 108

— our guardian God,   *Dry.* 7 : 265

— was ne'er the villain's prey,   *Gay* 2 : 282

— rarely rifes by virtue,   *Dry.* 7 : 241

— fhame of, then unimagin'd,   *Dyer* 22

— and poetry,   *Broome* 88

r, crows flee from fmell of,   *Butl.* 1 : 121

red glafs, to kill pigs,   *Butl.* 1 : 285

verfes to,   *Sav.* 188

 focial to all,   *Sav.* 190

           Powr'

Powel, by Nature form'd, without deceit, to pleafe, *Sav.* 190

Power, *Prior* 2 : 165

———— how obtained, *Gav.* 2 : 227

———— fprings from wealth, *Young* 3 : 280

———— is but to have one's fwing, *Gay* 2 : 24

———— none, can paft recal, *A. Phil.* 389

———— luft of fatal, *Dry.* 7 : 287

———— the general idol of mankind, *Gay* 2 : 129

———— tafte of, inflames thirft, *Duke* 90

———— all human, limited by fate, *Gay* 1 : 186

———— a curfe, if not a friend to right, *Young* 3 : 171

———— us'd, to juftify wrongs, *Pope od.* 4 : 122

———— can it fecure its owner's blifs ? *Prior* 2 : 174

———— difturb'd by fear, *Lytt.* 10

———— would it avert one penfive hour ? *Gay* 2 : 149

———— itfelf of juftice ftood in awe, *Cong.* 74

———— fubmits to juftice, *Dry* 1 : 28

———— from heaven derives, *Prior* 2 : 23

———— from above, fubordinately fpreads, *Parn.* 103

———— divine, whofe goodnefs knows no bound, *Mall.* 278

———— infinite muft act, *Garth* 69

———— and greatnefs to deftruction hafte, *Rowe L.* 46

———— of light and fhade, *Hughes* 249

———————— a new creation opens to our fight, *Hughes* 249

Powerful, what he takes not, beftows, *Dry.* 1 : 29

Powers, that refcued, fhall preferve the throne, *Prior* 1 : 101

Powis (Sir Thomas), epitaph on, *Prior* 2 : 300

Poyntz, verfes to, *Lytt.* 30

———————— under his picture, *Lytt.* 33

———————— whofe virtues warm, and whofe precepts guide, *ib.* 33

Poyntz,

tz, greatnefs to whom is power of being good, *Lytt.* 33

ice, living fermon, *Dry.* 3 : 209

e, defire to, *Parn.* 255

— general fong of to God, *Watts* 328

— for creation and providence, *Watts* 329

— for redemption, *Watts* 330

— for mercies fpiritual and temporal, *Watts* 332

— for birth and education, *Watts* 333

— for the Gofpel, *Watts* 334

— for learning to read, *Watts* 336

— a pure oblation, *Parn.* 174

— fincere, *Watts* 76

— only praife, when well addrefs'd, *Gay* 1 : 260

— when juft, one may commend, *Gay* 2 : 190

— where due, beftow, *Gay* 2 : 78

— immortal praife is virtue's claim, *Young* 1 : 264

— like a robe of ftate, to fit loofe, *Butl.* 2 : 200

— wounds a noble mind, when not due, *Young* 3 : 178

— undeferv'd, is fcandal in difguife, *Pope* 2 : 236

——————— who gives it or receives, may blufh, *id.* 336

— to venom turns, if wrong apply'd, *Fent.* 316

— the precept is, be thine the deed, *Pope od.* 3 : 52

— love of, ode or, *Aken.* 264

——————— the moft pleafing fpring of action, *Aken.* 264

— facred luft of, how men are urg'd ! *Pope* 1 : 112

— the valiant urges, *Pope il.* 1 : 367

— of thinking well, *Pope od.* 3 : 209

— of kings, to right whom they wrong'd, *Pope il.* 2 : 231

ng, harder than finding fault, *Buck.* 24

— all alike, is praifing none, *Gay* 1 : 163

Prattling women are defpis'd, *Gay* 2 : 73

Prayer, power of, *Cow.* 2 : 125

———— efficacy of, *Dry.* 1 : 301

———— confidence in, *Add.* 52

———— will prove the powerful charm of eafe, *Parn.* 144

———— draws down bleffings, *Cow.* 2 : 97

———— foul has an afylum in, *Young* 3 : 46

Prayer-book, verfes in, *Lanf.* 200

Prayers accepted through Chrift, *Milt.* 2 : 80

———— are Jove's daughters, *Pope il.* 1 : 285

Preaching, art of, *Pitt* 293

Precedence, charms of, *Shen.* 185

Precept may inftruct, but not delight, *Som.* 235

Preconceptions all our knowledge are, *Pom.* 338

Predeftin'd empires rife and fall, *Prior* 1 : 99

Prediction fuppofes means, *Milt.* 2 : 195

Pre-entail of providence, *Butl.* 2 : 6

Prejudice, worft foe to truth, *Lytt.* 27

———— for names to be avoided, *Pope* 1 : 108

———— fafe from, to keep the mind, *Rowe L.* 101

Prelacy, worldly pomp of, *Dry.* 3 : 210

Prepoffeffion, noble to get rid of, *Butl.* 2 : 265

Prepoffeffions and affections bind in chains, *Pom.* 342

Prerogative reftrained, *Thom.* 2 : 119

Prefbyter and Independent fall out, *Butl.* 1 : 5

Prefbyterian true blue, *Butl.* 1 : 15

———— fower, *Pope* 2 : 100

Prefbytery, commonwealth of popery, *Butl.* 1 : 145

Prefcience, to encreafe our pain, *Rowe L.* 81

Prefcription from the grave none can plead, *Young* 2 : 111

2

Prefent,

Present, full soon shall sleep, as sleeps the past, *Young* 3 : 224
———— food, a future grave, the wretched all, *Prior* 1 : 159
———— moment terminates our fight, *Young* 2 : 15
———— seems a thing of nought, *Parn.* 116
———— only, love demands, is love, *Gay* 1 : 240
Presents, fools and wife are caught alike, *Cong.* 137
———— made to Dean Swift, verses on, *Swift* 2 : 281
———— tokens of hospitality, *Pope od.* 4 : 51
———— with female virtue must prevail, *Gay* 1 : 110
Presiding power, one in every breast, *Fent.* 311
Prevenient grace, effects of, *Milt.* 2 : 85
——————— purchase of Christ, *Milt.* 2 : 85
Priam, palace of, described, *Pope il.* 1 : 201
———— sends a herald with Paris' proposal, *Pope il.* 1 : 232
———— asks a truce for burning the dead, *Pope il.* 1 : 232
———— sues for the body of Hector, *Pope il.* 2 : 347
———— lamentation and petition of, *Cong.* 33
———— slain by Pyrrhus, *Dry.* 5 : 375
Price, in his death, I see, *Young* 2 : 71
———— each man has his, *Aken.* 335
Pricking corns foretel the gathering rain, *Gay* 1 : 56
Pride debauches the judgement, *Cow.* 2 : 157
———— blinds man's erring judgement, *Pope* 1 : 100
———— the never-failing vice of fools, *Pope* 1 : 100
———— want of sense and thought, *Rosc.* 219
———— is born of ignorance, *Young* 2 : 140
———— is by ignorance increas'd, *Gay* 2 : 138
———— not made for man, { *Wall.* 238 { *Gay* 2 : 116
———— bestowed on all, a common friend, *Pope* 2 : 52

Pride,

Pride, named nobility of foul,   *Dry.* 2 : 94

—— that cafting weight, adds to emptinefs,   *Pope* 2 : 156

—— fate of, in Niobé,   *Gay* 1 : 35

—— chaftis'd by wrath divine,   *Pope il.* 2 : 352

—— nothing more deteftable,   *Cong.* 131

—— of numb'ring Ifrael,   *Milt.* 2 : 197

—— that bufy fin, fpoils all,   *Watts* 77

—— and fwells a haughty worm,   *Watts* 77

—— the univerfal paffion,   *Swift* 2 : 14

—— reigns through all,   *Young* 1 : 84

—— attends our glory, nor deferts our fall,   *Young* 1 : 84

—— brought low,   *Som.* 51

—— will have a fall,   *Gay* 2 : 198

—— elate with decent,   *Pope od.* 3 : 210

—— too wife for,   *Pope* 1 : 25

—— oppofe to fcorn,   *Lanf.* 178

—— in reafoning pride our error lies,   *Pope* 2 : 33

—— in religion is man's higheft praife,   *Young* 3 : 67

—— and avarice, who in the fair can cure,   *Young* 1 : 122

—— of words, and arrogance of mind,   *Pope od.* 3 : 70

—— in cloaths,   *Watts* 350

—— of May, and that of beauty, are but one, *Prior* 1 : 125

———— at morn both flourifh and at even fade, *Prior* 1 : 125

Prieft, who plagues, can never mend the world,   *Lytt.* 27

—— mine is thy daughter, and fhall remain, *Pope il.* 1 : 38

—— may pardon, and the God may fpare,   *Pope il.* 1 : 41

—— holy at Rome, here Antichrift,   *Prior* 1 : 35

Prieftefs of Delphos defcribed,   *Rowe L.* 210, 212

Priefts without grace,   *Dry.* 1 : 171

—— of all religions are the fame,   *Dry.* 1 : 128

Priests of poetic rage,   *Cow.* 1 : 192

Prince, the father of a people made,   *Pope* 2 : 63

———— can never lightly err,   *West* 200

———— and people, studious of their gain,   *Pope il.* 1 : 180

———— danger of, at Andero,   *Wall.* 15

———— more undaunted than Æneas, in a storm,   *Wall.* 18

———— of Orange,   *Wall.* 168

Princes, God's viceroys,   *Cow.* 2 : 226

———— have long hands,   *Buck.* 62

———— whose glory is from heaven,   *Pope il.* 2 : 147

———— like beauties, strangers are to truth,   *Gay* 2 : 29

Prior, poems of,   *Prior* 1 : 19

———— an ode,   1 : 43

———— part of Psalm lxxxviii,   1 : 23

———— to Dr. Turner,   1 : 24

———— to countess of Exeter,   1 : 28

———— on a picture of Seneca,   1 : 30

———— an ode,   1 : 30

———— to Fleet Shepheard,   1 : 33, 35

———— to countess of Dorset,   1 : 41

———— to lady Dursley,   1 : 41

———— to lord Buckhurst,   1 : 41

———— a Song,   1 : 44

———— despairing Shepherd,   1 : 45

———— to Charles Montague,   1 : 46

———— on Dr. Shaw's taking a degree,   1 : 48

———— translation,   1 : 48

———— on taking Namur,   1 : 49

———— ode in imitation of Horace,   1 : 49

———— hymn to the sun,   1 : 59

Prior, Lady's looking-glass,　　　　　　　　Prior 1 : 62
———— Love and Friendship,　　　　　　　　1 : 64
———— to the author of a Paftoral,　　　　　1 : 66
———— to a lady,　　　　　　　　　　　　1 : 67
———— on Ormond's picture,　　　　　　　1 : 69
———— Celia to Damon,　　　　　　　　　1 : 70
———— ode to the king,　　　　　　　　　1 : 76
———— imitation of Anacreon,　　　　　　1 : 83
———— ode fur la prife de Namur,　　　　　1 : 84
———— an Englifh ballad,　　　　　　　　1 : 85
———— an ode,　　　　　　　　　　　　1 : 98
———— to king on confpiracy,　　　　　　1 : 99
———— the Secretary,　　　　　　　　　1 : 102
———— Cloe weeping,　　　　　　　　　1 : 103
———— to Mr. Howard,　　　　　　　　　1 : 104
———— Love difarmed,　　　　　　　　　1 : 105
———— Cloe hunting,　　　　　　　　　1 : 107
———— Cupid and Ganymede,　　　　　　1 : 108
———— Cupid miftaken,　　　　　　　　1 : 111
———— Venus miftaken,　　　　　　　　1 : 111
———— a Song,　　　　　　　　　　　　1 : 112
———— the Dove,　　　　　　　　　　　1 : 113
———— a lover's anger,　　　　　　　　1 : 118
———— Mercury and Cupid,　　　　　　　1 : 119
———— on beauty,　　　　　　　　　　1 : 121
———— the queftion,　　　　　　　　　1 : 123
———— Lifetta's reply,　　　　　　　　1 : 123
———— the garland,　　　　　　　　　1 : 124
———— Lady, offering her looking-glafs to Venus,　1 : 126
———— Cloe jealous,　　　　　　　　　1 : 126
　　　　　　　　　　　　　　　　　Prior,

Prior, answer to Cloe,   *Prior* 1 : 128

—— a better answer,   1 : 129

—— Pallas and Venus,   1 : 130

—— to a young gentleman in love,   1 : 131

—— English padlock,   1 : 134

—— Hans Carvel,   1 : 137

—— a Dutch proverb,   1 : 142

—— Paulo Purganti and his wife,   1 : 142

—— the ladle,   1 : 148

—— verses written at Paris,   1 : 154

—————— written in Mezeray,   1 : 155

—————— written in the Nouveaux interets, 1 : 156

—— Adriani morientis ad animam,   1 : 157

                       by Fontenelle, 1 : 157

—— a passage in Erasmus's Moria,   1 : 158

—— to Sherlock on death,   1 : 159

—— Carmen Seculare,   1 : 161

—— remedy worse than the disease, 1 : 182

—— ode to memory of Villiers,   1 : 183

—— Prologue, spoken at court,   1 : 186

—— letter to Boileau,   1 : 188

—— a passage in Scaligeriana,   1 : 195

—— to a child of quality,   1 : 196

—— Partial fame,   1 : 197

—— plan of a fountain,   1 : 198

—— the camelion,   1 : 198

—— Merry Andrew,   1 : 200

—— a simile,   1 : 201

—— the flies,   1 : 202

—— from the Greek,   1 : 203

Prior, two epigrams,   *Prior* I : 204

———- to one writing ill, and fpeaking worfe,   I : 204

——— on the fame,   I : 205

——— quid fit futurum cras,   I : 205

——— Not-browne Mayde,   I : 205

——— Henry and Emma,   1 : 218

——— an ode to the queen,   I : 245

——— Her right name,   1 : 262

———- Cantata,   1 : 263

——— lines written in Ovid,   I : 264

——— a true maid,   I : 264

——— cafe of Florimel,   I : 265

——— reafonable affliction,   I : 265, 266, 267

——— Phyllis's age,   I : 267

———- forma, bonum fragile,   I : 268

——— epigram to duke of Noailles,   I : 268

——— epilogue to Phædra and Hippolytus,   1 : 269

———- critical moment,   I : 271

——— epilogue to Lucius,   I : 271

——— Thief and Cordelier,   I : 273

——— to Cloe,   I : 275

——— Epitaph,   I : 276

——— lines written in Montaigne's effays,   I : 278

——— Epiftle, defiring the queen's picture,   I : 279

——— to countefs of Devonfhire,   I : 280

——— fable from Phædrus,   I : 282

——— to Harley,   2 : 1, 2

——— invitation to earl Oxford,   2 : 4

——— Erle Robert's mice,   2 : 5

——— two poems in Chaucer's ftile,   2 : 7

                                                      Prior,

Prior, a flower painted by Varelst,   *Prior* 2 : 8

—— to lady Elizabeth Harley,   2 : 8

—— Protogenes and Apelles,   2 : 8

—— Democritus and Heraclitus,   2 : 12

—— on his birth-day,   2 : 12

—— epitaph extempore,   2 : 13

—— for his tomb ſtone,   2 : 13

—— for his monument,   2 : 14

—— Gualterus Daniſtonus ad Amicos,   2 : 15

——————————————— imitated,   2 : 16

—— firſt hymn of Callimachus,   2 : 17

—— ſecond hymn,   2 : 22

—— Charity,   2 : 27

—— Cupid in ambuſh,   2 : 29

—— lines on a column in church of Halſtead,   2 : 30

—— Alma,   2 : 31

—— -Solomon,   2 : 101

—— lines engraven on antique lamp,   2 : 196

—— turtle and ſparrow,   2 : 197

—— application,   2 : 212

—— Down Hall,   2 : 213

—— verſes to Henrietta Cavendiſh-Holles Harley,   2 : 220

—— prologue to the Orphan,   2 : 221

—— truth and falſehood,   2 : 222

—— the converſation,   2 : 225

—— the female Phaeton [by Mr. Harcourt],   2 : 228

—— the judgement of Venus [by the ſame],   2 : 229

—— Daphne and Apollo,   2 : 231

—— the mice,   2 : 235

—— two riddles,   2 : 239

Prior, epigram extempore,   *Prior* 2 : 240

—— Nell and John,   2 : 241

—— Bibo and Charon,   2 : 241

—— wives by the dozen,   2 : 241

—— fatal love,   2 : 242

—— a failor's wife,   2 : 242

—— on a f—t,   2 : 242

—— the modern Saint,   2 : 243

—— the parallel,   2 : 243

—— to a young lady, fond of fortune-telling,   2 : 244

—— Greek epigram imitated,   2 : 245

—— to a friend on his nuptials,   2 : 245

—— the wandering pilgrim,   2 : 246

—— Venus's advice to the Mufes,   2 : 248

—— Cupid turn'd ploughman,   2 : 248

—— Pontius and Pontia,   2 : 249

—— Cupid turn'd ftroller,   2 : 250

—— to a Poet of quality,   2 : 251

—— the Pedant,   2 : 251

—— cautious Alice,   2 : 252

—— the incurable,   2 : 252

—— to Fortune,   2 : 252

—— Nonpareil,   2 : 253

—— Chafte Florimel,   2 : 254

—— Doctors differ,   2 : 255

—— Epigram,   2 : 255

—— on Bp. Atterbury,   2 : 256

—— upon honour,   2 : 256

—— two enigma's,   2 : 257

—— the old gentry,   2 : 257

                        Prior,

Prior, the insatiable priest,   Prior 2 : 258

——— a French song imitated,   2 : 259.

——— a case stated,   2 : 259.

——— upon playing at Ombre,   2 : 260

——— Cupid's promise,   2 : 260

——— to earl of Oxford,   2 : 261

——— letter to lady Margaret Cavendish-Harley,   2 : 262

——— lines under the print to Tom Britton,   2 : 262

——— truth told at last,   2 : 263

——— lines in lady Howe's Ovid's epistles,   2 : 263

——— two epistles,   2 : 263

——— True's epitaph,   2 : 264.

——— epigram,   2 : 264

——— the Viceroy,   2 : 265.

——— songs for music,   2 : 273—292

——— Miscellanea,   2 : 293—300

——— th' admiring reader entertains,   Gay 1 : 215

——— simile in, applied,   Mall. 179

Priscian's head to break,   Butl. 1 : 198 | 2 : 201

Private family, in memory of,   Shen. 40

——— fears are in the public lost,   Rowe L. 294

——— grief is mine, the public yours,   Pam. 41

——— respects must yield to public good,   Milt. 3 : 36

——— reward sets God and state to sale,   Milt. 3 : 58

Probability, the easy purchase of the mind,   Pom. 344

——— the Vulgar's treasure,   Pom. 344

——— to be kept up in the epic,   Pope od. 3 : 3

——— to supply place of truth in poetry,   Prior 2 : 96

Probity be first, and parts the last,   Young 3 : 214

Problem,   Swift 1 : 31

Problem folved,   *Swift* 2 : 243

Procraftination, danger of,   *Cow.* 2 : 372, 374

——————— is the thief of time,   *Young* 2 : 16

Precris, a victim to her jealous fears,   *Gay* 1 : 37

Procruftes, to his bed by torture fits,   *Mall.* 165

Prodigal purfues expenfive vice,   *Broome* 43

——————— buys difhonour at a mighty price,   *Broome* 43

——————— to thee I come, my father and my home, *Prior* 1 : 24

Prodigies happening at Cæfar's death,   *Dry.* 5 : 113

Profeffions, all abound with difputes,   *Butl.* 2 : 98

——————— mountebanks in all,   *Butl.* 2 : 99

Profeffors in Agriculture,   *Cow.* 2 : 304

Profit, of myftic truth, conveyed in fables,   *Dry.* 7 : 189

Projectors are undone,   *Garth* 47

Projects pleafe,   *Garth* 47

Proletarian tything-men,   *Butl.* 1 : 36

Prologue, fpoken at court,   *Prior* 1 : 186

Prometheus, ill-painted,   *Cow.* 1 : 108

Promethean powder,   *Butl.* 1 : 123

Property, you fee it alter from you to me,   *Pope* 2 : 190

——————— is in the Saint,   *Butl.* 1 : 92

Prophecies, certain faith of,   *Pope od.* 4 : 9

Prophet,   *Cow.* 1 : 265

Profe, mould the future poem into,   *Pitt* 308

——————— of life, every fober hour,   *Young* 3 : 174

Profelytes to falfe perfuafions, many,   *Butl.* 2 : 323

Proferpine, Sicily configned to,   *Cow.* 2 : 17

——————— and Dis divide the regency of night, *Fent.* 249

Profpect, a poem,   *Thom.* 2 : 131

Profperity, a baneful ftate !   *Dyer* 23

Prosperity brings ease and soft delight,   *Dyer* 24

———— makes way for luxury,   *King* 302

Prostitute for bread,   *Prior* 1 : 234

Prostitutes abandon'd, who fall to avarice a prey,   *Lytt.* 43

Protecting care of heaven confide,   *Pope od.* 3 : 141

Protector, to memory of,   *Sprat* 149

————- panegyric on,   *Wall.* 134

————- on the death of,   *Wall.* 145

Protesilas in forty ships, the first Grecian slain,   *Pope il.* 1 : 95

Proteus, sea-born seer,   *Pope od.* 4 : 96

——— delegate of Neptune's watery reign,   *Pope od.* 3 : 122

——— various god,   *Pope od.* 3 : 124

——— who bound, will reveal futurity,   *Pope od.* 3 : 124

Prothous in forty barks led the Magnesians,   *Pope il.* 1 : 97

Protogenes, a painter of Rhodes,   *Prior* 2 : 9

————- and Apelles,   *Prior* 2 : 8

Proud man always wants respect,   *Gay* 2 : 186

—— what is not ?   *Young* 1 : 79

—— of folly, vice, disease,   *Young* 1 : 80

—— fall'n are, and the world is freed,   *Rowe* 20

—— unlamented pass away,   *Pope* 1 : 158

—— in spirit, speak with pride no more,   *Parn.* 149

—— to curb, and set the injur'd free,   *Prior* 1 : 166

—— man scorn, that is asham'd to weep,   *Young* 2 : 47

Proverb, power of,   *Butl.* 2 : 234

———— old, one rogue is usher to another,   *Pope od.* 4 : 99

Providence mysterious,   *Cow.* 1 : 171

———— paths of, hid,   *Dry.* 1 : 250

———— mists of, through which we cannot see, *id.* 1 : 312

———— thou great, unfathom'd deep !   *Parn* 152

Providence,

Providence, so various, perplexing,   Milt. 3 : 29

———— men lost in mazes of,   Milt. 3 : 17

———— over-rules all,   Cow. 2 : 89

———— dispensation of, unblameable,   Milt. 3 : 9, 10

———— cease ways of to blame,   Prior 3 : 252

———— deserts me not at last,   Pope od. 4 : 60

———— food and drink procures,   Pope od. 4 : 60

———— no control of,   Dry. 3 : 83

———— all things depend on,   Dry. 3 : 83

———— raises fit men to effect its purposes,   Cow. 2: 238

———— on mortals waits,   Swift 2 : 2

———— preserving what it first creates,   Swift 2 : 2

———— shall dust arraign ?   Pitt 255

———— to rolling worlds mark'd the space,   Pitt 256

———— all-wise, all-powerful,   Gay 1 : 277

———— none foresee turns of,   Pom. 278

———— kinder than we to ourselves,   Dry. 3 : 69

Prude sinks downward to a Gnome,   Pope 1 : 129

Prudence, on,   Den. 87

———— undeceiving, undeceiv'd,   Lytt. 70

———— nor too little, nor too much believ'd,   Lytt. 70

———— scorn'd unjust Suspicion's coward fears,   Lytt. 70

———— without weakness knew to be sincere,   Lytt. 70

———— guide you, and let honour bind,   Lytt. 99

———— Hymen's band should tie,   Lytt. 42

———— be thy guide,   Pope od. 3 : 309

———— shines through clear simplicity,   Fent. 309

———— confines to golden mean,   Den. 96

———— and wisdom to direct the wit,   Pom. 229

Prudent on the prosperous hill ascends,   Roscom. L. 353

Prudent

Prudent part is to wear interest next the heart,   *Gay* 2 : 162

Prudery, what,   *Pop.* 2 : 345

Prudes condemn the absent Prudes,   *Swift* 2 : 76

Prowels, active and paffive,   *Butl.* 1 : 138

Prytanæum, what,   *Weft* 209

Pfalm viii. tranflated,   *Pitt* 235

———— xx. tranflated,   *Pitt* 236

———— xxix. tranflated,   *Pitt* 239

———— xlvi. paraphrafed,   *Pitt* 240

———— lxxxviii. confiderations on part of,   *Prior* 1 : 23

———— xc. paraphrafed,   *Pitt* 242

———— cxxxix. paraphrafed,   *Pitt* 245

———— cxliv. paraphrafed,   *Pitt* 250

Pfalms,   *Milt.* 3 : 185

Pfaumis of Camarina, obtain'd three victories,   *Weft* 161

———— whom, on Alpheus, mules to conqueft bore, *Weft* 161

Pficharpax' foul lives in me,   *Parn.* 38

Pfyche, verfes on,   *Swift* 2 : 343

Pfyllians, proof againft the poifon of ferpents,   *Rowe L.* 420

———— manner of charming ferpents,   *Rowe L.* 421

———— cure the bites of ferpents,   *Rowe L.* 422

Ptolemy, Lagæan race, laft and worft of,   *Rowe L.* 360

Public only fwell'd the breaft, private apart,   *Dyer* 22

———— fpirit,   *Sav.* 116

———— ftill is learning's friend,   *Sav.* 120

———— vice portends a public fall,   *Young* 1 : 256

———— this is certain, this is fate,   · *Young* 1 : 256

———— zeal, firft paternal virtue,   *Thom.* 1 : 99

Pudding, native ingenuity,   *King* 216

———— and beef make Britons fight,   *Prior* 2 : 76

Pudding eat, and hold thy tongue, *Prior* 1 : 201

Puddings, art of making, *King* 415

Puker, rue, *Garth* 40

Pulpit, drum ecclesiaftic, *Butl.* 1 : 4

Pulteney, *A. Phil.* 361

————- poffeffing ftore, not folicitous for more, *A. Phil.* 361

————- elegantly wife, *A. Phil.* 361

————· epiftle to, *Gay* 1 : 171

————- put out of the council, 1731, *Swift* 2 : 223

————- (Margaret), daughter of Daniel, *A. Phil.* 363

———— bud of beauty, fairly blowing, *A. Phil.* 363

————- (Charlotte), *A. Phil.* 364

————- timely bloffom, infant fair,. *A. Phil.* 364

———— to Mrs. *Rowe* 71

Punic faith is infamous, *Add.* 292

Punifhment not to extend beyond crime, *Den.* 101

Punning, art of, *Swift* 1 : 250

Puns cannot form a witty fcene, *Swift* 2 : 151

Puppet-fhow, $\begin{cases} Add. & 95 \\ Swift\ 2: & 149 \end{cases}$

Puppy-water, beauty's help, whence diftill'd, *Swift* 2 : 219

Purcel, on the death of, $\begin{cases} Buck. & 97 \\ Dry.\ 2: & 194 \end{cases}$

Pure of hand and heart, *Pope od.* 4 : 39

Puritan and Papift, *Cow.* 1 : 343

Puritans hold mental refervation, *Cow.* 1 : 344

———— hold free-will, *Cow.* 1 : 345

————- preach blind faction,. *Cow.* 1 : 346

———— claim infallibility, *Cow.* 1 : 347

Purpofes to play at, *Butl.* 1 : 308

Purse to fill, our poet's work is done, *Pope* 2 : 229

———————— alike to them, by pathos, or by pun, *Pope* 2 : 229

Pursuing Care the sailing ship pursues, *Hughes* 104

Pursuit and flight, like swelling surges, *Dry.* 7 · 32

Purtenance, to gall in, *Butl.* 1 : 112

Pygmalion and statue, *Dry.* 4 : 32

Pygmies are pygmies still, tho' perch'd on Alps, *Young* 2 : 140

———— and Cranes, battle of, *Add.* 81

Pylœmenes, the Paphlagonians rules, *Pope il.* 1 : 101

Pym made Pope, *Cow.* 1 : 349

Pyræchmus the Pœonian troops attend, *Pope il.* 1 : 101

Pyramids of Egypt, *Thom.* 2 : 37

Pyramus in form all other youths surpass'd, *Hughes* 58

———— dispatches himself at the sight of the veil, *Hughes* 61

———— his sweetness, *Cow.* 1 : 55

Pyramus and Thisbe, { *Cow.* 1 : 55 { *Hughes* 58

———————————— epitaph on, *Cow.* 1 : 63

Pyrenean, huge hills of frost, *Rowe L.* 164

Pyres, thick-flaming shot a dismal glare, *Pope il.* 1 : 39

Pyrrhonians, objections answered, *Black.* 111

Pyrrhus like a snake, that casts its slough, *Dry.* 5 : 371

———— slays Priam, *Dry.* 5 : 375

———— prologue to, *Cong.* 84

Pythagoras, Samian sage, *Thom.* 2 : 58

———— fled Samos to avoid tyranny, *Thom.* 2 : 58

———— settled at Crotona, *Thom.* 2 : 58

———— taught the four cardinal virtues, *Thom.* 2 : 59

———— the transmigration of souls, *Thom.* 2 : 59

———— doctrine of transformation, *Gay* 1 : 119

Pythagoras, founder of the Italic school,   *Black.* 1

———— golden verses of,   *Rowe* 1

———— and the countryman,   *Gay* 2 : 91

Pythagorean philosophy,   *Dry.* 4 : 136

Pythian odes,   *West* 190

Q

Quacks of government,   *Butl.* 2 : 24

——— in politics a change advise,   *Som.* 271

Quadrille has murder'd sleep,   *Young* 1 : 153

———— ballad on,   *Gay* 1 : 267

Quails, a labouring tempest drives,   *Parn.* 114

Quaker, sly,   *Pope* 2 : 100

Quakers, like lanterns,   *Butl.* 1 : 198

Qualification, which makes a good writer,   *Pope* 1 : 9

Quality, to a child of,   *Prior* 1 : 196

———— a poet of,   *Prior* 2 : 251

Quandary, driven to,   *Buck.* 105

Quarrelling and fighting,   *Watts* 344

Quarrels decided with the pen,   *Butl.* 2 : 96

Quarter given, lawful to slay,   *Butl.* 1 : 95

Queen of Britain, queen of love,   *Wall.* 28

——— Waller to,   *Wall.* 158

——— on picture of,   *Lanf.* 134, 135

——— ode inscribed to,   *Prior* 1 : 245

——— picture desired,   *Prior* 1 : 279

——— Mary, essay on the death of,   *Pom.* 258

——— humble amidst the splendors of a throne,   *Pom.* 262

——— duties of religion were her felicity,   *Pom.* 163

——— virtue unmixt, without allay,   *Pom.* 163

——— mature for heaven, the fatal mandate came,   *Pom.* 264

Queen, faireſt nymph e'er grac'd the Britiſh plain, *Pom.* 265

—— on the death of, *Young* 3 : 149

—— of Arragon, prologue to, *Butl.* 2 : 211

—— Mary, prologue to, *Cong.* 81

—— of pleaſures, ſhares the toils of fight, *Pope il.* 1 : 127

—— reſcued Paris' forfeit life, *Pope il.* 1 : 127

—— her hours beſtow'd in curious works, *Pope od.* 3 : 171

Queen's theatre, prologue on opening, *Garth* 118

Querpo deſcribed, *Garth* 52

—— armed, *Garth* 68

—— expoſed in, *Butl.* 2 : 89

Queſter to the wood they looſe, *Rowe L.* 184

Quibbling elegy, *Swift* 1 : 281

Quiddity, ghoſt of defunct body, *Butl.* 1 : 11

Quinbus Fleſtrin, ode to, *Gay* 1 : 295

———————— the mountain-man, *Gay* 1 : 295

Quidnunc is an almanac of ſtate, *Young* 1 : 108

Quidnuncki's, *Gay* 2 : 23

———————— ſo Monomotapa calls monkies, *Gay* 2 : 23

Quidnuncs, clubs of, *Pope* 3 : 112

Quiet brooding o'er his future reign, *Prior* 1 : 171

—— treads, graſs and flowers, *Dyer* 6

—— in vain you ſeek on the marble floor, *Dyer* 6

—— along with pleaſure cloſe ally'd, *Dyer* 6

—— companion of obſcurity, *Cow.* 2 : 296

—— power ſerene, *Hughes* 102

—— mother of peace, and joy, and love, *Hughes* 102

—— which nor wealth nor honours give, *Hughes* 103

—— the univerſal wiſh, *Ot.* 72

—— life, and a good name, *Swift* 1 : 297

Quilca,

Quilca, Sheridan's country-house,   *Swift* 1 : 351

Quint of generals,   *Butl.* 2 : 73

Quintilian justest rules and clearest method join'd, *Pope* 1 : 119

Q's of answers,   *Butl.* 2 : 47

R

Rabble fickle,   *Butl.* 2 : 32

———— the supreme power,   *Butl.* 2 : 76

———— maintain church and state,   *Butl.* 2 : 319

———— support sects,   *Butl.* 2 : 320

Rabsheka, character of,   *Dry.* 1 : 171

Race run well, run twice,   *Cow.* 1 : 76

———— devour the way in,   *Pope od.* 3 : 206

———— of glory run, and race of shame,   *Mill.* 3 : 27

———— of transient life to run in useful ease,   *Broome* 54

Racine, softens to pity and to love,   *Lytt.* 28

Racy verses,   *Crw.* 1 : 130

Rage gnaw'd the lip,   *Pope od.* 4 : 172

———————————— and wonder chain'd the tongue, *id.* 3 : 55

———— appeased by music,   *Crw.* 2 : 85

———— so fierce can heavenly breast inflame,   *Pitt* 273

———— invades the wisest and the best,   *Pope il.* 1 : 287

———— begets rage,   *Lans.* 289

———— finds arms,   *Milt.* 1 : 194

———— rules all other passions,   *Lans.* 276

———— swelling like a torrent, drowns the rest,   *Lans.* 276

———— of craving hunger fled,   *Pope od.* 3 : 205

———— of thirst and hunger now supprest,   *Pope od.* 3 : 101

Rail, every man has equal strength to,   *Pope il.* 2 : 223

Railing a rule of wit, obloquy a trade,   *Swift* 1 : 12

Raillery, fineness of, must be inborn,   *Dry.* 7 : 193

                                   Rain,

Rain, figns of,   *Gay* 1 : 196

—— and fun-fhine mixt in April weather,   *Cong.* 85

Raleigh, voyage of,   *Dyer* 192

—— the fcourge of Spain,   *Thom.* 1 : 95

—— bled,   *Thom.* 2 : 113

Ralph, Squire of Hudibras,   *Butl.* 1 : 26

—— gifts of,   *Butl.* 1 : 27, & feq.

—— laid in the ftocks,   *Butl.* 1 : 136

Ralph (James), to Cynthia howls,   *Pope* 3 : 186

—— and makes night hideous, *ib.*

Ram, choice of,   *Dyer* 38

Ramilia's field, ten thoufand themes for verfe,   *Rowe* 15

—— plain Blenheim's fame renews,   *Prior* 1 : 155

Ramfay (Allan),   *Som.* 159

—— epiftle to,   *Som.* 210, 218

—— anfwer to Somervile,   *Som.* 215

Randal, low and mean,   *Dry.* 1 : 269

Ranters, a fect,   *Butl.* 1 : 149

Rants of Maximin to a wild audience pleafing,   *Lanf.* 234

Rape of the Lock,   *Pope* 1 : 127

—— tranflation of the firft part of,   *Pan.* 57

Raphael fent to Paradife,   *Milt.* 1 : 146

—— ordered to warn man,   *Milt.* 1 : 147

—— flight defcribed,   *Milt.* 1 : 148

—— Eve prepares for reception of,   *Milt.* 1 : 150

—— Adam proceeds to meet,   *Milt.* 1 : 151

—— entertained by Adam,   *Milt.* 1 : 152

—— a new creation raifes,   *Add.* 43

Rapine, with her harpy claws the bofom tears,   *Gay* 2 : 152

Rapture, carries above reafon, and beyond will,   *Buck.* 88

Rapture, to catch with poetic,   *Bud.* 1 : 156

────── works the finger's fancy high,   *A. Phil.* 312

Rapturous-songs, that breathe of wine,   *Broome* 188

Rascallion, used like,   *Bud.* 1 : 112

Rat-catcher and cats,   *Gay* 2 : 65

────────── sole guardian of a nation's cheese,   *Gay* 2 : 66

Ratiocination, to pay debt with,   *Bud.* 1 : 8.

Rats of amphibious nature,   *Bud.* 1 : 5

Raven sent out of the ark,   *Milt.* 2 : 113

───── Danish standard,   *Thom.* 2 : 104

───── of the law, loud croaks,   *Young* 2 : 124

─────────── and reads abundance into poverty, *id.* 2 : 124

───── the sexton, and earthworm,   *Gay* 2 : 190

Ready money makes the man,   *Som.* 306

───── commands respect where-e'er we go,   *Som.* 306

───── and gives a grace to all we do,   *Som.* 306

Real good, so little mortals know !   *Young* 3 : 122

Realm happy, which God vouchsafes to bless,   *Parn.* 175

Realms, housholds which the great must guide,   *Dry.* 1 : 84

────── the guilty victor's prize, suffice not,   *Pope* 1 : 286

Reaping described,   *Thom.* 1 : 111

Reason, a poem,   *Pom.* 338

────── is o'er-power'd in youth,   *Pom.* 338.

────── should over sense preside,   *Pom.* 338

────── correct our notions, and our judgement guide, *Pom.* 338

────── a taper, which but faintly burns,   *Pom.* 388

────── the comparing balance, rules,   *Pope* 2 : 43

────── form'd but to check, deliberate and advise, *Pope* 2 : 44

────── the card, passion is the gale,   *Pope* 2 : 45

────── discursive or intuitive,   *Milt.* 1 : 155

                                              Reason,

Reason, teach my best reason,   *Young* 2 : 5.

———— that common guide ordain'd,   *Wch* 233

———— leads man to solid bliss,   *Wch* 233

———— rightful empress of the soul,   *Pom.* 234

———— all exorbitant desires controls;   *Pom.* 234.

———— and love could ne'er agree,   *Pom.* 235

———— supported by sinewy force of argument;   *Pom.* 235

———— the voice of God,   *Thom.* 1 : 168

———— glory of, is to quell desire,   *Sav.* 39

———— how weak at best,   *Buck.* 82

———— glimmering ray of,   *Dry.* 1 : 244

———— discovers one first principle,   *Dry.* 1 : 245

———— sees not, who or what it is,   *Dry.* 1 : 245

———— groped for a future state,   *Dry.* 1 : 245

———— progressive,   *Young* 2 : 165.

———— use in divinity,   *Cow.* 1 : 134.

———— to rule,   *Dry.* 2 : 17

———— every passion sway,   *Pom.* 218

———— passion's foe,   *Young* 2 : 37

———— overwhelm'd by passion,   *Cow.* 1 : 62

———— betray'd by passion, shall resume her seat, *Prior* 2 : 145

———— heard, the sole mark of man,   *Young* 3 : 51

———— exerts her rays, to lead thro' error's maze, *Fent.* 314.

———— seems impertinence in love,   *Pom.* 222

———— great directress of our minds,   *Pom.* 225

———— conquers love,   *Lytt.* 13

———— restor'd, virtue reigns,   *Som.* 239

———— shadows of, betray,   *Den.* 47

———— pursued is faith,   *Young* 2 : 87

———— leads the judgement,   *Den.* 88

Reafon, lofs of, lefs piteous than depravation,   *Cow.* 2 . 363

———— once depofed, noife and folly take her place,   *Sav.* 40

———— cool at beft, but ferves when preft,   *Pope* 2 : 58

———— curioufly fpun, next to none,   *Butl.* 2 : 279

———— a fharp accufer, but a helplefs friend,   *Pope* 2 : 47

———— but removes weak paffions for the ftrong,   *Pope* 2 : 47

———— an ignis fatuus,   *Roch.* 319

———— downward, till we doubt of God,   *Pope* 3 : 248

———— fubmits to rhyme,   *Butl.* 2 : 242

———— paffion, anfwer one great aim,   *Pope* 2 : 84

———— and benevolence were law,   *Thom.* 1 : 12

————————— injurious act unknown,   *Thom.* 1 : 12

Reafons meafured by tale, not weight,   *Butl.* 2 : 348

Reafonable affliction,   *Prior* 1 : 265, 266, 267

Reafoning, falfe, of man,   *Milt.* 2 : 71

Reafoning-mule will neither lead nor drive,   *Matt.* 175

Rebel angels for ambition fell,   *Parn.* 269

———— nature holds out half my heart,   *Pope* 1 : 184

Rebellion fown by the Clergy,   *Cow.* 1 : 328

Rebus,   *Swift* 1 : 134

———— what,   *Swift* 1 : 134

———— anfwer to,   *Swift* 1 : 134

Recantation,   *Shen.* 34

Receipt, to reftore Stella's youth,   *Swift* 1 : 332

Receivers worfe than thieves,   *Butl.* 1 : 180

Receptacle of the chyle,   *Black.* 194

Recitative, an improved elocution,   *Hughes* 114

———————— pronouncing the words in mufical cadences, *id.* 114

———————— founded on a pleafing variety of accent,   *id.* 114

Reconcilement between Tonfon and Congreve,   *Rowe* 41

                    Reconciliation,

Reconciliation,   *Cong.* 52

Recovery of a lady,   *Sav.* 155

Recreant knight, no woman can endure,   *Dry.* 3 : 143

Rectitude, teach my best will,   *Young* 2 : 5

Recumbent Virtue's downy Doctors,   *Young* 2 : 84

Red-breast, sacred to the houshold-gods,   *Thom.* 1 : 161

Red-coat seculars,   *Butl.* 2 : 21

Red Sea, passage of,   *Cow.* 2 : 67

Redress of wrongs belongs to heaven,   *Pope od.* 3 : 69

Reds, blacks, and blues, got in fight,   *Butl.* 1 : 111

Redstreak, praise of,   *Phil.* 51

Reflections on state of the nation,   *Young* 1 : 247

————— on the Author's situation,   *Shen.* 65

Reformado saint,   *Butl.* 2 : 7 | 1 : 194

————— soldier,   *Butl.* 1 : 213

Reformation dispels ignorance,   *Dry.* 1 : 257

————— ills it gave occasion to,   *Dry.* 1 : 258

————— pretenders to,   *Butl.* 1 : 70

————— by fire and sword,   *Butl.* 1 : 15

Reformations, what,   *Butl.* 2 : 209

Refreshment after toil, ease after pain,   *Milt.* 1 : 145

Refusal, soften into grace,   *Young* 3 : 210

Regal state, deem'd no pre-eminence of ease,   *Thom.* 2 : 109

Regent of the southern sky, o'er my garden fly,   *Parn.* 203

Rehearsal, author of, sat to himself,   *Dry.* 7 : 108

Rehoboam, by young counsellors loses ten tribes, *Cow.* 2 : 121

Reign, how sweet a peaceful,   *Pope od.* 3 : 227

Rejoinder by the Dean,   *Swift* 1 : 243, 245

Re-judge his justice, be the God of God,   *Pope* 2 : 33

Relapse,   *Young* 2 : 91

Relentless

Relentless Destiny urges all that e'er was born,. *Prior* 1 : 188

Relieve us, poor,   *Pope ed.* 3 : 237

Religio Laici,   *Dry.* 1 : 244

Religion, queen of virtues,   *Cow.* 1 : 121

———— force,   *Young* 1 : 47

———— reigned mistress of her heart;.   *Young* 3 : 151

———— true, effects of,   *Black.* 66

———— guest of celestial race,   *Black.* 66

———— purge the mind of selfishness and brutal sense, *West* 317

———— and swell the heart with bless'd benevolence, *id.* 317

———— thou art all,   *Young* 1 : 15

———— crowns the statesman and the man,.   *Young* 1 : 264

———— sole source of public and of private peace, *id.* 1 : 264

———— the sole voucher man is man,   *Young* 2 : 80

———— the soul of happiness,   *Young* 2 : 81

———— best displayed in distress,.   *Young* 1 : 51

———— aids, where reason fails,   *Prior* 2 : 187

———— blushing, veils her sacred fires,   *Pope* 3 : 264

———— not sour'd by cant, nor stumm'd with merit, *Prior* 1 : 39

———— frights with a mien severe,   *Dry.* 2 : 87

———— forbids the persecuting, sword to draw,.   *West* 286

———— and free-created souls with terrors awe,.   *West* 286

———— not to be mended,   *Butl.* 1 : 16

———— a cloak for treason,   *Cow.* 1 : 348

————'s bright authority men dare,   *Garth* 38

Religions, all flock together,   *Butl.* 2 : 69

Religiously to follow Nature's laws,   *Rowe L.* 101

Remedy worse than the disease,   *Prior* 1 : 182

Remembrance builds delight on woe,   { *Pope ed.* 4 : 61
                                          { *Gay*   1 : 200

                                                        Remi,

'Remi, expert in javelins and the bow, *Rowe L.* 67

Renown is not the child of indolent repose, *Thom.* 1 : 241

Rent-charge on the rich to live, *Pope od.* 4 : 138

Repartees, *Butl.* 2 : 192

Repentance fierce rears her snaky crest,. *Thom.* 1 : 36

——————- inadequate in price, *Dry.* 1 : 248

Repetition, pleasing, when happily made, *Pitt* 366

Replies prompt in, but cautious to offend, *Pom.* 250

Repose, that temperance sheds, *Mall.* 253

—————— undeserving, undeserv'd, *Lytt.* 26

Representatives, laws by, binding, *Dry.* 2 : 31

Reproach, foul, has it a privilege from heaven ? *Pope il.* 1 : 50

——————— is infinite, and knows no end,. *Pope il.* 2 : 223

——————— arm'd, or with truth or falsehood, *Pope il.* 2 : 223

Reproachful speech want of argument supplies, *Gay* 2 : 194

——————— often ends the contest of disputing friends, *id.* 2 : 194

Reproof with decent silence bear, *Pope il.* 1 : 171

—————— those best can bear, who merit praise, *Pope* 1 : 115

Reputation dies at every word, *Pope* 1 : 138

Request, *Cow.* 1 : 223

Rescues met, beneath the mask of ill ? *Young* 3 : 122

Resentment just becomes the brave, *Pope il.* 1 : 290

Resign, and you remove the load of life, *Young* 3 : 103

Resignation, *Young* 3 : 87

——————— yet unsung, though claiming every Muse, *id.* 3 : 89

—————— thou sole support of age, *Young* 3 : 89

Resistance be repaid with blood, *Rowe L.* 303

Resolved to be beloved, *Cow.* 1 : 259

Resolution, *Cow.* 1 : 266

—————— suffering part of, *Dry* 2 : 278

Respect

Respect us human,   *Pope od.* 3 : 237

———— was never paid to pride,   *Gay* 2 : 169

Rest, too much, becomes itself a pain,   *Pope od.* 4 : 61

———— is a crime, when our Country calls,   *Browne* 74

Restless-passions, awed be,   *Browne* 54

Restoration,   { *Dry.* 1 : 19
                                       { *Roch.*   332

—————— ode on,   *Cow.* 1 : 179

—————— described,   *Thom.* 2 : 116

Restraint we all break through,   *Gay* 2 : 63

Resurrection,   { *Cow.* 2 : 22
                                      { *Add.*   86

—————— prospect of,   *Watts* 118

Retirement, advantages of,   *Walsh* 331

Retreat, described,   *Cow.* 2 : 385

———— thy joys content bestow,   *Sav.* 53

———— in war noble,   *Butl.* 1 : 123

Return, thou say'st, and bodies fall to clay,   *Parn.* 116

Revelation, necessity of,   *Dry.* 1 : 246

—————— discloses the forfeit,   *Dry.* 1 : 248

Revenge, bloody minister of ill,   *Dry.* 2 : 55

———— to methodize,   *Dry.* 3 : 223

———— costs our peace of mind,   *Dry.* 2 : 137

———— less sweet than forgiving,   *Dry.* 1 : 28

———— makes danger dreadless seem,   *Cong.* 17

———— may rest content with drums and parchm *Gay* 2 : 38

———— impatient rose,   *Collins* 272

———— and ambition beget war,   *Cow.* 1 : 92

Reverence of thyself thy thoughts control,   *Rowe* 3

Reverse,   ·   *Watts* 212

                                                  Review,

Review,   *Duke* 83

Revilings, growth of all nations,   *Dry.* 7 : 136

Revolt of the ten tribes,   *Cow.* 2 : 122

Revolutions ſtrange, time may bring,   *Gay* 1 : 276

Reward,   *Mall.* 297

———— of grace,   *Milt.* 2 : 70

Rhadamanth comes to quell the fray,   *Som.* 114

———— ſpeech of,   *Som.* 115

———— appeaſes the tumult,   *Som.* 117

Rhadamanthus, a judge of hell,   *Dry.* 6 : 138

Rhæbus, ſpeech to,   *Dry.* 6 : 311

Rheſus, the Thracian chief, ſlain,   *Pope il.* 1 : 314

———— horſes carried off,   *Pope il.* 1 : 314

———— ſwift as the wind, and white as ſnow, *id.* 1 : 315

Rhetoric ſleeks the tongue,   *Milt.* 2 : 201

Rhetorician, rules of,   *Butl.* 1 : 9

Rhine, parent of floods,   *Thom.* 2 : 65

Rhodes, with everlaſting ſunſhine bright,   *Pope il.* 1 : 93

———— beloved by Phœbus,   *Rowe L.* 206

———— tore from Chriſtians,   *Wall.* 56

Rhodope, the Bard torn in,   *Milt.* 1 : 203

Rhyme, barbarian,   *Roſc.* 225

———— fair barbarity,   *Dry.* 2 : 128

———— in needleſs bonds the poet ties,   *Smith* 193.

———— enervates poetry,   *Dry.* 2 : 153.

———— deſire of, taken for genius,   *Dry.* 1 : 261

Rhymes, he who writes in, dances in fetters,   *Prior* 2 : 97

———— miſ-ſpelt record a lover's flame,   *Gay* 1 : 225

Ribaldry, a poor pretence to wit,   *Buck.* 72

Ribalds, not one ſprig of laurel graced,   *Pope* 2 : 156

Rich.

I

Rich, on death of lady,   *Wall.* 65

—— grow, to give,   *Dyer* 141

—— is to be wife,   *Garth* 32

—— without bounty,   *Pope od.* 4 : 26

—— knave, a libel on our laws,   *Young* 1 : 82

—— offender escapes,   *Den.* 100

—— rival,   *Cow.* 1 : 273

—— and honest, would you be ?   *Gay* 2 : 148

—— the poor, the great, the small are level'd,   *Gay* 2 : 195

———————————— all by death confounded, *Gay* 2 : 195

Rich (John), rides in the whirlwind,   *Pope* 3 : 198

——————————————— and directs the storms, *ib.*

Richard, lion-hearted, unbelievers turn'd to flight,   *Phil.* 80

Richard III. the bristled boar,   *Gray* 357

Riches, the toil of fools, the wise man's snare,   *Milt.* 2 : 178

———— slacken virtue,   *Milt.* 2 : 178

———— the enamoured heart bewitch,   *Butl.* 1 : 172

———— that vex,   *Pope* 2 : 354

———— gathered, trouble,   *Prior* 1 : 160

———— possess'd, but not enjoy'd,   *Pope od.* 3 : 109

———— use of,   *Dry.* 7 : 360

———— some service may afford,   *Pitt* 396

———— but oftner play the tyrant,   *Pitt* 396

———— give meat, fire, and cloaths,   *Pope* 2 : 121

———— have wings, and man is but dust,   *Prior* 2 : 14

———— make pinions for themselves,   *Swift* 1 : 190

———— leave us, or we them,   *Cow.* 2 : 370

———— our chief desire,   *Dry.* 7 : 283

———— no grace of heaven, or token of th' elect, *Pope* 2 : 119

———— given to the fool, the mad, the vain, the evil, *id.* 2 : 119.
            . Riches

Riches cannot pay for faith or love,   Aken. 327

————— flow from bounteous heaven,   Pope od. 4 : 118

————— crown virtue,   Young 3 : 246

————— good or ill, as us'd by man,   Young 3 · 246

————— of my grace, like gems,   Parn. 197

————— of Nature,   Cow. 2 : 13

————— conjoined with meanness,   Cow. 1 : 50

Richmond lodge and Marble hill,   Swift 2 : 40

Rid thee of this Cæsar's gift, this life,   Rowe L. 108

Riddle,   Parn. 288

Riddles,   Swift 1 : 306

Riddling-sung the double-dealing priest,   Rowe L. 77

Ridicule, inquiry into,   Aken. 64

————— whether test of truth,   Aken. 102

————— sources of,   Aken.

————— end of,   Aken. 70

————— defined,   Aken. 98

————— object of,   Aken. 154

————— nature of,   Aken. 154

————— final cause of,   Aken. 155

————— rear'd on Reason's throne,   Pope 2 : 10

————— loaded with honours not her own,   Pope 2 : 10

————— has greater power to reform, than four, Swift 2 : 24

Ridley on Pitt's translations and poems,   Pitt 188

Right lives by law,   Dry. 1 : 185

————— whatever is,   Pope 2 : 39

————— too rigid, hardens into wrong,   Pope 2 : 62

————— independent of success,   Rowe L. 402

————— conquest cannot make it more or less,   Rowe L. 402

————— alone is bold and strong,   Young 3 : 2

Right,

5

Right, pray the gods to smile upon,   *Rowe L.* 108

——— hand a thief, the left receiver,   *Butl.* 2 : 69

——— name,   *Prior* 1 : 262

——— wits, grant I may be kept in,   *Swift* 1 : 89

Righteousness imputed,   *Dry.* 1 : 248

Rigidly honest, and severely just,   *Yal.* 445

Rills run gurgling o'er the sand,   *Rowe L.* 176

Rimmon, God of Damascus,   *Milt.* 1 : 20

Ring, tool of matrimony,   *Butl* 2 : 21

Riot agrees not with frugality,   *Cong.* 76

——— reared her lewd dishonest face,   *Rowe L.* 51

——— revenges the vanquished world,   *Dry.* 7 : 265

——— slower suicide,   *Young* 2 : 258

——— all, among the lawless train,   *Pope od.* 3 : 72

——— wastes the day,   *Pope od.* 3 : 228

Ripe, and yet thy life but green,   *Cow.* 1 : 121

Rise, but to sink,   *Garth* 93

Rising merit will buoy up at last,   *Pope* 1 : 110

Rival, nor love nor empire bears,   *Cong.* 133

River, flying at,   *Som.* 151

Rivers, how formed,   *Black.* 56

——— most celebrated,   *Black.* 58

——— carrying plenty with them,   *Black.* 59

——— through airy channels flow,   *Add.* 43

Roads Roman,   *Dyer* 17

Robe's geography, lines written in,   *Prior* 1 : 154

Robes, which blissful Eden knew not,   *Thom.* 1 : 89

Robin and Harry,   *Swift* 2 : 189

——— runs out in tongue as in estate,   *Swift* 2 : 189

Rochester, poems of,   *Roch.* 281

                                                                        Rochester,

Rochester, dialogue by,   Roch. 281

———— a pastoral dialogue,   284

———— the advice,   287

———— the discovery,   289

———— woman's honour,   290

———— Grecian kindness,   291

———— the mistress,   292

———— a song,   294, 297, 298, 301, 302

———— to Corinna,   295

———— on leaving his mistress,   299

———— on drinking in a bowl,   300

———— constancy,   304

———— a letter,   306

———— epistolary essay,   315

———— satyr on mankind,   318

———— maimed debauchee,   326

———— on nothing,   328

———— on Restoration,   332

———— death of princess of Orange,   333

———— an epilogue,   335

———— satire of Horace,   336

———— epilogue,   342

———— prologue,   344

———— character of,   Dry. 1 : 119, & seq.

———— epitaph on,   Dry. 2 : 200

———— elegy on,   Wall. 183

Rochfort, countess of, verses to,   Sav. 142

Rochfort, reply of,   Swift 1 : 235

Rock bursts, and rushing torrents flow,   Broome 17

———— divided, flows upon the plain,   Pan. 114

Rocks proclaim th' approaching Deity,   *Pope* 1 : 50

────── called Altars,   *Pitt* 277

Rod, scorn th' ungenerous province of,   *Pitt* 316

────── for which use softer means and milder ways,   *Pitt* 316

──────────── raise emulation in social studies,   *Pitt* 318

──────────── or gifts propose,   *Pitt* 318

Rogers, Waller to,   *Wall.* 114

Rolling-stone is ever bare of moss,   *A. Phil.* 304

Rolling-thunder grumbles in the skies,   *Broome* 27

Rolling year is full of God,   *Thom.* 1 : 191

Roman, a name should ever sacred be,   *Rowe L.* 354

────── Cæsar's foe, is a friend to virtue,   *Add.* 279

────── arts, from Roman bondage free,   *Hughes* 162

────── gaolers, chained to prisoners,   *Butl.* 1 : 293

────── hands have laid Hesperia waste,   *Rowe L.* 44

────── satire, of Roman growth,   *Dry.* 7 : 146

────── school,   *Thom.* 2 : 89

────── soul is bent to make man mild and sociable,   *Add.* 261

Romance, where fallacy in legends wildly shines,   *Sav.* 175

────── how framed,   *Wall.* 32

Romances, nothing but love and battles,   *Butl.* 1 : 47

Romans, character of,   *Milt.* 2 : 205

────── spread arts and civility,   *Den.* 104

────── who think like, like Romans fight,   *Tick.* 118

────── once free and virtuous, Britons beware !   *Dyer* 25

Rome, a poem,   *Thom.* 2 : 57

────── ruins of,   *Dyer.* 7

────── fall'n, a silent heap,   *Dyer* 7

────── even yet majestical,   *Dyer* 7

────── a solemn wilderness,   *Dyer* 10

Rome,

Rome, true name of, concealed,   *Dry.* 2 : 103

—— raised by ravishing women,   *Butl.* 2 : 119

—— mean beginnings of,   *Dyer* 22

—— gave jealousy to the neighbouring states,   *Dyer* 22

—— dictators of, rose from the plough,   *Dyer* 22

—— perseverance under difficulties,   *Dyer* 23

—— darling child of fate,   *Fent.* 199

—— kings of, elective,   *Dry.* 5 : 226

—— for wisdom, as for conquest fam'd,   *Lanf.* 157

—— queen of the earth,   *Milt.* 2 : 202

—— the world's imperial mistress,   *Rowe L.* 64

—— fated for liberty,   *Thom.* 2 : 59

—— labouring rose, and rapid fell,   *Thom.* 2 : 60

—— by Brutus free'd,   *Pitt* 230

—— virtuous poverty of,   *Pitt* 231

—— to a human shambles turn'd,   *Thom.* 2 : 71

—— had not virtue to be free,   *Thom.* 2 : 72

—— has its Cæsars,   *Add.* 323

—— contending parties' noblest prize,   *Rowe L.* 115

—— rent in twain,   *Tick.* 157

—— ever fond of war, was tir'd with ease,   *Rowe L.* 52

—— her ancient grandeur sunk,   *Hughes* 278

—— catch'd infection from the conquer'd East,   *Buck.* 90

—— sunk beneath her unwieldy weight,   *Rowe L.* 46

—— wrought her own destruction,   *Rowe L.* 47

—— the tomb of empire,   *Thom.* 2 : 17

—— by her fasces aw'd the subject world,   *Thom.* 2 : 18

—— senate, all head to counsel, and all heart to act, *Thom* 2 : 19

—— her forum, warm, popular, and loud,   *Thom.* 2 : 19

—— her own sad sepulchre appears,   *Pope* 2 : 144

Rome, magnificent in ruin,   *Add.* 42

—— died of luxury and pride, difeafes fell,   *Weft* 279

—— liberty's fair land to fhame and thraldom brought, *ib.*

—— trembling, flavifh, fuperftitious,   *Rowe L.* 309

—— and Pompey took up every thought,   *Rowe L.* 294

—— modern, ftands on the Campus Martius,   *Dyer* 16

—— thundering againft heathen lore,   *Pope* 3 : 179

—— fpiritual Sodom,   *Den.* 70

—— purple tyranny,   *Thom.* 1 : 69

—— no longer, but Babylon,   *P. ior* 2 : 66

—— fhines fupreme in arts, as once in power,   *Pitt* 358

Romulus reared by a wolf,   *Butl.* 1 : 54

—— tranflated,   *Butl.* 2 : 16

—— affumption of,   *Garth* 149

—— and Remus, where found at the teat of a wolf, *Dyer* 21

Rook, with harfh malignant caw,   *Swift* 2 : 201

—— at chuck,   *Som.* 297

Rooke on the fea afferts Anna's fway,   *Smith* 208

Rofamond, Jane Clifford,   *Dry.* 2 : 277

—— on opera of,   *Tick.* 115

—— let joy falute her fhade,   *Tick.* 115

Rofcommon, poems of,   *Rofc.* 213

—— on tranflated verfe,   213, & feq.

—— on 148th Pfalm,   227

—— prologue to duke of York,   231

—— Song,   232

—— Pfalm,   227

—— Virgil's Eclogue vi.   232

—— Ode on folitude,   238

—— Horace Ode xxii. b. i.   242

Roscommon, Guarini's Pastor Fido, _Rosc._ 242

———————— the dream, 244

———————— ghost of Commons, 245

———————— death of a lady's dog, 247

———————— epilogue to Alexander, 248

———————— on day of judgement, 249

———————— prologue to Pompey, 252

———————— Ross's ghost, 254

———————— corruption of times, 255

———————— Horace's Art of Poetry, 258

———————— makes rules a noble poetry, _Add._ 37

———————— best of critics and of poets, _Add._ 38

———————— translation of Horace, _Wall._ 172

———————— not more learn'd than good, _Pope_ 1 : 121

———————— only boasts unspotted lays, _Pope_ 2 : 225

———————— Dryden to, 2 : 127

———————— and Mulgrave rose like light, _Lans._ 234

———————— gave patterns and set bounds, _Lans._ 234

———————— for them forgoe the Stagyrite, _Lans._ 234

Rose, { _Watts_ 362
       { _Broome_ 171

——— the glory of the spring, _Broome_ 171

——— sweetest incense of the skies, _Broome_ 171

——— in Cytherea's cheeks, _Broome_ 172

——— keeps the fragrance of its prime, _Broome_ 172

——— birth of, _Hughs_ 106

——— queen of flowers, _Hughs_ 109

——— guarded by the pointed thorn, _Broome_ 22

——— short-lived, _Wall._ 99

Rose-bud, _Broome_ 59

Rose-bud,

Rose-bud,   *Shen.* 127

———— queen of fragrance,   *Shen.* 127

Rosemary used in making love,   *Butl.* 1 : 185

———— a riddle,   *Gay* 1 : 61

Roses rival, involv'd in blood the age,   *Yal.* 439

Rosicrucian lore,   *Butl.* 1 : 29

Rosicrusians, who,   *Pope* 1 : 126

Rosin'd bow torments the string,   *Gay* 1 : 87

Ross, ghost of,   *Rosc.* 254

—— ode on death of colonel,   *Collins* 262

—— man of, rise, honest Muse, and sing,   *Pope* 2 : 127

—— him portioned maids and 'prentic'd orphans blest, *id.* 128

—— the young who labour, and the old who rest,   *id.* 128

Rosy-beauty far outblush'd the morn,   *Gay* 1 : 244

Rosycross philosophers,   *Butl.* 1 : 248

Rot in sheep, how to prevent,   *Dyer* 39

Rover, a spaniel, verses on,   *Swift* 2 : 364

Roundelay,   *Dry.* 2 : 210

Round-table knights,   *Dry.* 3 : 200

Roundway-heath fight,   *Cow.* 1 : 339

Rout described,   *Dry.* 7 : 67

—— the thoughtless many,   *Dyer* 25

Rowe, poems of,   *Rowe* 1

———— Pythagoras, golden verses of,   2

———— on the success of her majesty's arms,   8

———— on Nicolini and Valentini,   30

———— epilogue to the Inconstant,   30

———— prologue to the Gamester,   32

———— epilogue, Love for love,   33

———————— to cruel gift,   35

Rowe, prologue to Non-juror,   *Rowe* 37
——— imitation of Horace,   39
——— reconcilement of Tonson and Congreve,   41
——— Horace to his cask,   42
——————— to Venus,   45
——————— imitated,   47
——— the union,   49
——— on contentment,   49
——— on last judgement, &c.   50
——— Colin's complaint,   51
——————— reply,   53
——— epigram,   56
——————— imitated in Latin,   56
——— Mæcenas,   57
——— epigram on prince of Wales,   58
——— verses to a simile of Pope,   58
——— song,   59, 65, 68
——— on a first visit to lady Warwick,   60
——— stanzas to lady Warwick,   60
——— the visit,   63
——— contented shepherd,   63
——— a lady singing,   67
——— to lord Warwick,   69
——— to lady Jane Wharton,   70
——— to Mrs. Pulteney,   71
——— ode for 1716,   71
——— birth-day 1716,   76
——— ode for 1717,   78
——————— to peace, for 1718,   82
——————— to the Thames, 1719,   84

Rowe,

Rowe, ſtory of Glaucus and Scylla,   *Rowe* 86

—— Lucan's Pharſalia,   41

—— (Thomas), verſes to,   *Watts* 191

—— verſes to (Benoni),   *Watts* 192

Royal highneſs, on approaching delivery of,   *Pitt* 192

—— maids, born victims of the ſtate,   *Lanſ.* 260

—— progreſs,   *Tick.* 118

—— Society, Cowley to,   *Cow.* 1 : 214

———— hiſtory of, by Sprat,   *Cow.* 1 : 220

———— ſatire on,   *Butl.* 2 : 187

Royaliſts commended,   *Butl.* 2 : 11

Royalty ſeized by the prieſthood,   *Milt.* 2 : 130

Rubicon, an humble river flows,   *Rowe L.* 54

———— the boundary between Gaul and Italy,   *Rowe L.* 55

Rudders govern, and the ſhips obey,   *Smith* 111

Ruddy evening ſkies foretel the morning fair,   *Rowe L.* 166

—— orient flames with day,   *Pope od.* 3 : 203

Ruffians brib'd, ne'er the cauſe enquire,   *Hughes* 305

Rufinus,   *King* 367

———— character of,   *King* 371

Rufus bleeds in the foreſt like a wounded hart,   *Pope* 2 : 60

Ruin'd abbey,   *Shen.* 259

Rule the rump, you rule the roaſt,   *Swift* 2 : 204

Ruler of nature, known in nature's laws,   *Parn.* 168

—— truſt with his ſkies,   *Pope* 2 : 204

—— to him commit the hour, the day, the year,   *Pope* 2 : 204

—— o'er the men of ſtring,   *Butl.* 1 : 53

Rules of ſpeech to ſtudy, no ignoble taſk,   *King* 272

—— are nature methodis'd,   *Pope* 1 : 94

—— derived from the practice of the ancents,   *Pope* 1 : 95

Ruling-

Ruling-passion, none diffemblers in, *Pope* 2 : 101

———— ftrong in death, *Pope* 2 : 104

———— conquers reafon ftill, *Pope* 2 : 124

Rum, rice's fpirit, *Phil.* 69

Rumbling of a coach, to write to, *Dry.* 2 : 286

Rump, what, *Butl.* 2 : 75

——— the commonwealth, *Butl.* 2 : 76

Rump-bone reprefents parliament, *Butl.* 2 : 76

Rumps roafted, *Butl.* 2 : 72

Rums rufty and dull, *Swift* 2 : 153

Run, as mice from a cat, *Butl.* 1 : 117

Rundle, bifhop of Derry, verfes on, *Swift* 2 : 344

——— has a heart, *Pope* 2 : 298

Running, no mean part in war, *Butl.* 2 : 91

————– a race between two legs, *Butl.* 1 : 304

Runnymede, infcription for a column at, *Aken.* 329

————— where the great charter was obtained, *Aken.* 329

Runny mead, charter of, *Den.* 18

Rural confufion, herds and flocks compofe, *Thom.* 1 : 60

——— games, *Som.* 95

——— maid, rich in poverty, enjoys content, *Gay* 1 : 15

——— ne'er feels the fpleen's imagin'd pains, *Gay* 1 : 16

——— nor melancholy ftagnates in her veins, *Gay* 1 : 16

——— fports, *Gay* 1 : 1

Rufhes ftrewed the ground, *Dry.* 3 : 139

Ruffel, his cannons thunder, *Add.* 14

————– like Homer's Hector, flung his fire, *Add.* 14

Ruther, youth's long locks in yellow rings defcend, *Rowe L.* 65

S.

Sabbath kept,	*Mih.* 1 : 228
———— was every day, .	*Dry.* 2 : 180
Sabines, chaste as,	*Dry.* 7 : 260
Sable, guard attended by,	*Swift* 2 : 87
Sachariſſa, ſleep bathes in her eyes,	*Wall.* 51
———— as coy as Daphne,	*Wall.* 54
Sacrament, what we receive in, .	*Dry.* 2 : 29
Sacred oracles can bear the ſearch,	*Duke* 137
——— thirſt of ſway, all ties of nature broke,	*Pope* 1 : 284
——— vows are bought and ſold,	*Fent.* 273
——— writ expreſſes great truths in few words,	*Wall.* 221
Sacrifice, ceremonies of,	*Dry.* 7 : 55
———— to time, fate dooms us all,	*Buck.* 17
Sacrifices, types of the promiſed ſeed,	*Milt.* 2 : 127
———— to Moloch,	*Cow.* 2 : 120
Sad to die, ſadder to live in woe,	*Prior* 2 : 200
—— to raiſe, and ſuccour the diſtreſſed,	*Prior* 2 : 149
Safe bind, and ſafe find,	*Prior* 2 : 10
Safe's the word,	*Swift* 2 : 305
Safety reſts on honeſt counſels,	*Young* 1 : 250
——— ſmiling, with her boſom bare, .	*Parn.* 271
——— ſecurely walks, .	*Parn.* 271
——— muſt man's liberty reſtrain,	*Pope* 2 : 65
——— placed in deſpair of ſafety,	*Den.* 17
Sagan of Jeruſalem, character of, .	*Dry.* 1 : 154
Sage, nor gain, nor fame purſues,	*Som,* 224
Sails wing the maſts,	*Pope od.* 3 : 131
Sailing compared to a chariot-race,	*Rowe L.* 338
Sailor ſly, made the maid a wife,	*Gay* 1 : 90
	Sailor's

Sailor's wife,   *Prior* 2 : 242
Saint, a peer of heaven,   *Butl.* 1 : 197
——— above confcience,   *Butl.* 1 : 199
——————— ordinances,   *Butl.* 1 : 199

St. Cecilia,
{
Add.   31
Dry. 2 : 203, 214
Pope   1 : 77
Tal.   286
}

St. Dennis, where proud Luxemburg defies,   *Hughes* 31
——————— forc'd to yield,   *Hughes* 31
St. George's Church,   *Ot.* 10
——————— Chapel, with trophies,   *Ot.* 11
——————— hall defcribed,   *Ot.* 16
St. James's Park,   *Wall.* 50
St. John, Englifh Memmius,   *Phil.* 25
——————— ode to,   *Phil.* 26, 29
St. Paul's, profpect from,   *Den.* 8
Saints, who,   *Butl.* 1 : 71
——— lead brothers by the nofe,   *Butl.* 1 : 39
——— reprefented by rumps,   *Butl.* 2 : 75
——— reformation termagants,   *Butl.* 2 : 61
——— of the firft grafs,   *Butl.* 1 : 209
——— may employ a conjurer,   *Butl.* 1 : 230
——— obedient to the laws of God,   *Parn.* 197
——— embrace thee with a love like mine,   *Pope* 1 : 194
Salacacaby, how made,   *King* 233
Salamander, defcription of,   *Swift* 1 : 33
——————— a reptile of the ferpent kind,   *Swift* 1 : 34
Salamanders, fiery termagants,   *Pope* 1 : 129
Salem, the realm of peace,   *Parn.* 231

                                                        Salient

Salient point, what, *Black.* 188

Salisbury plain fit for sheep, *Dyer* 31

————— adds grace to scepters and crowns adorns, *Lansf.* 141

Salisbury's garter shall for ever last, *Iansf.* 141

Sallé, on taking of, *Wall.* 24

Salmacis, story of, *Add.* 174

Salmon-fishing, *Gay* 1 : 9

Salt, use of, in diseases of sheep, *Dyer* 39

—— preventive of the rot, *Dyer* 39

—— to cast on a woman's tail, *Butl.* 1 : 165

Saltinbanco, to play, *Butl.* 1 : 261

Saltness of the sea, how to account for, *Black.* 61

Salvation, no name known for, but Christ, *Dry* 2 : 251

————— only from my God, my king, *Parn.* 226

Salvations, hymn for three great, *Watts* 56

Salve, to walk on fire, *King* 357

Samuel, child of prayers, *Parn.* 148

—— old, his sons behave ill, *Cow.* 2 : 175

Samian Y directs the steps, *Dry.* 7 : 331

—— letter points two ways, *Pope* 3 : 227

Samphire, to excite the gust of luxury, *Phil.* 37

Samson Agonistes, *Milt.* 3 : 7

—— birth of, foretold, *Milt.* 3 : 8

—— Nazarite, *Milt.* 3 : 8

—— strength of, *Milt.* 3 : 11

—— slays with jaw-bone of ass, *Milt.* 3 : 12

—— carries off the gates of Azza, *Milt.* 3 : 12

—— himself, an army, *Milt.* 3 : 13

—— called to deliver Israel, *Milt.* 3 : 14

—— pulls down Dagon's temple, and dies, *Milt.* 3 : 62

Sanctity not confined to place,   *Milt.* 2 : 113

Sand, storms of,   *Rowe L.* 397

Sandwich, wit piercing as her sparkling eyes,   *Lanf.* 145

Sandys, Waller to,   *Wall.* 107

Sapphira, emblem of,   *Cow.* 1 : 204

Sappho to Phaon,   { *Fent.* 277 / *Pope* 1 : 164

———- sings of ill-requited love,   *Fent.* 283

——- gentle, love-sick Muse,   *Swift* 2 : 317

———- melting rapture, soft desire infuses,   *Swift* 2 : 317

———-- yet once thy cares could employ,   *Pope* 1 : 167

———- inur'd to sorrow from my tender years,   *Pope* 1 : 168

———- hymn to Venus,   *A. Phil.* 398

———- fragment of,   *A. Phil.* 400

——— her melting airs,   *Aken.* 227

———- best instructs to love,   *Cong.* 125

Sarcasmous scandal,   *Butl.* 1 : 71

Sardinia, for yellow fields renowned,   *Rowe L.* 124

Sardonic smiles, by rancour rais'd,   *Swift* 2 : 200

Sarissa, verses to,   *Watts* 176

Sarmatia, nursery of nations,   *Thom.* 2 : 75

———— extent of,   *Thom.* 2 : 74

Sarpedon to Glaucus,   *Den.* 47

——— makes a breach in the wall,   *Pope il.* 1 : 373

——— is laid low in dust,   *Pope il.* 2 : 120

——— Jove's hapless offspring,   *Pope il.* 2 : 120

——— lies in dust,   *Pope il.* 2 : 121

——— stretch'd by Patroclus' arm,   *Pope il.* 2 : 121

——— in action valiant, and in council wise, *Pope il.* 2 : 121

Satan cast down from heaven,   *Milt.* 1 : 6

Satan, vain vaunt of,   *Milt.* 1 : 8, 9

——— described,   *Milt.* 1 : 11, 12, 14, 24

——— address to hell,   *Milt.* 1 : 13

————————— to evil spirits,   *Milt.* 1 : 25, 26

——— armour of,   *Milt.* 14, 15, 176

——— arrives at the gate of hell,   *Milt.* 1 : 56

——— address of, to death,   *Milt.* 1 : 57, 58, 62

——— death, reply of to,   *Milt.* 1 : 58

——— sin, reply of to,   *Milt.* 1 : 59, 60

——— address to Chaos and Night,   *Milt.* 1 : 67

——— lands in the sun,   *Milt.* 1 : 92

——— address to Uriel,   *Milt.* 1 : 95

——— lights on Niphates,   *Milt.* 1 : 97

——— tempter of mankind,   *Milt.* 1 : 101

——— accuser of mankind,   *Milt.* 1 : 101

——— hell within,   *Milt.* 1 : 103

——— self-reproach of,   *Milt.* 1 : 102, 103

——— pride of,   *Milt.* 1 : 103

——— supreme in misery,   *Milt.* 1 : 104

——— all good is lost to,   *Milt.* 1 : 104

——— evil good to,   *Milt.* 1 : 104

——— artificer of fraud,   *Milt.* 1 : 105

——— soliloquy of, on sight of Adam and Eve, *Milt.* 1 : 113, 118

——— hellish purpose of,   *Milt.* 1 : 114

——— search made of,   *Milt.* 1 : 127

——— found at the ear of Eve,   *Milt.* 1 : 127

——— abashed, on rebuke,   *Milt.* 1 : 129

——— overthrown by folly,   *Milt.* 1 : 131

——— proved a liar,   *Milt.* 1 : 132

——— hypocritical,   *Milt.* 1 : 133

Satan, vaunts of,   Milt. 1 : 133

———— prepares to refift,   Milt. 1 : 134

———— hindred by a fign in heaven,   Milt. 1 : 134

———— quits Paradife,   Milt. 1 : 135

———— envy of, againft the fon of God,   Milt. 1 : 161

———— fell through pride,   Milt. 1 : 161

———— drew after him, the third of heaven,   Milt. 1 : 162

———— wounded,   Milt. 1 : 184

———— routed,   Milt. 1 : 186

———— and his hoft thunder-ftruck,   Milt. 1 : 201

——————————— fall into the bottomlefs pit,   Milt. 1 : 202

———— bent on man's ruin,   Milt. 2 : 5

———— malice of,   Milt. 2 : 7

———— delights in ill,   Milt. 2 : 7

———— captious reafoning of,   Milt. 2 : 26

———— prevails by permiffion,   Milt. 2 : 46

———— perverts the prohibition to man,   Milt. 1 : 118

———— antagonift of heaven,   Milt. 2 : 58

———— return of to hell congratulated,   Milt. 2 : 60

———— recounts his feats and doom,   Milt. 2 : 60, 61

———— received with hiffes,   Milt. 2 : 62

———— and his mates turned to ferpents,   Milt. 2 : 63

———— deluded by fpecious fruit,   Milt. 2 : 64

———— under the controul of heaven,   Milt. 2 : 155, 159

———— loft to all hope,   Milt. 2 : 190

———— permitted to rule,   Milt. 2 : 207

———— loft to gratitude,   Milt. 2 : 207

———— God of this world,   Milt. 2 : 208

———— foiled,   Milt. 2 : 220

———— thief of Paradife,   Milt. 2 : 221

Satan enraged at difappointment,   *Milt.* 2 : 216

—— with his powers, fhall fink to endlefs doom,   *Pom.* 351

Satiety, from all things,   *Den.* 137

Satire, effay on,   { *Dry.* 1 : 112
                                                                { *Pope* 2 : 3

——— end of,   *Pope* 2 : 4

——— what,   *Dry.* 1 : 112

——— objeĉts of,   *Dry.* 1 : 113

——— fupplement of laws,   *Young* 1 : 77

——— true end of,   *Dry.* 1 : 125

——— origin of,   *Dry.* 7 : 135

——— extenfive fenfe of,   *Dry.* 7 : 163

——— how to be fpelled,   *Dry.* 7 : 163

——— nature of,   *Dry.* 7 : 173

——— heals with morals, what it hurts with wit, *Pope* 2 : 227

——— different among Greeks and Romans,   *Dry.* 7 : 137

——— proper fubjeĉts of,   *Dry.* 7 : 179

——— defined,   *Dry.* 7 : 203

——— confifts in fine raillery,   *Dry.* 7 : 193

——— well-writ, mortifies mankind,   *Buck.* 73

——— nicely to unfold human frailty,   *Buck.* 74

——— fmiles of, fharper than a frown,   *Buck.* 74

——— Dryden claims our praife in,   *Buck.* 74

——— all love, none the fatirift,   *Sav.* 165

——— calls for fenfe in every line,   *Young* 1 : 87

——— friends to Vice and Folly are thy foes,   *Young* 1 : 87

——— they dread, who defy the fkies,   *Young* 1 : 151

——— awes the brave, that earth and heaven defy, *Pope* 2 : 7

——— to guilt alone her vengeance is confin'd,   *Pope* 2 : 8

——— fhe only ftrikes to heal,   *Pope* 2 : 8

Satire delineates paffion, pictures man, *Pope* 2 : 15

—— friend to truth, to virtue and mankind, *Pope* 2 : 16

—— virtue firft armed with, *Dry.* 1 : 273

—— ftrike faults, but fpare the man, *Young* 3 : 205

—— on abufe of learning, *Butl.* 2 : 265

—— to a bad poet, *Butl.* 2 : 240

—— on French imitation, *Butl.* 2 : 244

—— on drunkennefs, *Butl.* 2 : 249

—— on marriage, *Butl.* 2 : 253

—— on plagiaries, *Butl.* 2 : 258

—— a court of chancery, *Dry.* 2 : 136

—— lafh the madnefs of a vicious age, *Gay.* 1 : 214

Satires, prologue to, *Pope* 2 : 148, & feq.

—— epilogue to, *Pope* 2 : 289, & feq.

Satisfaction for man's fin, neceffary, *Milt.* 1 : 80

—————— Son offers to give, *Milt.* 1 : 80, 81

Saturday, *Gay* 1 : 86

Satirical elegy, *Swift* 1 : 257

Satirique tragedy, *Dry.* 7 : 142

———————— different the Roman fatire, *Dry.* 7 : 144

——————— declination of, *Dry.* 7 : 144

Saturn civilized Latium, *Dry.* 6 : 210

—— brought golden times, *Dry.* 6 : 210

—— influence of, *Dry.* 3 : 112

—— ring of, *Mall.* 220

Saturnian days of lead and gold, *Pope* 3 : 216

—————— verfes, what, *Dry.* 7 : 149

Savage, the wanderer, *Sav.* 7

—————— the baftard, 84

—————— on lady Tyrconnel, 88

Savage, to Sir Robert Walpole,　　　　　　Sav. 92
―――― volunteer laureats,　　　　　　100—114
―――― of public spirit,　　　　　　115
―――― to Mr. John Dyer,　　　　　　127
―――― to Aaron Hill,　　　　　　130
―――― prologue to Henry VI.　　　　　　131
―――― the animalcule,　　　　　　132
―――― to Mrs. Haywood,　　　　　　135
―――― apology to Brillante,　　　　　　137
―――― epistle to Mrs. Oldfield,　　　　　　138
―――― on Mr. Hill's Gideon,　　　　　　140
―――― to lady Rochford,　　　　　　142
―――― to Miranda,　　　　　　144
―――― to a young lady,　　　　　　145
―――― the gentleman,　　　　　　146
―――― character of Mr. Foster,　　　　　　147
―――― the poet's dependance,　　　　　　149
―――― epistle to Damon and Delia,　　　　　　152
―――― to Miss M. H. with Pope's works,　　　　　　154
―――― on a lady's recovery,　　　　　　155
―――― the friend,　　　　　　157
―――― epistle to Mr. Dyer,　　　　　　161
―――― on the vice-president of St. Mary's Hall,　　　　　　163
―――― Fulvia,　　　　　　164
―――― epitaph on a young lady,　　　　　　166
―――― genius of liberty,　　　　　　167
―――― lines of Buchanan paraphrased,　　　　　　170
―――― the employment of beauty,　　　　　　171
―――― to Mrs. Jones,　　　　　　174
―――― on false historians,　　　　　　175
　　　　　　　　　　　　　　　　　　Savage,

Savage, a character,   *Sav.* 180
———— epitaph on Mrs. Jones,   182
———— Valentine's day,   183
———— to John Powell, Esq,   188
———— London and Bristol, delineated,   191
———— to Dyer,   142
———————————— an able critic, but a willing friend,   143
Savannahs, where the eye is in a verdant ocean lost, *Thom.* 1 : 67
Saucer-eyes,   *Butl.* 1 : 159
Saving be, that is, be wise,   *Som.* 390
Saviour comes, by ancient bards foretold,   *Pope* 1 : 50
———— golden rule of,   *Watts* 356
———— by Michael Angelo,   *Thom.* 2 : 88
Saul, like a raging lion,   *Cow.* 2 : 93
———— turned prophet,   *Cow.* 2 : 101
——— phrensy of,   *Cow.* 2 : 144
——— envy of, raised,   *Cow.* 2 : 154
——— daughters of, described,   *Cow.* 2 : 156
——— why chosen king,   *Cow.* 2 : 175
——— described,   *Cow.* 2 : 182
——— anointed,   *Cow.* 2 : 183
——— recrowned,   *Cow.* 2 : 191
——— invades the priesthood,   *Cow.* 2 : 196
——— chid by Samuel,   *Cow.* 2 : 196
Scab in sheep, cure for,   *Dyer* 40
Scaeva, bravery of,   *Rowe L.* 252
- ——— careless of the right, for hire fought,   *Rowe L.* 252
- ——— slain,   *Rowe L.* 259
Scale of sensual, mental powers adjusted,   *Pope* 2 : 36
——— of conquests ever wavering lies,   *Pope il.* 2 : 202

Scale,

Scale, furcharg'd with Hector's fate, low finks, *Pope il.* 2 : 272

———— with death it finks,   *Pope il.* 2 : 272

Scaliger, vain-glorious,   *Dry.* 7 : 169

Scaligeriana, on a paffage in,   *Prior* 1 : 195

Scamander attacks Achilles with all his waves, *Pope il.* 2 : 244

———— dried up by Vulcan,   *Pope il.* 2 : 248

Scandal ever gaping wide,   *Swift* 2 : 75

———— th' ignoble mind's delight,   *Pope* 1 : 287

———— meaner than a venal praife,   *Sav.* 42

———— with fquinting eyes,   *Ot.* 40

———— Fame's bufy hawker,   *Som.* 213

———— fpares no king,   *Dry.* 3 : 141

———— is converfation's fpirit,   *Gay* 2 : 54

———— fweetner of a female feaft,   *Young* 1 : 149

———— given, fin of,   *Milt.* 3 : 22

Scarborough (Dr.), Cowley to,   *Cow.* 2 : 37

Scars honourable,   *Butl.* 1 : 163

Scavengers, duty of,   *Gay* 1 : 101

Scent, ancients unacquainted with purfuing beafts by, *Som.* 6

Scenting, days good or bad for,   *Som.* 28

Scents, a phyfical account of,   *Som.* 25

Sceptics, opinions of,   *Butl.* 2 : 276

Sceptre, an enfign of the delegates of Jove,   *Pope il.* 1 : 47

———— unftain'd, immortal, and the gift of gods, *Pope il.* 1 : 69

Schedius, boldeft warriour, and the nobleft mind, *Pope il.* 2 : 149

Schellenberg, defcribed,   *Add.* 55, 56

Scheme of ambitious ftatefman, but a fhort vifion, *Gay* 2 : 16

Scheria fertile, alone and floating ifle,   *Pope od.* 3 : 146

———— where Science never rear'd her laurel'd head, *id.* 3 : 169

Scholar, relapfe of,   *Shen.* 126

                                                    Scholaftic

Scholaſtic pride, bold and blind, *Wiſt* 293

———————————— fierce in debate, and forward to decide, *id.* 293

School, no command ſo imperious, *Butl.* 2 : 347

——— and playhouſe the ſame, *Butl.* 2 : 269

——— for experimental philoſophy, *Cow.* 2 : 399

School-miſtreſs, *Shen.* 284

Schools, art of, what, *Butl.* 2 : 322

——— make artificial fools, *Butl.* 2 : 267

Schomberg, epitaph on, *Swift* 2 : 225

Science we ſeek, which ſtill deludes the mind, *Fent.* 216

——— not ſcience, till reveal'd, *Dry.* 7 : 312

——— phyſic of the ſoul, *Pope* 3 : 178

——— to raiſe and knowledge, be our care, *Prior* 1 : 177

——— dwindles, and how volumes ſwell, *Young* 1 : 161

——— become a trade, *Garth* 88

——— how to live, *Broome* 166

——— to bury ſorrows in the friendly draught, *Broome* 167

——— in attractive fable lies, *Fent.* 307

——— liberty ſtill attends, *Thom.* 2 : 144

——— whoſe piercing eye breaks each mental fetter, *id.* 2 : 145

——— hymn to, *Aken.* 356

——— firſt effuſive ray from the Great Source, *Aken.* 356

——— nor dive too deep, nor ſoar too high, *Aken.* 358

——— to faith, content thy beams to lend, *Aken.* 358

——— mix with the policies of men, *Aken.* 359

——— trace every action to its ſource, *Aken.* 359

——— form the heart, and rule the will, *Aken.* 359

——— hail, queen of manners, light of truth, *Aken.* 360

——— charm of age, and guide of youth, *Aken.* 360

——— ſweet of diſtreſs, *Aken.* 360

Science,

Science, fun of the foul,   *Akcn.* 360

———— ode on,   *Swift* 1 : 359

Scipio, highth of Rome,   *Milt.* 2 : 20

——— difmiffed the Iberian maid,   *Milt.* 2 : 169

——— great in triumph, in retirement great,   *Pope* 1 : 208

Scoffing and calling names,   *Watts* 346

Scold, one makes another ceafe,   *Rowe* 29

——— and parrot,   *Gay* 2 : 72

Scorn, daughter of Pride,   *Roth.* 289

——— torments more than fpight,   *Swift* 2 : 22

Scorpion, oil of, cures its wounds,   *Butl.* 2 : 50

Scotland, view of,   .   *Thom.* 1 : 136, & feq.

Scourge of wit,   *Dry.* 2 : 112

———— fhall lafh thee into fenfe,   *Pope od.* 4 : 130

Scowrers, a fet of rakes,   *Gay* 1 : 143

Scripture, authority of,   *Wall.* 205

———— - fufficiency of, in all needful things,   *Dry.* 1 : 254

———— contains every needful truth,   *Dry.* 2 : 31

———— plain in all things needful,   *Dry.* 1 : 256

———— abufe of,   *Dry.* 2 : 24

Scriptures, only rule of faith,   *Dry.* 2 : 42

———————— life,   *Dry.* 1 : 249

———— fhew, how God may be appeafed,   *Dry.* 1 : 249

———— ftile of, majeftic,   *Dry.* 1 : 249

Scrivener crucified,   *Butl.* 1 : 106

Sculpture taught her fifter Art correct defign,   *Thom.* 2 : 41

———— in the temple of Cumæ,   *Dry.* 6 : 113

Scurrility with gibing air,   *Swift* 2 : 75

Scut he left behind and half an ear,   *Swift* 2 : 224

Scylla, transformation of,   *Garth* 122

Scylla

Scylla, described,   *Pope od.* 3 : 315

————— dearly pays for Nisus' injur'd hair,   *Pope* 1 : 142

Scythian winter,   *Dry.* 5 : 163

Sea, a display of divine power and wisdom,   *Black.* 59

——— restrain'd within proper limits,   *Black.* 60

——— bounds set to,   *Cow.* 2 : 98

——— where all rivers end,   *Hal.* 220

——— where the proud horse and prouder rider fell,   *Parn.* 112

——— an emblem of mankind,   *Pitt* 289

——— where sharks, like lawyers, rob at will,   *Pitt* 289

——— where on the less the greater feed,   *Pitt* 289

Seamen riding,   *Butl.* 2 : 82

Sea-piece,   *Young* 3 : 223

Searcher follows fast, the object faster flies,   *Prior* 2 : 127

Searcloths to flea the face or hands,   *King* 314

Season, employment peculiar to each,   *Dry.* 5 : 106

Seasons,   *Thom.* 1 : 3

————— change us all,   *King* 205

————— resemble human life,   *Dry.* 4 : 143

————— picture the stages of man's life,   *Thom.* 1 : 189

Seat of the Almighty,   *Cow.* 2 : 82

Seats above, seats of eternal harmony and love,   *Hughes* 56

Secchia rapita, a Varronian satire,   *Dry.* 7 : 210

Secker is decent,   *Pope* 2 : 293

Second thoughts are best,   *Fent.* 277

————— vows my bridal faith profane,   *Pope od.* 4 : 164

Secret gripes a fool, till he lets it go,   *Pitt* 401

————— rare, between extremes to move,   *Pope* 2 : 127

Secretary,   *Prior* 1 : 102

Secrets to reveal, how heinous,   *Milt.* 3 : 23

Secu,

Sects, maggots of corrupted texts,   *Butl.* 2 : 4

—— factory of, how to improve,   *Butl.* 2 : 69

—— in extremes, abhor a middle way,   *Dry.* 2 : 37

Sedgwick, doomsday,   *Butl.* 1 : 241

Security, none so wretched as those beguiled by,   *Cong.* 56

Sedition, described,   *Cow.* 1 : 331

————— promoted by calumnies,   *Cow.* 1 : 342

————— to hum and hah,   *Butl.* 2 : 56

————— quell'd by authority of a grave person,   *Pitt* 279

Seed of the woman,   *Milt.* 2 : 131

—— of woman promised,   *Milt.* 2 : 90

—— consum'd in earth, multiplies its birth,   *Prior* 2 : 115

Seek not thyself, without thyself, to find,   *Dry.* 7 : 310

Self, see all in, and but for self be born,   *Pope* 3 : 249

—— inthrall'd to self,   *Milt.* 1 : 179

—— there is, of virtue fond,   *Young* 2 : 242

—————— as fond of every vice,   *Young* 2 : 242

—— to cry down,   *Butl.* 1 : 206

—— sordid, no shining deeds shoots up,   *Thom.* 2 : 139

Self-banished,   *Wall.* 98

Self-conceit, flattering,   *Den.* 89

—————— deceptious,   *Den.* 89

Self-consecration,   *Watts* 49

Self-defence, Nature's eldest law,   *Dry.* 1 : 140

Self-denying, gifted face,   *Butl.* 2 : 51

Self-disgrace, soured with,   *Fent.* 311

Self-esteem profitable at times,   *Milt.* 1 : 250

Self-existent being, necessary,   *Black.* 152

—————— a causeless cause, or nothing could be, *Black.* 152

—————— the world not that being,   *Black.* 152

                                        Self-

Self-existent, world not, because changeable,   *Black.* 152

Self-knowledge, in every view, directs our life,   *Gay* 2 : 138

Self-love, ambition, envy, pride,   *Swift* 2 : 257

————— their empire in our hearts divide,   *Swift* 2 : 257

————— in nature rooted fast,   *Swift* 1 : 124

————— attends us first, and leaves us last,   *Swift* 1 : 124

————— spring of motion, acts the soul,   *Pope* 2 : 43

————— bribes every sense,   *Som.* 343

————— still stronger, as its objects nigh,   *Pope* 2 : 44

————— drives through just and through unjust,   *Pope* 2 : 65

————— found the private in the public good,   *Pope* 2 : 65

————— and reason to one end aspire,   *Pope* 2 : 45

————— pain their aversion, pleasure their desire, *Pope* 2 : 45

————— and social are the same,   *Pope* 2 : 84

Self-opinion, active, rash, and blind,   *West* 215

Self-perusal, science rare !   *Young* 3 : 125

————— the Delphi of the mind,   *Young* 3 : 125

Self-violence sets man at variance with himself,   *Milt.* 3 : 60

Self-unread, may in vain their bibles read,   *Young* 3 : 125

Self-will with Satan fell,   *Young* 3 : 143

————— sacrifice supreme, be slain,   *Young* 3 : 135

Selfish heart deserves the pain it feels,   *Young* 2 : 13

Selim, the shepherd's moral,   *Collins* 233

Selli, race austere, their slumbers on the ground, *Pope il.* 2 : 108

Semele, delivered by thunder,   *Cow.* 2 : 9

Semi-gentleman of Inns of Court,   *Cow.* 1 : 77

Sena the Senones confines,   *Rowe L.* 102

Senate meet in Epirus,   *Rowe L.* 204

——— appoint Pompey general,   *Rowe L.* 206

——— echo of a thoughtless crowd,   *Dry.* 1 : 309

Senate,

Senate, void of order, as of choice,   *Pope* 1 : 230

———— hearts of, fearful, and confused their voice, *Pope* 1 : 231

———— recking with the slain,   *Rowe L.* 80

Seneffe's immortal fight, with martial terror charms, *Hughes* 31

Seneca short-lunged,   *Cow.* 1 : 98

———— dying in a bath,   *Prior* 1 : 30

Sensation, inlets of,   *Black.* 199

———————— all, but touch,   *Prior* 2 : 35

Sense, vassal of reason,   *Den.* 88

———— gives a grace to the homeliest face,   *Swift* 2 : 62

———— learn to rise in,   *Garth* 56

———— the less, the more my love appears,   *Pope* 1 : 171

———— meaner part of, to find a fault,   *Roch.* 335

———— to accompany rhyme,   *Dry.* 1 : 261

———— all ought to aim at;   *Dry.* 1 : 262

———— lies just 'twixt affectation and neglect,   *Pitt* 399

———— is our helmet, wit is but the plume,   *Young* 2 : 259

———— runs savage, broke from reason's chain,   *Young* 2 : 44

———— to forego, for a name,   *Roch.* 288

———— each vanity of, supply'd by pride,   *Pope* 2 : 52

———— joys of, health, peace, and competence,   *Pope* 2 : 72

Senses wandering to the verge of life,   *Pope il.* 2 : 65

———— submit to the soul,   *Dry.* 1 : 317

———— plung'd in the death of sleep,   *Pope od.* 3 : 197

———— act by pairs,   *Butl.* 1 : 301

———— intelligencers of the mind,   *Butl.* 1 : 301

Sentence in each look,   *Cow.* 1 : 80

Sentences not to appear embossed on,   *Dry.* 7 : 182

Sentimental allegory, what,   *Collins* 302

Separate souls of living touch impassive,   *Fent.* 255

                                                      Separate

Separate souls from elemental drofs difparted,   *Fent.* 255

Separation,   *Cow.* 1 : 308

Sepulture, rites of violated,   *Shen.* 62

Seraphina, ode to,   *Thom.* 2 : 191

———— to love, is to be pure, happy, and tender, *id.* 191

Serenata,   *Hughes* 200

Series endlefs of caufes and effects impoffible,   *Black.* 155

Sermon on the Mount, proteftant,   *Dry.* 2 : 59

Sermons are lefs read than tales,   *Prior* 2 : 203

Serpent, fubtleft beaft,   *Milt.* 2 : 6

——— fit imp of fraud,   *Milt.* 2 : 6

——— fubtleft of all beafts,   *Milt.* 2 : 21

——— made fpeakable of mute,   *Milt.* 2 : 22

——— flatters Eve,   *Milt.* 2 : 23

——— leads to the forbidden tree,   *Milt.* 2 : 24

——— defcribed,   *Milt.* 2 : 19

——— poffeffed by Satan,   *Milt.* 2 : 9

——— that author of all evil,   *Dry.* 5 : 209

——— deceived Eve,   *Milt.* 1 : 6

——— doom of,   *Milt.* 2 : 51

Serpents caft their fkins,   *Butl.* 2 : 37

——— origin of in Libya,   *Rowe L.* 405

——— various kinds of,   *Rowe L.* 409

——— kill many Romans,   *Rowe L.* 411

Septimius, ruffian flave, murders Pompey,   *Rowe L.* 356

——— cuts off his head,   *Rowe L.* 359

Sertorius vanquifh'd by Pompey,   *Rowe L.* 283

Servile flattery, oft harbours in courts,   *Phil.* 58

——— land, where tyrants ftill by turns command, *Pope* 1 : 287

——— mind well paid with fervile lot,   *Milt.* 3 : 21

                                  Servitude,

Servitude, what, *Milt.* 2 : 122

———— rife of, *Cow.* 2 : 262

———— gilded by riches, *Cow.* 2 : 268

———— in whatever degree, is fervitude, *Cow.* 2 : 269

Sequani, taught the horfe to guide, *Rowe L.* 67

Sefoftris, high on his car, drawn by fcepter'd flaves, *Pope* 1 : 206

———— yok'd monarchs to his chariot, *Phil.* 9

———— faw the fartheft Weft, *Hughes* 299

———— his chariots drawn by harnefs'd kings, *Hughes* 299

Setting, *Som.* 153

Setting-dog and partridge, *Gay* 2 : 81

Settle, city poet, *Pope* 3 : 85

Set phrafes, when you write, avoid, *Cong.* 130

Seven-dials, to feven ftreets count the day, *Gay* 1 : 113

Seventh day bleffed, *Milt.* 1 : 226

Severus, wall of, *Thom.* 2 : 103

Sewers, exact of tafte, *Pope od.* 4 : 80

———— maffy and firm, for ages, *Dyer* 9

Sex, ingenious to enfnare, *Som.* 293

——— part truth, part fiction, *Sav.* 145

——— fome thought, fome whim, and all a contradiction, *id.* 145

——— is ever to a foldier kind, *Pope od.* 4 : 31

Sextus, degenerate fon of Pompey, *Rowe L.* 267

———— confults the forcerefs Erichtho, *Rowe L.* 274

———— informs his elder brother of Pompey's death, *Rowe L.* 377

———— expreffes his horrour at the fight, *Rowe L.* 377

Shade, thrice we call'd on each unhappy, *Pope od.* 3 : 229

Shadow, privation of light, *Dry.* 2 : 152

———— ode on, *Pitt* 225

———— or a nothing in all hopes and fchemes, *Pitt* 225

Shadow

Shadow every where, no substance to be found,   *Pitt* 226

———— all, all on earth,   *Young* 2 : 7

———— in a glass, riddle on,   *Swift* 1 : 324

Shadwell nods the poppy on his brows,   *Pope* 3 : 173

Shaftesbury, character of,   *Duke* 87

Shakespeare, Fancy's child,   *Milt.* 3 : 103

———— had all from nature,   *Den.* 55

———— remonstrance of,   *Aken.* 249

———— alike the master of your smiles and tears, *id.* 250

———— the genius of our isle,   *Fent.* 234

———— sometimes stoop'd to please a barbarous age, *id.* 234

———— but wrote the play, th' Almighty made, *Young* 3 : 177

———— each passion drew,   *Mall.* 161

———— great above rule,   *Mall.* 161

———— yet unequal,   *Mall.* 161

———— join'd Tuscan fancy to Athenian force, *Collins* 276

———— felt for man alone,   *Collins* 276

———— wrote happily rather than justly,   *Dry.* 7 : 103

———— inscription for,   *Aken.* 327

———— for gain, not glory, wing'd his roving flight, *Pope* 2 : 2

———— and grew immortal in his own despight, *id.* 217

Shame, no greater torture,   *Butl.* 2 : 233

——— fear of,   *Pope* 2 : 4

——— perverted worst of evils,   *Pope* 2 : 4

——— lasting ! to our own fears a prey,   *Pope il.* 2 : 150

——— lives with guilt,   *Duke* 156

——— attends on prostituted praise,   *Pope* 2 : 14

——— suits but ill with the begging kind,   *Pope od.* 4 : 113

——— void of guilt,   *Thom.* 1 : 90

——— charming blush of innocence,   *Thom.* 1 : 90

Shame,

Shame, greateft evil and the greateft good,   *Pope il.* 2 : 329

Shamelefs they give, give what's not their own, *Pofc od.* 4: 109

———— woman is the worft of men,   *Young* 1 : 133

Shannon's waves lifted o'er thofe of Boyne,   *Prior* 1 : 57 .

Sharon rofe, a pleafing odour throws,   *Parn.* 198

She, every, appears a goddefs till enjoy'd,   *Prior* 2 : 205

She-Atheifts ne'er till now appeared,   *Young* 1 : 151

———————— a match for nothing but the Deity, *Young* 1 : 151

She-gallants, prologue to,   *Lanf.* 213

——————— epilogue,   *Lanf.* 215

Sheep, breed of, to fuit to foil and climate,   *Dyer* 36

—— choice of,   *Dyer* 38

——— difeafes of,   *Dyer* 39, 40

——— paftures fit for,   *Dyer* 30 .

——— inftinct of, to choofe their food and phyfic,   *Dyer* 40

——— cannot bear extremes,   *Dyer* 46

——— folding of,   *Dyer* 42

——— management of,   *Dry.* 5 : 160

——— cloath'd with fkins, to preferve their wool,   *Dyer* 60

——— cole or turnep, food for,   *Dyer* 60

——— in filence dies,   *Pope il.* 2 : 290

——— and bufh,   *Som.* 275

Sheep-fhearing,   { *Dyer*   49
                  { *Thom.* 1 : 56

——————— fong of,   *Dyer* 52

——————— fports of,   *Dyer* 59

——————— feaft of,   *Dyer* 55

Sheer-wit avoid, thar filly thing,   *Buck.* 78

Shell-fifh raifes Venus,   *King* 208

Shenftone, verfes to, in his illnefs,   *Shen.* 319

5   Shenftone,

Shenstone, verses written at the gardens of,   Shen. 316

———— verses to,   307—324

———— on death of,   314, 322

———— prefatory essay on elegy,   3

———— arrival at his retirement,   13

———— posthumous reputation,   15

———— untimely death of an acquaintance,   16

———— Ophelia's urn,   18

———— compares love with friendship,   20

———— to a lady,   21

———— describes a vision,   23

———— his early love of poetry,   26

———— his disinterestedness,   28

———— to fortune,   30

———— complains of the novelty of life being over,   32

———— his recantation,   34

———— to a friend,   35

———— declining an invitation to foreign parts,   37

———— in memory of a private family,   40

———— advantages of birth to merit,   43

———— indulges the suggestions of spleen,   47

———— repeats the song of Collin,   50

———— verses written in spring 1743,   53

———— compares his fortune with others' distress,   56

———— taking a view of his retirement,   59

———— verses written on the violation of sepulture,   62

———— reflections suggested by his situation,   65

———— the imperfect pleasure of a solitary life,   69

———— to Delia, with some flowers,   72

———— describing the sorrow of an ingenuous mind,   74

Shenſtone, odes, ſongs, ballads,　　　　　Shen. 79—149

———————— paſtoral ballad,　　　　　152—160

———————— levities,　　　　　161—195

———————— judgement of Hercules,　　　　　197

———————— progreſs of taſte,　　　　　215

———————— fate of delicacy,　　　　　215

———————— œconomy,　　　　　237

———————— the ruin'd abbey,　　　　　259

———————— effects of ſuperſtition,　　　　　259

———————— love and honour,　　　　　273

———————— the ſchool-miſtreſs,　　　　　284

———————— inſcriptions,　　　　　297—326

———————— verſes to,　　　　　307—324

Shepheard (Sir Fleetwood), letters to,　　　　　Prior 1 : 2

————————————————— epigram tranſlated by, Milt. 3 : 299

Shepherd of Iſrael, guide me right,　　　　　Parn. 197

————— diſarm'd, wolves the flock devour,　　　Dry. 1 : 185

————— ſcrip, its furniture,　　　　　Dyer 41

————— and philoſopher,　　　　　Gay 2 : 25

————— nor envy nor ambition knew,　　　　　Gay 2 : 26

————— ne'er the paths of Learning try'd,　　　Gay 2 : 26

Shepherd's dog and the wolf,　　　　　Gay 2 : 58

————— week,　　　　　Gay 1 : 51

————— of men, rulers of the land,　　　　　Tick. 173

Sheridan, anſwer to ſimile of,　　　　　Swift 2 : 322

————— to Jackſon,　　　　　Swift 1 : 247

————— Swift to,　　　　　Swift 1 : 349, 353

————— to Swift,　　　　　Swift 1 : 167, 352

————— prologue by,　　　　　Swift 1 : 212

————— reply of,　　　　　Swift 1 : 242

　　　　　　　　　　　　　　　　　　Sheridan,

Sheridan, submission of,	*Swift* 1 : 246
———— Latin verses to,	*Swift* 1 : 156
———— upon his verses,	*Swift* 1 : 231
———— on his circular verses,	*Swift* 1 : 232
———— to George-Nim-Dan-Dean,	*Swift* 1 : 224
———— his ballad on Ballyspellin,	*Swift* 2 : 332
Sherlock would clear the greatest mysteries,	*Pom.* 340
———— but perplex'd and made them darker,	*Pom.* 340
———— on Death,	*Prior* 1 : 159
Sheva, character of,	*Dry.* 1 : 195
Shew antique,	*Butl.* 1 : 211
Shield of Achilles, wrought by Vulcan,	*Pope il.* 2 : 187
———— his neck o'er shading, to his ancle hung,	*Pope il.* 1 : 196
Shifts of state, those jugglers' tricks,	*Swift* 1 : 4
Shilo sprung from Judah,	*Cow.* 2 : 75
———————— David,	*Cow.* 2 : 131
Shimei, character of,	*Dry.* 1 : 145
Ship in a tempest, like a foot-ball,	*Wall.* 16
Ship-money,	*Thom* 1 : 114
Ships, origin of,	*Dry.* 1 : 87
———— catalogue of,	*Pope il.* 1 : 86
Shipwreck, described,	{ *Mall.* 243 { *Pitt* 278
Shock, the pride of all his kind, here is laid,	*Gay* 1 : 252
———— who fawn'd like man, but ne'er like man betray'd,	*id.* 252
Shoe for walkers,	*Gay* 1 : 102
Shooting flying,	*Som.* 153
———— match,	*Dry.* 6 : 94
———— corns a shower presage,	*Swift* 1 : 60
Short by the knees, intreat for peace,	*Swift* 2 : 314

Short abfence, mutual joys increafe by,   *King* 297

—— life, well loft for endlefs fame,   *Pope* 1 : 316

Shortnefs of life,   *Cow.* 1 : 92

Shower (John), on his daughter's death,   *Watts* 285

Showers, the pearly daughters of the clouds,   *Weft* 180

Showery arch, the watery brede,   *Phil.* 71

Showery-bow, the Lord of nature fram'd,   *Broome* 97

Shrovetide cock,   *Dry.* 3 : 142

Sibyl, ftory of,   *Garth* 127

—— defcribed in her enthufiafm,   *Dry.* 6 : 115, 116

—— of Cumæ,   *Dry.* 6 : 21

—— Æneas's adventures foretold by,   *Dry.* 6 : 117

—— attends him to hell,   *Dry.* 6 : 125

—— defcribes various fcenes of it,   *Dry.* 6 : 125

—— conducts him to Anchifes,   *Dry.* 6 : 144

Sican to the Dean, on his birth-day,   *Swift* 2 : 340

Sicily, of old torn from Hefperia,   *Rowe L.* 123

—— and Italy, one continent,   *Dry.* 6 : 20

Sick are ever reftlefs,   *Hughes* 260

—— pain makes them impatient,   *Hughes* 260

—— in mind, covetous of more difeafe,   *Young* 3 : 2

—— half the cure, to know ourfelves,   *Young* 3 : 2

—— man and the Angel,   *Gay* 2 : 75

Sickle, each moment has,   *Young* 2 : 10

—— emulous of Time's enormous fcythe,   *Young* 2 · 10

Sicknefs,   *Swift* 2 : 149

—— on recovery from a fit of,   *Aken.* 284

—— ode after,   *Shen.* 103

—— fight of heaven in,   *Watts* 62

—— of long life, old age,   *Pope* 2 : 186

Sickness and pain wean from earth,   *Wall.* 222

Sicoris, running by Ilerda,   *Rowe L.* 161

Sicyon, swayed the most ancient sceptre,   *Aken.* 167

Sid Hamet, virtues of his rod,   *Swift* 1 : 65

—— character of,   *Dry.* 1 : 119

Sidney, thy beauty resistless,   *Lans.* 142

Sidon, capital of Phœnicia,   *Pope od.* 3 : 108

Sidrophel, a cunning man,   *Butl.* 1 : 227

————— Hudibras to,   *Butl.* 1 : 268

Siege described,   *Cong.* 16

—— exhibited in vision,   *Milt.* 2 : 107

—— of Troy, length of portended,   *Pope il.* 1 : 80

Sighs, that waft to heaven,   *Pope* 1 : 190

Sigismonda and Guiscardo,   *Dry.* 3 : 215

Silence described,   { *Cow.* 1 : 298 *Cong.* 30

—— under suffering, is best,   *Dry.* 3 : 158

—— becomes the wife,   *Som.* 373

—— Death's peculiar attribute,   *Young* 3 : 71

—— is the soul of war,   *Prior* 1 : 50

—— and Darkness, solemn sisters!   *Young* 2 : 4

———————— the grave, your kingdom,   *Young* 2 : 4

—— Rochester on,   *Pope* 1 : 350

—— coeval with eternity,   *Pope* 1 : 350

—— the knave's repute,   *Pope* 1 : 351

Silent grief, speaks but at the eyes,   *Dry.* 7 : 9

Silenus,   *Dry.* 5 : 49

—— youthful in decay,   *Pope* 1 : 335.

Silk, soft Persia yields,   *Dyer* 71

Silk-labourers of the mulberry wood,   *Black.* 74.

Silks come from maggots,   *Swift* 1 : 213

Silli of the Greeks, what,   *Dry* 7 : 144

Siloah, peaceful flood,   *Pitt* 240

Silver, simile on want of,   *Swift* 1 : 337

———— age,   *Dry.* 3 : 302

———— pen,   *Wall.* 95

Silurian cyder shall triumph o'er the vine,   *Phil.* 83

Simeon foretels what Christ should be,   *Milt.* 2 : 166

Simile, $\begin{cases} \textit{Shen.} \quad 184 \\ \textit{Prior } 1:201 \end{cases}$

·———— that solitary shines, sanctified whole poems, *Pope* 2 : 219

Similes describe, they nothing prove,   *Prior* 2 : 78

Simoisius, pierc'd by Ajax, lies,   *Pope il.* 1 : 145

Simony, to sing for gold,   *Young* 3 : 201

Simple I, and innocent of art,   *Tick.* 210

Simplicity, what,   *Pope il.* 1 : 24

———————— in perfection, in Scripture and Homer, *Pope il.* 1 : 24

———————— praise of,   *Shen.* 13

———————— ode to,   *Collins* 249

———————— by nature taught to breathe her genuine thought, *ib.*

———————— sister meek of Truth,   *Collins* 250

Sin, daughter of Satan,   *Milt.* 1 : 60

——— description of,   *Milt.* 1 : 61

——— one of the guards of Hell, described,   *Milt.* 1 : 56, 57

——— portress of Hell,   *Milt.* 1 : 63

——— opens to Satan,   *Milt.* 1 : 64

——— unable to shut the gate,   *Milt.* 1 : 64

——— effects of,   *Milt.* 2 : 38, 49

——— leaves naked and void of honour,   *Milt.* 2 : 39

——— pursues with guilt,   *Milt.* 2 : 40

Sin produces Death,   *Dry.* 2 : 193

—— makes the darken'd foul a fcene more fad,   *Young* 3 : 67

—— all comfort kills, nor leaves one fpark alive,   *Young* 3 : 67

—— made known, not removed by law,   *Milt.* 2 : 123

—— transferred on Chrift,   *Milt.* 2 : 152

—— to be repented of,   *Milt.* 3 : 24

—— and Death pave a way over Chaos,   *Milt.* 1 : 69

——————————— to Earth,   *Milt.* 2 : 55

——————— offspring of Satan,   *Milt.* 2 : 56

——————— congratulate Satan,   *Milt.* 2 : 57

——————— wafte the world,   *Milt.* 2 : 65

Sin and Satan, dragg'd captives, that captiv'd men, *Parn.* 181

Sinai, law given at,   *Watts* 67

—— bow'd and fhook beneath a God,   *Watts* 71

Sincere, what fo eafy as to be ?   *Pope od.* 4 : 91

Sing, afking leave to,   *Watts* 41

Singer (Mrs.), afterwards Mrs. Rowe, verfes to,   *Watts* 277

Single valour unequal to a numerous foe,   *Butl.* 1 : 103

—— life againft marriage,   *Den.* 57

Singularity, affectation of,   *Pope* 1 : 108

Sinking ftate, form fure plans to fave,   *Pope od.* 3 : 51

Sinners faved,   *Watts* 53

—— fubftituted for fuffering faints,   *Butl.* 1 : 204

Sinon, treachery of,   *Dry.* 5 : 353

—— unlocks the horfe,   *Dry.* 5 : 361

Sion, amidft her towers, her God appears,   *Pitt* 241

—— fmiles on the tumults of the world,   *Pitt* 241

Siphon to rack cyder,   *Phil.* 71

Sire murdered in the fon,   *Dry.* 6 : 312

—— fhall blefs his fon, the fon his fire,   *Pope od.* 3 : 295

Sirens,

Sirens, by their fongs entice their prey, *King* 322

—— to hear, warble in thy fong, *Gay* 1 : 1

Sires by fons, and fons by fathers die, *Tick.* 160

—— teach not your daughters to rebel, *Gay* 2 : 245

—— by counfel rein their wills, but ne'er compel, *Gay* 2 : 245

Sifters gave to Venus all my life to come, *Pope* 1 : 170

Sifyphus heaves a huge round ftone, *Pope od.* 3 : 301

———— rolls a ponderous ftone, *Fent.* 270

Six rows of lengthening pines the billows fweep, *Rowe L.* 146

Skill, greateft, is knowing when to praife, *Buck.* 117

—— and cozenage, thought the fame, *Buck.* 106

Skip of a lawyer, where did he grow; *Swift* 2 : 296

Sky, canopy of, a nobler covering than tombs, *Rowe L.* 325

Sky-lark, *Shen.* 119

Slander, direful trump of, founds, *Pope* 1 : 216

—— withers all before it, *Pope* 1 : 217

—— ftings the brave, *Pope od.* 3 : 210

—— like a magpie chatters, *Pope* 1 : 345

—— who deals in, lives in ftrife, *Gay* 2 : 72

Slave, can foldiers beg to wear the name of, *Rowe L.* 172

—— to fome hind, *Pope od.* 3 : 297

———————— to be, is better than monarch of the dead, *ib.*

—— firft to words, then vaffal to a name, *Pope* 3 : 250

Slave-trade, horror of, *Dyer* 111

Slaves of flaves, by fuperftition fool'd, *Thom.* 2 : 24

—— by vice unmann'd, *Thom.* 2 : 24

—— in guile ingenious, and in murder brave, *Thom.* 2 : 24

—— fuch thy fons, Oppreffion, are, *Thom.* 2 : 24

—— attempt in vain Freedom's caufe, *Rowe L.* 312

—— to their vices, can ne'er be free, *Thom.* 2 : 14

Slaves may obey, but they can never love,   *Lanf.* 254

———— extoll'd the hand that pay'd,   *Gay* 2 : 160

———— made citizens by turning round,   *Dry.* 7 : 349

Slaughter marks in blood his way,   *Broome* 18

———— vengeful, fierce for human blood,   *Pope od.* 3 : 221

Sleep, defcribed, $\begin{cases} \textit{Cow. } 1:281 \\ \textit{Dry. } 6:61 \end{cases}$

———— the bleffing of the night,   *Pope od.* 3 : 101

———— lazy owl of night,   *Cow.* 1 : 211

———— ode to,   *Aken.* 253

———— whofe fway charms every anxious thought,   *Aken.* 253

———— an elegy,   *Cong.* 106

———— a fweet forgetfulnefs of cares,   *Pope od.* 4 : 231

———— of all the powers the beft,   *Dry.* 4 : 62

———— O peace of mind, repairer of decay,   *Dry.* 4 : 62

———— care fhuns thy foft approach,   *Dry.* 4 : 62

———— thou balmy cure of ficknefs and of pain !   *Hughes* 259

———— foft oblivion of furrounding ills !   *Hughes* 259

———— fheds o'er all his balm,   *Broome* 25

———— fhed his fofteft balm,   *Broome* 63

———— grown a ftranger to my eyes,   *Broome* 71

———— two portals of,   *Pope od.* 4 : 156

———— gates of,   *Dry.* 6 : 155

———— cavern of,   *Dry.* 4 : 60

———— effects of,   *Wall.* 32

———— Death's brother,   *Butl.* 2 : 192

———— brother of Death,   *Broome* 146

———— Death's half brother,   *Pope il.* 2 : 49

———— friend to Life,   *Butl.* 2 : 192

———— the friend of Life,   *Broome* 146

. Sleep counterfeits **Death**,   *Butl.* 1 : 188

—— refembles Death,   *Den.* 140

—— dead.oblivion, lofing half a life too fhort,   *Thom.* 1 : 46

—— winds us up for the fucceding dawn,   *Young* 3 : 74

—— Nature's fweet reftorer,   *Young* 2 : 3

—— that tames the ftrong,   *Pope od.* 3 : 241

—— bathes in Sachariffa's eyes,   *Wall.* 51

—— fhuns the crown, vifits the weary fwain,   *Dyer* 130

—— we to wake, and only die to live,   *Prior* 2 : 186

—— and Death, two twins of winged race,   *Pope il.* 2 : 126

————————— of matchlefs fwiftnefs, but of filent pace, *ib.*

Sleep-compelling rod of Hermes,   *Dry.* 3 : 73

Sleeping laws the king's neglect revile,   *Prior* 2 : 154

Sleet of arrowy fhowers,   *Milt.* 2 : 194

Slender, Ghoft of,   *Shm.* 172

Slighteft fins, greateft crimes,   *Butl.* 1 : 76

Sloane, the foremoft toyman of his time,   *Young* 1 : 111

Sloth, coward, fitting in filence,   *Aken.* 129

—— ignoble charms of,   *Aken.* 211

—— mifchief of,   *Young* 3 : 243

—— 'tis a toil enervates man,   *Young* 3 : 243

—— unnerv'd with reft,   *Parn.* 59

—— turn her own difcafe,   *Parn.* 59

—— annals of,   *Garth* 26

—— God of,   *Garth* 22

—— reign of,   *Garth* 24

—— who's born for ?   *Gay* 2 : 154

Sloven and the fopling are the fame,   *Young* 1 : 95

Sloweft infects have moft legs,   *Butl.* 2 : 19

Slubber degullion bafe,   *Butl.* 1 : 132

                                                             Sluggard,

Sluggard,   *Watts* 361
Smarting, may convince a fool,   *Rosc.* 222
Smatterers, arrogant,   *Butl.* 2 : 274
Smec, legion,   *Butl.* 1 : 208
Smeck, canonical cravat of,   *Butl.* 1 : 143
Smedley (Dean), petition of,   *Swift* 1 : 258
——— answer to,   *Swift* 1 : 262
Smells, the breath of nature,   *Thom.* 1 : 22
Smiles flow from reason,   *Milt.* 2 : 11
——— lovely children of Content and Joy,   *Lytt.* 5
——— are radiant marks of man,   *Young* 3 : 102
——— of Fortune, as variable as woman's love,   *Lanf.* 279
Smith, Phædra and Hippolytus,   *Smith* 95
——— to the memory of Philips,   190
——— Charlettus Percivallo suo,   200
——— Percivallus Charletto suo,   201
——— Pocockius,   204
——— ode for the year 1705,   207
Smock-race,   *Som.* 133
Smooth and round in yourself,   *Swift* 2 : 129
Smyrna, ever sacred to the Muse,   *Dyer* 107
Snail was I born, and snail shall end,   *Gay* 2 : 72
Snails, house-bearing, yield salubrious water,   *Phil.* 47
——— pernicious to apples,   *Phil.* 47
——— spoil the verdure of the year,   *Gay* 2 : 173
——— near sweetest fruits abound,   *Gay* 1 : 75
Snake, to a lady playing with,   *Bronte* 90
Snow in whitening shower descends,   *Thom.* 1 : 161
——— men perishing in,   *Thom.* 1 : 163.
——— preserved,   *Wall.* 152
                                                 SNOW,

Snow, useful to the ground,   *Phil.* 67

——— riddle on,   *Swift* 1 : 327

——— (Thomas), epistle to,   *Gay* 1 : 195

——— whose wisdom found the South-Sea shelves, *Gay* 1 : 195

Snow-drop, a Fairy turned to,   *Tick.* 216

Snuff, pungent grains of titillating dust,   *Pope* 1 : 153

——— mundungus,   *Butl.* 2 : 49

——— or the fan, supplies each pause of chat, *Pope* 1 : 138

Sober prince, goverment of, is best,   *Dry.* 2 : 119

Social pleasure, ill-exchang'd for power,   *Pope* 2 : 290

Society, nurse of Art,   *Thom.* 1 : 110

Socrates, the Sent of Heaven,   *Mall.* 183

—————————— to whom its moral will was given, *ib.* 183

——— wisest of mankind,   *Thom.* 1 : 168

——— father of philosophy,   *Thom.* 2 : 42

——— tutor of Athens,   *Thom.* 2 : 42

——— here ever shines,   *Pope* 1 : 208

——— patience of,   *Butl.* 2 : 275

——— put to death for atheism,   *Black.* 6

————————— for asserting one God, *Black.* 6

Sodom, overthrow of,   *Cow.* 2 : 141

Sofola, thought to be Ophir,   *Dyer* 113

Soft looks, the silent eloquence of eyes,   *Hughes* 58

Soils, difference of,   *Dry.* 5 : 94

——— different natures of,   *Dry.* 5 : 125

——— to discover nature of,   *Dry.* 5 : 127

Soldier in love,   *Hughes* 140

——— should be modest as a maid,   *Young* 1 : 115

——— founder of jesuits,   *Butl.* 2 : 74

Soldier's end, all applaud, and weep,   *Hughes* 125

Soldier, desperately brave, falls a sacrifice to glory, *Hughes*125

———— if successful, deemed guardian genius of the state, *ib.*

———— admir'd when living, and when dead ador'd, *ib.*

Soldiers are perfect devils in their way, *Gay* 1 : 207

———— when once rais'd, they're cursed hard to lay, *id.* 207

Solemn council best becomes the old, *Pope il.* 1 : 139

Solemnity of proclaiming war, *Dry.* 6 : 185

———— is a cover for a sot, *Young* 1 : 93

Solicitude, *Shen.* 157

Soliloquies had need be few, *Buck.* 75

———— extremely short, *Buck.* 75

———— yet spoke in passion too, *Buck.* 75

———— occasion of, should naturally fall, *Buck.* 75

Soliloquy, { *Garth* 155
{ *Dry.* 1 : 318

———— of a beauty in the country, *Lytt.* 17

Solitude, *Cow.* 2 : 284

———— hymn on, *Thom.* 2 : 193

———— companion of the wise and good, *Thom.* 2 : 193

———— ode on, { *Rosc.* 238
{ *Pope* 1 : 85

———— who fit for, *Cow.* 2 : 286, 287

———— employment in, *Cow.* 2 : 288

———— nurse of sense, *Pope* 2 : 281

———— nurse of woe, *Parn.* 79

———— howe'er we range, in thee we fix at last, *Tick.* 107

———— divine retreat! *Young* 1 : 126

———— choice of the prudent! *Young* 1 : 126

———— there we court fair wisdom, *Young* 1 : 126

Solomon, *Prior* 2 : 101

Solomon,

Solomon, his writings, profound reasonings in, *Prior* 2 : 101

———— in his song, figures heavenly things, *Parn.* 193, 194

———— beguiled by women, *Milt.* 2 : 168

———— grandeur of, *Cow.* 2 : 121

Solon, last and wisest of Greece, *Aken.* 163

——— raised a temple to Liberty and Concord, *Aken.* 165

Solution, change of terms and scaffolding of words, *Prior* 2 : 117

Solymean rout, bold in treason, *Dry.* 1 : 142

Somers, character of, *Garth* 38

Somerset, duchess of, ode to, *Shen.* 79

Somerset-house alloted to the queen, *Cow.* 1 : 196

————————— new buildings of, *Wall.* 168

Sompner's prologue of Chaucer, answer to, *Gay* 2 : 1

Somervile, the Chace, *Som.* 13

————— Hobbinol, 95

————— Field-sports, 141

————— Ramsay (Allan), to, 159

————— Marlborough, duke of, ode to, 163

————————————— embarking for Ostend, 168

————— to Addison, 174

————— imitation of Horace, 180

————— to Dr. Mackenzie, 187

————— the wife, 189

————— memory of Mr. Moore, 191

————— epitaph on Hugh Lumber, 192

————— the Hip, 193

————— to a Lady, 195

————— presenting a white rose and a red, 196

————— bowling-green, 197

————— David's lamentation over Saul, &c. 204

Somervile,

Somerville, to a young Lady, with the Iliad,   *Som.* 207

———— to Allan Ramfay,   210, 218

———— Ramfay's anfwer,   214

———— on the Effay on Man,   221

———— to Mr. Thomfon, on his Seafons,   222

———— to lady Anne Coventry,   224

———— addrefs to his elbow-chair,   226

———— fong,   228.

———— paraphrafe of a French fong,   229

———— Hudibras and Milton reconciled,   230

———— on Miranda leaving the country,   231

———— to Phyllis,   234

———— to earl of Halifax,   235

———— fong for the lute,   237

———— the Coquette,   238

———— fuperannuated lover,   238

———— advice to the ladies,   240

———— Anacreontic,   240

———— to a difcarded toaft,   241

———— perjured miftrefs, from Horace,   242

———— to a young lady,   243

———— to Dr. M——, reading mathematics,   244

———— epigram from Martial,   244

———— to one who married his caft miftrefs,   246

———— new ballad,   247

———— Canidia's epithalamium,   250

———— hunting fong,   252

———— tranflat on of the tenth epiftle of Horace, 254

———— mifer's fpeech,   257

———— the captive trumpeter,   262

7

Somerville,

Somervile, bald-pated Welſhman and fly,   *Som.* 263

———— ant and fly,   265

———— wolf, fox, and ape,   267

———— dog and bear,   268

———— wounded man and flies,   270

———— wolf and dog,   271

———— the oyſter,   274

———— ſheep and the buſh,   275

———— frogs' choice,   276

———— Liberty and Love,   279

———— the two Springs,   282

———— bald batchelor,   288

———— fortune-hunter,   296

———— Devil outwitted,   335

———— officious meſſenger,   336

———— inquiſitive bridegroom,   346

———— Bacchus triumphant,   349

———— night-walker reclaimed,   352

———— happy diſappointment,   365

———— padlock for the mouth,   369

———— wiſe builder,   373

———— true uſe of the looking-glaſs,   374

———— Mahomet Ali Beg,   375

———— ſweet-ſcented miſer,   388

———— incurious bencher,   392

———— buſy indolent,   395

———— yeoman of Kent,   398

———— happy lunatic,   403

Son, effulgence of God's glory,   *Milt.* 1 : 195

———— ſent to finiſh the war,   *Milt.* 1 : 196

                                                  Son,

Son, image of God in all things,   *Milt.* 1 : 197

—— eternal, word Supreme,   *Parn.* 256

—— whofe tender love for all provides,   *Parn.* 256

———— power o'er all prefides,   *Parn.* 256

—— bright effulgence,   *Parn.* 261

—— goes to create,   *Milt.* 1 : 213

—— created all things,   *Milt.* 1 : 167

—— fent to judge fallen man,   *Milt.* 2 : 47

—— redeemer and ranfom of man,   *Milt.* 2 : 47

—— judge and interceffor,   *Milt.* 2 : 48

—— approbation of mercy to man,   *Milt.* 1 : 78

—— unexampled love of,   *Milt.* 1 : 86

—— the only peace for man,   *Milt.* 1 : 82

—— head, in Adam's room,   *Milt.* 1 : 82

—— merit of, imputed,   *Milt.* 1 : 82

—— men live in, tranfplanted,   *Milt.* 1 : 83

—— to judge angels and men,   *Milt.* 1 : 84

—— godhead of, denied by Socinus,   *Dry.* 2 : 33

—— redeem'd the honours of the race,   *Pope il.* 2 : 91

—— as generous as the fire was bafe,   *Pope il.* 2 : 91

—— lofs of an only,   *Buck.* 99

Song, expreffion eafy, and the fancy high,   *Buck.* 71

—— no part of poetry requires a nicer art,   *Buck.* 71

—— exact propriety of words and thought,   *Buck.* 71

—— there muft be art and fenfe in,   *Dry.* 1 : 275

—— inftructs the foul, and charms the ear,   *Pope od.* 3 : 314

—— laps the foul in Elyfium,   *Milt.* 3 : 130

—— fooths our pains,   *Young* 3 : 2

—— to gods and men is facred,   *Pope od.* 4 : 209

—— too daring, and the theme too great,   *Prior* 1 : 173

Song, is noife and impious the feaft,   *Pope od.* 3 : 72

—— imitated from the French,   *Shen.* 131

Songs and odes,   *Dry.* 2 : 201

—— fet to mufic,   *Prior* 2 : 273

Sonnet,   *Hughes* 77

—— hard to write well,   *Dry.* 1 : 271

Sonnets,   *Milt.* 3 : 169

Sons of a day, with each a brother at his back,   *Pope* 3 : 157

—— of God,   *Milt.* 2 : 105

—— of nobles are the fons of earth,   *Young* 3 : 264

—— to debafe, exalts the fires,   *Pope* 2 : 221

—— the hopes of all the years to come,   *Pitt* 252

—— their old unhappy fire defpife,   *Pope* 1 : 279

—— who with flagitious pride infult my darknefs, *Pope* 1 : 279

—— moft their fires difgrace,   *Pope od.* 3 : 71

Sophocles improved tragedy,   *Dry.* 1 : 278

Sorbonift, a rope of fand could twift,   *Butl.* 1 : 13

Sordid earth to fcorn, and mount the fkies,   *Broome* 93

Sorrow, foul in,   *Parn.* 248

—— of horrid parentage,   *Young* 3 : 102

—— fecond-born of hell,   *Young* 3 : 102

—— that privilege of men,   *Young* 2 : 110

—— from pang of, birth of endlefs joy,   *Young* 2 : 110

—— our lot, our portion pain,   *Prior* 2 : 175

—— the fine impos'd on length of days,   *Pope il.* 2 : 186

—— be thou hereforth my joy,   *Broome* 29

—— feem'd to wear one common face,   *Cong.* 37

Sorrows, which are our own, ferious heed we give,   *Weft* 207

—— for another's we foon ceafe to grieve,   *Weft* 207

—— which a friend would fhare,   *Pope il.* 2 : 100

Sot's hole, five Ladies at,   *Swift* 2 : 67

Sots, on a club of,   *Butl.* 2 : 350

Sovereign of the skies, who shall control?   *Pope Il.* 1 : 257

———— Being, but a sovereign good,   *Pope* 2 : 63

———— to contemn, charter of Jerusalem,   *Dry.* 1 : 161

Sovereignty, what women most desire,   *Dry.* 3 : 197

———————— and Grace,   *Watts* 112

Soul,   *Cow.* 1 : 243, 271

———— immortal substance, to remain,   *Prior* 2 : 180

———— conscious of joy, and capable of pain,   *Prior* 2 : 186

———— immortality of,   *Den.* 138

———— simple and indivisible,   *Den.* 139

———— escapes the wreck of worlds,   *Som.* 68

———— importance of,   *Young* 2 : 196

———— rescued from death,   *Young* 2 : 197

———— that busy thing, whence I know I am,   *Prior* 2 : 165

———— companion of the body's good or ill,   *Prior* 2 : 166

———— conscious of joy or pain,   *Prior* 2 : 166

———— pale it with rage, or redden it with shame, *Prior* 2 : 166

———— can scarce above the body rise,   *Pom.* 339

———— for great actions free,   *Pom.* 219

———— that justly thinks, would greatly dare,   *Sav.* 139

———— nothing but God can satisfy,   *Wall.* 218

———— in commerce with God, is heaven,   *Young* 2 : 237

———— can rest on nought but God,   *Young* 3 : 79

———————— here in full trust, hereafter in full joy, *Young* 3 : 79

———— anchor'd safe on Reason's peaceful coast, *Pope od.* 4 : 162

———— by tempests of wrath no longer tost,   *Pope od.* 4 : 162

———— by wisdom's noblest precepts crown'd,   *Rowe* 48

———— without reflection, to ruin runs,   *Young* 2 : 111

Soul saddens by the use of pain,   *Pope od.* 3 : 269

—— distemper'd, sport of passions,   *Add.* 253

—— deadly wound in,   *Dry.* 7 : 335

—— issued in the purple flood,   *Pope il.* 2 : 119

—— of pleasure reigns in rural seats,   *Parn.* 33

—— of the world,   *Dry.* 6 : 146

Souls must paint souls,   *Hughes* 271

—— the life of,   *Watts* 173

Sound, a comment to the sense,   *Rosc.* 225

—— must seem an echo to the sense,   *Pope* 1 : 106

—— learn to sink in,   *Garth* 56

Source of Being, hail,   *Thom.* 1 : 22

—— of woe, desire to know,   *Prior* 2 : 127

South beheld that master-piece of man,   *Pope* 3 : 228

—— opposed him out of zeal,   *Pom.* 340

—— shewing how well he could dispute and rail,   *Pom.* 340

South America, view of,   *Dyer* 124

South-Sea project,   *Swift* 1 : 200

———— at best a mighty bubble,   *Swift* 1 : 208

Southerne, epistle to,   *Fent.* 233

———— Dryden to,   *Dry.* 2 : 134

———— verses to,   *Pope* 2 : 355

Sow-geldering operation,   *Butl.* 1 : 181

Space immense beyond the stars,   *Aken.* 84

—— no midst, no centre in,   *Black.* 132

—— full, no motion in,   *Black.* 133

—— if interspers'd without matter, matter not necessary, *id.* 134

Spacious air, left to the wits,   *Swift* 1 : 42

———— there with licence to build castles,   *Swift* 1 : 42

Spade, learn to call a spade,   *Swift* 2 : 239

Spades be trumps, and trumps they were, *Pope* 1 : 139

Spadillio, unconquerable Lord, *Pope* 1 : 139

Spain, king of, *Garth* 112

———— haughty, soon shall hear and tremble, *Aken.* 356

———— numerous fleet perished on the coast, *Add.* 12

———— the fruitless strife gives o'er, *Hughes* 46

———— and claims dominion there no more, *Hughes* 46

Spaniel, use of in fowling, *Gay* 1 : 12

———— fawning slave to man's deceit, *Gay* 2 : 81

———— pimp of luxury, sneaking cheat, *Gay* 2 : 81

———— and cameleon, *Gay* 2 : 32

———— indulged to disobey command, *Gay* 2 : 32

———— how pretty were his fawning ways, *Gay* 2 : 32

Spanish Armada, defeat of, *Thom.* 2 : 112

———— war, folly of, *Cow.* 2 : 246

———— West-Indies, *Thom.* 2 : 111

Spark, each light gay meteor of a, *Pope* 2 : 106

Sparrow loves to chirp and talk, *Prior* 2 : 197

Sparrows treading, *Swift* 2 : 234

Sparta, surrounded by a range of hills, *Pope od.* 3 : 105

———— poor, *Duke* 143

———— sober, hard, and man-subduing city, *Thom.* 2 : 38

———— Lycurgus there built a temper'd state, *Thom.* 2 : 39

———— where mix'd each government, *Thom.* 2 : 39

———— there corruption lay wither'd at the root, *Thom.* 2 : 39

———— raised on Virtue's base, *West* 259

———— rough, in Virtue's love approv'd, *Rowe L.* 206

———— with female beauty gay, *Pope od.* 4 : 19

Spartan dame, prologue to, *Fent.* 332

Spartans not suffered to learn deceitful arts abroad, *West* 262

Spartans,

Spartans, by expofing to reclaim,   *Lanf.* 216

Specious gifts, no gifts, but guiles,   *Milt.* 2 : 176

Specious-good we court, and meet a real ill,   *Broome* 42

Speculation roofted near the fky,   *Young* 3 : 189

———— from garrets thunders,   *Young* 3 : 189

Speck of entity, how ftretches to man,   *Garth* 21

Spectator, to fuppofed author of,   *Tick.* 95

———— thy fpotlefs thoughts, unfhock'd prieft may hear, *ib.*

Speech, Thought's canal,   *Young* 2 : 35

———————— criterion too,   *Young* 2 : 35

———— that knows nor art nor fear,   *Pope il.* 1 : 278

Spell,   { *Step.* 192
    { *Gay* 1 : 73

———— 'fhall eafe my care,   *Gay* 1 : 73

———— ye right this verfe upon her ftone,   *Gay* 1 : 82

Spence, verfes to,   *Pitt* 389

Spenfer commended for paftoral,   *Pope* 1 : 22

———— too allegorical,   *Pope* 1 : 22

———— ftanza not always well chofen,   *Pope* 1 : 22

———— firft by Pifan poets taught,   *Smith* 193

———— himfelf affects the obfolete,   *Pope* 2 : 219

———— in his Shepherd's Calendar, not to be match'd, *Dry.* 5 : 18

———— in his dialect, imitated the Doric,   *Dry.* 5 : 18

———— excels in paftoral,   *Dry.* 1 : 264

———— in ancient tales amufed,   *Add.* 34

———— art predominates in,   *Den.* 55

———— like Aurora,   *Den.* 54

———— Milton's original,   *Dry.* 3 : 14

———— imitated,   *Pope* 1 : 344

———— imitation of,   *Pitt* 390

       Spenfer,

Spenser, no uniformity in his defign,   Dry. 7 : 116

———— borrowed his charaƈters from the then living, id. 116

———— his verfes numerous and various, .   id. 116

———— pearls in muddy waters lie,   Fent. 240

Sphinx, riddle of,   Prior 2 : 239

Sphinx's riddles durſt explain, .   Pope 1 : 278

Spice-iſlands, view of,   Dyer 117

Spick and fpan I have enough, . .   Swift 2 : 264

———————— I keep no antiquated ſtuff,   Swift 2 : 264

Spider only fpins on dark days,   Butl. 2 : 289

———— cunning and fierce, mixture abhorred,   Thom. 1 : 52

———— faints, what,   Butl. 1 : 324

Spiders never feek the fly,   Butl. 1 : 295

Spikenard, his grace,   . .   Parn. 198

Spinning, feveral methods of,   Dyer 85

Spinoſa, atheiſtical notions of,.   Black. 119

———— according to, univerfe, God, .   Black. 119

Spiral tops and copple-crowns,   Swift 2 : 176

Spirit, like a dove,   Milt. 2 : 152

———— the foul's eternal guide, .   Parn. 255

———— warm, poffefs and fill my mind,   Parn. 255

———— equally divine,. .   Parn. 261

———— with holy tranfports refine the breaſt, .   Parn. 261

Spirits die only by annihilation,   Milt. 1 : 184

———— light miſitia, of the lower ſky,   Pope 1 : 128

Spite, what will it not ?   Gay 2 : 107

Splay-foot rhymes in fmall poets,   Butl. 1 : 107

Spleen, parent of vapours, and of female wit,   Pope 1 : 146

———— who giveſt the hyſteric or poetic fit,   Pope 1 : 146

———— who ruleſt the fex to fifty from fifteen,   Pope 1 : 146

Q 3

Spleen, suggestions of, indulged, *Shen.* 47

——— gloomy cave of, *Pope* 1 : 145

——— pain at her side, and megrim at her head, *Pope* 1 : 145

——— bodies chang'd to various forms by, *Pope* 1 : 146

Splendid Shilling, *Phil.* 3

Splendor borrows all her rays from sense, *Pope* 2 : 142

Spoils and trophies shew epidemic woe, *Prior* 2 : 176

Sports, indications of the genius of a nation, *Som.* 91

——— of glory to the brave belong, *Pope od.* 3 : 209

Spots in the sun, are in his lustre lost, *Som.* 223

Spouse augments his joys, or mitigates his pain, *Pope* 1 : 228

——— endued with all the virtues of a horse, *Gay* 1 : 202

Sprat, on Cowley, 200

——— to Howard, on British princes, 162

——— history of Royal Society, *Cow.* 2 : 220

——— on his mistress drowned, *Sprat* 163

——— the plague of Athens, 174

——— to memory of Protector, 149

Sprightly chace the powers of life recruit, *Rowe L.* 168

Spring, { *Cow.* 1 : 229
{ *Broome* 167

——— described, *Dry.* 3 : 167

——— soft breezes with, *Broome* 167

——— in, olive struggles into birth, *Broome* 168

——— and youth will soon be going, *Hughes* 118, 119

——— wafted by the western gales, *Fent.* 322

——— youth of tender year, *Lytt.* 49

——— ode to, *Swift* 1 : 132

——— ode on, { *Gray* 325
{ *Hughes* 87

Spring,

Spring, season of desire,   Wall. 52

———— lovely season of desire,   Hughes 88

———— a pastoral,   Pope 1 : 25

———— descends in showers,   Pope od. 3 : 229

———— strows with flowers the meads,.   Hughes 192

———— nature blooming and benevolent,   Thom. 1 : 3, 4

———— influence on animate and inanimate nature,   id. 1 : 20

———— fair-handed, unbosoms every grace,.   id. 1 : 21

———— nipt with Winter's lagging rear,.   Milt. 3 : 60

———— without, and Winter all within,.   Fent. 292

———— new,   Shen. 53

———— of action to ourselves is lost,.   Pope 2 : 96

Springal, by his beauty curst to ills,.   Dry. 7 : 297

Springs of motion, from the seat of sense,.   Dry. 1 : 25

Sprouts to preserve green in boiling,   King 232

Squabble,   Gay 1 : 55

Squadrons, with spears erect, a moving iron wood, Pope il. 1 : 137

Squintisego maid,   Dry. 6 : 354

Squire, birth of,   Gay 1 : 219

———— a hopeful heir is born,.   Gay 1 : 219

———— and his cur,   Gay 2 : 142

Stafford, trial and death of,   Den. 39

Stag, on head of,   Wall. 102

——— death of, causes a war,   Dry. 6 : 179, 180

Stag-chace, described,   Som. 59

——— chac'd, repulsed by the herd,   Som. 63

Stage, ill be their fate who would corrupt,   King 262

———— true corrector of the age,   King 262

Stage-reformers, you stand the first,   Hughes 80

Stagirite, Reason betrayed to,.   Dry. 2 : 124

Stagirite,

Stagirite, his head a radiant Zodiac crown'd,   *Pope* 1 : 212

Stanhope, poems on the death of,   *Pitt* 297

———— the great, the brave, a prey to death,   *Pitt* 297

———— in arms and eloquence, like Cæsar, shone,   *Pitt* 297

———— Britannia mourn thy hero,   *Pitt* 298

———— the birth of years and labour of an age,   *Pitt* 299

———— his voice a senate, and his sword a war,   *Pitt* 299

———— his sword thro' legions cleaves his way,   *Pitt* 300

———— springs from the earth, and towers to heaven, *Pitt* 301

———— thy son, rise the Stanhope of the future age, *Pitt* 303

———— on his voyage to France,   *Tick.* 134

Stanley (Miss), epitaph on,   *Tham.* 2 : 179

———— here rest, above the joys, beyond the woes of life, *ib.*

Stanzas of the ancients, and their names,   *West* 117

Star guiding the wise men,   *Milt.* 2 : 151

—— each itself, a sun,   *Prior* 2 : 119

—— enliven worlds, deny'd to human sight,   *Prior* 2 : 119

—— primitive founts and origins of light,   *Prior* 2 : 119

Stars, spangles in the sky,   *Wall.* 31

———— suns, or centres to planets,   *Black.* 83

———— whether suns,   *Butl.* 2 : 153

———— not by reflection bright,   *Dry.* 2 : 124

———— at such a distance,   *Aken.* 85

———————————— that their light has not yet reach'd us, *ib.*

———— teach, as well as shine,   *Young* 3 : 22

———— unknown, appear'd to burn,   *Rowe L.* 72

———— and bad proud royalty for change prepare, *Rowe L.* 72

———— shall drop, the sun shall lose his flame,   *Gay* 1 : 278

———— by other sail,   *Add.* 13

———— to fribble with,   *Butl.* 1 : 224

Stare, for strangeness fit,   *Parn.* 6

Starve, badge of loyalty, to,   *Duke* 86

State after death, no alteration knows, .   *Pom.* 319

—— wife the man, who labours to secure a happy,   *Pom.* 319

—— all in proportion to,   *Pope* 2 : 35

—— pomps of, a trifle,   *Walsh* 332

—— Phaetons of, ..   *King* 384

State-artificer,   *Butl.* 2 : 26

State-camelion,   *Butl.* 2 : 25

State-lyes but little genius cost,   *Gay* 2 : 145

States, Atheists in their frame,   *Dry.* 1 : 41

—— must die,   *Thom.* 2 : 49

—— sink or rife, as govern'd well or ill,   *Young* 1 : 260

Statesman upright, who !   *Roch.* 325

——— creed of,   *Young* 1 : 260

——— found, but shoots of honest men, .   *Young* 1 : 2

Station, to stand in, till relieved,   *Den.* 136

Statius, noted for want of judgement,   *Dry.* 5 : 208

——— a Capaneus of a Poet,.   *Dry.* 5 : 209

——— teaches mean thoughts in founding words,   *Add.* 180

——— best verfificator, next Virgil,   *Dry.* 7 : 114

——— but knew not how to design,   *Dry.* 7 : 114

——— Thebais, first book,   *Pope* 1 : 273

——— part of the second book translated,   *Pitt* 211

Statue of the queen,   *Garth* 110

Stave and tail,   *Butl.* 1 : 105

Steadiness of soul and thought, by religion taught,   *Pom.* 270

Steal myself from life by slow degrees,   *Pope od.* 4 : 229

—— retiring to the dark grave, as to rest,   *Pope od.* 4 : 229

—— my people blessing, by my people blest,   *Pope od.* 4 : 229

                                                                          Steal

Steal from corroding care one tranfient day, *Pope od.* 3 : 208

Stealth, life by, *Cow.* 2 : 190

Steed, more fleet than thofe begot by winds, *Som.* 16

—— of bones and leather, *Butl.* 1 : 78

Steeds outfhine the fnow, outfly the winds, *Broome* 81

Steel could the works of mortal pride confound, *Pope* 1 : 144

—— now glitters in the Mufes' fhades, *Pope* 1 : 82

Stella to Swift, *Swift* 1 : 251, 253, 291

—— birth-day of, *Swift* 1 : 166, 168, 175, 254, 334

—— verfes, *Swift* 1 : 264

—— birth-day, March 13, 1726, *Swift* 2 : 1

—— at Wood-park, *Swift* 1 : 273

Stentor, endued with brazen lungs, *Pope il.* 1 : 183

—— furpaffed the force of fifty tongues, *Pope il.* 1 : 183

—— fpeech of, *Garth* 70

Stentorophonic voice, loud as, *Butl.* 1 : 283

Stephen Duck, threfher and poet, *Swift* 2 : 217

Stepney, poems by, *Step.* 245

—— to James II. 245

—— on Univerfity of Cambridge, 246

—— to Charles Montague, 248

—— on the confpiracy, 256

—— to Earl Carlifle, 257

—— to memory of Q. Mary, 260

—— the Auftrian eagle, 264

—— imitation of French verfes, 265

—— of Juvenal, Sat. viii. 267

—— of Horace, Book iii. Ode vii. 285

—— Book iv. Ode ix. 287

—— tranflation from Lucan, 290

Stepney,

Stepney, on death of Tibullus,   *Step.* 293

———- to the Evening Star,   296

Stepney's verse, with candour ever bleſt,   *King* 326

Stern juſtice and ſoft-ſmiling love embrace,   *Young* 2 : 69

——————— a wonder in Omnipotence,   *Young* 2 : 69

Sterling line, drawn to French wire,   *Roſc.* 215

——————————————— would thro' pages ſhine, *ib.*

Steſichorus, obſerver of the order in the ode,   *Cong.* 154

Still roving, ſtill deſiring, never pleaſed,   *Som.* 279

Stirom, embottled long, ere juſtly mild,   *Phil.* 73

——— ſoftened by age, it vigor gains,   *Phil.* 73

——— truſt not its ſmoothneſs,   *Phil.* 73

——— third circling glaſs of, ſuffices virtue,   *Phil.* 73

Stoiciſm, 'tis pride, rank pride,   *Ald.* 263

Stoics diſpute in their porch,   *Butl.* 1 : 190

——— all in the grave,   *Cow.* 1 : 147

——— philoſophic pride of,   *Milt.* 2 : 212

——— philoſophy of,   *Dry.* 7 : 173

Stock-dove cooes, mournfully hoarſe,   *Thom.* 1 : 64

Stock-doves plain amid the foreſt,   *Thom.* 1 : 200

Stocks, wooden jail,   *Butl.* 1 : 158

Stomach pulled down,   *Butl.* 1 : 122

Stomachs, to bring down,   *Butl.* 2 : 93

Stone and braſs our hopes betray,   *Hughes* 209

Stone henge, what,   *Dry.* 2 : 122

Stony-tempeſt, hail,   *Broome* 98

Stool, the dread of every ſcolding quean,   *Gay* 1 : 71

Stores ſtarve us or they cloy,   *Young* 3 : 247

Stork, ſworn foe of ſnakes   *Phil.* 46

Storm,   *Swift* 1 : 356

Storm defcribed, ⎰ *Dry.* 5 : 369 | 6 : 103, 18⅘
                Rowe L.   232, 368
                Pope   1 : 302
                Thom.   1 : 70
                Mall.   241

—— to terrify,   *Black.* 127
—— effects of,   *Garth* 73 | *Thom.* 158
—— figns of,   *Mall.* 241
Storms defcribed,   *Thom.* 1 : 156
——— prefages of,   *Thom.* 1 : 156
Stranger and the poor are fent by Jove,   *Pope od.* 3 : 177
——— to reft, who loves,   *Gay* 1 : 55
Stranger's due, give the ftranger-gueft,   *Pope od.* 3 : 192
Strangers perfecuted to be received,   *Dyer* 97
——— trade owing to,   *Dyer* 97
——— taught arras,   *Dyer* 98
Stratagem,   *Mall.* 315
——— in war, no deceit,   *King* 186
Stratton-fight,   *Cow.* 1 : 338
Stray, to be kept year and day,   *Butl.* 1 : 180
—— nymph,   *A. Phil.* 328
Stream grows wild by reftraint,   *Cow.* 2 : 73
Streams, fhallow, run dimpling all the way,   *Pope* 2 : 162
Strength confifts in fpirits and in blood,   *Pope il.* 1 : 292
——— and thofe are ow'd to generous wine and food, *id.* 292
——— is of the gods alone,   *Pope il.* 2 : 36
——— without wifdom, vain,   *Milt.* 3 : 9
——— wifdom, virtue, mighty Jove, are thine,   *Weft* 233
——— alike is felt from hope and from defpair, *Pope il.* 2 : 93
——— divided from truth, illaudable,   *Milt.* 1 : 185

                                 Strength

Strength of mind is exercise, not rest,   *Pope* 2 : 45

———— and pleasure rise from exercise,   *Parn.* 60

———— proportioned to the woes you feel,   *Pope il.* 2 : 349

Strenuous idleness, wasting strength in,   *Young* 2 : 8

Strephon and Chloe,   *Swift* 2 : 233

Strephon's love for Delia justified,   *Parn.* 248

Strict religion very rare,   *Watts* 182

Strife and debate thy restless soul employ,   *Pope il.* 1 : 45

Stroke of fate the bravest cannot shun,   *Pope il.* 2 : 174

Strollers, always on the wing,   *Swift* 1 : 210

———— prologue for,   *Pitt* 233

———— hasp'd in a coach came down,   *Pitt* 233

———— but shall in a cart, our old original, depart,   *Pitt* 233

———— we strut the fancy'd monarchs of an hour,   *Pitt* 234

———— duns, our emperors and heroes fear,   *Pitt* 234

Strolling mart,   *King* 215

Strong, if thou art, Jove hath made thee so,   *Tick.* 171

Strophé, what,   { *West* 117
                         { *Ong.* 153

———— and Antistrophe, why of the same measure,   *West* 117

Struggle of public care and private passion,   *Wall.* 29

Study, how to die, not how to live,   *Lansf.* 181

Stumbling-block,   *King* 427

Sturdy beggars intreat, then threat,   *Butl.* 2 : 126

Stygian coasts, the house of woe,   *Pitt* 212

Style proper for poetry,   *Pitt* 360

——— obscure to be avoided,   *Pitt* 360

——— different, as the images,   *Pitt* 361

——— metaphorical, lustre of,   *Pitt* 362

Styles different, for different subjects,   *Pope* 1 : 104

Styx in nine wide circles roll'd his flood,   *Pitt* 211

—— inviolable oath by,   *Dry.* 6 : 127

—— the dreadful oath of Gods,   *Pope il.* 1 : 97

—— that dreadful oath, which binds the thunderer, *Pope* 1 : 297

Subjects obey, when men of worth command,   *Broome* 72

Sublime, how rare in life or fong!   *Young* 3 : 285

Sublunary science, but guefs,   *Den.* 109

———— world, a vapour,   *Young* 2 : 218

———— all it holds, a vapour,   *Young* 2 : 218

———— a land of fhadows,   *Young* 2 : 218

———— a troubled ocean,   *Young* 2 : 218

Subordination neceffary in a confederacy,   *Pope od.* 3 : 5

Suborn our flight,   *Dry.* 3 : 275

Subftance, never treat beyond,   *King* 209

Subtleties come near nothing,   *Butl.* 2 : 228

Succefs is ftill from heaven,   *Pope il.* 2 : 124

—— 'tis not in mortals to command,   *Add.* 257

—— none can always hit,   *Butl.* 1 : 44

—— and fortune learn from Cæfar,   *Add.* 285

—— on vigour and difpatch depends,   *Garth* 66

—— no mark of a good caufe,   *Cow.* 1 : 184

—— too oft to guilt is given,   *Rowe L.* 142

—— juftifies all quarrels,   *Butl.* 2 : 336

Succeffes, poem on, to lord Godolphin,   *Rowe* 8

Succeffion, every kind lives by,   *Dry.* 3 : 135

—— art of,   *Thom.* 2 : 119

Suck a bull,   *Butl.* 1 : 43

Suckling, anfwer to,   *Wall.* 117

Suds, leaves my lady in,   *Swift* 2 : 196

Suffering, higheft fortitude,   *Mih.* 2 : 138

Suffering is the lover's part,   { Gay 1 : 306 / Hughes 127

Sufferings shew the generous mind,   Tal. 352

——— each his,   Gray 333

——— foretold Christ,   Milt. 2 : 214, 217

——— precede exaltation,   Milt. 2 : 189

——— light, give leisure to complain,   Dry. 3 : 104

——— greater make us dumb,   Dry. 3 : 104

Suffolk, inscription for bust of lady,   Lytt. 95

Suitor-powers in games divide their hours,   Pope od. 3 : 133

Suitors, number and country,   Pope od. 4 : 80

——— injuries of,   Pope od. 3 : 89

——— who lay in wait for Telemachus return, Pope od. 4 : 87

——— consult to destroy Telemachus,   Pope od. 3 : 134

——— gifts of,   Pope od. 4 : 128

——— their destruction foretold,   Pope od. 4 : 175

——— challeng'd to bend Ulysses' bow,   Pope od. 4 : 179

——— death of,   Pope od. 4 : 197

Sulpicia to Cerinthus,   Lytt. 95, 96

Sultan populace,   Butl. 2 : 93

Summer, a pastoral,   Pope 1 : 31

——— child of the sun, refulgent,   Thom. 1 : 43

——— with russet robes adorn'd,   Hughes 192

——— evening,   Watts 367

——— house, inscription on,   West 320

——— islands, battle of,   Wall. 68

——— fault to leap,   Butl. 2 : 106

——— seas are turn'd by sudden winds,   Prior 1 : 224

Sun, hymn to,   Prior 1 : 59

——— ode to,   Fent. 197

Sun, faireſt regent of the ſkies.　　　　　　*Fent.* 198

—— hours, thy offspring,　　　　　　　　*Fent.* 198

—— gentle joys on Albion ſhed,　　　　　*Fent.* 198

—— deſcribed,　　　　　　　　　　　*Milt.* 1 : 93

—— a red-hot iron,　　　　　　　　　*Butl.* 1 : 252

—— Nature's eye,　　　　　　　　　　*Dry.* 4 : 129

—— fountain of light and colour, warmth and life, *Mall.* 197

—— joy of earth, and glory of the ſkies,　*Pope od.* 3 : 322

—— by whoſe attractive force, thy ſyſtem rolls, *Thom.* 1 : 47

—— informer of the planetary train,　　　*Thom.* 1 : 47

—— parent of ſeaſons,　　　　　　　　*Thom.* 1 : 47

—— mineral kinds confeſs thy mighty power, *Thom.* 1 : 48

—— by thee the deſart joys,　　　　　　*Thom.* 1 : 49

—— great delegated ſource of light and life,　*Thom.* 1 : 49

—— by his ray the reptile young come wing'd abroad, *id.* 51

—— raiſed high, to diſperſe light,　　　　*Wall.* 28

——————————— to moderate heat,　*Wall.* 28

—— twofold his courſe, yet conſtant his career, *Prior* 2 : 118

—— regularity of his motion,　　　　　　*Black.* 75

—— adds colours to the world,　　　　　*Dry.* 6 : 251

—— divides the months, nights, and days,　*Hughes* 296

—— ſtands ſtill,　　　　　　　　　　*Milt.* 2 : 128

—— goes back ten degrees,　　　　　　*Parn.* 231

—— backward held the falling day,　　　*Broome* 17

—— ſhifted his ſetting and riſe,　　　　*Butl.* 1 : 255

—— thy wonders ſhall proclaim,　　　　*Pitt* 236

—— moon and ſtars, praiſe the Lord,　　*Watts* 74

——————————— formed,　　*Milt.* 1 : 218

——————————— for ſeaſons and times, *Milt.* 1 : 219

—— all is grief, beneath,　　　　　　　*Pope ad.* 3 : 270

Sun eclipfed at Cæfar's death, *Butl.* 1 : 250

—— in darknefs veil'd his face, *Rowe L.* 72

—— Satan's addrefs to, *Milt.* 1 : 102

—— put down by ladies eyes, *Butl.* 1 : 187

—— of righteoufnefs arofe ! *Parn.* 206

———————— and bid the church adore, *Parn.* 206

Sunday, new milk and mackarel only, fold on, *King* 215

—— fhines, no fabbath-day to me, *Pope* 2 : 149

Sundays profan'd by mackarel cries, *Gay* 1 : 125

Sunderland, ode to the earl of, *Tick.* 197

—————— Spencer, a name familiar to Windfor, *Tick.* 197

Suns of glory pleafe not, till they fet, *Pope* 2 : 214

Superannuated lover, *Som.* 238

Superior woes, fuperior ftations bring, *Broome* 44

Supernaculum was their jeft, *King* 360

Superftition, tyrannefs abhor'd, *Aken.* 127

—————— effects of, *Shen.* 259

—————— enflaves the mind, *Pope* 1 : 120

—————— makes love blind, *Cow.* 2 : 106

—————— from thy breaft repel, *Gay* 1 : 107

—————— o'er philofo; hy prevails, *Cong.* 65

—————— fhar'd the tyranny, *Pope* 2 : 64

—————— gods of conquerors, flaves of fubjects made, *ib.*

—————— deep o'er-hung the fkies, *Pope* 2 : 17

—————— beneath whofe baleful dews the poppy fprung, *ib.*

—————— fways the bulk of mankind, *Buck.* 95

—————— baleful charms of, *Aken.* 41

Superftitions, practice of, *Dry.* 7 : 323

Superftitious virtue is vice, *Rofc.* 220

Supper, preparatory thoughts for the Lord's, *Watts* 143

Suppofures hypothetical,   *Butl.* 1 : 149

Sure-defence on God we build,   *Pitt* 240

Sure-judge, how empty all, who all had tried,   *Lytt.* 28

Surety for th' unjuft, fuffers, who gives,   *Pope od.* 3 : 216

Surfeit in grief,   *Milt.* 3 : 59

Surly bull, the pride of Hockley-hole,   *Gay* 1 : 125

Surprife, a difh,   *King* 183

Surprifes fureft conduct fhew in war,   *Garth* 70

Surrey, the Granville of a former age,   *Pope* 1 : 69

———— numbers glow'd with warm defire,   *Fent* 240

Survey thy foul, and find the beggar there,   *Dry.* 7 : 342

Sufpenfe in news, torture,   *Milt.* 3 : 59

Sufpicion, againft,   *Aken.* 199

———— meditating plagues unfeen,   *Aken.* 199

Suum cuique,   *Dry.* 1 : 225

Swains, Trojans all, and vow but to deceive,   *Gay* 1 : 31

Swallow, Anacreontic,   *Cow.* 1 : 149

Swallows, whither they go,   *Dry.* 2 : 68

Swan rows in ftate on the fifhy river,   *Fent.* 319

—— contented with an humbler fate,   *Fent.* 319

—— fings her own elegy,   *Dry.* 4 : 193

Swanfwick, barrifter of,   *Butl.* 2 : 7

Sway, fift in, as firft in virtue,   *Pope od.* 3 : 227

Swear, or ftarve,   *Dry.* 7 : 352

Swearing and curfing,   *Watts* 347

Sweet as a rofe her breath and lips,   *Gay* 1 : 272

——- babe, fair beauty's bud,   *Broome* 92

————- what fruits thy bloffoms fhall produce,   *Broome* 92

————- may no vice o'ercloud thy future day,   *Broome* 93

—— William's farewell, &c.   *Gay* 1 : 253

                                                     Sweeteft

Sweeteſt ſhe, who ſtinks the moſt,   *Prior* 2 : 64

———— before you ſee, you ſmell,   *Prior* 2 : 64

Sweetner, ſaſſafras,   *Garth* 40

Sweet-ſcented miſer,   *Som.* 388

Swift, his ode to Temple,   *Swift* 1 : 1

————— to the Athenian Society,   1 : 9

—— lines in a table-book,   1 : 20

—— Mrs. Harris's petition,   1 : 21

—— ballad on the game of traffic,   1 : 26

—— another,   1 : 28

—— the diſcovery,   1 : 29

—— problem,   1 : 31

—— deſcription of a ſalamander,   1 : 33

—— to the earl of Peterborow,   1 : 36

—— on the union,   1 : 37

—— on Mrs. Biddy Floyd,   1 : 38

—— Apollo outwitted,   1 : 39

—— Vanbrugh's houſe,   1 : 41

————————— hiſtory of,   1 : 46

—— Baucis and Philemon,   1 : 48

—— elegy on Partridge,   1 : 54

—— Merlin's prophecy,   1 : 58

—— deſcription of the morning,   1 : 59

———————— city ſhower,   1 : 60

—— on the houſe by Caſtleknock,   1 : 62

—— virtues of Sid Hamed's rod,   1 : 65

—— Atlas, or the miniſter of ſtate,   1 : 68

—— town eclogue,   1 : 69

—— fable of Midas,   1 : 71

—— new ſong,   1 : 74

Swift, Windsor prophecy,   *Swift* 1 : 77
—— epigrams,   1 : 77, 79, 99, 212 | 2 : 278, 346, 370
—— Corinna,   1 : 79
—— Toland's invitation to Difmal,   1 : 80
—— peace and Dunkirk,   ·1 : 82
—— Horace, Book i. Ep. vii.   1 : 84
———————— Book ii. Sat. vi.   1 : 89
—— on himfelf,   1 : 93
—— the faggot,   ·.   1 : 96
—— Catullus to Lefbia,   1 : 98
—— on a curate's complaint,   1 : 99
—— inventory of his goods,   1 : 100
—— Cadenus and Vaneffa,   ·1 : 101
—— to love,   1 : 131
—— ode to fpring,   1 : 132
———————— to wifdom,   1 : 133
—— a rebus,   ·1 : 134
—— Horace, Book ii. Ode i.   1 : 135
———————— Book i. Ep. v.   ·1 : 140
———————— Book iii. Ode ii.   1 : 152
———————— Book iv. Ode ix.   1 : 158
—— to Harley,   1 : 146
—— in ficknefs,   1 : 149
—— fable of the bitches,   1 : 150
—— Phyllis,   1 : 158
—— to Delany,   1 : 159
—— left-handed letter,   1 : 163
—— motto for Mr. Hafard,   1 : 164
—— to Sheridan,   1 : 165, 349
—— Stella's birth-day,   1 : 166, 168, 334

4

Swift, Sheridan to,	*Swift* 1 : 167
—— answer,	1 : 167.
—— to Stella,	1 : 170, 175, 291
—— elegy on Demar,	1 : 179.
—— epitaph on a miser,	1 : 181.
—— to Mrs. Houghton,	1 : 181
—— verses on windows,	1 : 182
—— Apollo to,	1 : 183
—— news from Parnassus,	1 : 186
—— run upon the bankers,	1 : 189
—— description of an Irish feast,	1 : 192
—— new song,	1 : 193
—— progress of beauty,	1 : 195
—————— poetry,	1 : 199
—— South-Sea,	1 : 200
—— dog and shadow,	1 : 209
—— to a friend,	1 : 209
—— billet to the players,	1 : 210
—— the prologue,	1 : 210.
—— prologue to a play,	1 : 212
—— epilogue,	1 : 214 .
—— poem,	1 : 216
—— on Gaulstown-house,	1 : 218 .
—— country life,	1 : 219
—— Sheridan to Nim-Dan-Dean,	1 : 224 .
—— answer,	1 : 225
—— Nim-Dan-Dean's invitation,	1 : 227
—— to Nim-Dan-Dean,	1 : 229
—— to Sheridan,	1 : 231, 250
—— on Sheridan's circular verses,	1 : 232

R 3

Swift, on Dan Jackson's picture,   *Swift* 1 : 233
———— verses on the same,   1 : 234, 235
———— Dan Jackson's defence,   1 : 236
———— Rochfort's reply,   1 : 238
———— Delany's reply,   1 : 241
———— Sheridan's reply,   1 : 242
———— rejoinder by,   1 : 243, 245
———— Sheridan's submission,   1 : 246
———— to Dan Jackson,   1 : 247
———— Stella to,   1 : 251
———— to Stella,   1 : 253
———— on the buried bottle,   1 : 253
———— epitaph,   1 : 254
———— satirical elegy,   1 : 257
———— Smedley's petition,   1 : 258
———— answer by,   1 : 262
———— verses by Stella,   1 : 264
———— jealousy,   1 : 264
———— Delany's villa,   1 : 264
———— on a window at Delville,   1 : 266
———— Carberiæ rupes,   1 : 267
———— Carbery rocks,   1 : 268
———— on the plot,   1 : 270
———— Stella at Woodpark,   1 : 273
———— copy of birth-day verses,   1 : 276
———— Joan cudgels Ned,   1 : 280
———— quibbling elegy,   1 : 281
———— Pethox the great,   1 : 283
———— Mary the cook-maid's letter,   ' 1 : 286
———— New-year's gift,   1 : 289
                                            Swift,

Swift, Dingley and Brent,   *Swift* 1 : 290

—— on dreams,   1 : 292

—— Whitſhed's motto,   1 : 294

—— verſes to,   1 : 295

—— anſwer,   1 : 295

—— a quiet life and a good name,   1 : 297

—— birth of Manly Virtue,   1 : 300

—— verſes on a judge,   1 : 305

————— on the ſame,   1 : 305

—— riddles,   1 : 306—331

—— receipt to reſtore Stella's youth,   1 : 332

—— epigram on Wood's braſs-money,   1 : 336

—— a ſimile,   1 : 337

—— Wood, an inſect,   1 : 338

—— on Wood, the iron-monger,   1 : 340

—— Will Wood's petition,   1 : 341

—— ſong on Wood's half-pence,   1 : 343

—— a ſerious ſong upon William Wood,   1 : 346

—— to Quilca,   1 : 351

—— bleſſings of a country life,   1 : 352

—— plagues of a country life,   1 : 352

—— Sheridan to,   1 : 352

—— anſwer,   1 : 353

—— portrait from the life,   1 : 354

—— on ſtealing a crown,   1 : 355

—— the ſtorm,   1 : 356

—— ode on ſcience,   1 : 359

—— on Stella's birth-day,   2 : 1

—— Horace, Book i. Ode xiv.   2 : 4

—— on St. Patrick's well ſudden drying up,   2 : 7

Swift, on Young's Univerfal Paffion,   *Swift* 2 : 13

——— dog and thief,   2 : 15

——— Grubftreet writers, advice to,   2 : 16

——— to a lady,   2 : 17

——— young lady's complaint,   2 : 27

——— letter to the Dean,   2 : 28

——— Palinodia, Horace, Book i. Ode xvi.   2 : 31

——— Bec's birth-day,   2 : 33

——— on Tiger's collar,   2 : 35

——— epigrams on windows,   2 : 35—38

——— to Janus,   2 : 39

——— paftoral dialogue,   2 : 40, 64

——— defire and poffeffion,   2 · 45

——— on cenfure,   2 : 47

——— furniture of a woman's mind,   2 : 48

——— Tom Clinch going to be hanged,   2 : 50

——— to Pope,   2 : 51

——— love poem by a phyfician,   2 : 52

——— at Sir Arthur Achefon's,   2 : 54

——— on an old glafs,   2 : 55

——— anfwer extempore,   2 : 55

——— on cutting down the old thorn,   2 : 56

——— my lady's lamentation and complaint,   2 : 60

——— on the five ladies at Sot's hole,   2 : 67

——— five ladies' anfwer,   2 : 69

——— beau's reply,   2 : 70

——— journal of a modern lady,   2 : 71

——— a dialogue,   2 : 81

——— Tim and the fables,   2 : 90

——— Tom Mullinix and Dick,   2 : 91

                                                     Swift,

Swift, Dick, a maggot,   *Swift* 2 : 93

—— clad all in brown,   2 : 94

—— Dick's variety,   2 : 95

—— epitaph on general Gorges and lady Meath,   2 : 96

—— verses on I know not what,   2 : 97

—— complaint on his deafness,   2 : 98

—— to himself, on St. Cecilia's day,   2 : 99

—— Paddy's character of the Intelligencer,   2 : 99

—— parody on a character of Smedley,   2 : 101

—— Paulus,   2 : 103

—— answer,   2 : 103

—— dialogue,   2 : 109

—— on burning a dull poem,   2 : 111

—— epistle to lord Carteret,   2 : 112

—— epistle upon an epistle,   2 : 116

—— libel on Delany and Carteret,   2 : 121

—— to Delany,   2 : 128

—— directions for a birth-day song,   2 : 134

—— bouts rimés,   2 : 143

—— helter skelter,   2 : 145

—— logicians refuted,   2 : 147

—— puppet-show,   2 : 149

—— grand question debated,   2 : 152

—— to the Dean,   2 : 159

—— Drapier's-hill,   2 : 160

—— reasons for not building at Drapier's-hill,   2 : 161

—— panegyric on,   2 : 165

—— twelve articles,   2 : 178

—— revolution at Market-hill,   2 : 179

—— Traulus, part i.   2 : 183

                                       Swift,

Swift, Traulus, part ii.   *Swift* 2 : 187

———— Robin and Harry,   2 : 189

———— to Betty the Grifette,   2 : 191

———— Death and Daphne,   2 : 192

———— Daphne,   2 : 196

———— pheafant and lark,   2 : 198

———— anfwer,   2 : 203

———— on the Irifh club,   2 : 207

———— progrefs of marriage,   2 : 208

———— a new ballad,   2 : 214

———— on Stephen Duck,   2 : 217

———— lady's drefling-room,   2 : 218

———— power of time,   2 : 223

———— on Pulteney's being out of the council,   2 : 223

———— epitaph on duke of Schomberg,   2 : 225

———— Caffinus and Peter,   2 : 226

———— a beautiful young nymph going to bed,   2 : 230

———— Stephen and Chloe,   2 : 233

———— Apollo,   2 : 243

———— place of the damned,   2 : 245

———— Judas,   2 : 246

———— epiftle to Gay,   2 : 247

———— on the Irifh bifhops,   2 : 253

———— on his death,   2 : 255

———— his works with moral views defign'd,   2 : 273

———— to pleafe and to reform mankind,   2 : 273

———— epiftle to two friends,   2 : 274

———— Helfham's anfwer to,   2 : 276

———— prefent to,   2 : 279

———— verfes to,   2 : 280

    Swift,

Swift, verfes occafioned by the preceding,   *Swift* 2 : 281

—— beaft's confeffion,   2 : 282

—— advice to a parfon,   2 : 289

——- parfon's cafe,   2 : 290

——- hardfhip upon the ladies,   2 : 291

—— love fong,   2 : 292

—— on the words, brother proteftants,   2 : 293

—— Yahoo's overthrow,   2 : 296

—— on the archbifhop of Cafhel,   2 : 299

—— on poetry,   2 : 300

—— Horace, Book iv. Ode xix.   2 : 316

—— new fimile for the ladies,   2 : 319

—— anfwer,   2 : 322

—— vindication of the libel,   2 : 328

—— friendly apology,   2 : 330

—— Sheridan's ballad on Ballyfpellin,   2 : 332

—— anfwer,   2 : 335

—— Horace, part of Book i. Sat. vi.   2 : 337

—— on a printer's being fent to Newgate,   2 : 339

—— day of judgement,   2 : 339

—— verfes to the Dean on his birth-day,   2 : 340

—— on Pfyche,   2 : 343

—— Dean and Duke,   2 : 343

—— on Dr. Rundle,   2 : 344

—— charaĉter, &c. of the legion-club,   2 : 347

—— an apology, &c.   2 : 355

——- Dean's manner of living,   2 : 361

—— verfes made for fruit-women,   2 : 361

—— on Rover, a fpaniel,   2 : 364

——- ay and no,   2 : 366

Swift,

Swift, anfwer to a friend's queftion,   *Swift* 2 : 366

———— Apollo's edict,   2 : 367

———— on birth-day,   2 : 371

———— epiftle to Nugent,   2 : 374

———— infcription for the Dean's monument,   2 : 378

———— epigram, occafioned by it,   2 : 378

———— makes a wretch fhift to deafen with puns and rhyme, 1 : 27

———— had the fin of wit,   1 : 94

———— humour and mirth in all he writ,   1 : 94

———— reconcil'd Divinity and Wit,   1 : 94

———— turns to politics his dangerous wit,   1 : 94

———— not the graveft of divines,   2 : 1

———— on the death of,   2 : 255

———— on his birth-day,   *Parn.* 275

———— in judgement folid, as in wit refin'd,   *Parn.* 275

———— how fure you wound, when ironics deride,   *Parn.* 276

———— for clofer ftyle,   *Pope* 2 : 273

———— Hibernian politics, thy fate,   *Pope* 3 : 206

———— fav'd the rights, a court attack'd,   *Pope* 2 : 225

Swifs Cantons, feat of liberty,   *Thom.* 2 : 92

———— ficknefs,   *Thom.* 2 : 92

———— no longer pay, no longer friend,   *Gay* 2 : 160

———— fight on any fide for pay,   *Dry.* 2 : 58

Swinifh gluttony ne'er looks to heaven,   *Milt.* 3 : 148

———————————— crams and blafphemes his feeder, *id.* 148

Swithin nor Paul rule the clouds and winds,   *Gay* 1 : 107

Swold mutton, what,   *King* 182

Sword of violence fhall right confound,   *Rowe L.* 79

———— o'er Noble and Plebeian rang'd,   *Rowe L.* 87

Swore, how he fwore,   *Swift* 2 : 297

                                                        Sydney's

Sydney's verfe halts ill on Roman feet,   *Pope* 2 : 219
Syene, where Meridian funs no fhadow give,   *Rowe L.* 111
Sylla, Pompey's mafter,   *Rowe L.* 61
—— with no lefs cruelty returns,   *Rowe L.* 89
—— to crufh a hated faction fought,   *Rowe L.* 93
Sylphs, dæmons of air, well-conditioned,   *Pope* 1 : 126
—— and Sylphids, the aerial kind,   *Pope* 1 : 135
—————————— who tend the fair,   *Pope* 1 : 135
—— as when women, are mighty fond of place,   *Pope* 1 : 139
—— and Gnomes, are but a woman's heart,   *Parn.* 54
Sylvia, of,   *Wall.* 92
Sympathetic fpeed,   *Butl.* 1 : 17
Sympofium of Julian, Varronian fatire,   *Dry.* 7 : 163
Synalepha, what,   *Dry.* 3 : 292
Synod, a fair,   *Butl.* 1 : 142
Synods fhew a zeal for nothings,   *Garth* 22
—— myftical bear-gardens,   *Butl.* 1 : 140
—— whelps of inquifition,   *Butl.* 1 : 142
Syracufans effaced the memory of tyrants,   *Cow.* 2 : 221
Syria, ifland of, defcribed,   *Pope od.* 4 : 61
Syrinx changed to reeds,   *Dry.* 3 : 330
Syrtes faithlefs, as the moving fands,   *Pope* 1 : 323
—— mountains of fand,   *Pitt* 277
Syrts defcribed,   *Rowe L.* 387
Syftems only form'd, to difagree,   *Prior* 2 : 39

T

Tabernacle fet up,   *Milt.* 2 : 127
Tabitha, reputation of for fpeed,   *Som.* 131
—— fall of,   *Som.* 133

Table,

Table, not more than seven at,   *King* 212

—— not lefs than three,   *King* 212

Tables, like pictures to the fight,   *King* 219

Tænarus gives paſſage to the realms below,   *Pitt* 213

—— whence cries and groans, and din of hell are heard, *ib.*

Tages taught to abuſe mankind,   *Rowe L.* 77

Tail ſteers birds and fiſhes,   *Butl.* 2 : 75

—— of worſhip,   *Butl.* 1 : 78

Tails meant for ornament,   *Butl.* 1 : 182

Taint, left by Adam on all,   *Dry.* 2 : 193

Talbot, to Gallia's power eternal foe,   *Prior* 1 : 257

—— chancellor, to memory of,   *Thom.* 2 : 164

—— in him we ſaw the piercing eye,   *Thom.* 2 : 164

———————— the virtues and the force of Rome, *ib.*

—— deſpiſing frowns or ſmiles of power,   *Thom.* 2 : 167

Tale, the whiſper of the babbling vulgar,   *Smith* 104

—— all who told, added ſomething new,   *Pope* 1 : 224

—— is blunt, but honeſt is my mind,   *Pope* 1 : 252

—— from falſehood free, not free from woe,   *Pope od.* 4 : 56

Talent diſcern, and Jove's laws adore,   *Fent.* 319

Talents miſapply'd and croſt, Nature's intent is foil'd, *Gay* 2 : 182

———————— a taylor or a butcher ſpoil'd, *id.* 182

—— for converſation fit,   *Swift* 1 : 159

—— humour, breeding, ſenſe, and wit,   *Swift* 1 : 159

Tales, not true nor falſe, till heard,   *Butl.* 1 : 282

—— the lenitives of age,   *Young* 1 : 197

Talgol deſcribed,   *Butl.* 1 : 59

—— prowefs of,   *Butl.* 1 : 59

Taliacotius ingrafts noſes, &c.   *Butl.* 1 : 19

Taliſmanic louſe,   *Butl.* 1 : 289

Talk,

Talk, food of the mind, *Milt.* 2 : 11

—— moſt, who have the leaſt to ſay, *Prior* 2 : 60

Talking wife, that prime ill, *Prior* 2 : 61

Tallard, unhappy in death of his ſon, *Add.* 63

———————— in rout of his troops, *Add.* 63

———————— in his own bondage, *Add.* 63

—— the chief, the father, and the captive wept, *Add.* 63

—— greatly diſtreſt ! *Add.* 63

—— ill abides his boaſt, *Phil.* 13

Talus, ſtory of, *Broome* 105

—— a giant, ſprung from giant-race, *Broome* 105

Tamarind, fever-cooling fruit, *Thom.* 1 : 66

Tame elephant inveigles the wild, *Butl.* 1 : 72

—— ſtag, *Gay* 2 : 51

Tamerlane, prologue to, *Garth* 115

Tantalus a doleful lot abides, *Fent.* 270

—— pines with thirſt amidſt the waves, *Pope ed.* 3 : 301

Tapeſtry, taught by the Saracens, *Dyer* 99

———— antiquity of, *Dyer* 99

———— of Blenheim, deſcribed, *Dyer* 98

Taphians, a duteous people and induſtrious iſle, *Pope ed.* 3 : 46

———— to naval arts inur'd, and ſtormy toil, *Pope ed.* 3 : 46

Tarchon leads the Tuſcans, *Dry.* 6 : 223

—— joins the Trojans, *Dry.* 6 : 277

—— author of the roving war, *Rowe L.* 382

—— reprov'd by Cato, . *Rowe L.* 382

Tardy juſtice will o'ertake the crime, *Dry.* 3 : 148

Tarentum famous for its wool, *Dyer* 68

Tarquin and Tullia, *Dry.* 1 : 220

Tartarus deſcribed, *Broome* 145

Tartary,

Tartary, deferts of,   *Mall.* 208

Tafk delightful! to rear the tender thought,   *Thom.* 1 : 42

———————————— to teach the young idea how to fhoot, *id.* 42

——- hard, to queftion wifely men of years,   *Pope od.* 3 : 82

Taffo regular in the unities,   *Dry.* 7 : 115

—— unhappy in his action,   *Dry.* 7 : 115

—— too lyrical,   *Dry.* 7 : 115

—— full of conceits and points,   *Dry.* 7 : 115

—— in his Amyntas, exceeds Paftor fido,   *Dry.* 5 : 18

—— tranflation from,   *King* 425

—— of duchefs, verfes writ in,   *Wall.* 200

Tafte, what,   *Aken.* 79

—— progrefs of,   *Shen.* 215

——- that eternal wanderer,   *Pope* 2 : 230

—— talk what you will of, you'll find,   *Pope* 2 : 253

—— two of a face, as foon as of a mind,   *Pope* 2 : 253

—— may erf,   *Gay* 2 : 194

—— different may pleafe, different vermin,   *Gay* 2 : 195

—— to lead through the maze of,   *King* 216

Tautology, great prophet of,   *Dry.* 2 : 110

Taxes appear like legal duns,   *Gay* 1 : 206

Taylor, once fwan of Thames,   *Pope* 3 : 172

Tea, of,   *Wall.* 161

—— aids fancy,   *Wall.* 161

—— repreffes vapours,   *Wall.* 161

—— to talk of modes and fcandal, over,   *Pitt* 269

——- and run through all the female politics,   *Pitt* 269

Tea-table,   *Gay* 1 : 228

Tears againft,   *Watts* 216

—— the eloquence of forrow,   *Sav.* 33

                                                        Tears,

Tears, sign of contrition, _Milt._ 2 : 82
———— sooth the soul's distress, _Young_ 3 : 184
———— heart-relieving, _Mall._ 280
———— make sorrow bright, _Pope_ 1 : 349
———— silver drops, like morning dew, _Pope_ 1 : 349
———— flow nobly, shed for all mankind, _Tick._ 117
———— from sweet Virtue's source, benevolent to all, _Lytt._ 69
———— rain'd copious in a shower of joy, _Pope od._ 4 : 71
———— but indulge the sorrow, not repress, _Pope od._ 4 : 124
———— in mortal miseries are vain, _Pope od._ 3 : 158
———— none suffice, a dying world to weep, _Rowe L._ 317
———— heart's disguise, _Roch._ 284
Teeth, twofold hedge of, _Prior_ 2 : 67
Telamon in twelve ships leads the Salaminians, _Pope il._ 1 : 89
Telemachus, the care of Pallas, _Pope od._ 3 : 42
——————— goes in quest of Ulysses, _Pope od._ 3 : 43
——————— sets sail in quest of his father, _Pope od._ 3 : 76
——————— arrives at Pylos, _Pope od._ 3 : 81
——————— under the conduct of Minerva, _Pope od._ 3 : 81
——————— finds Nestor sacrificing on the shore, _id._ 3 : 81
——————— is lodg'd by Nestor, _Pope od._ 3 : 98
——————— with Pisistratus set out for Sparta, _Pope od._ 3 : 101
——————————— arrives at Sparta, _Pope od._ 3 : 105
——————— entertain'd by Menelaus, _Pope od._ 3 : 107
——————— return'd, _Pope od._ 4 : 65
——————— repairs to Eumæus, _Pope od._ 4 : 67
——————— relates his travels, _Pope od._ 4 : 95
Telescopes enlarge our knowledge, _Cw._ 1 : 219
Tell-tale out of school, of wits the greatest fool, _Swft_ 2 : 242
Tempe, fam'd in song, _Lytt._ 21

Temperance, good effects of,   Milt. 2 : 102, 103

———— gives health,   Pope 2 : 185

Temperate sleeps, and spirits light as air,   Pope 2 : 185

Tempest described,   { Dry. 5 : 316 / Pitt 276

———— enough to live in, die in port,   Young 2 : 113

Temple (Sir William), ode to,   Swift 1 : 1

———— verses on Miss,   Cong. 149

———— of Death,   Buck. 11

———— of Fame,   Pope 1 : 201

———————— seated high, on a rock of ice,   Pope 1 : 202

Temples cast a lustre on the throne,   Young 3 : 151

Temptation, not to be despised,   Milt. 2 : 73

Temptations throng, thicker than arguments,   Pope 2 : 44

Ten censure wrong, for one who writes amiss,   Pope 1 : 91

——— commandments,   Watts 356

——— tribes, fall and restoration,   Milt. 2 : 197

Tender conscience, what,   Butl. 1 : 317

Tenderness and social love, holiest of things,   Aken. 43

———————————— by which all things are link'd,   ib. 43

Term fix'd to all the race of earth,   Pope il. 1 : 212

Terrenes what,   King 183

Terrours, that wither'd even the strong,   Pope il. 2 : 37

Teucer slays many Trojans,   Pope il. 1 : 250

———— screen'd by his brother Ajax,   Pope il. 1 : 250

Teutates dire, human blood demands,   Rowe L. 67

Texts, to cap,   Butl. 2 : 58

Thales, founder of the Ionic school,   Black. 10

Thame and Isis,   King 426

Thames, Isis and Thame, authors of his name,   Pope 1 : 71

Thames

Thames defcribed,   { *Den.* 13 / *Dyer* 102

————— addrefs to,   *Crw.* 1 : 198

————— England's pride,   *Hal.* 219

————— mild and ferene,   *Hal.* 220

————— boaft of merchants, and the failor's theme, *A. Phil.* 342

————— richer than Pactolus' ftreams,   *Saw.* 108

————— up, the world's abundance flows,   *Tick.* 132

————— with gentle courfe devolving fruitfulnefs, *Prior* 1 : 172

————— rich prefents in his hand, traverfes the land, *Hughes* 18

————— ferene, with fruitful tide,   *Hughes* 150

————— free from extremes of ebb and flow,   *Hughes* 150

————— foft and ftill, the filver furface glides,   *Cong.* 26

————— great father of the Britifh floods,   *Pope* 2 : 65

————— future navies on thy fhores appear,   *Pope* 2 : 65

————— had a Churchill, Heber, Mare,   *Fent.* 199

————— roll, fovereign of the ftreams,   *Fent.* 199

Thammuz, a Syrian god,   *Milt.* 1 : 20

————— called Adonis,   *Milt.* 1 : 20

Thamyris, whofe pride defy'd the Mufes,   *Pope il.* 1 : 91

Thanks, enlarg'd by gladnefs, and infpir'd with love, *Parn.* 153

Tharfis deem'd Portugal,   *Dyer* 156

Thaw, defcription of,   { *Gay* 1 : 124 / *Thom.* 1 : 187

Theatre in the Hay-market, Epilogue in,   *Cong.* 83

Thebais of Statius,   *Pope* 1 : 273

Theban friends, Pelopidas and Epaminondas,   *Thom.* 2 : 51

————— Pindar's lofty ftrain,   *Swift* 2 : 317

Thebans, of a flavifh difpofition,   *Aken.* 295

————— of remarkable dulnefs,   *Aken.* 295

The

Thebe sacred to Apollo's name,   *Pope il.* 1 : 53

Thebes, with a hundred gates,   *Pope il.* 1 : 281

———— great empress on the Egyptian plain, *Pop: il.* 1 : 281

———— by alternate sway to govern,   *Pope* 1 : 285

Theme chuse proportion'd to your Muse,   *Pitt* 307

———— each to have a proper stile,   *Dry.* 1 : 263

Themis, prophecy of,   *Gay* 1 : 330

———— who humbles, or confirms the wise, *Pope od.* 3 : 63

———— then could speak in polish'd prose,   *Fent.* 237

Thenot, Colinet,   *A. Phil.* 301

Theocritus excels in simplicity,   *Pope* 1 : 20

———— deficient in manners,   *Pope* 1 : 21

———— his dialect has a secret charm,   *Pope* 1 : 21

———— inimitable by a Roman,   *Dry.* 5 : 17

———— translations from,   *Dry.* 4 : 299

———— Cyclops of,   *Duke* 99

Theodore and Honoria,   *Dry.* 3 : 241

Theoxenia, what,   *West* 155

Thermopylæ, the famed pass,   *Thom.* 2 : 41

Theron praised,   *Cow.* 2 : 13

———— hospitable, just, and great,   *West* 146

———— so fam'd for bounteous deeds, and love of mankind, *ib.* 154

———— fam'd Agrigentum's honour'd king,   *West* 154

Thersites, loud and turbulent of tongue,   *Pope il.* 1 : 75

———— aw'd by no shame, by no respect control'd, *id.* 1 : 75

———— in scandal busy, in reproaches bold,   *Pope il.* 1 : 75

———— glories, the great to lash,   *Pope il.* 1 : 75

———— his figure such, as might his soul proclaim, *id.* 1 : 76

———— much he hated all, but most the best, *Pope il.* 1 : 76

———— royal scandal, his delight supreme,   *Pope il.* 1 : 76

                                            Thersites,

Therfites, who acts the leaft, upbraids the moft, *Pope il.* 1 : 77

————— by the dam from lordlings fprung, *Tick.* 225

————— by the fire exhal'd from dung, *Tick.* 225

Thefeus, endued with more than mortal might, *Pope il.* 1 : 48

Thefpis, inventor of tragedy, *Dry.* 7 : 142

————— firft exhibited tragedy, *Rofc.* 269

————— fung ballads from a cart, *Dry.* 2 : 239

Theffaly defcribed,. *Rowe L.* 263

————— mountains of, *Rowe L.* 263

————— rivers of, *Rowe L.* 264

————— inhabitants of, *Rowe L.* 265

————— famous for forcery,. *Rowe L.* 268

————— abounds in herbs for charms, *Rowe L.* 268

————— an invective againft, *Rowe L.* 326

Thetis, filver-footed queen, { *Tick.* 184 / *Pope il.* 1 : 61

————— filver-footed dame, *Pope il.* 2 : 185

————— preferves Patroclus' body from corruption, *id.* 2 : 196

————— obtains from Achilles Hector's body, *Pope Il.* 2 : 333

Thick lips, the fate of Auftria,. *Tick.* 142

Thief, { *Cow.* 1 : 252 / *Watts* 363

————— and cordelier, *Prior* 1 : 273

Thieves never feel the quiet hour,. *Gay* 2 : 80

————— afcendant in the cart, *Butl.* 1 : 236

Thing of things ! *Swift* 2 : 69

————— impoffible, *Cong.* 169

Things below capricious ftate of, *Hughes* 277

————— changeful, no fix'd duration know, *Hughes* 277

————— beft, grow by corruption worft, *King* 262

S 3

Third,

Thirſt, which virtuous envy breeds, *Pope il.* 1 : 45

———— of glory, quells the love of life, *Add.* 60

———— of fame, vice of great ſouls, *Tick.* 107

———— of boundleſs ſway, greatly to ſcorn, *Tick.* 119

———— and pale Famine, Death's forms, ariſe, *Rowe L.* 175

Thirty, to a lady of, *Broome* 91

———— reigns a toaſt at, *Broome* 91

Thiſbe had charms unequal'd in the Eaſt, *Hughes* 58

———— falls on Pyramus's ſword, *Hughes* 63

———— her beauty, *Cow.* 1 : 55

Thiſtles wear the ſoftest down, *Butl.* 2 : 325

Thoas leads the Etolians in forty ſhips, *Pope il.* 1 : 93

Thomas, Angelic doctor, *Butl.* 1 : 12

Thomſon, Spring, *Thom.* 1 : 3

———————— Summer, 1 : 43

———————— Autumn, 1 : 106

———————— Winter, 1 : 153

———————— a hymn, 1 : 191

———————— Caſtle of indolence, 1 : 199

———————— Britannia, 2 : 1

———————— ancient and modern Italy, 2 : 13

———————— Greece, 2 : 33

———————— Rome, 2 : 57

———————— Britain, 2 : 79

———————— Liberty, a poem, 2 : 13

———————— the proſpect, 2 : 129

———————— Newton, a poem ſacred to, 2 : 157

———————— Talbot, a poem ſacred to, 2 : 164

———————— Wales, prince, poem to, 2 : 176

———————— Aikman, verſes on death of, 2 : 177

Thomson, ode, Thom. 2 : 178

——— Stanley, epitaph on Miss, 2 : 179

——— Murdoch, verses to, 2 : 181

——— Matthew, paraphrase on 6th chapter, 2 : 181

——— Doctor, the incomparable soporific, 2 : 182

——— happy man, 2 : 183

——— wooden bridge at Westminster, 2 : 185

——— songs, 2 : 185—188

——— nuptial song, 2 : 189

——— Ode, 2 : 190

——— to Seraphina, 2 : 191

——— on Æolus's harp, 2 : 192

——— hymn on solitude, 2 : 193

——— prologue to Mustapha, 2 : 195

——— Dennis to, 2 : 196

——— epitaph on, 2 : 197

——— Seasons are his monuments of fame, 2 : 197

——— ode on death of, Collins 281

——— epistle to, on his Seasons, Som. 222

Thorn cut down, Swift 2 : 56

Thornhill, on his rape of Helen, Pitt 205

——— thy swift art imitates Nature's work, Pitt 206

——— thy figures give the passion, they seem to feel, Pitt 206

——— unite the pleasing discord of shade and light, Pitt 209

Thought, quickness of, Black. 209

——— retrieves the spirits of the brave, Pope il. 2 : 8

——— must delineate thought, Hughes 271

——— who indulges, encreases pain, Prior 2 : 127

——— brings the weight, that sinks the soul, Prior 2 : 155

——— of death, shall like a god inspire, Young 2 : 53

Thought of death alone, the fear deſtroys,   *Young* 2 : 113

———————— heaves us from the duſt,   *Young* 2 : 114

——————— each nobler, now buried in luxury or avarice, *Aken.* 351

——————— lengthen'd, gleaming through many a page, *Pope* 2 : 219

Thoughtleſs mortals ! ever blind to fate,   *Pope* 1 : 141

Thoughts, quickneſs of,   *Den.* 139

——————— tormentors,   *Milt.* 3 : 28

——————— of labour paſt, increaſe joy,   *Phil.* 73

——————— of glory paſt, loſer's greateſt curſe,   *Rowe* 12

——————— what debaſe, and what exalt the ſoul,   *Sav.* 8

——————— veering, loſt between good and ill,   *Thom.* 1 : 189

——————— the ſoul, deeds the body train,   *Parn.* 103

——————— raiſed on truth, as on a rock ſhall ſtand, *Lanſ.* 233

——————— that breathe,   *Gray* 349

——————— that earthly pomp deſpiſe,   *Sav.* 22

Thouſand miſeries we feel, till ſunk in miſery, *Young* 3 : 123

Thouſands err, when few may know,   *Milt.* 1 : 178

——————— to murder, gives immortal fame,   *Young* 1 : 160

Thunder-ſtorm,   *Mail.* 200

Thraldom of love,   *Cow.* 1 : 226

Thracian courſers deſcribed,   *Dry.* 7 : 51

Thracians tame the ſavage horſe,   *Pope il.* 2 : 3

Threats urge the fearful,   *Pope il.* 1 : 367

——————— ſinner oft hard to,   *Dry.* 3 : 208

Three, ineffable, coequal,   *Tom.* 327

Threnodia Auguſtalis,   *Dry.* 1 : 298

Thriſty nature how little craves,   *Rowe L.* 130

——————— no great coſt requires,   *Som.* 256

Throne made a ſtye,   *Milt.* 2 : 204

——————— fatal to two contending kings,   *Pope* 1 : 276

         Thus, &c.

Thrones, the penance and the guilt of tyrants,   *Fent.* 218

Thule, fable of,   *A. Phil.* 375

Thumbs bent back, to kill,   *Dry.* 7 : 234

Thunder, composition of,   *Dry.* 6 : 215

————— marrs small beer and weak discourse, *Young* 1 : 109

————— rumbling from the mustard-bowl,   *Pope* 3 : 148

————— and lightning, use of,   *Black.* 92

Thunder-storm described,   *Thom.* 1 : 81

————————— effects of,   *Thom.* 1 : 81, 85

Thursday,   *Gay* 1 : 73

Thyrsis,   *Walsh* 100

————— and Delia,   *Lans.* 158

Thyself revere, and yet thyself despise,   *Young* 2 : 134

Tiber, dear to Rome,   *Rowe L.* 103

————— encourages Æneas,   *Dry.* 6 : 197

————— his neglected wave mournfully rolls,   *Dyer* 7

Tiberius, old and lascivious,   *Milt.* 2 : 204

Tibullus writes from the heart to the heart,   *Ham.* 204

————— parts of an elegy of,   *Lytt.* 50

Tick, to fight upon,   *Butl.* 1 : 129

Tickell, poems of,   *Tick.* 95

————— to the supposed author of the Spectator,   95

————— poem on prospect of peace,   97

————— to Addison, on his Rosamond,   115

————————————— on his Cato,   117

————— the royal progress,   118

————— imitation of Nereus's prophecy,   124

————— epistle from a lady, &c.   127

————— an ode,   134

————— prologue,   136

Tickell, original picture of Charles I. 138

———— fragment of a poem on hunting, . 140

———— Apollo making love, 146

———— fatal curiofity, 147

———— defcription of the Phœnix, 147

——————————————— from Claudian, . 148

———— verfes to Mrs. Lowther, . 153

———— to a lady with flowers, 154

———— on a lady's picture, 155

———— part of Lucan's 4th book tranflated, 156

———— firft book of Homer tranflated, 161

———— to earl of Warwick, on Addifon's death, . 187

———— Colin and Lucy, . 191

———— to Kneller, 194

———— on the death of earl of Cadogan, . 196

———— ode to the earl of Sunderland, . 197

———— Kenfington-garden, 200

———— to a lady before marriage, . 218

———— on the horn-book, . 221

———— Therfites, 225

Tide to fave, . Butl. 2 : 25

——— of life, various flows, . Weft 149

——————— obnoxious ftill to Fortune's veering gale, Weft 149

——————— now rough with anguifh, care, and ftrife, Weft 149

——————— now glides ferene and fmooth, . Weft 149

Tides, ufes of, Black. 61

———— actuated by the moon, . Black. 63

———— myfterious flow of, Dry. 1 : 88

———— of luft, that fwell their boiling veins, Pope od. 4 : 168

Ties from conftraint can never bind, Lanf. 255

Tillage, .

Tillage, different kinds of,   *Dry.* 5 : 94

Tiger, king playing with,   *Pitt* 280

———— a lap-dog, motto on his collar, .   *Swift* 2 : 35

Tigris and Euphrates join their ftreams,   *Rowe L.* 133

———————————— and foon divide, .   *Row: L.* 133

Tim and the Fables,   *Swift* 2 : 90

Timbrels lively pleafure gave, .   *Parn.* 113

Time,   *Milt.* 3 : 93

———— in perpetual flux, .   *Dry.* 4 : 142

———— all things obey,   *Dry.* 4 : 150

———— fire of years,   *Parn.* 133

———— power of, .   *Swift* 2 : 223

———— 'twixt inftant now, and fate's approach, is all, *Prior* 2 : 17

———— what, compar'd with long eternity,   *Parn.* 116

———— no change of motion knows,   *Fent.* 324

———— gently affuages pain, .   *Prior* 2 : 141

———— for all things,   *Milt.* 2 : 189

———— than gold more facred,   *Young* 2 : 20

———— more a load than lead to fools, .   *Young* 2 : 20

———— its worth afk death-beds,   *Young* 2 : 21

———— we wafte, not ufe,   *Young* 2 : 24

———— redeem we,   *Young* 2 : 21

———— this fubtle thief of life,   *Pope* 2 : 242

———— the father, who produces all,   *A. Phil.* 389

———— appointed Lord of all futurity,   *Cong.* 21

———— lays kings and kingdoms wafte,   *Cong.* 23

———— appears a moment, as it is,   *Young* 3 : 46

———— imperious judge,   *Aken.* 217

———— above revenge, or fear or pity juft,   *Aken.* 217

———— hung his unexpanded wings,   *Broome* 18

Time, univerfal cure of every grief,   *Buck.* 14

—— the wretch's friend,   *Mall.* 238

—— life's great phyfician,   *Mall.* 238

—— high time, to fhift this difmal fcene,   *Young* 2 : 55

—— once loft, is never found,   *Gay* 2 : 180

—— truly underftood, the moft precious earthly good, *id.* 180

—— we never can recal,   *King* 309

—— fure deftroyer, filent and flow,   *Mall.* 171

——that makes you homely, make you fage,   *Parn.* 64

—— relentlefs ! power deftroying !   *Parn.* 73

—— impairs all things,   *Rofc.* 257

—— the fubtle thief of life,   *Pope* 2 : 242

—— confumes alike the afhes and the urn,   *Hughes* 208

—— the blooming outfide will decay,   *King* 286

—— born of Fate,   *Aken.* 301

—— devouring many fons,   *Aken.* 301

—— conquers all, and we muft Time obey,   *Pope* 1 : 43

—— alike brings to duft mankmd,   *Buck.* 17

—— only can mature the labouring brain,   *Young* 3 : 204

—— the father, and the midwife, pain,   *Young* 3 : 204

—— on this head has fnow'd,   *Young* 2 : 111

—— powder'd o'er his head with fnow,   *Som.* 290

—— changes thought,   *Prior* 1 : 224

—— loftinefs abafes,   *Dyer* 68

—— lifts the low, and level lays the lofty,   *Dyer* 4

—— as well as Cupid is blind,   *Prior* 1 : 31

—— to kill, dire labour, and weary woe,   *Thom.* 1 : 223

—— if trifling kills, fure vice muft butcher,   *Young* 2 : 29

—— of all burdens, feems moft galling,   *Gay* 2 : 174

—— Death, and Friendfhip,   *Young* 2 : 19

Time and Industry bring our wishes nearer,   *Prior* 1 : 223

—— and Thought, those foes to fair ones,   *Pope* 2 : 109

—— and Tide, for no man stay,   *Som.* 391

—— riddle on,   *Swift* 1 : 325

Times in the hand of God,   *Milt.* 2 : 189

—— on,   *Buck.* 106

Timon, Silli of,   *Dry.* 7 : 145

Timotheus touch'd the lyre,   *Hughes* 175

—————— began the song from Jove,   *Hughes* 175

—————— could swell the soul to rage, or kindle soft desire, *ib.*

—————— rais'd a mortal to the skies,   *Hughes* 180

Tin, Britain famous for,   *Dyer* 68

Tindal, who virtue and the church alike disowns, *Pope* 2 : 207

Tiresias, oraculous seer,   *Fent.* 248

—————— transformed,   *Add.* 157

—————— rises from the shades,   *Pope od.* 3 : 279

—————— relates Ulysses' future fate,   *Pope od.* 3 : 281

—————— phantom-prophet,   *Pope od.* 3 : 283

Tirzah, a regal place,   *Parn.* 211

Tisiphone described,   *Pope* 1 : 282

—————— one of the Furies,   *Dry.* 6 : 138

Titans of portentous size,   *Broome* 143

—— rush'd with fury uncontrol'd,   *Broome* 143

—— fell from the realms above,   *Broome* 146

Tithe-pig metropolitan,   *Butl.* 1 : 145

Tithonus to a grashopper contracted,   *Prior* 2 : 201

Titian, Nature's favorite,   *Hughes* 83

Title and profit I resign,   *Gay* 2 : 126

—— the post of honour shall be mine,   *Gay* 2 : 126

Titles claim honour, when they crown the wise,   *Sav.* 161

Titles are marks of honeſt men and wiſe,   *Young* 1 : 82

———— no deference claim, when merit pleads,   *Broome* 76

———— deriving from their ſwords alone,   *Yal.* 438

Titus, delight of men !   *Thom.* 2 : 73

Tityrus and Meliboeus,   *Dry.* 5 : 21

Tityus, earth-born, covering nine acres,   *Fent.* 269

———— in fetters bound, o'er-ſpreads nine acres, *Pope od.* 3 : 300

Tlepolemus from Rhodes led nine ſhips,   *Pope il.* 1 : 93

Tmolus, crown'd with ſnow,   *Pope il.* 2 : 227

Toaſters,   *Hughes* 162

Toaſts, that round the table ſail,   *Som.* 213

Tobacco, filthy concomitant of claret,   *Prior* 1 : 145

———— uſes of,   *Phil.* 45

———— in whoſe fumes I loſe the toil of life,   *Phil.* 29

To-day here, to-morrow gone,   *Prior* 2 : 210

Tofts and Margaretta,   *Hughes* 162

Toil ſtrings the nerves,   *Dry.* 2 : 147

——-- and purifies the blood,   *Dry.* 2 : 147

——-- and be glad,   *Thom.* 1 : 243

——-- created gains, the beſt and ſweeteſt far,   *Thom.* 1 : 232

——-- hardy love of, to inſpire,   *Rowe L.* 393

——-- was not then,   *Thom.* 1 : 211

Toilet, deſcribed,   *Pope* 1 : 131

Toilette,   *Gay* 1 : 224

———— nurſery of charms,   *Gay* 1 : 23

———— ſacred myſteries of,   *Gay* 1 : 27

Toils of law, to perplex the truth,   *Thom.* 1 : 166

————— and lengthen juſtice to a trade,   *Thom.* 1 : 166

Toland and Tindal, prompt at prieſts to jeer,   *Pope* 3 : 165

Toland's invitation to Diſmal,   *Swift* 1 : 80

Tom Britton, lines on, *Hughes* 125

———— music warbled in her sweetest strain, *Hughes* 125

Tom Mullinix, and Dick, *Swift* 2 : 91

Tomb, a thousand ways lead mortals to, *Pope od.* 3 : 320

Tombstone for Prior, *Prior* 2 : 13

To-morrow where ? in another world, *Young* 2 : 16

———— is a satire on to-day, *Young* 3 : 215

———— till, defer not to be wise, *Cong.* 148

————'s sun, to thee may never rise, *Cong.* 148

————'s wiser than to-day, *Pope* 13 108

———— cheats us all, *Hughes* 203

Tones used to win women, *Butl.* 1 : 72

Tongue, so voluble a weapon, *Pope il.* 2 : 223

———— of man is blister'd o'er with lies, *Gay* 1 : 239

———— mov'd by flattery, or with scandal hung, *Gay* 1 : 2

———— windy satisfaction of, *Pope od.* 3 : 141

———— Marcellus of our, *Dry.* 2 : 162

Tonson counts writers' merits by the sheet, *Prior* 1 : 38

———— turn'd upholsterer, *Young* 1 : 89

———— yield to Lintot's lofty name, *Gay* 1 : 216

Tool that knaves work with, call'd a fool, *Butl.* 1 : 6

Tormenter Conscience finds man out, *Milt.* 2 : 205

Torrid zone, summer in, *Thom.* 1 : 65

Tortur'd tears, to speak our sense, are made, *Young* 1 : 161

Torture forces to tell untruths, *Dry.* 2 : 29

Tournament described, *Dry.* 3 : 119

Tower, head mounted with, *Dry.* 7 : 273

Town, a winged war upon, *Rowe L.* 143

———— bulwark'd with walls and lofty towers, *Cong.* 15

———— eclogue, *Swift* 1 : 69

2

Towns,

Towns, like crocodiles, vulnerable in belly,   *Butl.* 2 : 306

Townshend (honourable Charles), ode to,   *Aken.* 231, 257

————— to Mrs. Elizabeth,   *Broome* 62.

Trade, advantages of,   *Dyer* 78

————— of the elder Tyre,   *Dyer* 79.

————— springs from peace,   *Young* 3 : 280

————— source, sinew, soul of all,   *Young* 3 : 269

————— warn'd by, Tyre, O! make religion thine, *id.* 3 : 270 .

————— to circulate like blood,   *Dry.* 1 : 61

————— natural to Britain,   *Young* 3 : 244

————— cherish'd by her sister, Peace,   *Young* 3 : 244

————— gay Freedom's smile,   *Young* 3 : 250

————— inhuman ! spoiling Guinea of her sons, *Thom.* 1 : 78

————— men over-reach in,   *Gay* 2 : 76

————— two of, can ne'er agree,   *Gay* 2 : 66

Tradesmen, to cheat,   *Garth* 36

Tradition, species of,   *Dry.* 2 : 33

————— to try by Scripture,   *Dry.* 2 : 34

————— set quite aside,   *Dry.* 2 : 36

————— makes only probability,   *Dry.* 1 : 256

————— written, authentic,   *Dry.* 1 : 256

————— vanity and insufficiency of,   *Dry.* 1 : 253

Traduction, mind comes by,   *Dry.* 2 : 163

Traerbach besieged and taken,   *Add.* 66

Traffic, probable extent of,   *Dyer* 127

————— is intercourse of ill,   *Buck.* 90

————— game of,   *Swift* 1 : 26.

Tragedians, Greek, simplicity of their plans, *Collins* 308

Tragedy, miniature of human life,   *Dry.* 5 : 210

————— why the most perfect work of poetry, *Dry.* 7 : 133

       Tragedy,

Tragedy, more for the paffions,   *Dry.* 5 : 213
———- provokes our hopes and fears,   *Dry.* 1 : 275
———- raifes pity,   *Dry.* 1 : 276
———- origin of,   *Dry.* 1 : 277
———- love, reigning paffion in,   *Dry.* 1 : 278
———- Thefpis, author of,   *Dry.* 1 : 277
Tragic Mufe, province of,   *Dry.* 2 : 143
———- fpirit, full in Shakefpear fhone,   *Pope* 2 : 228
Traitor once, betrays no more,   *Pope il.* 1 : 312
———- to the vices regnant,   *Swift* 2. : 186
Traitors barter liberty for gold,   *Pope* 4 : 13
Trance, what,   *Butl.* 1 : 313
Transfufion of the blood,   *Butl.* 1 : 270
Tranflated verfe,   *Rofc.* 213
Tranflation, glory of not fmall, when well done,   *Pitt* 357
Tranflations,   *A. Phil.* 379
———- of the beft ancients,   *Rofc.* 214
Tranflators generally traducers,   *Dry.* 5 : 80
Tranfmigration,   *Dry.* 4 : 141
———- taught by Pythagoras,   *Den.* 56
———- taught,   *Dry.* 6 : 147
Tranfport is the language of the fkies,   *Young* 3 : 107
———- to kindle into, at a grave,   *Young* 1 : 14
Trap, the den of filent fate,   *Parn.* 39
——- rape of,   *Shen.* 166
Travelling, abufe of,   *Weft* 259
Travels, bad effects of,   *Ot.* 16
Traulus, a dialogue,   *Swift* 2 : 183
———- fecond part,   *Swift* 2 : 187
Treachery, the ftain of war,   *Rowe L.* 106

Treachery, the foldier's fhame,   *Rowe L.* 106

———— you women ufe to men,   *Pope* 1 : 248

Treacle, vipers yield,   *Wall.* 148

Treafon, to thrive by,   *Dry.* 2 : 248

Treat, three courfes be the moft,   *King* 212

Treble and bafe, in wanton fugues each other chace, *Hughes* 144

———————— by turns they rife and fall,   *Hughes* 144

Tree,   .   *Cow.* 1 : 309

—— of knowledge,   { *Cow.* 1 : 133

                        { *Milt.* 1 : 108

—— in the midft of garden, forbidden,   *Milt.* 2 : 25

—— recommended by the ferpent,   *Milt.* 2 : 25

—— of knowledge forbidden,   *Milt.* 1 : 115, 225, 242

—— of life,   *Milt.* 1 : 108

—— is diftinguifhed by the fruit,   *Gay* 2 : 167

—— cut in paper,   *Wall.* 165

Trees, life of, in the bark,   *Butl.* 2 : 281

—— the methods of raifing,   *Dry.* 5 : 117

—— foils proper for,   *Dry.* 5 : 122

Trent and Severn may be joined,   *Dyer* 102

———————— both joined to the Thames,   *Dyer* 102

Treffes like the morn,   *Milt.* 3 : 147

Tricks, worfe than a mule,   *Butl.* 1 : 112

Trifle, think nought,   *Young* 1 : 144

Trifles make life,   *Young* 1 : 144

Trifling the theme, not fo the poet's praife,   *Add.* 17

———— head, and a contracted heart,   *Pope* 3 : 250

Triple combat,   *Wall.* 182

Tripods, inftinct with fpirit, roll'd on living wheels, *Pope il.* 2 : 183

Triton defcribed,   *Dry.* 6 : 279

                             Trivia,

Trivia,   *Gay* 1 : 101

———— by thee transported, I securely stray,   *Gay* 1 : 101

———— goddess of streets or ways,   *Gay* 1 : 101

Trivial basting, not despond on,   *Butl.* 1 : 122

Triumph, what, but madness, shouts, and noise, *Prior* 2 : 175

———————— held it, to forgive,   *Sav.* 73

Triumphs sink into a coin,   *Pope* 2 : 145

———————— vain,   *Dry.* 7 : 288

Triumvirate of desolation,   *Cow.* 1 : 183

————————— preserved peace, but short,   *Rowe L.* 47

Troja, sport of,   *Dry.* 6 : 98

Trojan matrons, solemn procession,   *Pope il.* 1 : 203

———— ships, transformation of,   *Garth* 139

———— war,   *Dry.* 4 : 76

———— women burn the ships,   *Dry.* 6 : 100

Trojans, enumeration of,   *Pope il.* 1 : 100

———— rush with shouts,   *Pope il.* 1 : 105

———— attack the Greeks,   *Pope il.* 1 : 135

———— dread not the vaunts of Peleus' son,   *Pope il.* 2 : 227

———— rush into Xanthus,   *Pope il.* 2 : 236

———— twelve taken as victims,   *Pope il.* 2 : 236

———— attack the Grecian rampart,   *Pope il.* 1 : 360

Tros, of whom the Trojan name,   *Pope il.* 2 : 222

Trotter, a pye,   *King* 207

Troubles of the state behold the end of ambition, *Rowe L.* 201

Troubles spring more from fancy than the thing, *Prior* 2 : 207

Trout, angling for,   *Thom.* 1 : 16

Trouts tickled best in muddy waters,   *Butl.* 2 : 289

Troy, walls of, built by Apollo,   *Duke* 148

———— destruction of,   *Den.* 20

Troy,

Troy, destruction by the gods,   Dry. 5 : 377
—— fall of, like a felled oak,   Dry. 5 : 378
—— taken after a ten years siege,   Dry. 5 : 358
—— fled, unmindful of her former fame,   Pope il. 2 : 113
—— driven by flight and terror,   Pope il. 2 : 113
True to our own o'erbearing pride,   Prior 2 : 79
——, and false to all the world beside,   Prior 2 : 79
—— to virtue, and as warm as true,   Pope 2 : 193
——'s epitaph,   Prior 2 : 264
—— blue, fair emblem of unstained breast,   Gay 1 : 189
—— English dean,   Swift 2 : 214
—— free-thinking what,   Young 2 : 204
—— greatness lies in daring to be great,   Young 3 : 162
—— happiness consists alone in doing good,   Som. 187
—— joy, the sun-shine of the soul,   Young 3 : 271
—— liberty, what,   Dry. 7 : 350
—— love's knots,   Butl. 1 : 175
—— maid,   Prior 1 : 264
—— monarchy,   Watts 187
—— courage,   Watts 189
—— riches,   Watts 203
—— wisdom is the price of happiness,   Young 1 : 83
—— wit, everlasting, like the sun,   Buck. 69
Trulla described,   Butl. 1 : 61, 62
—— conquers Hudibras,   Butl. 1 : 130
Truly great, for others live, and for others die, Thom. 2 : 166
Trump of aye or no,   Butl. 2 : 46
Trumpet, signal of onset,   Phil. 13
——— inspiring firm resolution,   Phil. 13
——— sounds harsh in the Muses' grove,   Fent. 327

Trumpet, found of the laft,   *Cow.* 2 : 24

———— dead raifed by,   *Rofc.* 250

———— the dead awakes,   *Young* 1 : 10

Trumpets fleep, while chearful horns are blown,   *Pope* 1 : 72

———— feaft of,   *Cow.* 2 : 111

———— fpiritual,   *Butl.* 2 : 215

Truft is a trial,   *Butl.* 1 : 174

——— fix on nothing here below,   *Parn.* 153

Trufty-ftaff her feeble limbs fuftains,   *Gay* 1 : 334

Truth, fpecies of,   *Aken.* 139

———— virtue not to be disjoined from,   *Aken.* 143

———— has greateft ftrength,   *Cow.* 1 : 186

———— I revere, wifdom never lies,   *Pope od.* 3 : 296

———— that looks the very foul,   *Thom.* 2 : 17

———— fevere delights of,   *Dry.* 1 : 252

———————— fhall dictate to my tongue,   *Pope od.* 3 : 120

———— fhews the real eftimate of things,   *Young* 2 : 102

———— bids me look on men, as autumn leaves,   *Young* 2 : 102

———— will at laft remove the fcreen,   *Gay* 2 : 145

———— ever naked will appear,   *Prior* 2 : 224

———— decks our fpeeches and our books,   *Prior* 2 : 225

———— needs no flowers of fpeech,   *Pope* 2 : 203

———— oppreffed by confidence,   *Butl.* 2 : 290

———— Time's daughter,   *Butl.* 1 : 248

———— told at laft,   *Prior* 2 : 263

———— never yet went in difguife,   *Prior* 2 : 247

———— is always plain,   *Prior* 2 : 269

———— plain truth, is welcome to the wife,   *Young* 1 : 264

———— immortal, celeftial born,   *Hughes* 205

———— the band of love,   *King* 325

Truth.

Truth be your guide,　　　　　　　　　　　　Pope 2 : 14

—— guards the poet, fanctifies the line,　　　Pope 2 : 305

—— like a fingle point, efcapes the fight,　　Pom. 343

—— lies hid, and life is o'er, ere we explore it,　Pom. 344

—— fpeaks too low,　　　　　　　　　　　　Dry. 2 : 244

—— let every line endure teft of,　　　　　　Lanf. 234

—— cherifh, ye Mufes, the forfaken fair,　　　Lanf. 234

—— take to your train this beauteous wanderer,　Lanf. 234

—— foils falfehood,　　　　　　　　　　　　Milt. 2 : 198

—— itfelf light, fhuns darknefs,　　　　　　Dry. 2 : 101

—— ftamps conviction,　　　　　　　　　　Rofc. 220

—— is one,　　　　　　　　　　　　　　　Rofc. 220

—— brighteft thro' the plaineft drofs,　　　Lanf. 220

—— fhould not always be reveal'd,　　　　　Gay 2 : 60

—— in fpite of manners, to be told,　　　　Parn 63

—— in rhyme,　　　　　　　　　　　　　Mall. 288

—— fhines the brighter, clad in verfe,　　　Swift 1 : 172

—— never was indebted to a lye,　　　　　Young 2 : 233

—— whofe voice alone is praife,　　　　　　Mall. 291

—— to contend for, not victory,　　　　　　Broome 12

—— is depofited with man's laft hour,　　　Young 2 : 90

—— keen vibration of, is hell,　　　　　　Young 2 : 90

—— to be loved, needs only to be feen,　　　Dry. 2 : 9

—— lends the Stoic courage,　　　　　　　Dry. 7 : 311

—— prefer to friendfhip,　　　　　　　　　Den. 95

—— veil'd in plaufible difguife,　　　　　　Pope od 4 : 13

—— huge and overgrown, admired,　　　　Butl. 2 : 165

—— to make by votes,　　　　　　　　　　Butl. 2 : 163

—— is ever read in woman's eyes,　　　　　Gay 1 : 239

—— and candour fhew in all you fpeak,　　　Pope 1 : 114

　　　　　　　　　　　　　　　　　　　　　　　Truth

Truth and falsehood,   *Prior* 2 : 223

—— and juftice, with uprightnefs dwell,   *Rowe L.* 402

Tub-holders-forth,   *Butl.* 2 : 48

Tuck bail'd from rufty durance,   *Butl.* 1 : 50

Tuefday,   *Gay* 1 : 62

Tuke's tragi-comedy,   *Cow.* 1 : 205

Tulip, queen of flowers,   *Garth* 85

—— bluſhing in diverſities of day,   *Pope* 1 : 348

Tully, Rome's other glory,   *Pitt* 322

—— for happy eloquence renown'd,   *Rowe L.* 290

—— ſpeech to Pompey,   *Rowe L.* 291

—— eloquence arrays,   *Dyer* 11

—— immortal, ſhone with equal rays,   *Pope* 1 : 212

—— great father of his country,   *Pope* 1 : 212

—— firen-power of,   *Fent.* 237

—— publiſhed what Lucretius wrote,   *Broome* 65

Tupping-time, care of ſheep in,   *Dyer* 41

Turenne with York could glory ſhare,   *Buck.* 109

Turf lie lightly on the grave,   *Dry.* 7 : 312

—— o'er virtue charms,   *Young* 1 : 238

Turk ſpreads thraldom and defolation,   *Dyer* 109

Turkey and the ant,   *Gay* 2 : 94

——— trade, decay of,   *Dyer* 108

Turkiſh empire, prefage of ruin of,   *Wall.* 197

Turks, invaſion and defeat of,   *Wall.* 155

Turn-ſtile more certain than Fortune,   *Butl.* 1 : 101

Turner, Prior to,   *Prior* 1 : 24

Turnus infpired by Alecto to oppofe Æneas,   *Dry.* 6 : 176

——— arms, and breaks the peace,   *Dry.* 6 : 178

——— defcribed,   *Dry.* 6 : 193

Turnus fends to Diomedes,   *Dry.* 6 : 196
———— like a lion,   *Dry.* 6 : 267
———— kills Pallas,   *Dry.* 6 : 292
———— fires Æneas' fhips,   *Dry.* 6 : 233
———— like a wolf,   *Dry.* 6 : 232
———— armour of,   *Dry.* 7 : 26
———— like a wanton courfer,   *Dry.* 7 : 26
———— challenge of,   *Dry.* 7 : 47
———— challenges Æneas,   *Dry.* 7 : 50
———— in armour,   *Dry.* 7 : 51
———— like the bull in female's fight,   *Dry.* 7 : 51
———— difpirited,   *Dry.* 7 : 57
———— flaughter by,   *Dry.* 7 : 64
———— like Boreas,   *Dry.* 7 : 65
———— forced to the combat,   *Dry.* 7 : 80
———— breaks his fword,   *Dry.* 7 : 82
———— flies,   *Dry.* 7 : 83
———— purfued by Æneas,   *Dry.* 7 : 84
———— flain,   *Dry.* 7 : 93
Turtle and fparrow,   *Prior* 2 : 197
Twangdillo defcribed,   *Som.* 100
———————— laments his fiddle broken,   *Som.* 122
Tweed no more divides the Britons,   *King* 384
Twelve articles,   *Swift* 2 : 178
Twickenham, on grotto at,   *Pope* 2 : 353
Twins, oppofite in minds and manners,   *Dry.* 7 : 359
———— ev'n from the birth are mifery and man, *Pope od.* 3 : 193
Twitters amorous,   *Butl.* 1 : 277
Two friends, epiftle to,   *Swift* 2 : 274
——— mice,   *Prior* 2 : 235

Two

Two monkeys,   Gay 2 : 97
——- owls and the sparrow,   Gay 2 : 84
————— Athens, seat of learned fame, rever'd our name, id. 85
——- riddles,   Prior 2 : 239
——- springs,   Som. 282
————————— from the same parent hill,   Som. 282
Twysden, how lov'd he liv'd, how deplor'd he fell, Smith 196
Tyburn,   Mall. 302
——— finisher of care and pain,.   Mall. 305
Tyber now no longer Roman,   Pope 3 : 238
——— vain of Italian arts, Italian souls,   Pope 3 : 238
Tydeus, heir of Calydon,   Pope 1 : 322
——————— little body lodg'd a mighty mind,   Pope il. 1 : 184
Typhoeus, sprung from Tartarus and Earth,   Broome 147
——————— a match for gods in might,.   Broome 147
——————— blasted by Jove's thunder,   Broome 148
——————— impious foe of gods,.   West 194
——————— plung'd in the horrid dungeons of deepest hell, ib.
Tyranny, fly, no more be known,   Cong. 160
——————— wants subjects for its reign,   Rowe L. 298
——————— ecclesiastical,   Thom. 2 : 83
——————— civil,   Thom. 2 : 82
——————— enslaves the body,   Pope 1 : 120
——————— the worst, that persecutes the mind,   Dry. 2 : 16
——————— of the Puritans,.   Cow. 1 : 351
Tyrant, what,   Cow. 2 : 225
——————— arm'd with insolence and pride,.   Pope il. 1 : 43
——————— inglorious slave to interest,   Pope il. 1 : 43
——————— suffers, and the world is freed,   Som. 178
Tyrant-joy of hearing slaves complain,   Lytt. 13
                                                                 Tyrant-

Tyrant-power fits enthron'd with blood, *Aken.* 41
Tyrants devour, not rule, *Butl.* 2 : 324
———— fancy mankind made for them, *Dry.* 7 : 20
———— think men were born for flaves, *Gay* 2 : 114
———— are but princes in difguife, *Garth* 103
———— under perpetual fears, *Cow.* 2 : 223
———— govern with an iron rod, *Pope od.* 3 : 70
———— and be the fcourge of God, *Pope od.* 3 : 70
Tyrconnel, on vifcountefs of, *Sav.* 88
———————— droops, and pleafure is no more, *Sav.* 89
Tyre fat an emprefs, aw'd the flood ! *Young* 3 : 252
——— golden city was her name, *Young* 3 : 252
——— mother of crafts, *Young* 3 : 253
——— pilot of kingdoms, *Young* 3 : 253
——— great mart of nations, *Young* 3 : 253
——— her fall, *Young* 2 : 156
Tyrian Gades fees the fetting fun, *Rowe L.* 296
Tyro, daughter of Salmoneus, *Fent.* 256
———— had Pelias and Neleus by Neptune, *Fent.* 169

V

Vacuum prevented by water and air, *Black.* 169
Vagellius, defcribed, *Garth* 54
Vain to hope to cheat th' allfeeing eyes of heaven, *Weft* 140
——— all we act, and all we think, *Prior* 2 : 101
——— of life expofe, *Young* 2 : 52
——— hope ! to leave one's felf behind, *Fent.* 293
————————— and live a thoughtlefs exile from the mind, *ib.*
——— love, *Cow.* 1 : 241
——— man ! boldly vies with his God, *Broome* 24

Vain

in would trace the maze of providence,   *Tick.* 139

rld, abode of guilt and forrow,   *Add.* 337

, Petrarch's retreat,   *Aken.* 90

e, when birds their partners take,   *Gay* 1 : 74

e-day,   { *Shen.* 225   *Sav.* 183

-fon, from a valiant fire,   *Lytt.* 76

few o'ermatch an hoft of foes,   *Pope od.* 3 : 70

foars above affliction,   *Add.* 284

is a moufe-trap,   *Butl.* 1 : 114

and Beauty ftill were Britain's claim,   *Hughes* 161

———— both are her great prerogatives of fame, *ib.*

nts grace, who never wanted wit,   *Pope* 2 : 229

gh, houfe of,   *Swift* 1 : 41

—— hiftory of his houfe,   *Swift* 1 : 41

is, blue, tranfparent,   *Pope* 1 : 71

yck, Waller to,   *Wall.* 47

ke, death of,   *Cow.* 1 : 107

a, not in years a fcore,   *Swift* 1 : 118

— dreams of a gown of forty-four,   *Swift* 1 : 118

— as years increafe, fhe brighter fhines, *Swift* 1 : 119

— reafon'd without plodding long,   *Swift* 1 : 119

— nor ever gave her judgement wrong, *Swift* 1 : 119

i, Atheiftic opinions of,   *Black* 116

es, that tire,   *Pope* 2 : 354

forbids thee to be vain,   *Young* 2 : 141

. with pocket-glafs,   *Swift* 2 : 75

. mirror of,   *Thom.* 1 : 215

. of the world,   *Prior* 2 : 101

. deaf to reproof,   *Mall.* 166

Vanquifh

Vanquish in words, be mine the prize in fight,   *Gay* 1 : 313

Vanquished love,   *Young* 1 : 47

Vapours, maggots in the brain,   *Swift* 1 : 213

———— a fit of, clouds this demi-god,   *Pope* 2 : 202

Variety is all our bliss,   *Buck.* 41

———— endearing,   *Den.* 15

———— alone gives joy,   *Prior* 2 : 205

———— kind source of joy!   *Som.* 289

———— it is, that gives delight,   *Pitt* 341

Variety's the source of joys below,   *Gay* 1 : 214

Various climes with various fruits are fraught,   *West* 263

———— objects various passions move,   *West* 233

———— readings, burthens of modern editions,   *Broome* 8

Varronian satire, what,   *Dry.* 7 : 159

Veal, blown up,   *Butl.* 1 : 80

———— receipt for stewing,   *Gay* 1 : 298

Vegetables, wisdom of God, in,   *Black.* 92

———— uses of,   *Black.* 93

Veil of Thisbe torn by a lioness,   *Hughes* 60

———— observed bloody by Pyramus, who supposes her slain, *ib.*

Veins, structure of,   *Black.* 190

Venal art, that vice of Courts,   *Mall.* 169

———— fair, bid her adieu,   *Aken.* 197

———— unworthy she your bliss to prove,   *Aken.* 197

Venetia first emerg'd from barbarous waste,   *Dyer* 69

Vengeance, goddess never sleeping,   *Swift* 2 : 222

———— aloud for justice cries,   *Gay* 2 : 91

———— hour of, lies ripening in fate,   *Pope od.* 3 : 89

———— hard as it is, suppress,   *Pope il.* 1 : 46

———— be left to powers divine,   *Dry.* 2 : 62

       Vengeance

ance I vow, and for your crimes you die, *Pope od.* 3 : 66

—— ftrikes, whom heaven has doom'd to fall, *id.* 4 : 81

—— refolv'd, 'tis dangerous to defer, *Pope od.* 4 : 82

—— waits th' unhallow'd tongue, · *Weſt* 139

—— divine, daring hearts controuls, *Rowe L.* 323

—— certain ftrikes the perjur'd breaſt, *Gay* 2 : 290

Creator Spiritus, *Dry.* 1 : 316.

deſcribed, *Thom.* 2 : 91

riſe of, *Thom.* 2 : 91

roſe from dirt and ſea-weed, · *Pope* 2 : 80

neck, to gain a fortune, · *Butl.* 1 : 174.

greater, to give your perſon than goods away, *Pope* 1 : 233

ſets, ere Mercury can riſe, *Pope* 1 267

goddeſs of deſire, · *Cong.* 177.

can tame ſtubborn race of men to love, *Cong.* 177

far as life exiſts, her care extends, *Cong.* 179

genial power of love, *Dry.* 3 : 103

companion of the ſun, *Dry.* 3 : 104

nfluence of, *Dry.* 3 : 103

prung from the ſea,
{ *Wall.* 18
{ *Gay* 1 : 21.

wanton Loves and Graces round her wait, *Gay* 1 : 28.

aughter-loving dame,
{ *Wall.* 38.
{ *Pope il.* 1 : 121

girdle deſcribed, *Pope il.* 2 : 49

—— effect on Jove, *Milt.* 2 : 170.

ttribute of, *Shen.* 121

miſtaken, *Prior* 1 : 111

led, yet could not die, *Broome* 20

ures Æneas, *Dry.* 7 : 67.

Venus

Venus, no fantaſtic goddeſs,　　　　　　　*Hughes* 66

—— painted from every colour in nature,　　*Hughes* 66

—— judgement of,　　　　　　　　　*Prior* 2 : 229

—— deals the Nectar round,　　　　　　*Hughes* 85

—— her advice to the Muſes,　　　ᵉ　*Prior* 2 : 248

—— and Adonis,　　　　　　　　　*Hughes* 168

—— temple of,　　　　　　　　　　*Dry.* 3 : 92

—— vigil of,　　　　　　　　　　*Parn.* 29

—— of Medici,　　　　　　　　　*Thom.* 2 : 87

Verbal criticiſm, what,　　　　　　　*Broome* 9

———————— evils of,　　　　*Broome* 9

Verſe comes from heaven, like inward light,　*Prior* 1 : 36

—— can gild inſtruction with delight,　　*Sav.* 42

—— power of,　　　　　　　　　　*Walſh* 311

—— majeſty of debaſed to rhyme,　　　*Dry.* 2 : 187

—— is the laſt of human works that dies,　*Hughes* 209

—— not confined to any one meaſure,　　*Pitt* 306

—— at its birth it ſung the gods alone,　*Pitt* 306

—— religion claim'd it for her own,　　*Pitt* 306

—— hence call'd heroic,　　　　　　*Pitt* 307

—— beſt befits a mind devoid of woe,　　*Fent.* 278

—— trifling care and empty ſound of,　　*Dry.* 7 : 313

—— vileſt, at court thrives beſt,　　　*Swift* 2 : 306

—— curſt be, that makes one worthy man my foe, *Pope* 2 : 161

—— gives Virtue ſcandal, Innocence a fear,　*Pope* 2 : 161

—— and ſculpture bore an equal part,　　*Pope* 2 : 146

Verſeman or proſeman, term me, which you will, *id.* 2 : 174

Verſes on I know not what,　　　　　*Swift* 2 : 97

—— to the king,　　　　　　　　　*Prior* 1 : 99

—— in a lady's ivory table-book,　　　*Swift* 1 : 20

Verſes

Verfes by a lady to the Author,   *Lanf.* 182

—— anfwered,   *Lanf.* 183

—— in a leaf of the Author's poems,   *Lanf.* 238

Verfify in fpite,   *Dry.* 7 : 222

Vertù, what,   *Weft* 276

Vertumnus and Pomona, ftory of,   *Garth* 143

———— and Pomona,   *Pope* 1 : 334

———— changes forms, to gain Pomona,   *Pope* 1 : 336

Very good wife, prologue to,   *Cong.* 89

Vefpafian daub'd with dirt,   *Butl.* 1 : 222

Vefper chaces the light,   *Cow.* 1 : 57

—— lights up the fky,   *Dry.* 3 : 181

Ufens, head of the Equicolæ,   *Dry.* 6 : 191

Vice, origin of,   *Aken.* 63, 151

—— horror of,   *Aken.* 151

—— felf-love in a miftake,   *Young* 2 : 243

—— is only varied in the drefs,   *Cong.* 149

—— is the act of man, by paffion toft,   *Weft* 233

—— what it diforders, can God compofe,   *Weft* 233

—— each a loader,   *Dry.* 7 : 251

—— how it unmans a nation !   *Aken.* 351

—— engenders fhame,   *Prior* 2 : 159

—— pours forth the troubled ftreams of hell,   *Thom.* 1 : 237

—— from hell rear'd up its hydra-head,   *Hughes* 81

—— a monfter of a frightful mien,   *Pope* 2 : 50

—— like fome monfter, feized the town,   *Lanf.* 214

—— in pulpits and at bar fhe wears a gown,   *Lanf.* 214

—— transforms man's reafon into beaft,   *King* 266

—— enfeebling, withers each nerve,   *Dyer* 24

—— with giant-ftrides comes on amain,   *Pope* 2 : 296

Vice

Vice at stand, and at highest flow,   *Dry.* 7 : 229

—— become an art,   *Butl.* 2 : 231

—— affectation in,   *Butl.* 2 : 231

—— defies the juggler,   *Gay* 2 : 102

—— a guinea in her hand takes every shape, but charity, *ib.*

—— can bolt her arguments,   *Milt.* 3 : 148

—— triumphs here,   *Dry.* 1 : 246

—— in its first approach, with care to shun,   *Mall.* 177

—— fetter'd-in, seek not to be free,   *Rowe* 7

—— win us from, and laugh us into sense,   *Tick.* 113

—— he lash'd, but spar'd the name,   *Swift* 2 : 267

—— must be or ridicul'd, or lash'd,   *Swift* 2 : 267

—— and faction held in awe,   *Fent.* 220

—— is dull,   *Young* 1 : 194

Vice-principal of St. Mary-Hall,   *Sav.* 163

Viceroy,   *Prior* 2 : 265

Vices lashed by Juvenal,   *Dry.* 7 : 182

Vicious love depraves the heart,   *Thom.* 2 : 191

—— hearts fume phrenzy to the brain,   *Young* 2 : 209

Vicissitude attends every worldly state,   *Lanf.* 144

—— of fall and spring,   *Young* 1 : 12

Vicissitudes strange of human fate,   *Dry.* 3 : 129

—— alternate, like day and night,   *Dry.* 3 : 129

Victor o'er life, and all her train of woes,   *Prior* 2 : 173

—— oft triumphs, but to fall,   *Pope il.* 2 : 181

Victors are by conquest curst,   *Broome* 31

—— the bravest are the worst,   *Broome* 31

—— by victories undone,   *Dry.* 2 : 149

Victoria, march of,   *Hughes* 86

—— her flying camp of loves prepare for the march, *ib.*

Victories, like fame, before th' invader fly,   *Hughes* 86

Victorious ravagers, human comets, vanish,   *Thom.* 2 : 167

Victory to tug for,   *Butl.* 1 : 117

———— to stop the victor's way,   *Rowe L.* 106

———— to know to use,   *Butl.* 1 : 121

———— the curse of those that win,   *Rowe L.* 181

———— fatal end, where still new woes begin,   *Rowe L.* 181

———— o'er one's self the greatest conquest,   *Hughes* 50

Vida, art of poetry,   *Pitt* 305

Vida immortal, poet and critic,   *Pope* 1 : 121

Villain, one condemned to drudgery,   *Butl.* 1 : 295

———— with usury swell'd,   *Thom.* 2 : 68

———— tho' he 'scape a while,   *Swift* 1 : 152

———— feels slow vengeance at his heels,   *Swift* 1 : 152

———— to call great, absurd,   *Pope* 2 : 78

———— his censure is extorted praise,   *Pope* 2 : 9

Villains of fame,   *Rowe* 87

Villainy, nothing sacred but,   *Pope* 1 : 295

———— steps in,   *Cong.* 72

———— to establish by law,   *Dry.* 1 : 224

Villers, that life of pleasure, and that soul of whim, *Pope* 2 : 130

Villiers, ode to memory of,   *Prior* 1 : 183

———— for wisdom as for beauty fam'd,   *Lans.* 145

Vine planted by Noah,   *Butl.* 2 : 253

——— hates the ivy,   *Phil.* 42

——— clasps the tall elm,   *Phil.* 42

Vines, rules for,   *Dry.* 5 : 129

——— their liquid harvest yield,   *Pope il.* 2 : 45

Vintage,   *Broome* 169

Vineyard,   *Thom.* 1 : 129

Violence hallow'd by the name of Right,   *Rowe L.* 41

Violet, fair daughter of Ajax's blood,   *Young* 3 : 162

Viper envy revel'd in my veins,   *Fent.* 292

———— ſpite, cruſh'd by thy virtue, at thy feet lay dead, *Hughes* 49

Virago minx,   *Butl.* 1 : 213

Virbius, name of Hippolytus,   *Dry.* 6 : 192

Virgil, panegyric on,   *Pitt* 385

———— Phœbus' undoubted ſon,   *Pitt* 313

———— thought, and ſpoke in every word a god,   *Pitt* 313

———— nought can match his genius but his art,   *Pitt* 313

———— ſince him, degenerate ſouls ſucceed,   *Pitt* 313

———————— and give us ſound, when we call for ſenſe, *ib.*

———— ſuperior in judgement to Theocritus,   *Pope* 1 : 21

———— abounds in variety,   *Pope* 1 : 21

———— in his Georgic has a ruſtic majeſty,   *Add.* 208

———— toſſes the dung about with grace,   *Add.* 208

———— takes his prognoſtications from Aratus,   *Add.* 208

———— metaphorical in ſecond book,   *Add.* 209

———— vigorous and ſpirited in third book,   *Add.* 209

———— highly pleaſed among his bees,   *Add.* 210

———— conteſts the praiſe of judgement,   *Pope il.* 1 : 1

———— ſublime in epic ſtrains,   *Fent.* 238

———— tfuly great, and muſt pleaſe,   *Dry.* 7 : 316

———— dignity of expreſſion, ornament of,   *Dry.* 7 : 106

———— excellence of, in diction,   *Dry.* 7 : 185

———— extracted gold from dung,   *Butl.* 2 : 261

———— did not give the finiſhing to Æneid, vii. & xii. *Dry.* 7 : 97

———— expreſſes much in little,   *Dry.* 3 : 294

———— combined Homer's two poems,   *Dry.* 3 : 19

———— of a ſedate temper,   *Dry.* 3 : 19

Virgil, Æneis of,   *Dry.* 5 : 312

———- Georgics of,   *Dry.* 5 : 91

———- paftorals of,   *Dry.* 5 : 21

———- tranflation of,   *Wall.* 128

———- imitation of,   *Walfh* 361

———- fifth eclogue of,   *Duke* 128

——— praife of a country life,   *Cow.* 2 : 308, 310

Virgin, fkill'd in labours of the loom,   *Pope od* 4 : 14

——— in the fpider ftill remains,   *Gay* 1 : 341

——— fhall conceive, a virgin bear a fon,   *Pope* 1 : 47

——— flies from hateful truth,   *Broome* 47

——— honour, once, is always ftain'd,   *Prior* 1 : 229

——— voice offends no virgin ear,   *Hughes* 80

Virginia, improvement of,   *Dyer* 123

Virginity, no precept for,   *Pope* 1 : 256

Virgins fcornful, who their charms furvive,   *Pope* 1 : 144

——— like harmony,   *King* 322

——— we form like wax,   *Pope* 1 : 231

——— are virgins ftill, while 'tis unknown,   *Gay* 1 : 32

Virtue, what ! but repofe of mind,   *Thom.* 1 : 204

——— a pure etherial calm,   *Thom.* 1 : 204

——— is Self-love in her wits,   *Young* 2 : 243

——— practifed, gives a habit,   *Wall.* 220

——— fovereign good,   *Aken.* 138, 150

——— will of God, the perfect,   *Aken.* 145

——— for ever frail below,   *Young* 2 : 95

——— only a name,   *Cow.* 2 : 36

——— pride of, humbled by Chrift,   *Cow.* 2 : 37

——— true, lies in the midft,   *Buck.* 55

——— has immortal charms,   *Prior* 2 : 212

Virtue,

Virtue, pleafed by being fhown, *Swift* 1 : 121

———— knows nothing, which it dares not own, *Swift* 1 : 121

———— can make us without fear difclofe, *Swift* 1 : 121

———— our inmoft fecrets to our foes, *Swift* 1 : 121

———— fparkles near a tomb, *Young* 3 : 149

———— alone has majefty in death, *Young* 2 : 41

———— with immortality, expires, *Young* 2 : 202

———— vices to abhor, *Pope* 2 : 195

———— confirm'd by ferious thought, *Pom.* 291

———— with exercife hardened, *Dry.* 2 : 183

———— alone is happinefs below, *Pope* 2 : 80

———— no real joy, fave her's, *Thom.* 2 : 139

———— from Virtue's bands is ne'er remov'd, *King* 286

———— take care how you ftray from, *King* 264

———— conceal'd, obfcurely dies, *Som.* 184

———— tho' neglected, reigns, *Som.* 186

———— local find, *Pope* 3 : 249

———— come, thou heavenly gueft, *Broome* 41

———— fix thy empire in my breaft, *Broome* 41

———— funk to poverty, meets fcorn, *Thom.* 1 : 113

———— often dwells with woe, *Aken.* 236

———— ftands the teft of fortune, *Add.* 323

———— like gold, tortured in the furnace, comes brighter out, *ib.*

———— repulfed, yet knows not to repine, *Swift* 1 : 152

———— affailed, but never hurt, *Milt.* 3 : 142

———— a goddefs we confefs, *Cong.* 112

———— only, and her friends, a friend to, *Pope* 2 : 177

———— it is, Virtue to commend, *Cong.* 109

———— can brook the thoughts of age, *Gay* 2 : 191

———— lafts the fame through every ftage, *Gay* 2 : 191

Virtue

Virtue feek, to Providence refign the reft, _Gay_ 2 : 97

———— arm'd muft conquer lawlefs pride, _Prior_ 1 : 193

———— fteel'd with, to view death or want undifmay'd, _Fent._ 309

———— improves, when fhaded by difgrace, _Som._ 164

———— alone is free, _Milt._ 3 : 158

———— makes the blifs, where-e'er we dwell, _Collins_ 233

———— flies, as to her home, to Cato's breaft, _Rowe L._ 94

———— to full profperity gave way, _Rowe L._ 51

————- in youth, no ftable footing finds, _Rowe L._ 341

———— fcorns on coward terms to pleafe, _Rowe L._ 392

——————— or cheaply to be bought, or won with eafe, _id._ 392

———— glorious danger makes her truly great, _Rowe L._ 392

———— fole furvives, _Thom._ 1 : 189

———— immortal, never-failing friend of man, _Thom._ 1 : 189

———— prefers glory to liberty or life, _Smith_ 120

———— praife awaits, _Aken._ 265

———— from, the pureft joys out-well, _Thom._ 1 : 237

———— is a joy, that will for ever laft, _Pom._ 321

———— rich in itfelf with folid joys, _Fent._ 202

———— to follow, ev'n for virtue's fake, _Pope_ 1 : 218

———— pure, in receffes of the foul, _Dry._ 7 : 325

———— hard fate, to be diftreft, _Swift_ 1 : 70

———— dryly praifed and ftarves, _Dry._ 7 : 225

———— fuffers here, _Dry._ 1 : 246

———— tho' diftrefs'd is ftill the fame, _Rowe L._ 403

————- I follow ; where fhe fhines, I praife, _Pope_ 2 : 299

———— I pant for, _Add._ 285

———— kindles living joys, _Young_ 1 : 194

———— the child of fenfe, _Young_ 1 : 194

———— at firft fubdues, then keeps, our hearts, _King_ 321

Virtue,

Virtue, which Chriſtian motives beſt inſpire, *Young* 2 : 56

———— alone engenders us for life, *Young* 2 : 37

———— is the path to Praiſe, *Pope od.* 4 : 191

———— the path to Peace, *Dry.* 7 : 300

———— the root, and Pleaſure is the flower, *Young* 2 : 232

———— plant, Content's the fruit, *Gay* 2 : 153

———— virtue loves, *Gay* 1 : 186

———— not rolling ſuns, the mind matures, *Young* 2 : 117

———— what ſhews more, than a humble mind, *Gay* 1 : 230

———— virtues can impart, *Gay* 2 : 57

———— like Janus, bears a double face, *Swift* 2 : 3

———— looks back with joy where ſhe has gone, *Swift* 2 : 3

———— and therefore goes with courage on, *Swift* 2 : 3

———— ſhe at your ſickly bed will wait, *Swift* 2 : 3

———— and guide you to a better ſtate, *Swift* 2 : 3

———— woman's frail defence, *Yal.* 382

———— the paint, that can with wrinkles ſhine, *Young* 1 : 134

———— that and that only can old age ſuſtain, *Young* 1 : 135

———— is beauty, *Young* 1 : 47

———— ſtyl'd its own reward, *Swift* 2 : 2

———— the chief of human good, *Swift* 2 : 2

———— the nutriment of the mind, *Swift* 2 : 3

———— is amiable, mild, ſerene, *Lytt.* 41

———— without, all beauty, and all peace within, *Lytt.* 41

———— weak, an empty form, *Thom.* 2 : 166

———— conceal'd, is inactivity at beſt, *Swift* 1 : 158

———— be then your firſt purſuit, *Gay* 2 : 167

———— diſtinguiſhes mankind, *Gay* 2 : 195

———————————— man from man, *Dry.* 3 : 232

———— without wealth exerts leſs power, *Prior* 2 : 21

Virtue

Virtue and defcent no inheritance,   Dry. 5 : 84.

—— cómes not by inheritance,   Dry. 3 : 201

—— of a lover is excefs,   Lytt. 42

—— by the charms of wit refin'd,   Lytt. 25

—— at once exalts and polifhes the mind,   Lytt. 25

—— with beauty, femblance of a form divine, Prior 2 : 221

———————— ftill fhare the fway,   Hughes 96

—— and Fame,   Lytt. 79

—— and happinefs depend on ftaid precaution, Weft 174

—— and Vice are Empire's life or death,   Young 1 : 260

—— and wealth ! what are ye but a name ! Pope 2 : 131

—— was taught in verfe, and Athens rofe, Prior 1 : 188

—— to verfe immortal luftre gives,   Prior 1 : 53

—— is her own reward,   Prior 1 : 54

—— 'tis virtue makes a king,   Pope 2 : 197

—— to perifh for our country's good,   Swift 1 : 112

—— apology of,   Young 2 : 213

Virtues moral and intellectual,   Cow. 2 : 240

—— how to be judged of,   Cow. 2 : 240

—— conquer with a fingle look,   Thom. 2 : 100

—— improving by defcent his own,   Yal. 441

—— daughters of Truth,   Collins 290

—— fhould rife as fortunes fwell,   Young 3 : 259

—— of humanity are Cæfar's,   Add. 322

—— keep the middle line,   Dry. 2 : 178

—— confcious of, and not vain, raifes them, Dry. 2 : 179

Virtuofo's, to,   Shen. 169

Virtuous be, fave yourfelves from fhame,   Gay 2 : 166

—— every man his brother,   Swift 2 : 288

—— man in danger from company,   Cow. 2 : 361

U 4.

Virtuous, nothing fear, but life with fhame,　　　Lanf. 184

———— none but, are of noble blood,　　　Garth 103

———— be, and happy for your pains,　　　Pope 2 : 206

———— actions confcience of,　　　Den. 112

———— friendfhip, is aught fo fair ?　　　Akin. 149

———— man, having nothing, has all,　　　Cow. 2 : 350

———— minds, the nobleft throne for Jove,　　　Rowe L. 403

———— poverty does great things,　　　Milt. 2 : 177

———————— deem'd difgrace,　　　Lytt. 99

———— and vicious every man muft be,　　　Pope 2 : 51

Vifigoths fall fierce on Spain and Gaul,　　　Pope 3 : 179

Vifion,　　　{ Buck. 51
　　　　　{ Lanf. 175
　　　　　{ Parn. 89

———— to David,　　　Cow. 2 : 119

———— futurity revealed in,　　　Milt. 2 : 99

———— manifeft of future fate,　　　Pope od. 3 : 141

———— of God, happinefs in,　　　Milt. 1 : 75

———— defcribed,　　　Shen. 23

Vifions not always vain,　　　Dry. 3 : 151

Vifit,　　　Rowe 63

———— in winter,　　　Shen. 102

Vital fpirit fled, returns no more,　　　Pope il. 1 : 282

Vitilitigation, oppofed to found reafon,　　　Butl. 1 : 147

Vixen I hate, that her mind affails,　　　Cong. 121

———— and fcratches with her bodkin or her nails,　Cong. 121

Ulcers, one of the Egyptian plagues,　　　Cow. 2 : 61

Ulyffes, for wifdom's various arts renown'd,　　Pope od. 3 : 39

———— long exercifed in woes,　　　Pope od. 3 : 39

———— entertain'd by Circe,　　　Pope od. 3 : 264

　　　　　　　　　　　　　　Ulyffes,

Ulyſſes, his men recover their human ſhape,   *Pope od.* 3 : 266

———— taught by labours to be wiſe,   *Pope od.* 3 : 269

———— for counſel, like the gods renown'd,   *Pope il.* 1 : 74

———— fir'd with praiſe, or with perſuaſion mov'd,   *id.* 74

———— check'd with reproof the vile, or tam'd with blows, *id.* 75

———— follow'd in twelve gallies,   *Pope il.* 1 : 92

———— a chief in wiſdom, equal to a god,   *Pope il.* 1 : 92

———— detain'd by Calypſo,   *Pope od.* 3 : 39

———— an exile from his paternal coaſt,   *Pope od.* 3 : 39

———— learn'd in all the wiles of human thought,   *id.* 153

———— enur'd to perils, to the worſt reſign'd, *Pope od.* 3 : 154

———— builds a ſhip,   *Pope od.* 3 : 155

———— ſets ſail,   *Pope od.* 3 : 156

———— oppoſes the eſcape by night,   *Pope il.* 2 : 44

———— ſeconded by Diomed,   *Pope il.* 2 : 45

———— great in the counſel, glorious in the field, *Pope il.* 1 : 78

———————— action, and in council wiſe,   *Pope il.* 1 : 140

———— for his art renown'd,   *Pope il.* 2 : 316

———— encompaſs'd and wounded,   *Pope il.* 1 : 338

———— reſcued by Ajax,   *Pope il.* 1 : 340

———— comes, and Death his ſteps attends,   *Pope od.* 3 : 67

———— his woes, a countleſs train,   *Pope od.* 3 : 68

———— twice ten years he roams,   *Pope od.* 3 : 68

———————— are paſt, and now he comes,   *id.* 68

———— knew the ſerpent mazes of deceit,   *Pope od.* 3 : 116

———— may boaſt a title to the loudeſt fame, *Pope od.* 3 : 117

———— in battle calm,   *Pope od.* 3 : 117

———— wiſe to reſolve, and patient to perform, *Pope od.* 3 : 117

———— gentle of ſpeech, beneficent of mind, *Pope od.* 3 : 135

———— people's parent,   *Pope od.* 3 : 135

Ulyſſes

Ulyffes rul'd his fubjects with a father's love,   *Pope od.* 3 : 145

———— the patient man,   *Pope od.* 3 : 145

———— fhipwreck'd,   *Pope od.* 3 : 158

———— gets afhore on Phæacia,   *Pope od.* 3 : 164

———— much-afflicted, much-enduring man,   *Pope od.* 3 : 208

———— relates his adventures to Alcinous,   *Pope od.* 3 : 227

———— Ithaca, the fair, his native foil,   *Pope od.* 3 : 227

———— verfed in the turns of various human-kind,   *id.* 238

———— bores the Cyclop's eye,   *Pope ode* 3 : 242

———— efcapes by means of Polyphemus' rams, *Pope ed.* 3 : 244

———— defcent to hell,   *Pope od.* 3 : 278

———— fhades, apparition to,   *Pope od.* 3 : 278

———— ftops the ears of the failors,   *Pope od.* 3 : 314

———— is himfelf lafh'd to the maft,   *Pope od.* 3 : 314

———— efcapes Sirens, Scylla, and Charybdis, *Pope od.* 3 : 315

———— lands on Sicily,   *Pope od.* 3 : 319

———— companions feize on and kill the oxen of the fun, *id.* 321

———————————— perifh by fhipwreck,   *Pope od.* 3 : 323

———— himfelf efcapes on the maft to Calypfo's ifle,   *id.* 324

———— takes leave of Alcinous,   *Pope od* 4 : 5

———— embarks,   *Pope od.* 4 : 6

———— arrives at Ithaca,   *Pope od.* 4 : 6

———— laid fleeping on the fhore,   *Pope od.* 4 : 7

———— awakes, but knows not his native Ithaca, *Pope od.* 4 : 16

———— in ufeful craft refin'd,   *Pope od.* 4 : 14

———— artful in fpeech, action, and in mind, *Pope od.* 4 : 14

———— in the difguife of a beggar,   *Pope od.* 4 : 18

———— entertained by Eumæus,   *Pope od.* 4 : 25

———— feigned hiftory,   *Pope od.* 4 : 30

———— man of woes,   *Pope od.* 4 : 59

Ulyffes conducted by Eumæus to the palace,   Pope od. 4 : 98

———- palace of, defcribed,   Pope od. 4 : 101

——— difcovers himfelf to Telemachus,   Pope od. 4 : 78

——— changed in perfon and drefs by Minerva, Pope od. 4 : 77

——— removes the weapons out of the armory, Pope od. 4 : 135

——— in converfation with Penelope,   Pope od. 4 : 141

——— gives a feign'd account of his adventures,   id. 141

——— defcribes Ulyffes to Penelope,   Pope od. 4 : 143

——— affures her of his fpeedy return,   Pope od. 4 : 146

——— difcover'd by Euryclea to be Ulyffes, Pope od. 4 : 150

——— owns himfelf,   Pope od. 4 : 153

———- how he came by the fcar on his knee, Pope od. 4 : 152

———- orders Euryclea to conceal him,   Pope od. 4 : 153

———-- is witnefs to the diforders of the women, Pope od. 4 : 161

———- renewed by Pallas,   Pope od. 4 : 224

———- and Penelope recount what paft during feparation, id. 230

———- goes to his father's retirement,   Pope od. 4 : 242

———-- difcovers himfelf to Eumæus and Philætius,   id. 186

———- bends the bow, to the confufion of the fuitors, id. 194

———- fam'd for warlike wiles,   Fent. 271

——— lov'd by Pallas, his wifdom points the way, Broome 76

———- and Tirefias,   King 424

Umber'd arms thick flafhes fend,   Pope il. 1 : 261

Umbra, character of,   Garth 54

Umbrella, ufe of,   Gay 1 : 108

Umbria, green retreats,   Add. 42

Umbril, a dufky, melancholy fprite,   Pope 1 : 145

Umbro, at the head of the Marrubians,   Dry. 6 : 191

Unbelief,   Cow. 1 : 310

——— what   Young 2 : 201

Unbelief is blind, *Milt.* 3 : 139

Unbelievers impiously despise the sacred oracles, *Cong.* 67

Unblemish'd let me live, or die unknown, *Pope* 1 : 226

Unbodied souls, images of air, *Pope od.* 4 : 235

———————— impassive semblance, *Pope od.* 4 : 235

Unchang'd the lion's valiant race remains, *West* 181

Uncommon worth is still with fate at strife, *Pitt* 394

———————— still inconsistent with a length of life, *ib.*

Undoing ! still to love and love in vain, *Hughes* 221

Unequal fight ! when youth contends with age, *Pope od.* 4 : 118

Unfading youth, with impotence of mind, *Fent.* 294

Unfaithful maid-servants executed by Ulysses, *Pope od.* 4 : 214

Unfather'd product of disgrace, *Pope od.* 4 : 141

Unforeseen is unprepared, *Dry.* 3 : 78

Unfortunate lady, elegy on, *Pope* 1 : 157

Unguarded virtue human arts defies, *Smith* 189

Unhappy Dryden ! *Pope* 2 : 225

———————— Great ! in love with cares, *Broome* 41

Union, { *Swift* 1 : 37
{ *Rowe* 49

———— one stem the thistle and the rose shall bear, *Rowe* 49

———— verses on, *Fent.* 220

———— the bond of all things, *Pope* 2 : 60

———— mysterious of the human with the divine nature, *Pom.* 333

Union-crosses o'er the Seine shall wave, *Fent.* 221

Unison strings sound alike, *Cow.* 2 : 87

Unities give plays their grace, *Buck.* 75

Universal apparition, *Gay* 2 : 82

———————— cures, to quack off, *Butl.* 1 : 285

———————— frame, is man's short span, capacious of ? *Aken.* 42

Universal medicine, a cheat, *Butl.* 2 : 347

———— prayer, *Pope* 2 : 87

Universe, a wide machine, *Black.* 82

———— one whole, *Black.* 104

Unlearned men of books assume the care, *Young* 1 : 89

———— as eunuchs are guardians of the fair, *id.* 89

Unnatural flights, an essay on, *Lansf.* 231 [*Life*, p. 45]

Unrewarded lover, *Walsh* 310

Unripen'd age, weak its counsels, *Pope il.* 2 : 311

———— headlong is its rage, *ib.*

Unruly murmurs, or ill-tim'd applause, *Pope il.* 2 : 198

———— wrong the justest cause, *Pope il.* 2 : 198

Unthinking men no scruples make, *Buck.* 114

Untriumphable fray, *Butl.* 1 : 68

Unwash'd-knight of Bath, *Gay* 1 : 269

Unwelcome revelers, flown with insolence and wine, *Pope od.* 3:48

Unwilling willing fair he storms, *Broome* 170

Vocal lay, responsive to the strings, *Pope od.* 3 : 204

Voice is powerful of a faithful friend, *Pope il.* 2 : 80

Voiture, trifles are elegant in him, *Pope* 2 : 335

———— excels in the irony, *Swift* 1 : 160

———— hint from, *Shen.* 177

Voltaire the wise, Voltaire the gay may blame, *Young* 3 : 138

Voluntary faults, effect of, *Cow.* 2 : 11

Volunteer laureat, *Sav.* 100

Voluptuous man, a slave, *Cow.* 2 : 274

———— species of, *Cow.* 2 : 274

Vote, *Cow.* 1 : 73

Votes, not controul establifhed power, *Dry.* 1 : 158

———— make a part exceed the whole, *Dry.* 1 : 158

Vow, though delayed, not violated,   *Butl.* 2 : 112

—— strained, is broken,   *Butl.* 1 : 200

Vowels, riddle on,   *Swift* 1 : 326

Vows nor tears can fleeting life prolong,   *A. Phil.* 314

—— you never will return, receive,   *Pope* 1 : 171

—— impious,   *Dry.* 7 : 322

Upright judge, verses on,   *Swift* 1 : 305

Upstart sectary,   *Butl.* 1 : 209

Upstarts, to support their station, cancel obligation, *Gay* 2 : 91

—— —— insolent in place,   *Gay* 2 : 71

Urania,   *Hughes* 250

—— heavenly born,   *Milt.* 1 : 207

—— Wisdom, the sister of,   *Milt.* 1 : 207

Uriel apprises Gabriel of Satan's descent,   *Milt.* 1 : 119

—— reply to Satan,   *Milt.* 1 : 96, 97

Urim, character of,   *Garth* 24

—— and Thummin, what,   *Milt.* 2 : 183

Urns, two, by Jove's throne ever stood,   *Pope il.* 2 : 349

—— source of evil one,   *Pope il.* 2 : 349

—— and one of good,   *Pope il.* 2 : 349

—— thence the cup of mortal man he fills,   *Pope il.* 2 : 349

Usurpation,   *Cow.* 1 : 294

—— effects of,   *Cow.* 1 : 329

Usurping croud, that worst of tyrants,   *Pope il.* 1 : 75

Use bounds delight,   *Cow.* 2 : 94

—— alone, sanctifies expence,   *Pope* 2 : 142

Usury, to pay back with,   *Butl.* 1 : 130

Vulcan, the black sovereign of the skies,   *Pope il.* 2 : 214

—— sovereign of the fire,   *Pope il.* 2 : 185

—— the artist-god,   *Pope il.* 2 : 186

        Vulcan,

1, the architect divine,   *Pope il.* 1 : 62.

— hurl'd headlong from th'etherial height, *Pope il.* 1 : 62

— makes arms for Æneas,   *Dry.* 6 : 215

— hurl'd from heaven,   *Tick.* 186

— palace, master-piece of skill,   *Tick.* 187

no described,   *Mall.* 212

r, inquisitive and loud,   *Pope od.* 3 : 185

— death too harsh appears to,   *Garth* 45

— justly fear'd, when Pompey fled,   *Rowe L.* 72

— ever discontent,   *Pope* 1 : 287

— still prone to change,   *Pope* 1 : 287

— sure, the monarch, whom they have, to hate, *ib.*

re Hopkins ruins thousands for a groat,   *Gay* 1 : 196

r, sparrow, and other birds,   *Gay* 2 : 123

th become leprous,   *Cow.* 2 : 124

W.

er, verses lost on,   *Cow.* 1 : 318

ing-maid,   *Cow.* 1 : 306

s, prince of, verses to,   *Thom.* 2 : 176

—— princess of, ode,   *Hughes* 231

ter (Mrs.) on poems of,   *Pitt* 290

— a female Muse, without one guilty line,   *Pitt* 290

cers, looks of, shew their business,   *Gay* 1 : 120

—— happiness of,   *Gay* 1 : 128

—— free from diseases,   *Gay* 1 : 128

king advantageous to learning,   *Gay* 1 : 129

l, to stick one to,   *Buth.* 2 : 104

lace, great patriot-hero,   1 : 137

—— ill-requited chief,   *Thom.* 1 : 121

                Waller,

Waller, poems of,   *Wall.* 15

———— danger of his majesty at Andero,   *Wall.* 15

———— on Buckingham's death,   21

———— to the king on his navy,   22

———— on the taking of Sallé,   24

———— on his majesty repairing Paul's,   25

———— on the queen's picture,   28

———— of the queen,   30

———— apology of sleep,   32

———— puerperium,   34

———— to the queen-mother of France,   35

———— country to lady Carlisle,   36

———— countess of Carlisle in mourning,   37

———— answer to a libel against Carlisle,   39

———— Carlisle's chamber,   40

———— to Phyllis,   41

———— to lord Northumberland,   42

———— to lord Admiral,   44

———— song,   46, 55, 76, 82, 90, 91, 96, 99

———— on lady Dorothy Sidney's picture,   46

———— to Van Dyck,   47

———— at Pens-hurst,   49

———— to lord Leicester,   50

———— of the lady, who can sleep at will,   51

———— misreport of being painted,   52

———— of passing thro' a crowd,   53

———— story of Phœbus and Daphne,   54

———— to mistress Braughton,   56

———— at Pens-hurst,   58

———— to lady Lucy Sidney,   59

Waller to Amoret,   *Wall.* 60, 63

———— on friendſhip of Sachariſſa and Amoret,   62

———— à la Malade,   64

———— on death of lady Rich,   65

———— battle of the Summer iſlands,   68

———— of love,   77

———— to Phillis,   79

———— to lord Falkland,   80

———— for drinking healths,   81

———— of Iſabella playing on lute,   83

———— to a lady ſinging,   84

———— of Mrs. Arden,   84

———— marriage of dwarfs,   85

———— Love's farewel,   86

———— from a child,   86

———— on a girdle,   87

———— to the mutable fair,   87

———— the fall,   91

———— of Sylvia,   92

———— the bud,   92

———— on diſcovery of a lady's painting,   94

———— to a lady, who gave a ſilver pen,   95

———— Chloris,   96

———— of loving at firſt ſight,   97

———— the ſelf-baniſhed,   97

———— Thyrſis, Galatea,   100

———— on the head of a ſtag,   102

———— to a lady in retirement,   103

———— miſer's ſpeech,   104

———— on Ben Jonſon,   104

Waller, on Fletcher's plays,   *Wall.* 106

———— to Sandys, on his tranflation of the Bible,   107

———— to Henry Lawes,   108

———— to Davenant on Gondibert,   109

———— to Wafe, on Gratius,   110

———— to Evelyn, on Lucretius,   112

———— to Higgins, on Venetian triumph,   113

———— verfes to Dr. Rogers,   114

———— Chloris and Hylas,   116

———— anfwer of Suckling's verfes,   117

———— to a friend on fuccefs of love,   120

———— apology for having loved before,   121

———— to Zelinda,   122

———— to lady Morton,   123

———— to a lady playing with a fnake,   125

———— Night-piece,   126

———— tranflation of part of Virgil's 4th Æneis, 128

———— on picture of a fair youth,   133

———— on a brede of divers colours,   133

———— panegyric to Protector,   134

———— of a war with Spain, &c.   141

———— on death of Protector,   145

———— to the king, on his return,   146

———— on St. James's park,   150

———— of invafion and defeat of Turks,   155

———— to the queen on her birth-day,   158

————————————— fong on her birth-day,   159

———— of her majefty, on New-year's-day,   160

———— of tea, commended by her majefty,   161

———— prologue for the lady-actors,   161

Waller, of mother to prince of Orange, *Wall.* 162

—— to dutchefs of Orleans, 163

—— on new-buildings at Somerfet-houfe, 163

—— of a tree cut in paper, 165

—— to a lady, who recovered the above copy, 166

—— of Mary, princefs of Orange, 166

—— to prince of Orange, 168

—— of Englifh verfe, 171

—— on Rofcommon's Ars Poetica of Horace, 172

—— ad comitem Monumetenfem, 174

—— to Killigrew, on altering Pandora, 175

—— on Monmouth's expedition to Scotland, 176

—— to a friend of the author, &c. 178

—— to author of Britifh princes, 179

—— to Creech, on his Lucretius, 180

—— triple combat, 182

—— of an elegy on Rochefter, 183

—— to Chloris, 184

—— on lofs of D. of Cambridge, 184

—— inftructions to a painter, 185

—— to the king, 196

—— prefage of ruin of Turks, 197

—— to the dutchefs, 199

—— verfes written in the Taffo of the dutchefs, 200

—— on Higgins, 201

—— Divine poems, 203

—— epigrams, epitaphs, and fragments, 233

—— to Lanfdowne, *Lanf.* 131

—— Lanfdowne to, 131

—— to memory of, 132

X 2

Waller fhall never die,   *Lanf.* 133

———— the Mufe's darling,   133

———— a poet, with a plentiful eftate,   133

———— like Cato's was his fpeech,   134

———— like Ovid's was his fong,   .   134

———— firft gave weight and meafure,   .   *Dry.* 1 : 265

———— imitated,   *Pope* 1 : 346

———— was fmooth,   *Pope* 2 : 228

———— courtly,   *Add.* 37

———— harmonious,   *Add.* 37

———— can fhew Cromwell's innocence,   *Add.* 37

———— compliment the ftorm, that bore him hence,   *Add.* 37

———— verfe fmooth as the fair,   *Fent.* 240

———— fung of Sachariffa's pride,   *Fent.* 317

———— taught the lute to breathe his pain,   *Fent.* 328

———— his mufe by Nature form'd to pleafe,   *Fent.* 328

———— maker, and model, of harmonious verfe,   *Fent.* 328

———— politely form'd, to profit and to pleafe,   *Fent.* 329

Wall-fruit,   *Thom.* 1 : 129

Wallington-houfe, lines in a window at,   *Hughes* 270

Walls have tongues, and hedges ears,   *Swift* 2 : 41

Walnut, in rough-furrow'd coat fecure,   *Phil.* 7

———— impairs all generous fruit,   *Phil.* 42

Walpole (Sir Robert),   *A. Phil.* 365

———————— minifter of England's weal, *A. Phil.* 365

———————— epiftle to,   { *Young* 3 : 209
                                   { *Sav.*   92

———————— innocence diftrefs'd flies to,   *Sav.* 93

Walfh, poems by,   *Walfh* 309

———— to his book,   309

                                                    Walfh,

Walsh, unrewarded lover,   *Walsh* 310

———— epigram by,   311

———— power of verse,   311

———— death,   317

———— to his false mistress,   317, 325

———— the antidote,   320

———— on a favour offered,   321

———— the reconcilement,   322

———— dialogue,   322

———— Lyce,   324

———— fair mourner,   324

———— love and jealousy,   325

———— the petition,   326

———— on quitting his mistress,   327

———— against marriage,   328

———— epigrams,   329

———— to Cælia,   330

———— retirement,   331

———— despairing lover,   333

———— song,   334, 339

———————— to Phyllis,   335

———— to a lady, resolved against marriage,   336

———— pastoral eclogues,   343

———— best critic,   *Dry.* 7 : 97

———— the Muses's judge and friend,   *Pope* 1 : 121

Watts, Horæ Lyricæ,   *Watts* 10

———— worshiping with fear,   39

———— asking leave to sing,   41

———— divine judgements,   42

———— earth and heaven,   44

Watts, felicity above, Watts 46
———— God's dominion and decrees, 47
———— self-confecration, 49
———— Creator and creatures, 50
———— God glorious, and finners faved, 53
———— humble enquiry, 54
———— penitent pardoned, 55
———— hymn for three great falvations, 56
———— the incomprehenfible, 59
———— death and eternity, 60
———— fight of heaven in ficknefs, 62
———— univerfal Hallelujah, 63
———— the Atheift's miftake, 65
———— law given at Sinai, 67
———— remember thy Creator, 72
———— fun, moon, and ftars, praife the Lord, 74
———— welcome meffenger, 75
———— fincere praife, 76
———— true learning, 78
———— true wifdom, 80
———— fong to creating wifdom, 82
———— God's abfolute dominion, 85
———— condefcending grace, 87
———— the infinite, 88
———— confeffion and pardon, 89
———— young men, &c. praife the Lord, 92
———— flying fowl, &c. praife the Lord, 93
———— comparifon and complaint, 94
———— God fupreme and felf-fufficient, 96
———— Jefus, the only Saviour, 97

Watts

Watts, looking upward,   Watts 99

————— Chrift, dying, rifing, and reigning,   100

————— the God of thunder,   101

————— day of judgement,   102

————— fong of angels above,   103

————— fire, air, earth, and fea, praife the Lord,   107

————— the farewel,   109

————— God only known to himfelf,   109

————— pardon and fanctification,   110

————— fovereignty and grace,   112

————— law and gofpel,   113

————— feeking a divine calm,   114

————— happy frailty,   115

————— launching into eternity,   117

————— profpect of the refurrection,   118

————— ad Dominum noftrum Jefum Chriftum,   119

————— fui ipfius increpatio,   122

————— excitatio cordis cœlum verfus,   123

————— breathing towards heaven,   124

————— in Sanctum Ardalionem,   125

————— proteftant church at Montpelier demolifhed,   126

————— two happy rivals,   127

————— hazard of loving the creatures,   131

————— defiring to love Chrift,   132

————— heart given away,   133

————— meditation in a grove,   134

————— faireft and only beloved,   135

————— mutual love ftronger than death,   138

————— fight of Chrift,   139

————— love on a crofs and on a throne,   142

Watts, preparatory thought for the Lord's fupper, *Watts* 143

———— converfe with Chrift, 144

———— grace fhining and nature fainting, 146

———— love to Chrift, prefent or abfent, 148

———— abfence of Chrift, 149

———— defiring his defcent to earth, 151

———— afcending to him in heaven, 152

———— prefence of God, worth dying for, 153

———— longing for his return, 154

———— hope in darknefs, 155

———— come, Lord Jefus, 157

———— bewailing my own inconftancy, 159

———— forfaken, yet hoping, 161

———— the conclufion, 162

———— to her majefty, 164

———— Palinodia, 168

———— to John Locke, 168

———— to John Shute, 169

———— to William Nokes, 170

———— to Nathaniel Gould, 171

———— to Thomas Gibfon, 173

———— to Milo, 175

———— to Sariffa, 176

———— to Thomas Bradbury, 179

———— ftrict religion very rare, 182

———— to C. and S. Fleetwood, 184

———— to William Blackbourn, 186

———— true monarchy, 187

———— true courage, 189

———— to Thomas Rowe, 191

Watts,

Watts, to Benoni Rowe,   *Watts* 192

——— to John Howe,   194

——— difappointment and relief,   196

——— hero's fchool of mortality,   198

——— freedom,   200

——— on Locke's Annotations, &c.   202

——— true riches,   203

——— adventurous Mufe,   206

——— to N. Clark,   209

——— afflictions of a friend,   211

——— the reverfe,   212

——— to John lord Cutts,   213

——— burning feveral poems, Martial, &c.   214

——— to Mrs. B. Bendyfh,   216

——— few happy matches,   217

——— to David Polhill,   219, 235

——— the celebrated victory of the Poles,   221

——— to Henry Bendyfh,   229

——— the happy man,   232

——— to the difcontented and unquiet,   240

——— to John Hartopp,   243, 248

——— to Thomas Gunfton,   245

——— to Mitio,   249

——— the fecond part,   254

——— the third part,   262

——— on the death of the duke of Gloucefter, &c.   265

——— epigram of Martial to Cirinus,   265

——— epiftola fratri, R. W.   266

——— fratri olim navigaturo,   269

——— ad Johannem Pinhorne,   270

Watts, ad Johannem Hartoppum, *Watts* 275

———— to Mrs. Singer, 277

———— an epitaph on king William, 279

———— an elegiac fong on Mrs. Peacock, 281

———— epitaphium Nathanielis Matheri, 283

———— elegiac thought on Anne Warner, 287

———— on the death of Mrs. M. W. 290

———— funeral poem on Thomas Gunſton, 294

———— elegy on the reverend Mr. Gouge, 312

———— divine fongs for the ufe of children, 323—359

———— a fpecimen of moral fongs, 361

———— a cradle hymn, 368

Wanderer, *Sav.* 7

———————— and alone, where ſhall I turn, *Sav.* 10

Wandering beauty, *Hughes* 163

———————— error quite miſguides the world, *Rowe L.* 78

———————— pilgrim, *Prior* 2 : 246

Want, an amorous thing, *Butl.* 1 : 309

———— ſcorn of every fool, *Dry.* 7 : 240

———— the great teacher, *Dry.* 7 : 308

———— virtues of, *Dry.* 3 : 204

———— what can it not ? *Pope od.* 4 : 102

———— and ſhame, how ill agree ? *Pope od.* 4 : 105

———— too oft betrays the tongue to lie, *Pope od.* 4 : 28

Wantly's dragon by valiant Moore, *Gay* 1 : 91

Wants relieve and ſpare our bluſhes, *Young* 1 : 148

———— brood of voluptuouſneſs, *Dyer* 24

War, exhibited in vifion, *Milt.* 2 : 106

———— that mad game of the world, *Swift* 1 : 4

———— the victualling a camp, *Butl.* 2 : 95

War

War is toil and trouble,   *Hughes* 177

——— that ſupreme tribunal,   *Mall.* 305

——— fees lawyers by ten thouſands,   *Mall.* 305

——— that fierce lion, long diſdaining law,   *Hughes* 19

——— rang'd uncontrol'd, and kept the world in awe, *Hughes* 19

——— goary jaws of,   *Broome* 68

——— ſcourge of men,   *Wall.* 192

——— artificial plague of man,   *Butl.* 2 : 224

——— lays waſte,   *Milt.* 2 : 111

——— comes, and ſavage ſlaughter muſt abound, *Rowe L.* 79

——— is the death of commerce and increaſe, *Young* 3 : 280.

——— our conſumption, gainful trade of chiefs, *Dry.* 1 : 15

——— of crimes and ruffian idleneſs the child, *Thom.* 1 : 233

——— the needy bankrupt's laſt reſort, *Rowe L.* 53

——— ſolemnity of,   *Dry.* 6 : 185

——— preparation for,   *Dry.* 6 : 186

——— horrid wa , thoughtful walks invades, *Pope* 1 : 82

——— how keen, if dulneſs draw the ſword, *Pope* 3 : 181

——— in heaven,   *Milt.* 1 : 173

——— of the gods,   *Pope il.* 2 : 250

——— raiſed by ſlander,   *Cow.* 1 : 327

——— for the king againſt him,   *Butl.* 1 : 69

——— great in the praiſe, rich in the ſpoils of, *Pope od.* 4 : 32

——— taſk of, is in glorious action, *Pope il.* 2 : 124

——— makes the valiant ſecure,   *Dry.* 1 : 89

——— made for peace,   *Parn.* 98

——— modern way of,   *Butl.* 2 : 93, 94

——— with Spain,   *Wall.* 141

Wards, court of,   *Thom.* 2 : 116

Warner (Mrs. Anne), elegy on,   *Watts* 287

3.

Warrior

Warrior-hero, how great to see him fight for liberty, *Hughes* 124

Warriors by flying gain fame, *Wall.* 169

————— to beard, *Butl.* 1 : 103

Wars and horrours are thy savage joy, *Pope il.* 1 : 45

—— deemed only heroic subjects, *Milt.* 2 : 4

Warton (Dr.), ode by, on occasion of West's Pindar, *West* 130

Warwick (lord), on his birth-day, *Rowe* 69

————— (lady), on a first visit to, *Rowe* 60

————— to, on Addison's going to Ireland, *Rowe* 61

Warwick gives and resumes sceptre, *Wall.* 16

————— king-maker, *Thom.* 2 : 110

Wase, *Wall.* 110

Washing, head to give for, *Butl.* 1 : 109

Wasps, how destroyed, *Phil.* 48

Wasting years wither human race, *Pope il.* 1 : 139

Water claims the highest praise, *West* 135

———— chief of Nature's works divine, *West* 135

———— inspiration of, sober, *Akin.* 308, 310

———— danger of being on, *Gay* 1 : 128

———— mouth to make, *King* 170

Waters, how assembled in one cavity, *Black.* 145

————— turned to blood, *Cow.* 2 : 57

Ways of heaven for ever just and wise, *Akin.* 57

Waves in restless errors roll, *Add.* 12

Weak, a prey unto the strong, *Som.* 276

———— how can subdue the stronger, *Gay* 2 : 18

Weakness, woman's excuse, *Milt.* 3 : 34

————— all wickedness is, *Milt.* 3 : 35

Weal, public and private, not to be parted, *Aken.* 225

Wealth is power, *Young* 3 : 252

Wealth,

Wealth, 'tis navies, armies, empire,   *Young* 3 : 252
——— springs from trade,   *Young* 3 : 280
——— the secret spoils of peace,   *Dry.* 2 : 95
——— ill-fated,   *Pope* 2 : 80
——— enjoins new toils,   *Young* 2 : 146
——— and murders peace,   *Young* 2 : 146
——— much is disease,   *Young* 2 : 147
——— seed of luxury and pride,   *Wall.* 143
——— brings luxury and disease,   *Butl.* 2 : 226
——— provocative to amorous heat,   *Butl.* 1 : 172
——— to look on, with undesiring eyes,   *Dry.* 7 : 351
——— is disturb'd by care,   *Lytt.* 10
——— is a cheat,   *Young* 1 : 130
——— in the grofs is death,   *Pope* 2 : 127
——— but life, diffus'd,   *Pope* 2 : 127
——— a servant,   *Den.* 96
——— may feek us, but Wisdom must be fought, *Young* 2 : 234
——— true ufe of, to know,   *Rowe* 48
——— with nobler Virtue join'd,   *West* 150
——— in glory's chace must aid the mind, *West* 150
——— enlarges not the narrow mind,   *Mall.* 341
——— brings the beauties or the faults to light, *Hughes* 274
——— hath power of doing,   *Gay* 2 : 128
——— hard fate of,   *King* 223
——— if alone, can make and keep us blest, *Pope* 2 : 208
——— still, still be getting, never, never rest, *Pope* 2 : 208
——— without virtue, avails not,   *Prior* 2 : 21
——— dims the eyes of crowds,   *Dyer* 142
——— allures war,   *Dry.* 2 : 51
——— is it the potent fire of peace ?   *Prior* 2 : 174

Wealth

Wealth-give to heaven, by aiding the diftreft, *Pope od.* 3 : 291

—— fole patron of the building trade, · *Swift* 1 : 42

—— for frugal hands heaven decrees, *Tick.* 120

—— by the bounteous only is enjoy'd, *Weft* 205

—— treafures of, in diffufive good employ'd, *Weft* 205

—— procures returns of fame and friends, *Weft* 205

—— claim'd diftinction, favour, grace, *Gay* 2 : 165

—— thus loft, with that our friends, *Som.* 325

—— within, the mind's immortal ftore, *Hughes* 173

—— to recompence flender dividend of fenfe, *Fent.* 228

—— and beauty lefs than virtue pleafe, *Pope od.* 3 : 69

Wealthy kings are loyally obey'd, *Pope od.* 3 : 291

Weapon-falve heals, *Butl.* 2 : 50

Weary nature craves the balm of reft, *Pope od.* 4 : 225

Weather, changes of, *Dry.* 5 : 108

—— prefages of, $\begin{cases} Dry.\ 5:108 \\ Garth\ \ \ 98 \end{cases}$

—— figns of, *Gay* 1 : 105

—— and our wills agree, *Dry.* 2 : 246

Weaving defcribed, *Dyer* 86

—— hiftory of, *Dyer* 95

—— fettlement of in Britain, *Dyer* 95

Weazel, when you torment, *Swift* 1 : 32

—— his paffion by his fcent you find, *Swift* 1 : 32

Wedding-day, *Mall.* 184

—— my life be fuch, *Mall.* 191

Wedlock honeft, is a glorious thing, *Pope* 1 : 228

—— worfe than any loop-hole, *Butl.* 1 : 178

Wednefday, *Gay* 1 : 66

Weep, fhepherds, and remember flefh is grafs, *Gay* 1 : 83

Weeping,

Weeping,   { *Cow.* 1 : 304 / *Pope* 1 : 349

Weigh anchor, and some happier clime explore, *Young* 2 : 32

Well-bred, and yet sincere,   *Pope* 1 : 117

Welcome,   *Cow.* 1 : 268

———— the coming, speed the parting guest, *Pope od.* 4 : 50

———— messenger,   *Watts* 75

———— death has lost his sting,   *Watts* 75

———— guilt gives it its fierce array, *Watts* 76

———— fame, virtue, freedom,   *Aken.* 355

Well-meaners think no harm,   *Dry.* 3 : 106

Welsted, flow, like thine inspirer, beer,   *Pope* 3 : 186

Welwyn, epitaph at,   *Young* 1 : 238

West, olympic odes,   *West* 133—190

—— first Pythean,   196

—— first Nemean,   202

—— eleventh Nemean,   209

—— second Isthmian,   216

—— song of Orpheus,   221

—— story of Phineus,   225

—— hymn of Cleanthes,   232

—— triumphs of the gout,   235

—— on the abuse of travelling,   259

—— Education,   281

—— Father Francis' prayer,   318

—— inscription in a summer-house,   320

West, verses to,   *Lytt.* 54

—— whose gentle warmth discloses earth's womb, *Phil.* 34

Western wonder,   *Den.* 64, 65

———— world, believe and sleep,   *Pope* 3 : 179

Westminster-

Weftminfter-abbey, kings crowned and fleep in, *Wall.* 153

Weftminfter-hall, feat of juftice, *Wall.* 154

Wey, that rolls a milky wave, *Pope* 1 : 71

Whacum, employment of, *Butl.* 1 : 235

Whale, like a huge carrack, *Waller* 74

Whales fport in woods, and dolphins in the fkies, *Pope* 3 : 197

Wharton, the fcorn and wonder of our days, *Pope* 2 : 101

————— flagitious, yet not great, *Pope* 2 : 102

————— drunk twelve years together, *Pitt* 281

————— to lady Jane, *Rowe* 70

What is, that ought to be, *Pope il.* 1 : 61

————- muft be, muft be, *Pope il.* 2 : 350

————- right, what true, what fit, be all my care, *Pope* 2 : 193

————— d'ye-call-it, *Gay* 1 : 255

Whatever is, is right, *Pope* 2 : 39

Wheat, ftrength of human life, *Phil.* 52

Wheel of fops ! that faunter of the town, *Young* 1 : 85

——————— call it diverfion, and the pill goes down, *ib.* 1 : 85

Whelps, litter of, *Som.* 71

————— number to be reared, *Som.* 71

————— not to hunt too foon, *Som.* 72

————— fet out to their feveral walks, *Som.* 72

————— broken from running at fheep, *Som.* 73

Whigs would reform the ftate, *Dry.* 2 : 249

Whiggifh plots, fource of, *King* 384

Whimfy, not reafon, is the female guide, *Lanf.* 178

Whipping, virtue's governefs, *Butl.* 1 : 84

————— fympathetic, *Butl.* 1 : 205

————— poft, *Butl.* 1 : 98

Whirlwinds roar from every quarter of the fky, *Pitt.* 216

Whistle, for want of thought,   *Dry.* 3 : 259

———— to bring to one's,   *Butl.* 2 : 223

White, do penance in,   *Butl.* 2 : 199

White-hall, raised by a prelate,   *Wall.* 153

White-lead to repair a lady's face and China-ware, *Swift* 1 : 197

White rose and a red presented to a lady,   *Som.* 196

White witches mischievously good,   *Dry.* 1 : 211

Whitmore, epitaph on,   *Dry.* 2 : 195

Whitshed, motto of,   *Swift* 1 : 294

Whole stupendous, all are but parts of,   *Pope* 2 : 38

Whores are women of unguarded hours,   *Gay* 2 : 19

———— and silver born in one age,   *Dry.* 7 : 253

Wicked have no right to the Creature,   *Butl.* 1 : 92

———— punishment of,   *Dry.* 6 : 138

———— hence depart to torments,   *A. Phil.* 393

———— ears are deaf to Wisdom's call,   *Pope od.* 4 : 81

———— man was never wise,   *Pope od.* 3 : 71

———— ministers oppress,   *Gay* 2 : 145

Wickedness is blind,   *Dyer* 112

———— and folly, kindred powers,   *Thom.* 2 : 166

Wickliff struck at papal usurpation,   *Thom.* 2 : 111

Widdrington fights on his stumps,   *Butl.* 1 : 103

Widow, a witch engrafted on a scold,   *Prior* 2 : 210

———— wile of,   *Fent.* 272

———— rarely wants a foe, or finds a friend,   *Pom.* 283

———— and virgin-sisters,   *Broome* 159

Widows too wise for batchelors to wed,   *Pope* 1 : 230

———— wed as often as they can,   *Dry.* 3 : 206

Wife,   *Som.* 189

———— a termigant, insulting jade,   *Som.* 189

Wife, to leave parents and country,   Milt. 3 : 36

——— how to choofe,   Pom. 272

——— peculiar gift of heaven,   Pope 1 : 229

——— how precarious the bleffing,   Gay 2 : 96

——— the heavier clog,   Butl. 1 : 179

——— who would not yield, and could not rule, Prior 2 : 204

——— will was chang'd with every wind,   Prior 2 : 204

——— now could chide, now laugh, now cry, Prior 2 : 204

——— now fing, now pout,   Prior 2 : 204

——— how much dearer than the bride,   Lytt. 62

——— glad to oblige, and pleafed to pleafe, Prior 2 : 204

——— of Bath,   { Dry. 3 : 186
    { Pope 1 : 255

——— of fnow, enamoured of,   Butl. 1 : 169

Wife's pleafure caufes hufband's pain,   Prior 1 : 138

Wight, mirror of knighthood,   Butl. 1 : 5

Wild afs defcribed,   Young 1 : 219

——— boar and ram,   Gay 2 : 37

——— fig-tree fplits the rock,   Dry. 7 : 312

——— fallies to be ftri&ly examin'd o'er,   Pitt 353

Will, free by nature,   Milt. 1 : 156

——— not over-ruled by fate,   Milt. 1 : 156

——— left free by God,   Milt. 2 : 14

——— obeying reafon is fecure,   Milt. 2 : 15

——— may fwerve, if reafon be off its guard, Milt. 2 : 15

——— of heaven is ever good for all,   Aken. 53

——— and a&, word and work of God, the fame, Prior 2 : 123

——— the bully of the mind,   Ot. 62

——— the only faculty of women,   Butl. 2 : 333

——— refufed, grieves a woman moft,   Dry. 3 : 122

Will, none want reasons to confirm,   *Pope* 1 : 227

—— is curb'd by tyrant Want,   *Sav.* 59

—— resolved, nothing hard to,   *Duke* 91

William, second, fills Henry's place,   *Hughes* 46

———- sicken'd soon and sudden dy'd,   *Hughes* 46

———- leaving his bride, daughter of Britain, pregnant, *ib.*

———- founder of the Belgic state,   *Hughes* 41

———- III. epitaph on,   *Watts* 279

————- inscription for,   *Aken.* 328

———- how conquer'd, and how France retir'd, *Prior* 1 : 101

———- like Alcides, crush'd faction,   *Hughes* 49

———- a greater name than any age can boast, *Prior* 1 : 58

———- the scourge of France,   *Prior* 1 : 87

———- his genius shall look down and bless this isle, *Hughes* 54

———- his life untouch'd be, as is his fame, *Prior* 1 : 100

———- and Margaret,   *Mall.* 153

Winchester, epitaph on,   *Dry.* 2 : 199

————- (Benjamin, bishop of), ode to,   *Aken.* 267

Wind to beat, at three lengths,   *Butl.* 1 : 267

—— out of,   *Butl.* 1 : 106

Wind-bound with horror,   *Butl.* 1 : 210

Windham, master of our passions and his own, *Pope* 2 : 299

Window, like a pillory,   *Butl.* 1 : 238

—— verses on a,   *Swift* 1 : 182

Windows, epigrams on,   *Swift* 2 : 35—39

Winds burst their dark mansions in the clouds, *Pope il.* 1 : 73

——- uses of,   *Black.* 89

——- nor seasons guide, nor order binds, *Prior* 2 : 185

——- howl o'er the main, and thunder in the sky, *Broome* 26

——- lose their force, that unresisted fly, *Rowe L.* 138

Winds whistling, what they foretel, *Gay* 1 : 107

Windsor built by Charles II. *Ot.* 9

———— described, { *Ot.* 10 *Den.* 9

———— antiquity of, *Den.* 9

———— where Edward enroll'd the red-crofs knight, *Tick.* 197

———— fair heaven, that doft the ftars inclofe, *Prior* 1 : 175

Windsor-caftle, *Ot.* 3

———————— antiquity of, *Ot.* 13

———————— paintings of, *Ot.* 14

Windsor-foreft, *Pope* 1 : 57

Windsor prophecy, *Swift* 1 : 77

Windsor's towery pride, *Pope* 1 : 346

Wine, a poem, *Gay* 1 : 282

———— whofe fovereign power revives decaying nature, *ib.*

———— cordial reftorative to mortal man, *Gay* 1 : 282

———— warms our chilly blood, *Gay* 1 : 283

———— incorporate with light and heat, *Cong* 49

———— effects of, *Rowe* 43

———— happy effects of, *Broome* 169

———— fovereign cure of human woes, *Broome* 169

———— gives a kind releafe from care, *Broome* 169

———— whets the wit, *Pom.* 217

———— gives difcourfe a pleafant flavour, *Pom.* 217

———— can of their wits the wife beguile, *Pope od.* 4 : 40

———— make the fage frolic, and the ferious fmile, *ib.* 4 : 40

———— fweet poifon of, mifufed, *Milt.* 3 : 122

———— infpires, 'tis fweet to rave, *Broome* 165

———— infpiration of, frantic, *Aken.* 309

———— makes cowards brave, *Som.* 190

Wine

Wine cheers the heart, *Milt.* 3 : 25

———— overturns the brave, *Milt.* 3 : 25

———— give the debtor, *Phil.* 74

———— adds courage and mirth, *Phil.* 74

———— puts our time and care to flight, *Gay* 2 : 176

———— warms the blood, adds luftre to the eyes, *Cong.* 141

———— and Love have always been allies, *Cong.* 141

———— heightens defamation, *Gay* 1 : 257

———— generous, which thoughtful Sorrow flies, *Pope od.* 3 : 72

———— pernicious to mankind, *Pope il.* 1 : 202

———— unnerves the limbs, and dulls the noble mind, *id.* 202

———— powerful wine can thaw the frozen cit, *Swift* 1 : 144

———— and fashion him to humour and to wit, *Swift* 1 : 144

———— rofy-bright the brimming goblets crown'd, *Pope od.* 4 : 171

Wines work, when vines are in flower, *Butl.* 1 : 165

———— unmixt, to chear the grave and warm the poet, *Pope od.* 4 : 3

Winter, { *Shen.* 128
{ *Thom.* 1 : 153

———— fullen and fad, *Thom.* 1 : 153

———— approach of, *Thom.* 1 : 155

———— fends down the wolves from the mountains, *id.* 166

———— defcribed, *Cong.* 48

———— beginning of, defcribed, *Gay* 1 : 101

———— within the Polar circle, *Thom.* 1 : 180

———— a paftoral, *Pope* 1 : 40

———— all his fnowy ftores difplays, *Black.* 74

———— furly paffes of, *Thom.* 1 : 4

———— laggard, like feeble age, *Hughes* 192

———— evening, *Thom.* 1 : 174

———— folftice, *Aken.* 191

Winter

Winter folftice, fun's wintery goal,   *Aken.* 191

———— winds loofen the roots of trees,   *Phil.* 67

Winter's coolnefs, fpite of fummer's rays,   *Pope* 1 : 348

———— day,   *Mall.* 335

Winters fevere in America,   *Dyer* 124

Winter, to Thomfon on,   *Mall.* 341

Wifdom,   *Cow.* 1 : 247

———— - ode to,   *Swift* 1 : 133

———— to be fool no more,   *Pope* 2 : 195

———— calls, feek virtue firft,   *Pope* 2 : 196

———— by experience bought,   *King* 303

———— never lies,   *Pope od.* 3 : 82

———— has its date, affign'd by heaven,   *Pope il.* 1 : 231

———— alone can pureft friendfhip know,   *Gay* 2 : 263

———— never works in vain,   *Thom.* 1 : 28

———— true,   *Watts* 80

———— bleft, whom fhe guides,   *Watts* 80

———— by which God is more diftinctly known,   *Yal.* 444

———— the nobleft power of man,   *Yal.* 444

———— creating, fong to,   *Watts* 82

———— in the motion of the heavenly bodies,   *Black.* 68

———— in the pofition of the fun,   *Black.* 69

———— in the fucceffion of the feafons,   *Black.* 71

———— infinite muft know,   *Garth* 69

———————— form the beft fyftem,   *Pope* 2 : 30

———— learn from the wife,   *Pope od.* 3 : 314

———— children of, make her known,   *Den.* 92

———— the defect of form fupplies,   *Pope od.* 3 : 209

———— of numbering our days,   *Cow.* 2 : 368

———— is in age,   *Dry.* 3 : 196

    Wifdom,

Wisdom, sphere of, is the sphere of age,   *Parn.* 64

———— what can it not ?   *Pope od.* 3 : 146

———— in youth and beauty, is but rare,   *Pope od.* 3 : 197

———— ennobles man,   *Young* 2 : 99

———— secret streams of, flow calm and flow,   *West* 215

———— to know our duty,   *Milt.* 1 : 237

———— the sole artificer of bliss,   *Young* 1 : 140

———— and delight, if they part, they die,   *Young* 2 : 34

———— is above suspecting wiles,   *Swift* 1 : 107

Wise lived yesterday,   *Cow.* 2 : 376

—— is but to know, how little can be known,   *Pope* 2 : 79

—— how prone to doubt, how cautious! *Pope od.* 4 : 15 | 3 : 113

—— distrust the too fair-spoken man,   *Thom.* 1 : 206

—— instruct the wise,   *Broome* 75

—— in more than words or notion,   *Pom.* 270

—— to consult, and active to defend,   *Pope il.* 1 : 194

—— with courage bear, what heaven ordains, *Pope od.* 3 : 283

—— who in love is,   *Broome* 139

—— are the only wretched,   *Prior* 1 : 47

—— the only happy,   *Som.* 260

—— through time, and narrative with age,   *Pope il.* 1 : 111

—— man never will be sad,   *Young* 2 : 239

—— builder,   *Som.* 373

—— child better than a foolish king,   *Prior* 2 : 161

—— and good receive the stranger as a brother, *Pope od.* 3 : 223

—— kings by love and mercy reign,   *Gay* 2 : 31

—— to look,   *Butl.* 1 : 253 | 2 : 31

—— man's power's the limit of his will,   *Cong.* 71

Wisely who acts, can never act by fate,   *Black.* 163

————————— means and ends must understand, *Black.* 163

Wisely to spend is the great art of gain,   *Young* 3 : 152

Wish,   { *Cow.* 1 : 249
                 { *Hughes* 151

—— ardent ever wrong,   *Young* 3 : 113

—— refignation's full reverfe,   *Young* 3 : 113

Wifhes leap the bounds of man,   .   *Dyer* 140

—— folly of,   *Prior* 1 : 153

—— all are a ladle,   *Prior* 1 : 154

—— reftlefs,   *Yal.* 364

—— like painted landfcapes,   *Yal.* 364

—— wildly rolling, banifh quiet,   *Dyer* 5

—— remedied by cutting fhorter,   *Cow.* 2 : 373

Wifhing, of all employments, is the worft,   *Young* 2 : 64

Wit, what it is not,   *Cow.* 1 : 97

—— what it is,   *Cow.* 1 : 98

—— a luxuriant vine,   *Cow.* 1 : 208

—— defined,   *Add.* 194

—— diftinguifhed,   *Add.* 194

—— well conceived, though not defin'd,   *Swift* 1 : 159

—— and humour differ quite,   *Swift* 1 : 159

—— gives furprize,   *Swift* 1 : 159

—— is only to turn agreeably a proper thought,   *Buck.* 78

—— excites gay furprize,   *Thom.* 1 : 174

—— is but a fecond praife,   *Mall.* 160

—— a gin,   *Butl.* 1 : 114

—— fhy of ufing it,   *Butl.* 1 : 6

—— never to be learned,   *Butl.* 2 : 259

—— petty larceny of,   *Butl.* 2 : 264

—— mifprifions of,   *Butl.* 2 : 210

—— brighteft far, funk in good fenfe,   *Young* 3 : 140

                           Wit,

Wit, a gay prerogative from common sense,   *Young* 3 : 203

—— little of, mix'd with a great deal of pains,   *Swift* 1 : 29

—— triumphs over age and fate,   *Som.* 241

—— that gloomy cares beguiles,   *Som.* 213

—— talks most, when least she has to say,   *Young* 2 : 254

—— precious, as the vehicle of sense,   *Young* 2 : 254

—— but as its substitute, a dire disease,   *Young* 2 : 254

—— shines through rough cadence of a rugged line, *Dry.* 2 : 161

—— the life-refining soul,   *Thom.* 1 : 109

—— twenty men of, for one of sense,   *Pope* 1 : 5

—— life of, a warfare upon earth,   *Pope* 1 : 6

—— more than women need,   *Dry.* 3 : 216

—— that knows no gall,   *Thom.* 1 : 57

—— is by politeness sharpest set,   *Young* 1 : 91

—— fed by vice and folly,   *Roch.* 342

—— a just share given to each,   *Roch.* 317

—— to starve by,   *Dry.* 2 : 248

—— is prais'd, but hungry lives and cold,   *Gay* 1 : 181

—— in rags ridiculed,   *Dry.* 7 : 240

—— o'er love prevails,   *King* 253

—— with solid judgement, rarely united,   *Tal.* 443

—— want of beauty well supplies,   *Fent.* 278

—— blame the false and value still the true,   *Pope* 1 : 107

—— true, is nature to advantage dress'd,   *Pope* 1 : 103

—— to nick,   *Butl.* 2 : 88

—— modes in, take their turn,   *Pope* 1 : 109

—— current folly proves the ready,   *Pope* 1 : 109

—— unhappy, atones not for the envy it brings,   *Pope* 1 : 111

—— by fools 'tis hated, and by knaves undone,   *Pope* 1 : 112

—— as the chief of virtue's friends,   *Swift* 2 : 131

Wit difdains to ferve ignoble ends,   *Swift* 2 : 131

—— mix with pomp, and dignity with eafe,   *Tick.* 123

—— like wine, intoxicates the brain,   *Lytt.* 40

—— too ftrong for feeble woman to fuftain,   *Lytt.* 40

—— men of, panders to a vicious mind,   *Swift* 2 : 122

—— and judgement often are at ftrife,   *Pope* 1 : 94

—— and virtue ne'er decay,   *Som.* 241

—— and wifdom,   *A. Phil.* 372

Witch's prayer, faid backway,   *Butl.* 1 : 112

Withers, immortal rhyme of,   *Butl.* 1 : 229

Witnefs-judge precludes a long appeal,   *Pope od.* 4 : 154

Witneffes go like watches,   *Butl.* 1 : 203

Witney broad-cloth proper for horfemen,   *Gay* 1 : 102

Wits, different kinds of,   *Dry.* 1 : 261

—— have fhort memories, and dunces none,   *Pope* 3 : 261

—— who like owls, fee only in the dark,   *Pope* 3 : 191

—— are game-cocks to one another,   *Gay* 2 : 47

—— the Atheifts of the age,   *Swift* 1 : 12

—— who would the pulpit, as they rule the ftage,   *id.* 12

Witty want refin'd the huntfman's wiles,   *Tick.* 144

Wives, a random choice,   *Pope* 1 : 258

—— freakifh when well, fretful when fick,   *Pope* 1 : 258

—— by the dozen,   *Prior* 2 : 241

Woe in filence moft appears,   *Cong.* 101

Woes in embryo ripening into life,   *Pom.* 266

—— are from above,   *Pope ed.* 3 : 176

—— tread each other's heel,   *Young* 2 : 45

—— I endure, which none but kings can feel,   *Broote* 71

—— load of, united falls on me,   *Broome* 71

—— prevailing eloquence,   *Pope ed.* 3 : 181

           Wolf

Wolf within, sheep without, a monster,   *Den.* 99

—— and dog,   *Som.* 271

—— fox and ape,   *Som.* 267

Wolves, a tribute of, imposed on Wales,   *Som.* 48

Woman taken from man,   *Milt.* 1 : 247

———— described,   *Milt.* 1 : 247

———— fairest of all God's gifts,   *Milt.* 1 : 247

———— of one flesh with man,   *Milt.* 1 : 248

———— led to the nuptial bower,   *Milt.* 1 : 248

———— fair defect of nature,   *Milt.* 2 : 74

———— cause of much mischief,   *Milt.* 2 : 75

———— deplores her fault,   *Milt.* 2 : 76

———— persuades to suicide,   *Milt.* 2 : 77, 78

———— dissuaded from it,   *Milt.* 2 : 79, 80

———— snare to man,   *Milt.* 2 : 90

———— good lovely in,   *Milt.* 2 : 10

———— doom of,   *Milt.* 2 : 51

———— rise of,   *Parn.* 5

———— is the worst of every ill,   *Lanf.* 263

———— enticing crocodile, whose tears are death, *Lanf.* 263

———— Syren, that murders with enchanting breath, *id.* 263

———— to one sin confin'd ! strange,   *Gay* 2 : 19

———— pride is this day her darling passion,   *Gay* 2 : 19

———— the next, slander,   *Gay* 2 : 19

———— gaming succeeds,   *Gay* 2 : 19

———— virtue's mortgaged for her losses,   *Gay* 2 : 19

———— woman, when to ill inclin'd,   *Pope od.* 3 : 294

———— all hell contains no fouler fiend,   *Pope od.* 3 : 294

———— Greece lies a desart land, by,   *Pope od.* 3 : 295

———— hate of, implacable,   *Yal.* 390

                                Woman,

Woman, wit dangerous too little, as too much,   *Pom.* 273

———— muſt burſt with, or blab a ſecret,   *Dry.* 3 : 194

———— by nature, importune to know,   *Fent.* 264

———— nauſeous rule of,   *Pom.* 225

———— loves herſelf alone,   *Som.* 234

———— oft ſhifts her paſſions, like the wind,   *Gay* 2 : 236

———— who knows the ways inconſtant, of ?   *Gay* 2 : 242

———— a various and a changeful thing,   *Dry.* 6 : 64

———— loves nothing, or not long,   *Milt.* 3 : 41

———— meek and demure, proves a thorn,   *Milt.* 3 : 41

———— one virtuous rarely found,   *Milt.* 3 : 42

———— furniture of her mind,   *Swift* 2 : 48

———— caught, nothing bolder than,   *Dry.* 7 : 265

———— if you wiſh ill, turn her over to her will,   *Young* 1 : 131

———— a creature, fair and vain,   *Parn.* 9

———— the fondling miſtreſs and the ruling wife,   *Parn.* 9

———— young Pandora ſhe,   *Parn.* 10

———— form divine,   *Prior* 2 : 18

———— falſe, o'er the wife prevails,   *Pope od.* 3 : 284

———— thinks all compliments ſincere,'   *Gay* 1 : 248

———— in body weak, more impotent in mind,   *Hughes* 80

———— with men goes with the worſt in argument,   *Milt.* 3 : 37

———— leſs than, in the form of man,   *Pope il.* 1 : 245

———— chief is maſter of the war,   *Prior* 1 : 258

———— nobleſt ſtation is retreat,   *Lytt.* 41

———— important buſineſs of, is love,   *Lytt.* 41

———— honour of,   *Rowb.* 290

———— ſcorn'd, with eaſe wrought to vengeance,   *Smith* 111

———— hard to ſay, what wins her love,   *Milt.* 3 : 41

———— love in, made of ſubtle intereſt,   *Dry.* 2 : 237

Woman,

Woman, on a mischievous,   *Broome* 118

———— in nothing should be naked,   *Young* 1 : 145

———— but veil her very wit with modesty,   *Young* 1 : 141

———— counsel of, brought woe,   *Dry.* 3 : 158

———— sex to the last,   *Dry.* 3 : 268

———— and fool are two things hard to hit,   *Pope* 2 : 109

———— to man his sovereign bliss,   *Dry.* 3 : 153

———— is seen in private life alone,   *Pope* 2 : 113

———— bred to disguise, in public 'tis you hide, *Pope* 2 : 113

———— at best a contradiction still,   *Pope* 2 : 115

———— envy, what magic can assuage,   *Lanf.* 142

———— eyes her very soul express,   .   *Gay* 1 : 243

———— frailty, always to believe,   *Pope il.* 1 : 121

———— fraud should meet woman's vengeance,   *Smith* 139

———— hate, 'tis vain to shun,   *Som.* 370

———— heavy the blow, and sure as fate,   *Som.* 370

———— meaning to be read backwards,   *Lanf.* 251

Womankind, nature prodigal to,   *Duke* 105

———— never knows a mean,   *Dry.* 7 : 268

———— thinks no pleasure too dear,   *Dry.* 7 : 268

———— in ills ever bold,   *Dry.* 7 : 256

———— aspire to dominion,   *Dry.* 7 : 262

———— vanity rules,   *Gay* 2 : 251

———— love is the weakest passion of their mind, *id.* 251

Women,   *Lanf.* 198

———— made for men,   *Butl.* 2 : 120

———— satire on,   *Young* 1 : 117

———— own ambition,   *Young* 1 : 117

———— through every scene of vanity they run, *Young* 1 : 118

———— have no characters at all,   *Pope* 2 : 105

5

Women have but one faculty, the will,   *Butl.* 2 : 333

———— paint their imperfections,   *Butl.* 1 : 299

———— tempers as artificial, as their faces,   *Butl.* 1 : 299

———— a parrot's privilege forbidden,   *Gay* 2 : 73

———— try and condemn without jury,   *Gay* 2 : 73

———— place and birth, their paradise,   *Butl.* 1 : 303

———— wifeſt men deceived by,   *Milt.* 3 : 14

———— wed one man, to wanton with a ſcore, *Young* 1 : 150

———— practiſed but to roll an eye,   *Young* 3 : 254

———— with varying vanities,   *Pope* 1 : 130

———————————— ſhift toy-ſhop of the heart, *ib.*

———— will be wavering,   *Fent.* 231

———— their love is with the lover paſt,   *Pope od.* 4 : 48

———— ſucceeding flame expels the laſt,   *Pope od.* 4 : 48

———— when they liſt, can cry,   *Pope* 1 : 253

———— free gifts ſcorn, and love what coſts us pains, *id.* 263

———— itch of news,   *Dry.* 7 : 269

———— the fame of every ſtreet,   *Dry.* 7 : 269

———— itch to know their fortune,   *Dry.* 7 : 277

———— ruling paſſions of,   *Pope* 2 : 113

———————————— love of pleaſure and of ſway, *ib.*

———— they ſeek the ſecond, not to loſe the firſt, *ib.*

———— power all their end, but beauty all the means, *ib.*

———— on dotage build their ſway,   *Prior* 2 : 159

———— alone, perhaps, in the wordy war excel, *Pope il.* 2 : 223

———— and vent their anger, impotent and loud, *id.* 223

———— like cowards, tame to the ſevere,   *Lanſ.* 179

———— only fierce, when they diſcover fear, *Lanſ.* 179

———— prove ungrateful, as men prove true, *Cong.* 52

———— the joys they give, few, ſhort and unſincere, *Cong.* 61

Women love like cats,   *Dry.* 2 : 269

———— thofe fair diffemblers, fly,   *Lanf.* 148

———— obnoxious to the priefts,   *Dry.* 7 : 274

———— deal in philtres,   *Dry.* 7 : 278

———— their revenge,   *Dry.* 7 : 251

———— anger, impotent, and loud,   *Dry.* 2 : 154

———— weak of reafon, impotent of will,   *Dry.* 7 : 279

———— fiends, who meditate ill,   *Dry.* 7 : 280

———— where they will, are all in hafte,   *Dry.* 3 : 255

———— an eafy prey to the brave,   *Dry.* 3 : 123

———— follow fortune, where fhe leads,   *Dry.* 3 : 123

———— power of,   *Butl.* 2 : 132

———— ill confequence of gazing on,   *Gay* 1 : 135

———— like princes, find few real friends,   *Lytt.* 40

———— your heart's fupreme ambition to be fair,   *Lytt.* 40

———— chufe their men, like filks, for fhow,   *Gay* 1 : 173

———— of every nation are the fame,   *Gay* 1 : 173

———— by nature love th' intriguing trade,   *Gay* 1 : 176

Women's armour,   *Cow.* 1 : 127

———— fuperftition,   *Cow.* 1 : 270

Wonder implies novelty, but not *vice verfâ*,   *Aken.* 86

———— by clear knowledge deftroyed,   *Roch.* 310

Wonders of creating-power endlefs,   *Mall.* 215

———— wrought in Egypt,   *Milt.* 2 : 125

Wonderful, pleafure from,   *Aken.* 20

———— men fonder of, than of true,   *Butl.* 2 : 164

Wood, an infect,   *Swift* 1 : 338

———— the iron-monger,   *Swift* 1 : 340

———— petition of,   *Swift* 1 : 341

———— new fong on his half-pence,   *Swift* 1 : 343

            Wood,

Wood, serious poem on,   *Swift* 1 : 346

Wood's money, epigram on,   *Swift* 1 : 336

Wood, that will hold tack,   *Butl.* 1 : 110

———- wall of,   *Wall.* 168

———- of stars,   *Cow.* 1 : 211

Woodcock, of times intelligent,   *Phil.* 67

Wooden bridge to be built at Westminster,   *Thom.* 2 : 185

——————— must it my waves disgrace,   *Thom.* 2 : 185

Wooden horse, stratagem of,   *Dry.* 5 : 359

Woodland retreat,   *Thom.* 1 : 59

Wood-nymph,   *Aken.* 329

Woods, where little warblers tune their lay,   *Broome* 52

——— have ears,   *Dry.* 3 : 78

——— haunt of the Druids,   *Phil.* 53

Woodstock, here Henry lov'd,   *Tick.* 106

——————— and Chaucer learn'd to sing, *ib.*

——————— doft Edward's cradle claim,   *Fent.* 206

——————— receives an equal hero for thy Lord,   *Fent.* 206

Wool, winding of,   *Dyer* 58

——— diversity of, in the fleece,   *Dyer* 59

——— skill, in assorting,   *Dyer* 59

——————— among the Dutch,   *Dyer* 59

——— different uses of,   *Dyer* 59

——— lightest in common fields,   *Dyer* 61

——— none good in cold or wet pastures,   *Dyer* 61

——— Phœnicia, Syria, and Judea, famous for,   *Dyer* 64

——— twice ting'd with the Murex,   *Dyer* 64

——— Tarentum famous for,   *Dyer* 68

——— Bætica famed for,   *Dyer* 68

——— Coraxi, noted for,   *Dyer* 68

Wool, Coraxi, ram of, valued at a talent, *Dyer* 68

—— now Caftile and Segovia famous for, *Dyer* 69

—— in hot climes, only on the tail, *Dyer* 71

—— Arica in Peru, famous for, *Dyer* 72

—— called the Comber's lock, value of, *Dyer* 72

—— methods to prevent its exportation, *Dyer* 73

—— of Atlas' vales, *Dyer* 111

—— combing, inventor of, *Dyer* 75

—— dying of, *Dyer* 76

Woolen manufactures carried to China, *Dyer* 118

Wooton, death of, *Cow.* 1 : 101

Word to keep, old-fashioned trick, *Butl.* 2 : 113

Word-catcher, that lives on fyllables, *Pope* 2 : 156

Words, images of thoughts, *Butl.* 2 : 281

—— power of, to affuage grief, *Milt.* 3 : 13

—— that burn, *Gray* 349

—— warm, but warm without offence, *Pope od.* 3 : 212

—— congealed in Northern air, *Butl.* 1 : 11

—— as fafhions, alike fantaftic, if too new or old, *Pope* 1 : 105

—— obfcene, too grofs to move defire, *Buck.* 72

—— are like leaves with little fruit, *Pope* 1 : 104

—— are but wind, *Butl.* 1 : 194

—— flow readily to the notions, *Dry.* 1 : 265

—— different, as the various kinds of poetry, *Pitt* 367

—— be cull'd with niceft care, *Pitt* 368

—— fweet as honey from his lips diftill'd, *Pope il.* 1 : 48

—— to coin, no laws forbid, *Pitt* 371

—— in which your tongue is poor, *Pitt* 372

—— coined allowable, *Rofc.* 261

—— are the Poet's paint, *Lanf.* 231

Words so strong, we see the subject figur'd,   *Pitt* 348

_____ barbarous to be smoothed to the ear,   *Pitt* 374

_____ made subservient to the sense,   *Pitt* 374

_____ their strength, extent, and nature know,   *Pitt* 374

_____ found a picture of the sense,   *Pitt* 376

_____ proportioned to the subject,   *Pitt* 376

Work, to make completely fine,   *Swift* 1 : 226

_____ number and weight and measure join,   *Swift* 1 : 226

_____ perfected, the joy was past,   *Prior* 2 : 131

_____ so vast, to raise the Roman name,   *Pitt* 274

_____ the metal far surpass'd,   *Garth* 67

Work-house described,   *Dyer* 90

Works of gods what mortal can survey ?   *Pope od.* 4 : 222

_____ not titles, must prove our worth,   *Pope il.* 1 : 297

World, the work of love,   *Duke* 119

_____ harmonious frame of, bespeaks God,   *King* 367

_____ governed by geometry,   *Butl.* 1 : 255

_____ best and fairest of unnumber'd,   *Aken.* 44

_____ a well-set clock,   *Cow.* 2 : 96

_____ a great family,   *Roch.* 317

_____ an inn,   *Som.* 398

_____ and death the journey's end,   *Dry.* 3 : 129

_____ a great stage,   *Dry.* 2 : 241

_____ consists of puppet-shows,   *Swift* 2 : 85

_____ like a regular poem,   *Cow.* 2 : 86

_____ like a wood,   *Lansf.* 186

_____ where wanderers lose themselves,   *Lansf.* 186

_____ is all title-page,   *Young* 2 : 224

_____ without contents,   *Young* 2 : 224

_____ in nature's ample field, a point,   *Young* 2 : 93

_____ is no neuter,   *Young* 2 : 226

     World,

World, it will wound or fave,   *Young* 2 : 226

———— well-known, will give our hearts to heaven,   *id.* 226

———— has ills, and fuch may find thee,   *Parn.* 206

———— made of fighting and of love,   *Butl.* 1 : 47

———— that gulf of fouls,   *Young* 2 : 31

———— defpife, who venerate themfelves,   *Young* 2 : 31

———— was made for Cæfar, but for Titus too,   *Pope* 2 : 74

———— fcarce the firm philofopher can fcorn,   *Thom.* 1 : 114

———— a diftaff fhould obey,   *Hughes* 290

———— cataftrophe of,   *Cow.* 2 : 51

———— end of,   *Milt.* 2 : 137

———— conflagration of,   *Milt.* 1 : 84

———— moft enjoy, who leaft admire,   *Young* 2 : 252

———— fit loofe to, nor aught admire,   *Som.* 256

———— forgetting, by the world forgot,   *Pope* 1 : 190

———— whofe beauties perifh, as they blow,   *Parn.* 100

———— enjoyed by fenfe, and God by thought,   *Parn.* 153

———— to know,   *Swift* 1 : 115

——————— a phrafe for vifits, ombre, balls, and plays, *ib.*

World's bravery, liveries of light,   *Cow.* 1 : 212

———— the main, how vext, how vain,   *Young* 1 : 201

Worlds, millions of, hang in the fpacious air,   *Gay* 1 : 5

Worldly-wife is but half-witted,   *Young* 2 : 139

Worms, the great, the vile, are food alike for,   *I anf.* 181

Wor'fter fight,   *Cow.* 1 : 330

Worth is more than power,   *Broome* 76

———— unboaftful, oft dwells in humble ftation,   *Thom.* 1 : 66

———— in mifery, a reverence pay,   *Pope ad.* 3 : 291

———— of politenefs is the needful ground,   *Young* 1 : 104

———— makes the man,   *Pope* 2 : 77

Worthy should receive recompence of virtuous praise, *West* 257

Wortley Mountague, lady Mary, verses to, *Pope* 2 : 366

Wound round, hard to cure, *Butl.* 2 : 325

Wounded, they wound, . *Pope il.* 2 : 93

——— man and swarm of flies, . *Som.* 270

Wounds healed by wider wounds, *Butl.* 2 : 34

——— how fair, in our country's cause ! *Pitt* 262

——— all before, honourable, *Butl.* 1 : 109

——— all glorious, all before, *Pope il.* 2 : 15

——— to cure, and conquers to forgive, *Prior* 1 : 57

Wrangling, a consequential ill of freedom, *Prior* 1 : 195

——— science taught noise and show, *Pope* 1 : 350

Wrath awaked, signs of, *Mil.* 1 : 175

——— of Jove, what so dreadful, *Pope od.* 3 : 151

——— of princes ever is severe, *Pope od.* 4 : 98

——— suppress, and heaven obey, *Tick.* 172

——— and revenge from men and gods remove, *Pope il.* 2 : 173

——— far, far too dear to every mortal breast, *ib.*

——— sweet to the soul, as honey to the taste, *ib.*

Wrath's ready hands are never at a loss, *Rowe L.* 153

Wreaths familiar to the letter'd race, *Fent.* 306

Wren with sorrow to the grave descends, *Pope* 3 : 205

Wrestler sacred conquers heaven, *Wall.* 21

Wretch unfriendly to the race of man, *Pope od.* 4 : 168

——— no words can move, *Tick.* 212

——— by beauty dazzled and bewitched by love, *Tick.* 212

——— was born to want, whose soul is poor, *Gay* 1 : 196

Wretched hear, and the gods revere, *Pope il.* 2 : 348

——— man ! unmindful of thy end, *Pope il.* 2 : 144

——— man by impious pride undone, *West* 139

Wretched

Wretched mortals ! loft in doubts below,   *Pope il.* 1 : 86

————— but guefs by rumour, and but boaft we know,   *ib.*

————— when from thee, vex'd when nigh,   *Prior* 1 : 64

Wretches hang, that jurymen may dine,   *Pope* 1 : 138

————— once deceas'd, to woes confign'd,   *A. Phil.* 392

Wrinkles of threefcore fhall make you vainly wife, *Hughes* 127

Write well, or not at all,   *Dry.* 1 : 121

————— with fury, and correct with phlegm,   *R-fc.* 223

Writer, the moft fevere to himfelf,   *Dry.* 1 : 266

————— to confult faithful friends,   *Dry.* 1 : 267

Writers, rehearfals of,   *Dry.* 7 : 311

————— will be, who never will be read,   *Cong.* 87

Writing well, nature's mafter-piece,   *Buck.* 69

————— a difeafe,   *Cong.* 88

————— of men,   *Cotu.* 2 : 95

Wrong, black, hovering clouds appal,   *Young* 3 : 233

————— fwift vengeance waits on,   *Pope od.* 3 : 215

————— and oppreffion no renown can raife,   *Pope od.* 4 : 191

————— I feel, tends to public weal,   *Sav.* 20

————— fow by the ear,   *Butl.* 1 : 245

Wrongs, my fole oracles, infpire my rage,   *Pope il.* 2 : 101

————— of bafe mankind unmoved beat,   *Pope od.* 4 : 15

Wrong-doing Great, violent will of,   *Prior* 2 : 172

Wycherley, character of,   *Lanf.* 234

————— excels in true comedy,   *Lanf.* 235

————— with pointed wit and energy of fenfe,   *Fent.* 236

X

Xanthus, called Scamander by the fons of earth, *Pope il.* 2 : 216

Xenocrates, victor in the Ifthmian games,   *Weft* 216

Xenocrates, to all benevolent, by all revered, *West* 219

Xerxes laid o'er the Hellespont a bridge, *Rowe L.* 116

———— through mid Athos found his fleet away, *Rowe L.* 116

Y

Yahoo, overthrow of, *Swift* 2 : 296

Yalden, poems of, *Yal.* 351

———— against grief, 351

———— hymn to morning, 353

———————— darkness, 355

———— human life, 359

———— against enjoyment, 363

———— curse of Babylon, 365

———— to Congreve, 371

———— the insect, 374

———— to Chamberlain, 376

———— to Watson, 378

———— rape of Theutilla, 380

———— St. Cecilia, 386

———— force of jealousy, 389

———— to his mistress, 392

———— imitation of Horace, 394

———————— Homer, 396

———— on reprinting Milton, 399

———— to Mackworth, 400

———— Ovid's art of love, 408

———— essay on Sir Willoughby Aston, 436

Yea and no in senates hold debate, *Tick.* 96

Years following years steal something every day, *Pope* 2 : 242

———— at last they steal us from ourselves away, *Pope* 2 : 242

Years,

Years, like ftealing waters glide,   *Cong.* 114

———— that fweep the tolling race of man,   *Thom.* 1 : 45

———————————— all their laboured monuments away, *ib.*

Yeoman of Kent,   *Som.* 398

———— liv'd on his own, and paid no rent,   *Som.* 398

Yielded reafon fpeaks the foul a flave,   *Thom.* 2 : 37

Yoke may yoke, and blood may blood repay,   *Sav.* 126

York, duke of,   *Buck.* 106

———— praife of,   *Ot.* 5

———— dutchefs of, Dryden to,   *Dry.* 1 : 42 | 2 : 130

———— duke of, verfes to,   *Lanf.* 128

Young, laft day,   *Young* 1 : 1

———— religion, force of,   1 : 47

———— vanquifhed love,   1 : 47

———— love of fame,   1 : 69

———— fame, love of,   1 : 69

———— univerfal paffion,   1 : 69

———— on women,   1 : 117

———— ode to the king,   1 : 169

———— on Lyric poetry,   1 : 177

———— ocean,   1 : 187

———— Job, paraphrafe on part of,   1 : 219

———— Notes on the paraphrafe,   1 : 225

———— Angelo, piece of the crucifixion,   1 : 233

———— to Addifon, on his Cato,   1 : 234

———— epilogue to the brothers,   1 : 235

———— epitaph on lord Aubrey Beauclerk,   1 : 237

———————— on Dr. Young's fervant,   1 : 238

———— on the death of Addifon,   1 : 239

———— reflections on the ftate of the kingdom,   1 : 245

Young,

Young, complaint,   *Young* 2 : 3

———— refignation,   3 : 83

———— on death of queen Anne,   3 : 147

———— inftalment,   3 : 157

———— to lord Laufdowne,   3 : 165

———— to Mr. Pope,   3 : 187

———— Mr. Doddington to Walpole,   3 : 209

———— old man's relapfe,   3 : 215

———— lord Melcombe to,   3 : 219

———— fea-pieces,   3 : 226

———— imperium pelagi,   3 : 235

———— verfes to, by lord Melcombe,   3 : 219

———— epiftle to,   *Pitt* 189

———— his fatires, verfes on reading,   *Swift* 2 : 13

———— Ammon fcorns to run with lefs than kings, *Som.* 265

———— Dryden fpare, for his father's fake,   *Cong.* 88

———— gentleman, on death of,   *Pitt* 278

———————— fair was thy frame and beautiful thy foul, *ib.*

———————— his years told by virtues, not by days, *ib.*

———————— in love,   *Prior* 1 : 134

Young lady in tears,   *Som.* 243

———————— to, with the Iliad tranflated, *Som.* 207

———————— epiftle to,   *Gay* 1 : 208

———————— epitaph on,   { *Sav.* 166
                                           { *Mall.* 157

———————— fcap'd from life, fafe on the fhore, *Mall.* 157

———————— ode to,   *Shen.* 93

———————— verfes to, with Venice preferved, *Lytt.* 92

———————— verfes to,   *Sav.* 145

———— man and cat,   *Pitt* 267

Young men soon give and soon forget affronts,   *Add.* 293

Youth, spring of life,   *Gay* 1 : 225

—— fair virtue's season,   *Shen.* 245

—— dare to be happy, but dare and be,   *Pom.* 238

—— calls for pleasure,   *Aken.* 348

—— devours pleasures,   *Dry. e* : 146

—— only lays up sighs for age,   *Young* 1 : 83

—— of frolics, an old age of cards,   *Pope* e : 114

—— is apt to err,   *Pope il.* 2 : 344

—— an empty wavering state,   *Pope il.* 1 : 110

—— of itself, to numerous ills betray'd,   *Pitt* 315

—— requires a prop, and wants a foreign aid, *Pitt* 315

—— small cause to plain,   *A. Phil.* 302

—— does one smiling hope attend,   *A. Phil.* 302

—— be train'd, to bear the stings of poverty, *Pitt* 261

—— in sickness, impotent as age,   *West* 238

—— and white age pour along,   *Pope od.* 3 : 204

—— wedded to stooping age,   *Pope* 1 : 238

—— seduc'd give up age to want and shame, *Prior* 1 : 136

—— by steel unmann'd,   *Hughes* 293

—— and frail beauty, how they die!   *Bronme* 103

—— is the best time for action mortals have, *Pom.* 234

Z

Zacynthus, green with ever-shady groves, *Pope od.* 4 : 140

Zadoc, character of,   *Dry.* 1 : 154

Zeal, a dreadful termagant,   *Butl.* 2 : 37

—— fanatic, unappeasable,   *Butl.* 2 : 39

—— a pestilent disease,   *Butl.* 2 : 325

—— ardor of,   *Milt.* 2 : 188

                             Zeal,

Zeal, by perfecution's rage, refines,   *Sav.* 29

—— hot, yet dark and blind,   *Duke* 114

—— blind conductor of the will,.   *Dry.* 2 : 66

—— curft ungodlineſs of,.   *Young* 2 : 49

—— bitterneſs of faintly,   *Mall.* 257

—— how blind its fury,   *id.* 266

—— not charity, became the guide,   *Pope* 2 : 64

—— for their country, and thirſt. of virtuous praiſe, *Hughes* 49

—— for worth diftreſt,   *Dry.* 1 : 188

—— warmed not fcorched with,   *Dry.* 2 : 179

—— and Humility,. wings of the foul,.   *Young* 2 : 153

Zealous crouds in ignorance adore,   *Rowe L.* 140

————— the leſs they know, they fear the more, *id. ib.*

Zelinda, Waller to,   *Wall.* 122

Zenobia, in learning, beauty, and in virtue ſhone, *Sav.* 104

—— beneath her rofe Longinus,   *Sav.* 104

Zephyr,   *Mall.* 315

—— weſtern wind,.   *Mall.* 315

Ziloah, praife of,   *Dry.* 1 : 198

Zimri, character of,   *Dry.* 1 : 143

Zodiac, ftars in, fhift,   *Butl.* 1 : 257

Zopirus, ambition of,   *Cow.* 2 : 267

Zounds ! what a fall had our dear brother ?   *Gay* 2 : 24

F I N I S.

CPSIA information can be obtained
at www.ICGtesting.com
Printed in the USA
BVHW091701201118
533618BV00017B/897/P